Lecture Notes in Computer Science　9768

Commenced Publication in 1973
Founding and Former Series Editors:
Gerhard Goos, Juris Hartmanis, and Jan van Leeuwen

Editorial Board

More information about this series at http://www.springer.com/series/7412

Lucio Tommaso De Paolis · Antonio Mongelli (Eds.)

Augmented Reality, Virtual Reality, and Computer Graphics

Third International Conference, AVR 2016
Lecce, Italy, June 15–18, 2016
Proceedings, Part I

Editors
Lucio Tommaso De Paolis
University of Salento
Lecce
Italy

Antonio Mongelli
University of Salento
Lecce
Italy

ISSN 0302-9743   ISSN 1611-3349   (electronic)
Lecture Notes in Computer Science
ISBN 978-3-319-40620-6   ISBN 978-3-319-40621-3   (eBook)
DOI 10.1007/978-3-319-40621-3

Library of Congress Control Number: 2016941288

LNCS Sublibrary: SL6 – Image Processing, Computer Vision, Pattern Recognition, and Graphics

Printed on acid-free paper

This Springer imprint is published by Springer Nature
The registered company is Springer International Publishing AG Switzerland

Preface

This book contains the contributions to the Third International Conference on Augmented Reality, Virtual Reality and Computer Graphics (SALENTO AVR 2016) that has held in Otranto (Italy) during June 15-18, 2016. We cordially invite you to visit the SALENTO AVR website (http://www.salentoavr.it) where you can find all relevant information about this event.

SALENTO AVR 2016 intended to bring together researchers, scientists, and practitioners to discuss key issues, approaches, ideas, open problems, innovative applications, and trends on virtual and augmented reality, 3D visualization, and computer graphics in the areas of medicine, cultural heritage, arts, education, entertainment, and the industrial and military sectors.

We are very grateful to Patrick Bourdot, co-chair of the conference, as well as the Program Committee and local Organizing Committee members for their support and for reviewing and discussing the submitted papers in a timely and professional manner. We would like to sincerely thank the keynote and tutorial speakers who willingly accepted our invitation and shared their expertise through illuminating talks, helping us to fully meet the conference objectives.

In this edition of SALENTO AVR we were honored to have the following keynote speakers:

- Antonio Emmanuele Uva - Polytechnic Institute of Bari, Italy
- Leo Joskowicz - University of Jerusalem, Israel
- Matteo Dellepiane - ISTI-CNR, Pisa, Italy
- Stefano Baldassi - Meta Company, California, USA

We extend our thanks to the University of Salento and the Department of Engineering for Innovation for the enthusiastic acceptance to sponsor the conference and to provide support in the organization of the event.

SALENTO AVR attracted high-quality paper submissions from many countries. We would like to thank the authors of all accepted papers for submitting and presenting their works at the conference and all the conference attendees for making SALENTO AVR an excellent forum on virtual and augmented reality, facilitating the exchange of ideas, fostering new collaborations, and shaping the future of this exciting research field.

For greater readability of the two volumes, the papers are classified into five main parts that include contributions on: Virtual Reality, Augmented and Mixed Reality, Human–Computer Interaction, Applications of VR/AR in Medicine, and Applications of VR/AR in Cultural Heritage.

We hope the readers will find in these pages interesting material and fruitful ideas for their future work.

June 2016

Lucio Tommaso De Paolis
Antonio Mongelli

Organization

Conference Chair

Lucio Tommaso De Paolis   University of Salento, Italy

Conference Co-chair

Patrick Bourdot   CNRS/LIMSI, University of Paris-Sud, France

Honorary Chair

Giovanni Aloisio   University of Salento, Italy

Scientific Program Committee

Andrea Abate	University of Salerno, Italy
Selim Balcisoy	Sabancı University, Turkey
Vitoantonio Bevilacqua	Polytechnic of Bari, Italy
Monica Bordegoni	Politecnico di Milano, Italy
Davide Borra	NoReal.it, Turin, Italy
Andrea Bottino	Politecnico di Torino, Italy
Pierre Boulanger	University of Alberta, Canada
Andres Bustillo	University of Burgos, Spain
Massimo Cafaro	University of Salento, Italy
Sergio Casciaro	IFC-CNR, Italy
Bruno Carpentieri	University of Salerno, Italy
Marcello Carrozzino	Scuola Superiore Sant'Anna, Italy
Mario Ciampi	ICAR/CNR, Italy
Pietro Cipresso	IRCCS Istituto Auxologico Italiano, Italy
Lucio Colizzi	CETMA, Italy
Jean-Marc Cieutat	ESTIA Recherche, France
Arnis Cirulis	Vidzeme University of Applied Sciences, Latvia
Yuri Dekhtyar	Riga Technical University, Latvia
Matteo Dellepiane	National Research Council (CNR), Italy
Giorgio De Nunzio	University of Salento, Italy
Francisco José Domínguez Mayo	University of Seville, Spain
Aldo Franco Dragoni	Università Politecnica delle Marche, Italy
Italo Epicoco	University of Salento, Italy
María José Escalona Cuaresma	University of Seville, Spain

Krzysztof Walczak   Poznan University, Poland
Anthony Whitehead   Carleton University, Canada

Organizing Committee

Ilenia Paladini   University of Salento, Italy
Valerio De Luca   University of Salento, Italy
Antonio Meo   University of Salento, Italy
Pietro Vecchio   University of Salento, Italy

Contents – Part I

Virtual Reality

Augmented and Mixed Reality

Contents – Part II

Applications of VR/AR in Cultural Heritage

Human-Computer Interaction

Virtual Reality

Simulation of Tsunami Impact upon Coastline

Aristotelis Spathis-Papadiotis and Konstantinos Moustakas$^{(\boxtimes)}$

Electrical and Computer Engineering Department,
University of Patras, Patra, Greece
moustakas@upatras.gr

Abstract. This paper presents a simulation of a tsunami impact upon an urban coastline. Emphasis was given to the conservation of momentum, as its distribution in space and time is the main factor of the wave's effects on the coastline. Due to this, a hybrid simulation method was adopted, based on the Smoothed Particle Hydrodynamics (SPH) method, enriched with geometric constraints and rigid body interactions. The implementation is the result of cooperation between the Bullet physics engine and our custom SPH engine, which successively process the dynamic state of the fluid at every timestep. Furthermore, in order to achieve better performance a custom data structure (LP grid) was developed for the optimization of locality in data storage and minimization of access time. Simulation data is exported to VTK files, allowing interactive processing and visualization. Experimental results demonstrate the benefits of impulse recording at potential hazard estimation and evaluation of defense strategies.

Keywords: Fluid simulation · Tsunami · SPH · Tsunami-coastline interaction · Force visualization

1 Introduction

Simulations of natural phenomena are a precious tool for analysis and understanding of the processes behind them as well as the implications of those. Especially fluid dynamics is one of the fields most benefited by the explosive growth of high performance parallel computing architectures of the last years. Tsunamis are one of the most devastating natural disasters, with much attention drawn to them lately, especially after the 2004 Indian Ocean tsunami and the 2011 Tōhoku earthquake and tsunami, two of the largest incidents in modern history. Multiscale modelling of tsunami generation, propagation and impact is a trending research area, as respective simulations give valuable insights into the underlying mechanisms and relations between the various stages of an unfolding tsunami incident, while also facilitating the assessment of potential hazard it poses upon impact on a coastline.

A tsunami is a series of waves in a water body caused by an impulsive disturbance that vertically displaces a large volume of water. Tsunamis are generated by earthquakes, volcanic eruptions, landslides and other such events which have

L.T. De Paolis and A. Mongelli (Eds.): AVR 2016, Part I, LNCS 9768, pp. 3–15, 2016.
DOI: 10.1007/978-3-319-40621-3_1

the potential to transmit a huge amount of mechanical energy to an overlying or adjacent water volume. On a macroscopic level, tsunami propagation across the ocean as well as coastline inundation and runup are usually simulated through methods based on various versions of the shallow water equations, which are derived from the Navier-Stokes equations if the horizontal length scale is much greater than the vertical one. Conversely, the aforementioned methods are not appropriate in smaller scale simulations of the impact upon the coastline, since in order to obtain a reliable estimation of the forces exerted on the terrain, complex dynamics of fluid-structure interactions have to be accounted for. One of the most used methods for simulating complex flows with multiple boundary interactions is Smoothed Particle Hydrodynamics, initially proposed in the 1970s for the treatment of compressible flows in astrophysical problems. The method has enjoyed extensive adoption, having been applied to numerous fields ranging from aerodynamics and geology to engineering and computer graphics with exceptional results, lending itself well to adaptations and extensions. The main contribution of our approach is the emphasis given to the explicit conservation of momentum and the detailed data collection and visualization relating to its distribution upon the coastline during the tsunami impact. Towards this end, we adopted SPH enriched with geometric constraints as our method of choice due to the unparalleled advantages it offers, directly linked to its properties as a lagrangian method.

2   Related Work

Computational fluid dynamics is a very active area of research, as it relates to a wide spectrum of applications in computer graphics, engineering and science. The SPH method was developed independently by Gingold and Monaghan [8] and Lucy [14] in 1977. Since then, it has been employed in a wide variety of problems and applications, proving itself to be a flexible and attractive method for the simulation of complex, multicomponent/multiphase flows. Its flexibility is shown by the numerous adaptations and customizations it has undergone to suit many diverse problem domains.

Tsunami simulations have been shown to be a valuable tool in the literature, aiding in estimation of key parameters of a tsunami incident, such as its propagation course and coastal inundation. Simulations of the devastating 2004 Indian Ocean tsunami have been carried out by Wang and Liu [20] and Ioualalen et al. [11], using nonlinear shallow water equations and nonlinear Boussinesq models respectively. In both cases, good agreement between calculations and field measurements of inundation and runup indicate the robustness of these approaches. Using two different models, Kakinuma [12] reproduced a past incident with sufficient accuracy. The governing equations for both were the continuity and Reynolds equations for incompressible fluids in porous media, while water surface displacement was determined by the vertically integrated continuity equation for the first and the 3D Volume of Fluid method for the second model. Lastly, Samaras et al. [17] used a 2D horizontal model based on the higher oder Boussinesq equations to simulate tsunami-induced coastal inundation in two relevant areas of interest in the Mediterranean.

Relating to the SPH method, Desbrun and Gascuel [6] used it to animate highly deformable bodies of various stiffness and viscosity, while proposing important extensions like the "spiky" pressure smoothing kernel and discussing implementation issues such as the fluid surface reconstruction from density iso-surfaces. Later, Müller et al. [16] used this work as a basis for fluid simulation in interactive applications. Becker and Teschner [2] developed Weakly Compressible SPH, where the ideal gas equation of state is replaced with the much more strict Tait equation to reduce compressibility to a user-defined upper bound, thus avoiding an inefficient explicit Poisson equation solver. In recent years, Solenthaler and Pajarola [18] improved WCSPH by proposing Predictive-Corrective Incompressible SPH, where a prediction-correction scheme is used to compute particle pressures through iterative density constraint satisfaction and propagation through the fluid, until the final tolerance conditions are met. Implicit Incompressible SPH was then proposed by Ihmsen et al. [10], in which the density is predicted using a discretized form of the pressure Poisson equation, as obtained from the combination of a direct discretization of the continuity equation and symmetric pressure forces.

SPH has been employed in many simulations involving wave-coastline interactions. Debroux et al. [5] used SPH for the simulation of tsunami impact on real coastline topography, where important features like the energy and speed of the wave were measured over the course of time. Gómez-Gesteira and Dalrymple [9] simulated the impact of a wave generated by a dam break against a tall structure with a 3D SPH method, showing good agreement with lab measurements of velocities and forces. Dalrymple and Rogers [3] gave a comprehensive overview of techniques regarding usage of SPH for simulation of water waves and their interaction with structures, while also highlighting its suitability for close-up examinations of small regions. Many studies have considerably improved upon this line of research, yielding exceptional results. For example, St-Germain et al. [19] used a 3D WCSPH model to examine and analyze spatially and temporally forces exerted by tsunami-like hydraulic bore upon freestanding structures.

Due to its generality and adaptability, SPH has been the method of choice for many applications and relative extensions. Macklin and Müller [15] enriched SPH with positional geometric constraints, thus enforcing incompressibility while maintaining stability and allowing for large timesteps. Rigid-fluid interaction is one of the strong aspects of the method, as is shown by Akinci et al. [1], where rigid surfaces are sampled by boundary particles, which adaptively contribute to fluid properties to address boundary region deficiencies and inhomogeneities, in order to incorporate rigid bodies to a unified hydrodynamic framework. Finally, a thorough overview of various implementation algorithms and data structures for SPH, together with their advantages and drawbacks is provided by Domínguez et al. [7].

3   Proposed Framework

Our proposed simulation framework is based on SPH, a lagrangian fluid simulation method whose core notion is the discretization of the fluid into particles, which serve as interpolation points for the estimation of fluid properties in space. Advantages of this method include the exact treatment of advection, the natural way of dealing with special interface interactions, the inherent conservation of significant quantities (mass, momentum, energy) and the self-adaptivity of computational load to the fluid location and state in the flow domain. To efficiently ensure incompressibility in degenerate cases and undersampled boundary regions while maintaining relatively large timesteps, SPH was enhanced with explicit solving of geometric constraints between particles. These constraints are solved by the Bullet physics engine, within which fluid particles are represented as rigid bodies, while also being subject to SPH forces as computed at each timestep of the simulation.

3.1   SPH Method

Starting from the identity:

$$f(\boldsymbol{r}) = \int_V f(\boldsymbol{x})\delta(\boldsymbol{r} - \boldsymbol{x})d\boldsymbol{x},$$

where $\delta(\boldsymbol{r})$ the Dirac delta function and $\boldsymbol{x} \in V$, one can obtain a more general interpolation rule by substituting $\delta(\boldsymbol{r})$ with a smoothing kernel $W(\boldsymbol{r}, h)$:

$$f(\boldsymbol{r}) \approx \int_V f(\boldsymbol{x})W(\boldsymbol{r} - \boldsymbol{x}, h)d\boldsymbol{x}$$

whose limit when $h \to 0$ approaches the delta function and is normalized to unity:

$$\lim_{h \to 0} W(\boldsymbol{r}, h) = \delta(\boldsymbol{r}) \quad \text{and} \quad \int_V W(\boldsymbol{r}, h)d\boldsymbol{x} = 1$$

The smoothing radius h serves as a cutoff radius in the smoothing process, as particles beyond that distance have no contribution to the sum, i.e. $W(r, h) = 0$ when $r > h$. For the discrete case, where f is discretized to particles with density ρ and mass m, the weighting ratio m/ρ can be used to construct a weighted sum interpolant for any field A:

$$A(\boldsymbol{r}) = \sum_i \frac{m_i}{\rho_i} A(\boldsymbol{r}_i)W(\boldsymbol{r} - \boldsymbol{r}_i, h) \tag{1}$$

which lies at the heart of the SPH formulation. According to this, the gradient can be computed by the following approximation:

$$\nabla A(\boldsymbol{r}) = \sum_i \frac{m_i}{\rho_i} A(\boldsymbol{r}_i)\nabla W(\boldsymbol{r} - \boldsymbol{r}_i, h) \tag{2}$$

The obvious advantage of this is the exclusive dependence on the smoothing kernel gradient, which can be precomputed for sensible kernel choices. However, this formula can lead to unsymmetric pair forces, compromising the conservation of linear and angular momentum of the system. To symmetrize these forces depending on gradients (like those originating from pressure differences), we can use the product rule:

$$\nabla\left(\frac{P}{\rho}\right) = \frac{\nabla P}{\rho} - \frac{P}{\rho^2}\nabla\rho \quad \Leftrightarrow \quad \nabla P = \rho\left[\frac{P}{\rho^2}\nabla\rho + \nabla\left(\frac{P}{\rho}\right)\right]$$

to obtain an alternative approximation of gradient

$$\nabla P = \rho\left[\frac{P}{\rho^2}\sum_i \frac{m_i}{\rho_i}\rho_i\nabla W(\boldsymbol{r}-\boldsymbol{r}_i,h) + \sum_i \frac{m_i}{\rho_i}\frac{P_i}{\rho_i}\nabla W(\boldsymbol{r}-\boldsymbol{r}_i,h)\right]$$
$$= \rho\sum_i m_i\left(\frac{P}{\rho^2}+\frac{P_i}{\rho_i^2}\right)\nabla W(\boldsymbol{r}-\boldsymbol{r}_i,h) \tag{3}$$

which is antisymmetric for all interacting particle pairs. Viscosity forces on the other hand are proportional to the laplacian of the velocity field:

$$\nabla^2\boldsymbol{v} = \sum_i \frac{m_i}{\rho_i}(\boldsymbol{v}_i-\boldsymbol{v})\nabla^2 W(\boldsymbol{r}-\boldsymbol{r}_i,h) \tag{4}$$

and are always antisymmetric, since they depend on velocity difference $\boldsymbol{v}_i - \boldsymbol{v}$ between particles. In each timestep of the simulation, the density of all particles is first computed according to Eq. (1):

$$\rho = \sum_i m_i W(\boldsymbol{r}-\boldsymbol{r}_i,h) \tag{5}$$

as it depends only on the relative position of those. The pressure at each particle location is then obtained from its respective density through an equation of state. After this step, the pressure and viscosity forces are computed from the particle data and integrated back into the position and velocity of the particles.

3.2 Implementation

Simulation Initialization. Each simulation under our implementation consists of two elements, the coastline terrain (static) and the tsunami wave (dynamic). For the simulation setup, terrain is imported from a suitable 3D geometry definition file format, the initial conditions of the impacting wave (position and velocity) are configured and the desired discretization resolution for the fluid (i.e. the number of particles it is discretized into) is set. From these conditions, the terrain and fluid are initialized and key parameters are computed as subsequently described. Terrain geometry is uniformly scaled by a user-supplied factor and docked to the origin of coordinates and the particle effective radius r is determined such that the specified discretization resolution is achieved. Fluid particles are initially placed on a Hexagonal Close-Packed lattice covering the fluid initial position, in order to accomplish the densest possible packing and symmetry:

$$[x, y, z] = \left[2i + [(j + k) \bmod 2], \sqrt{3}[j + \frac{1}{3}(k \bmod 2)], \frac{2\sqrt{6}}{3}k \right] r \qquad (6)$$

In this configuration, the smoothing radius h is computed such that each particle has approximately 50 neighbours (following the empirical rule established in the literature). The timestep is calculated according to the Courant-Friedrichs-Lewy criterion:

$$\delta t_{\text{CFL}} = C \frac{\delta x}{v_{\text{max}}}, \qquad (7)$$

for values of Courant number $C \approx 0.5$ with characteristic length δx equal to the particle effective radius and maximum velocity v_{max} determined by the maximum mechanical energy in the initial configuration.

SPH Parameters. Following standard practice, we used three different smoothing kernels for density, pressure gradient and velocity laplacian computation, respectively:

$$W_{\text{poly6}}(r, h) = \frac{315}{64\pi h^9} \begin{cases} (h^2 - r^2)^3 & 0 \le r \le h \\ 0 & \text{otherwise} \end{cases} \qquad (8)$$

$$W_{\text{spiky}}(r, h) = \frac{15}{\pi h^6} \begin{cases} (h - r)^3 & 0 \le r \le h \\ 0 & \text{otherwise} \end{cases} \qquad (9)$$

$$\nabla W_{\text{spiky}}(r, h) = \frac{-45}{\pi h^6}(h - r)^2$$

$$W_{\text{viscosity}}(r, h) = \frac{15}{2\pi h^3} \begin{cases} -\frac{r^3}{2h^3} + \frac{r^2}{h^2} + \frac{h}{2r} - 1 & 0 \le r \le h \\ 0 & \text{otherwise,} \end{cases} \qquad (10)$$

$$\nabla^2 W_{\text{viscosity}}(r, h) = \frac{45}{\pi h^6}(h - r)$$

In each simulation step iteration, W_{poly6} is used as smoothing kernel for the fluid density estimation at each particle, based on its neighbour particle locations. W_{spiky} and $W_{\text{viscosity}}$ are substituted into Eqs. (3) and (4), in order to compute forces arising from pressure differences and viscosity, respectively. Fluid pressure is obtained from the estimated fluid density through the ideal gas equation of state:

$$P = k(\rho - \rho_0), \qquad (11)$$

according to which the pressure is proportional to the difference of the current from the rest density. The major problem with this equation of state are the compressibility issues that have been shown to exist in simulations using it.

A frequently proposed solution is to replace the above with the Tait equation of state:

$$P = B \left(\left(\frac{\rho}{\rho_0} \right)^{\gamma} - 1 \right), \tag{12}$$

where usually $\gamma = 7$ and B is a proportionality constant controlling the tolerance for density fluctuations. This equation is much more punishing on density fluctuations away from the rest density, therefore requiring significantly smaller timesteps to ensure stability.

Enhancements to SPH. In our framework we opted for a different solution, inspired by Position Based Fluids [15], in which particles are represented by spherical rigid bodies. The most important advantage of this technique is the elegant handling of boundary, undersampled and degenerate fluid regions that tend to arise very frequently in simulations of free flows. The adoption of this approach allows to treat boundary collisions in a simple manner, while naturally enforcing incompressibility near boundaries and free surfaces. In these regions, estimators fail to describe the actual flow regime due to neighbour particle shortage. This undersampling creates the need for correction procedures, usually involving ghost/boundary particles, to avoid pressure instabilities, particle clustering and other artifacts. On the contrary, no such method is necessary under our representation, where degenerative cases are handled through geometric constraints, thus selectively preventing unreliable estimations from affecting the flow.

Data Organization and Export. Rigid body dynamics are handled by the Bullet physics engine. A custom cell list data structure (LP grid) was implemented in order to optimize particle dynamic storage and access time. The simulation domain is divided by a regular 3D grid of spacing equal to the smoothing radius into cubic cells containing the fluid particles. Particles are generated as Bullet objects and are stored in the LP grid, which consists of three storage vectors. As shown in Fig. 1, particles are accessed by following pointers through

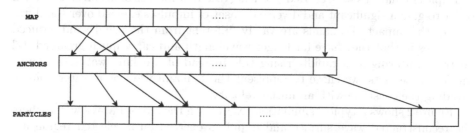

Fig. 1. Organization of the custom data structure designed for the efficient storing and interaction scanning between simulation particles. From top to bottom, `map` encodes the 3D to linear locality preserving mapping onto `anchors`, which in turn points to each cell's particles in `particles`.

those vectors in order. The map vector contains pointers to anchors and in turn anchors pointers to particles, which contains the simulation particles. Each cell's particles are continuously stored in the particles vector. Each element of anchors represents a cell and contains a pointer to the start of the region that contains that cell's particles in particles. Since SPH access patterns are heavily reliant on neighbour searching, increasing the locality in the linear order in which cells are stored is clearly beneficial to performance, due to better utilization of cache memory. For that reason, cells are represented spatially sorted along a space-filling curve in anchors (and consequently, particles), in order to maximize locality preservation from the 3D simulation domain to the linear storage. To efficiently address the cells, one extra layer encoding the locality preserving mapping has to be added, in the form of the first vector map. To access a cell, the three indices i_x, i_y, i_z specifying its position in the grid are converted to a linear index i (a simple way is through the formula $i = i_z * N_y * N_x + i_y * N_x + i_x$, where N_x N_y N_z is the number of cells along the x, y and z axis in the grid respectively). The map vector serves as a lookup table, so that its i-th element contains a pointer to that cell's representation on anchors. LP grid advantages include cohesive storage, quick neighbour search and interaction scanning, exploitation of the SPH algorithm access patterns and fast, in-place update.

Simulation is following the Bullet framework, with the SPH code being embedded as an internal timestep tick callback function. We took advantage of the Bullet infrastructure to extract detailed information about the collisions between fluid and terrain regarding the resulting impulse, time and location. Impulse and particle data are then written to multiple VTK files per frame. Samples of the smoothed color field (common name in the literature for the field having the value 1 at particle locations and 0 everywhere else) on the regular cell lattice are also exported, which are then used to reconstruct the fluid surface as an isosurface of that field. At the end of the simulation a cumulative impulse heatmap along with the scaled and docked terrain model is also provided.

4 Results

Multiple simulations were carried out using different models of urban coastline, in order to gain a significant and diverse dataset of impulses exerted over the duration of the impact. Tsunamis are vastly different from the usual wind-induced sea waves in that they have far longer wavelength and carry much greater total energy, appearing as a rapidly rising tide instead of breaking waves. Accounting for these facts, we chose to represent the tsunami wave as a water volume invading the coastline with an initial velocity.

Figure 2 shows a typical simulation result with the aid of Paraview^{TM}, where the reconstructed wave surface and impulses exerted on a selected region are visualized along the 3D terrain model and plotted on a histogram. Figure 3 shows impulse heatmaps generated by simulation of tsunami impact upon three different urban terrain models. The base ground width and depth of the models are in the order of 100 m and the fluid is discretized into 80 k particles, having

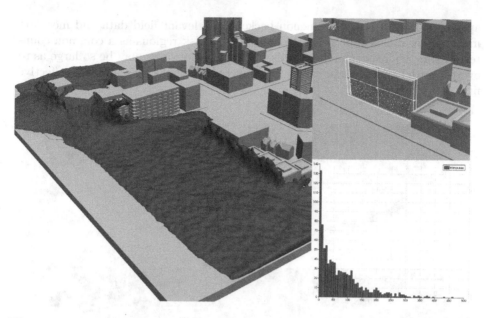

Fig. 2. Example visualization of impact data in Paraview^{TM}. Fluid surface is reconstructed as an isosurface of the color field, while impulses on the selected region are visualized as points on the 3D terrain model and in a histogram grouped by their magnitude.

Fig. 3. Tsunami impulse heatmaps for three different urban models visualized under Paraview^{TM}. Most of the wave's energy is absorbed by the first obstacle in its way.

an initial velocity of 10 m/s. Simulation time for each model was about 40 min on a x86_64 GNU/Linux desktop computer with an Intel^{TM} i7-3770 processor and 8 GB of main memory, accounting for 5 s of simulated time.

A comparison of the resulting impulse heatmap from the same tsunami impact upon an exposed coastline and one with a protective seawall is shown in Fig. 4. These heatmaps confirm a well-documented observation in the literature, i.e. that tsunami energy is absorbed mostly by the first obstacle in its way. This has been noted by Danielsen et al. [4] and Kathiresan and Narayanasamy [13], who both emphasized the protective role coastal vegetation (mangrove forests) played in mitigating the impact effects of the 2004 Indian Ocean tsunami. The same conclusion has been reached by Yanagisawa et al. [21] through theoretical approximation of the phenomenon backed by relevant field data and measurements. Seawalls have been constructed in high-risk regions as a common countermeasure against tsunami hazards. Although the waves may be so large as to overtop such barriers, these cases are somewhat rare, making seawalls an effective first line of defense.

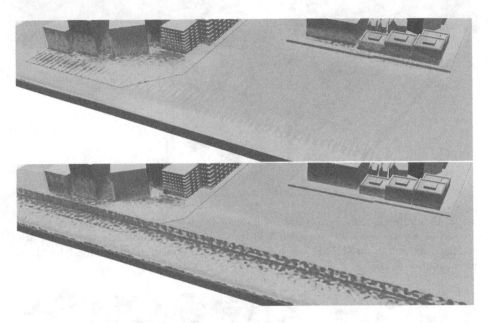

Fig. 4. Comparison between the impulse heatmap of a tsunami hit on the same urban coastline model, without (top) and with (bottom) the protection of a seawall. Seawalls are commonly found in high-risk areas, as they reduce impact effects significantly.

The performance of the simulation program was satisfactory, there is however a substantial margin for improvement. Figure 5 shows a plot of the mean computation time per internal timestep for variable fluid resolution. It is important to note that a higher number of simulation particles imposes a shorter internal timestep due to their smaller effective radius. These measurements are also representative of the worst-case scenario, as due to the initial fluid conditions the particles are closely packed in a single body of fluid, thus having maximum number of mutual interactions and reducing the performance gains from our spatial hashing data structure. About 75 % of runtime is spent in single-threaded code consisting mostly of Bullet and I/O operations, while the rest corresponds to multi-threaded code of our SPH engine.

Although our framework provides rich and detailed data, a quantitative comparison to either field measurements or results of other methods utilizing different versions of the SPH formulation couldn't be reliably made. We haven't yet implemented a way to configure the wave's initial conditions and coastline terrain to

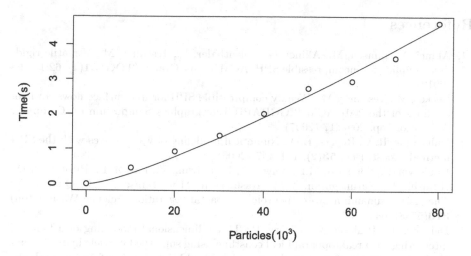

Fig. 5. Plot showing the mean simulation time (in seconds) per internal timestep for the first 10 output frames (each frame was set to 0.05 s of simulated time), for 10 k to 80 k particles (continuous line represents $O(nlog_2 n)$ growth).

model the impact according to predictions of large scale simulations or data from past incidents. Qualitatively, our method seems to compare well to similar codes utilizing SPH to simulate small scale tsunami interactions with coastline structures. Other methods usually make use of SPH enhancements originating from the CFD literature, which aim to improve some aspect of the flow (for example incompressibility, regarding WCSPH). In this particular application domain though, boundary interactions can be arguably considered more important than the flow itself. Our approach, enriching SPH with direct positional constraint solving, shows promise as an efficient way for dealing explicitly and exactly with momentum preservation and detailed fluid-structure impulse recording.

5   Conclusions

We presented the theoretical background and implementation of an enriched SPH framework, whose main purpose was the faithful simulation and detailed recording of the forces exerted upon the coastline during a tsunami impact. The chosen output file format lends itself to rich visualizations, allowing for a quick overview of complex simulation data. Multiple simulations have been carried out, resulting in interesting visualizations of impact data and evaluation of defense mechanisms. Furthermore, detailed impulse logs are provided, which can then be processed to extract relevant high level information. Possible future extensions could be the incorporation of wider, dynamic terrain models, including nearby seabed, the adjustment of the fluid initial conditions to match those predicted by large scale shallow water or Boussinesq models and performance optimizations in the implementation towards a more integrated dataflow scheme.

References

1. Akinci, N., Ihmsen, M., Akinci, G., Solenthaler, B., Teschner, M.: Versatile rigid-fluid coupling for incompressible SPH. ACM Trans. Graph. (TOG) **31**(4), 62:1–62:8 (2012)
2. Becker, M., Teschner, M.: Weakly compressible SPH for free surface flows. In Proceedings of the 2007 ACM SIGGRAPH/Eurographics Symposium on Computer Animation, pp. 209–217 (2007)
3. Dalrymple, R.A., Rogers, B.D.: Numerical modeling of water waves with the SPH method. Coast. Eng. **53**(2), 141–147 (2006)
4. Danielsen, F., Sørensen, M.K., Olwig, M.F., Selvam, V., Parish, F., Burgess, N.D., Hiraishi, T., Karunagaran, V.M., Rasmussen, M.S., Hansen, L.B., Quarto, A.: The Asian tsunami: a protective role for coastal vegetation. Science(Washington) **310**(5748), 643 (2005)
5. Debroux, F., Prakash, M., Cleary, P.: Three-dimensional modelling of a tsunami interacting with real topographical coastline using smoothed particle hydrodynamics. In: Proceedings of the 14th Australasian Fluid Mechanics Conference, Adelaide, Australia, pp. 311–314 (2001)
6. Desbrun, M., Cani, M.P.: Smoothed particles: a new paradigm for animating highly deformable bodies. In: Boulic, R., Hégron, G. (eds.) Computer Animation and Simulation 1996. Eurographics, pp. 61–76. Springer, Wien (1996)
7. Domínguez, J.M., Crespo, A.J., Gómez-Gesteira, M., Marongiu, J.C.: Neighbour lists in smoothed particle hydrodynamics. Int. J. Numer. Meth. Fluids **67**(12), 2026–2042 (2011)
8. Gingold, R.A., Monaghan, J.J.: Smoothed particle hydrodynamics: theory and application to non-spherical stars. Mon. Not. R Astron. Soc. **181**(3), 375–389 (1977)
9. Gómez-Gesteira, M., Dalrymple, R.A.: Using a three-dimensional smoothed particle hydrodynamics method for wave impact on a tall structure. J. Waterw. Port Coast. Ocean Eng. **130**(2), 63–69 (2004)
10. Ihmsen, M., Cornelis, J., Solenthaler, B., Horvath, C., Teschner, M.: Implicit incompressible SPH. IEEE Trans. Vis. Comput. Graph. **20**(3), 426–435 (2014)
11. Ioualalen, M., Asavanant, J., Kaewbanjak, N., Grilli, S.T., Kirby, J.T., Watts, P.: Modeling the 26 December 2004 Indian Ocean tsunami: case study of impact in Thailand. J. Geophys. Res. Oceans **112**(C7) (2007)
12. Kakinuma, T.: 3D numerical simulation of tsunami runup onto a complex beach. In: Advanced Numerical Models for Simulating Tsunami Waves and Runup, pp. 255–260 (2008)
13. Kathiresan, K., Rajendran, N.: Coastal mangrove forests mitigated tsunami. Estuar. Coast. Shelf Sci. **65**(3), 601–606 (2005)
14. Lucy, L.B.: A numerical approach to the testing of the fission hypothesis. Astron. J. **82**, 1013–1024 (1977)
15. Macklin, M., Müller, M.: Position based fluids. ACM Trans. Graph. **32**(4), 104:1–104:12 (2013)
16. Müller, M., Charypar, D., Gross, M.: Particle-based fluid simulation for interactive applications. In: Proceedings of the 2003 ACM SIGGRAPH/Eurographics Symposium on Computer Animation, pp. 154–159 (2003)
17. Samaras, A.G., Karambas, T.V., Archetti, R.: Simulation of tsunami generation, propagation and coastal inundation in the Eastern Mediterranean. Ocean Sci. **11**(4), 643–655 (2015)

18. Solenthaler, B., Pajarola, R.: Predictive-corrective incompressible SPH. ACM Trans. Graph. (TOG) **28**(3), 40:1–40:6 (2009)
19. St-Germain, P., Nistor, I., Townsend, R., Shibayama, T.: Smoothed-particle hydrodynamics numerical modeling of structures impacted by tsunami bores. J. Waterw. Port Coast. Ocean Eng. **140**(1), 66–81 (2014)
20. Wang, X., Liu, P.L.F.: Numerical simulations of the 2004 Indian Ocean tsunamis-coastal effects. J. Earthq. Tsunami **1**(3), 273–297 (2007)
21. Yanagisawa, H., Koshimura, S., Goto, K., Miyagi, T., Imamura, F., Ruangrassamee, A., Tanavud, C.: The reduction effects of mangrove forest on a tsunami based on field surveys at Pakarang Cape, Thailand and numerical analysis. Estuar. Coast. Shelf Sci. **81**(1), 27–37 (2009)

Design and Implementation of a Low Cost Virtual Rugby Decision Making Interactive

Alan Cummins[✉] and Cathy Craig

School of Psychology, Queen's University of Belfast, Belfast, UK
a.cummins@qub.ac.uk

Abstract. The paper describes the design and implementation of a novel low cost virtual rugby decision making interactive for use in a visitor centre. Original laboratory-based experimental work in decision making in rugby, using a virtual reality headset [1] is adapted for use in a public visitor centre, with consideration given to usability, costs, practicality and health and safety. Movement of professional rugby players was captured and animated within a virtually recreated stadium. Users then interact with these virtual representations via use of a low-cost sensor (Microsoft Kinect) to attempt to block them. Retaining the principles of perception and action, egocentric viewpoint, immersion, sense of presence, representative design and game design the system delivers an engaging and effective interactive to illustrate the underlying scientific principles of deceptive movement. User testing highlighted the need for usability, system robustness, fair and accurate scoring, appropriate level of difficulty and enjoyment.

Keywords: Perception and action · HCI · Game design · Interactive · Sport

1 Introduction

This paper describes the design and implementation of a rugby side step interactive for use in an education and heritage visitor centre in Belfast, N.Ireland. This interactive is based on ground breaking deceptive movement research conducted by [1] and allows users to attempt to virtually block animated rugby players running towards them. The virtual rugby players are carrying out different side steps (deceptive movements) of varying levels of difficulty. The paper will briefly describe the research and the design of the system with reference to the psychological principles underpinning the work.

Original work by Brault et al. [1] explored how coordinated body movement can be used to not only communicate action intention but also to deceive an opponent. The researchers made use of an interactive VR environment to present real body movement (deceptive and non-deceptive), captured from real rugby players using motion capture. These body movements were then used to animate virtual rugby avatars that make side-step movements to try and beat a defender. Participants were asked to predict the final running direction of the virtual attacker (See Fig. 1). An analysis of the participants' responses showed that expert players focused more on the visual information that specified true running direction (i.e. the avatar's centre of mass) compared to the novice users

© Springer International Publishing Switzerland 2016
L.T. De Paolis and A. Mongelli (Eds.): AVR 2016, Part I, LNCS 9768, pp. 16–32, 2016.
DOI: 10.1007/978-3-319-40621-3_2

who tended to focus more on the deceptive movement signals (upper trunk yaw and out-foot placement) that fooled them into thinking the avatar was running in the opposite direction. Further, it was found that experts waited significantly longer before making a decision. This delay in movement initiation allowed experts to pick-up more visual information which in turn allowed them to be more accurate in their decisions. It should be noted, however, that this delay was possible due to the superior action capabilities of the experts (i.e. their ability to cover the distance quicker than novices). This cutting edge experiment made use of expensive virtual reality equipment and a large laboratory space to fully immerse the participant in the virtual environment. The current work highlighted in this paper, aims to transpose the essence of the aforementioned research into an interactive that can be employed in a public space with the associated limitations in complexity, practicality and cost of the equipment used.

Fig. 1. Original work by Brault et al. [1]. (A) Participant wears custom VR backpack. (B) Deceptive MOCAP animation of French rugby players within Virtools. (C) Participant moves to intercept the virtual player. (D) Makes use of Intersense IS-900 tracking with Cybermind Visette45 HMD.

The interactive aimed to provide a physical and cognitive experience of a key component of the game of rugby (namely blocking an attacking player), while additionally, illustrating the importance of the dynamics of human movement in signaling action intentions. Meaningful participation for visitors in a museum setting is challenging [2]. In order to provide such meaningful participation fundamental psychological research was adapted to engage, entertain and educate the user.

2 Design

Psychological principles underlying design choices will be outlined, followed by a description of the system designed.

2.1 Egocentric Viewpoint

In order to measure perception and action we need a methodology that can adequately and accurately recreate this perception/action loop from the player's perspective (e.g. head mounted cameras [3]). In other words, we need to use technology that allows us to recreate an athlete's (egocentric) 3D viewpoint of an unfolding sports related event that can be updated in real time. An egocentric viewpoint is essential to provide players with the relevant information necessary to act in a natural manner. In the original work a head mounted display combined with a low latency tracking system was used (Cybermind Visesette45 with an Intersense IS-900 ultrasonic positioning system). This methodology has been adapted for use in other context such as cricket bowling, gap perception in rugby and goal-keeping [4–7]. However, in adapting the work for use in a visitor centre setting, use of such equipment was cost-prohibitive and does not lend itself to long-term practical use. Furthermore, it does not allow other visitors to share the experience in a satisfactory way, with head mounted display ego-motion resulting in a very jittery image. To overcome these limitations a large screen was used to present the action, geometry sized to provide a one to one mapping of movement in the real world to movement in the virtual display. This provided a perceptual window of the virtual stadium, where the virtual player could be perceived as moving towards the visitor playing the game. A Microsoft Kinect camera system was used to update the viewpoint in real-time with the image moving left or right as the visitor moved. Although the projection was not in 3-D, having a depth cue such as motion parallax generated by the ego-motion of the visitor, offered a much more compelling experience.

2.2 Immersion

Immersion is related to the technical capability that a system has. It aids sense of presence but is distinct in that it relates to technical specification. The system designed for the visitor centre acknowledged that the technical specification of the original work would need to be reduced but that this does not necessarily have to impact on the sense of presence perceived by the user. i.e. there may be a low level of immersion but a high level of presence.

2.3 Sense of Presence

Sense of presence is highly related to immersion, although a discrete concept, defined by [8] subjective perception in which an individual's experience is generated by technology but that that experience is perceived without acknowledging the role of the technology i.e. an individual is present in a virtual experience but feels that it is real in some subjective sense. It has been argued that VR systems provide the potential, through improving, technology to immerse an individual and provide a sense of presence. However, sense of presence is not solely defined or constrained by the complexity or technical capability of the hardware used. As previously discussed, a reduced technological solution was deemed most appropriate in the context of use. Therefore a number of factors were combined into the design to improve the sense of presence based on the factors highlighted in the work of Schuemie et al. [9].

- Immediacy of control: The Microsoft Kinect makes use of a camera-based system to estimate body position and as such the user does not need to wear any additional sensors. With this minimum abstraction between movement and movement-based feedback, an immediacy of control was provided.
- Anticipation: It was paramount to capture the real movement of players as the provision of naturalistic performance provides the best source of information to allow players to anticipate direction of travel. With sufficient control, immediacy and anticipation, perception of movement also contributed to the sense of presence.
- Mode of control: The user interface was purposefully simplified to avoid any complicated gestures. This included reducing any initial input to the system via player selection or otherwise. Rather than make use of gestures to control the game, a simple button press was used to start the interactive. Further, calibration was included within the game mechanic and hidden from the end-user. Interaction was only provided via body movement (stepping side to side) in a natural manner.
- Modality of Information and multimodal presentation: Information was provided for both the visual and auditory sensory channels to draw the user more into the interactive. The stadium was recreated and actual sounds from an Ulster rugby game were captured. Realistic game commentary and feedback were recorded from a well-known sports commentator and embedded throughout the game to further enhance the user experience. Clear sound and visual information were also combined to provide clear playing instructions and provide performance feedback during game play.
- Environmental richness: High-resolution models of known objects (e.g. Kingspan stadium), realistic player avatar movement and recognisable stadium sounds all contributed to an environmentally enriched experience.
- Reduction of distraction features: The experience was designed to provide an augmented reality i.e. the player movement in the real world has an effect on the virtual world laid out. This was enhanced through the use of grass flooring which stretched from the real world through to the virtual pitch. Further, the game is played within a semi-enclosed space, reducing outside distraction and drawing the visitor into the interactive experience.
- Meaningfulness of the experience: The experience attempts to provide a means of interacting with professional rugby players, watching their real movement while attempting to block them as they attempt to deceive and pass. Essentially, the meaningfulness of the experience should relate to the real world [A]. The system provided the capability to do so with players reporting that they felt immersed within the experience, albeit without any physical contact.
- Realistic performance: Sense of presence was enhanced through the presentation and measurement of real performance of both virtual character and the player (i.e. performance feedback score (block = 10 points, half-block = 5 points, miss = 0 points) at the end of each trial).

2.4 Representative Design

An important factor when designing a system is to maintain an interactive relationship between an organism and his/her environment so that the behaviour observed in an experimental context mirrors, as closely as possible, the behaviour observed in a realistic sport setting [10]. The concept of representative design introduced by Brunswik emphasised the need to have experimental tasks that allow the player to pick up perceptual information that specifies a property of the environment actor system [11, 12]. The system made use of real captured movement to ensure that behaviour elicited would closely match those found in a realistic sporting setting.

2.5 Perception and Action

Related to representative design, is the notion of perception and action coupling. Gibson said that "We must perceive in order to move but we must also move in order to perceive" [10]. In the context of sport, players are active (rather than passive) perceivers who continuously engage in exploratory behaviours that allow them to pick up important information to guide their decisions about when and how to act. In other words, their behaviour emerges from their egocentric perception of what the environment affords at a given moment in time (active perception) and what the actor is capable of doing (action capabilities) [13]. The system maintains the perception-action loop, allowing players to act upon the perceived heading direction. A mere button-press would miss this important concept. Decision-making emerges from the constraints in the player-environment interaction. Affordances emerge as a player interacts with the system. This unfolding dynamic allows each player to obtain a unique performance, based on their own action capabilities. This perception-action loop should be maintained through mapping of movement in the real world in the virtual [14].

2.6 Functional Fidelity

In a review by Miles et al. [15] noted that the most important factor for using virtual reality technology in a sporting context is functional fidelity. Research suggests that picture realism is not a determining factor when trying to use virtual reality technology to elicit realistic sporting behaviours [16, 17]. Rather, it is the extent to which the user can interact with the environment and respond as they would in the real world that predominates [18]. However, work by Vignais et al. [19] highlights that visual fidelity can play a factor with a need for sufficient communication of the simulated movement within an animation. An observer's own movement (action) must be incorporated into changes in the display (perception). By maintaining this aspect from real-life, the perception/action loop experienced will be carried over from real to virtual and the level of behavioural realism, or functional fidelity, in a virtual environment will be significantly increased [20]. Functional fidelity includes aspects such as accurate representation of player movement, time and place appropriate interaction which maintains real time response, captured via natural interaction with the environment and replication of the physical properties of those interactions.

2.7 System Design

Game Design. The operational definition of a computer game as defined by Pauli et al. is playful interaction with a computer which involves an effort to overcome unnecessary obstacles [21]. There are many benefits of game playing: Enjoyment and pleasure, sense of structure, motivation, activity, flow since games are adaptive, learning as games have outcomes and provide feedback, ego gratification, excitement, creativity, emotion and social learning [22]. Flow experience is defined as consisting of eight fundamental elements [23]. These are that a task can be completed, that there is an ability to concentrate on the task, that there are clear goals and immediate feedback to facilitate this, that a sense of control over actions emerges which is effortful but achievable, that concern for self disappears but emerges more strongly after the task is complete and that the sense of duration of time is altered. Flow has been identified as a major reason for the attractiveness of a game [24]. They state that dual-flow is required to keep a player in a state of flow. This comprises of the dual flow of attractiveness and effectiveness. Good game design comes out of four main principles: the designer, context, participants and meaningful play [25]. Building on this, Salonius-Pasternak and Gelfond suggested that effective game design should meet the needs of its intended audience in terms of expectations and characteristics of the audience [26]. The audience was defined as young people from age six upwards with a wide range of exposure to rugby. With these considerations in mind, the aim was to provide an informative, realistic but playful movement game interactive to illustrate the aforementioned psychological components involved in deceptive movement in rugby. The following sections describe the design and implementation of the interactive based on the game design concepts discussed.

Game Mechanics. To play the interactive users must attempt to block an approaching virtual player. A total of six different players perform a pre-recorded deceptive movement to either the left or right side of the user. The user attempts to block the virtual player by anticipating the correct running direction and then moving to the correct side. The game algorithm determines if a full, half or no block has occurred by detecting the user body position relative to the avatar as the avatar passes the user. Performance feedback is given after each attempted block and a final score is presented to user at the end of the six trials.

Scoring. Scoring was based on a 0 (no tackle), 5 (partial tackle) and 10 (full tackle) point scale. Initial conception was based on scoring related to a higher number of body markers but this proved to have little impact on the end score achieved and complicated the scoring dynamic. Rather only six tracked components were taken into account to determine if there was a collision between the virtual player and the user. These were left, right and centre shoulder, left, right and centre hips. A half block was scored if the user collided with the virtual player bounding box (See Fig. 2) with either the left or right hip and/or left or right shoulder (depending on the correct end running direction) while a full block was scored if the centre of the user's body collided with the virtual player. This provided sufficient complexity and granularity of score to provide a range of scores for each play of the interactive. The scoring system chosen focuses on providing effective, simple feedback based on clear objectives to maximise engagement and motivation [27]. Additionally, a focus on simulation misses an opportunity to engage the player's fantasy and as such pure accurate simulation was adapted to allow for better user engagement. This simplification of the collision detection algorithm avoided a complex interaction between the user's various body parts and those of the virtual player i.e. in real-life it becomes important to consider whether an arm or leg and associated contact points, among many other factors, would result in a successful tackle. This gamification of this rugby playing scenario allowed for non-rugby experts to engage more readily with the interactive. Score therefore could not be equated to rugby playing ability. Instead, this interactive looks only at whether a successful movement decision was made with a successful stopping tackle being filled in via user fantasy.

Fig. 2. (A) Kinect Points (blue dots) which represent the user's body segments. (B) Simple bounding box on the virtual player to inform collision detection between the user and the virtual player. (C) One to one mapping between the physical and the virtual space. (Color figure online)

Player Movement. Player movement within the game was detected using a low cost movement sensor (Microsoft Kinect V1) (See Fig. 2). This hardware provided sufficient speed of movement detection and processing (25 fps) to allow for the detection of the player's movement response in real-time. Although the Microsoft Kinect can detect multiple users, it was decided to simplify control by always detecting the last player in the predefined playing space. Although the Microsoft Kinect allows for gestural control, it was decided to minimise complex interactions within the interactive by ignoring this functionality. This meant that users were not required to learn any calibration movements or use gestural control to navigate the game environment. Movement was reduced to a one-to-one mapping of movement in the virtual space and detected displacement in the physical game playing space. As mentioned above, a reduced set of body points were also used to simplify scoring and to ensure that a wide range of body sizes and morphologies could be tracked. The tracked positions were head, shoulders (mid, left and right) and hips (mid, left and right) with side-to-side movement being mapped via detection of the user's head position. By in turn mapping this movement to a virtual camera a motion parallax effect was produced which enhanced both the sense of movement and immersion in the game. In agreement with Isbister and Mueller, the game provided feedback on the end result of the movement, i.e. whether a block was made or not, rather than on the quality of the actual movement itself [28]. This ambiguity allowed for the sensor to provide sufficient feedback while allowing individual users to use a range of different movements to achieve similar results. Within the context of the interactive, this type of tracking provided sufficient complexity to allow for the user's accurate detection of deceptive movement without adding other more sport specific factors such as correct body position required for a real rugby tackle.

Sound Design. As previously mentioned, audio was recorded by a well-known commentator. A script was provided with a series of responses to various game actions. The commentator was also asked to adapt the script accordingly to ensure his own unique style of presentation was captured. This was then edited with Adobe Audition to create clear, volume-levelled audio for use in-game. Throughout the game a random selection of appropriate audio segments were used to ensure players did not become fatigued by repeated audio, with the instructions, the only consistent component. Audio was used to entice players, clearly explain rules of the game, provide positive reinforcing feedback during game play and provide a summary at the end of each game session. Stadium ambiance was captured during a regular season game to capture crowd chants and supporter band songs.

Visual Presentation. As mentioned above, consideration was given to the presentation of the interactive, making use of a low-cost head mounted display. However, this was ruled out to reduce health and safety risks (VR sickness, movement in a virtual space with physical constraints, loose wiring), the inability for other users to simultaneously share the experience and also due to costs (hardware maintenance and durability, initial hardware investment). Curved projection was also considered but ruled out, due to costs, space limitations and weighting of improved experience versus a flat screen. Additionally, passive 3D projection was considered to aid immersion. However, this was ruled out for several reasons. Firstly, the nature of animations produced with regard to speed and time on screen would not benefit from 3D presentation. Secondly, users would be required to wear 3D glasses which were deemed impractical in an unmanned exhibition space. Thirdly, the interactive was designed to be viewed simultaneously by other visitors and therefore 3D projection would have appeared blurred without everyone wearing passive glasses. The space dedicated to the interactive was defined prior to consultation with the design team. As such, there was limited fixed space, within which to fit an interactive. That being said, the play space was designed to optimise the visual display screen to encompass and immerse the player within the interactive. A screen of size of 3.5 m × 2.625 m was installed to produce as large an image as possible that would span the entire play area (wall to wall and floor to ceiling). A Panasonic PT-EX510, fitted with short throw lens, was used to display images.

Physical Layout. The play space measured a total of 3.5 m × 3.95 m. Within this, a dedicated action zone was demarcated via floor markings and lighting control (See Fig. 3). This helped the user to position himself/herself in the ideal playing position. There was initial concern that the player would not reposition themselves at the centre of the game-play area at the end of each movement. However, the players, in the majority of cases automatically repositioned themselves in the centre of the game area with an inherent understanding of how the game worked and how placement in the centre would best optimise their chances of success. A run-off space either side of the main game zone was incorporated to ensure physical risk to players was minimised while they engaged with the interactive [28]. Artificial grass flooring was used to extend the perception of the virtual pitch out into the physical space, increasing the level of presence within the virtual environment. In order to cater for the greatest range of user characteristics careful consideration was given to the positioning of both the player tracking sensor (the Kinect) and the projector. The play space was limited by the capabilities of the Kinect Sensor (1.2 m - 3.5 m) and the physical limitations imposed by the space available in the visitor centre.

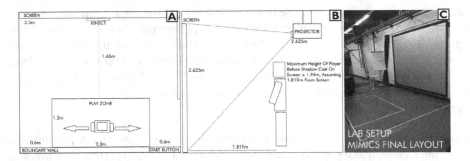

Fig. 3. Physical layout of the play space. (A) Overhead view of the space (B) overhead front projection (C) final physical space layout mocked in the movement innovation lab

Front-projection was used and therefore the possibility of a shadow being cast on screen by a user needed careful consideration. Optimum placement was made to allow players ranging in height, from 0.6 m to 1.93 m, to play the game. Those that fell outside this range could still play although body tracking became less reliable as body segments began to fall outside the tracked volume and a shadow was cast on the screen for those greater in height. A virtual representation of the player on screen was considered but it was decided to use the real-world one-to-one mapping to provide players with a sense of position i.e. the player position was not manipulated to fit the game mechanic.

Virtual Player Likenesses. Player likenesses were recreated by South West College making use of Autodesk Maya. Reference images of player faces were captured during motion capture sessions and sample shirt images were used to add player clothing. Anthropometric measurements were taken of every player to include head, neck, chest, waist, bicep, calf and thigh circumference alongside weight, height and length of main body segments. These were then incorporated into each model to closely match the real rugby player's dimensions. Each player had a skeleton attached. Models were saved in the fbx file format and imported into Unity, following standard naming conventions (See Fig. 4). Motion capture was carried out over a number of sessions making use of 22 Qualisys Motion Capture cameras (Oqus 3 and Oqus 3+) arranged to capture a 6 m × 10 m action space (See Fig. 4). Joints and body segments were markered-up providing a total of 56 passive reflective markers on each player. Their motion was then captured while carrying out a number of set movements which included walks, jog, run, idle, celebration, deceptive and non-deceptive side-steps. Side-steps were carried out against an opponent to aid timing and encourage realistic movement. Multiple trials were captured and from these a subset was selected for labelling and conversion into animation files. Labelled files were imported into Autodesk Motionbuilder software tied to an actor and subsequently to the custom 3D player likeness. For animations requiring additional length, the player's own run was merged and hand adjusted to create a seamless complete animation. Finally, finger position was manipulated for each player to ensure a rugby ball appeared to correctly sit in-hand during the virtual animations of the deceptive movements (side-steps). Each movement lasted approximately four seconds. By capturing the professional rugby player's real movements, it was possible to capture a number of deceptive movements. These deceptive movements are unique to each player and involved different relevant orientation/reorientation parameters, medio-lateral displacement of the center of mass (COM), foot, head, upper trunk, and lower trunk yaw; and upper trunk roll as described in the precursor work [1]. Essentially, by use of false exaggerated parameters of movement combined with postural stabilisation, each rugby player was able to produce deceptive movements that could deceive a defender with varying levels of success. These varying levels of success were harnessed to create an interactive that catered to a large range of capabilities.

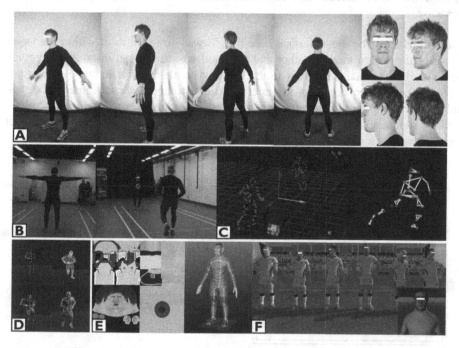

Fig. 4. Player likeness. (A) Reference photography of all players. (B) MOCAP using Qualisys. (C) Data cleanup and labelling. (D) Mapping in Autodesk Motionbuilder. (E) Texturing for normal, specular and diffuse. (F) In-game player rendering

3D Environment. The 3D environment consisted of a recreation of the Kingspan Stadium, Ulster Rugby (See Fig. 5). Initial architecture concept had been developed within Google SketchUp by Ulster Rugby Architecture and Design Contractors. This model was imported into Unity 3D and further refined to include necessary elements such as rugby posts, stadium hoardings, flood lights, home and away player seating, field markings etc.

Fig. 5. Final interactive (A) Nevin Spence Centre with the bottom panel showing a visitor playing the interactive (B) user interface instruction elements (C) final virtual player depictions within the interactive

User Interface. The user interface (See Fig. 5) was designed to fit within the larger visitor centre design motif (Mather and Co.) and was developed in-house to provide clear visual and textual guidance to users. This was combined with auditory instructions to ensure that all users could quickly interact. The instructions chosen aimed to be clear and concise while providing sufficient information for any user to begin play without need for additional assistance. In addition use of iconography was made to ensure that users were given a visual indication of actions required.

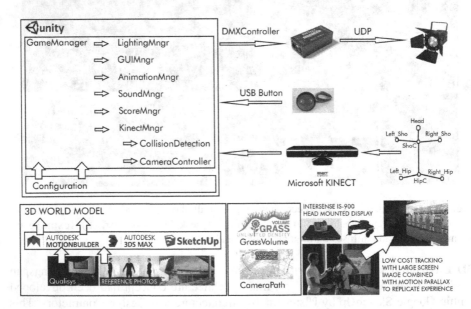

Fig. 6. System elements that enable the interface with the external hardware elements

System. The system was developed using the game engine Unity Professional 4.0. Third party assets were used which included grass pitch (VolumeGrass), stadium flyover camera manager (CameraPath) and the Microsoft KinectWrapper V1.7 Unity plugin. The program consists of a main manager class which handles game mechanics and is supported by a number of specialised classes to handle player animation, player collision, audio, user interface and lighting interface (See Fig. 6). A custom Unity plugin was written to communicate over UDP with a DMX Control unit to control lighting (fading, flashing, colour change). Configuration parameters were provided to control the game which included timing (audio, in-game, idle components), sound volume, lighting configuration (speed, intensity, colour), scoring metric and default user position relative to the virtual environment. A Microsoft Windows 7 PC (Intel core i7, Nvidia GT700 series card, 16 Gb RAM) was used to run the program connecting to a Microsoft Kinect V1 via USB. A USB start button was used to trigger game start.

3   User Testing

Previous research has shown that virtual deceptive movement can be shown to a user and can illicit natural behaviours in response to those stimuli, albeit within an experimental laboratory settings. However, in adapting the original research work for a visitor centre interactive there were a number of unknowns that required user testing. Testing was carried out in a cyclical manner with input from both end users and subject matter experts (VR, Rugby, Exhibition Design). Testing was carried out via prototyping, in-lab (Movement Innovation Lab, Queen's University of Belfast), in large-scale public testing (Make it Digital, Northern Ireland Festival event, BBC BlackStaff Studios) and in final production settings (Ulster Rugby, Kingspan Stadium, Nevin Spence Centre). Aspects considered during testing included:

3.1   Motion Perception Using Parallax Motion

Initial design proposed that user movement alone would provide sufficient connection between the virtual and physical environment. However, additional movement queues were required to engage the user and provide a perception of physical movement mapped into the virtual space.

3.2   Sufficiently Accurate Body Segment Detection

As the system made use of reduced segment tracking it was important to understand if users perceived this as acceptable within the confines of the game mechanics. The users perceived tackling as responsive and accurate to their own expectations of play. Further, testing highlighted the flexibility of body tracking used in that users of many different heights, wearing different types of clothing were sufficiently tracked to allow for game-play throughout. The design essentially made use of the limitations of the Microsoft Kinect to help ensure relevant appropriate movement detection within the game confines

[28]. By allowing for ambiguity in movement and collision an appropriate balance was created to ensure users felt gameplay reacted in an expected way.

3.3 Unexpected Actions

Testing was paramount to understand unexpected or unplanned events that might occur during game use. Examples included users attempting to cheat the system (moving towards screen before virtual player runs past them), swapping users mid-game, a user helping another user to play (e.g. holding a younger player). Users did attempt to run forward within the play space to intercept the player before a deceptive movement was made. This was counteracted by creating a virtual zone, within which collision detection occurred. This minimised the effect of cheating the system.

3.4 User Experience of Virtual Tackle

This ties to the previous section but relates to the user experience of tackling and whether users perceived correctly that a tackle should have been made or missed. Initial testing was carried out in the laboratory using subject matter experts (experienced with VR systems, original system, experienced rugby players and coaches). This testing led to movement of fixed camera position relative to the z-direction in the virtual space. This meant that virtual player made their deceptive movement within screen space and then proceeded to virtually run past the physical point where the user was stood.

3.5 Level of Difficulty

Games should be challenging but not so much as to feel frustrating with [29] suggesting that there should be an attempt made to keep players in 'flow' which is a balance between challenge and ability. The level of difficulty of the movements was assessed through play-testing in-lab and in testing as part of the BBC Make It Digital Festival 2015. Initial design proposals considered balancing the game difficulty by combining a set of known player movements based on their average level of difficulty so as to provide a consistent level of difficulty to each and every user. However, during play-testing it became apparent that the level of difficulty was sufficiently set via randomisation of player movements that no further grouping of movements was required. Figure 7 shows the average score per virtual player for a total of 242 individual tackles, averaged over both, left and right final direction heading. The average score across all users for all virtual players is 5.8 (Std dev 2.9), indicating that, typically, users can make some connection with the virtual player. It is clear that players 3 and 4 were found to be more deceptive (and more difficult to block) as average scores are much lower (4.5 and 3 respectively). However, because every user faces deceptive movements from all six virtual players, the level of difficulty is sufficiently mixed to allow users to experience sufficient challenge while also rewarding play.

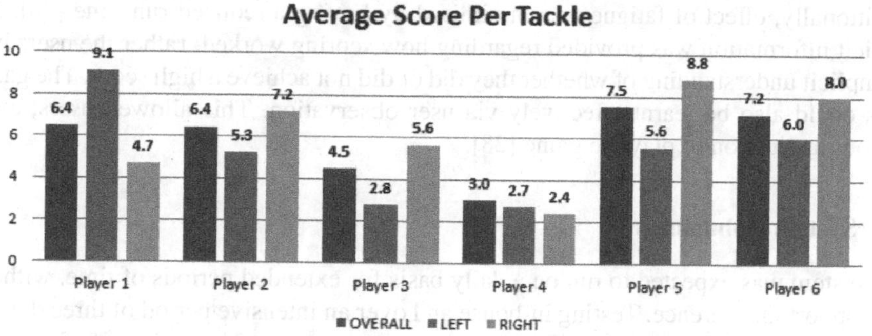

Average Score Per Tackle

Fig. 7. Average score per tackle for each virtual player

Further, consideration was given to the level of difficulty as it applied to the physical capabilities of the user i.e. would a younger player find the interactive more or less challenging than an older user. It was found that both younger and older players found the interactive equally difficult. The physical movement required to block a player was minimal so the challenge lay in attempting to perceive and anticipate the final running direction of the player and act upon it in a timely manner. This allowed users from five years upwards to play. It is important to note that challenge and difficulty are intended in games but this does not mean that the style of interaction should be the overriding means of challenge [30]. The skills required to perform in-game were directly related to the perceived affordances made available to players. The interactive aimed to high-light the skill of the professional players involved and the skill required to anticipate or react to that deceptive movement by the user. Therefore, the game difficulty needed to remain fairly high. However, the game also aimed to provide an engaging yet enjoyable experience so a balance was struck via choice of user body position and collision detection to achieve a score.

3.6 Understanding Usability

Usability testing was carried out in the lab by (i) domain experts (interactive design subject matter experts, VR systems experts), (ii) several groups of younger users within a controlled lab environment (three groups of twenty users, ranging in age from eight to sixteen), (iii) three hundred plus users of all ages at the NI Science Festival and (iv) via a soft opening of the visitor centre for a period of three months. Instructions were made to be self-explanatory as the interactive would not be manned by staff. Further, the instructions provided sufficient visual information to allow play with or without hearing accompanying auditory instructions. Several hard of hearing users tested the interactive and were able to understand and play the game without any assis-tance. Each tackle was preceded by a graphic and whistle sound to prepare the user. As the interactive was part of a larger visitor centre tour, it was important that total playtime was not excessive to avoid bottlenecks. Input from experienced visitor centre concept designers suggested that the game should run for no longer than one minute and thirty seconds (note this varied slightly depending on duration of audio feedback).

Additionally, effect of fatigue was minimised by having a reduced run-time [28]. No explicit information was provided regarding how scoring worked; rather the users had an implicit understanding of whether they did or did not achieve a high score. The game rules could also be learnt effectively via user observation. This allowed users, even without instruction to play the game [28].

3.7   System Robustness

The system was expected to run on a daily basis for extended periods of time, without any support interference. Testing in-house and over an intensive period of three days at the BBC NI Science Festival indicated that the program could run for sufficient time without issue. Final lighting control was not known prior to final production installation. However, in-lab testing had highlighted appropriate ranges of lighting to ensure the Microsoft Kinect sensor would effectively pickup user movement.

3.8   User Engagement and Enjoyment

Engagement and enjoyment of a system is difficult to capture, particularly with a large range of expectations from novice users of all ages through to those experienced in playing rugby. Malone suggests that fun can be achieved via the inclusion of three components [31]. These are challenge, fantasy and curiosity. Challenge is created by the inclusion of a simple goal which should be practical or fantasy rather than the achievement of a skill in of itself. This allows for informative performance feedback regarding attainment of that goal. Fantasy is provided by inserting the user in the virtual rugby world and pitting them against professional players. Curiosity is defined as the motivation to learn independent of any goal or fantasy fulfilment and this can be achieved by sensory means, informational complexity or cognitively. Feedback is core to curiosity to help the player delve further into how to play the game. The scoring system employed is simple yet sufficient to provide this feedback. By including users (novice and expert) of all ages throughout the design process the interactive remained educational, instructive while entertaining as witnessed during extended play-testing with multiple users, requests for repeat play and via the visitor centre management report.

4   Discussion

The work highlighted that despite limitations in implementation; underlying design principles can be adopted to ensure that the important components of an interactive tool can be implemented to create an innovative interactive display. Presence is well understood so as not to be limited by the technological implementation and as such the work focused on the elements that could potentially increase levels of presence and end user engagement and enjoyment. Transformative work such as this is important to help illustrate scientific work within a relevant context to a broad range of users. This allows educators to use the fun elements of a visitor centre space as a jumping-off point to explore underlying scientific principles. The interactive design made use of low-cost components, which although have limitations, do have capabilities that allow for a suitable interaction. It provides an example of how fundamental research could potentially be adapted to be used in a non-laboratory setting.

As technology improves and also becomes more robust, there is the potential for the use of head mounted displays within public space areas. Hardware such as the Oculus Rift, HTV Vive and others can provide suitable interaction to produce other types of immersive, interactive public gaming. However, work is required to understand and improve the acceptance of such technology, particularly with regard to the desire for shared visitor experiences and the practicality of high usage within a visitor centre environment.

Acknowledgements. The project described was carried out on behalf of Ulster Rugby, as part of their new Nevin Spence Centre which is dedicated to Nevin Spence. Funding was provided by the Department of Culture, Art and Leisure and the Northern Ireland Executive. The project also acknowledges Image Studio, South West College, Enniskillen. The project also acknowledges the precursor work carried out by [1].

References

1. Brault, S, Bideau, B, Kulpa, R, Craig, C.M.: Detecting deception in movement: the case of the side-step in rugby. PLoS One (2012). 10.1371/jounral.pone.0037494
2. MacDonald, G.F., Alsford, S.: The museum as information utility. Mus. Manag. Curatorship **10**, 305–311 (2001)
3. Croft, H., Kardin Suwarganda, E., Faris Syed Omar, S.: Development and application of a live transmitting player-mounted head camera. J. Sports Technol. **6**(2), 97–110 (2013)
4. Dhawan, A., Cummins, A., Spratford, W., Dessing, J.C., Craig, C.: Development of a novel immersive interactive virtual reality cricket simulator for cricket batting. In: Chung, P., Soltoggio, A., Dawson, C.W., Meng, Q., Pain, M. (eds.) 10th International Symposium in Computer Science in Sports (ISCSS 2015). Advances in Intelligent Systems and Computing, pp. 203–210. Springer, Heidelberg (2015)
5. Watson, G., Brault, S., Kulpa, R., Bideau, B., Butterfield, J., Craig, C.: Judging the 'passability' of dynamic gaps in a virtual rugby environment. Hum. Mov. Sci. **30**(5), 942–956 (2011)
6. Correia, V., Arajújo, D., Cummins, A., Craig, C.M.: Perceiving and acting upon spaces in a VR rugby task: expertise effects in affordance detection and task achievement. J. Sport Exerc. Psychol. **34**(3), 305–321 (2012)
7. Craig, C., Bastin, J., Montagne, G.: How information guides movement: intercepting curved free kicks in soccer. Hum. Mov. Sci. **30**(5), 931–941 (2011)
8. Lombard, M., Ditton, T.: At the heart of it all: the concept of presence. J. Comput. Mediated Commun. **3**, 0 (1997). doi:10.1111/j.1083-6101.1997.tb00072.x
9. van der Schuemie, M.J., Straaten, P., Krijn, M., van der Mast, C.: Research on presence in virtual reality: a survey. Cyberpsychol. Behav. Soc. Network. **4**(2), 183–201 (2001)
10. Gibson, J.J.: The Ecological Approach to Visual Perception. Houghton Mifflin, Boston (1979)
11. Brunswik, E.: Perception and the Representative Design of Psychological Experiments, 2nd edn., rev. & enl. University of California Press, Berkeley (1956)
12. Araújo, D., Davids, K., Serpa, S.: An ecological approach to expertise effects in decision-making in a simulated sailing regatta. Psychol. Sport Exerc. **6**(6), 671–692 (2005)

13. Craig, C., Watson, G.: An affordance based approach to decision making in sport: discussing a novel methodological framework. Revista de psicología del deporte: RDP; revista semestral de psicología (Palma) **20**(2), 689–708 (2011)
14. Craig, C., Cummins, A.: New methods for studying perception and action coupling. In: Baker, J., Farrow, D. (eds.) Routledge Handbook of Sport Expertise. Routledge, London (2015)
15. Miles, H.C., Pop, S.R., Watt, S.J., Lawrence, G.P., John, N.W.: A review of virtual environments for training in ball sports. Comput. Graph. **36**(6), 714–726 (2011). In 2011 Joint Symposium on Computational Aesthetics (CAe), Non-Photorealistic Animation and Rendering (NPAR), and Sketch-Based Interfaces and Modeling (SBIM)
16. Bideau, B., Kulpa, R., Menardais, S., Fradet, L., Multon, F., Delamarche, P., Arnaldi, B.: Real handball goalkeeper vs. virtual handball thrower. Presence Teleoperators Virtual Environ. **12**(4), 411–421 (2003)
17. Vignais, N., Bideau, B., Craig, C., Brault, S., Multon, F., Delamarche, P., Kulpa, R.: Does the level of graphical detail of a virtual handball thrower influence a goalkeeper's motor response? J. Sports Sci. Med. **8**(4), 501–508 (2009)
18. Zahorik, P., Jenison, R.L.: Presence as being-in-the-world. Presence: Teleoperators Virtual Environ. **7**(1), 78–89 (1998)
19. Vignais, N., Kulpa, R., Craig, C., Brault, S., Multon, F., Bideau, B.: Influence of the graphical levels of detail of a virtual thrower on the perception of the movement. Presence Teleoperators Virtual Environ. **19**(3), 243–252 (2010)
20. Craig, C.: Understanding perception and action in sport: how can virtual reality technology help? Sports Technol. **6**(4) (2013, 2014). doi:10.1080/19346182.2013.855224
21. Pauli, K.P., May, D.R., Gilson, R.L.: Fun and games: the influence of a playful pre-training intervention and microcomputer playfullness on computer-related performance. J. Educ. Comput. Res. **28**(4), 407 (2003)
22. Prensky, M.: Computer games and learning: digital game-based learning. In: Raessens, J., Goldstein, J. (eds.) Handbook of Computer Game Studies, p. 99 (2005)
23. Csikszentmihalyi, M.: Flow: The Psychology of Optimal Experience. Harpers Perennial (1990)
24. Sinclair, J., Hingston, P., Masek, M.: Considerations for the design of exergames. In: GRAPHITE 2007, Perth, Western Australia, 1–4 December 2007
25. Preece, J., Rogers, Y., Sharp, H.: Interaction Design, 2nd edn. Wiley, Hoboken (2007)
26. Salonius-Pasternak, D.E., Gelfond, H.S.: The next level of research on electronic play: potential benefits and contextual influences for children and adolescents. Hum. Technol. **1**(1), 5 (2005)
27. Neal, L.: Implications of computer games for systems design. In: Diapeer, D., Gilmore, D., Cockton, D., Shackel, B. (eds.) Proceedings of the IFIP TC13 Third International Conference on Human-Computer Interaction. Elsevier Science Publishers (1990)
28. Isbister, K., Mueller, F.F.: Guidelines for the design of movement-based games and their relevance to HCI. Hum. Comput. Interact. **30**(3–4), 366–399 (2015). doi: 10.1080/07370024.2014.996647
29. Chen, J.: Flow in games (and everything else) - a well-designed game transports its players to their personal flow zones, delivering genuine feelings of pleasure and happiness. Commun. ACM **50**(4), 31 (2007)
30. Jorgensen, A.H.: Marrying HCI/usability and computer games: a preliminary look. In: NordiCHI 2004, Tampere, Finland, 23–27 October 2004
31. Malone, T.W.: What makes things fun to learn? A study of intrinsically motivating computer games. Cognitive and Instructional Sciences Series (1980)

Immersive Virtual Reality-Based Simulation to Support the Design of Natural Human-Robot Interfaces for Service Robotic Applications

Federica Bazzano[1]([✉]), Federico Gentilini[1], Fabrizio Lamberti[1], Andrea Sanna[1], Gianluca Paravati[1], Valentina Gatteschi[1], and Marco Gaspardone[2]

[1] Dip. di Automatica e Informatica, Politecnico di Torino,
Corso Duca degli Abruzzi, 24, 10129 Torino, Italy
{federica.bazzano,federico.gentilini,fabrizio.lamberti,
andrea.sanna,gianluca.paravati,valentina.gatteschi}@polito.it
[2] TIM JOL Connected Robotics Applications LaB,
Corso Montevecchio 71, 10129 Torino, Italy
marco.gaspardone@telecomitalia.it
http://areeweb.polito.it/grains-group/
http://jol.telecomitalia.com/jolcrab/

Abstract. The increasing popularity of robotics and related applications in modern society makes interacting and communicating with robots of crucial importance. In service robotics, where robots operate to assist human beings in their daily life, natural interaction paradigms capable to foster an ever more intuitive and effective collaboration between involved actors are needed. The aim of this paper is to discuss activities that have been carried out to create a 3D immersive simulation environment able to ease the design and evaluation of natural human-robot interfaces in generic usage contexts. The proposed framework has been exploited to tackle a specific use case represented by a robotics-enabled office scenario and to develop two user interfaces based on augmented reality, speech recognition as well as gaze and body tracking technologies. Then, a user study has been performed to study user experience in the execution of semi-autonomous tasks in the considered scenario though both objective and subjective observations. Besides confirming the validity of the devised approach, the study provided precious indications regarding possible evolutions of both the simulation environment and the service robotic scenario considered.

Keywords: Service robotics · Adjustable autonomy · Natural user interfaces · Human-robot interaction · Augmented reality · Virtual reality

1 Introduction

In recent years, *service robotics* has received much attention due to its useful contributions to humans' daily life. In 1997, the International Federation of

L.T. De Paolis and A. Mongelli (Eds.): AVR 2016, Part I, LNCS 9768, pp. 33–51, 2016.
DOI: 10.1007/978-3-319-40621-3_3

Robotics (IFR) defined a service robot as a "robot which operates semi or fully autonomously to perform services useful to the well being of humans and equipment, excluding manufacturing operations". Examples of service robots include personal/domestic robots, entertainment robots, multimedia/remote presence robots, education and research robots, elderly and handicap assistance robots, professional robots, medical robots, etc. [1].

As suggested by the above definition, in order to assist human beings, service robots may require two different levels of autonomy (LOAs): *semi* and *full* autonomy. These terms are used to discriminate situations where robot's skills are sufficient to perform a given task in complete autonomy from situations where human intervention may be required. The additional ability of a robot which is often required in collaborative scenarios to flexibly support both semi and full autonomous operations by letting the user switch between the two configurations is generally referred to *adjustable* autonomy [2].

The number and type of LOAs available for a robot directly translate into requirements for the human-robot interaction (HRI) strategies to be implemented [3]. HRI is about "understanding, designing, and evaluating robotic systems for use by or with humans" [4]. This definition includes the analysis of the context in which robots operate and of which modalities are used to implement this interaction. Depending on the proximity degree of the human to the robot, the interaction may be *remote* or *proximate*. The former term refers to situations in which people are not present in the same environment as robots, whereas the latter is used when people and robots are co-located [4].

An important aspect to take into consideration when studying HRI is the type of information exchanged between human and robot. The different ways of combining this information result into *unimodal* or *multimodal* interfaces. Unimodal interfaces let users interact with robots by using one single modality at a time including, besides traditional devices like keyboard, mouse, joypad, etc., visual and auditory techniques. Visual techniques exploit computer vision methods to process data from one or more camera sensors in real-time and extract relevant information about the user such as facial expressions, body movements, head and gaze directions, etc. Auditory techniques process acoustic signals to implement speech or speaker recognition functionalities. Multimodal interfaces merge two or more modalities in a redundant or complementary way. Inputs must be recognized from different sources and combined according to temporal and contextual constraints in order to allow for their interpretation [5].

Both approaches have their advantages and drawbacks. Unimodal interaction may not be the most intuitive way of communicating for human beings and may not give the same possibilities to any user to interact with robots. However, it generally produces the shortest reaction times [6]. Multimodal approaches could provide more flexible interactions between humans and robots, thanks to the ability of the underlying technologies to recognize natural forms of human communicative principles and behavior [7]. Thus, not surprisingly, natural user interfaces (NUIs) are often built upon such techniques, even though simultaneity of different modalities may produce ambiguities due to imprecisions, noise or other factors [8].

Although a number of works studied the applicability of many unimodal and multimodal interaction paradigms for controlling the various LOAs of service robot, there is not an approach that can be regarded as the ultimate natural HRI solution for service robotics, especially taking into account the great variety of possible application scenarios that may be considered.

By leveraging the above considerations, this paper presents the work that has been carried out at Politecnico di Torino and TIM JOL Connected Robotics Applications LaB[1] with the aim to extend the interaction capabilities of a mobile telepresence robot named *Virgil* originally meant to be used in cultural heritage scenarios. Interfaces natively available to control the robot include a Web-based desktop application managed through mouse and keyboard, as well as a touch-based mobile app.

The interest of involved parties was to study other possible applications for the robot, by properly supporting the design of requested interfaces and enabling an effective evaluation of their performance before actually passing to a possible hardware renovation and/or integration phase.

Previous works demonstrated that simulated environments can be successfully exploited to evaluate the efficiency of interaction [9], the user's cognitive or mental workload [10], the degree of situational awareness [11] and the level of shared understanding between humans and robots [12,13] in the execution of HRI tasks. Thus, a virtual reality (VR) simulation framework based on the Unity platform was firstly developed, allowing to potentially experiment with any desired hardware modification.

Then, by taking into account current robot's characteristics, an office scenario was considered as a use case, and possible tasks to be carried out by interacting with the robot were defined.

Afterwards, two alternative natural interfaces for controlling the above tasks were devised. The first interface assumes that the user is wearing a head-mounted display and gets information about robot's status and available commands though Augmented Reality (AR) visual hints. Inputs are passed to the robot either through voice or gaze-based stimuli. In the second interface, visual hints are displayed on a tablet screen mounted on top of the robot, and commands are issued through voice and body movements, thus removing the need to wear or operate an additional device. User's inputs are collected using sensors embedded in the Microsoft Kinect V2 device and a DualShock3 controller. For the output, the Oculus Rift DK2 has been considered, in order to provide users with an immersive experience [14].

A user study was carried out with 36 volunteers, who were asked to carry out defined tasks by interacting with the robot in the simulated office environment using the two interfaces, and to evaluate them in subjective terms by filling in a questionnaire. Objective data were also collected regarding tasks completion time. Measurements allowed to identify positive and negative aspects of the two interfaces, which will be considered for designing the next generations of the considered robot.

---

[1] http://jol.telecomitalia.com/jolcrab/.

The rest of the paper is organized as follows. In Sect. 2, significant works in the area of HRI are reviewed. In Sect. 3, technologies adopted for implementing the designed simulation framework are introduced. Section 4 provides an overview of the architecture of the proposed framework, whereas Sect. 5 illustrates the VR-based office environment created to study the selected use case by also analyzing robotics interaction tasks considered. Section 6 provides details about the two user interfaces. Section 7 introduces the methodology adopted to perform the experimental tests and discusses results obtained. Finally, Sect. 8 concludes the paper by providing possible directions for future research activities in this field.

2   Related Work

Many works in the field of HRI focused on the design and evaluation of different types of natural interfaces exploiting, among others, voice commands, (multi)touch inputs, body and hand gestures, eye and gaze tracking, haptic feedback, etc.

In [15], Bolt showed that multimodal interfaces, in the specific case merging voice and gesture commands, provide a more natural form of interaction between humans and robots. In [16], Skubic et al. studied how human-robot spatial dialogue combined with a multimodal robot interface produce better interactions and enable robots to adjust their level of autonomy in an appropriate way. In [17], Fong investigated the collaborative relationship between humans and robots, and investigated benefits that could possibly derive from this interaction, e.g., in terms of an increased robot's performance due to human intervention.

Other studies investigated how to enhance multimodal interfaces with AR techniques with the goal to improve the effectiveness of resulting HRI. As a matter of example, in [18], Green described a system in which humans collaborate with robots by using an AR-based multimodal interface. The adoption of AR technology allowed to achieve an intuitive information exchange between humans and robots, by also improving user's awareness of the surrounding environment. Similarly, in [19], Maida et al. showed that the use of AR can enhance robot control operations.

In parallel to these studies, other works focused on proving that even simulators could represent valid tools for designing and assessing human-robot interfaces. For instance, in [20], a 2D robotic simulator named *Stage* was used to investigate how multi-robot systems could be operated. Authors concluded that a 2D simulator may be effective for handling multiple robots in a simplified environment, but 3D robotic simulators (such as *Gazebo*[2], *Webots*[3] or *RoboLogix*[4], to name a few) are needed for more complex scenarios. Thus, to make an example, in [21], a service robot named *Cero* and meant to develop a new communication paradigm based on social dialogue is designed and tested in a 3D virtual environment. Simulation was used to evaluate user's reactions and to understand

---

[2] http://gazebosim.org.
[3] https://www.cyberbotics.com/overview.
[4] https://www.robologix.com/.

how to shape robot's aspect in order to improve the communication model. Similarly, in [22], the use of a service called robot *Virbot* in a 3D virtual house was experimented, with the aim to prove the efficacy of simulation environments in this field.

In many cases, professional simulation environments designed to manage complex robot's dynamics may be replaced by tools originally developed to support the creation of 3D games and interactive applications. In general, in these tools it is easier to implement the required logic (e.g., by integrating different types of natural input devices, using natively-available gameplay bricks to describe robot's behavior, etc.), though it could be much more difficult, if not impossible, to reproduce all the physical elements in a faithful way. An example of this approach is reported in [23], where the *Modular Open Robots Simulation Engine (MORSE)* tool based on the open-source Blender Game Engine (BGE)[5] is presented.

The aim of this paper is to report on the work that has been carried out towards the development of a simulation framework based on the an off-the-shelf game engine to be used for supporting the design and assessment of natural human-robot interfaces. A specific field is tackled, represented by service robotics, and different natural interaction means are combined to create two alternative interfaces meant to enable the control of three possible robotic office tasks in an adjustable autonomy configuration.

3   Technologies

This section briefly presents the technologies considered in this work and illustrates how they have been used in the development of the proposed framework. More specifically, the Unity environment exploited for developing the 3D simulation will be firstly described. Then, the Oculus Rift DK2 used for producing a sense of immersivity will be introduced, by also discussing the Microsoft Kinect and DualShock3 technologies used to gather user's input. Lastly, details about the Virgil robot and its hardware and software characteristics will be provided.

3.1   Unity

Unity[6] is a development platform including an editor and a game engine (or player) that can be used to create video games and interactive applications running on multiple platforms. The editor allows developers to manage project assets (including 3D models, materials, textures, fonts, etc.) and create the necessary interaction logic, e.g., by laying out levels and scenes, creating the graphics interfaces, preparing animations, writing scripts, etc. When ready, games can be built and deployed as standalone applications meant to execute the designed gameplay on a variety of desktop operating systems, mobile platforms, gaming consoles and websites.

---

[5] https://www.blender.org/.

[6] https://unity3d.com/.

3.2 Oculus Rift DK2

The Oculus Rift DK2[7] is a virtual reality head-mounted display developed by Oculus VR. It is an input/output device, where the input captured by internal sensors and external infrared camera is sent to a suitable processing logic in order to determine user's head pose in the real world. The output is used to move the virtual camera in the 3D environment in real-time and render the graphics content to be sent to the head-mounted display and viewed by the user. Oculus Rift DK2, like other VR devices, is natively supported by the Unity environment through proper assets.

3.3 Microsoft Kinect

The Microsoft Kinect[8] is an input device created for allowing users to interact with their gaming console without the need for specific controller but simply using a natural user interface based on gestures and voice commands. The Microsoft Kinect V2 sensor used in this work consists of a horizontal bar including a RGB camera, a depth sensor and an array of microphones that can be used to capture users' full-body poses, facial expressions and speech. When used in body tracking mode, the device is capable to detect simultaneously up to six people and to extract joint-based skeleton data for two of them. In this work, the Microsoft Kinect V2 has been used to track user's arms and recreate their movement in Unity.

3.4 DualShock3 Controller

The DualShock3 controller[9] is vibration-feedback gamepad developed by Sony for PlayStation consoles. It comes equipped with a USB port and Bluetooth wireless connectivity that makes it possible to use it also on desktop computers. It provides the users with thirteen digital buttons, two analog sticks and four directional buttons. In the context of this work, it has been connected to the machine running the simulation framework and exploited to let the user move his or her avatar and explore the immersive virtual environment.

3.5 Virgil

Virgil is a wheeled mobile robot initially designed to allow museum visitors to experience areas not included in the itineraries planned for the visit or closed to the public (Fig. 1). At present, it is meant to be piloted remotely by the tour guide and stream a live video of the visited area over WiFi and 4G networks [24]. It is about 120 cm tall, and weights approximately 14 Kg. Its Li-Fe 12 V battery provides it with an autonomy of 4 h. Its maximum velocity is 1 m/s. It mounts

---

[7] https://www.oculus.com/en-us/dk2/.
[8] https://www.xbox.com/kinect/.
[9] https://www.playstation.com/en-us/explore/accessories/dualshock-3-ps3/.

a pan-tilt camera and a laser sensor, which is capable to detect obstacles at a distance of up to 30 m with an horizontal field of view (FOV) of 270°. Its control software provides it with autonomous navigation with local and global path planning and obstacle avoidance functionalities.

Fig. 1. The Virgil robot in a museum installation.

With the aim to explore other application opportunities for the robot, the goal of this work is to support the design of suitable user interfaces capable to improve the effectiveness of human-interaction in relevant scenarios. In particular, an office use case is considered, and several collaborative HRI tasks defined. Then, two alternative interaction methods making use of augmented reality, speech recognition as well as gaze and body motion tracking technologies are experimented. Thanks to the devised simulation environment, designers are provided with the possibility to evaluate alternative solutions before possibly moving to physically implementing modifications to actual robot's configuration.

Thus, to make an example, in the virtual environment robot's camera has been replaced by a tablet device mounted on a pan-tilt support that makes it possible to recreate the current robot's setup while at the same time introducing the possibility for the robot to display information useful for supporting human-robot interaction.

4   Simulation Framework

The proposed simulation framework has been deployed on a laptop computer equipped with Microsoft Windows 8 operating system. The logical components that were assembled and/or developed to implement the framework are illustrated in Fig. 2, whereas framework configuration used for experimental tests is reported in Fig. 3.

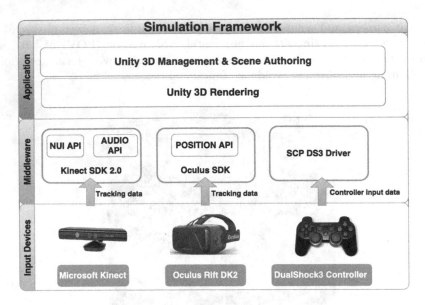

Fig. 2. Logical architecture of the simulation framework.

In the devised architecture, the lowest layer is represented by devices used to collect user's interaction (though, in some cases, they are also exploited to present system output). The DualShock3 controller is used to gather motion input to be used for letting the virtual avatar move in the simulated office environment. The Oculus Rift DK2 provides head rotation information, which is used to adjust the avatar's FOV and, in one of the interfaces to be studied, as a means for selecting scene objects to interact with. Lastly, Microsoft Kinect V2 is used to gather voice commands and, in one of the designed interfaces, to track user's arms and recognize selection by pointing gestures.

The middleware layer includes APIs used to process raw data produced by the input devices and to convert them in meaningful information for the top layer. For instance, speech processing has been implemented using the Microsoft Kinect for Windows SDK 2.0[10], whereas user's body movements have been tracked using the Zigfu Development Kit[11] for Unity. APIs provided by the Oculus SDK have been used to obtain the information from motion sensors, determine user's head pose in the real world and synchronize virtual camera's view in the simulation environment. Lastly, DualShock3 controller input has been handled though the SCP DS3 management software drivers.

Framework stack is completed by the application layer. The structure of this layer recalls, from a logical point of view, the phases devoted to the creation of the virtual environment (scene authoring) and the actual execution of the simulation (scene rendering), which in the context of this work have been implemented using

---

[10] https://www.microsoft.com/en-us/download/details.aspx?id=44561.
[11] http://zigfu.com/en/zdk/overview/.

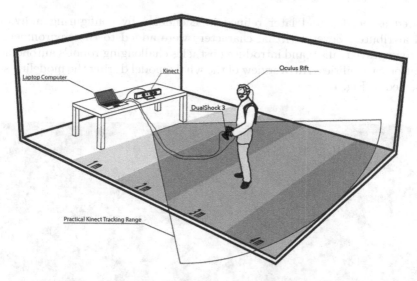

Fig. 3. Configuration of technologies used to manage user's interaction with the simulation framework and perform the experiments.

two elements of Unity, i.e., the editor and the game engine. In the authoring phase, the virtual office environment has been created, and the gameplay logic defined. That is, 3D objects have been loaded and positioned in the virtual space, by also specifying their visual appearance. Then, intelligence of scene objects, both in terms of autonomous or user-controlled behaviors, has been specified by means of scripted procedures. In the rendering phase, interactions and objects' behavior are managed in real-time to virtually simulate user's experience with the robot.

5   The Virtual Environment

This section presents the steps that led to the generation of the virtual environment representing the office scenario selected as a use case for this work. In particular, description will focus on the operations required to create the 3D models and to endow them with the necessary intelligence.

5.1   Modeling

When 3D assets are not available in advance, modeling is the first phase any virtual reality development process. In this work, the 3D environment consists of a model representing the TIM JOL Connected Robotics Applications LaB headquarters. The model is composed by different parts, such as walls, doors, furniture, etc. that were created separately in SketchUp[12] in order to be

---

[12] http://www.sketchup.com.

animated as needed and later refined in Blender[13] by configuring individual visual attributes. Several virtual characters were added to the environment in order to improve realism and introduce obstacles challenging robot's autonomous navigation capabilities. An overview of the whole model during the modeling step is reported in Fig. 4.

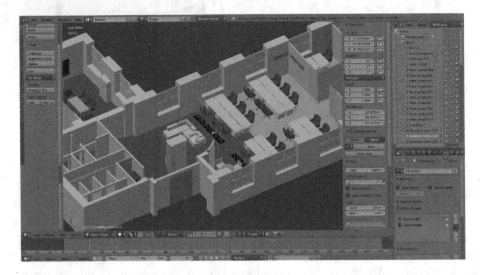

Fig. 4. 3D model of the office environment in Blender.

A comparable approach was pursued also for the Virgil robot, which was modeled in separate parts, namely chassis, wheels, tablet, camera and other sensors. Lastly, a humanoid avatar was introduced to let the user receive a feedback of his or her arm movements. Models created have been imported in Unity and added as game objects in the process of defining the scene and configured in such a way to be considered by collision detection/avoidance algorithms. Virgil model configuration in Unity is illustrated in Fig. 5.

5.2 Programming

In Unity, gameplay logic can be defined by means of scripts. In this work, C# scripts have been associated to different game objects to manage responses to user input, ensure that internal events of the simulation occur at the appropriate time and define robot's autonomous behaviors.

For instance, scripts associated with the scene are exploited to process speech input (by converting recognized keywords into commands) and manage body and head tracking data to drive avatar's motion. They also handle information displayed on a TV screen located at the entrance of the virtual environment, which

---

[13] https://www.blender.org.

Fig. 5. 3D model of the Virgil robot and configuration of its collision properties in Unity.

is used to provide the user with basic information about interaction possibilities available.

Scripts linked to the robot are used, among others, to make it reach a given destination by avoiding obstacles, to track a moving character in the environment and detect its pose and gestures, to update content displayed on the tablet screen or as AR hints at status changes, to keep the tablet oriented towards the avatar, etc. It is worth observing that navigation algorithms implemented in the simulation environment only approximate those that are actually used to control the real robot, since a precise reconstruction of Virgil's behavior in Unity was out of the scope this work. Similar considerations apply for the tracking functionality, which has been implemented using basic ray casting. Nonetheless, it is worth mentioning that activities are in progress to implement fine-grained simulations requested in the next design steps by moving technologies presented in this work under Gazebo[14], by exploiting its native link with Virgil's Robot Operating System (ROS)[15]-based control logic.

Robot's scripts additionally control the state machines that have been designed to describe, based on the above capabilities, three usage scenarios for the considered robot. Each scenario refers to a possible task (later referred to also as function) the robot could be involved into, namely, *robotic guide*, *follow me* and *free destination*.

---

[14] http://gazebosim.org/.

[15] http://www.ros.org/.

The *robotic guide* function is meant to help office visitors reach a given location in an unknown environment. Instead of using a map, the idea is to ask the robot to serve as a guide. To simulate this scenario, the user is positioned close to the entrance door of the considered environment. One or more robots are waiting in their docking (recharge) stations. The user chooses the robot he or she wants to control, specifies the destination he or she want to reach by giving the name of a specific room or of the person to be visited, the meeting to attend, etc. The robot moves towards the destination by waiting for the user when he or she is too far (that is, it tries to keep his or her avatar in its FOV at a given distance). When the destination is reached, the robot returns to the waiting area.

The *follow me* function can be used to move the robot to a given location. In this case, it is the user that moves in the environment while the robot tries to follow him or her.

Lastly, the *free destination* function refers again to a scenario in which the user needs to control robot's motion. However, in this case, destination is indicated explicitly by giving its coordinates in the 3D space. Depending on the interaction modality adopted, coordinates are obtained though gaze or hand tracking using head and body motion data gathered by the Oculus Rift DK2 or the Microsoft Kinect V2 devices, respectively.

6   User Interfaces

In this work, two user interfaces were experimented, which differ in the way information useful for controlling the robot (commands available, current status, etc.) are presented to the user and in the way selection interactions (required to select the robot and specify destination coordinates) are gathered.

One of the interfaces assumes that the user is wearing a see-through AR device. In the following, it will be referred to as the *AR interface*. Information visualization can rely on AR visual hints, whereas selection can be implemented using gaze/head tracking functionalities offered by the wearable device. It is worth noticing that, basically, in this configuration a head-mounted VR device is used to simulate a see-through AR scenario.

In the other interface, information is displayed on the robot tablet, rather than as AR hints. Hence, it will be referred to as *non-AR*, or *NAR interface*. Given the key role played by the tablet, robot is programmed to keep always its screen oriented towards the user's avatar as they reciprocally move in the virtual environment. In this interface, to perform a selection operation the user is requested to use his of her arms, whose direction is tracked relative to the robot's pose.

In both the interfaces, all the other functionalities are managed through voice commands. As said, basic information about interface usage is reported on the screen at the entrance of the virtual office environment. In the following, a detailed description of the two interfaces will be provided. A video showing user interaction with the three robot's functions using the two interfaces is also available[16].

6.1 AR Interface

This configuration assumes that the user can make selections by using his or her gaze by means of a see-through head-mounted AR device with head tracking capabilities. Hence, in all the scenarios considered, he or she firstly selects the robot to work with by framing it in his of her FOV. Proximity to the robot is used as an additional criterion for actually enabling interaction with such robot. The robot reacts by entering a state in which it can be asked to carry out one of the functions above (or to deactivate itself). A yellow light indicates that it is ready to receive commands, while commands available are displayed as AR hints on top of it (Fig. 6a).

When the *robotic guide* function is activated, the robot starts moving toward the selected destination (a green light indicates that the robot is actually executing a given function). The path followed is displayed on the ground through an AR-based polyline. Commands available to interact with the robot (e.g., to stop it) are displayed, together with actual status and distance from destination (Fig. 6b).

When the *follow me* function is selected, visual hints are used to display, independent of where user's gaze is actually directed, the location and distance of the robot relative to avatar's position (Fig. 6c). This way the user does not have to repeatedly look back to see whether the robot is actually following him or her or not.

Lastly, when the *free destination* function is used, user is requested to frame a given location in the 3D environment in his or her FOV and use a vocal command to make the robot move towards such location (Fig. 6d).

6.2 NAR Interface

In this configuration, before issuing any command, the user needs to specify the robot he or she wants to use by pronouncing the keyword "Virgil", followed by the robot ID (printed on the chassis). The use of this activation method is justified by the assumption that, in real life, more than one robots could be in service simultaneously and commands from other users to their robot could generate "interferences". This approach allows to preserve the user-robot association. Once the robot has been activated, commands and status are displayed on the tablet screen. Given the small size of the display, additional information generally required to let the user fully understand how to use the interface are reported on the TV screen (Fig. 7a).

When the *free destination* function is activated and robot is moving, commands available and distance to destination are displayed on the tablet screen, which is kept oriented towards the user (Fig. 7b).

---

[16] https://www.dropbox.com/s/oc8nhe970iqp6v3/video.mp4?dl=0.

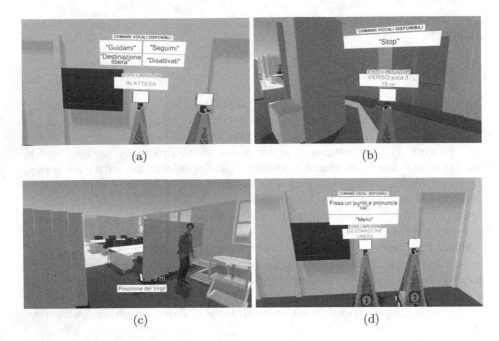

Fig. 6. Aspect of the AR interface for (a) function selection, and (b)–(d) during operation in each of the three tasks considered.

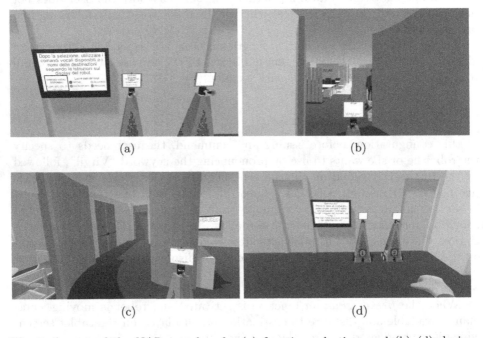

Fig. 7. Aspect of the NAR interface for (a) function selection, and (b)–(d) during operation in each of the three tasks considered. (Color figure online)

For the *follow me* function, with this interface no information about robot's position can be provided to the user (Fig. 7c).

Lastly, when the *free destination* function is used, the user specifies destination coordinates by pointing a given location in the 3D space with his or her arm (Fig. 7d).

7 Experimental Results

Evaluation of the proposed AR and NAR interfaces was carried out based on objective and subjective observations collected through a user study that involved 36 participants selected from Politecnico di Torino students (28 males and 8 females). According to declarations collected, 54 % of them had used already 3D applications and games, 24 % had experimented with VR or AR applications (by using Google Cardboard[17], Google Glass[18] or Samsung Gear[19]) and 23 % had previous experience with natural interfaces (mainly with Microsoft Kinect, Leap Motion Controller[20] as well as with Apple Siri[21] and Microsoft Cortana[22] voice assistants).

Participants were invited to use the three functions defined for the robot either through the AR or NAR interface (with an equal distribution on the two interfaces). The order in which robot's functions had to be used by a given participant was selected in a random way.

During the experiment, time required to complete the task assigned with the particular function was measured. At the end, each participant was asked to fill in a usability questionnaire (in Italian, available for download[23]) split in two parts.

The first part included, for each function, three questions based on the after-scenario test developed in [25]. Questions were aimed to determine whether participant was satisfied, overall, with the ease of use in completing the task, with the amount of time requested and with support information provided (as AR hints or on the tablet screen for the AR and NAR interfaces, respectively). This part was the same for both participants who used the AR interface and for those who used the NAR one.

The second part was created by considering the SASSI methodology [26] for the assessment of a speech interface (which, in this work, represents the central way for interacting with the robot, actually common to both AR and NAR configurations) and adapting it to let participants consider also the other interaction means. SASSI requests participants to evaluate 34 statements referring to six usability factors, i.e., System Response Accuracy (SRA), Likeability

---

[17] https://www.google.com/get/cardboard/.
[18] http://www.google.it/glass/start/.
[19] http://www.samsung.com/us/mobile/wearable-tech.
[20] https://www.leapmotion.com/.
[21] http://www.apple.com/ios/siri/.
[22] http://windows.microsoft.com/en-us/windows-10/getstarted-what-is-cortana.
[23] https://www.dropbox.com/s/q2s82c0zezoxkyv/questionnaires.zip?dl=0.

(LIKE), Cognitive Demand (CD), Annoyance (AN), Habitability (HAB) and Speed (SPE) by expressing their agreement on a 7-point Likert scale. This part of the questionnaire was slightly differentiated based on the interface actually used by the considered participant to carry out the tasks, in order to provide him or her with concrete examples meant to ease understanding of individual statements.

Results obtained in terms of completion time as well as of overall satisfaction based on after-scenario questions are reported in Fig. 8. At first sight, it is evident that completion times obtained with the AR interface are significantly lower than those experimented with the NAR one (Fig. 8a). Statistical significance was confirmed by running independent samples t-test on collected data (P largely lower than 0,05). Average values obtained with the subjective evaluation based on the after-scenario test appear to describe an almost comparable situation also for what it concerns ease of use, time and support information provided in completing the task assigned (Fig. 8b–d). However, t-test analysis confirmed a statistical significance concerning ease of use only for the *robotic guide* and *follow me* tasks. Despite numerical observations, there was not a statistical evidence in different satisfaction about task duration. Regarding satisfaction with

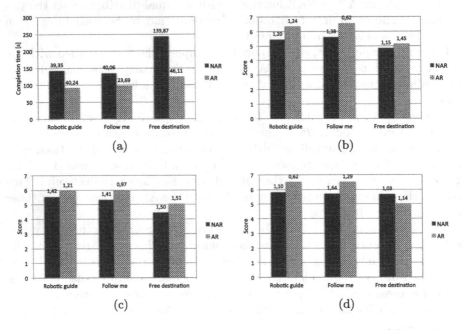

Fig. 8. Results for the three functions using the two interfaces about (a) completion time and overall satisfaction (after-scenario evaluation) in terms of (b) ease of use, (c) perceived time requested and (d) support information provided in completing the task. Bar height reports average value. For (a), lower is better. For (b)–(d), higher is better. Labels indicate standard deviation.

information provided, t-tests confirmed a better score of the AR interface for the *robotic guide* task.

Results concerning subjective observations gathered through the adapted SASSI methodology are reported in Fig. 9 (using a worse to better scale). Independent samples t-test analysis returned a statistical significance only for the Speed factor, confirming, on the one side, improved performance in terms of completion time with the AR interface (obtained also through numerical measurements), as well as a higher interaction frequency (number of commands that can be issued in a given time interval) possible with such interface.

Based on the outcomes of statistical significance analysis, it was not possible to draw definitive conclusions about the other SASSI factors when considering statements in an aggregate way. However, by looking at individual statements for the various factors it appears that interaction with the system is considered more efficient with AR (statement SRA.9). With the NAR interface, interaction appears to be more repetitive than with AR (statement AN.24) and it is easier for the user to loose track of where he or she is in the interaction (statement HAB.32). Based on feedback collected during the tests, this seems to be due to fact that, with the NAR interface, the user needs to use his or her voice to repeatedly activate the robot, whereas with the AR he or she simply has to frame it in the FOV. Similarly, with the NAR interface information useful for keeping track of the actual state in the interaction is available only on the tablet screen mounted on the robot, whereas with the AR interface they are either always available (e.g., when the robot is following) or easy to obtain (by looking at the robot even at distance).

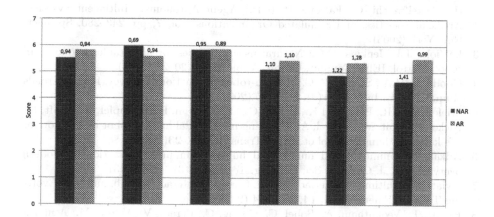

Fig. 9. Results obtained by applying the adapted SASSI methodology in terms of System Response Accuracy (SRA), Likeability (LIKE), Cognitive Demand (CD), Annoyance (AN), Habitability (HAB) and Speed (SPE) for the two interfaces. Bar height reports average value (higher is better), whereas labels are used to show standard deviation.

8 Conclusions and Future Work

In this work, the creation of a simulation framework aimed to support the study of interaction paradigms for robotic applications was presented. The proposed framework was exploited to help the development of natural user interfaces to be exploited in a service robotic scenario. Interfaces designed, based on voice commands, AR as well as head/gaze and body motion tracking were tailored to the control of a set of selected office-oriented robotic tasks. Experimental results obtained through a user study provided precious indications about user experience with the two interfaces, both in objective and subjective terms.

Results are expected to be used to drive next design and implementation steps planned for the robotic platform considered in the study. Future work will additionally focus on integrating the technologies developed and assembled in this work into other simulation environments considering also robot's dynamics in order to gather further indications about feasibility and suitability of the proposed interfaces before actually passing to the production and/or renovation phases.

References

1. International Federation of Robotics. Service robots. In: World Robotics 2015, pp. 12–14. IFR (2015). http://www.ifr.org/service-robots/
2. Acquisti, A., Feltovich, P., Hoffman, R., Jeffers, R., Prescott, D., Suri, N., Uszok, A., Van Hoof, R., Bradshaw, J.M., Sierhuis, M.: Adjustable autonomy and human-agent teamwork in practice: an interim report on space applications. In: Hexmoor, H., Castelfranchi, C., Falcone, R. (eds.) Agent Autonomy. Multiagent Systems, Artificial Societies, and Simulated Organizations, vol. 7, pp. 243–280. Springer, New York (2003)
3. LaViola, J.J., Jenkins, O.C.: Natural user interfaces for adjustable autonomy in robot control. IEEE Comput. Graph. Appl. **35**(3), 20–21 (2015)
4. Goodrich, M.A., Schultz, A.C.: Human-robot interaction: a survey. Found. Trends Hum. Comput. Interact. **1**(3), 203–275 (2007)
5. Stiefelhagen, R., Ekenel, H.K., Fügen, C., Gieselmann, P., Holzapfel, H., Kraft, F., Nickel, K., Voit, M., Waibel, A.: Enabling multimodal human-robot interaction for the karlsruhe humanoid robot. IEEE Trans. Robot. **23**(5), 840–851 (2007)
6. Adkar, P.: Unimodal and multimodal human computer interaction: a modern overview. Int. J. Comput. Sci. Inf. Eng. Technol. **2**(3), 1–8 (2013)
7. Oviatt, S.: Multimodal interfaces. Hum. Comput. Interact. Handb. Fundam. Evolving Technol. Emerg. Appl. **14**, 286–304 (2003)
8. Kollar, T., Vedantham, A., Sobel, C., Chang, C., Perera, V., Veloso, M.: A multimodal approach for natural human-robot interaction. In: Ge, S.S., Khatib, O., Cabibihan, J.-J., Simmons, R., Williams, M.-A. (eds.) ICSR 2012. LNCS, vol. 7621, pp. 458–467. Springer, Heidelberg (2012)
9. Crandall, J.W., Goodrich, M.A., Olsen Jr., D.R., Nielsen, C.W.: Validating human-robot interaction schemes in multitasking environments. IEEE Trans. Syst. Man Cybern. Part A Syst. Hum. **35**(4), 438–449 (2005)
10. Sheridan, T.B.: Humans and Automation: System Design and Research Issues. John Wiley and Sons Inc., New York (2002)

11. Endsley, M.R.: Designing for Situation Awareness: An Approach to User-Centered Design. CRC Press, Boca Raton (2011)
12. Johnston, J.H., Fiore, S.M., Paris, C., Smith, C.A.: Application of Cognitive Load Theory to Developing a Measure of Team Decision Efficiency. Technical report, DTIC Document (2002)
13. Klein, G., Feltovich, P.J., Bradshaw, J.M., Woods, D.D.: Common ground and coordination in joint activity. Organ. Simul. 53, 139–184 (2005)
14. Nechvatal, J.: Immersive Ideals/Critical Distances, pp. 48–60. LAP Lambert Academic Publishing, Saarbrücken (2009)
15. Bolt, R.A.: "Put-that-there": Voice and Gesture at the Graphics Interface, vol. 14(3), pp. 262–270. ACM (1980)
16. Skubic, M., Perzanowski, D., Blisard, S., Schultz, A., Adams, W., Bugajska, M., Brock, D.: Spatial language for human-robot dialogs. IEEE Trans. Syst. Man Cybern. Part C Appl. Rev. 34(2), 154–167 (2004)
17. Fong, T., Thorpe, C., Baur, C.: Multi-robot remote driving with collaborative control. IEEE Trans. Ind. Electron. 50(4), 699–704 (2003)
18. Green, S.A., Chen, X., Billinghurst, M., Chase, J.G.: Collaborating with a mobile robot: an augmented reality multimodal interface. In: 17th World Congress of the International Federation of Automatic Control, pp. 15595–15600 (2008)
19. Maida, J.C., Bowen, C.K., Pace, J.W.: Enhanced Lighting Techniques and Augmented Reality to Improve Human Task Performance. Technical report, NASA (2005)
20. Gerkey, B., Vaughan, R.T., Howard, A.: The player/stage project: tools for multi-robot and distributed sensor systems. In: 11th International Conference on Advanced Robotics, pp. 317–323 (2003)
21. Severinson-Eklundh, K., Green, A., Hüttenrauch, H.: Social and collaborative aspects of interaction with a service robot. Robot. Auton. Syst. 42(3), 223–234 (2003)
22. Savage-Carmona, J., Billinghurst, M., Holden, A.: The virbot: a virtual reality robot driven with multimodal commands. Expert Syst. Appl. 15(3), 413–419 (1998)
23. Echeverria, G., Lemaignan, S., Degroote, A., Lacroix, S., Karg, M., Koch, P., Lesire, C., Stinckwich, S.: Simulating complex robotic scenarios with MORSE. In: Noda, I., Ando, N., Brugali, D., Kuffner, J.J. (eds.) SIMPAR 2012. LNCS, vol. 7628, pp. 197–208. Springer, Heidelberg (2012)
24. Giuliano, L., Ng, K., Efrain, M., Lupetti, M.L., Germak, C.: Virgil, robot for museum experience: study on the opportunity given by robot capability to integrate the actual museum visit. In: 7th International Conference on Intelligent Technologies for Interactive Entertainment, pp. 222–223 (2015)
25. Lewis, J.R.: IBM computer usability satisfaction questionnaires: psychometric evaluation and instructions for use. Int. J. Hum. Comput. Interact. 7(1), 57–78 (1995)
26. Hone, K.S., Graham, R.: Towards a tool for the subjective assessment of speech system interfaces. Nat. Lang. Eng. 6(3–4), 287–303 (2000)

Multi-Resolution Visualisation of Geographic Network Traffic

Berkay Kaya and Selim Balcisoy[✉]

Sabanci Univeristy, Orhanli, 34956 Tuzla, Istanbul, Turkey
{berkayk,balcisoy}@sabanciuniv.edu
http://www.sabanciuniv.edu

Abstract. Flow visualization techniques are vastly used to visualize scientific data among many fields including meteorology, computational fluid dynamics, medical visualization and aerodynamics. In this paper, we employ flow visualization techniques in conjunction with conventional network visualization methods to represent geographic network traffic data. The proposed visualization system integrates two visualization techniques, flow visualization and node-link diagram. While flow visualization emphasizes on general trends, node-link diagram visualization concentrates on the detailed analysis of the data. A usability study with multiple experiments is performed to evaluate the success of our approach.

Keywords: Network visualization · Data visualization · Flow visualization

1 Introduction

Extracting useful patterns and exploring important details in the data is impossible by just reading it in a textual form. The need for information visualization emerges in this step. Information visualization satisfies this need by offering the data in various forms with differing interactions. Information visualization aims to provide graphical representations and user interfaces for interactively exploring large sets of items [4]. Visualizations can give an overview of the data, they can filter the data according to the user's needs, summarize data and help identifying important patterns [6].

In today's digital world, one of the most elegant collected data is network traffic data. Some typical examples of network traffic data are telephone calls, electronic mails, flight traffic etc. Networks are generally based on simple graphs, which are formed by the connecting lines that represent binary connections between nodes. In binary connections, the properties of the relationships between the members are disregarded. Ignoring the important features of the relationships can lead to reduction of potentially valuable information. Traffic density is an appropriate example of a quantitative value that can be assigned with each relationship. Encoding every connection with traffic density value is crucial in

© Springer International Publishing Switzerland 2016
L.T. De Paolis and A. Mongelli (Eds.): AVR 2016, Part I, LNCS 9768, pp. 52–71, 2016.
DOI: 10.1007/978-3-319-40621-3_4

analyzing the important features of the network. In a geographic network, node positions are of key importance. Hence, layout of the network should be stable, such that geographic properties are not lost.

Visualizing geographic network traffic is a challenging task for several reasons. In geographic networks, the positions of the nodes play an important role. Although dealing with geographic data on 2D displays looks like a trivial process, there are many important issues. If number of records are too high, visualization gets cluttered due to the limited pixel count of the displays. The cluttered view yields to misleading results, thus clear views should be supplied.

Supporting both global and local views is another significant challenge. Users should be able to comment on global trends while working on the overview mode. On the other hand, specific details can be detected when detailed view is enabled. Likewise, users should be able to examine regions with high level of detail. In brief, successful visualizations must allow users to obtain important, insightful patterns from an overview as well as to investigate the details of each node and links [13].

To summarize the problem definition, the network traffic should be visualized in such a way that, geographic properties are not lost. Moreover, supporting both global and local views is mandatory for data analysis. It becomes easier to detect global patterns in the large scale layout, whereas individual traffic information can only be examined in the detailed view. Therefore, level of detail should be navigable through the program by interactive techniques like zooming.

In this paper, we employed two visualization techniques, node-link diagrams and flow visualization, in the context of geographic network visualization. We integrated flow visualization techniques to network visualization problem. Our visualization system is based on level of detail framework, which is controlled by the camera distance. In the detailed view, network traffic is visualized by node-link diagrams. In the overview, visualization system benefits from the flow visualization techniques to represent high density traffic. The novelty comes from the presentation of a visualization system for network data, where UFLIC method is used to visualize flows and produce animations, and LOD is view dependently applied. Finally, we evaluated the success of our visualization system with usability experiments.

The main contributions of this research can be classified into two categories: (i-) Integration of flow visualization techniques in geographic network visualization context. (ii-) Combination of two different visualization techniques, performing level of detail.

2   Exposition

Network layout is a fundamental point in the network visualization. For a visualization method to convey information as effectively as possible, good layout is crucial. The literature on network layout has been dominated by force-directed strategies because they produce clever spreading of nodes and reasonable visibility of links [13]. A second common layout strategy, which generates familiar and comprehensible layouts, uses geographical maps, in which the node locations are fixed [1]. Edges are drawn between locations denoting the relationships between the entities. A third strategy uses circular layout for nodes. This visualization places nodes in a circular layout and it produces an elegant presentation with criss-crossing lines through the center of the circle [2,8]. In geographic networks, node positions are important, therefore, layout cannot be altered in a straightforward fashion. Small changes in the layout can be negligible if they don't reduce the perception of relationships.

As a subfield of scientific visualization, flow visualization is a popular field in visualization. Flow visualization covers a variety of applications such as weather simulation, meteorology, computational fluid dynamics and medical visualization [9]. The coverage of flow visualization solutions spans multiple technical challenges like 2D vs. 3D solutions. The data type also plays an important role on designing the flow visualization application. Visualization of time-dependent unsteady data may face different challenges than steady data representations.

2.1 Dense Texture-Based Flow Visualization

These visualizations are built on the concept of computation of texture values to generate a dense representation of the flow [9]. Flow motion is incorporated through the related texture values along the vector field. These methods provide full spatial coverage of the vector field.

Spot Noise Based Methods: Spot noise, first introduced by van Wijk [15], is one of the first dense texture based methods in the flow visualization literature. The resulting texture is generated by distribution of a set of intensity functions called spots. These spots represent a particle that warps over a small step in time. After a period of time, these particles form a streak in the direction of the local streamline. For further details on spot noise based methods, a state of the art report can be found in [9].

Line Integral Convolution: First introduced by Cabral and Leedom [3], a large community of flow visualization researchers dedicated themselves for developing better methods. In the original LIC algorithm a white noise image is taken as input. Texels are convolved along the path of streamlines. The convolution process is actually a low-pass filter, which creates smoothened textures. In order to create a dense representation, post-processing steps like high-pass filtering is used. Several extensions are developed in several directions like extending LIC to 3D, applying LIC to unsteady flow data, improving the performance of LIC to real time and etc. Details can be found in the state of the art report on dense texture-based flow visualization by Laramee et al. [9].

In the design process of our flow visualization technique, we reviewed several constraints in network visualization such as traffic direction and density. In order to represent traffic direction, providing an understandable flow animation was crucial. Furthermore, dense representations should be preferred in order to highlight traffic density. With these motivations, we decided on building our algorithm on dense-texture based methods. The algorithm used for generating flow textures in our approach is mainly based UFLIC (Unsteady Flow Line Integral

Convolution). UFLIC maintains the coherence of flow animation by successfully updating convolution results. UFLIC uses LIC as the underlying approach.

2.2 Level of Detail

LOD attempts to balance complexity and performance by managing the amount of detail presented in the visualization [10]. According to the measures like camera distance, object with the corresponding level of detail is drawn. Performance is increased by eliminating unimportant geometry. Controlling the detail level as the viewing parameters change, is referred to view-dependent level of detail control [5,7]. In network visualization problem, level of detail can be maintained by regulating the underlying graph structure. In this paper, level of detail is controlled by the camera distance.

3 Flow Visualization for Geographic Networks

The proposed visualization system is based on two different visualization techniques. The first approach, which is node-link diagrams applied to geographic networks, achieves high level of detail. In this view, each relationship in the geographic network is represented as individual edges. The second approach incorporates flow visualization into network visualization framework when level of detail is low. The regions having high density traffic are represented as flow textures.

Flow visualization approaches are built upon 2D vector fields. We claim that it is not convenient to involve every pixel in the flow area. In the case of network visualization, some nodes may not have any traffic at all. Therefore, we rejected the idea of defining global vector field to denote network structure. Instead, we present small texture patches representing edges in the network.

3.1 Line Integral Convolution

Our algorithm for visualizing flow is based on Line Integral Convolution (LIC) algorithm [3]. In this algorithm, an input image, which is generally a white noise image, is convolved along streamlines that are retrieved from the underlying

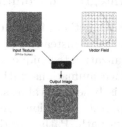

Fig. 1. LIC Pipeline

Fig. 2. Convolution path. Source pixel (blue) and visited pixels (red). Note that there are four red pixels in opposite directions. (Color figure online)

vector field. In Fig. 1, flow of the LIC pipeline is illustrated. LIC algorithm is based on value gathering scheme, where each pixel value of the output image is dependent on the local streamlines that originate from a given pixel. In the process of calculating the output image's pixel values, the contributing pixels are gathered from bidirectional advected streamlines. The length of these local streamlines defines the convolution length. Increasing the convolution length leads to the reduction in contrast; thus, flow lines can hardly be depicted. On the contrary, if the convolution length is too small, flow patterns disappear due to insufficient filtering. Therefore, it should be defined proportionally to the size of the vector field.

Only directional component of the vector field is used in the advection process. Values are gathered from the corresponding pixels and averaging is used to get the convolved value. Figure 2 demonstrates the convolution path of a given pixel, when convolution length is 4. The LIC output pixel value for a given point p is given by the Eq. 1:

$$F(p) = \frac{\int_{-L}^{L} F(P(p, s)) k(s) ds}{\int_{-L}^{L} k(s) ds} \tag{1}$$

where L is the convolution length, P(p, s) is a parametric curve defining the local streamline, s is some distance between (0,L) in both directions and k(s) is the weighting function.

3.2   Unsteady Flow Line Integral Convolution - UFLIC

There are many extensions to LIC method, including UFLIC [12], FastLIC [14], EnhancedLIC [11], and etc. UFLIC (Unsteady Flow Line Integral Convolution) forms the basis of our flow visualization technique, main reason being that it has the ability to effectively produce animations with spatio-temporal coherence. Unlike the basic LIC, UFLIC is based on value scattering scheme. Instead of gathering pixel values from opposite directions on the local streamlines, each pixel scatters its value along its path. Paths are defined by the corresponding streamlines. This natural phenomenon of leaving footprints around their flow traces creates the output image by successively scattering and convolving the values.

UFLIC algorithm is consisted of two steps; time-accurate value scattering process and successive feed forward scheme. Given an initial input texture image, every pixel serves as a seed particle. Every active seed particle advects forward in the vector field, following a pathline that originates from the center of the pixel. The pathline is computed with the Eq. 2:

$$p(t + \Delta t) = p(t) + \int_{t}^{t+\Delta t} v(p(t)dt)$$ (2)

where p(t) is the position of the particle at time t, p(t+Δt) is the new position after time Δt, and v(p(t),t) is the velocity of the particle at p(t) at time t.

In the time-accurate value scattering process, each pixel deposits its value and the current integration step along the pathline it travels. Due to the depositing seed particles, every pixel keeps a buffer structure called C-Buffer (Convolution Buffer) for the purpose of convolving scattered values. Each C-Buffer holds several buckets, which correspond to different integration steps. The number of buckets that a C-Buffer holds is dependent on the number of integration steps. Each bucket in a C-Buffer has a field of intensity value and a field of the accumulated weight. According to the computation time, corresponding bucket is selected and the computed intensity value is written to the output image. Accumulated intensity and weight values in a C-Buffer are computed in a cumulative fashion as follows:

$$I_{accum} = I_{accum} + I_{current}$$

$$W_{accum} = W_{accum} + W_{current}$$

Each seed particle has a global life span, which in fact defines the lifetime of a pixel in terms of integration steps. This parameter, Life Span, also defines the number of buffers in a C-Buffer. When computing the convolution, the necessary buffer index is obtained from the equation:

$$BufferIndex = ComputationalTime(modLifeSpan)$$

Since each pixel advects its value along their path during their life span, there exist some buckets with future timestamps. These buckets will be used when their time comes. Animation is carried by successively increasing buffer indexes, which satisfies the iterative convolution of values from the C-Buffers.

Successive feed forward scheme defines the workflow of the algorithm. Initially, the input image is given as input to value scattering process. After value scattering process advects and convolves the input image, it generates an output image for the current time step. For the further steps, instead of using the initial white noise texture, the output image that is computed from the previous time step is fed forward as an input image to the current value scattering process.

This successive feed forward scheme is a kind of low-pass filtering process. Therefore, after some time, since we use low-pass filtered output images as inputs, the resulting images get blurred. As a result, the contrast among the flow lines will be lost. One solution for this problem is to apply high pass filter to input image before scattering process.

3.3   Path Generation

In our flow visualization technique, only regions that have flow properties are filled with vectors. This is supported by using an alpha mask. If a pixel on the input texture is not an active seed, its alpha value is set to 0. In path generation process, visited pixels are defined as active seeds. Using this alpha mask also benefits the system by increasing performance in the convolution process. Consequently, only active seeds are visible and they are included on the convolution phase.

A single record in a geographic network dataset is specified by two entities, source and destination nodes. Since flow textures are mapped onto 2D plane, the position of source and destination nodes are also transformed into 2D coordinates and they are mapped to the corresponding texture coordinates. We used quadratic Bezier curves to define paths. A parametric form of a quadratic Bezier curve is defined as:

$$p(t) = (1 - t)^2 P_0 + 2(1 - t)t P_1 + t^2 P_2, t \epsilon [0, 1]$$

where P_0 and P_2 define the end points and P_1 represents the control point. Parameterization is controlled by the value t. The curve passes through P_0 at t = 0 and P_2 at t = 1. Points between P_0 and P_2 are calculated with the equation above. In our case, the end points are represented by source and destination nodes. Calculation of the control points is illustrated in Fig. 3. In this figure, source and destination nodes are denoted with red circles. The orange line is the line connecting the source and destination nodes. Orange circle is the point which stands at equal distances from the red circles, computed by taking the mean of the end points. In order to give the feeling of 3D, instead of using orange circle as the control point, the median point is computed in terms of geospatial coordinates, i.e. latitude and longitude. The blue circle denotes the geospatial median point. The blue curve denotes the curvilinear path of the expected flow.

Fig. 3. Calculation of control points (Color figure online)

Similar to source and destination points, control point is also mapped to 2D coordinates. After projecting the control point to 2D coordinate system, a

number of curves are defined to generate the path of the flow. The number of
curves generated is dependent on the flow width. For instance, if the width of
the flow is 10, 10 different curves are generated with their respective control
points. Source and destination points remain the same; however, control points
are altered in opposite directions. New control points stand on the line that is
orthogonal to the line connecting the end points, Fig. 4.

Fig. 4. Calculation of new control points depending on the width of the flow (Color
figure online)

In Fig. 4, the black thick line $L_{perpendicular}$ denotes the line that is orthogonal
to the line connecting the end points. Depending on the width of the flow,
each new control point is placed in opposite directions with incremental steps
along $L_{perpendicular}$. Green and orange circles represent the new control points
generated in opposite directions. When the end points and control points are
defined, quadratic Bezier curves are formed. Specific positions in a path are
calculated as follows. In the para-metric form of Bezier curves, t varies between
0 and 1. Starting from 0, we increment t value by $1/L$ in each step, where L
denotes the path length. Finally, we obtain an array of positions, called PathLine,
in which the size of the array is equal to path length. In the following pseudocode, path index is denoted by i. i varies between 0 and L. Paths are defined in
a recursive fashion such that pixels jump to first position after they reach the
end. This precaution is taken for the continuous animation of flows (Fig. 5).

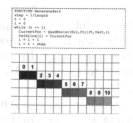

Fig. 5. Example path in terms of pixel positions. Numbers above pixels denote the
path indexes.

In the path generation process, the length of the path has an important role.
Path length is a predefined value, which is defined with respect to the resolution
of the texture. In our application, the resolution of the 2D plane is 600×600.

There are two parameters that affect the path length, which are life span and convolution length.

$$PathLength = LifeSpan x ConvolutionLength$$

By experimental results, Life Span is set to 30 and Convolution Length to 10, making path length equal to 300.

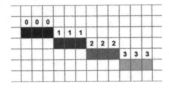

Fig. 6. Value scattering process. Numbers above pixels denote depositing timestamps.

3.4 Value Scattering Process

In this step, every seed pixel scatters its intensity value along its path. At each time step in their life span, they leave their foot-prints, i.e. deposit their values in the visited pixel's buckets. For each seed pixel, their alpha value is set to a predefined transparency value. This value is set to 80 % transparency but if more opaque flows are desired, higher opacity values can be set. Each seed pixel follows their paths in structures called PathLine. This PathLine structure is simply an array of 2D vectors, representing 2D coordinates in the texture. Life Span and Convolution Length parameters play an important role in this process. As each pixel moves towards their path, they deposit their values via structures called buckets. Depositing time is incremented from 0 to Life Span. For each time step t, the number of pixels visited is equal to Convolution Length. After depositing values with the same time step, time step is incremented by 1. Same procedures are followed for further steps. Illustration can be found in Fig. 6.

Each bucket holds accumulated intensity I_{accum} and accumulated weight W_{accum}. When a pixel deposits its value in the visited pixels' bucket, time index is used for reaching the corresponding bucket. In a pixel's C-Buffer, there are n buckets with time indexes i from 0 to Life Span. Consequently, the size of each C-Buffer is equal to Life Span. The Fig. 7 illustrates these structures.

C-Buffers are used in the convolution process. After every seed pixel deposits its value, not only for the current step, but for future steps, value scattering process is terminated.

3.5 Convolution Process

Convolution process is triggered after value scattering process terminates. Value scattering process is executed when flow locations are altered. Unlike value scattering process, convolution process is called in real time. The main reason is

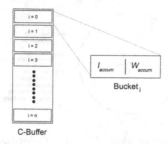

Fig. 7. C-Buffer and Bucket Structures

that the animation of the flow is carried out in this step. The output of the convolution process is a new 2D texture with the new values acquired from the scattering process. Therefore, this convolution function has to be called with increasing time steps, in order to animate during the runtime. The time step parameter of the convolution process is calculated by:

$$CurrentTimeStep = BufferIndex(modLifeSpan)$$

BufferIndex is increased by 1 after each convolution process. The convolution is initialized by reaching the bucket with timestamp value equal to CurrentTime Step. After reaching the corresponding bucket, accumulated intensity and weight values are read. Convolution is performed by dividing the accumulated value to the accumulated weight. The computed value is then written to the output texture.

4   Level of Detail for Geographic Networks

We performed our level of detail study depending on the camera distance. In high level of detail, flow visualization is disabled. Geographic network traffic is visualized by node-link diagrams in this state. When the camera distance reaches or exceeds the threshold value, flow visualization is enabled revealing high density traffic. In both levels of detail, node-link diagram visualization is enabled. In Node-Link Diagram visualization technique, each edge in the network is represented as trails, which are arcs drawn over the surface of the globe. Nodes in the network, which are locations with geographic properties, are represented as spheres. Elements drawn in this visualization are working on 3D coordinate space.

Trails are drawn by quadratic Bezier curves over the surface of the Earth. After depicting the nodes' 3D coordinates, a median point is calculated in the middle of these nodes. This is done in three steps. First, the mean of these nodes' 3D coordinates is calculated. Secondly, this vector is normalized to the unit vector. Finally, it is scaled to fit on the surface of the Earth; hence it is multiplied by the radius of the Earth. Resulting point is referred as median point. You can see the illustration of this process in the Fig. 8.

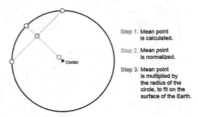

Fig. 8. Path Generation of Trails. (Color figure online)

Fig. 9. Bidirectional trails. (Color figure online)

After calculating the median point, a quadratic Bezier curve is drawn in 3D coordinate space. This curve denotes the path of the trail. When there is a bidirectional traffic relation between two nodes, paths are modified to avoid overlapping. In this case, the median points of the two trails are moved in opposite directions along the orthogonal vector defined at the median point. Algorithm used for calculating new control points is the same as in the case of path generation of flows, see Fig. 4.

In Fig. 9, the trail at the center is the original path defined between two locations. Since there is bidirectional traffic between them, new paths are defined in opposite directions. Bidirectional paths are drawn with higher opacity.

The length of the trail defines the number of pieces (line segments) that are needed to draw this curve. In other words, a curve is consisted of an arbitrary number of line segments. For animation purposes, these line segments can be encoded with several visual parameters like opacity value and color.

Trails are designed to support many useful visual parameters. Visual attributes that are supported in our representation are explained below in subheadings. Properties of the traffic relations are encoded with various visual parameters. Trails are encoded with gradient colors. Nodes in the same region (i.e. continent) are colored with the same colors.

Fig. 10. Region Coloring Scheme. (Color figure online)

Fig. 11. Gradient Coloring of Trails. (Color figure online)

In Fig. 10, region coloring scheme is shown. Locations that belong to the defined regions, i.e. continents, are colored according to this setting. The following figure shows a singular trail that is colored with gradient coloring option. Source location in this traffic relation is in North America; therefore it is colored as blue. Destination location is in Europe; thus making it red. Gradient coloring is done by linearly interpolating colors between source and destination colors, see Fig. 11.

Width is one of the visual parameters that can be used to encode traffic density. As traffic density increases, the width of the trail increases. Figure 12 shows two trails width different width settings.

Fig. 12. Trails with different widths, 1 (top) and 5 (bottom).

Branching is the other visual parameter that is used for representing traffic density. Instead of drawing a singular trail, the trail is split into a number of branches. The number of branches, i.e. thin singular trails, is directly proportional to the traffic density (Fig. 13).

Fig. 13. A trail split into 4 branches.

Animating bubbles are used to stress traffic direction. During the execution of the application, bubbles are animated from source node to destination node. Speed of the animating bubbles is not encoded with a variable in the dataset (Figs. 14 and 15).

Fig. 14. A trail with animating bubbles. Accompanying video is illustrating this technique in detail.

Fig. 15. Comparison of two visualizations in low level of detail. Node-link diagram visualization with branching enabled (left) and flow visualization (right).

5   Usability Study

The usability experiments were on measuring legibility of the flow visualization technique, identification of locations that are involved in high density traffic, perception of global trends and subjective comments about the visualization techniques. 20 graduate students participated in the experiments, only five of them had any experience in data visualisation.

We used a randomly generated flight data. Entries in the data set indicate number of flights occurred between locations. Each record in the traffic data set is consisted of source and destination indexes and the density of the traffic between them. Scaling of density parameter is a crucial step in defining trail properties. When traffic density is below 10, a single trail is drawn. If traffic density is in between 10–100, trails are encoded with width or branching factor, depending on the density mapping mode. For example, if traffic density is 50, depending on the mapping scheme, trail width is set to 5 or 5 branches are drawn. When camera distance exceeds the threshold distance value, flow visualization is enabled. Trails having density above 50 are clustered into flow locations, if they satisfy the clustering property. In order to form a cluster, locations that are close to each other have to exceed the cumulative density threshold value, 150. After defining the flow locations, flows are drawn while cluster-forming trails are hidden. In other words, trails are replaced with flows to emphasize high density traffic.

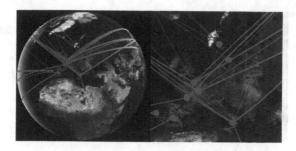

Fig. 16. Camera distance is set to maximum distance (left), camera is zoomed into nearest perspective (right).

5.1 Legibility of the Flow Visualization Technique

In the first experiment, effectiveness of the flow visualization technique is evaluated. The trail visualization technique is not taken into consideration. The visibility of a flow is decided on its length with respect to a threshold value, in terms of screen coordinates. If the length of the flow is smaller than the threshold length, it will be hidden. In this experiment, participants are expected to rate the legibility of the flow direction with respect to the different threshold values, 25, 100 and 200 pixels. Rating of the legibility is defined on a scale from 1 to 5, 1 being the most difficult and 5 being the easiest. In the first step, participants are presented with a flow having length equal to 25 pixels. Afterwards, same procedures are followed with length values 100 and 200 pixels.

5.2 Identification of Locations with High Traffic Density

In this experiment, participants are expected to count the number of locations with high traffic density in Europe, where node-link visualization is analyzed in terms of density encoding. Since the scope of this study includes only node-link visualization, flow visualization is disabled at all zoom levels. In node-link diagrams, edges may cross over nodes or other edges. This situation may lead to visual clutter that would reduce the legibility of relationships.

Density encoding in our node-link representation is managed by two different methods; branching and width coding. These methods yield to different views in terms of different levels of detail. The experiment is performed in four steps. In the first step, width coding is enabled and camera stays on the maximum distance. After the user counts the number of locations with high density traffic, camera is zoomed into nearest perspective, which forms the second step. These two steps are shown in Fig. 16. Following these two steps, remaining steps are carried out when branching method is enabled Fig. 17. Same zoom levels are used in this state as well.

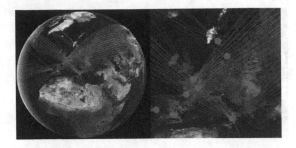

Fig. 17. Branching is enabled. Camera distance is set to maximum distance (left), camera is zoomed into nearest perspective (right).

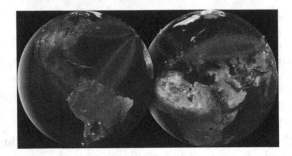

Fig. 18. Global trends highlighted with red. (Color figure online)

5.3   Recognition of Global Trends

In the third experiment, the perception of global trends around the world is evaluated. Participants are expected to count the number of regions that imply high density traffic such as from Europe to Asia, etc. Initially, all trails are drawn with width coding enabled. After completing this task, they are expected to repeat same procedure with branching enabled. Following these two tasks, participants are encouraged to analyze the global trends when flow visualization is enabled Fig. 18.

5.4   Subjective Comments

In the last step of the experiment, participants are encouraged to give subjective comments about the visualization techniques that they have experienced in previous steps. Instead of asking their opinion on pre-defined subjects, they are expected to evaluate the success of different visualization techniques regarding their experiences. Critical discussion issues from the participants' feedbacks can be summarized as: i- Identification of locations in different levels of detail, ii- Perception of traffic direction and density, iii- Understanding of global trends, iv- Legibility, visual clarity.

6   Discussion and Results

In the first experiment, legibility of the flow direction is addressed. In all cases, majority of the participants were able to detect flow direction without difficulties. The legibility feature is not a quantitative measure; therefore, results vary significantly. When flow length is 25 pixels, 9 participants out of 20 (45 %) voted for 5, 3 participants out of 20 (15 %) voted for 4, 6 participants out of 20 (30 %) voted for 3, 1 person out of 20 (5 %) voted for 2 and 1 person out of 20 (5 %) voted for 1. In the second case, when flow length is set to 100 pixels, results are much clearer. 13 participants out of 20 (65 %) have chosen 5, where 6 of them (30 %) have chosen 4 and 1 person have chosen legibility as 3. In the last case, 20 participants out of 20 have agreed that the legibility of flow direction is 5 (easiest) when flow length is 200 pixels. The Fig. 19 depicts results. We concluded that the legibility of flow direction is proportional to the flow width.

In the second experiment, identification of the locations with high traffic density in Europe is analyzed. Each method, branching and width coding is tested with different zoom levels. The Fig. 20 shows the number of locations predicted by the participants when branching method is used. The Fig. 21 indicates the same situation when width coding method is used. In both figures, the columns at the front represent the results when zoom level is high.

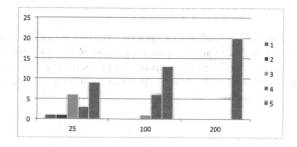

Fig. 19. Legibility of flow direction. The horizontal axis represents the flow length in pixels and vertical axis shows the number of participants that agreed on the legibility scores. (Color figure online)

Although it is impossible to derive specific conclusions from these results, it is evident that in both methods, majority of participants have agreed that the number of locations varies between 4 and 6. In both methods, it's improbable to analyze the effect of zoom level. In branching method, some of the participants have counted more locations when zoom level is increased. However, the opposite situation, where participants counted fewer locations when camera stands on maximum distance, holds as well. When width coding method is enabled, thick lines overlap and the locations below those edges become hidden. The most important result obtained from this study is that, changes in the zoom level cannot be directly related to the identification of locations.

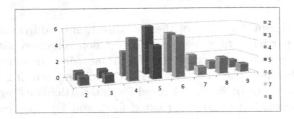

Fig. 20. Identification of the number of locations with high density traffic in Europe when branching method is enabled. The horizontal axis represents the number of locations counted and the vertical axis shows the number of participants. Columns at the front represent high zoom level and vice versa. (Color figure online)

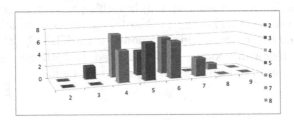

Fig. 21. Identification of the number of locations with high density traffic in Europe when width coding is enabled. The horizontal axis represents the number of locations counted and the vertical axis shows the number of participants. Columns at the front represent high zoom level and vice versa. (Color figure online)

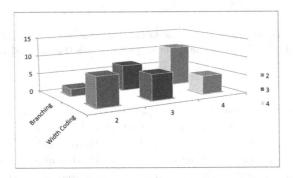

Fig. 22. Identification of global trends. The horizontal line represents the number of regions counted, the vertical axis show the number of participants. Width coding is represented with the columns at the front, branching is represented with the columns at the back. (Color figure online)

The third experiment focuses on the global trends in such a way that participants are expected to find the number of regions with high density traffic. There are four regions detected in the clustering algorithm used in the application. These regions are the traffic from Europe to Asia, from North America to Europe, from North America to South America and from Europe to South America, also shown in Fig. 18. It is beneficial to remind that clustered regions form flow locations and flows are drawn between these locations to denote very high density traffic. Multiple trails having traffic density value above 50 are clustered into flow locations. In the application, these regions are calculated automatically and flows are drawn; however, participants are expected to find the regions with very high density traffic when flows are not visible. In other words, participants are encouraged to detect those regions in node-link visualization with branching and width coding methods. Figure 22 presents the results.

It is reasonable to deduce a conclusion that participants were more comfortable in detecting the regions with high density traffic when branching method is enabled. 11 out of 20 participants (55 %) found 4 regions in branching method; whereas in width coding method, only 5 out of 20 participants (25 %) identified 4 regions.

In the final experiment, flow visualization is demonstrated and participants were encouraged to draw conclusions from the tasks they have accomplished in previous steps of the experiment considering all visualization methods presented. The results of the user study can be summarized as:

i- Majority of the participants (60 %) preferred flow visualization technique for evaluating global trends. They claimed that node-link visualization technique suffer from visual clutter in terms of legibility of global structure. Using a completely different visual technique for displaying very high density traffic also attracted participants' attention.

ii- Legibility of traffic direction is best perceived by flow visualization technique. The response time needed to analyze traffic direction is too low in flow visualization technique when compared to node-link diagram technique.

iii- Traffic density is best examined by flow visualization and branching enabled node-link diagram.

iv- Participants experienced difficulties on detecting locations in node-link diagrams when width coding is enabled, due to the fact that some locations were exposed to overlapping edges. Some participants also faced this uncertainty when branching method is used; however, those cases were negligible when compared to the cases when width coding is enabled.

v- In high levels of detail, participants favored branching method over width coding method. Their main concern was the comparability of width parameter. They argued that making decisions between trails having different numbers of branches is much easier than comparing their widths, especially if their density values are close.

7 Conclusions

In this paper, we present a visualization tool that incorporates flow visualization techniques in the context of geographic network visualization. An overview of the whole data while encouraging participants to discover and analyze patterns in detail is achieved by performing LOD. It is managed by altering the layout of the network structure and modifying employed visualization techniques. In high level of detail, node-link visualization is enabled to provide detailed information. When level of detail is low, general trends can be easily depicted in flow visualization.

The results of the usability study experiments have shown that some visualization techniques performed better than others on certain aspects. One conclusion we derived is that our flow visualization technique gave promising results in representing network traffic. Participants have agreed that our technique was able to convey valuable information about traffic direction and density. Moreover, participants have preferred flow visualization technique over conventional node-link diagram visualization in terms of visual clarity. It is also essential to mention that clustering algorithms are not in the scope of this paper. However, with suitable clustering algorithms, excelling results can be achieved.

While studying LOD we conclude that providing unambiguous images is a fatal concern when dealing with global context. Avoiding visual clutter by the removal of trails with high density traffic helped flow visualization technique to outperform other visualization techniques in the identification of global trends. In high LOD, the visual parameters that are used to encode traffic density in node-link visualization are analyzed. We obtained that participants found width coding method unsuccessful in interpretation of traffic density. On the other hand, branching method gave promising results in terms of representing traffic density and comparability in high LOD.

References

1. Becker, R.A., Eick, S.G., Wilks, A.R.: Visualizing network data. IEEE Trans. Visual Comput. Graphics **1**(1), 16–28 (1995)
2. Breitkreutz, B.J., Stark, C., Tyers, M., et al.: Osprey: a network visualization system. Genome Biol. **4**(3), R22 (2003)
3. Cabral, B., Leedom, L.C.: Imaging vector fields using line integral convolution. In: Proceedings of the 20th Annual Conference on Computer Graphics and Interactive Techniques, pp. 263–270. ACM (1993)
4. Dykes, J., MacEachren, A.M., Kraak, M.J.: Exploring Geovisualization. Elsevier, Amsterdam (2005)
5. Engin, B., Bozkaya, B., Balcisoy, S.: Introducing level of detail to 3d thematic maps. In: ICA GeoViz (2009)
6. Fayyad, U.M., Wierse, A., Grinstein, G.G.: Information Visualization in Data Mining and Knowledge Discovery. Morgan Kaufmann, San Francisco (2002)
7. Hoppe, H.: Smooth view-dependent level-of-detail control and its application to terrain rendering. In: Visualization 1998, Proceedings, pp. 35–42. IEEE (1998)

8. Huffaker, B., Nemeth, E., Claffy, K.: Otter: A general-purpose network visualization tool. In: Proceedings of the 9th Annual Conference of the Internet Society (1999)
9. Laramee, R.S., Hauser, H., Doleisch, H., Vrolijk, B., Post, F.H., Weiskopf, D.: The state of the art in flow visualization: Dense and texture-based techniques. In: Computer Graphics Forum, vol. 23, pp. 203–221. Wiley Online Library (2004)
10. Luebke, D.P.: Level of Detail for 3D Graphics. Morgan Kaufmann, Boston (2003)
11. Scheuermann, G., Burbach, H., Hagen, H.: Visualizing planar vector fields with normal component using line integral convolution. In: Proceedings of the Conference on Visualization 1999: Celebrating Ten Years, pp. 255–261. IEEE Computer Society Press (1999)
12. Shen, H.W., Kao, D.L.: A new line integral convolution algorithm for visualizing time-varying flow fields. IEEE Trans. Visual Comput. Graphics 4(2), 98–108 (1998)
13. Shneiderman, B., Aris, A.: Network visualization by semantic substrates. IEEE Trans. Visual Comput. Graphics 12(5), 733–740 (2006)
14. Stalling, D., Hege, H.C.: Fast and resolution independent line integral convolution. In: Proceedings of the 22nd Annual Conference on Computer Graphics and Interactive Techniques, pp. 249–256. ACM (1995)
15. Van Wijk, J.J.: Spot noise texture synthesis for data visualization. In: ACM Siggraph Computer Graphics, vol. 25, pp. 309–318. ACM (1991)

Methodology for Efficiency Analysis of VR Environments for Industrial Applications

Jana Dücker(✉), Polina Häfner, and Jivka Ovtcharova

Institute for Information Management in Engineering,
Karlsruhe Institute of Technology, Karlsruhe, Germany
{jana.duecker, polina.haefner,
jivka.ovtcharova}@kit.edu

Abstract. Companies are keen on using novel technologies like Virtual Reality (VR) in order to achieve competitive advantages. However, the economic impact of the integration of such technologies in a company is difficult to quantify. Especially small and medium enterprises encounter difficulties when trying to quantify the benefits of instruments like VR. During the decision process, companies need extensive support and expensive consulting. In this paper a methodology for an efficiency analysis of industrial VR integration is presented. It includes both cost- and utility-based considerations. The user-friendly analysis allows the decision-maker to access a deeper understanding of VR and it results in a customised VR solution. The proposed economic assessment methodology is being validated by two companies in the mechanical engineering sector and it is proved to be a very useful tool to enable the decision for VR integration.

Keywords: Virtual reality · Efficiency analysis · Cost-benefit · Industrial applications

1 Introduction

The key for a company in context of globalisation is to prove their innovation ability in order to attain competitive advantages. However, required investments in new technologies are often associated with high costs. Especially if small and medium enterprises (SME) disinvest, it may have serious consequences.

Using Virtual Reality (VR) technologies companies can achieve next to front-loading other competitive advantages in their respective fields. The development of these technologies has been growing quickly in recent years, in the entertaining industry as well as in industrial applications. A forecast for 2018 based on data from 2014 predicts that sales of VR products (hardware and software) will increase from US $90 million (in 2014) to US$5,200 million [1]. This represents a growth of nearly 5800 % and indicates that quite some companies do see benefits (however hard to quantify) in the tools provided by the VR technology.

Nevertheless, the initial investments of industrial VR applications are a major barrier for SME. Industrial VR systems are complex product-service-systems consisting of hardware, software and services (henceforth referred to as VR configuration or

© Springer International Publishing Switzerland 2016
L.T. De Paolis and A. Mongelli (Eds.): AVR 2016, Part I, LNCS 9768, pp. 72–88, 2016.
DOI: 10.1007/978-3-319-40621-3_5

VR solution). Their entire beneficial consequences are hard to quantify. Moreover the user acceptance of these technologies has increased significantly over the past twelve years. A study conducted in 2015 revealed that the companies have great concerns regarding the accompanied high investments and lack of access to information for VR integration [2]. For this reason, a systematic economic analysis is required, which allows companies without prior VR experience to evaluate the potential of VR systems in general and gives guidelines on which VR systems suits their individual requirements best.

The following chapter gives an overview of related works on classification of VR systems, investment appraisal models and approaches for economic and efficiency analyses. It is followed by a short description of the developed methodology for efficiency analysis of VR environments. For better understanding a detailed description of each methodology step is described on the basis of the validation. The paper is then concluded with a proposition for future work.

2   Related Work

The result of a servery in 2015 with 51 German SME without any prior VR experience [2] shows that SME face two main challenges, which complicate the VR integration: The high investment costs and the lower level of information about VR.

One main challenge is that companies without any VR experience need methods to evaluate VR systems in regard to technical parameters and company-specific benefits. One possible solution is the classification scheme for VR systems from Weidig et al. [3]. In this approach "Non-VR experts" can formulate requirements of those technologies on the basis of a scheme and evaluate them. It is based on linked tables, which is constructed in several stages. The model provides a good approach to classify VR interaction technologies due to the combined knowledge from different technical areas. This method is suitable for the classification of VR functions, but it could be extended by a concrete usage of VR technology.

Methods for evaluation of VR usability and benefits already exist, especially for special application areas. For example, Rizzo and Kim conducted a SWOT analysis of the field of Virtual Reality rehabilitation and therapy [4]. There is also a computerised diagnostic tool for usability evaluation of virtual environment systems [5]. In this application, a participant can evaluate an existing VR system based on 100 questions derived from 10 usability factors. However, specific economic analyses for VR in companies prior to the installation of the VR system are still missing.

The other main challenge for SME is the high investment combined with uncertain profit. Almost every investment appraisal is built on methods like net present value and payback method [6]. The most reused benefit methods are use-value analysis (like analytic hierarchy process [7]) and cost-benefit analysis [8]. There are specific analyses for different industries as well. The VR investments are comparable to general IT investments. Therefore *OTT* developed an economic analysis with risk levels (WARS), which analyses the cost-effectiveness of IT investments [9]. The model includes not only a statement about the costs and benefits, but evaluates the stability of potential results as well. It is based on the cost-benefit analysis of IBM. The risk levels reflect the probability, which costs and benefits can realise. The benefits and costs can be represented over the increasing risks levels in a diagram. Therefore the intersection of the two curves can be assessed at the corresponding level of risk with the payment [9]. A direct transfer of this method to industrial VR applications is not possible. However, an adaption for virtual reality technology was developed and is presented in this publication (see Sect. 3).

There are only a few methods, which combine solutions for the two challenges described above. A general approach is to use experience-based knowledge of companies with VR systems. This exchange of experience is the most important requirement for information acquisition [2]. The experience-based knowledge was surveyed in 2015 with participants, who had already been working with VR systems in their company. In this way 17 companies provided an insight into the everyday business with VR environments. The aim was to highlight actual important VR applications for different businesses and to reveal the development of usage by a comparison of a study by Klocke *et al.* conducted in 2003 [10] and a study by Dücker taken in 2015 [2]. It turned out that the companies used the technology very intensively [2], compared with 2003 [10]. However, the companies continue to use intense basic functions of VR technologies such as design reviews or early error detection, but also use advanced applications like simulations. These results improved the basis for discussion and enabled as well as accelerated the decision making process. However, only qualitative statements about the economy could be obtained in this study. Statements about precise economic improvements were only made by a few companies, because companies have either no capacity to gather this data or they protect their internal company secret.

A methodology for economic analysis of VR technologies was developed by Kunst [11] in 2005, where he focused on virtual factories. *KUNST* recognised the problem that classic investment calculations are difficult to apply in this context. In particular, the potentials of VR applications in his work are well-structured. He divides the analysis in different parts, but he did not discuss the relationship between the results. It is difficult to assess the relevance of this model in practice, because the key components for a practical implementation and interpretation were not described in detail.

SME have less time to get involved in the technology specification and usage in their particular company, so they are often compelled to engage an expensive consultant to guide them through the integration process. There exist many solutions only for partial aspects and there is no holistic method to easily, fast and cost effective analyse their VR potential prior to VR integration.

3 Efficiency Analysis of VR Environments for Industrial Applications

The amount of the initial investment for VR integration in a company usually can be estimated very accurately. However the companies assume high and difficult to predict consequential costs. The developed Efficiency Analysis of VR Environments so called WAVE methodology (German acronym: *Wirtschaftlichkeitsanalyse für Virtual Engineering*) should create transparency for companies on their way to the technology adaptation. When companies think about the integration of VR at the first time, they usually face the following questions:

- Can my company take more opportunities in the relevant market through the usage of VR technologies?
- How can VR be used in practise? Which use cases are relevant for my company?
- Which parameters should be considered by choosing a suitable VR technology?
- What investments, benefits and monetary success can my company expect by analysing different VR systems?

The WAVE model allows a step by step approximation of this complex issue without the need of initial knowledge about VR technologies. It also involves a lot of interdisciplinary divisions in order to obtain comprehensive statements about a future VR usage. In addition to the insights on possible improvements in the company, a concrete VR solution is also identified by a risk-based efficiency analysis optimised for the specific company.

3.1   General Approach of the WAVE Methodology

This chapter describes the general approach of the Efficiency Analysis of VR environments, so called WAVE methodology (see Fig. 1). The evaluation of the VR technology potential is divided in 8 steps followed by the integration of the optimal VR system.

Step 1: Needs Identification. The aim of the first step is to develop a general understanding of the current situation of the company. Therefore, an internal interdisciplinary team analyses the actual situation. The identification of the general needs is based on a SWOT analysis [12]. The further analysis is continued only if the identified needs can be satisfied using VR technologies (see Sect. 4).

Step 2: Requirement Analysis. For the requirements analysis an extensive questionnaire ware developed. Employees from all relevant departments should participate in the survey, so that the result is as representative as possible. The questionnaire is intended for participants with a little background knowledge regarding VR. Thus questionnaire is designed for the participants to develop a deeper understanding of VR technologies during reading and answering the survey.

It begins with the questions about basic and general trends of the particular company. These include the extent of the hardware and the desired level of support by using the novel technology (11 questions).

The second part of the questionnaire deals with the applications and their benefits (90 questions). This part is based on an extensive literature review and is heavily influenced by the work of Kunst [11]. A nearly complete list of all applications sorted by the product life cycle phases utilise this previous findings. The applications comprise from the design phase through product development to sales and recycling. It highlights issues such as the early internal collaboration, the visualisation of assembly processes, the use of VR at fairs and the testing of services in respective environments.

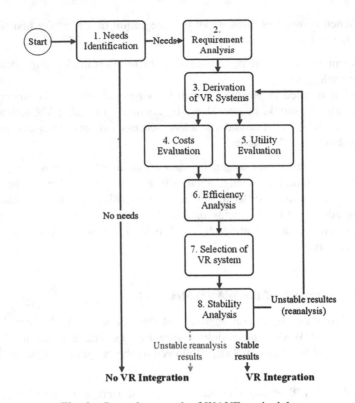

Fig. 1. General approach of WAVE methodology

Table 1. Profiling Approach

	Average profile	Maximum profile	Minimum profile
Nominal scale	Percentage evaluation	At least once selected	Selected by all
(Quasi-) metric scale	Average	Maximum	Minimum
Ordinal scale	Most frequently selected	Highest category which been selected at least once	Lowest category, which been selected at least once

Besides the identification of relevant applications, participants can examine the relevance of benefits as well.

In the third part the participant evaluates the function and features of VR software with the principle of the classification scheme for VR systems from Weidig et al. [3] (41 questions). Finally, additional comments can be specified (3 questions).

The evaluation of the requirement analysis uses profiling (Average, Maximum and Minimum profile). The approach of profiling is different for the different types of scale (see Table 1). How to apply the profiling is described in Sect. 4 (see Table 3).

Step 3: Derivation of VR Systems. The third step involves the evaluation of the requirements analysis. For this step one or more VR experts (e.g. provider, consulting or research institution with focus on VR technologies) analyse the response profile (average, maximum, minimum) and create different scenarios. The methodology is scalable in its design, because the number of different evaluation scenarios is unrestricted. In this way a company can evaluate only one VR system or compare various VR systems.

Step 4: Costs Evaluation. The determination of costs includes both one-time and ongoing costs. For example, maintenance and external support are a part of running costs. They were estimated by the VR system provider with 5 % of the one-time hardware cost and 15–20 % of software costs both for updates and training. However, the estimates are increased hardware costs due to unplanned outages by involving risk levels which are illustrated in Table 2. Further cost aspects were derived on the basis of the response profile. For example, a profile that focused the company as a pure user of VR (not developer) included lower costs for training and instruction. However, in this case cost factors such as the data preparation should be applied higher assessment. Attention should be paid to the one-time hardware cost. The VR system providers calculated not only the costs for hardware, but planning and implementation costs.

On this basis, further analysis will be carried out under optimistic and pessimistic aspects. The pessimistic case assumes that for instance a projector lamps used-up before the end of operating life. These additional potential costs are dependent on the levels of risk. This concept of risk levels distinguishes form *OTT's* method [9]. So the costs data are transferred to another array. For each VR configuration the costs are divided into largely known, estimable and hard tangible costs with respect to realisation opportunities (high, medium, low). Table 2 illustrates the segmentation. This procedure corresponds to Ott [9] method, except the allocation and structuring of costs were adjusted to VR technology. For the subsequent analysis the risk levels (1–9) are added to each other. Risk level 1 considers all possible costs. With increase of risk levels (optimistic view) only the largely known and estimable costs with high realisation chance are involved.

Step 5: Utility Evaluation. The benefits of using Virtual Reality (VR) can be assessed both in monetary and qualitative terms. For this reason, the benefit is calculated in two different ways, with monetary and qualitative focus. For monetary consideration a standardised procedure is not recommended, because the design and the amount vary for each business context. On the one hand there are different benefits depending on the industry sector, e.g. using of product prototypes. On the other hand, the collection of data through the company's internal documentation and various data quality can be difficult. The problems are often the mere lack of availability of information, such as for costs, projects, events and resources. Basically, the company-specific dimensions can be calculated with the direct, indirect and strategic benefit categories. This calculation is structured like the cost evaluation. Only the sum of the risks levels are

Table 2. General structure of the cost for one VR configuration with illustration of risk levels (1–9)

Cost category ↓		Realisation chance →	High	Medium	Low
Largely known costs	One -time (O)	Consulting fees, Hardware Software Training + manpower Data preparation	**9**	**8**	**7**
	Currently (C)	Manpower Room costs Software licence Rent of technology (for VR Sharing) Energy costs			
Estimable costs	O	Decision making, actions Manpower	**6**	**5**	**4**
	C	Maintenance Further Training			
Hard tangible costs	O		**3**	**2**	**1**
	C	Adaptation of business processes			

exactly the other way round. In the pessimistic case (risk level 1) only largely known benefits consider with most realisable opportunities.

The second way to evaluate utility is a non-monetary benefit analysis. This based on the requirement analysis from step 2. The benefit factors are assessed for each VR system of one or more experts on a scale from 0 to 100 using the questionnaire already used in step 2. The evaluation of each VR system forms the basis of the analysis and determination of the utility values in step 6. A purely utility-based analyse is reasonable, because it is difficult to estimable monetary aspects.

Step 6: Efficiency Analysis. All necessary data are collected in the previous steps. The efficiency analysis is now divided in three analytical parts:

1. *Pure cost-based consideration*: involves a comparison of net present value (NPV) of the various VR systems (see Fig. 2 and Table 5).
2. *Pure utility-based consideration*: includes benefit analyses based on requirements analysis and involves a comparison of a developed capital-benefit value of the various VR systems (see Figs. 3 and 4).
3. *Mixed benefit- and cost-based consideration with inclusion of risk levels*: inspired by the WARS model [9] and includes more analysis like amortization of the various VR systems (see Figs. 5, 6, 7, 8, 9 and Table 6).

A deeper understanding of the efficiency analysis could be gained in Sect. 4.6 where it is applied and described in details.

Step 7: Selection of VR System. A preliminary decision is made in this step. The resulted rankings of last step are compared. The selection is easy if all rankings of the analysis parts follow the same pattern. If different rankings exist, there are various options. In the second analysis part, the alternatives were sorted by an index called capital-benefit value. This index results from division of utility value by NPV. Because of low costs, the called capital-benefit values can be very high despite small utility values. However, alternatives with utility values below 50 do not fulfil the requirements. This guideline will help in final decision. Furthermore alternatives with lower costs and benefits are to be preferred if the company is risk-averse.

Step 8: Stability Analysis. The stability analysis is used to check the robustness of the results. The stability of the model is essential, because the required data is collected under high uncertainty. Many of the cost factors and especially the benefit factors are based on estimations. Therefore, relevant parameters of the model are varied in order to check whether they affect the decision. The following list is a selection of parameters that can be used:

- Stability of the present values:
  - variation of interest rate
  - variation of the duration of use of a VR configuration
- Stability of the cost-benefit analysis:
  - variation of weighting of the utility analyses
  - change of expert reviews in the most important features
- Stability of the WARS model: variation in risk assessment
  - costs are probably and benefits improbably
- Stability of the payback period:
  - Pessimistic: costs exist earlier and benefits generate later
  - Optimistic: cost generate later and benefits exist earlier

If the selection of the VR configuration does not change after the stability test, this configuration is the optimal solution. If the stability analysis results in a changing configuration by only a small variation of parameters, the reason of the volatile result should be identified. In the simplest case the selection always changes between two models. This suggests that both VR systems are suitable for the given requirements. In this case the decision should be taken in regard to qualitative aspects. A review of each step is necessary if the variation causes a random change between the different alternatives. One possible explanation for that phenomenon is that for the company the use of VR is not economical. There is also the possibility that the company has placed demands on a VR system that cannot be realised by any particular configuration. In this case a combination of several solutions is possible.

Virtual Reality Integration. After the selection of the optimal VR system the integration starts. Therefore, indicators, which are specific to the company, should be designed to check the efficiency. Thus, an easier analysis is possible in case the VR system does not become reliable and profitable. Therefore, problems and obstacles can be solved at early stage of development. After all, the experts agree: The correct use of a VR system brings great benefits, which are often difficult to quantify.

4 Validation of the WAVE Methodology

The following section describes explicitly the approach on the basis of a validation. The general validation is based on one company (see company A in Table 3) from mechanical engineering sector. Only in one part of the validation (step 2: requirement analysis) another company from the same trade is involved in order to demonstrate variety of results.

Step 1: Needs Identification. The findings of the validated company derived from a group discussion with employees from the departments of sales, market analysis, IT and technical production. The following areas were identified as needs:

Table 3. Comparison of requirements analysis between two companies

	Company A	Company B
Precipitants	5	5
Identify application	Product development, marketing, sales, R&D	Product development, sales
Expected group size	>5	<5
Relevant applications (average evaluation, [0,10])	Support to events\trade shows (10), visualisation for product demonstration (9.5), clientele expansion (9.25)	Design Review (8.6), dimensionally correct consideration of the products in the early product development (8.4), customers expansion (8)
Relevant benefits (average evaluation, [0,10])	Image improvement (9), Intuitive integration of untrained persons (8.6), Internal conferences (local independence) (8)	Increasing productivity and quality of employees (7.8), employee creativity (7.8), employee motivation (7.6), better basis for discussion (7.6)
Mandatory functions	Explore, present, visual feedback, display 3D models, 3DOF	Present

- Image improvement and sales support
- Knowledge collection
- Knowledge transfer
- New services

In those areas VR can be used to improve the actual situation of the company. So the analysis can continue.

Step 2: Requirement Analysis. In carrying out the WAVE model at different companies, it came to different requirements and therefore also to different profiles. As an example Table 3 demonstrates a comparison between two companies of a same sector. The numbers in brackets describe the average of participant's evaluation on a scale where 10 represents perfect matching and 1 represents the opposite.

It can be seen that the requirements are set differently to the VR systems. In particular, the applications and benefits differ.

Step 3: Deduction of VR Systems. Five possible VR systems were configured in the validation (for company A). These are based on offers from VR system providers, according to the results of the requirement analysis:

1. *High End*: A customised three-sided CAVE with wide-ranging software based on the *Maximum profile*.
2. *Mobile*: a mobile system consisting of a 3D projector, tracking system, screen and software with basic functions on the basis of the *Average profile*.
3. *Low Cost*: an inexpensive self-assembled system consisting of 84-inch 3D TV, tracking system and open source software on the basis of M*inimum profile*.
4. *VR Sharing*: No purchase of hardware. In this particular case the company rents VR technologies next to company's location and for trade shows.
5. *3D*: Just a 3D system consists of a 3D projector without tracking (for verification of the added value of VR).

Step 4: Costs Evaluation. The cost evaluation involves both company-internal and external cost. The external consideration includes hardware, software and service costs. Experts estimated the costs for each VR configuration on basis of offers (High End, Mobile, Low Cost, VR Sharing, 3D). It is important to differ between one-time and running cost.

The company-internal cost includes especially manpower for system integration and reorganisation actions. Moreover the company had to calculate the running costs for example room and energy cost.

Step 5: Utility Evaluation. Following use cases with important benefit aspects are included from the company (see Table 4). They are derived from the requirement analysis. The company sells large, complex machines and presents them on fairs. If a VR system is used, direct cost savings by fairs are, for example, lower transport costs, lower costs for personnel (staff, travel, accommodation costs, fees, etc.) and smaller stand space at the fair. In addition, it also increases the chance of new orders (indirect benefits), because of the unique selling point.

In addition, other strategic benefits arise. The innovative technique can go along with an improved image and increased awareness. If a company use VR for customer presentations, it can also improve the image. In both cases the image improvement is estimated by increased sales.

The bracketed fields could not be considered on the basis of the collected data. The monetary evaluation was based on internal information. Then the risk levels are considered in the same way as in the cost evaluation.

Table 4. Use cases with important benefit aspects included in the validation

Use cases	Trade show	Presentation to customers	Internal meeting
Direct	Cost reduction	Time reduction	Time reduction
Indirect	More prospects and potential new contracts	Improvement of orders	(Error reduction)
Strategical	Image improvement	Image improvement	(Higher level of transparency)

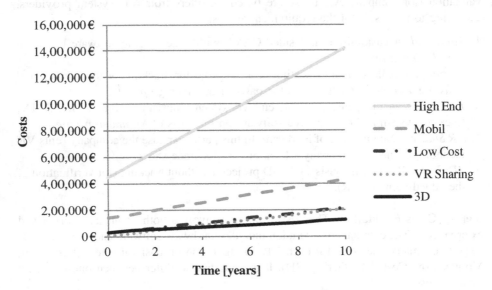

Fig. 2. Cost trends of VR alternatives

Step 6: Efficiency Analysis. After collection of all relevant data the efficiency analysis, which is divided in three parts, can be applied.

1. Pure cost-based consideration

The first step is to create a visualisation to get a first impression of the cost of the VR systems. Hence, the costs of each configuration are displayed over time (see Fig. 3).

Furthermore the present value should be determined (see Table 5). This corresponds to the calculation of the net present value (NPV) except that deposits are not observed. Configurations with small negative NPV are more advantageous. In this example the *3D, VR Sharing* and *Low Cost* perform well.

Table 5. Present value of VR alternatives

	High end	Mobile	Low cost	VR sharing	3D
10 Years	−1.196.928	−365.172	−171.930	−160.523	−103.513
Endless use	−2.387.060	−721.180	−400.990	−411.000	−215.798

2. Pure utility-based consideration

The utility-based consideration includes three (classical) benefit analyses, which are combined by weighting. The appraisal criteria (of any cost-benefit analysis) bases on the requirement analysis. The weighting of the evaluation criteria set by the participants (company) in the questionnaire. A high weighting of appraisal criteria concerns in a greater assessment of this aspect in step 2. The assessment of experts was carried out in the previous step on a scale from 0 to 100. A spider chart is created for the most important five to ten properties. This underlines the advantages and disadvantages of the different alternatives. In Fig. 4, the results are shown.

Now a ranking of the resulting utility values of each VR configuration, which range between 0 and 100, can be established. This analysis part enables first interpretations to the suitability of a VR model. We developed an index to concretise the results, which relate utility values to NPV of the cost-based consideration. This capital-benefit value (German acronym: Kapital-Nutzen-Wert) is illustrated in Fig. 5. Therefor the capital-benefit value is resulting from division of utility value by NPV. High negative capital-benefit values are interpreted positively.

High End was excluded based on these results, because the *Mobile* solution has a similar utility and in the same time is much cheaper.

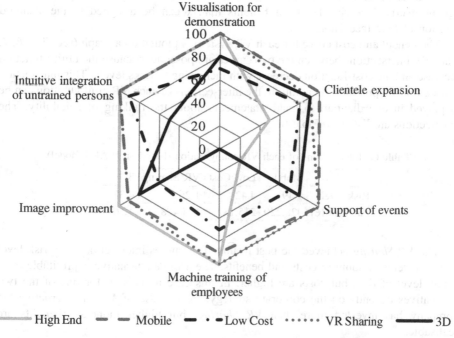

Fig. 3. Spider chart of the 6 most important properties (0- inadequate; 100- perfect)

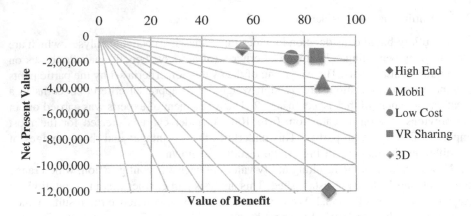

Fig. 4. Visualisation of capital-benefit value of the VR configuration

3. Mixed benefit- and cost-based consideration

The benefit- and cost-based consideration bases on WARS model [9]. This analysis is realised by the calculation of costs and utility from step 4 and 5.

The monetary benefits are based on one year. We have to calculate the present values to compare them with the costs. The result of this step is a slightly different benefit matrix. The risk levels of benefits matrix can be assigned to the standard division of *OTT* (see Table 2).

The benefit and cost curve for each VR system is plotted on a graph (see Figs. 6, 7, 8 and 9). Intersections between the two curves are possible, because the utility-function increase and the cost-function decrease with increasing of risks levels. This intersection is used for interpretation. In addition, the intersections of each VR configuration can be displayed in one diagram to make statements about the ranking of suitability. The intersections are listed in Table 6.

Table 6. Intersections of each VR configuration (based on WARS model)

	Mobile	Low Cost	VR Sharing	3D
Risk level	1.49	4.42	1.26	4.37
Payment [€]	428,220	215,181	194,428	127,976

The *VR Sharing* achieved the best results. The curves intersect at a low risk level and a moderate amount of costs and benefits. The *Mobile* alternative is profitable from a low level of risk, but costs are higher. In this case a decision for one of the two alternatives depends on the corporate strategy. In the case of *Mobile* alternative the company has invested more than *VR Sharing*, but higher monetary benefits are realisable.

Moreover an amortization calculation is realised. The data of annual costs and benefits have already been completed. They are depending both on the risk level. For each risk level the payoff time is calculated. It is important that the values of final stages

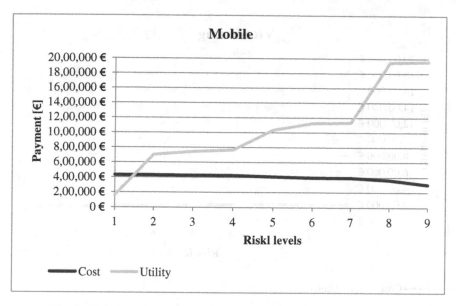

Fig. 5. Benefit and cost consideration of *Mobile* based on WARS model

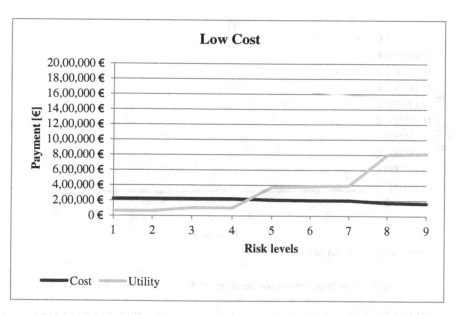

Fig. 6. Benefit and cost consideration of *Low Cost* based on WARS model

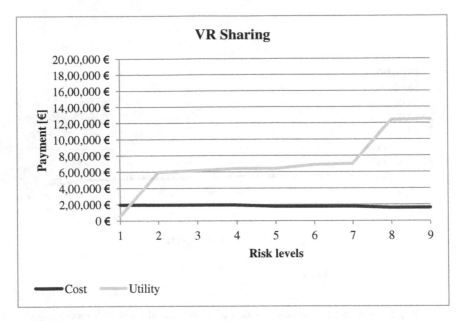

Fig. 7. Benefit and cost consideration of *VR Sharing* based on WARS model

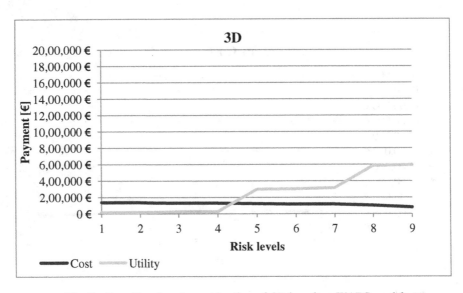

Fig. 8. Benefit and cost consideration of *3D* based on WARS model

of the WARS model are not used, because they are present values and don't concern on years. For the interpretations of each payoff time all risk levels are relevant (for each VR configuration). Optionally, this can be represented in a graph (see Fig. 10). So it is easier to compare the curves of VR alternatives on the risk levels (x-axis) and amortization year (y-axis).

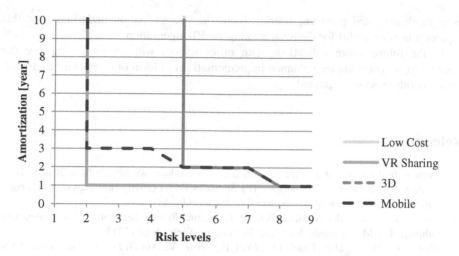

Fig. 9. Comparison of payback periods of VR alternatives

The *VR Sharing* alternative amortizes from the second risk level in the first year. The system is fastest profitable in comparison to the other alternatives with the highest probability.

In summary *VR Sharing* compare favourably with the other alternatives. *Mobile* achieved second best results. *3D* and *Low Cost* achieved only moderate to poor results.

Step 7 & 8: Selection of VR System and Stability Analysis. *High End* was excluded for the particular company due to the poor results in the utility-based consideration. The prime selection is *VR Sharing* followed by *Mobile, Low Cost* and *3D*.

At last, the stability analysis supports the previously made selection and the organisation can begin the process of integration. In the validation, some examples for stability parameters are variation of estimated useful life of each VR alternatives, interest rate of present value, weightings and expert assessments of benefit analysis. The selection was stable over all variations.

5   Conclusion and Further Work

This paper shows that the economic analysis of VR investments includes complex aspects. Already existing approaches support VR investment decisions, but they are not yet qualified to be applicable for SME. The qualitative economic statements from VR users are not sufficient valid.

In this paper a methodology for an efficiency analysis of industrial VR integration was presented. The user-oriented analysis allows companies to access a deeper understanding of VR, while working on the analysis. The result is a customised VR system, which was compared with other VR systems derived from the internal company requirements. So the proposed economic methodology is scalable. Moreover SMEs can easily apply the cost-effective method. It was validated with two companies from machinery and plant engineering industry. The validation underlines that this approach is very useful for decision making of VR integration.

In the future, more validations with other sectors will follow to improve the methodology. There are also planned implementations in form of computer-based tool. So a smooth process is granted.

References

1. Nunatak (n.d.). Forecast revenue for virtual reality products worldwide from 2014 to 2018 (in million U.S. dollars). In Statista - The Statistics Portal (2016). http://www.statista.com/statistics/426276/virtual-realiy-revenue-forecast-worldwide/
2. Dücker, J.: Analyse der Wirtschaftlichkeit der Virtual Reality Technologie im Kontext von Industrie 4.0. Master thesis, Karlsruhe Institute of Technology (2015)
3. Weidig, C., Mestre, D.R., Israel, J.H., Noel, F., Perrot, V., Aurich J.C.: Classification of VR interaction techniques, based on user intention. Eurographics Digital Library (2014)
4. Rizzo, A.A., Kim, G.J.: A SWOT analysis of the field of virtual reality rehabilitation and therapy. Presence **14**(2), 119–146 (2005)
5. Kalawsky, R.S.: VRUSE—a computerised diagnostic tool: for usability evaluation of virtual/synthetic environment systems. Appl. Ergon. **30**(1), 11–25 (1999)
6. Favaro, J.: A comparison of approaches to reuse investment analysis. In: ICSR, p. 136. IEEE (1996)
7. Saaty, T.L.: How to make a decision: the analytic hierarchy process. Eur. J. Oper. Res. **48**(1), 9–26 (1990)
8. Mishan, E.J., Quah, E.: Cost-Benefit Analysis. Routledge, London (2007)
9. Ott, H.J.: Wirtschaftlichkeitsanalyse von EDV-Investitionen mit dem WARS-Modell am Beispiel der Einführung van CASE. Wirtschaftsinformatik **35**(6), 522531 (1993)
10. Klocke, F., Straube, A.M., Pypec, C.: Vorsprung durch Virtual Reality. Management Summary. IPT, Aachen (2003)
11. Kunst, S.: Konzeption eines Modells zur Bewertung der Wirtschaftlichkeit von Virtual-Reality-Systemen in der Digitalen Fabrik. Diploma thesis, Hochschule Wismar (2005)
12. Hill, T., Westbrook, R.: SWOT analysis: it's time for a product recall. Long Range Plan. **30**(1), 46–52 (1997)

Unity3D Virtual Animation of Robots
with Coupled and Uncoupled Mechanism

Víctor Hugo Andaluz[1,2](✉), Jorge S. Sánchez[1], Jonnathan I. Chamba[3], Paúl P. Romero[3],
Fernando A. Chicaiza[1], Jose Varela[2], Washington X. Quevedo[1],
Cristian Gallardo[2], and Luis F. Cepeda[1]

[1] Universidad de las Fuerzas Armadas ESPE, Sangolquí, Ecuador
{vhandaluz1,jssanchez,fachicaiza,wjquevedo,lfcepeda}@espe.edu.ec
[2] Universidad Técnica de Ambato, Ambato, Ecuador
jazjose@hotmail.es, cmgallardop@gmail.com
[3] Escuela Superior Politécnica de Chimborazo, Riobamba, Ecuador
{jonnathanchamba,p_romero}@espoch.edu.ec

Abstract. This paper presents the development of the animation of robots in virtual reality environments, whose mechanisms can be coupled -the movement relies on mechanical principles-; and uncoupled mechanisms, *i.e.*, the degrees of freedom are controlled independently via a control unit. Additionally, the present phases to transfer the design of a robot developed in a CAD tool to a virtual simulation environment without being lost the physical characteristics of the original design are showed, for which it is considered the various types of motions that the robot can perform depending on the design. Finally, shows the results obtained from the simulation of motion of a robot hexapod 18DOF and Theo Jansen mechanism.

Keywords: Virtual reality · Robot simulation · Unity3D · Coupled and uncoupled mechanism

1 Introduction

In recent years, robotics research has experienced a significant change. Research interests are moving from the development of robots for structured industrial environments to the development of autonomous mobile robots operating in unstructured and natural environments [1–8]. The advancement of technology has allowed the development of computers that support increasingly real and complex simulations in different areas of research and industry. Based on this progress, tools are designed continuously to replicate reality in completely virtual environments. One such tool is the graphic engine developed by Unity Technologies, Unity3D, which allows to develop virtual environments for a wide range of platforms [9] and operating systems.

The simulation process begins with the creation of the 3D model of the robot, considering the aspects of modeling, translation of the format and application. In *modeling phase* is designed the three-dimensional structure of each of the parts and elements of the robot using a tool Computer Aided Design (CAD) [10], which pursues

© Springer International Publishing Switzerland 2016
L.T. De Paolis and A. Mongelli (Eds.): AVR 2016, Part I, LNCS 9768, pp. 89–101, 2016.
DOI: 10.1007/978-3-319-40621-3_6

the physiognomic credibility of the robot taking into account the considerations that facilitate mobility for future animation effects. While the *Translation CAD format phase* to a supported format for Unity3D animation is achieved by additional software, due to hierarchy requirements it must contain certain elements. Finally, *application phase* represents the controlled movement of the 3D model in a similar way to a real environment, taking into account that certain parts move and rotate with respect to each other, for which you should consider animation techniques.

For the simulation of the 3D model, the hierarchy of the elements of the model are consider [10]. This consideration represents a set of rigid parts that are attached to other (anterior and posterior) through joints, so that in the articulated hierarchy is considered: *(i) Control by fixed points,* taking into account that the position of the root segment in space can be allocated independently and allow to move the entire articulated figure for the space; however, sometimes the position of another segment of the hierarchy can be directly determine and hold it in place during movement; for example, when walking one foot remains in contact with the ground while the other foot is moving, and then the other foot support is changed; to reproduce this behavior can begin assigning the node representing the fixed foot as the root node, from which the position of the other segments is calculated; the root node can be change from one foot to another and rearrange the hierarchy, given that the changes made in each joint will be invested; *(ii) Additional restrictive ligatures,* in this case the articulated structures can be combined with parameter values of the joints, so the number of degrees of freedom is reduced and it is easier to get the movements in the different parts of the structure; for example, the two arms of a human figure can move together, linking their angles by transfer functions that match.

In this context, this paper proposes the animation of coupled and uncoupled robotic mechanisms. Additionally, the phases for moving the robot from a design CAD tool to a virtual environment simulation is presented, maintaining the physical characteristics of the original design. Finally, the simulation results are presented in the Unity3D platform, where the different types of motion for a hexapod robot 18DOF (uncoupled mechanism) and other robot based on the mechanism of Theo Jansen (coupled device) formed by three mechanisms system by side and independently controlled by two DC motors are showed.

This paper is divided into 6 Sections including the Introduction. In Sect. 2 the control problem is formulated. Next in Sect. 3 the modeling of the mobile manipulator robot and the controllers design for path following are presents. While the bilateral communication between MatLab-Unity3D is present in Sect. 4. In Sect. 5 the experimental results for of autonomous control and tele-operated for a robotic arm are presented and discussed. Finally, the conclusions are given in Sect. 6.

2   Problem Formulation

The designs of robotic prototypes developed in software Computer Aided Design CAD, SolidWorks, Autodesk Inventor, among others, do not provide all the necessary conditions for a graphic simulation of a realistic 3D model and its environment. The need for simulation focused on the interaction between the human operator, the robot and a more realistic and immersive environment, has made the simulation function of the CAD software are not sufficient to achieve this objective, because the CAD software does not have a high quality graphics compared to professional digital animations and video game made in other simulation software.

Unity3D is one of the main commercial graphics engines oriented to video games that have graphics quality in the simulation and the processing in the physical environment variables (gravity, collisions and deformations among others) that needs a 3D model for a more realistic interaction between robot-environment, enabling integration of software and hardware, *e.g.*, Leap motion, Oculus, Novint Falcon^{MT}, ROS, among others.

Limiting of support of Unity files from CAD software is not direct, therefore, is necessary to carry out intermediate modifications to integrate operation model designed. In this context, this work proposes a simple methodology to generate 3D movement of robots depending on their mechanism of movement and/or degrees of freedom, for this is considered a robot based on the mechanism of Theo Jansen, and hexapod robot with 18 DOF. The latter robot hasn't degrees of freedom related to joints, but with rotations that obeying the mechanics of the 3D model, as shown in Fig. 1.

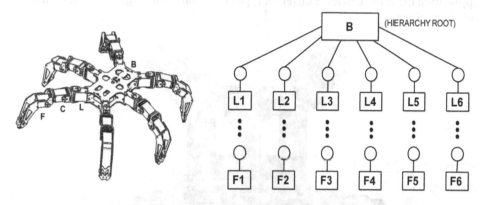

Fig. 1. Hierarchy scheme

The simulation in function of the hierarchy considers each rigid segment is defined with respect to a reference system centered on the origin of the joint. Therefore, each time is changed the position of a joint belonging to the hierarchy you should: *(i)* move the coordinate system from its previous position to the point where it will connect the next segment; *(ii)* once there, you have to rotate the coordinate system according to the state of the joint, that is, according to the target values.

3 Modeling 3D, CAD

The software Automation Mechanical Design SolidWorks is a design tool parametric solid modeling based on operations that leverages the ease of learning the graphical interface. This tool can create 3D solid models fully associative with or without restrictions, while simultaneously using automatic reactions or user defined to capture design intent. A geometric solid model contains all surface geometry and wireframe necessary to describe in detail the edges and model faces [11].

For this work, the design of a hexapod robot and other based on the mechanism of Theo Jansen are considered. The hexapod robot consists of 18 servomotors Dynamixel AX-12A, which have the ability to feed back to the control unit: speed, temperature, position, torque, to be controlled independently according to control criteria implemented [12]. The structure of the hexapod robot has a central base in which is located the control system, feed, and six servo motors that serve for tips axis robot are fixed, as illustrated in Fig. 1.

The Fig. 2 shows one of the six extremities of hexapod robot, the same which has three degrees of freedom (including the servomotor located in the central base). This design is done with the objective that the robot moves on smooth or uneven surfaces, *i.e.,* wooded uneven surfaces, environments, rocks, sand environments, among others (Fig. 3).

By having the central base of the robot with fixed servomotors for each of the limbs, these provide independent movement there between therefore according to the application the robot can have different types of locomotion, e.g., non-holonomic or omnidirectional.

Fig. 2. Hexapod robot: central base

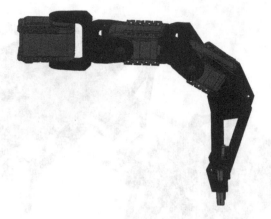

Fig. 3. Hexapod robot: assembly of an extremity

The final result of the assembly of robot shown in Fig. 4(a); while the physical construction of the robot shown in Fig. 4(b). The hexapod robot is based on a polymethylmethacrylate structure because it is lightweight and has high resistance to deformation.

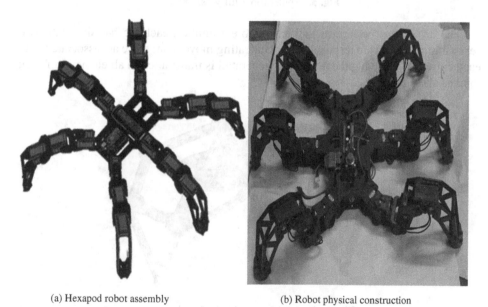

(a) Hexapod robot assembly   (b) Robot physical construction

Fig. 4. Hexapod robot 18DOF

The design of a robot based in the *Theo Jansen* mechanism consists of a group of linked bars strategically, such that the movement generated is similar to the limbs of a spider, as shown in Fig. 5.

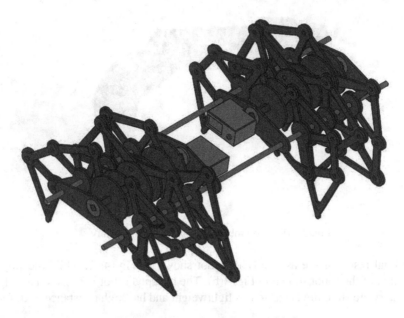

Fig. 5. Spider robot fully assembled

The design has performed will have two extremities, each leg has six joints, two servo motors which are responsible for generating movement; these are associated with each extremity allowing the movement generated is transmitted to all elements of each joint as shown in Fig. 6.

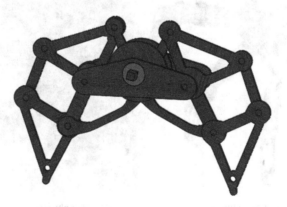

Fig. 6. Extremity assembled of spider robot

4   Export the 3D Model to Unity3D

The process to generate animation of 3D model of a robot in a virtual environment is divided into 6 stages: obtaining 3D model, addition of hierarchies, establish the kind of movement, add textures, generate the motion and finally, apply the animation, view Fig. 7:

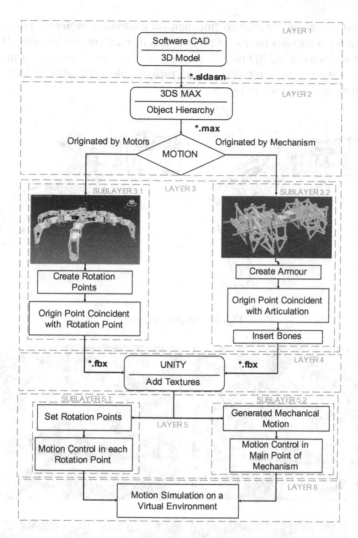

Fig. 7. Process diagram

The step of obtaining the 3D model presents the process of assembling the robot in SolidWorks, which exports the 3D model file with an extension *.sldasm. Given that Unity does not support files with the extension generated by SolidWorks, the step of addition of hierarchies makes use of Autodesk 3DS MAX software. 3DS MAX can import the file generated by CAD software, also create hierarchies, which allow you to have the relationship of positions of each one of them elements of the model. When importing, each component of the 3D model maintains its position in the assembly space of but their relations and constraints of placement are lost during the process, which is necessary to use hierarchies and get a file with extension *.max. At the stage of establishing the type of movement, considering the type of locomotion that has the 3D model, which can be coupled mechanical movement (locomotion system based on caterpillars);

or mechanical movement uncoupled (mechanism composed engines). The uncoupled mechanical motion requires the use of pivot points that are created by using 3DS MAX software. In all joints of the 3D model, each point of origin of movement must match the location of the points of rotation, and in turn, should preferably be located in the axes of each motor, as shown in Fig. 8.

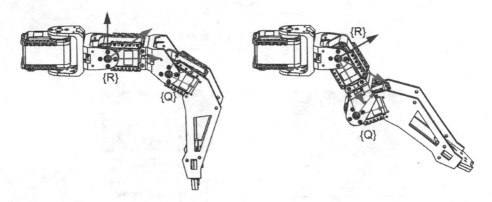

Fig. 8. Rotation points

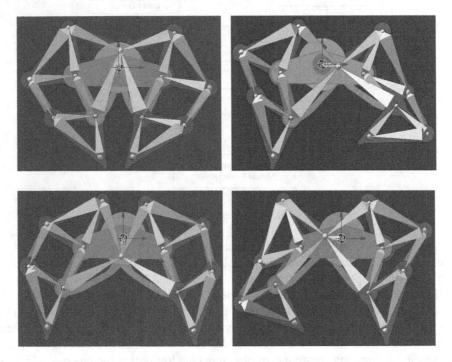

Fig. 9. Coupled motion

The coupled mechanical movement it was developed in Blender because it allows do this kind of armor. An armature acts as a skeleton which can move bones, these in turn, transmit the movement to each object that forms the 3D model. The location of the reference system should be the same as the point where the mechanical movement is generated -main articulation-, from this point, the movement will be transmitted through the bones to the various components of the 3D model as shown in the Fig. 9.

In the step of adding textures is imported the file generated in Blender or 3D MAX. The Fig. 10 shows a file that does not have textures, which have added by Unity to generate a similar actual appearance.

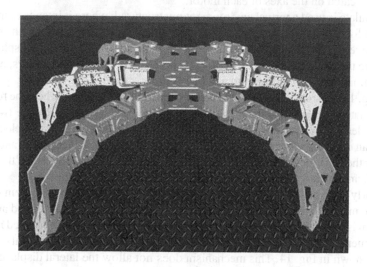

Fig. 10. Untextured hexapod robot

In the step of generating movement, it considering the use of pivot points, wherein the motion control in each of these points is established; and the use of armor where the motion control is set to the point where locomotion mechanism is generated. Finally, in the simulation stage, is added physical variables to the control set in the motion generation layer by integrating haptic devices, audio and video variables.

5   Simulation Experimental Results

The feasibility of the proposed structure for the simulation of designs for the developed robots, it has been proven through experiments in real form using a haptic device Novint Falcon[MT], to control movement of the hexapod robot and the other based on the mechanism of Theo Jansen. The simulation is performed in a desktop computer that has the following characteristic I7 2.3 GHz processor, 8 GB of RAM and a graphic card NVIDIA GeForce GT 630M.

5.1 Environment 3D Simulation

The platform on which the 3D simulation environment develops is Unity; on this simulation platform is built the robots and displacement thereof based on the control haptic device shown. Figure 11 shows the environment created for simulation, in this environment can generate the physical variables involved in a real environment.

In this environment is performed the movement of hexapod robot, which has 18 DOF. In the Fig. 12 is observed the principle of mechanical movement uncoupled, which is based on establish a point of origin of motion in each joint of the 3D model, these points are located on the axes of each motor.

To simulate is used a virtual environment unstructured, where it intends to make the inspection for which you can select between two types of displacement through the haptic device (Novint Falcon^{MT}). In the Fig. 12 is noted non-holonomic displacement type, where the robot has only perpendicular speeds to the axis of the motors, allowing a unidirectional movement, forward and backward.

The Fig. 13 shows the omni-directional movement of the hexapod, where the robot can be moved laterally, with this the displacement of the robot is guided by the two linear velocities, defined in a rotating right-handed spatial frame, and the angular velocity. The operator can drive the robot at will depending on the type of movement you want to do to move over the work area. The operation mode selection is performed by one of the buttons has the Novint Falcon^{MT}, also control in three-dimensional to drive the robot.

Similarly was made the robot simulation based on the mechanical system of Theo Jansen, the mechanism of each limb is formed by 7 solids, 5 joints and 2 fixed areas, the mechanism is driven by a pair of motors, the movement is based on the coupled mechanical movement, its principle is the armor, this acts as a skeleton can move joints mechanically, as shown in Fig. 14. This mechanism does not allow the lateral displacement of the joints, which is limited to a linear velocity perpendicular to the axis from the limbs and an angular velocity, like a mobile robot type unicycle. That can rotate freely around its axis. The term unicycle is often used in robotics to mean a generalized cart or car moving in a two-dimensional world; these are also often called unicycle-like or unicycle-type vehicles. On the other hand, the non-holonomic velocity constraint of the robot determines that it can only move perpendicular to the legs axis.

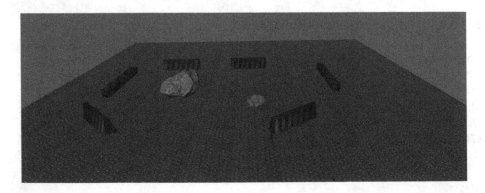

Fig. 11. Virtual environment

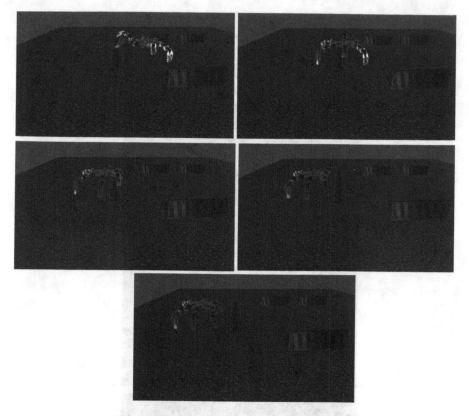

Fig. 12. Hexapod robot non-holonomic displacement

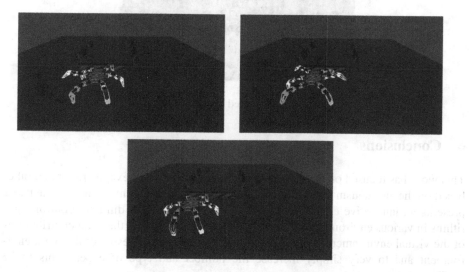

Fig. 13. Hexapod robot omni-directional displacement

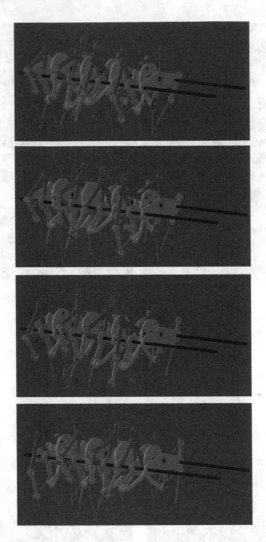

Fig. 14. Displacement of robot based on the of Theo Jansen mechanism

6   Conclusions

This work has focused on developing motion simulation of a hexapod robot and other based on the mechanism Theo Jansen in a virtual unstructured environment. The paper presents an innovative environment that facilitates the assays different control algorithms in various environments that can develop safely. Among the main contributions of the virtual environment is the ease you have to change the design of the work environment and to very simply increase the number and type of experiments to be performed.

Acknowledgment. The authors would like to thanks to the Consorcio Ecuatoriano para el Desarrollo de Internet Avanzado -CEDIA-, Universidad de las Fuerzas Armadas ESPE, Universidad Técnica de Ambato and the Escuela Superior Politécnica del Chimborazo for financing the project *Tele-operación bilateral cooperativo de múltiples manipuladores móviles – CEPRAIX-2015-05*, for the support to develop this paper.

References

1. Andaluz, V.H., Quevedo, W.X., Chicaiza, F.A., Varela, J., Gallardo, C., Sanchez, J.S.: Transparency of a bilateral tele-operation scheme of a mobile manipulator robot. In: SALENTO AVR International Conference on Augmented and Virtual Reality (2016)
2. Shekhar, H., Guha, R., Juliet, A.V., Kumar, J.: Mathematical modeling of neuro-controlled bionic arm. In: International Conference on Advances in Recent Technologies in Communication and Computing, pp. 576–578 (2009)
3. Andaluz, V.H., et al.: Nonlinear controller of quadcopters for agricultural monitoring. In: Bebis, G., et al. (eds.) ISVC 2015. LNCS, vol. 9474, pp. 1–12. Springer, Heidelberg (2015). doi:10.1007/978-3-319-27857-5_43. ISBN 978-3-642-25485-7
4. Ison, M., Vujaklija, I., Whitsell, B., Farina, D.: High-density electromyography and motor skill learning for robust long-term control of a 7-DoF robot arm. In: IEEE Transactions on Neural Systems and Rehabilitation Engineering (2015)
5. Andaluz, V.H., Ortiz, J.S., Sanchéz, J.S.: Bilateral control of a robotic arm through brain signals. In: De Paolis, L.T., Mongelli, A. (eds.) AVR 2015. LNCS, vol. 9254, pp. 1–14. Springer, Heidelberg (2015). ISBN 978-3-642-25485-7
6. Kiguchi, K., Hayashi, Y.: Estimation of joint torque for a myoelectric arm by genetic programming based on EMG signals. In: WAC World Automation Congress, pp. 1–4 (2012)
7. Ranky, G.N., Adamovich, S.: Analysis of a commercial EEG device for the control of a robot arm. In: IEEE Annual Northeast Bioengineering Conference (2010)
8. Gauthaam, M. Kumar, S.S.: EMG controlled bionic arm. In: NCOIET Innovations in Emerging Technology, pp. 111–114 (2011)
9. Indraprastha, A., Shinozaki, M.: The investigation on using Unity3D game engine in urban design study. J. ICT Res. Appl. **3**(1), 1–18 (2009)
10. Zwart, S.F.P., McMillan, S.L., van Elteren, A., Pelupessy, F.I., de Vries, N.: Multi-physics simulations using a hierarchical interchangeable software interface. Comput. Phys. Commun. **184**(3), 456–468 (2013)
11. SolidWorks Corporation. Conceptos básicos de SolidWorks Piezas y ensamblajes (2006)
12. http://support.robotis.com

A Scalable Cluster-Rendering Architecture for Immersive Virtual Environments

Giovanni Avveduto$^{(\boxtimes)}$, Franco Tecchia, Marcello Carrozzino, and Massimo Bergamasco

Percro Laboratory, Scuola Superiore Sant'Anna, Pisa, Italy
g.avveduto@sssup.it

Abstract. Complex virtual environments often require computational resources exceeding the capabilities of a single machine. Furthermore immersive visualization can exploit multiple displays fostering the needing of computational power. We hereby present a system, called *XVR Network Renderer*, allowing rendering load to be distributed throughout a cluster of workstations operating concurrently. The proposed solution consists in a set of software modules structured as a single-master multiple-slaves architecture. The master software intercepts all the graphical commands performed by an OpenGL application, without any modification of the source code. The commands are then streamed and executed individually by each slave client. The Network Renderer can be seen as a virtual OpenGL context with high capabilities. The system can be configured to work with a wide range of complex visualization setups, like CAVEs, automatically handling stereoscopy, performing perspective corrections and managing projection-related common problems. Any number of displays can be simultaneously managed by the cluster.

Keywords: Cluster rendering · Immersive virtual environments · Visualization systems

1 Introduction

Nowadays, VR applications are increasingly hungry in terms of computational resources. They may require performances exceeding the computational power that a single workstation, even if exploiting multiple processors and multiple graphics cards, is able to deliver. Additionally, immersive visualization systems requires multiple rendering passes to handle stereoscopy.

Our proposed system, called *XVR Network Renderer*, takes advantage of a network of calculators to perform rendering, according to the "cluster rendering" approach. Each cluster's node takes care of a subset of the rendering task, thus allowing large output resolution and multiple channels to be handled without requiring high-end or dedicated hardware. We ensured that our solution works using commodity hardware: the various calculators involved are not required to be identical, are connected by means of ordinary LAN devices, and may be safely equipped with low-end graphics cards.

© Springer International Publishing Switzerland 2016
L.T. De Paolis and A. Mongelli (Eds.): AVR 2016, Part I, LNCS 9768, pp. 102–119, 2016.
DOI: 10.1007/978-3-319-40621-3_7

The Network Renderer can be seen as a virtual OpenGL context with very high capabilities, completely transparent to the original application. The virtualization of the graphical context is performed by a software layer that intercepts all the OpenGL API calls issued by the original application, called *master* application, and sends them to a set of programs, called *slaves*, running on the networked machines. In our approach, the master workstation is in charge of distributing the rendering load among the slave workstations directly connected to output devices. In this way the rendered images do not need to be sent back to the master node, which can be a reasonable limitation when the resolution and the number of the managed displays grow up.

The Network Renderer have been designed with complex immersive visualization systems in mind. In particular, we have targeted PowerWall-like [1] and CAVE-like [2] setups. This means that our system is able to handle many of the usual real-life problems that arise when using multiple projectors together, such as adjusting brightness and colors and handling overlapping regions. Furthermore it is possible to distort the projected images in order to exploit non-perpendicular projection or curved surfaces. A perspective correction can be performed allowing also to add head tracking capabilities to every application. This viewpoint's change is performed independently by the slave programs, without affecting the computational resources of the master machine. The Network Renderer configuration is centralized on the master machine.

2   Related Work

The rendering phase is notoriously one of the most demanding operations from a computational point of view of a graphical application, especially when photorealistic quality and high frame rates are required. Virtual Reality is a multimodal interaction with dynamic and responsive virtual environments. Providing immersion to the user is usually achieved by covering his field of view typically surrounding him with several displays, or putting displays near his/her eyes. Both the increasing number of managed displays and the real-time constraints further increase the computational load requirements. A considerable number of solutions have been developed to manage applications with high rendering-load [3,4]. A typical strategy to approach the problem is *divide et impera*, that is splitting the rendering task into subsets and processing each of them concurrently. This approach is usually called "parallel rendering".

A possible classification of parallel rendering systems is based on the employed hardware components. Systems having multiple graphics pipelines inside a single calculator are called multipipe rendering systems [5]. Conversely, systems employing a cluster of networked calculators, each with its own pipeline working concurrently with the others, are called cluster rendering systems [6–8]; in this case, network communication has to be used to perform task assignments and combination of the various outputs, in order to obtain the final image.

Clusters have long been used for parallelizing traditionally non-interactive graphics tasks, but in the last years, there has been growing interest in using clusters for interactive rendering tasks. Thanks to the impressive improvements in the performance of commodity graphics hardware occurred in recent years and to the appearance of networks with gigabit bandwidth, cluster architectures have become a valid and cost-effective alternative to former proprietary multi-processor systems.

2.1   WireGL

In 2001 Stanford University developed WireGL [6], a scalable platform for cluster rendering of graphics applications. WireGL provides the OpenGL API to each node in a cluster, virtualizing multiple graphics accelerators into a sort-first [4] parallel renderer with a parallel interface. The sort-first approach consists in distributing primitives early in the rendering pipeline — during geometry processing — to processors that can do the remaining rendering calculations. This generally is done by dividing the screen into disjoint regions and making processors responsible for all rendering calculations that affect their respective screen regions.

WireGL follows the well established client-server approach: one or more clients send OpenGL commands to one or more servers, called *pipeservers*. Pipeservers follow the sort-first approach, and collectively manage the rendering of the whole image. Each pipeserver exploits the capabilities of his own graphics hardware and is linked to all clients through a high speed network. The image is split into several tiles, and each server manages one or more of them. The final image is obtained re-assembling the output from each pipeserver. Without special hardware to support image reassembly, the final rendered image must be read out of each local framebuffer and redistributed over a network. A simpler and more efficient way to perform the reassembling operation is to make each pipeserver deal with a single display for each of the partitions it manages. The displays can then be physically joined together in order to obtain the final image. This kind of approach may lead in principle to a non-balanced distribution of the rendering load between the graphics servers. To partially solve this problem, a number of algorithms have been developed. They can be executed by a dedicated module, that could be implemented both in software and in hardware, as for the Lighting-2 system [9].

2.2   Chromium

Chromium [7] is a further development of WireGL. Chromium inherits from WireGL the codification used to store the OpenGL commands, the interception mechanism and the client-server architecture. It allows to perform more transformations on API streams, and to arrange cluster nodes in a more generic topology than WireGL's many-to-many-to-few arrangement. The Chromium user decides which nodes of the cluster are involved in a given distributed rendering session, and what kind of communication they are going to use. These parameters are specified through a centralized configuration system, represented as an acyclic graph. Each node of the graph represent a computer of the cluster, whereas the edges symbolize the network traffic. Each node is made of two parts: *transformation* and *serialization*.

Transformation is performed by modules called *Stream Processing Units* (SPUs); they specifie how to modify an OpenGL call sequence, in a completely configurable way, usually carried out according to particular stream processing algorithms. This operation generates one or more different sequences of OpenGL commands. SPUs are implemented by a runtime library, in the same way as the WireGL driver.

Serialization is the elaboration of one or multiple command sequences, in order to generate a single output stream. The whole system is initialized by a special component called mothership. It accomplishes the task of configuring and managing the Chromium processes, and it is capable of dynamically reconfiguring the system's components. It also manages the resource distribution and verifies that every SPU chain and every network connection are created as requested by the application. Mothership configuration is not only a matter of setting number of parameters but it requires a dynamic scripting language, making the configuration a demanding task.

3   System Description

The main purpose of *XVR Network Renderer* [10] is to perform OpenGL cluster rendering exploiting the sort-first approach [4] using a a LAN. It employs a single-master multiple-slaves architecture. The system consists of a single module called *Network Driver* (see Sect. 3.1) running on the *master* workstation, and one or more *slave programs* (see Sect. 3.2) running on the same and/or on other workstations. All the machines are connected to the same local network. The module running on the master node intercepts all the OpenGL API calls, executes them locally and sends them to the slave programs through the network. The slave programs perform the rendering tasks according to a centralized configuration (see Sect. 3.5); they may also perform additional operation on their outputs (see Sect. 3.6). Master and slaves are synchronized on a per-frame basis (see Sect. 3.4). Intercepting graphical commands does not require any modification to the OpenGL master application. Our approach is based on sending graphical commands instead of rendered images over the network. This typically lead to lower bandwidth usage without quality loss: the approach of sending high resolution pre-rendered images would require an extremely high performance network or a lossy images compression.

OpenGL APIs are constantly evolving, so, although all functions can be potentially intercepted by the driver, not all functions are currently managed. During the development of the system we have focused on supporting applications developed using XVR. XVR is a flexible and efficient framework, that allows to easily develop Virtual Reality applications while maintaining a fine-grained control on the basic aspects of visualization and interaction [11].

The XVR Network Renderer has been carried out in order to provide a cluster rendering architecture suitable to manage visualization systems for Virtual

Environments. This kind of facilities can greatly vary in terms of number, kind and physical arrangement of the output devices, and consequently of required computational power. The architecture can scale from a single display setup, to a PowerWall exploiting multiple displays, up to big CAVE-like systems exploiting multiple walls enlightened by multiple projectors. The XVR network renderer has been also successfully used to implement global illumination in CAVEs architectures [12].

The network renderer has been employed in a number of EU projects [13–15].

3.1   Network Driver

The Network Driver is the module running on the master node, performing different tasks. First of all, it intercepts all the OpenGL API calls performed by the master application. Similarly to WireGL and Chromium, the interception mechanism relies on a fake OpenGL dynamic library deployed on the master machine instead of the true one.

The collected commands are passed to a module called *packetizer*, which is in charge of encoding them and storing the commands into a buffer. The encoding is performed in a custom, optimized way, by assigning a unique identifier to each function and attaching its parameters. Every time a frame ends or the buffer exceeds a threshold, the data are sent through the network to a cluster of slave hosts (see Sect. 3.3), in order to get them actually executed. OpenGL is a state machine [16]. In order to keep consistent the OpenGL state, the graphical commands are executed on the master node too. It ust be noted that the resolution of the master OpenGL context is totally unrelated from the slaves ones; this allows the master node to keep low its resolution, limiting performance hit due to this "useless" visualization.

In principle, the Driver may also filter or modify the intercepted commands according to some user-defined criteria or in order to reduce network load. Due to the fact that the task of maintaining the OpenGL state consistent is performed by the master node, some of the commands — like all the *glGet* API functions — can be safely executed only on the master node. This allows to save network bandwidth and computing performances by avoiding to send such commands to slave nodes. To further reduce the network load, the Driver exploits data compression; details are provided in Sect. 4. Low network utilization and system scalability are ensured by using broadcast or multicast addresses: the network load remains the same, except for the synchronization overhead, when the number of the slave nodes increases. The overall working scheme of the cluster rendering mechanism employed by XVR Nework Renderer is shown in Fig. 1.

3.2   Slave Programs

Every host of the cluster manages the information exchange with the Network Driver through a slave program. Each slave is identified by a unique name within the cluster. The slave program listens on a connectionless socket and waits first for the cluster configuration sent by the master, then for the OpenGL commands

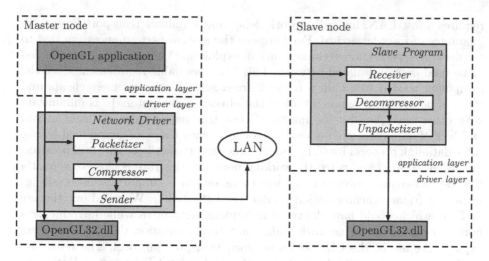

Fig. 1. Overall scheme of the system's architecture.

stream. Each slave initialize its own graphical context by extracting its configuration from the cluster's one (see Sect. 3.5). After the initialization phase, the slave starts to decode the received command stream and to execute them locally. The slave program may be configured to perform additional calculations such as camera transformations or attenuation and distortion effects (see Sect. 3.6).

Each slave's OpenGL context may have a different resolution and exploit different camera transformations. The most useful implication of this feature is that each slave may be configured to replicate just a subset of the master's context, as well as to handle the whole or a part of a bigger virtual context, provided that the original application does not perform any pre-culling phase. Combining the resulting rendering together, a very high resolution output can be obtained without being constrained by the fill rate of a single graphics card. This configuration is intended to work with visualization setups where each slave is directly connected to one or more output devices, in order to avoid sending the rendered images back through the network. This approach is particularly effective when dealing with high-resolution output: sending high-resolution images over the network especially when interactive frame rates are required would not be a negligible problem. Many immersive visualization systems exploits multiple output devices, e.g. CAVEs use multiple projectors in order to surround the user. Projectors are physically arranged to compose a unique seamless visualization. Some of the problems which typically raises in this cases, like overlapping zones or non-perpendicular projections, are handled by our software.

3.3   Network Protocol

Network traffic generated by the Network Driver has soft real-time requirements and is not tolerant of data loss. Proper functioning of the XVR Network renderer requires a fast LAN, limited network delay and a reliable transport layer with guarantee of in-order arrival. Furthermore the system performances are tied to the network speed. Though the system can exploit any kind of LAN, it is intended to be used over an isolated network. This is a reasonable requirement since the equipment needed to set up a network from scratch are extremely cheap, and there is no practical reason to allow the clustered computers to communicate with other hosts besides the master. Given this requirement, in-order arrival and lack of duplicates are no longer a concern since they are guaranteed by the LAN data-link protocol itself, including Ethernet. Packet losses are still possible, but on an isolated and correctly working network, this rate is close to zero. By the way, an error-recovery mechanism turns out to be important especially as far as per-frame synchronization is concerned (Sect. 3.4). We ruled out the use of TCP, which would have delivered redundant guarantees while introducing a noticeable overhead in network traffic and communication delay. Our system exploits the use of the UDP as its network transport protocol. The reliability of the communication is demanded to the higher-level Fragmented Datagram Protocol (FDP). In order to lower the network load, all the data are sent to a broadcast or a multicast address.

Two application-layer protocols have been developed to manage the cluster's functioning, each of them dealing with a different aspect of the communication. The Network OpenGL Protocol (NOGLP) is the high-level protocol that handles information exchange, per-frame synchronization and data compression. First of all, a NOGLP packet containing the cluster configuration is sent to the slave nodes allowing for cluster initialization. Each slave application extracts the needed informations and answers to the master node. The master ensures that all the clients are ready before starting to send the graphical stream. Following packets contain the commands stream. Sending single-command packets would flood the network, while collecting too many commands to be sent would introduce a high latency. For this reason it is possible to set a threshold: when the collected commands stored in the buffer exceed this threshold the buffer is sent, and the collection continues. Either way, the buffer is also sent every time a frame ends. This approach is a reasonable trade-off allowing to exploit the network bandwidth while limiting the latency. At the end of each frame, the cluster is synchronized in order to present all the images at the same time (see Sect. 3.4).

The Fragmented Datagram Protocol is the low-level protocol that handles the fragmentation of those NOGLP packets exceeding UDP's maximum transmission unit (MTU). Through the introduction of acknowledgement messages, FPD prevents possible data loss due to slave-side buffer overflow or network packet loss. The Driver sends a number of packets defined by the window size, and waits for ACKs from all slaves; in case of packet or ACK losses it re-sends the missing informations.

3.4   Per-Frame Synchronization

Typically, the various output images from the different slave programs have to be merged into a single consistent image, either on a flat screen or on a more complex surface. In order to avoid inconsistencies in the resulting image, a per-frame synchronization has to be performed. Not only the slave programs need to be synchronized with each other, but the master node needs to be synchronized with the rest of the cluster as well. This is to maintain a global consistency between input devices, which are connected to the master node, and output devices, connected to the slave nodes. Synchronization is performed by the NOGLP protocol in a simple fashion. Each slave broadcasts a UDP datagram to every node of the cluster, including the master node. The message is sent just before the end of the frame: the command to display the rendered image (*SwapBuffers*) is issued only after receiving the synchronization message from each and every other slave programs. This scheme avoids to experience cluster de-synchronizations, at least at frame level. Please note that we do not try to perform fine vertical synchronization, as this is out of scope of our software. For this, we either rely on hardware support where available, or ignore it altogether. In our tests we never experienced any visible artifact in this respect when using passive stereo projection. However when using active stereo projection the use of hardware synchronization mechanism is strongly suggested in order to synchronize the rendering on a per-eye basis.

3.5   Cluster Configuration

The cluster can be configured through a set of configuration files, specifying the slave nodes which compose the cluster, the *views* belonging to each slave, and the *tiles* which are managed by each view. Each slave program initializes his own OpenGL context according to the size specified by the configuration. For each slave it is possible to define one or more views; each view conceptually represents an OpenGL viewport with its own perspective matrices, with no perspective-continuity requirements. The possibility for a slave to render multiple views allows a single slave to manage a complex visualization system. Although discouraged for performances reason, it would be possible to connect all the displays of a CAVE-like system to a single slave node, assuming it is physically possible. Furthermore, it is possible to split the output of each view into multiple tiles. Tiles allow to split view's output among multiple displays, without the performance hit that would be caused by rendering the application multiple times with different perspective matrices. The flexible configuration allows both to manage a complex visualization system using a single node, or to balance the same rendering load among multiple nodes.

Configuring the system consists in specifying the size of the virtual walls, their locations and orientations according to a reference system and the load distribution by choosing the slaves/views/tiles arrangement. Using this data, the system is able to calculate the transformation matrices needed to compose a unique coherent visualization. It is furthermore possible to configure several additional slave-side feature like stereo-rendering, tracker-driver camera transformations, overlapping compensation and more.

In our system we decided to employ a centralized configuration scheme in order to avoid to access and configure each node individually. Almost all parameters are configurable on the master node; the only parameter that needs to be set on a slave is its unique identifier, which, anyway, is set once and for all. The Network Driver parses the configuration parameters locally and sends them to the slaves through the first NOGLP message. Each slave, then, extracts from this configuration packet only the information pertaining itself.

3.6   Additional Features

The collected OpenGL commands belonging to each frame can be processed and modified in order to provide additional features, without the needs to modify the original application.

Stereoscopy. XVR Network Renderer provides software support to several stereoscopic visualization schemes. This feature is particuarly important since most commodity graphics cards do not provide hardware support for stereoscopy. Our software-managed stereoscopy supports anaglyphs, side-by-side channels and active stereoscopy if hardware supported. It is also possible to obtain the reverse, that is to display only a single channel when the application uses two of them. The master application is not required to be aware of the availability of stereoscopic modes. If the application is originally monoscopic anyway, it is possible to render it in stereoscopic mode nonetheless. This conversion is achieved by buffering the commands composing a frame during the execution of the left eye and after displacing the point of view executing them again for the right eye. Only necessary commands are executed twice, the others are optimized away. This way, we relieve the application developer from taking care of stereoscopic code. The inter-pupillary distance is configurable too.

Perspective Correction. The ability of each slave to independently modify the perspective matrices of the original OpenGL scene is useful for two purposes. First to take into account the data sent from a head-tracker connected to the system. Secondly, it is possible to adapt to the geometry of a complex visualization system, particularly when slaves are far apart or not coplanar. This way, it is possible to set up a head-tracked CAVE-like system, where each slave handles a single wall, a single channel of a single wall or even a tile of a single wall, as described below. Tracking data can be forwarded by the master node to the cluster. It is furthermore possible to send head-tracking data directly to the cluster in order to minimize the latency. As a mere consequence, the system allows to simply render the application from a different point of view without modifying the original application.

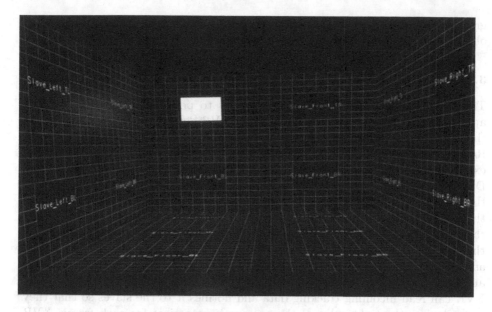

Fig. 2. Calibrating a 18-projectors CAVE system. Test grids allow for fine distortion compensation.

Projection Correction. As stated before, the system has been developed also as a platform to build immersive virtual reality systems, exploiting multiple screens. The system therefore provides tools to obtain a smooth continuity between different projected images. It is possible to compensate in software optical flaws or projection overlapping by configuring a 2D distortion mesh for each tile. A visual tool to create the distortion meshes have been developed; it projects test patterns (grids) that can be manually deformed to obtain a seamless image (see Fig. 2).

Future works include the development of an automatic calibration procedure. It is furthermore possible to specify custom attenuation areas and attenuation profiles. Finally the system allows the projection on curved surfaces, which are managed as 3D meshes on which a virtual viewport is projected according to the user's point of view.

Capturing OpenGL Videos. A useful feature of our system is the ability to capture the OpenGL commands streams and execute it later on, as if it would be a video record of a particular run of the master application. The recording is obtained by saving on disk the same data that the master would send to the slaves. Similarly, the playback is implemented by sending the recorded data on the network as if it were generated on the fly. As a result, the recorded file is very compact, and its size is independent of the output resolution. It can also be played with different slave configurations, applying, for instance, additional graphical effects on the output, or modifying the point of view according to data obtained from a head tracker, or running on a different screen geometry.

3.7   Integration with XVR

The main aim of XVR Network Renderer is to perform cluster rendering of applications generated and managed by the XVR development environment. At the same time, XVR is capable of interacting automatically with the Network Renderer, in order to take advantage of its features in the simplest way. For example in XVR is possible to manually disable and after re-enable the Network Driver if we want to prevent a portion of OpenGL code to be executed by the slaves. This kind of communication between the master application and the Network Driver is obtained through the injection of placemarkers inside the OpenGL data stream. Placemarkers are a particular set of OpenGL calls that do not have any effect on OpenGL status. This implementation scheme assures that the master applications works without any modification also when an ordinary OpenGL driver is present instead of the Network Driver. In addition, XVR can read incoming tracking data and notifies it to the slaves so that they can calculate the right value of the perspective matrices for each frame. XVR Network Renderer can be used even with other frameworks based on OpenGL, assuming that the used APIs are supported by the Driver or by implementing the missing functions. Assuming that the support is experimental, we have been able to successfully run some applications running on the Unity framework.

4   Parallelism

XVR Network Renderer intends to be a cluster rendering architecture suitable for Immersive Virtual Environments.

The system have been designed paying attention to performances. Both the system's main components — the Network Driver and the slave programs — exploit paradigms of parallel programming. Our architecture adopts a N-stage pipeline model to speed-up performances. Each stage refers to a software module of the system. The number of the pipeline stages is configurable and can vary between 1 and 3 both for the master and for the slave programs.

The three master's modules — the *packetizer*, the *compressor* and the *sender* — correspond to their dual stages on the slave program — the *unpacketizer*, the *decompressor* and the *receiver*. The packetizer is in charge of intercepting and buffering the graphical commands, the compressor shrinks the size of the data sent over the network, while the sender actually sends them. On the slave side, once the data have been received by the receiver module, thay are unshrinked by the decompressor and finally unpacketizer is in charge of decoding the stream and executing the commands in the graphical context.

Multiple compression stages are performed on the stream in order to reduce the network load, and speed-up the performances in case of bandwidth bottlenecks. The overall data compression relies on different compressor modules which applies different shrinking techniques according to the type of the data. If the frame contains geometry description commands, a geometric compression module will handle them [17]. Similarly, compressible images are reduced in size by a JPEG compressor, whose compression level can be configured to achieve desired ratio.

The beginning of an OpenGL application usually starts with a loading phase, where all the assets are loaded in memory. After that the following frames often consist in the exploration of the model itself. Each frame is mainly a collection of drawing calls and calls to change the camera placement. To exploit frame-to-frame coherence the system uses a diff algorithm [17,18] in order to avoid sending a large percentage of each frame data (all the geometry information). The above compression stages happens in-place and are performed sequentially by the packetizer, which is single-threaded up to now. If the output of the previous operations does not fit the MTU size, then it is compressed with a general purpose compressor (LZO or Zlib). Indeed, in case of small packets the compression is automatically turned off because the impact of the compression in terms of required time would overcome the benefit of sending a smaller packet. This compression stage is performed by a compressor module in parallel to the packetizer. On the slave node the original data is reconstructed by performing all the stages presented above in reverse order with respect to the master's side. An overall scheme of the parallel architecture is shown in Fig. 4.

Even if most of the compression modules internally exploits multi-threading, they necessarily introduce additional latency during the production stage of the frame. Under certain circumstances, the delay is completely overcome by the time saved in sending less data. When the underlying LAN technology allows high transmission rates, compressing data would require more time than transmitting it outright. On the contrary, using slower networks leads to sending times which overcome the compression times. Each compression stage can be enabled or disabled by configuring the Driver in order to obtain the maximum performance from each application, according to its traits.

4.1   Test-Bed IVE Setup

In order to fully exploit the system and to be able to deeply test it, we have intentionally used a complex CAVE^{TM} setup for conducting our performance tests. The CAVE is composed by four projected walls arranged in the shape of a room, with a $4 \times 4m^2$ floor and walls $2.4m$ high. Each wall is back-projected using 4 projectors, while the floor is front-projected by 6 of them, see Fig. 4. In this setup the cluster consists of 5 nodes, running slave programs, in addition to a master node on which the Driver is installed and running the XVR application. The 4 projectors belonging to each wall are connected to a single node, running a single slave managing a single view divided into 4 tiles (see Sect. 3.5). The 6 projectors belonging to the floor are instead connected to two different nodes, each one running one slave program configured as a single-view with 3 tiles. Each projector has a 1280x720 resolution.

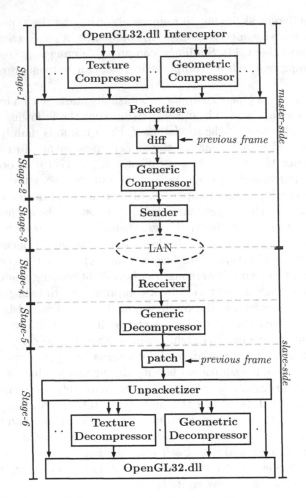

Fig. 3. Overall scheme of the system's architecture. The system exploit a 6-stages pipepline parallel strategy to speed-up performances.

The system exploits active stereo rendering performed at 60 Hz, and the per-eye syncronization of the cluster relies on hardware capabilities. All nodes are connected to the same isolated gigabit LAN, capable of a maximum transmission unit of 64 kB.

4.2   Test-Bed Applications

In order to conduct our tests we have chosen a set of four applications (see Fig. 5), which differ in terms of complexity, number and size of the assets and average frame size; these characteristics are summarized in Table 1. The *Rollercoaster* demo is characterized by a mid-low rendering load and by a small average frame size. The *CAD* demo's average frame size is small as well, but the rendering load

Fig. 4. The 6-nodes and 18-projectors CAVE^{TM} setup used to run performance tests.

is far higher. We have therefore chosen two applications characterized by large frame sizes due to the continuous streaming of video contents: *Kinect* and *Virtual Museum*. The two differ in terms of computational load, the former performs a far demanding GLSL shader which generates on-the-fly the geometry by processing the input stream. Screenshots of the application are shown in Fig. 5.

4.3   Method

The applications used to perform each test have been chosen according to the feature we want to test. Performances have been measured in terms of frames

Table 1. Statistics showing the different characteristics of the test-bed applications.

	Rollercoaster	CAD	Kinect	Virtual Museum
Models complexity (*triangles*)	330 K	4.8 M	0	234 K
Streaming video (*pixels per second*)	0	0	23 Mpixelps	30.7 Mpixelps
Frame size	13 kB	223 kB	1.49 MB	3.67 MB
Compressed size (LZO)	13 kB	57 kB	920 kB	2.67 MB
Compressed size (Jpeg + LZO)	13 kB	57 kB	250 kB	688 kB
OpenGL cmds	2105	38136	324	2145
Display lists	514	18992	4	471
Bound Textures	2	1	10	18
Transformations	10	3	14	41

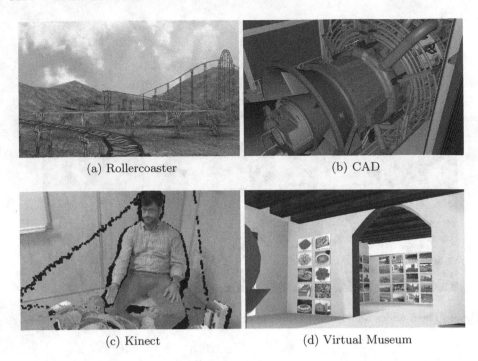

(a) Rollercoaster   (b) CAD

(c) Kinect   (d) Virtual Museum

Fig. 5. Screenshots of test-bed applications.

per second that the system have been able to run at. The frame rate have been obtained by averaging one minute of each applications' runs. Graphs reports average, minimum and maximum values. All the measures have started after that each application had ended to load all the assets, in order to avoid that the start-up phase would greatly influence the results.

The cluster configuration used to conduct all tests exploits the above described CAVE setup. The master runs the application at VGA resolution in order to limit the master rendering's impact on cluster performances. The distortion correction have always been turned on. Even if the vertical sync needs to be turned always on in order to avoid tearing problems, we have decided to disable the V-Sync for the test, in order to be able to register the maximum performances reachable by the system.

All the results referred to the *Local* configuration, have been collected by running the application locally on a slave workstation. The context resolution is the same as if configured as a node of the cluster (WQHD). The local results can be considered as the maximum performance reachable by the system. The master node is more powerful than a slave node and is asked to run the application at lower resolution; in this way it cannot behave as a system's bottleneck.

4.4   Impact of the Architecture

In order to assess the impact of the cluster rendering on performances, we have firstly executed each test-bed application locally on a slave node; secondly we have executed it exploiting the network rendering. Figure 6 shows how the cluster rendering negatively influences the applications performances, due to the communication and synchronization overheads. We need to take into account that the cluster rendering has been performed in a stereoscopic way, negatively affecting the performances. Considering all, we have been able to turn a "simple desktop" application into a "fully immersive VR" application without even the needs of modifying it, by degrading and the performances by less than half compared to the local run.

We would also like to assert the impact of the system parallelism exploiting a pipeline paradigm on performances. We have therefore conducted tests on the system configured to run first in sequential mode and then exploiting the pipeline paradigm. Figure 7 shows that all test-bed applications have benefited of the higher parallelism. The higher parallelism have led to better results, thanks to the reduction of the waiting time spent for the cluster synchronization.

When the frame size is low, and consequentially the network load is low as well, the pipeline load results to be extremely unbalanced. In this case the impact of the higher parallelism is negligible. On the opposite, when the pipeline load is well balanced — like in the *Kinect* and *Virtual Museum* demos — the performance gain reaches it's maximum. However, we expect a slightly higher latency when the pipeline parallelism is exploited, but we plan to carry out more tests about this aspect as future work.

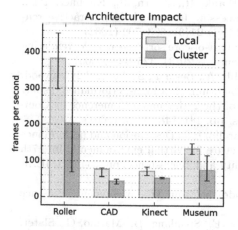

Fig. 6. Impact of LAN speed and compression on system performances.

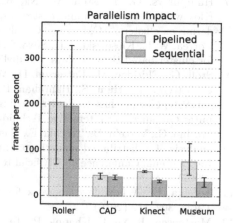

Fig. 7. Impact of parallel pipeline paradigm on system performances.

5 Conclusion and Future Work

We have presented the *XVR Network Renderer*, a software system used to perform cluster rendering of OpenGL applications developed using the XVR environment. This software allows a single master workstation to control complex visualization systems such as PowerWalls or CAVE-like systems. Future work includes the introduction of heuristics for performances optimization, by dynamically adapting the system configuration to the running application. Support for other common development environments like Unity is under investigation.

References

1. University of Minnesota: PowerWall. http://www.lcse.umn.edu/research/powerwall/powerwall.html. Accessed 21 Feb 2016
2. Cruz-Neira, C., Sandin, D.J., DeFanti, T.A., Kenyon, R.V., Hart, J.C.: The cave: audio visual experience automatic virtual environment. Commun. ACM **35**(6), 64–73 (1992)
3. Crockett, T.W.: An introduction to parallel rendering. Parallel Comput. **23**(7), 819–843 (1997)
4. Molnar, S., Cox, M., Ellsworth, D., Fuchs, H.: A sorting classification of parallel rendering. IEEE Comput. Graph. Appl. **14**(4), 23–32 (1994)
5. Molnar, S., Eyles, J., Poulton, J.: Pixelflow: high-speed rendering using image composition. ACM SIGGRAPH Comput. Graph. **26**, 231–240 (1992). ACM
6. Humphreys, G., Eldridge, M., Buck, I., Stoll, G., Everett, M., Hanrahan, P.: Wiregl: a scalable graphics system for clusters. In: Proceedings of the 28th Annual Conference on Computer Graphics and Interactive Techniques, pp. 129–140. ACM (2001)
7. Humphreys, G., Houston, M., Ng, R., Frank, R., Ahern, S., Kirchner, P.D., Klosowski, J.T.: Chromium: a stream-processing framework for interactive rendering on clusters. ACM Trans. Graph. (TOG) **21**(3), 693–702 (2002)
8. Corrêa, W.T., Klosowski, J.T., Silva, C.T.: Out-of-core sort-first parallel rendering for cluster-based tiled displays. Parallel Comput. **29**(3), 325–338 (2003)
9. Stoll, G., Eldridge, M., Patterson, D., Webb, A., Berman, S., Levy, R., Caywood, C., Taveira, M., Hunt, S., Hanrahan, P.: Lightning-2: a high-performance display subsystem for pc clusters. In: Proceedings of the 28th Annual Conference on Computer Graphics and Interactive Techniques, pp. 141–148. ACM (2001)
10. Marino, G., Vercelli, D., Tecchia, F., Gasparello, P.S.: Description and performance analysis of a distributed rendering architecture for virtual environments. In: 17th International Conference on Artificial Reality and Telexistence, pp. 234–241. IEEE (2007)
11. Tecchia, F.: A flexible framework for wide-spectrum vr development. Presence **19**(4), 302–312 (2010)
12. Mortensen, J., Yu, I., Khanna, P., Tecchia, F., Spanlang, B., Marino, G., Slater, M.: Real-time global illumination for vr applications. IEEE Comput. Graph. Appl. **6**, 56–64 (2008)
13. Steed, A., Tecchia, F., Bergamasco, M., Slater, M., Steptoe, W., Oyekoya, W., Pece, F., Weyrich, T., Kautz, J., Friedman, D., et al.: Beaming: an asymmetric telepresence system. IEEE Comput. Graph. Appl. **6**, 10–17 (2012)

14. Pérez Marcos, D., Solazzi, M., Steptoe, W., Oyekoya, O., Frisoli, A., Weyrich, T., Steed, A., Tecchia, F., Slater, M., Sánchez-Vives, M.V.: A fully immersive set-up for remote interaction and neuro rehabilitation based on virtual body ownership. Front. Neurol. **3**, 110 (2012)

15. Normand, J.M., Spanlang, B., Tecchia, F., Carrozzino, M., Swapp, D., Slater, M.: Full body acting rehearsal in a networked virtual environment – a case study. Presence: Teleoperators Virtual Environ. **21**(2), 229–243 (2012)

16. Shreiner, D., Group, B.T.K.O.A.W., et al.: OpenGL Programming Guide: The Official Guide to Learning OpenGL Versions 3.0 and 3.1. Pearson Education, New Jersey (2009)

17. Marino, G., Gasparello, P.S., Vercelli, D., Tecchia, F., Bergamasco, M.: Network streaming of dynamic 3D content with on-line compression of frame data. In: 2010 IEEE Virtual Reality Conference (VR), pp. 285–286. IEEE (2010)

18. Hunt, J.W., MacIlroy, M.: An algorithm for differential file comparison. Computing science technical report. Bell Laboratories, New Jersey (1976). https://books.google.it/books?id=zJ2LMwAACAAJ

The Effect of Emotional Narrative Virtual Environments on User Experience

Claudia Faita[✉], Camilla Tanca, Andrea Piarulli, Marcello Carrozzino, Franco Tecchia, and Massimo Bergamasco

PERCRO Perceptual Robotics Laboratory,
Institute of Communication Information and Perception Technologies,
Scuola Superiore Sant'Anna, Pisa, Italy
{c.faita,c.tanca,a.piarulli,m.carrozzino,f.tecchia,m.bergamasco}@sssup.it

Abstract. The surrounding world has a strong impact on the way we feel and perceive the events that happens in daily life. The power of environments to elicit emotions in humans has been widely studied in experimental psychology by using exposure to photographs or real situations. These researches do not reproduce the vividness of events in ordinary life and do not permit to control the situations that happen within. By reproducing a realistic scenario similar to daily life and by controlling the social narratives happening within, Virtual Reality (VR) is a powerful tool to investigate the effect of environments on humans' feelings and emotions. In this study we have animated the emotional content of a realistic virtual scenario with a dynamic scene in order to introduce a novel approach to investigate the effect of environments in human feeling based on the Emotional Narrative Virtual Environment (ENVE) paradigm. A sample of 36 subjects experimented 3 ENVEs with a Fear, Disgust and Happy emotional content, made to live with a social narratives, in an immersive VR setup. Results showed the ability of ENVE to elicit specific emotional state in participants and corroborate the idea that the ENVE approach can be used in environmental psychology or to treat persons with mental disease.

Keywords: Virtual Reality · Virtual environment · Emotion perception · Emotional virtual reality · Environment perception

1 Introduction

Emotions are one of the central aspects in the life of human beings because they influence daily choices, social relationships and the general approach to life itself. A lot of studies have shown that a high level of emotional skills, i.e. the ability to manage and control own and others' emotions (Emotional Intelligence), contributes to improve personal well-being, to enhance job performance and life satisfaction [1,2].

An important factor that influences the emotional state of a person is the surrounding environment. The impact of the environment on the emotional state

© Springer International Publishing Switzerland 2016
L.T. De Paolis and A. Mongelli (Eds.): AVR 2016, Part I, LNCS 9768, pp. 120–132, 2016.
DOI: 10.1007/978-3-319-40621-3_8

of humans has been widely studied by using the environmental psychology app-roach [3]. A great deal of experimental research demonstrate that there is an effect of the emotional context on memory, moral judgment and behavioral reac-tion [4,5]. According to the results of such studies the design of the daily life contexts as work-office, cities, supermarket have radically changed in order to make them more pleasant. The major limitation in the environmental psychology approach is the study of the effect of the environment in an ecological way.

Virtual Reality (VR) can be a helpful tool as it recreates realistic scenarios in which social dynamics develop. VR, unlike conventional methods like exposure to real situations or to photographs, simulates the user's presence in a digital environment and permits to control the events that happen within. Because of the ecological validity and control-based environments, VR has become a useful methodology for the experimental psychology research, especially to treat different kinds of mental health disease [6,7].

Moreover, it has been shown that participants in VR-experiences perceive and feel strong emotions both during the human-avatar and the human-environment interaction. Several studies have been conducted to investigate the emotional stimuli elicited by VR by using both 3D avatars [8,9] and affective environments [10,11]. This research showed that participants in VR experiences perceived spe-cific emotions corresponding to the valence of VR or Avatar Mood. Banos et al. [12] have also investigated the relationship between the perception of emotion and the sense of presence in VR experience. They found that the affective content of Virtual Environments (VEs) has impact on the sense of presence especially for the target of engagement which results higher in emotional environment respect to the neutral one. Due to these features, VEs with emotional content can be useful tools to investigate mental disorder and body image distortion [13].

All the research investigating the emotional aspect of VEs do not pay atten-tion to the social dynamics developed in the virtual context with the risk of playing down the ecological validity of VR. According to the Narrative Theories approach [14] dynamic and storytelling VR increases the sense of being physi-cally located within the VE and the sense of interaction with the environment. For this reason, this kind of VR applications are widely used in education [15], VR games for training [16,17], to acquire ethical skills [18] and for dissemination of culture [19,20].

In our study we have combined the emotional content of virtual scenarios with specific social narratives in order to replicate a daily life situations able to elicit an emotional affective state in an ecological way. The aim of this research is to introduce a novel paradigm to study environmental emotional perception by using the Emotional Narrative Virtual Environment (ENVE) approach. For this purpose we have created three different VEs endowed with disgust, fear and happy emotional contents and animated with specific social narratives. A prelim-inary research, to evaluate the ability of the ENVE to elicit specific emotions, was carried out on 36 subjects. In this research we have used VR-immersive technology (Oculus-Rift) to recreate a strong sense of immersion in the virtual space and a high sense of presence in the emotional scene [12]. By measuring the similarity between the users response to real and virtual situation, it has been showed that VR-immersive technology can enhance emotional and psychological responses arousing the feeling to be present in a real situation rather than virtual [21]. Moreover, immersive technologies increase the sense of being physical located in virtual space with own body [22].

Based on the results of our study, ENVE will be improved and used to further investigate the effect of the emotional content on the user experience, especially related to the avatar interaction in the virtual emotional situation.

In this paper the social scenario and social narratives of each ENVE will be presented with a brief description of the technology used to create them. Then the experimental design is described focusing on the participants, procedure and material used in the experiment. The results are presented and discussed in the last part of the manuscript. A conclusion will provide the guidelines for further investigation of emotion perception in VR.

2 Emotional Narrative Virtual Environment

The purpose of this research is the creation of Emotional Narrative Virtual Environments endowed with a specific emotional content. The main characteristics of this kind of environments are the following:

- *emotional*: the environment has specific emotional content and the virtual scenario must elicit in the participant the corresponding emotion
- *narrative*: the scene is animated with a social narratives similar to what could happen in a real situation, enhancing the emotional content of the scenario.

In this study we have created three ENVEs, happy, disgust and fear, each one characterized by an emotional scene. The virtual environments and scenarios are described in the following paragraphs.

2.1 Scenario

In order to evoke in the participants specific emotions we have created three different virtual scenarios starting from the photographs of the International Affective Picture System (IAPS) [23]. Figure 1 show the three different kinds of virtual scenario with emotional valence.

The three virtual environment are designed as followed:

1. Happy Environment (HE) is a green area with two swings, a slide, a big playground and an hot-air balloon that flies in a blue sky. Is placed in a big open garden with some trees and a field of grass that waves softly to the wind. In order to increase the joyfulness of the scenario a background sound of birds chirping and slight rustling was added.
2. Disgust Environment (DE) is a dark alley surrounded by buildings. All over the muddy ground lie bins completely full of garbage and a lot of trash outside. In the sky, a lot of moving clouds colour the entire scenario gray. To increase the realism of DE a murmur background and cars noise were added.

Fig. 1. In the left panel the three virtual scenarios visualized by participants in the experiment. From top to bottom: the Happy Environment (virtual playground), the Disgust Environment (dark alley) and the Fear Environment (mountain scenario). In the right panel the three virtual scenarios with the animations. From top to bottom: the children playing volleyball in the playground, the man which loose balance walking on the Tibetan Bridge and the mice turn all around in the alley.

3. Fear Environment (FE) is a mountain scenario in which a Tibetan Bridge is located. The bridge connect two mountains that are divided by a lake and a man is walking on it. The sky is cloudy and there is a lot of mist. In the background sounds of thunders and strong wind enhance the frightening appearance of the scenario.

2.2 Social Narratives

In order to mimic daily-life situations in a realistic way each VE was animated with a specific dynamic scene that should enhance the emotional content of the scenario. The aim was to introduce a social narratives coherent with the valence of the context. In the virtual environment an event transforms the scenario into a *social narrative* by developing a *dynamic scene*. The *social narratives* are three, one for each environment and they develop in the following way:

1. HE: two children start playing with a ball in the playground. The sound of children voices drives the scene ;
2. DE: a lot of small mice start to move all around the virtual space and two big rats move around the garbage. The squeaking sound of several mice was used to accompany the development of the scene;
3. FE: an earthquake produces a strong oscillation of all the environment and of the bridge. The man walking on the bridge loses balance. A strong sound of explosion accompanies the earthquake.

3   Experimental Design

The goal of this study was to investigate the ability of ENVE to elicit specific emotion in the user experience. The ENVE approach is based on the creation of emotional environment and emotional scene in which participants are completely immersed in a real life situation. An experiment to evaluate the effectiveness of ENVE to affect emotional state of users was carried out.

In this section the experimental set up, participants and procedure are detailed. The measures used in the evaluation of ENVE are also followed explained.

3.1   Apparatus for ENVE and Technological Set up

The virtual environments were modeled by using the game engine Unreal Engine 4. Small animations for the static part of the exploration, as the wind through the grass and trees and the hot-air balloon movement according to the clouds, were added through UE4s visual scripting-language Blueprint. In order to create the social narratives the same UE4s visual scripting-language Blueprint was used. The avatars were taken from Rocketbox library (www.rocketbox-libraries. com) animated through motion capture data from The Carnegie Mellon University Motion Capture Database (http://mocap.cs.cmu.edu/) retargeted, mounted and looped in order to fit our purposes. The same language was also used to spawn an editable number of mice and to move them along a number of arbitrary points. The sound in the environments was used to increases the isolation from the outside world and feel the noises as they were real (located in the ambient in correspondence of the sources). In order to provide a strong sense of immersion in the environments a Head Mounted Display was used in the experiment. The application that runs the ENVE and the animations was realized through the game engine Unreal Engine 4 on a PC with Oculus Rift DK2. UE4 facilitates the design of complex custom environments using low poly models and complex materials through a visual editing interface and a visual scripting-language. Oculus Rift integration is native to UE4 and provides binocular vision into the virtual scenarios via HDMI input. It provides also rotational head tracking with 6dof and a front-face tracking that allows the user to look around the virtual environment and to move in it (in a short range). The dark foam surrounding the goggles blocks out most of the external light and enhance the isolation from the outside world and the related immersion in the VE.

3.2   Participants

A sample of 38 subjects were recruited to participate in the experiment. In the preliminary phase they read and signed a consent form in which the experiment was briefly explained. Prior to start the experiment a questionnaire to rate the level of depression of each subject, Beck Depression Inventory questionnaire (BDI), was used as exclusion criterion. Based on the results of BDI 2 subjects were excluded in the study because they rated a score equal or higher than 14. A total of 36 participants (28 male and 8 female) performed the experiment. They were healthy subjects with no history of mental disease, aged 30.22 ± 6.66 y.o. with a level of education equal or higher then high school diploma. They self-rated in a 5-point Likert scale their level in the use of personal computer (average 40.80 ± 0.58), videogames (average 3.33 ± 1.41) and virtual reality (average 3.19 ± 1.45).

3.3   Measures

For each subjects tree different types of questionnaire were used to assess their emotional state and the sense of presence in the ENVE: i- The pre-experimental questionnaire to assess generic and demographic information; ii- the self-report measure to rate if participants have a level of depression prior to start the experiment (exclusion criteria) and the sense of presence at the end of the experience; iii- the self-rate questionnaire to assess the emotional state and sense of presence elicited by the ENVE.

   i- A generic questionnaire was used to collect demographic information of participant and exclude from the study subjects with mental disease and history of depression. Moreover, a self-rated questionnaire about the use of videogames, virtual reality and personal computer was given.

   ii- BDI questionnaire was used as a selection criterion in pre-experimental phase. It is a self-report questionnaire to assess the cognitive aspect of depression and measure the depressive symptom. It consist in 21-questions multiple-choice relating to symptoms of depression. Participants had to chose the statement that better described his/her mood state.

   Selected questions of Reality Judgment and Presence Questionnaire (RJPQ) were used as self-measure to assess the sense of presence and reality judgment of participants [24]. A 10-point Likert scale was used to answer all items. 17 of these questions were used to assess Reality Judgment (Q2, Q6, Q7, Q12, Q13, Q16), sense of Presence (Q9, Q10, Q11, Q15, Q17), Emotional Involvement (Q8, Q4), Control, an important characteristic of immersion, (Q14), Realism, both perceptual and interactive, including perceptual clarity and natural modes of interaction (Q1), Expectations and the possibility of Anticipation and prediction in the virtual environment (Q3, Q5). Two additional Questions were added in order to assess the emotional involvement of the environment and the emotional involvement of the social narrative: (-*To what extent did the virtual scenario was emotional?; -To what extent did the virtual scene viewed in the virtual environment was emotional?*).

iii- The emotional effect of the ENVE experience was evaluated by rating on a 5-point Likert scale to what extent the experience induces in a subject a sense of fear-happiness-disgust. Also the sense of Presence elicited by each environment and social narrative was evaluated by rating on a 5-point Likert scale the feeling experienced in the virtual scene (*Did you feel like you are in the alley-in the virtual play area-in mountain scenario?*) and the feeling to be involved in the social narrative (*Do you feel like the mice were actually rotating around the garbage-the man on the bridge were really losing balance-the children were really play in the play area?*)

3.4   Procedure

36 subjects participated to the study. None of them had a history of depression and completed a Back Depression Inventory (BDI) as exclusion criteria. 2 subjects were excluded in preselected phase as they scored less than 14 in BDI Questionnaire. The aim of the experiment is to evaluate the emotional content of ENVEs, and if whether ENVEs induce in the participant the emotional state corresponding to the emotional content of the environment. The experiment will be divided in three phases.

In the *Baseline phase* participants were instructed about the entire procedure of the experiment. Prior to start the ENVEs visualization they had to complete the BDI questionnaire. Then the experimenter explained them to dress the helmet, to wear stereo headphones and how to explore the environments.

In the *Experimental phase* the participants were completely immersed in the Virtual Scenario for a period of 50 s. During this period they could explore the environment, looking all around and "let themselves go" to what they see in the virtual scenario without performing any specific task. After this time the environment "comes alive" with a dynamic scene having a duration of 20 s. The three environments are presented to each participant for one time following 6 different sequences: HE-DE-FE; HE-FE-DE; DE-HE-FE; DE-FE-HA; FE-DE-HE; FE-HE-DE. In order to reset the emotional state elicited by an ENVE a rest time of 120 s between each scenario was given to participants during which they answered to a questionnaire composed by 5 questions related to the emotional state and the sense of presence perceived within the ENVE. At the end of the three experiences the *Self-Experience evaluation phase* started. First the participants had to answer to a final Questionnaire about the sense of presence and emotional valence of the environment (RJPQ). Secondly a brief interview were conducted by the experimenters concerning the overall impressions and comments about the experience.

4   Data Analysis and Results

Data was collected by considering two experimental factors: the emotional content of ENVE ($E_{content}$) and the emotion elicited in the participants ($E_{elicited}$, Happiness, Disgust, Fear). A repeated measure ANOVA with ENVE as a

Table 1. Results of Repeated Measure Anova.

Repeated Measure Anova				
Score $E_{elicited}$	within factor	df	F	p-value
Happiness	ENVE	2	76.54	< 0.001
Disgust	ENVE	1.21*	60.31	< 0.001
Fear	ENVE	1.76*	27.88	< 0.001
Congruence	ENVE	2	11.57	< 0.001
Presence VE	ENVE	2	2.24	< 0.114
Presence SN	ENVE	2	1.01	< 0.373

Note.*Greenhouse-Geisser Correction (Sphericity could not be assumed on the basis of Mauchly's test)*

Table 2. Results of Post-Hoc Test.

Score $E_{elicited}$	mean difference	95 Confidence Interval*	p-value
HE-DE			
Happiness	1.86	[1.45 2.27]	< 0.001
Disgust	-1.72	[-2.24 -1.21]	< 0.001
Fear	-1.06	[-1.54 -0.57]	< 0.001
Congruence	0.47	[-0.03 0.98]	< 0.072
HE-FE			
Happiness	1.53	[1.09 1.97]	< 0.001
Disgust	-0.17	[-0.35 0.02]	< 0.092
Fear	-1.22	[-1.70 -0.74]	< 0.001
Congruence	0.89	[0.42 1.36]	< 0.001
DE-FE			
Happiness	-0.33	[-0.68 0.01]	< 0.062
Disgust	1.56	[1.04 2.07]	< 0.001
Fear	-0.17	[-0.52 0.19]	< 0.569
Congruence	0.42	[0 0.83]	< 0.050

Note.*Confidence Interval on Mean Difference estimated performing 1000 bootstraps*

within-group factors was conducted for each $E_{elicited}$. It is worth underlying that Repeated Measures ANOVA has been demonstrated to be an appropriate statistical test even for ranked variables as those based on Likert Scales are [25]. The aim was to investigate if the $E_{content}$ elicited specific emotion in participants. A Greenhouse-Geisser Correction was used for the $E_{elicited}$ fear and disgust ANOVA, as sphericity could not be assumed (as resulting from Mauchly's test, [26]). The congruence effect was also investigated between each $E_{content}$ of ENVE and the corresponding $E_{elicited}$ in participants. A repeated measure ANOVA was also conducted by considering Sense of Presence in Virtual Environment ($SoPinVE_{elicited}$) and Sense of Presence in Social Narratives ($SoPinSN_{elicited}$) as dependent variable. Results of ANOVA are reported in Table 1. A significant effect of $E_{elicited}$ for the $E_{content}$ of each ENVE was found in all of emotions elicited (p < 0.001). We also found a significant effect of congruence effect between $E_{content}$ and the corresponding $E_{elicited}$ (p < 0.001). For those ANOVA yielding a significant ENVE effect, differences between each couple of ENVE were estimated using *Post-hoc* tests with Sidak correction for multiple comparisons [27]. For each *Post-hoc*, the confidence interval on mean difference was estimated performing 1000 bootstraps. Results are presented in Table 2 and observed means with indicator of significantly different conditions are reported in Fig. 2. Significant differences in the comparisons of HE-DE and HE-FE were found for the Happiness effect $E_{elicited}$, for the HE-DE and DE-FE when considering the Disgust effect $E_{elicited}$, (p < 0.001 for both). Regarding Fear $E_{elicited}$ a significant effect was found in the HE-DE (p < 0.001) and HE-FE (p < 0.001) comparisons but not for DE-FE. As shown in Fig. 2c, very similar score were obtained for Fear in FE (2, 36±0.9) and in DE (2, 19±1, 06). A significant difference (p < 0.001) was found between the unexpected high mean score obtained by Fear in DE (2, 19±1, 06) and that obtained in HE (1, 14±0, 42). The *Post-hoc* tests on congruence effect between specific $E_{elicited}$ in corresponding $E_{content}$ yielded a significant difference (p < 0.001) only for the couple HE-FE with a significantly higher happiness score in HE (3, 15 ± 0, 9) when compared with fear in FE (2, 36 ± 1, 07). A high mean score of SoP in both SN and VE was observed for all the ENVEs; no statistical difference was found either for the $E_{content}$ of ENVE, p < 0.114, or for $SoPinVE_{elicited}$, p < 0.373.

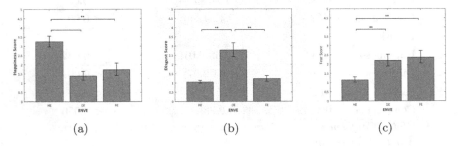

(a)   (b)   (c)

Fig. 2. Mean Score obtained for Happiness (a), Disgust (b), Fear (c), in each Emotional Narrative Virtual Environment. The bars represent the standard deviation and the stars show the significant difference found in pairwise *Post-hoc* test.

5   Discussion

In the present research a novel methodology was presented to investigate the effect of the environment in the emotional perception by using an ecological approach based on Emotional Narrative Virtual Environments. The aim of the study was to create and evaluate three different scenarios animated with emotional scenes able to elicit in VR-users specific emotions. For this purpose an experiment was carried out on 36 participants who have made experience of happy, fear and disgust ENVEs and they rate their level of happiness, fear and disgust for each environment. The mean score obtained for each answer ($E_{elicited}$ in participants) was considered as dependent variable to investigate if $E_{content}$ of ENVE elicited specific emotion in participants. Results showed no statistical difference for the mean score of $E_{elicited}$ in the ENVE. A *Post-hoc* test was carried out to investigate if $E_{elicited}$ shows a significant different in the pairwise comparison between $E_{content}$. We found a relevant difference between HE-DE and HE-FE for happiness. This results corroborate our hypothesis that HE elicit "more happiness" than DE and FE. As we supposed, similar results was found also for the $E_{elicited}$ Disgust, because it obtained a relevant major mean score in DE respect to HE and FE. A comparable result was obtained by Fear in the comparison between FE and HE, but not for FE-DE. The mean score of Fear in FE $2, 36 \pm 1, 07$ was similar to mean score obtained by Fear in DE $2, 19 \pm 1, 06$. This result supports the idea that FE do not elicit a fear emotion more than DE. This is not completely in line with previous research that supports the idea that specific VEs induce more corresponding target emotion than other kind of emotion [11]. However, Banos et al. [11] do not consider the correlation between Fear and Disgust Environments in the ability to elicit the corresponding emotions. We suppose that disgust is an emotion that in some cases is strictly related with fear. In fact several participants in the brief interview after experiment stated that they have fear of mice. Moreover, some of them told us that they perceive a feeling of fear to be in a enclosed environment as the alley. In future investigations we will take into account the difference between enclosed and open environments in order to investigate their influence on the emotional perception. The analysis of congruence in which the mean of each $E_{elicited}$ was compared with corresponding $E_{content}$ of ENVE found a significant different for both HE-FE (p-value< 0.001) and for DE-FE (p-value< 0.050). This means that the HE was able to elicit "more happiness" than the FE was to elicit fear. At the same time DE elicit disgust more than FE elicit fear. In conclusion the congruence effect for FE $(2, 36 \pm 1, 07$ mean score) was significantly lower than the DE $(2, 78 \pm 1, 2$ mean score) and HE $(3, 25 \pm 0, 9$ mean score). We argue that there are two main reasons to explain this result: the design of the environment and the third person perspective. FE is a mountain open scenario with a man walking on a Tibetan Bridge. This kind of scenario is usually associated with an idea of "game experience" instead of serious activity. Secondly, participants observed the scene and they didn't feel a sense of fear toward the man on the bridge because they couldn't interact with him. In the after experience interview a lot of participants said that *they wanted to go on the bridge to save the man, but they couldn't do it* and for this reason the experience was *like a movie*. Conversely, in DE the participants were completely immersed in the scene in first person perspective and the mice turned all around them. However the third person perspective in HE did not influence the emotional feeling elicited because the environment itself was joyful. Almost all participants said that *it was pleasant to stay in the park and hear the chirping of birds.*

The sense of presence felt during the experiences of Virtual Scene and Virtual Scenario did not statistically differ for the $E_{content}$ of environment (see Table 1). The mean score for $SoPinVE_{elicited}$ and $SoPinSN_{elicited}$ was > 3 in all ENVEs. This is in line with the trend of median score obtained in the RJPQ Questionnaire (see Fig. 3). In particular the high score obtained by Q4 and Q9 (*To what extent did things in the virtual world have impact on you?* and *To what extent did you feel like you went into the virtual world, and you almost forgot about the world outside?*) corroborate the suggestion that participants felt a sense of presence in ENVE. Moreover additional question Q18 (*To what extent did the virtual scenario was emotional?*) and Q19 (*To what extent did the virtual scene viewed in the virtual environment was emotional?*) are in line with the mean score results of $E_{elicited}$ in virtual environments and demonstrate that VEs are able to elicit emotion in participants. A high score obtained in the Q5 answer (*To what extent what you experienced in the virtual world fitted your expectations about what could happen in a real world?*) is in line with the idea that the animation of the scene is similar to what could happen in a real life situation and that SN enhance the valence of the scenario.

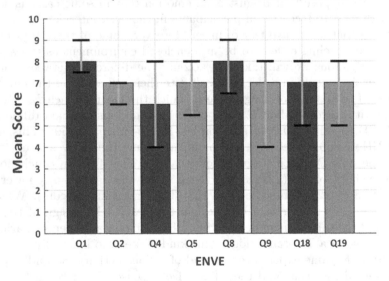

Fig. 3. Answers to the Reality Judgment and Presence Questionnaire and to two additional questions (AQ18 AQ19) about the sense of presence in the environment and in the social narratives. The height of each bar represents the median value, while the upper and lower whiskers are the 25*th* and 75*th* percentiles respectively

6 Conclusion and Future Work

The overall results of this research showed that the ENVE was able to elicit specific emotions related to the emotional content of the virtual environment. We believe that the reason of these results depends on the features of the Emotional Narratives Virtual Environment, i.e. the social narratives combined with specific content of the emotional environment. These findings it is corroborate the idea that the ENVE approach can be used in the field of environmental psychology to study the effect of the surrounding environment in a ecological way. However this study present two limitations. The first one is the small samples and the difference between the number of male and female that could limit the possibility of a solid statistical analysis. The second one is that during the ENVE experience participants did not interact actively with the object and people in the environment. In order to strengthen the value of our results the experiment will be tested with a wider group of subjects and the number of male and female will be conformed. Moreover, in the future the ENVEs will be improved including both human-avatars and human-objects interaction in order to create condition more similar to daily life activities.

References

1. Cherniss, C., Extein, M., Goleman, D., Weissberg, R.P.: Emotional intelligence: what does the research really indicate? Educ. Psychol. **41**, 239–245 (2006)
2. Palmer, B., Donaldson, C., Stough, C.: Emotional intelligence and life satisfaction. Pers. Individ. Differ. **33**, 1091–1100 (2002)
3. Proshansky, H.M., Ittelson, W.H., Rivlin, L.G.: Environmental Psychology: Man and his Physical Setting. Holt, Rinehart and Winston, New York (1970)
4. Valdesolo, P., DeSteno, D.: Manipulation of emotional context shape moral judgment. Psychol. Sci. **17**, 476–477 (2006)
5. Erk, S., Kiefer, M., Grothe, J., Wunderlich, A.P., Spitzer, M., Walter, H.: Emotional context modulates subsequent memory effect. Neuroimage **18**, 439–447 (2003)
6. Gregg, L., Tarrier, N.: Virtual reality in mental health. Soc. Psychiatry Psychiatr. Epidemiology **42**, 343–354 (2007)
7. Vanni, F., Conversano, C., Del Debbio, A., Landi, P., Carlini, M., Fanciullacci, C., DellOsso, L.: A survey on virtual environment applications to fear of public speaking. Eur. Rev. Med. Pharmacol. Sci. **17**, 1561–1568 (2013)
8. Faita, C., Vanni, F., Lorenzini, C., Carrozzino, M., Tanca, C., Bergamasco, M.: Perception of basic emotions from facial expressions of dynamic virtual avatars. In: De Paolis, L.T., Mongelli, A. (eds.) AVR 2015. LNCS, vol. 9254, pp. 409–419. Springer, Heidelberg (2015)
9. Krumhuber, E.G., Kappas, A., Manstead, A.S.: Effects of dynamic aspects of facial expressions: a review. Emot. Rev. **5**, 41–46 (2013)
10. Riva, G., Mantovani, F., Capideville, C.S., Preziosa, A., Morganti, F., Villani, D., Gaggioli, A., Botella, C., Alcañiz, M.: Affective interactions using virtual reality: the link between presence and emotions. CyberPsychol. Behav. **10**, 45–56 (2007)

11. Baños, R., Botella, C., Liaño, V., Guerrero, B., Rey, B., Alcañiz, M.: Sense of presence in emotional virtual environments. In: Proceedings of Presence, pp. 156–159 (2004)
12. Baños, R.M., Botella, C., Alcañiz, M., Liaño, V., Guerrero, B., Rey, B.: Immersion and emotion: their impact on the sense of presence. CyberPsychol. Behav. **7**, 734–741 (2004)
13. Gutiérrez-Maldonado, J., Ferrer-García, M., Caqueo-Urízar, A., Letosa-Porta, A.: Assessment of emotional reactivity produced by exposure to virtual environments in patients with eating disorders. CyberPsychol. Behav. **9**, 507–513 (2006)
14. Aylett, R., Louchart, S.: Towards a narrative theory of virtual reality. Virtual Reality **7**, 2–9 (2003)
15. Clandinin, D.J.: Narrative and story in teacher education. In: Russell, T., Munby, H. (eds.) Teachers and Teaching: From Classroom to Reflection, pp. 124–137. Falmer Press, London (1992)
16. McCoy, J., Treanor, M., Samuel, B., Tearse, B., Mateas, M., Wardrip-Fruin, N.: Authoring game-based interactive narrative using social games and comme il faut. In: Proceedings of the 4th International Conference & Festival of the Electronic Literature Organization: Archive & Innovate, Citeseer (2010)
17. Lorenzini, C., Faita, C., Carrozzino, M., Tecchia, F., Bergamasco, M.: VR-based serious game designed for medical ethics training. In: De Paolis, L.T., Mongelli, A. (eds.) AVR 2015. LNCS, vol. 9254, pp. 220–232. Springer, Heidelberg (2015)
18. Lorenzini, C., Faita, C., Barsotti, M., Carrozzino, M., Tecchia, F., Bergamasco, M.: Aditho–a serious game for training and evaluating medical ethicsskills. In: Chorianopoulos, K., Divitini, M., Hauge, J.B., Jaccheri, L., Malaka, R. (eds.) Entertainment Computing-ICEC 2015. LNCS, vol. 9353, pp. 59–71. Springer, Heidelberg (2015)
19. Ruffaldi, E., Evangelista, C., Neri, V., Carrozzino, M., Bergamasco, M.: Design of information landscapes for cultural heritage content. In: Proceedings of the 3rd International Conference on Digital Interactive Media in Entertainment and Arts, pp. 113–119. ACM (2008)
20. Carrozzino, M., Bruno, N., Bergamasco, M.: Designing interaction metaphors for Web3D cultural dissemination. J. Cult. Heritage **14**, 146–155 (2013)
21. Slater, M., Frisoli, A., Tecchia, F., Guger, C., Lotto, B., Steed, A., Pfurtscheller, G., Leeb, R., Reiner, M., Sanchez-Vives, M.V., et al.: Understanding and realizing presence in the presenccia project. IEEE Comput. Graph. Appl. **27**, 90–93 (2007)
22. Normand, J.M., Spanlang, B., Tecchia, F., Carrozzino, M., Swapp, D., Slater, M.: Full body acting rehearsal in a networked virtual environment a case study. Presence: Teleoperators Virtual Environ. **21**, 229–243 (2012)
23. Lang, P.J., Bradley, M.M., Cuthbert, B.N.: International affective picture system (iaps): Technical manual and affective ratings. NIMH Center for the Study of Emotion and Attention, pp. 39–58 (1997)
24. Baños, R.M., Botella, C., Garcia-Palacios, A., Villa, H., Perpiñá, C., Alcaniz, M.: Presence and reality judgment in virtual environments: a unitary construct? CyberPsychol. Behav. **3**, 327–335 (2000)
25. Zimmerman, D.W., Zumbo, B.D.: Relative power of the wilcoxon test, the friedman test, and repeated-measures anova on ranks. J. Exp. Educ. **62**, 75–86 (1993)
26. Mauchly, J.W.: Significance test for sphericity of a normal n-variate distribution. Ann. Math. Stat. **11**, 204–209 (1940)
27. Šidák, Z.: Rectangular confidence regions for the means of multivariate normal distributions. J. Am. Stat. Assoc. **62**, 626–633 (1967)

User Based Intelligent Adaptation of Five in a Row Game for Android Based on the Data from the Front Camera

Jan Novotny, Jan Dvorak, and Ondrej Krejcar[(✉)]

Faculty of Informatics and Management,
Center for Basic and Applied Research, University of Hradec Kralove,
Rokitanskeho 62, 500 03 Hradec Kralove, Czech Republic
jan.novotny.17@uhk.cz, dvorakj@gmail.com,
ondrej@krejcar.org

Abstract. Playing games on mobile phones is very popular nowadays. Many people prefer logic games such as chess, five in a row, checkers etc. This work aspires to come up with a concept of such game, in which the user will not have to deal with setting the opponent's difficultness – the application will automatically optimize itself. In order to that it will use a shot acquired by the front camera and suitable algorithms of a computer vision. On the smartphone front camera shots these algorithms are able not only to recognize a human face, but as well to estimate an indication about the particular person (for example age, sex, mood). This work brings the concept and an implementation of the game five in a row for Android mobile platform. The paper suggests an applicable algorithm coming out of a Minimax method with its own evaluating function. To design this function there are utilized genetic algorithms – precisely a tournament selection method. Therefore the result of this work is a concrete algorithm of the opponent in the game five in a row implemented into the Android application, which optimizes itself to the user according to the data from the smartphone front camera.

Keywords: Android · Five in a row · Minimax · Alfa-beta pruning · Genetic algorithms · Face recognition

1 Introduction

Nowadays a large number of people own a smartphone. Many of them don't use it just for the basic purposes, but also for fun and playing games. For sure we could find many users as well that would like to play on their smartphone a game known mainly from school desks – five in a row. Playing five in a row on the smartphone has a big advantage, that the user doesn't need a real opponent. The opponent can be some algorithm of an artificial intelligence.

For the best possible enjoyment of the game it is important that the user can choose the opponent to play with the equable emulator possible. And even better is, if the suitable opponent for the user is set automatically and the user can simply enjoy the experience of the game with the opponent and does not have to deal with any application settings.

© Springer International Publishing Switzerland 2016
L.T. De Paolis and A. Mongelli (Eds.): AVR 2016, Part I, LNCS 9768, pp. 133–149, 2016.
DOI: 10.1007/978-3-319-40621-3_9

For the automatic selection of the opponent's level can be used the data from the smartphone front camera. Presently there exist a number of algorithms of computer vision, which are able not only to identify a human faces (face-detection), but also to analyze the found face and gain different specifications (face-recognition), such as sex, age, race etc. However, these specifications don't have to serve only to change the opponent's level in the five in a row, but as well for the overall adjustment of the application to the user.

Therefore the main goal of this work is the conception of the suitable opponent algorithm in the game five in a row that can intelligently change its difficulty according to the front camera data. Thus the work handles with two main topics:

(1) *formation of the algorithm for the opponent in the game five in a row with a possibility to modify its difficulty*
(2) *work with the image from the front camera and application of the computer vision algorithms with the purpose of recognition the shot faces*

The formation of the new algorithm for recognition of the shot faces is beyond the scope of this work. It is a difficult problem, which is well described in an article [1]. Though, this work resumes information about currently used technologies. Consequently the technologies are used and compared.

In this work there is suggested the algorithm of the artificial intelligence for the opponent in the game five in a row. The paper does not contain explanation of the game rules. Concretely there are considered game rules of Gomoku with a playing field sized 15×15, see [6].

According to [2] there generally exist two types of algorithms for five in a row (and similar games such as chess) – no-searching and searching. The first, easier of them, is mostly based on several rules that result from experience of the algorithm's author. This way in contrary to the other does not use any searching. The second way is more sophisticated and uses space searching of all the possible rolls into a certain depth. Principally it comes from already existing algorithms such as Minimax or its enhancement – Alfa-Beta pruning. These algorithms are described in detail for example in articles [3, 4] and in the work they will be represented in the next chapter. For this work it is more suitable to use the second way with searching, because it is possible to easily change the performance of the algorithm by customizing the searching depth.

The basis of the Minimax algorithm is an evaluating function. Its task is to evaluate a specific position by a concrete numeric value. The evaluating function is the most important part of the whole algorithm. It is applied for evaluating nodes in the searching tree. The concept of the evaluating function is a subject of next chapters.

2 Problem Definition

The work targets two problems – especially the creation of the new algorithm for five in a row and then also utilization of shots from the smartphone front camera. This chapter contains both of the problems.

2.1   Opponent Algorithm in the Game Five in a Row

One of the work goals is to suggest the suitable artificial intelligence algorithm for the opponent in the game five in a row. As it was said in the previous chapter already, the competent candidate to solve the algorithm is minimax.

This algorithm uses a "game tree". It is a tree of all the possibilities, how the specific game can further progress. The algorithm calculates with the game tree limited by a certain preset depth, because the whole tree would be huge. Minimax evaluates every tree leaf using the evaluating function. The evaluation of each node is defined as the best value of its successor. The best value is defined different way in the case of odd and even tree levels. In the odd levels there's tendency to choose the maximum value of the evaluating function, on the contrary in the even levels to choose the minimum value. For the root position is not important its evaluation, but the discovered roll leading to its best evaluated successor. [5] The principal of minimax method is shown in the Fig. 1.

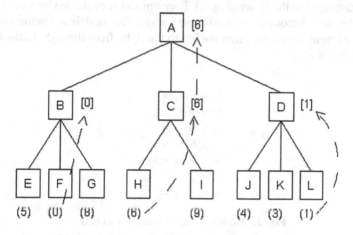

Fig. 1. Minimax algorithm (overtaken from [2])

A simple pseudo code of this method can be displayed for example as below [7]:

```
int maxi( int depth ) {
    if ( depth == 0 ) return evaluate();
    int max = -oo;
    for ( all moves) {
        score = mini( depth - 1 );
        if( score > max )
            max = score;
    } return max;
}

int mini( int depth ) {
    if ( depth == 0 ) return -evaluate();
    int min = +oo;
    for ( all moves) {
        score = maxi( depth - 1 );
        if( score < min )
            min = score;
    } return min;
}
```

This principle uses many algorithms for the game five in a row. The fundamental point, where it differs, is the evaluating function. Below there are presented several evaluating functions from different authors.

An article [8] suggests total of 6 methods to implement the evaluating function. Through a tournament it was found out, that in a competition stands the best an algorithm called "Simple (Line Based)". It evaluates every unblocked tuple of a specific player with value 4n and again every unblocked tuple of an opponent with value -4n. Then the function result becomes a sum of these values.

Evaluating function by author [9] searches for every quadruplet, triplet and couple on the playing field and to these values it assigns a certain weight, whereas the weight of the quadruplet is the highest and the weight of the couple is the lowest. Generally it applies, that the more of such consecutive quadruplets, triplets and couples the player has, the bigger is his chance to win.

Next author [10] mentions an evaluating function based on searching models. The models are displayed in the figure (Fig. 2). Every model is evaluated by a certain value; the result afterwards becomes a sum of these values. The models are being searched in all possible different directions (from the left to the right, from the right to the left, from the top way down etc.)

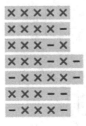

Fig. 2. Models in the evaluating function

Next evaluating function was designed by author [11]. The principal is locating all the quintuples of consequent fields, whereas every quintuple is evaluated according to its content. For evaluation of all the quintuples are used rules listed below [11]:

- If all the fields are empty, the evaluation is 0
- If there is at least one sign by each of the players in the quintuple, the evaluation is 0
- If there are signs by just one player in the quintuple, the player gains
    - 1 point, if he has one sign in the certain quintuple
    - 73 points, if he has two signs in the certain quintuple
    - 511 points, if he has three signs in the certain quintuple
    - 1751 points, if he has four signs in the certain quintuple

This idea seems to be very good and the result algorithm, which may be tested directly on the author's web site, plays subjectively very well. However, the author of the algorithm doesn't explain anywhere, how he got to the applied numbers 1, 73, 511 and 1751.

This work utilizes the last mentioned algorithm of the evaluating function and tries to improve it. The numbers 1, 73, 511 and 1751 suggested by the author [11] are not supported by any objective analysis. Therefore this work aims to find out the optimal values for this evaluating function.

2.2 Customization of the Game According to the Shots from the Front Camera

As it was mentioned in the first chapter, for setting the difficulty of the five in a row it is possible to use the shots from the front camera on the mobile device. These shots can be analyzed and out of them it is possible to obtain various information about the user, who plays the game. Among the obtained information range user's age, sex and mood. Concretely it is possible to use the data in the game this way:

- Automatic setting of the easiest level in the case the user is a child.
- Adaptation of a graphic interface and the game level regarding to sex and age of the user.
- If the user thinks too long and the application recognizes he is sad, it displays a help option with the best roll

Part of this work is therefore a summary of existing technologies for the face recognition in the image, which can be used on the Android platform, and their comparison.

In the August 2015 Google Company introduced a new version of Google Play services, specifically version 7.8. A component of this version is new Mobile Vision API, which contains a support for the face recognition in the image and a real-time recognition of the barcodes. The new API for the face recognition in the image has 4 functionalities for now [14]:

- Face detection in the image
- Face tracking – i.e. extension of face detection also for video. API manages to track the face in the face detection and it knows, that it is still the same person
- Discovering areas of concern in the face (Facial landmarks) - for example position of left and right eye, nose, mouth etc. (total 8)
- Classification – for now API can only estimate a probability of smile and a probability that left and right eyes are open

Unfortunately Google Play services are not able to guess sex, age and race etc. out of the image. But for this issue it is possible to neatly exploit various web services available on the internet. The principal of these services is sending a request with an attached image file and following answer of the web service, mostly in JSON format, which contains various specifications about the found person/people in the picture.

The first of such web services distributes Microsoft Company as a part of "Project Oxford", specifically it is a service called "Face APIs" [15]. This service can classify information about the found person listed below:

- Different facial landmarks – many times more than Google Play services (total 27)
- Age and sex

Though the Microsoft service is free (after registration and a key generation), but unfortunately it is limited by up to 20 requests in a minute and 5000 requests in a month.

Next service, which is free, but in contrary with no limits, is called Face++ [16]. It can classify following data about the identified person:

- Various facial landmarks – less then Microsoft service (total 6)
- Probability of smile
- Sex – including its probability
- Race – including its probability
- Age – including from-to range

Next there exist several other similar services, but an overwhelming majority of them is charged. For the purpose of this work there will be used just the mentioned services.

3 New Solution

This chapter concerns with suggesting the new opponent algorithm in the game five in a row and results from the algorithm described in the second chapter. To find a suitable quadruplet of aforementioned values there are used genetic algorithms in the work.

Genetic algorithms are inspired by natural evolution process in the nature. The fundamental is Darwin's theory of natural selection and Mendel's genetics theory. The intention of the genetic algorithms is seeking through the space and discovering the optimal solution of the specific function, for which doesn't exist (or is too difficult) an exact algorithm. Every possible solution is represented by an individual in a population. The population then is a set of individuals – a set of possible solutions. Over time the population evolves. The poor individuals die out; better individuals appear and replace them.

Such algorithm can be written in pseudo code this way:

```
k = 0
Initialization P(k)
Evaluation P(k)
Repeat
    k = k+1
    Selection P(k) from individuals in P(k-1)
    Recombination P(k)
    Evaluation P(k)
Until the terminal condition is fulfilled
```

The step Recombination P(k) means executing two genetic operators – crossing and mutation. Evaluation P(k) is realized by fitness function calculation, which evaluates each individual in the population according to his quality [12].

The selection in the genetic algorithms may be realized using several selection methods. These include for example different alternatives of roulette selection and a tournament selection. In this work it is used the tournament selection that picks the best individuals from the population on the base of an arranged tournament between the individuals.

3.1 Realized Tournament Selection

Within this work it was arranged a tournament between algorithms for five in a row. Every individual was represented by a quadruple of values (a, b, c, d), where

- a represents number of points for one sign in a quintuple
- b represents number of points for two signs in a quintuple
- c represents number of points for three signs in a quintuple
- d represents number of points for four signs in a quintuple

in the evaluating function described supra.

The tournament was realized using all-play-all method. The matching rivals were algorithms with different values (a, b, c, d) in the evaluating function with scanning of the minimax tree into depth 2. In every match of two individuals:

- the winner gained 1 point
- the loser gained 0 points
- both players gained ½ point in the case of draw (filling the whole playing field 15 × 15)
- Further tournament specification:
- In every round total 10 individuals matched each other; in that round they competed each other two times; every time different player started the match.
- Total 21 rounds of the tournament were arranged.
- In every round there were played total 90 matches.
- Fitness function of an individual means a sum of points gained during a specific tournament round.
- Into the next round principally progressed:
- 2 individuals with the highest fitness function (without crossing and mutation),
- 5 individuals originated by mutation of an individual with the highest fitness function,
- 3 randomly generated individuals
- In the zero generation there were generated ten individuals by a generator of pseudorandom numbers.

3.2 Tournament Results

The process of the arranged tournament is captured by table (Table 1 – 1st selection).

There was chosen a winner from the results displayed in the table (Table 1) - a quadruple (23, 342, 2132, 40125). This individual was compared with the original individual (1, 73, 511, 1751), but that one lost both of the two matches. The chosen procedure should lead to find an optimal individual, however 21 rounds are apparently not enough. Since the calculation is quite difficult (21 rounds take ca. 45 min using a usually powerful laptop) it was arranged a second tournament, where the zero generation included also the original individual (1, 73, 511, 1751). This way guarantees that yet the zero generation contains a quality individual, which is a good basis for consequent uprising of better individuals by mutation. The process of the second tournament is captured by table (Table 1 – 2nd selection).

Table 1. Tournament selection nr. 1 (2nd column) and 2 (3nd column)

Round	Winner of the round (1st)	Winner of the round (2nd)
1.	(12362, 19815, 41587, 43100)	(1, 73, 511, 1751))
2.	(8786, 14601, 50000, 33367)	(2, 34, 189, 817)
3.	(153, 7455, 46919, 22063)	(2, 34, 189, 817)
4.	(64, 2518, 34758, 13620)	(2, 34, 189, 817)
5.	(61, 4794, 20165, 18829)	(2, 34, 189, 817)
6.	(25, 1734, 10356, 31796)	(1, 4, 193, 1079)
7.	(26, 336, 5698, 50000)	(1, 4, 193, 1079)
8.	(26, 336, 5698, 50000)	(1, 4, 193, 1079)
9.	(26, 336, 5698, 50000)	(1, 4, 193, 1079)
10.	(34, 244, 3095, 22952)	(1, 4, 193, 1079)
11.	(34, 244, 3095, 22952)	(1, 4, 193, 1079)
12.	(34, 244, 3095, 22952)	(1, 4, 193, 1079)
13.	(23, 342, 2132, 40125)	(2, 7, 24, 456)
14.	(23, 342, 2132, 40125)	(2, 7, 24, 456)
15.	(23, 342, 2132, 40125)	(1, 4, 193, 1079)
16.	(23, 342, 2132, 40125)	(1, 4, 193, 1079)
17.	(23, 342, 2132, 40125)	(1, 4, 193, 1079)
18.	(23, 342, 2132, 40125)	(1, 4, 193, 1079)
19.	(23, 342, 2132, 40125)	(1, 4, 193, 1079)
20.	(23, 342, 2132, 40125)	(2, 7, 24, 456)
21	(23, 342, 2132, 40125)	(1, 4, 193, 1079)

As a winner quadruple of values for the evaluating function according to this tournament was chosen a quadruple (1, 4, 193, 1079).

4 Implementation

4.1 Implementation of the Five in a Row Algorithm

The whole application is implemented in Java language and is intended for Android platform. The main logic of the algorithm is divided into two classes displayed in the Fig. 3.

The most important class is the class GomokuMiniMaxEngine with the method play, which receives as an input a two dimension field of values representing an actual game position and also a numeric value, which represents the specific symbol (a cross or a circle). The method returns coordinates of the best found roll. The second considerable class is GomokuGame, which represents a certain game position (implemented by a two dimension field). The class includes a method checkGameEnd, which returns value 0 in the case that it's not end yet, 1 in the case the cross wins, 2 in the case the circle wins and 3 in the case of draw (filling the whole playing field).

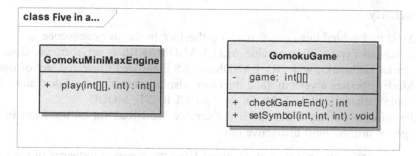

Fig. 3. Class diagram

The basic minimax algorithm was improved in this work with the alfa-beta pruning, which is very well described for example in the article [2]. This algorithm accelerates the slow minimax by pruning the minimax tree by redundant branches. This way it gives the same result with a shorter calculation time. For easier imagination the calculation with the classic minimax algorithm with searching into depth 3 took approximately 1.5 min on a common laptop.

Using alfa-beta pruning the calculation was reduced to ca. 6 s. With alfa-beta pruning it depends on an order of searching the rolls, in which they are being searched through – therefore in the work it was implemented also simple sequencing of the rolls. With this sequencing of the rolls the calculation was reduced from 6 s to ca. 1 s, which is already an acceptable calculation time.

4.2 Implementation of the Technologies for the Face Recognition

The technologies applicable for the face recognition in the image were mentioned in the second chapter. This chapter handles with their practical use.

(1) *Google Play services*

The first technology applicable for the Android platform is Faces API in Google Play services. A fundamental class of this API is a class FaceDetector. While creating the class it is possible to set how much the API shall recognize in the detected face. The following code demonstrates how this can be realized:

```
FaceDetector detector =
new FaceDetector.Builder(context)
.setTrackingEnabled(true)
.setLandmarkType(FaceDetector.ALL_LANDMARKS)
.setClassificationType(FaceDetector.ALL_CLASSIFICATIONS)
.setMode(FaceDetector.FAST_MODE)
.setProminentFaceOnly(true)
.build();
```

Concretely:

- setTrackingEnabled turns on/off tracking the face in the shots sequence
- setLandmarkType – when a value ALL_LANDMARKS is set, there are detected the facial landmarks, with NO_LANDMARKS there aren't detected any of them
- setMode regulates a velocity (and therefore also accuracy) of the calculation. The possible variants are FAST_MODE and ACCURATE_MODE
- setProminentFaceOnly estimates, if the service shall look for all the faces in the image, or just the most distinctive one

The concrete values can be then obtained from the concrete instances of the class called Face, which contains methods such as *getIsSmilingProbability()*, *getIsLeftEyeOpenProbability()*, *getIsRightEyeOpenProbability()*, or *getLandmarks()*.

(2) *Face APIs (Microsoft)*

For the API by Microsoft [15], it is possible to set demanded parametres similarly as with Google Play services:

- analyzesFaceLandmarks – turns on/off the facial landmarks detection
- analyzesAge – turns on/off the age estimation
- analyzesGender – turns on/off the sex estimation

Furthermore while requesting the web service it is necessary to use a key (subscription-key), which can be generated while registration on the web. Afterwards the web service returns the calculated values in the JSON format.

(3) *Face++*

To simplify the use of API Face++ in the Java language there exist an elementary library directly from authors of Face++, which can be downloaded at the project web site [16]. Then its use can be as follows:

JSONObject result = httpRequests
.detectionDetect(new PostParameters().
setImg(new File("picture.jpg")));

While creating an instance httpRequests of the class HttpRequests it is required to enter the generated key, similarly as with the Microsoft product.

4.3 The Implementation of the Game Five in a Row on the Android Platform

Since the calculation of the five in a row algorithm is computationally difficult, it is necessary that the calculation is carried out in the background. That is implemented in the work using an IntentService.

The playing field for the five in a row of size 15×15 is realized in the graphic interface by 225 instances of an ImageView class. In the case the square is empty, it's selected empty white area while rendering, if the square isn't empty, it's selected the image of a cross or a circle. For each square it is applied an onClickListener, which operates a certain event (a click).

In Picture 4 it's showed a designed graphic interface. In the left top corner there is visualization of the actual player (a person) with a name and a symbol for which he plays. In the right top corner there is the opponent (the artificial intelligence) with his symbol. After ending a game there appears a button for beginning a new game.

The technologies for the face detection were implemented into the application this way:

(1) If the user is
    (a) 0–11 years, it is set the easiest (the first) level
    (b) 12–14 years, it is set the second level
    (c) 15–70 years, it is set the third level
    (d) 70–120 years, it is set the easiest (the first) level
    (e) the fourth (the most difficult) level can be set only manually
(2) If the user is
    (a) a man, the symbols on the playing board are rendered black
    (b) a women, the symbols on the playing board are rendered red
(3) If the user thinks too long and is sad (applies only in the real-time detection - see the following paragraph), there appears a help button for the next roll

The face detection is demanding for the consumption of the device. That's why in the application there are implemented two possibilities of use:

(a) The detection will take place only once – in the beginning of a new game – the acquired information as age and sex are used for the whole game
(b) It is executed a real-time face detection. In this case it is displayed the user's face below the playing board to him and there are showed the detected information in real time. See figure (Fig. 4).

5 Testing of Developed Solution

This chapter describes testing of the newly designed opponent algorithm in the game five in a row and also there are compared the technologies for the face detection in the image mentioned supra.

5.1 Testing of the Newly Designed Algorithm

The third chapter describes a way used to design the new quadruple of values for evaluating function of the minimax algorithm. This chapter targets to compare the original algorithm by author [11] with the algorithm suggested in this work.

The easiest comparison of the two algorithms for the game five in a row is to let them play against each other. But this comparison resulted with a draw – every time became a winner the player who started the game.

For a better comparison of the two algorithms this work employs a game opening called SWAP. While opening with SWAP the starting player places 3 signs on the playing board; 2 crosses and one circle or 1 cross and 2 circles. The second player

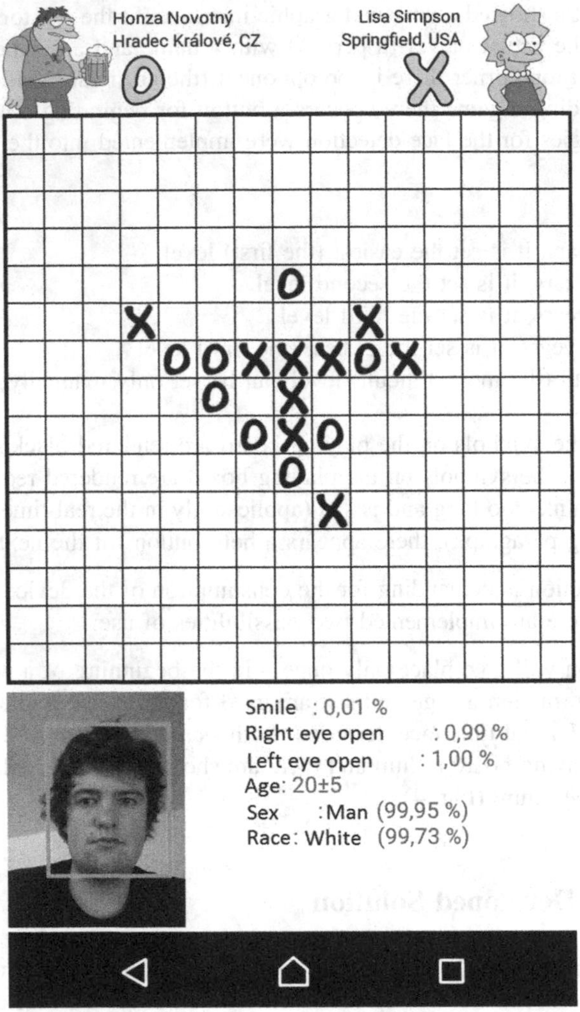

Fig. 4. GUI

picks, which sign he wants to take. The first roll takes the player that has less signs on the playing board. This way guarantees that the game is more equable than with the classic opening the five in a row game (called surewin) [13].

To compare the algorithms there were suggested total 4 signs locations to open the game that are more equable than the classic opening the game. The four opening types are visualized on the following pictures (Fig. 5).

The test consisted of 8 games of the algorithms mentioned supra. Every algorithm played each opening type two times – ones with crosses and for the second time with circles. The game results are displayed in Table 2.

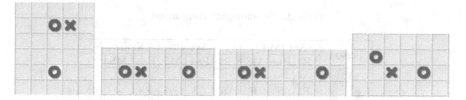

Fig. 5. Opening for test nr. 1, 2, 3, 4

Table 2. The results of the comparison

	(1, 73, 511, 1751)	(1, 4, 193, 1079)
Opening 1	0 wins	2 wins
Opening 2	0 wins	2 wins
Opening 3	0 wins	2 wins
Opening 4	1 win	1 win

The original algorithm with the quadruple (1, 73, 511, 1751) made it only once to win - in the fourth opening. Concretely in that case the algorithm played with circles (that is two signs in the SWAP opening). This result approves that the new suggested solution is better than the original one.

5.2 Comparison of the Technologies for the Face Detection in the Image

In the second chapter there were mentioned existing technologies for the face detection in the image. This chapter brings their comparison by concrete examples. For the testing there were used total 10 pictures of people taken from public web servers. The information detected using Face++, Face API by Microsoft and Google Play services are showed in Table 3.

It's visible in the Table 3, that both of the web services (Face++ and Microsoft Face API) successfully managed to recognize sex of the photographed people in all the cases.

The person's age estimation was also very good in all the cases; the largest diversion from the real age was made by Face++ service in the last photo (diversion of 24). An average diversion was similar for both of the services: Face++ 5.8 years and the Microsoft service 5.9 years.

Considering the probability of the certain person's smile is a subjective matter. The measured values are only informative. But taken subjectively we can say that both of the algorithms work very well. The largest difference between the algorithm values is within the penult person, though neither a human would say if this person does smile or not.

Table 3. Technologies comparison

Person	Sex (M/F)			Age			Smile (%)		
	R	F++	MS	R	F++	MS	F++	MS	G
	F	F	F	18	23	20	88	–	45
	M	M	M	24	35	39	3	–	0
	F	F	F	26	25	27	95	–	98
	M	M	M	29	21	31	1	–	1
	F	F	F	31	30	27	5	–	1
	F	F	F	32	30	23	1	–	1
	F	F	F	34	34	38	4	–	12
	M	M	M	39	36	35	0	–	27
	M	M	M	62	65	71	58	–	10
	M	M	M	76	52	67	94	–	98

* Explanatory notes: R ... real entry, F++ ... Face++, MS ... Microsoft Face API, G ... Google Play services, M ... masculine, F ... feminine.

6 Discussion

Results presented in part 5 (Testing of Developed Solution) provide a reasonable level of developed solution according the defined parameters in part 2 (Problem Definition), unfortunately there are still some limitations for real and efficient use of the developed solution by the use of APIs from third part developers - such described in part 2.2.). Developed solution is open for implementation of own algorithm for face detection in the images based on existing solutions presented in major journals and international conferences in last 4 years as the problem is widely spoken in the computer science community [17–23].

Very interesting paper [17] deal with a problem of games which are boring when they are too easy and frustrating when they are too hard. A game in which the challenge level matches the skill of the human player has the greatest entertainment value. Authors introduced a simple and fast method for adjusting a difficulty level of a computer opponent. The results show that proposed method matches the difficulty level of an opponent to a player's skill level even without full information about player's abilities. This solution has many useful ideas which can be taken into account for new algorithm development. Another ideas can be found also in [18] and patent [19], while in [20] authors deal with a problem how to achieve flow and increase player retention. Being able to evaluate how people play a game is a crucial component for detecting gamer's strategies. Authors provide a study on Real Time Strategy (RTS) game. They are extracting a real-time information about the players strategies, while after it, the model is evaluated in terms of unsupervised learning (concretely, K-Means). Other publications [21–23] dealt with a problem of player's strategy from psychology point of view, where we can found also several ideas, which can be useful in our algorithm. These will be investigated in future versions of our developed solution.

7 Conclusions

This project brings a successful finding of the new algorithm for an opponent in the game five in a row. It was compared with the original algorithm and in the comparison it became a winner. So it can be indicated as a better one. The algorithm was created in the Java language and consequently used in the application for Android.

Furthermore the project resumes and compares the actual technologies for the face detection in the image. In the coming days we can expect improvements of these technologies, particularly API by Google Play services, which will definitely find their assertion in certain applications.

Acknowledgement. This work and the contribution were supported by project "SP-2102-2016 - Smart Solutions for Ubiquitous Computing Environments" Faculty of Informatics and Management, University of Hradec Kralove, Czech Republic. We also acknowledge the technical language assistance provided by Pavlina Simkova.

References

1. Yang, M.H., Kriegman, D.J., Ahuja, N.: Detecting Faces in Images: A Survey. http://vision. ai.illinois.edu/publications/pami02a.pdf (2002). Accessed 11 Nov 2015
2. Fialka, L.: Advanced environment for playing board games). Praha, Bachelors work. Czech Technical University in Prague. https://dip.felk.cvut.cz/browse/pdfcache/fialkl2_2006bach. pdf (2006). Accessed 11 Nov 2015
3. Pearl, J.: The Solution for the Branching Factor of the Alpha-Beta Pruning Algorithm and its Optimality. Programming Techniques and Data Structures. http://wiki.cs.pdx.edu/ wurzburg2009/nfp/abavg.pdf (1982). Accessed 11 Nov 2015
4. Knuth, D.E., Moore, R.W.: An Analysis of Alpha-Beta Pruning. Artificial Intelligence. http://www-public.tem-tsp.eu/~gibson/Teaching/CSC4504/ReadingMaterial/KnuthMoore 75.pdf (1974). Accessed 11 Nov 2015
5. Kuhr, T.: Algorithm minimax. Palacky University Olomouc, Olomouc. http://www.inf.upol. cz/downloads/studium/PS/minimax.pdf. Accessed 27 Nov 2015
6. Gomoku. Game Rules. http://gamerulesguru.com/gomoku.shtml (2009). Accessed 27 Nov 2015
7. Minimax. Chess programming. https://chessprogramming.wikispaces.com/Minimax (2015). Accessed 27 Nov 2015
8. Kulev, V., WU, D.: Heuristics and Threat-Space-Search in Connect 5. http://isites.harvard. edu/fs/docs/icb.topic707165.files/pdfs/Kulev_Wu.pdf (2009). Accessed 27 Nov 2015
9. Kim, J.: Gomoku agent using Minimax/Alpha-beta pruning, Gomoku. https://github.com/ janecakemaster/gomoku (2013). Accessed 27 Nov 2015
10. Loos, A.: Machine Learning for k-in-a-row Type Games Using Random Forest and Genetic Algorithm. University of Tartu, Tartu. http://comserv.cs.ut.ee/forms/ati_report/downloader. php?file=5D52AF13A55F51ADB1F03E3C1EEAF628BA1BC580 (2012). Accessed 27 Nov 2015
11. Description of the five in a row algorithm. Trixi blog. http://blog.trixi.cz/2013/02/popis-piskvorkoveho-algoritmu/. Accessed 27 Nov 2015
12. Posik, P.: Genetic algorithms. Czech Technical University in Prague, Praha. http://labe.felk. cvut.cz/~posik/pga/theory/ga-theory.htm (2000). Accessed 27 Nov 2015
13. The five in a row rules. The tutorial center of five in a row and renju. http://www.vcpr.cz/ napoveda-a-pravidla/pravidla-piskvorek/ (2015). Accessed 27 Nov 2015
14. Mobile Vision. Google developers: Find objects in photos and video, using real-time on-device vision technology. https://developers.google.com/vision/ (2015). Accessed 28 Nov 2015
15. Face APIs. Microsoft Project Oxford. https://www.projectoxford.ai/face (2015). Accessed 28 Nov 2015
16. Face++ API. Face++: Leading Face Recognition on Cloud. http://www.faceplusplus.com/. Accessed 28 Nov 2015
17. Lach, E.: A quick method for dynamic difficulty adjustment of a computer player in computer games. In: Rutkowski, L., Korytkowski, M., Scherer, R., Tadeusiewicz, R., Zadeh, L.A., Zurada, J.M. (eds.) ICAISC 2015. Part II. LNCS, vol. 9120, pp. 669–678. Springer, Heidelberg (2015)
18. Balas, B., Thomas, L.: Competition makes faces look more aggressive. J. Vis. **15**(12), 1217 (2015). doi:10.1167/15.12.1217

19. Kang, H.S., Kwon, H.: Method for providing service fighting game, involves choosing multiple characters, requesting electric charge between characters, registering pinhole free skill, determining character attack order and renewing strength of opponent character. Patent Number: KR2015055150-A, SMILEGATE INC. (2015)
20. Palero, F., Ramirez-Atencia, C., Camacho, D.: Online gamers classification using K-means. In: Camacho, D., Braubach, L., Venticinque, S., Badica, C. (eds.) Intelligent Distributed Computing VIII. SCI, vol. 570, pp. 197–204. Springer, Heidelberg (2014)
21. Vermeulen, L., Castellar, E.N., Van Looy, J.: Challenging the other: exploring the role of opponent gender in digital game competition for female players. Cyberpsychology Behav. Soc. Networking 17(5), 303–309 (2014). doi:10.1089/cyber.2013.0331
22. MacKay, T.L., Bard, N., Bowling, M., Hodgins, D.C.: Do pokers players know how good they are? Accuracy of poker skill estimation in online and offline players. Comput. Hum. Behav. 31(1), 419–424 (2014). doi:10.1016/j.chb.2013.11.006
23. Slezak, D.F., Sigman, M.: Do not fear your opponent: suboptimal changes of a prevention strategy when facing stronger opponents. J. Exp. Psychol.-Gen. 141(3), 527–538 (2012). doi:10.1037/a0025761

Modeling of Complex Taxonomy: A Framework for Schema-Driven Exploratory Portal

Luca Mainetti, Roberto Paiano, Stefania Pasanisi[✉], and Roberto Vergallo

Department of Innovation Engineering, University of Salento, Lecce, Italy
{luca.mainetti,roberto.paiano,
stefania.pasanisi,roberto.vergallo}@unisalento.it

Abstract. This paper discusses an evolution of exploratory portal for an advanced and easy construction of an exploratory portal, through a simplification of the data loading process by a modeling of complex taxonomies. The main requirement for achieving this goal has been to make the schema-driven portal through a modeling of taxonomy, the data and the portal layout on Excel. A framework is proposed in which we implement an application that can build the exploratory portal from this Excel model. We have validated the portal population process, first "in vitro", then "in vivo".

Keywords: Exploratory portal · Data visualizations · Taxonomy · Knowledge discovery

1 Introduction

An exploratory portal takes advantage of the principles and the aims of exploratory computing technique. Exploratory Computing (EC) [2] is a process supported by the system which, at each user request, gives her feedback by emphasising the interesting properties of the current result and possibly suggesting one or more possible actions that can be taken in her next exploration step. Thus starting by a specific realm, Rich Datasets, we have a specific approach, Exploratory Computing, and a specific solution, Exploratory Portals [3].

The first generation of exploratory portals for rich datasets (where objects are classified according to powerful taxonomies) has already provided a way to support effective user experiences, where traditional approaches (like query, search, faceted search, data mining, logical reasoning, data visualizations, …), instead, would only partially satisfy "exploratory" needs [1]. HOC-LAB has developed, over the years, a number of portals (on archeology, tourism, education) exploiting the EC approach: their actual use, by real-life users, has highlighted new, advanced, requirements that will inform a forthcoming new generation of portals. A specific portal, Learning4All – L4ALL, is an example of "first-generation" portal. The L4ALL portal was developed in the frame of a national research project about how technology impacts education at school [1].

A Rich Data Set, from now on RDS, can be defined as a set of "objects" where each object is associated to a set of values belonging to a "taxonomy", i.e. a set of predefined "facets". The RDS of our application consists of a number of educational experiences

© Springer International Publishing Switzerland 2016
L.T. De Paolis and A. Mongelli (Eds.): AVR 2016, Part I, LNCS 9768, pp. 150–161, 2016.
DOI: 10.1007/978-3-319-40621-3_10

carried on at school with a strong support by ICT. Each experience has some formatted data (location, school level, etc.) some multimedia data (various text files, audio files, video files, etc.) and is classified according to nearly 60 facets.

All the objects were classified by pedagogy experts according to a complex taxonomy consisting of 28 attributes' categories and more than 300 attributes. Categories and attributes are organized into widgets supporting both selection and exploration. Each widget shows the value of the attributes for the current state of the dataset; different visualization strategies can be chosen by the user: absolute value, percentage, word-cloud, histogram, etc. The current set of objects is shown on a "canvas". The properties determined by the EC system should be shown to users in a comprehensive way. Thus, efficient and effective visualizations are needed [2].

This paper discusses an evolution of exploratory portal for an advanced and easy construction of a portal, through a simplification of the data loading process by a modeling of complex taxonomies [3].

To achieve the aims described the portal of the evolution of optical activity are:

- Simplification of the data loading process, by using simple Excel files;
- The portal multi-tenant management: anyone can instantiate a copy of populating portal with classified data according to a custom taxonomy.

To get to these objectives, the portal generation will become schema-driven.

The paper is organized as follows: Sect. 2 discusses the existing research and similar approaches. Section 3 sets a modeling of complex Taxonomy. Section 4 describes a Framework development for effective building of exploratory portal. Section 5 draws the conclusions and highlights possible future work.

2   Related Works

By Exploratory Portal, we mean a highly interactive delivery environment, where the exploration can take place through a number of strongly interconnected (and interdependent) interactions.

In this context "exploration" is not search, nor faceted search, nor data mining, nor logic reasoning, nor data visualization: it is a combination of all these approaches, and something more.

Thanks to advanced Human-Computer Interaction mechanisms, the portal can support sophisticated exploration activities in the cycle <selection, feedback, selection>. Sub-sets of the "universe" (i.e. the initial set of objects) can be easily created via selection or manual operations; sets and subsets can be saved (according with their intensional or extensional definition) for later usage.

Exploratory Data Analysis (EDA) is another example of an information exploration activity: is an approach to analyzing data sets to summarize their main characteristics, often with visual methods [5]. Exploratory Data Analysis, or EDA for short, is a term coined by Tukey in the book "Exploratory Data Analysis" in 1977 [5]. In contrast to statistical approaches aimed at testing specific hypotheses, Exploratory Data Analysis (EDA) is a quantitative tradition that seeks to help researchers understand data when little or no statistical hypotheses exist, or when specific hypotheses exist but supplemental representations are needed to ensure the interpretability of statistical results.

In this way, EDA seeks to answer the broad scientific questions of "what is going on here" and "how might I be fooled by my statistical results" [6]. In 2006, Marchionini [7] postulate the idea of Exploratory Search as a model in which the user learns and investigates information after a first step of Lookup. Exploratory Search, as Marchionini state, is similar to learn search activity and social searching where people use the same strategy for locating, comparing and assessing results. In exploratory search people usually submit a tentative query to get them near relevant documents then explore the environment to better understand how to exploit it, selectively seeking and passively obtaining cues about where their next steps lie. Exploratory search can be considered a specialization of information exploration, a broader class of activities where new information is sought in a defined conceptual area; exploratory data analysis is another example of an information exploration activity. Exploratory search systems (ESSs) capitalize on new technological capabilities and interface paradigms that facilitate an increased level of interaction with search systems. Examples of ESSs include information visualization systems, document clustering and browsing systems, and intelligent content summarization systems. ESSs go beyond returning a single document or answer in response to a query, and instead aim to instigate significant cognitive change through learning and improved understanding [8].

Exploratory computing is an innovative and more recent paradigm that is possible to describe as the step-by-step "conversation" of a user and a system that "help each other" to refine the data exploration process, ultimately gathering new knowledge that concretely fulfills the user needs [9]. Using this new paradigm, have been developed some Exploratory Portal in several field of interest (archeology, tourism, education, etc.) [10–12]. The Exploratory Computing approach as explained in [2] and in its manifesto [3] allows users to investigate of complex dataset composed of rich information. The user can interact with the data and can discover information features that he/she didn't see at a first lookup. The innovation of the Exploratory Computing has several features such as serendipitous discovery, at-a-glance understanding, niche finding, raise of interest, sense-making.

3   Modeling of Complex Taxonomy

To achieve the aims described, it was carried out a preparatory activity but necessary to the advanced management of information and the establishment of appropriate digital formats. Then, we have worked on the modeling of a complex taxonomy for EDOC project experiences in order to feed exploratory portals, with the aim to develop the knowledge about how technology and pedagogy affect the quality of educational experiences. On the basis of empirical evidence (experiences) conducted by real teachers in real contexts, in real situations, it has built an online repository of hundreds of experiments, conducted in classrooms of each school level, where the technology has been cleverly combined with solutions pedagogies in order to generate substantial educational benefits.

The framework implemented has as main objective the effective construction of an exploratory portal, sustaining the adaptivity of the portal to the different uses. The main requirement for achieving this goal has been to make the schema-driven portal: the first generation of the portal is not schema-driven, it was therefore necessary to make a schema-driven portal through a modeling of taxonomy, the data and the portal layout on Excel.

The general scheme proposed consists of two files excel: one relating to the data and one relating to the annexes of the experiences.

The data file consists of the following types of sheets

- WIDGET: only one sheet, defines the overall layout and the number of columns in which subdivide the widgets in the interface (Fig. 1).
- DEFINE W#: one sheet for each facet, defines the structure of each widget, the labels displayed for each widget and shows the translation into English (Fig. 2).
- W# LABEL: one sheet for each facet, defines the data of experience (Fig. 3).
- TPACK: one sheet for each facet of interest, with the selected/entered values (Fig. 4).

The connection between the sheets is via the WIDGET ID. The schema presented defines all aspects of the data of our case study in the portals.

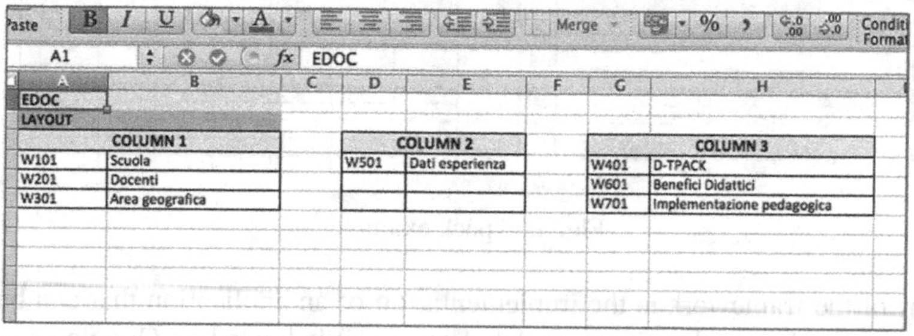

Fig. 1. Widget example

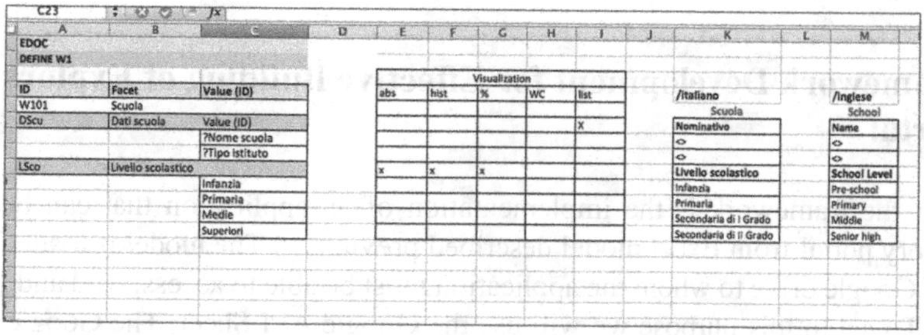

Fig. 2. Define W# example

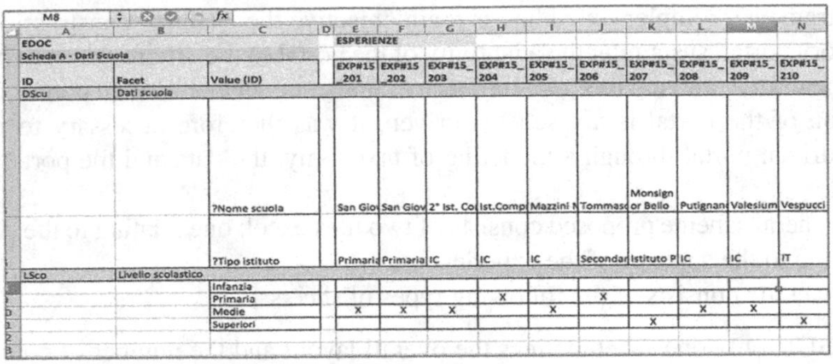

Fig. 3. W# Label example

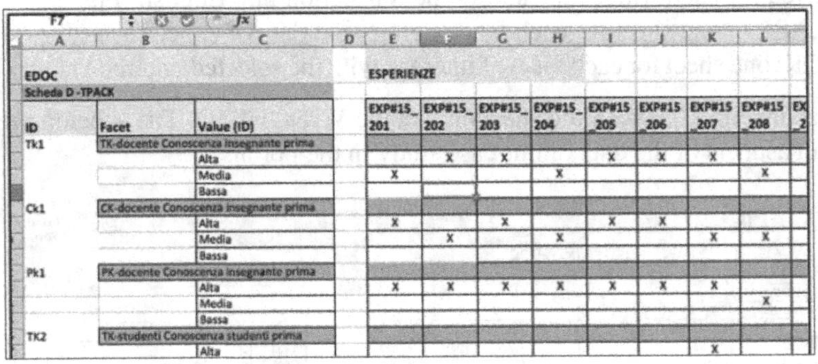

Fig. 4. Tpack example

Focus of the framework is the implementation of an application that can build the exploratory portal from this Excel model. The model is loaded on Google drive space to which the application must be able to access, read and process the file. In order you will use the Google Sheet API described below.

4   Framework Development for Effective Building of Exploratory Portal

Focus of the framework is the implementation of an application that can build the exploratory portal from Excel model described previously. The model is loaded on the space of Google drive to whom the application must be able to access, read and process the file. To get to this purpose we will use the Google API Sheet. The Google Sheets API (formerly called the Google Spreadsheets API) lets you develop client applications that read and modify worksheets and data in Google Sheets. This API is useful for: managing the worksheets in a Google Sheets file, consuming the rows of a worksheet, managing cells in a worksheet by position [4].

4.1   Framework Architecture

The Fig. 5 following describes the logical architecture of the system:

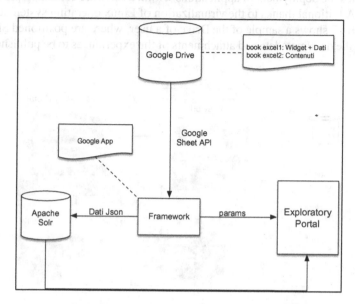

Fig. 5. Architectural proposal: logical view

As seen from the figure, the exploratory portal is just the element closest to the end user. In reality, there are several other blocks that allow you to achieve the pre-set objectives. In particular:

- the Google Drive block, where Excel schemes - transformed into Google Sheet items - are instantiated. The sheets can be shared in a group to ensure even synchronous collaboration on the same data (experiences).
- the Framework block, an application that loads data from Google Drive (by Google App Engine Framework) and that instantiates the template of the portal. This then exports the data of the experiences on the instance of Apache Solr and the part of interface configuration directly on the portal.

The following Fig. 6 shows the corresponding physical architecture.

We see in particular that, by the side exploratory portal, it has been enriched with the REST Web Service (implemented with library Jersey then with JAX-RS specification). This fact will allow you to configure the portal according to user preference specified in the book Excel (Sheet). The View of the portal will be made dynamic, so that dynamically draw facets (rather than forecast the facets statically in HTML code). A further software component provided in the portal is the Free Marker Template (FMT) engine. This will allow to fully customize the portal view, enabling to specify a template 'ftl' format for rendering custom of the experience card.

The portal runs on Apache Tomcat 7.0 Servlet Container. To allow cloning of the portal through Web interface will use Docker [13]. Docker is an open-source project that automates the deployment of applications within a software container, providing an abstraction Additional thanks to the virtualization of Linux operating system level. The following Fig. 7 shows a sample of the Drive of a user, where are positioned Sheet files that contain the data/metadata and attachments of the experiences to be published on the portal.

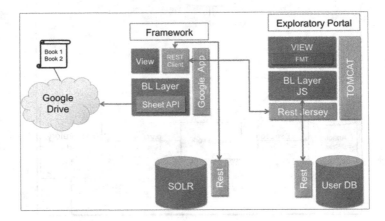

Fig. 6. Architectural proposal: physical view

Fig. 7. Detail of book drive

4.2 Implementation

To transfer data to the portal, is not sufficient to read the incoming data from Google Drive. It is necessary to design an apposite data model, taken over directly from the present context. Thus, are defined the Data Transfer Object (DTO), or a class structure whose purpose is to wrap the data to be transferred to the portal. The following Fig. 8 shows the UML diagram of the dependency of the DTO model.

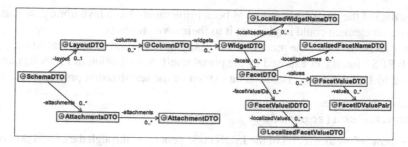

Fig. 8. Data model

The model was taken directly from the analysis of the Excel book provided by the Fondazione Politecnico di Milano. In detail, the schema consists of a layout and of a list of attachments. The layout consists of a set of column objects, each of which, groups a set of widget objects. The widget includes both the facet list for that widget, and their location. Similarly, the set of facets includes a facet names, localized for different languages, and a set of values for the facets, seen as the ID-value pairs (e.g. "ScuolaPrimaria" - TRUE, "teacher" - "M. red"). The IDs are also localized, e.g. ScuolaPrimaria can be located in "primary school" or "Primary school".

```
{
    "layout": {
        "columns": [{
            "widgets": [{
                "id": "W101",
                "name": "Scuola",
                "localizedNames": [{
                    "lang": "/italiano",
                    "value": "Scuola"
                }, {
                    "lang": "/inglese",
                    "value": "School"
                }].
                "facets": [{
                    "id": "DScu",
                    "name": "Dati scuola",
                    "visualizationAbs": false,
                    "visualizationHist": false,
                    "visualizationPercent": false,
                    "visualizationWC": false,
                    "visualizationList": true,
                    "localizedNames": [{
                        "lang": "/italiano",
                        "value": "Nominativo"
                    }, {
                        "lang": "/inglese",
                        "value": "Name"
                    }].
                    "facetValueIDs": [{
                        "ID": "?Nome scuola",
                        "localizedValues": []
                    }, {
                        "ID": "?Tipo istituto",
                        "localizedValues": []
                    }].
                    "facetvalues": [{
                        "experienceID": "EXP#15_201",
                        "values": [{
                            "facetValueID": "?Nome scuola",
                            "facetValue": "San Giovanni Bosco"
                        }, {
                            "facetValueID": "?Tipo istituto",
                            "facetValue": "Primaria"
                        }]
                    },
                    ...
```

Fig. 9. An excerpt of the JSON code

The data of the described model has been implemented as a Java library, so that any architectural element could implement it to their own purposes.

After instantiation of the model, this is ready to be serialized and sent to the portal through REST interfaces exposed by the portal itself. Serialization in JSON format was designed by GSON library. Below is an extract of the serialization process:

```
Gson gson=new Gson();
gson.toJson(schemadto);
```

We show below an excerpt of the JSON code generated through the export procedure described (Fig. 9):

The portal is easily cloned, as a matter of fact so it can have different instance the Web application itself populated by the same exporter.

5 Validation and Test

Part of our effort has been spent to validate the portal population process, first "in vitro", then "in vivo". In Fig. 10 the validation scenario is depicted; in particular:

- The EDOC partner contacts the school's authorities (e.g. the teachers and the principle) that have accepted to share their educational experience.

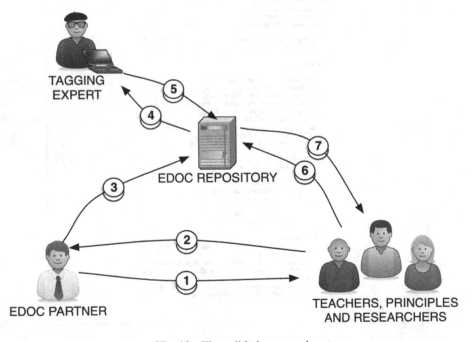

Fig. 10. The validation scenario

- The school's authorities are interviewed about the experience, so they answer the questions asked by the EDOC partner (results interview). They also give the partner all the electronic material produced as a result of the experience (e.g. a multimedia presentation, a database, a movie, a website).
- The EDOC partner arranges and processes the material collected from the interview according to the conceptual model defined within the EDOC project. So the partner can connect to the EDOC repository and uploads such material.
- The tagging expert obtains the package containing all the information and the material regarding the experience.
- The tagging expert analyzes the information and the material about the experience and uses the software installed on his own PC to tag the experience, according to the defined taxonomies. Then the tagging information about the experience is attached to the experience object stored onto the repository.
- Other teachers, principles and researchers interested in implementing new educational and/or reusing best educational concrete practices connect to the repository and select some keywords from the defined taxonomies.
- A subset of experiences is proposed to the users, so they can download all the needed information for re-implementing the educational experiences.

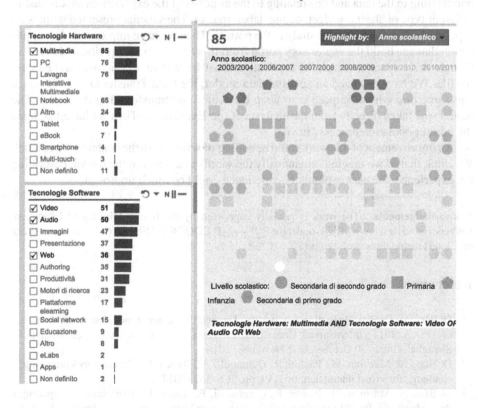

Fig. 11. A portal screenshot

In the next picture it is shown the result of a search over the portal. It is simulated the research of learning experiences involving multimedia technologies, in which audio/video or Web content has been delivered. On the left side, the user can act over the widgets in order the select the wanted options. On the right side, the experiences map gets updated in real time as soon as new widget values are selected (Fig. 11).

6 Conclusions

This paper proposes an evolution of exploratory portal through a simplification of the data loading process by a modeling of complex taxonomies.

To achieve the aim, it was carried out a preparatory activity but necessary to the advanced management of information and the establishment of appropriate digital formats. We worked on the modeling of a complex taxonomy for EDOC experiences in order to feed exploratory portals. We have implemented a framework with the objective of the effective construction of an exploratory portal, sustaining the adaptivity of the portal to the different uses. The main requirement for achieving this goal has been to make the schema-driven portal. The general scheme proposed consists of two files excel: one relating to the data and one relating to the annexes of the experiences subdivided in different type of sheets (widget, define, label, tpack). The schema presented defines all aspects of the data of our case study in the portals. Then we have implemented an application that can build the exploratory portal from this Excel model, previously loaded on Google drive space to which the application must be able to access, read and process the file. We have designed an apposite data model, the Data Transfer Object (DTO), a class structure whose purpose is to wrap the data to be transferred to the portal. The model was taken directly from the analysis of the Excel book. Then we have validated the portal population process "in vivo".

An improvement of this work could be adding of semantic to the content of the model. We think that, if we tagging semantically the words contained in the model, describing the experience, the user exploratory experience could be much improved.

Acknowledgements. The work is partially supported by the Italian Ministry of Education, University and Research (MIUR) under the PON4a2_B EDOC@WORK3.0 (Education and Work on Cloud) national research project.

References

1. Di Blas, N., Paolini, P.: Exploratory portals. The need for a new generation. In: Proceedings of DSAA 2014 (International Conference on Data Science and Advanced Analytics), Shanghai, China, 30 October 30–1 November 2014
2. Di Blas, N., Mazuran, M., Paolini, P., Quintarelli, E., Tanca, L.: Exploratory computing: a challenge for visual interaction. In: AVI, pp. 361–362 (2014)
3. Di Blas, N., Mazuran, M., Paolini, P., Quintarelli, E., Tanca, L.: Exploratory computing: a draft Manifesto. In: 2014 International Conference on Data Science and Advanced Analytics (DSAA), pp. 577–580. IEEE, October 2014
4. https://developers.google.com/google-apps/spreadsheets/

5. Tukey, J.W.: Exploratory Data Analysis, pp. 2–3. Addison-Wesley (1977). ISBN 0-201-07616-0
6. Behrens, J.T., Yu, C.H.: Exploratory data analysis. In: Schinka, J.A., Velicer, W.F. (eds.) Handbook of Psychology: Research Methods in Psychology, Vol. 2, John Wiley & Sons, Inc., New Jersey (2003)
7. Marchionini, G.: Exploratory search: from finding to understanding. Commun. ACM **49**(4), 41 (2006)
8. White, R.W., Muresan, G., Marchionini, G.: Report on ACM SIGIR 2006 workshop on evaluating exploratory search systems. In: ACM SIGIR Forum, vol. 40, no. 2, pp. 52–60. ACM, December 2006
9. Buoncristiano, M., Mecca, G., Quintarelli, E., Roveri, M., Santoro, D., Tanca, L.: Exploratory computing: what is there for the database researcher? In: SEBD, pp. 128–135 (2015)
10. Bucciero, A., Mainetti, L., Vergallo, R.: Structuring repositories of educational experiences: a case study. In: Proceedings of the IEEE Collaborative Learning and New Pedagogic Approaches in Engineering Education (EDUCON) 2012 Conference, pp. 772–780, Marrakech, Marocco, 17–20 April 2012
11. Ferrari, L., Di Blas, N., Paolini, P., Arpetti, A., Lanzillotti, R., Falcinelli, F., Vergallo, R., Ierardi, M.G., Pacetti, E.: "Learning for all": is everyone learning?. In: Bastiaens, T., Marks, G. (eds.) Proceedings of World Conference on E-Learning in Corporate, Government, Healthcare, and Higher Education, pp. 1782–1792 (2012)
12. Paolini, P., Di Blas, N., Mainetti, L., Ierardi, M.G., Costabile, F., Falcinelli, F., Guerra, L., Leo, T., Ferrari, L.: Assessing and sharing (technology-based) educational experiences. In: Bastiaens, T., Ebner, M. (eds.) Proceedings of World Conference on Educational Multimedia, Hypermedia and Telecommunications 2011, pp. 3150–3157. AACE, Chesapeake (2011)
13. http://www.docker.com

Audio-Visual Perception - The Perception of Object Material in a Virtual Environment

Ryan Anderson, Joosep Arro[✉], Christian Schütt Hansen, and Stefania Serafin

Aalborg University Copenhagen, Copenhagen, Denmark
{rjan15,jarro15,csha15}@student.aau.dk, sts@create.aau.dk

Abstract. A digital approach to audio-visual perception of object material and mass within unimodal and multimodal conditions. Similar research has been executed regarding the perception of physical object material, however little has been accomplished relating to virtual perceptions of object material. This study evaluates the effects of manipulating specific stimuli when inducing cross modal augmentation, intersensory biases and cross modal transfers. Three test conditions were established in order to determine perceptual accuracies and mass type dominance: auditory only stimuli, visual only stimuli and audio-visual stimuli.

The results indicated that multimodal perception was more accurate when perceiving object material and that vision was most dominant within unisensory conditions. No dominance was found within a multimodal environment when there was object incongruency, however when the visual stimuli was obscure, the auditory modality confirmed the final perception.

Keywords: Audio-visual · Virtual environment · Multimodal · Object material · Perception

1 Introduction

There is a strong relationship between information received through sensory modalities and the final perception of object materials and mass. This report explores the combined use of auditory and visual perception in a digital educational game. The aim is to understand how user experience can be enhanced or skewed by altering specific perceptual modalities. In the experiment, participants were given a three-phase test, in an attempt to measure perceptual accuracy for each specific stimuli condition. The testing environment utilizes differing stimuli conditions, in order to investigate which sense is most dominant when perceiving object mass or material in a virtual environment. The first phase focused on auditory perception; the participant was presented with five objects that aesthetically, looked the same. However only differing in auditory feedback when each item was dropped. The second phase utilised only visual stimuli, the participants were able to pick up five aesthetically different objects. Each were textured to represent their corresponding material. The final phase combined both, auditory and visual stimuli in a multimodal perceptual experience. The environment consisted of 10 objects. Six objects possessed congruency in relationship between auditory and visual representation, whereas the other four objects were incongruent between audio and visual appearance.

© Springer International Publishing Switzerland 2016
L.T. De Paolis and A. Mongelli (Eds.): AVR 2016, Part I, LNCS 9768, pp. 162–171, 2016.
DOI: 10.1007/978-3-319-40621-3_11

2 Background Work

We are able to determine a number of object properties through only a unisensory experience. Numerous physical objects have distinct or unique physical and auditory properties specific to their material, typically their properties can be conceptualised based on previous experiential interactions. The object's mass, texture and estimated auditory impact sound that is produced upon being dropped, can be determined by using solely the visual modality. These perceptual skills are crucial in order to understand the environment we are contained in. For example, when walking, the ability to determine whether the floor surface is fragile or slippery is critical in order to avoid harm.

Studies have shown that the human observers are extremely adept at material recognition, even when materials are presented to them briefly [1]. While Fleming agrees and even enforces that the humans are remarkably good at determining materials by visual perception, he also states that, "despite its subjective ease, material perception poses the visual system with some unique and significant challenges, because a given material can take on many different appearances depending on the lighting, viewpoint and shape [2]."

The visual perception of materials is composed of two factors: First is the material categorization, second the property estimation [2].

Material categorization is the assignment of a material to a category or label. These categories can be very broad such as textile and stone and does not need to be very precise, but specific categories like a silk scarf from Thailand can be used. Categorization is used to connect the given material a set of information based on stored knowledge.

Perception through the use of material property estimation is the identification of specific characteristics for a material [2]. These characteristics are vast: reflection, glossiness, translucency, opacity and elasticity; and are by humans further defined, e.g. matte, shine or glossiness. Therefore, property estimation is useful for detecting subtle differences between aesthetically similar materials.

It is commonly believed that vision is the most dominant modality in multisensory perception. An experiment performed by L. Shams et al. found that the visual perception could be manipulated by other sensory modalities [3]. They discovered a visual illusion that, "when a single visual flash is accompanied by multiple auditory beeps; the single flash is incorrectly perceived as multiple flashes." This research showed that it was evident that in multimodal perception, the brain can experience intercessory biases when there is conflicting information.

An experiment done by Waka Fujisaki et al. looks into human perception of materials when the visual appearance of one material is combined with the impact sound of another. The results from this test indicated a strong interaction between audio-visual material perceptions. For example, the results showed that, when a glass image was coupled with the impact sound of a glass, participants perceived the object correctly. However, when the same visual stimulus was coupled with a pepper sound, participants perceived the visual material to be plastic, therefore influencing the phenomena of cross modal transfers [4].

There was a limited number of scientific papers written regarding auditory and visual perception in a virtual environment; most research had focused on real world materials.

A study conducted by Bonneel et al. focuses on audio and visual perception of materials in the virtual environment [5]. The paper explores whether the auditory and visual modality mutually interact in the perception of material rendering quality, in particular when varying the level of rendering quality for audio and graphics. The results from this research conveyed that better quality sound improves the perceived similarity of a lower-quality visual approximation to the reference. The paper concluded that the auditory perception in the virtual environment was valued more than the higher level of rendering quality. The purpose for proposing object material within a virtual environment was to investigate whether it were possible to produce a change to the visual appearance of the virtual material by pairing the object with an incongruent impact sound.

3   Experiment Design

We conducted an experiment exploring how the effect of specific auditory and visual stimuli have on determining and perceiving the material and mass of an object in a virtual environment. The goal of the experiment was to see if it was possible to skew or enhance the participants' perception of particular object materials.

3.1   Methods

Test participants were chosen using mostly convenience sampling, all subjects who volunteered also stated that they had normal hearing and visual ability. It was also made sure that participants were made naive towards the purpose and goal of the experiment. The test consisted of nine participants with the age range being between 21 and 61, five of which were female and four being male. The results were obtained in quantitative format. The data was obtained through a three-phase questionnaire that was presented to the participant during each relevant phase. The data was compiled through quantifying the results. The accuracy of perception was measured by the percentage of the occurrences of user input matching the material of the object. Additionally the most accurate modality within a unisensory condition was defined through comparing the means of both visual and auditory accuracies. Therefore, sensory dominance in multimodal perception was defined by comparing the occurrences of user input matching either the texture or sound of the object.

3.2   Selection of Materials, Audio and Shape

A collection of six audio samples and textures were organised into six distinct categories including: glass, metal, clay, paper, plastic and wood, which can be seen in Fig. 1. The shape and surface area of the object (cube, $10 \times 10 \times 10$ units) was kept consistent as the geometric shape of the item can alter the perceived material and mass of the object and produce unwanted variability in results [6].

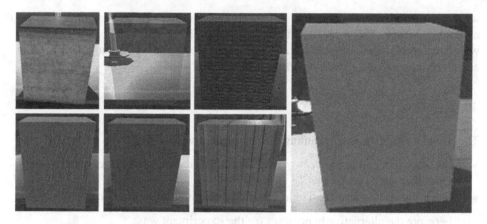

Fig. 1. Textures used in the testing environment. From top left to bottom right: clay, glass, metal, paper, plastic and wood. Far right: untextured.

3.3 Virtual Environment

Lighting intensity, position and bounce intensity were kept constant in each test scene in order to make sure light consistencies did not affect texture aesthetics, therefore interfering with accuracy of results.

3.4 Procedure

Before presenting the experiment to an official test participant, we performed a pilot test on two people. The intent was to test that the audio and material textures accurately represented their desired material.

The study was carried out using three desktop PC's, each test participant were also given the same pair of headphones (Sennheiser HD 335s). This would ensure that the audio representation of each material would remain consistent. The experiment was structured into three linear stages, where the same materials were presented using different modalities. In each stage, all objects were completely randomised and had no particular order. The experiment consisted of three conditions (two unisensory and one multimodal):

- Auditory Stimuli
- Visual Stimuli
- Audio-visual Stimuli

Test participants were firstly introduced to the audio only stimuli in which they were presented with five untextured cubes, all maintaining consistent geometric shape. The participant was able to interact with each cube by picking up and dropping the item. The intent was to produce audio feedback emulating the event of the material being dropped onto the floor. This was done similarly in regards to the visual only stimuli condition, except that all five cubes were textured with materials and had no auditory feedback when dropped. The final condition introduced audio-visual stimuli to support a multi-modal experience. This time 10 textured cubes complemented with auditory feedback were presented to the player. Six cubes possessed a congruent relation between audio and texture, whereas the remaining four were incongruent.

4   Results

The initial null hypotheses regarding the experiment was:

- "The mean perception accuracy of both auditory and visual modalities were the same within unisensory conditions."
- "There was no dominance of either modality within multimodal conditions"

    Therefore the alternative hypotheses for the experiment was:

- "The mean perception accuracy of visual modality was higher than that of audition within unisensory conditions."
- "The visual modality is dominant within multimodal conditions"

    The experiment was executed in order to observe two aspects: which sensory modality is most efficient when determining the material and mass of an object within a unisensory condition? Moreover, in the case of incongruence between vision and audition, which modality would be most dominant when determining the material and mass of the object?

    The mean perceptual accuracies of the unisensory modalities were calculated based on the user input that was equal to the texture or audio applied to the objects. The visual mean percentage accuracy is 75.5 % and the auditory mean percentage accuracy is 68.8 %. The difference in accuracies can be seen in Fig. 2.

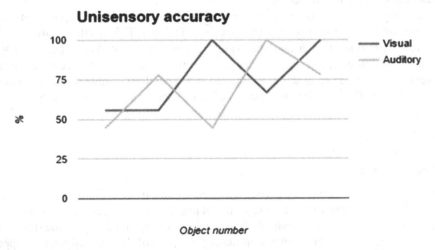

Fig. 2. Unisensory accuracies between visual and auditory modalities (Color figure online)

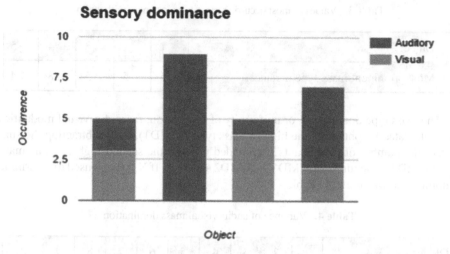

Fig. 3. Sensory dominance for incongruent objects within multimodal conditions (Color figure online)

Figure 3 shows the dominance of one modality over another in multimodal perception where textures and audio are incongruent. Sensory dominance (SD) is the difference between the correctly perceived materials favouring visual (V) or auditory (A) modality: SD = V − A (see Table 1).

Table 1. Calculated sensory dominance

Object	7	8	9	10
Sensory Dominance	3-2 = 1	0-9 = -9	4-1 = 3	2-5 = -3

To find the uniform perception (UP) of one modality regarding mass perception, the function UP = SV − SA was used. SV equals the sum of the most prominent perception for each object with textures (Table 2). SA equals the sum of the most prominent perception for each object with audio (Table 3). If negative it is audio with more uniform perceptions of the objects, if positive it is vision. UP = (4 + 5+7 + 5+9) − (6 + 5+5 + 8+4) = 2.

Table 2. Values of most occurring mass-type instances with visual

Object	1	2	3	4	5
Most prominent mass-type instances	4	5	7	5	9

Table 3. Values of most occurring mass-type instances with audio

Object	1	2	3	4	5
Most prominent mass-type instances	6	5	5	8	4

The mass type domination, or uniformity of perception, for audio-visual modalities was calculated by obtaining the highest mass type (MMD1), then subtracting the sum of half the number of participants (n, rounded up) and the second highest value mass type (MMD2). The function $MMD1 - (MMD2 + n) = X$. If $X \geq 0$ was used to determine if dominance was present (Table 4).

Table 4. Variance of audio-visual mass domination

Object	1	2	3	4	5	6	7	8	9	10
Light mass	3	0	5	9	5	7	4	0	3	3
Medium mass	3	1	4	0	4	2	4	1	5	4
Heavy mass	2	8	0	0	0	0	1	8	1	2

5   Discussion and Conclusion

Virtual environments have the opportunity to alter, skew and enhance the human perception in a wide variety of methods. The purpose of the experiment conducted was to better understand which specific modality was most precise and dominant. More specifically when determining and perceiving the material and mass of an object in a virtual environment, in both unisensory and multimodal conditions.

The mean perceptual accuracy of the visual modality in a unisensory environment was greater than audition (visual, 75.8 % | audio, 68.8 %). This result could be expected, as vision is polymodal within the virtual environment. In comparison with the auditory modality, this is not the case as it only has access to one stimuli (sound). Therefore, it would be fair to consider that a visual representation in a virtual environment delivers a better perception of the object in question.

Both visual and auditory modalities were compared in multimodal perception with the intent to declare the most dominant sense. Four objects had incongruent textures and sound. Two objects were perceived as their visual texture, while the other two, their audio sound. Therefore, the final verdict in this case would be; both modalities are equally dominant when perceiving objects. However, in the extreme case of the clay-textured object being paired with metal audio feedback, this convinced all participants that they perceived a metal texture. Observations conveyed that the auditory modality was primarily dominant when there was visual uncertainty about the object's material.

Previous research supporting the test results state that by removing the congruence between vision and audition, and by altering the sound of the object, the person's perception could be altered into perceiving another material than the visual modality is seeing [4].

It is important to note that it is likely that participants perceived the objects differently in the virtual environment than they would have in a real world setting. This could be due to the absence of the somatosensory system in a virtual environment. Therefore participants could not utilise all modalities efficiently, (such as touch, pressure, temperature) therefore reducing the accuracy of information perceived regarding each object.

The results between auditory and visual modalities, when comparing the opinions of perceived mass, suggests there is more uniformity amongst visual perception.

Results regarding the perceived mass in a multimodal environment resulted in 40 % of the cases being mass type dominant. In 50 % of cases, participants had a varied perception and 10 % had high variation. In most cases participants agreed on one or two masses for an object. Therefore it can be interpreted that in utilising multimodal perception, mass is accurately and uniformly perceived based on people's knowledge.

Incongruent shapes 7 and 10 convey the possibility of intersensory biases being present due to the disparity in choice between the audio and visual stimuli, which therefore could be due to conflicting information between the two stimuli (Table 5).

Table 5. Analysing intersensory biases between incongruent objects

Object (Audio-visual)	7	8	9	10
Texture (T)	Metal	Clay	Wood	Glass
Audio (A)	Wood	Metal	Wood	Plastic
Predicted Accuracy (T | A)	3 | 2	0 | 9	4 | 1	2 | 5
Accuracy (%)	33.33	0.00	44.44	22.22

When comparing perceptual accuracies between unisensory and multimodal conditions, it can be assumed that cross modal augmentation was present in the case of perceiving metal. The perception of metal within a visual only environment was 55.55 %, audition only 77.77 % and in multimodal conditions 88.88 %, therefore the presence of both modalities enhanced the perception of metal; strangely, in two cases the perceptual accuracy was decreased within a multimodal environment. These two cases were in relation to wood (visual only 100 %, auditory only, 44 %, multimodal 88 %) and paper (visual only 66 %, auditory only 100 %, multimodal 88 %). These results could be due to intersensory biases, as two stimuli were present and therefore perhaps conveying conflicting stimuli.

Lastly, the phenomena of cross modal transfers was observed when presenting the incongruent objects. In particular objects 8 (texture - clay, audio - metal) and 10 (texture - glass, audio - plastic) were successful in skewing the majority of participants perception. Therefore, participants perceived the visual material of the object as the same impact sound of the material they heard being dropped, thus inducing an illusion (Table 6).

Table 6. Analysis cross modal transfers amongst affected incongruent objects

Object	8	10
Texture (T)	Clay	Glass
Audio (A)	Metal	Plastic
Predicted Accuracy (T | A)	3 | 2	2 | 5 (6)
Accuracy (%)	0.00	25.00

Accuracy of results could have been made more reliable by utilising a greater quantity and variation of material textures and audio. This would prevent participants influencing their opinions regarding the perception of the similar object based on prior experience.

As the experiment was conducted on a small number of participants, the validity of the results could be improved by increasing the pool of participants. By doing so this would enable us to make valid generalised conclusions drawn from the experiment. The results could also be made more specific via the use of quota sampling instead of convenience sampling. This therefore would allow us to analyse characteristics that would be of relevance to the experiment.

It was determined that multimodal perception leads to a more accurate perception of objects in a virtual environment.

Moreover, it can be proved that vision is the primary modality. Despite this, there was no dominance between either modality when there was incongruency between visual and auditory stimuli. However in cases where there was uncertainty regarding the visual modality, the auditory modality was used to confirm the finalised perception.

Acknowledgments. We would like to thank The Study Board for the Media Technology at the Aalborg University for funding our project. In addition, we would like to thank our supervisor Stefania Serafin and all the test participants.

References

1. Adelson, E., Rosenholtz, R., Sharan, L.: Material perception: what can you see in a brief glance? **9** (2009)
2. Fleming, R.W.: Visual perception of materials and their properties. **94**, 62–75 (2013)
3. Shams, L., Kamitani, Y., Shimojo, S.: What you see is what you hear. **408**, 788 (2000). Macmillan Magazines Ltd.
4. Fujisaki, W., Goda, N., Motoyoshi, I., Komatsu, H., Nishida, S.: Audiovisual integration in the human perception of materials. **14** (2014)
5. Bonneel, N., Suied, C., Viaud-Delmon, I., Drettakis, G.: Audio-visual perception of materials for virtual environments. (2009)
6. Martín, R., Iseringhausen, J., Weinmann, M., Hullin, M.B.: Multimodal Perception of Material Properties. 33–40 (2015)

Facial Landmarks for Forensic Skull-Based 3D Face Reconstruction: A Literature Review

Enrico Vezzetti[1], Federica Marcolin[1(✉)], Stefano Tornincasa[1],
Sandro Moos[1], Maria Grazia Violante[1], Nicole Dagnes[1],
Giuseppe Monno[2], Antonio Emmanuele Uva[2],
and Michele Fiorentino[2]

[1] Department of Management and Production Engineering,
Politecnico di Torino, Corso Duca degli Abruzzi 24, 10129 Turin, Italy
{enrico.vezzetti, federica.marcolin,
stefano.tornincasa, sandro.moos,
mariagrazia.violante}@polito.it,
s180683@studenti.polito.it
[2] Department of Mechanics, Mathematics and Management,
Politecnico di Bari, Via Amendola 126/B, 70126 Bari, Italy
{giuseppe.monno, antonio.uva,
michele.fiorentino}@poliba.it

Abstract. Recent Face Analysis advances have focused the attention on studying and formalizing 3D facial shape. Landmarks, *i.e.* typical points of the face, are perfectly suited to the purpose, as their position on visage shape allows to build up a map of each human being's appearance. This turns to be extremely useful for a large variety of fields and related applications. In particular, the forensic context is taken into consideration in this study. This work is intended as a survey of current research advances in forensic science involving 3D facial landmarks. In particular, by selecting recent scientific contributions in this field, a literature review is proposed for in-depth analyzing which landmarks are adopted, and how, in this discipline. The main outcome concerns the identification of a leading research branch, which is landmark-based facial reconstruction from skull. The choice of selecting 3D contributions is driven by the idea that the most innovative Face Analysis research trends work on three-dimensional data, such as depth maps and meshes, with three-dimensional software and tools. The third dimension improves the accurateness and is robust to colour and lightning variations.

Keywords: Landmarks · Fiducial point · 3D face · Forensic · Reconstruction

1 Introduction

A facial landmark is a key point of the face with a specific biometric and geometrical meaning. Landmarks have been originally introduced by Farkas [1] and extensively applied to different disciplines involving human face. In particular, landmarks are daily used by maxillo-facial surgeons in pre- and post-surgical phases to keep track of facial shape behaviour.

© Springer International Publishing Switzerland 2016
L.T. De Paolis and A. Mongelli (Eds.): AVR 2016, Part I, LNCS 9768, pp. 172–180, 2016.
DOI: 10.1007/978-3-319-40621-3_12

Landmarks may be skeletal-based or skin-based, depending on whether they lie on bones or directly on the skin. In the first case they are *hard-tissue*, in the second they are called *soft-tissue* landmarks. It is out of the scope of this paper to report all anthropometric and morphometric definitions of respectively osseous and soft-tissue landmarks. But extensive handbooks and reference works have been written within the context of Anthropometry discipline, such as [2–4], which report the truthful and medical meaning of each landmark. Figure 1 shows the most adopted facial soft-tissue landmarks. In this work we will refer to landmarks also as 'fiducial points'.

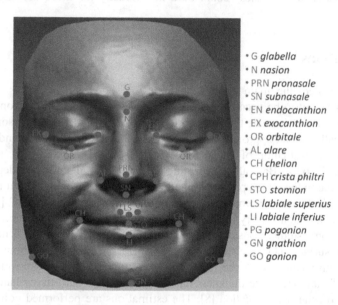

- G *glabella*
- N *nasion*
- PRN *pronasale*
- SN *subnasale*
- EN *endocanthion*
- EX *exocanthion*
- OR *orbitale*
- AL *alare*
- CH *chelion*
- CPH *crista philtri*
- STO *stomion*
- LS *labiale superius*
- LI *labiale inferius*
- PG *pogonion*
- GN *gnathion*
- GO *gonion*

Fig. 1. Popular soft-tissue landmarks in frontal view face acquired via 3D scanner [5, 6].

Facial hard-tissue landmarks partially correspond to soft-tissue ones, meaning that some points which lie on the skin have a corresponding one under the tissue depth, be lying on the respective part of the skull. Among the ones presented in Fig. 1, these landmarks are *glabella*, *nasion* (corresponding to *posterior nasal spine* bony landmark), *subnasale* (corresponding to *anterior nasal spine*), *orbitale*, *pogonion*, *gnathion*, *gonion*. The coordinates of the soft-tissue and hard-tissue landmarks do not correspond, but they are called with the same anthropometric name, as they represent the conceptually-equal facial point.

The reason why these fiducial points are core in the context of human face is that a landmark set of an individual forms a univocal mapping of his/her face. Landmark positions could be registered, stored, and used to compare the face with another, study the face itself, provide specific medical features. In other words, a landmark set represents a face and offers a sketched and compact version of it.

This work is intended as a brief survey of the recent literature on 3D facial landmarks-based forensic research works. Contributions have been chosen among the years 2014 and 2015, in order to provide the most up-to-date view of the latest frontier of landmarks' applicability. Works have also been chosen within the context of 3D to stress the attention towards new technologies and favour latest and most innovative methodologies. This is also to support those research groups who have undertaken the investigation of the third dimension, which in the future will be the core one.

The reason of surveying forensic applications of facial landmark is that the scientific community lacks a literature review with these features. Landmarks are significant elements for Face Analysis subfields; thus, providing researchers with a survey about "landmarks for forensics" could be a key remedy for those investigating this branch.

2   Applications

In forensic science, the main application adopting facial landmarks as a working framework turns out to be **reconstruction**. Facial shape reconstruction from skulls of dead bodies is used to recreate the ante-mortem face of an unidentified person [7]. This technique is called facial approximation or (cranio) facial reconstruction and is strictly connected to the evaluation of Facial Soft-Tissue Thickness (FSTT) [8], also called Tissue Depths (TD) [9]. Basically, "accepting that craniofacial soft tissue depths play a fundamental role in the development of an effective facial approximation, it is essential that tissue depth datasets appropriately approximate modern populations" [[10]: page 146e8]. This evaluation is very often undertaken among landmark locations.

Although some studies considered a fixed skin thickness (of about 1.5 mm) for the whole facial surface [11], several others performed evaluations about how this soft-tissue depth changed over the facial zones, relying on landmark positions. Bulut et al. built a facial soft-tissue thickness database among 31 hard-tissue landmarks for forensic craniofacial reconstruction [8]. The estimations are performed point by point and the overall study provides a valuable contribution in the understanding of how a face could be shaped and modelled by relying only on the skull. Similarly, Duan et al. studied the relationship between facial skin and skull in order to reconstruct facial shape only with the osseous part for both forensic purposes [12]. Tissue depths were estimated also by Guyomarc'h et al. depending on age, sex, and corpulence by working on 87 hard-tissue and 102 soft-tissue landmarks. Among the skin landmarks adopted for this study, some were manually positioned on face, others were projected on the skin from the corresponding osseous landmark [13]. Parks et al., supported by Federal Bureau of Investigation (FBI) Laboratory Division, aimed at building a detailed tissue depth database among 25 landmarks and compared it with previous relevant studies [10]. Similarly, sex-, age-, and weight-differentiated tissue depths have been investigated by Shrimpton et al. [9], who used a large set of quasi-landmarks in a spatially-dense scenario. Relevant investigations about Tallied Facial Soft Tissue Depth Tables (T-Tables) have been undertaken by Stephan relying on the same 25 landmarks [14]. Inada et al. investigated nose region for reconstruction purposes, showing that the location of cephalometric nasal skin landmarks could be predicted based on skeletal ones [7].

Table 1. Table highlighting details (method, results, software, database,…) of each paper.

reference	(Bulut, Sipahioglu, & Hekimoglu, 2014)	(Duan, Huang, Tian, Lu, Wu, & Zhou, 2015)	(Guyomarc'h, Dutailly, Charton, Santos, Desbarats, & Coqueugniot, 2014)	(Inada, et al., 2014)
results	build-up of a facial soft-tissue thickness database	learn the relationship between the face skin and the skull and reconstruct a person's face from his skull using the relationship	estimating face shape	investigate relationship between nasal soft-tissue and hard-tissue landmarks
# soft-tissue landmarks	0	9	102	25
# hard-tissue landmarks	31	22	87	
which landmarks	G N LS LI GO GN SN OR CPH AL + others	AL EN EX CH PRN OR N SN LS LI GN + others	EN EX AL LS LI CH STO CPH…	PRN SN N PG GN G GO
landmarking method	single practitioner	\	Five sets of landmarks were taken five times by one observer with a week interval between each set, and 20 sets of landmarks were taken by two observers.	marked individually by the same investigator for 3 times with mechanical 3-D digitising system (Micro Scribe G2X)
landmarking accuracy	\	\	0.3-3.2 mm intra-observer dispersion; 0.6-6.1 mm Inter-observer dispersion	0.47 mm mean error
type of data	DICOM (Digital Imaging and Communications in Medicine) by Computer Tomography (CT)	triangle meshes including about 150,000 and 220,000 vertices for skull and skin, respectively, obtained via CT	DICOM (Digital Imaging and Communications in Medicine) by Computer Tomography (CT)	Cephalograms
support software	Amira 5.2.2 (Visage Imaging, Burlington, USA)	\	MorphoJ + MakeHuman	C++
database dimension — #people	320	114	500	60
age	18-80	20–60	18-96	20-25
females	160	52	235	30
males	160	62	265	30
population	Turkish vs European vs Korean	mostly coming from Han ethnic group in the North of China	\	Japanese

Table 1. *(Continued)*

reference	*(Parks, Richard, & Monson, 2014)*	*(Shrimpton, et al., 2014)*	*(Stephan, 2014)*	*(Mehta, Saini, Nath, Patel, & Menon, 2014)*	*(Short, Khambay, Ayoub, Erolin, Rynn, & Wilkinson, 2014)*
results	build-up of a facial soft-tissue thickness database	detailed description of tissue depths	LITERATURE REVIEW discuss the utility of 2008 and 2013 Tallied Facial Soft Tissue Depth Tables (T-Tables)	craniofacial indices are helpful parameters for the determination of origin of the skeletal remains	assess the accuracy of a computer modelled facial reconstruction technique using CBCT data from live subjects
# soft-tissue landmarks	25	7500	25	0	24
# hard-tissue landmarks				11	0
which landmarks	G GN LI LS N PG SN	spatially-dense set of quasi-landmarks	G N LS LI GO PG	N EN AL OR AL GN	N EX EN AL PRN SN CH CPH LS LI PG GN
landmarking method	using Mimics 14.11 and following common guidelines	\	\	marked	identified twice with 4 weeks interval time
landmarking accuracy	\	\	\	\	0.2- 2.4 mm reduction
type of data	3D models from CT scans	CT converted into 3D face	\	CT scans of neuro-cranium	STL from DICOM from CBCT
support software	Mimics 14.11	\	\	\	VRMesh + Matlab
database dimension — #people	388	156	\	100	10
age	18-62	7-86	\	21-40	18-40
females	\	89	\	47	5
males	\	67	\	53	5
population	Asian African European Hispanic	Caucasian	\	Gujarati, India	\

Mehta *et al.* also worked within the forensic scenario by studying differences among different Indian populations in terms of 11 osseous landmark-based craniofacial indexes [15]. Short *et al.* adopted 24 soft-tissue landmarks to assess the accuracy of a computer modelled facial reconstruction technique using CBCT data from live subjects, for both forensic and archaeological purposes [16].

Table 1 outlines detailed features of each of these research contributions.

3 Landmark Allocation

Landmark localization is a key step. Despite recent contributions have shown that automatic landmarking, even if soft-tissue-based, is possible [17–28], for many applications landmarks are manually localized.

In particular, in the forensic context, landmarks are completely manually allocated. Manual localization methods are **digitization** [7, 29], physical **markers** placing [15], and **software-aided** localization [10]. Related supporting **tools** and **software** are Microscribe G2X digitizer [29], Mimics 14.11 [10], Amira 5.2.2 [8], MorphoJ [13], VRMesh [16], MakeHuman [13].

The **number of observers** positioning landmarks in this context is always single user-based [7, 8, 13, 29]. Thus, no intra- nor inter-individual errors are computed. Nonetheless, even if only one user makes the allocation, different **observations** are registered sometimes: two [16], three [7], five [13, 29]. And a **time period** can pass between different localizations: one week [13] or four weeks [16].

4 Outcomes

Some interesting outcomes concerning the relationship between a hard-tissue landmark and its corresponding soft-tissue one under TD emerged. Analysis of FSTT [8] in correspondence to landmark locations showed that males generally had greater values than females, and that Body Mass Index (BMI) had strong influence of FSTT. Similarly, Guyomarc'h *et al.* indicated that corpulence had the major effect on soft-tissue thicknesses, compared to age, sex, and ethnicity [13]. Body mass and weight have also be taken into consideration by Parks *et al.*, who, given the documented prevalence of obesity in U.S.A. area, purposely assembled U.S. population to consider escalating weight of them [10]. BMI was also taken into consideration by Shrimpton *et al.* [9], together with sex and age. Nonetheless, specific studies showed that a correlation exists between soft-tissue depth thickness and underlying craniometric dimension regardless to diet, age, and sex [29]. This preserves the possibility of comparing results concerning skin and bony parts, by guaranteeing a quantitative relationship between the dimensions of the two. A correlation was also confirmed by Inada *et al.*, who investigated the nasal region [7] and showed that osseous landmarks predicted the position of each soft-tissue landmark both in males and females. Other studies concerning tissue depths [14] show how relevant this subject is in this scenario.

Given that the skeleton is used as a basis for these researches, we can see that in the forensic context hard-tissue landmarks are more commonly addressed as a starting point for the research, even if in correlation with soft tissues and skin. These researches also proved that a correlation between hard- and soft-tissue landmarks existed and that TD was mostly influenced by corpulence, rather than sex and age. This and other features of current research on 3D forensic reconstruction are summed up in Fig. 2.

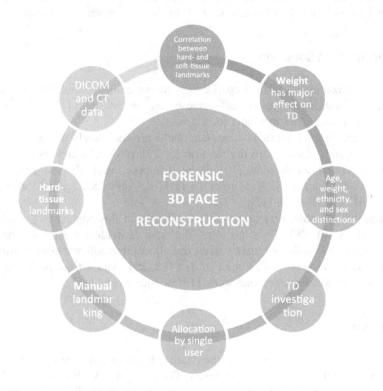

Fig. 2. Emerging features of landmark adoption in the context of 3D forensic reconstruction.

5 Conclusion

A compact literature review is presented including recent papers about facial 3D landmarks in the forensic area. In particular, this study has showed that **reconstruction** was the core forensic subfield in which landmarks were investigated by the scientific research community. Facial shape is reconstructed by manually positioning landmarks on the skull of an unidentified person and, then, by estimating soft-tissue thicknesses. Different allocation techniques, tools, timings, users are registered. The emerging common feature of the investigated landmark-based forensic researches is that the allocation of hard-tissue landmarks was always manual, typically performed by only one observer. Also, the quantitative evaluation of tissue depth brings some considerations about sex and corpulence, which seems to be the major element determining soft-tissue thickness.

References

1. Farkas, L.: Anthropometry of the Head and Face in Medicine. Elsevier North Holland Inc., New York (1981)
2. Farkas, L.: Anthropometry of the Head and Face, 2nd edn. Raven Press, New York (1994)
3. Swennen, G., Schutyser, F., Hausamen, J.: Three-Dimensional Cephalometry: A Color Atlas and Manual. Springer Science & Business Media, Berlin (2005)
4. Preedy, V.: Handbook of Anthropometry Physical Measures of Human Form in Health and Disease. Springer, New York (2012)
5. Vezzetti, E.: Adaptive sampling plan design methodology for reverse engineering acquisition. Int. J. Adv. Manufact. Technol. **42**(7–8), 780–792 (2009)
6. Vezzetti, E.: Computer aided inspection: design of customer-oriented benchmark for noncontact 3D scanner evaluation. Int. J. Adv. Manufact. Technol. **41**(11–12), 1140–1151 (2009)
7. Inada, E., Saitoh, I., Murakami, D., Kubota, N., Takemoto, Y., Iwasaki, T., Yamasaki, Y.: Relationship between nasal and skeletal landmarks on lateral cephalograms of adults. Aust. J. Forensic Sci. **46**(3), 339–347 (2014)
8. Bulut, O., Sipahioglu, S., Hekimoglu, B.: Facial soft tissue thickness database for craniofacial reconstruction in the Turkish adult population. Forensic Sci. Int. **242**, 44–61 (2014)
9. Shrimpton, S., Daniels, K., De Greef, S., Tilotta, F., Willems, G., Vandermeulen, D., Claes, P.: A spatially-dense regression study of facial form and tissue depth: towards an interactive tool for craniofacial reconstruction. Forensic Sci. Int. **234**, 103–110 (2014)
10. Parks, C., Richard, A., Monson, K.: Preliminary assessment of facial soft tissue thickness utilizing three-dimensional computed tomography models of living individuals. Forensic Sci. Int. **237**, 146.e1–146.e10 (2014)
11. Flynn, C., Stavness, I., Lloyd, J., Fels, S.: A finite element model of the face including an orthotropic skin model under in vivo tension. Comput. Methods Biomech. Biomed. Eng. **18**(6), 571–582 (2015)
12. Duan, F., Huang, D., Tian, Y., Lu, K., Wu, Z., Zhou, M.: 3D face reconstruction from skull by regression modeling in shape parameter spaces. Neurocomputing **151**, 674–682 (2015)
13. Guyomarc'h, P., Dutailly, B., Charton, J., Santos, F., Desbarats, P., Coqueugniot, H.: Anthropological facial approximation in three dimensions (AFA3D): computer-assisted estimation of the facial morphology using geometric morphometrics. J. Forensic Sci. **59**(6), 1502–1516 (2014)
14. Stephan, C.: The application of the central limit theorem and the law of large numbers to facial soft tissue depths: T-Table robustness and trends since 2008. J. Forensic Sci. **59**(2), 454–462 (2014)
15. Mehta, M., Saini, V., Nath, S., Patel, M., Menon, S.: CT scan images to determine the origin from craniofacial indices for Gujarati population. J. Forensic Radiol. Imag. **2**(2), 64–71 (2014)
16. Short, L., Khambay, B., Ayoub, A., Erolin, C., Rynn, C., Wilkinson, C.: Validation of a computer modelled forensic facial reconstruction technique using CT data from live subjects: a pilot study. Forensic Sci. Int. **237**, 147.e1–147.e8 (2014)
17. Calignano, F., Vezzetti, E.: Soft tissue diagnosis in maxillofacial surgery: a preliminary study on three-dimensional face geometrical features-based analysis. Aesthetic Plast. Surg. **34**(2), 200–211 (2010)

18. Vezzetti, E., Calignano, F., Moos, S.: Computer-aided morphological analysis for maxillo-facial diagnostic: a preliminary study. J. Plast. Reconstr. Aesthetic Surg. **63**(2), 218–226 (2010)
19. Vezzetti, E., Moos, S., Marcolin, F.: Three-dimensional human face analysis: soft tissue morphometry. In: Proceedings of the InterSymp 2011, Baden-Baden, Germany (2011)
20. Vezzetti, E.: Exploiting 3D ultrasound for fetal diagnostic purpose through facial landmarking. Image Anal. Stereology **33**(3), 167 (2014)
21. Moos, S.: Cleft lip pathology diagnosis and foetal landmark extraction via 3D geometrical analysis. Int. J. Interact. Des. Manufact. (IJIDeM), 1–18 (2014)
22. Vezzetti, E., Marcolin, F.: F., M.: Geometrical descriptors for human face morphological analysis and recognition. Robot. Auton. Syst. **60**(6), 928–939 (2012)
23. Vezzetti, E., Marcolin, F.: Geometry-based 3D face morphology analysis: soft-tissue landmark formalization. Multimedia Tools Appl., **68**(3), 895–929 (2014)
24. Vezzetti, E., Marcolin, F.: 3D human face description: landmarks measures and geometrical features. Image Vis. Comput. **30**(10), 698–712 (2012)
25. Vezzetti, E., Moos, S., Marcolin, F., Stola, V.: A pose-independent method for 3D face landmark formalization. Comput. Methods Programs Biomed. **198**(3), 1078–1096 (2012)
26. Vezzetti, E., Marcolin, F., Stola, V.: 3D human face soft tissues landmarking method: an advanced approach. Comput. Ind. **64**(9), 1326–1354 (2013)
27. Vezzetti, E., Marcolin, F., Fracastoro, G.: 3D face recognition: an automatic strategy based on geometrical descriptors and landmarks. Robot. Auton. Syst. **62**(12), 1768–1776 (2014)
28. Vezzetti, E., Marcolin, F.: 3D landmarking in multiexpression face analysis: a preliminary study on eyebrows and mouth. Aesthetic Plast. Surg. **38**, 796–811 (2014)
29. Hünemeier, T., Gómez-Valdés, J., Azevedo, S., Quinto-Sánchez, M., Passaglia, L., Salzano, F., González-José, R.: FGFR1 signaling is associated with the magnitude of morphological integration in human head shape. Am. J. Hum. Biol. **26**(2), 164–175 (2014)

Virtual Reality Applications with Oculus Rift and 3D Sensors

Edi Ćiković, Kathrin Mäusl, and Kristijan Lenac[✉]

Faculty of Engineering, University of Rijeka, Rijeka, Croatia
klenac@riteh.hr

Abstract. In this paper we describe our experiences with skeletal tracking using Unreal Engine 4 with Oculus Rift and Xbox 360 Kinect while building a tool for rehabilitation of patients with impaired motor skills. We give an overview of the implemented solution, describe the problems encountered and how they were solved.

1 Project Goals

The goal of this project was to create a Virtual Reality experience using the *Oculus Rift* and any available 3D sensor. We decided to combine the *Oculus Rift* and the *Xbox 360 Kinect* sensor in order to create an immersive experience where the partaker sees virtual arms in Virtual Reality which correspond to his own. An example of this can be seen in Fig. 1.

Fig. 1. Virtual arms used in the project

2 Choice and Configuration of the 3D Sensor

As we wanted to implement skeletal tracking the logical choice was to use the *Xbox 360 Kinect* as it had skeletal tracking implemented in the driver. However, installing all the necessary drivers proved to be intricate. Our first attempt was to install the latest *Kinect for Windows 2.0* drivers, however the device was not recognized because in the 2.0 version *Microsoft* dropped support for the original

L.T. De Paolis and A. Mongelli (Eds.): AVR 2016, Part I, LNCS 9768, pp. 181–185, 2016.
DOI: 10.1007/978-3-319-40621-3_13

Xbox 360 Kinect, (which we failed to realize). We have also considered using open source drivers, however they did not work well on *Windows*. Furthermore, in the open source driver, skeletal tracking was absent. Upon further investigation, the latest version of the *Kinect for Windows* drivers with the support for the *360* version of the device was 1.8. After installing 1.8 version of the Runtime and SDK, development on the *Kinect* was possible.

3   Choice and Configuration of the Game Engine

Currently two of the mainstream Game engines have fully implemented support for *Oculus Rift*:

– Unity 5
– Unreal Engine 4

We decided we were going to use *Unreal Engine 4* as it's source code is available to the developers. Furthermore, the integration and the documentation is in the authors' opinion superior to *Unity 5*. Both engines were compatible with *Kinect for Windows SDK* as the SDK available in *C++* and *C#* which *Unreal Engine 4* and *Unity 5* use respectively.

After choosing the engine and getting familiar with the *Kinect SDK* we attempted to implement the skeletal tracking functionality in the engine, however there were numerous problems.

First problem that we encountered were *Windows Data Types. Unreal Engine 4* is partially incompatible with the *Windows Data Types*. It uses the same Data Type names for it's purposes, which makes it impossible to include the *Kinect SDK*. Fortunately, the engine includes header files which enable the use of *Windows Data Types*.

Secondly, *Kinect SDK* requires you to include the `windows.h` file without using the `WIN32_LEAN_AND_MEAN` definition, however as it was already defined deep inside the engine, it was necessary to manually include all the libraries which were excluded.

Thirdly, problems occurred with linking the *Kinect SDK* libraries, so it was required to manually edit the build script to include the missing library.

Finally, despite overcoming all of the above problems, the code would build, but the engine experienced major and spontaneous instability issues. The most serious issue was that when the code to get data from *Xbox 360 Kinect* was implemented, the device would get recognized, but not properly initialized. Furthermore, when compiling that code for a hot-reload[1] it would compile and load successfully, however when trying to load the project again at a later time the project would crash, without a clear way to resolve the issue short of removing the code used for skeletal tracking.

---

[1] The *Unreal Engine 4's* method of compiling and loading the latest iteration of your project without the need to restart the *Unreal Editor*.

4   Implementing the Shared Memory Solution

It soon became clear that there are a lot issues between the *Kinect SDK* and *Unreal Engine*, which meant that other solutions had to be found. After debating the possible solutions it was agreed to use two processes. One of the processes would communicate with the *Kinect* and pass through the skeletal tracking data to the engine using named shared memory. *Skeleton Basics-D3D C++ Sample* from the *Kinect for Windows Developer Toolkit* was used to create the first process. Afterwards shared memory was implemented in the engine as well.

5   Displaying the *Kinect* Data in the Engine

The goal was to render arms inside the engine, which would use the partaker's hand, elbow and shoulder positions to set the bone positions of the virtual arms. As the *Unreal Engine's* animation framework uses *Blueprints* it was necessary to create an interface so that the *Animation Blueprint* use the data retrieved from shared memory. After the data was retrieved it was used to transform the bones in the virtual arms. Scaling factor of 100 had to be used as the *Kinect* measures distance in Meters and *Unreal Engine* uses Centimeters as the default unit. Also the *Unreal Engine* uses an atypical coordinate system where Y and Z axes are inverted, i.e. Y axis is depth and the Z axis is height.

Furthermore, the data transferred only included the joint positions. Fortunately, *Unreal Engine's Blueprint* system includes a node[2] called *Find look at rotation*, shown in Fig. 2, which uses vector arithmetic to calculate what the rotation would be if you positioned yourself at the first point and looked at the second point. Then the translation and rotation transforms were used to display the arms within the engine.

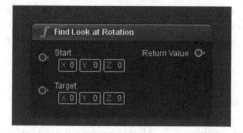

Fig. 2. The example of the *Find look at rotation* node.

---

[2] Objects such as events, function calls, flow control operations, variables, etc. used in the *Blueprint* system.

6   *Oculus Rift* Adaptation

As the engine has a built in plugin for *Oculus Rift* launching the project within it was trivial. However in order to combine both the data from both devices further work needed to be done. The arms appeared dislocated from the body, rotating the *Oculus Rift* rotated the arms as well. That meant that *Oculus Rift's* movements had to be disconnected from the player controller and then properly configured so that when the project is started arms are properly rotated to appear that you are facing straight. Also the head position from the *Oculus rift* and the head position from *Kinect* had to be synchronized, meaning that the locations of the arms are relative to the position of the head.

7   3D Projector Adaptation

An additional goal was to port the project for use on a 3D projector. *Unreal Engine 4* however, does not support stereoscopic 3D rendering. Hence, a plugin was created to alleviate the problem. *SimpleHMD* plugin used for rendering on simple *Head Mounted Displays* such as *Google Cardboard* etc. was forked in order to expedite the implementation. After resolving the mathematical and logical inconsistencies within the forked plugin, such as the interpupillary distance, expectations were met and the plugin was finished. The port is operational, however does not provide nearly the same level of immersion as the *Oculus Rift* version of the project.

8   Making the Virtual Arms Scalable

One of the issues was that when using both the translation and rotation transforms, the sensor would report the joints being too far away and that would cause parts of the virtual arms to appear dislocated, which is immersion breaking. This issue is resolved by excluding the translation in the transform, which results in the bones always being connected to their parent bone and it being independent of the size of the partaker's arms.

9   Discussion and Future Work

One of the potential problems is the inaccuracy of the *Kinect 360*. It often occurred during testing that the *Kinect 360* would fail to lock on to some of the joints. The joints would then appear to flicker, or would be placed completely wrong, which is both immersion breaking and even nauseating. Also it looses tracking when crossing your arms. The possible solution would be to use a newer iteration of the *Kinect* device which would be the *Kinect for Windows v2*. However, that means that porting to the newer version of the *Kinect SDK* is required. An alternative solution would be to use some other sensor for skeletal tracking, however that usually means implementing your own skeletal tracking solution.

The first thing partakers usually try to is to see their hands in Virtual Reality. That is of course problematic as *Kinect 360* does not support finger tracking and is not precise enough to be able to handle finger tracking. This problem can also be resolved by replacing the *Kinect 360* sensor with the *Kinect for Windows v2*. However the finger tracking on that device is still not precise enough to insure immersion. The second solution would be to combine yet another sensor such as the *Leap Motion* which handles the finger tracking fairly well. A hierarchy of sensors should then be established so that when a more precise sensor looses track, another less precise sensor takes over. That would be useful for when the hands of the partaker are too far away from the *Leap Motion*. Another problem that should be resolved is how to synchronize the sensors, for situations when one of the sensors reports a false position of a joint.

The presented solution can be used as a tool for rehabilitating patients with impaired motor skills. It can help in the cure of conditions such as *Phantom limb*[3]. Missing limbs, or parts of it, can be simulated by mirroring existing limbs. The movement of limbs can be increased in the simulation. With help of experts in the medical field, we plan to develop and implement special exercises which will hopefully increase and improve the rehabilitation of afflicted patients.

---

[3] A phantom limb is the sensation that a missing limb is still attached to the body and moving synchronously with other body parts.

The Virtual Experiences Portals — A Reconfigurable Platform for Immersive Visualization

Ian D. Peake[✉], Jan Olaf Blech, Edward Watkins, Stefan Greuter, and Heinz W. Schmidt

RMIT University, Melbourne, Australia
ian.peake@rmit.edu.au

Abstract. Virtual Experience Portals are mobile stereoscopic ultra high definition LCD displays with human interface sensors, which can be combined into a reconfigurable development platform for shared immersive virtual and augmented reality experiences. We are targeting applications in, for example, industrial automation, serious games, scientific visualization and building architecture. The aim is to provide a framework for natural and effortless interfaces for shared small group experiences of interactive 3D content, combining selected existing elements of computer aided virtual environments and virtual reality. In this short paper we report on efforts to date in developing the platform, integration with an existing visualization framework, SAGE2, some short application case studies, one in an industry-sponsored research context in industrial automation, and some ideas for future work.

1 Introduction

The Virtual Experiences Laboratory (VXLab) at RMIT is being used as a specialised facility by disciplines such as Media and Communications, Computer Science, Software Engineering, Architecture and Design and eResearch (also known as e-Science). The VXLab is being used as a platform to support and showcase research capabilities, including by the founding Australia-India Research Centre for Automation Software Engineering (AICAUSE) in industrial automation, and in learning and teaching for both internal and external stakeholders such as industry bodies, corporations, government agencies and international institutions, including in cross-disciplinary project collaborations and multi-national collaboration such as with our industry partner ABB[1].

Within the VXLab we have designed and implemented the "virtual experience portals" (VXPortals). A VXPortal is a window into an interactive and immersive experimental virtual 3D space. The display system allows participants to experience a changing perspective as they walk in front of the portal and look

---

[1] www.abb.com.

L.T. De Paolis and A. Mongelli (Eds.): AVR 2016, Part I, LNCS 9768, pp. 186–197, 2016.
DOI: 10.1007/978-3-319-40621-3_14

into a 3D space as if it was viewed through a glass panel. The portals are intended for use in a mix of applications, several but not all of which may be classed as virtual or augmented reality usages. In particular the VXPortals are intended to be compatible with specific 3D application platforms of interest to lab users, currently SAGE2 and Unity 3D. Requirements focus on enabling immersive visualization through a combination of multiple large displays with realistic output suitable for viewing by more than one user: Display pitch at least matching conventional displays to suit groups and individuals moving within the observation space both close to and distant from display surfaces, while reducing distractions of excessive tiling of displays; Display output supporting spanning multiple physical devices without complex synchronisation of viewing equipment; Flexibility of movement of displays, into varying configurations, to explore dynamically changing viewpoints into possibly-dynamic environments, even possibly in real time.

In this paper we describe: the planned architecture and realization of our VXPortals framework including SAGE2 and extensions, developed in the RMIT Virtual Experiences Laboratory; the SmartSpace 3D application running on the VXPortals and its research context in the Australia-India Research Centre for Automation Software Engineering; some concept demonstrators; and further planned applications and the user interaction design possibilities afforded by the framework.

Fig. 1. VxPortals in VXLab Gallery (Field Carr, used by permission)

2 Design and Implementation

The virtual experience portals (VXPortals) are 6 units of 84 in. stereoscopic ultra high definition display panels mounted on mobile carts. The aim is to provide immersive stereoscopic multi-perspective visualization, as well as more traditional uses. For example the portals may be arranged in a polygon facing outwards to enable participants to view virtual exhibits in (stereoscopic) 3D, walking around the exhibit to view it from different perspectives. Each panel is driven by a single high performance personal computer (PC). The primary display mode is with a single central quasi-circular arrangement with users "looking inward" — square (4 large panels), hexagon (6), triangle (6) with the remainder of panels at walls. The cluster may be either central or in a position gravitating towards one wall in order to create open space nearby. Figure 1 shows the gallery area with a cluster of portals in use. Figure 2 shows the architecture of the VxPortals system.

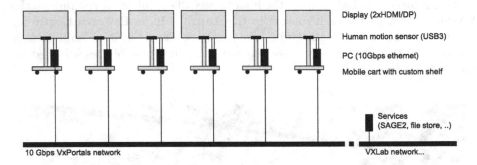

Fig. 2. VxPortals Architecture

To support these use cases, the gallery area has been enlarged to provide an approximately 12×12 m space to accommodate a central cluster of panels while providing adequate viewing area surrounding it. The gallery doubles as work space, with portable tables and conventional workstations provided for short term projects, and as a presentation space with a large conventional HD projection screen and stackable chairs. To support flexible layout, power and data ports are provided throughout the space via ceiling ports. Two power and data floor service boxes support the main use cases involving large central clusters of portals, and to avoid wherever possible the distraction of wiring hanging from the ceiling. Older, smaller high-end screens have been preserved for off-facility experimentation with drivers and software and signage and engagement for the public passing by (through windows of the facility).

The physical size of the displays (84 in.) is exactly offset by the display resolution, providing a highly usable dot pitch similar to conventional displays at close range without the need for tiling. Indeed, the panels are constructed by seamless 2×2 tiling of 42 in. displays.

2.1   Hardware

Workstations for portals are Dell Precision T5610 with an NVidia Quadro K5000 video adapter. Commercial mobile carts suitable for the panels are retrofitted with a simple shelf, and hook and loop fasteners to accommodate workstations.

Display panels, being a composite of four standard 42 in. HD subpanels, offer four separate DisplayPort/HDMI inputs to drive subpanels individually, as well as several composite modes where the system renders signals to a mosaic of subpanels. One mode accepts a single 30 Hz 3840×2160 signal which is displayed over the entire physical panel. We are using another mode which accepts a pair of 60 Hz 1920×2160 signals and displays each over the left or right half of the whole panel respectively (column of two sub panels). This enables us to generate a 60 Hz display at 3840×2160. The display panel is capable of displaying horizontal-interlaced stereoscopic signals suitable for viewing on standard passive polarized display glasses.

To maximize options for delivering content to displays, 10 Gbps network infrastructure is supported throughout, including workstations, switch and cabling.

We selected the NVidia Quadro series card based on its professional support, mosaic tiling, and suitability for conventional workstation class rendering for engineering applications, at the possible expense of raw performance. For human motion sensing at least one Microsoft Kinect sensor is mounted per portal.

2.2   Software and Services (SAGE2)

The VXPortals are integrated into our distributed lab environment to provide centralised user position tracking and smart application deployment. Initially support has been integrated into SAGE2, Scalable Adaptive Graphics Environment 2 [13], with support for Unity3D planned. The VXPortals could be incorporated into any lab environment which provides 10 Gbit networking and a SAGE2 service with the modifications described in this paper.

SAGE2 provides a web-based service for deployment and coordination of regular, rectangular tiled video wall applications. A SAGE2 server accepts websocket-based connections from display tiles, user interface applications and content-generation applications, and coordinates the generation and routing of content and user interface events to display tiles. Display tiles run as ordinary (maximized) web browsers connected to a SAGE2 server with their specific display ID designating their position in a regular, rectangular tiled (2D) array of screens which have a common size, resolution and dot pitch. SAGE2 applications are HTML5-based with a common abstract class making them SAGE2-aware and tileable. After display tiles are connected, the server manages the deployment of applications to relevant tiles depending on whether and where an application, or a segment of an application, is deemed visible on a given tile. GPU-accelerated 3D rendering within SAGE2 applications is directly supported, via WebGL and 3JS, albeit with some porting to the SAGE2 architecture required, and management of aspects of local clipping needed to display correctly and scalably in the tiled context.

Our use of SAGE2 for the VXPortals is unconventional, perhaps arguably a generalization of SAGE2, which presents some potential problems and tradeoffs. SAGE2 is designed to support multi-user collaboration through service-based coordination of regular tiled display walls, and this assumption about 2D display tiling is reflected throughout the architecture. However there is also significant power and flexibility, for example, multiple display tiles can all act as the "same" (logical) tile, so in principle several independent display walls could be operated in synchronization. Also, the rectangular-display assumption is not yet deeply integrated into the architecture display of display clients and applications. Finally, since SAGE2 provides a means to automatically deploy HTML-based applications to multiple displays, using it for prototyping is attractive. Elsewhere in the VXLab we are using SAGE2 to drive a more conventional SAGE2 tiled display wall.

We modify the SAGE2 server to relay head tracking information from sensors to displays, and modify standard SAGE2 3D applications with perspective correction and metadata with locations of portal display corners and sensor position and pose. For our VXPortals we run a dedicated SAGE2 server with a single logical tile ("0") with all display tiles set with this tile ID.

A Kinect face tracking application is used to determine the position of the front-most user for each given sensor, if any, which is then relayed to the SAGE2 server via a websocket connection. The SAGE2 server is extended with a dedicated message type for head tracking updates which is in turn broadcast to all known displays hosting a VXPortal application. The data also includes other sensor information, most importantly, a unique sensor ID, as well as data harvested by the Kinect libraries such as user pose and engagement.

We modify SAGE2 applications to deliver their perspective-corrected view of a scene based on the physical position of the user in relation to selected user-visible display tile and some filtering based on spatial reasoning. Individual applications contain metadata with positions of all known displays and sensors. Based on the sensor ID and portal ID, the system filters events to determine whether the event is relevant to a given portal. For example, for some user positions, certain portals (display tiles) are not visible and therefore should not be updated. It is possible for one or more users to have logically exclusive access to a set of portals that only they can see, in which case all portals can be made available to their respective sole user. In more complex cases, when two users can see one portal, the system will make choices such as allocating each user their closest portal, while portals in their peripheral vision may be preferentially allocated to other users.

We use a method documented by Robert Kooima [12] to calculate perspective correction, which requires the tracker-space location of the viewer and the given display via three corner points uniquely identifying it. This has the advantage that position data for multiple displays may provided within a single unified frame of reference for metadata. However it also seems to include the assumption that tracker space origin lies at the camera; then the head position is offset from the actual camera position and a projection matrix is calculated on that

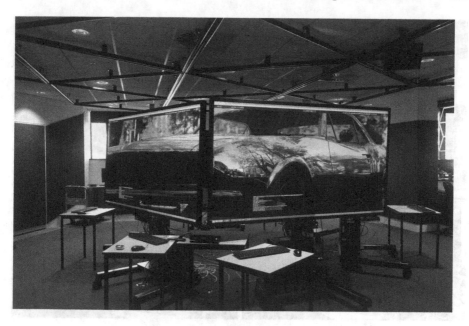

Fig. 3. VXPortal Demonstrator (Camaro)

basis, which includes rotation and translation from the origin. We had difficulty applying the method to a scene-graph based application such as 3JS where the position of the camera directly determines other effects such as material shading, e.g. reflections. We chose to align head and camera position and dynamically align tracker space origin per update, recalculating other display positions accordingly.

As a proof of concept for the above we have ported one of the SAGE2 demonstrator applications (Camaro from Car_3JS) to the VXPortals[2]. Figure 3 shows one user's view of a virtual car displayed in the VXLab. Figure 4 shows the parallax effect apparent to the user moving from left to right past one screen in four successive positions, respectively shown at top left, top right, bottom left and bottom right. An obvious improvement of such a demonstrator would be to use a cube mapped photograph or realistic model of the VXLab gallery to generate reflections instead of the outdoor image provided in the sample application.

3   SmartSpace 3D

The SmartSpace 3D application[3] is a SAGE2 user interface for a decision support platform. Figure 5 shows SmartSpace 3D running on a flat tiled SAGE2 display wall and the VXPortals, respectively.

---

[2] A recent video of this demonstrator can be seen at https://youtu.be/CYh9hFJW JDo.

[3] http://3dclouds.wix.com/3dclouds.

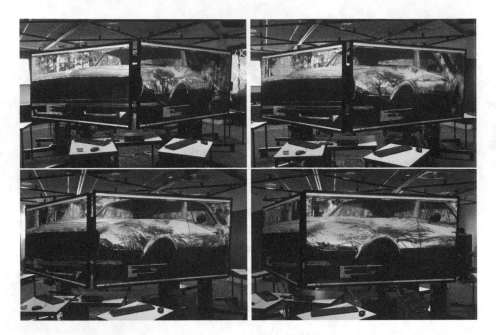

Fig. 4. VXPortal Demonstrator (user perspective moving from left to right)

Based on incoming events such as consultancy requests or automatically generated events triggered by sensors, relevant information is processed, selected and displayed to relevant stakeholders. Here with SmartSpace 3D we support the 3D visualization of graphical information needed in the decision support process. Such information comprises, for example, cloud coverage, ultraviolet radiation and power station location data.

There are various methods of interaction with the SmartSpace 3D app. The primary method is to use a mouse or keyboard for pan (orbit around model) and zoom functions. In the portals version of SmartSpace 3D, these pan and zoom functions are no longer used; instead the user can move around the portal and thereby get the effect of panning and zooming. The application is rendered to a cubic volume (space above square map), Therefore for the portal version we have demonstrated the use of four portals so that the user experience is that the map is exactly contained within the space bounded by the four portal screens.

SmartSpace 3D is a demonstrator related to the collaborative engineering project [1]. The collaborative engineering project supports stakeholders in their decisions by retrieving, filtering and visualizing appropriate information in case as a response to incidents.

SmartSpace 3D uses the BeSpaceD language and tool [2] for spatiotemporal modeling and contextual reasoning. Here we are primarily concerned with visualization of the spatio-temporal models. BeSpaceD is implemented in Scala, thus runs in a Java environment.

Fig. 5. SmartSpace 3D on tiled video wall and on VXPortals

Below we show an example of a BeSpaceD model. The `OccupyPoint` command refers to a position in a 2D cartesian plane. A 2D position is translated to a 3D position and object shape/size such as depending on the associated `Owner`, for example `Cloud`.

```
...
BIGAND(List(
  IMPLIES(AND(TimePoint(1453173062565),Owner(Cloud)),
    BIGAND(List(OccupyPoint(129,283), ..., OccupyPoint(414,486)))),
  IMPLIES(AND(TimePoint(1453173782565),Owner(UV Index)),
    IMPLIES(OccupyBox(0,0,511,511),ComponentState(4.4))),
  IMPLIES(AND(TimePoint(1453174142565),Owner(Cloud)),
    BIGAND(List(OccupyPoint(412,286), ..., OccupyPoint(222))))
))
...
```

SmartSpace 3D has been implemented in our framework using ThreeJS and OpenCTM JS libraries based on a standard template in our framework. SmartSpace 3D parses BeSpaceD data, which is then stored as an associative array of the form `timeStamp → owner → data` where `data` may for example refer to a sequence of 2D points. The application iterates through the array, processing each of the time-stamped data sets, rendering each of the frames of data inside the 3D environment. The application then animates each time-stamped frame of data automatically until it reaches the end of the data set.

4   Other Applications

The VXPortals have also been used for student projects in internships and advanced game design (Fig. 6). One such application is Big Sky which uses six portals to depict a six-season view of Australian geography.

5   Related Work, Evaluation and Future Work

Our work is clearly related to, and benefiting from, extensive and long standing work on CAVEs [5] and more recent variants such as Varrier [18]

Fig. 6. Big Sky and Temple student projects using VXPortals

and CAVE2 [7] which commonly support viewing of 3D content with GPU-accelerated perspective-correction and head tracking. There are several commercial CAVE platforms such as those by MechDyn[4] and EON reality[5] which have in particular been applied to the engineering domain. However to the best of our knowledge CAVEs are not usually designed to have reconfigurable display elements, nor provide a unified framework for so-called hybrid virtual reality content suited both to tiled display walls as well as 3D content normally displayed in CAVEs [6]. The published work on CAVE2 identifies and seeks to address the need for hybrid virtual reality frameworks. This effort appears to have been continued in the design for SAGE2, which appears to be one of the few applications supporting both projection-based VR as well tiled display walls [15]. However we are not aware of any other CAVE-based SAGE2 deployments which provide perspective-corrected head-tracked applications.

The VROOM [4,10] is also an antecedent of our work. A VROOM at RMIT previously occupied our VXPortals gallery space [20], consisting of several high definition active stereo video projectors. However VROOM has a fixed layout and was not conceived of as providing flexible layout or perspective-corrected displays. Experience with the VROOM at RMIT motivated our VxPortal requirements expressed as an extension of the VXROOM, including for compact, mobile, higher definition displays.

3D scanning technology such as Microsoft Kinect and similar devices have been used for various research projects. Examples comprise indoor localization (e.g., [9,11]), gesture recognition (e.g., [16]) and academic approaches, e.g., in robotics [14]. The Kinect appears provides adequate head tracking precision to provide perspective correction [8,15]. However the Kinect's range and field of view, while generous for other applications, combined with issues seen in our setup (Windows 8.1) make it difficult to exploit for distributed head tracking over large areas beyond that suited to a single sensor. We have demonstrated that multiple Kinects can be combined to cover a large area with small amounts of overlap in field of view. However in our setup it appears that a 1–2s registration delay occurs whenever a user enters or leaves the field of view. This

---

[4] http://www.mechdyne.com/hardware.aspx?name=CAVE.

[5] http://www.eonreality.com/eon-icube/.

applies particularly when users move between Kinects. Also in our implementation occasionally the Kinect application will appear to drop out for short periods, possibly identifying another user in the same field of view, before re-acquiring the same user again. The overall created by dropouts for users depends on the application. For creating photographs of the results, the dropouts are minor, however for normal uses dropouts create the impression of discontinuity and the user experiences a discontinuity. Due to architectural restrictions requiring a single dedicated USB3.0 controller per Kinect we have yet to investigate whether Kinects can be combined with field of view overlapping without interference and loss of quality.

The work presented in this paper is aligned with our VXLab facility, we have explained details of the underlying SAGE2 visualization with a focus on network architecture and applications in industrial automation [3,17]. The immersive visualization and Kinect work presented in this paper was not covered by this previous work. Leap-motion-based control of robots was studied by us in [19]. Elsewhere in the VXLab we are using SAGE2 to drive a more conventional video wall, with the prospect to provide a unifying framework to support 3D web-based applications which may be ported cheaply, or even automatically migrated between, different kinds of visualization platforms, including mobile devices, VR headsets, tiled display walls and future immersive group environments such as the VXPortals. In this paper we have not evaluated the impact of a web-based architecture on rendering performance or usability.

Although the portals have been used to display stereoscopic output, with our current hardware we have yet to adjust our SAGE2 applications such stereoscopy is usable with acceptable update rates in real time. Position data for displays and sensors is manually entered, which means that any physical reconfiguration requires manually reconfiguring the application. We have developed several predefined data sets of position data, expressed in a room geometry relative to a designated portal and sensor orientation, so that common layouts (e.g. square, hexagon) can be approximately supported. We are planning for a more seamless approach requiring the automatic precise tracking of display units, which would enable dynamic change of perspective. A last more serious limitation is due to the display, which can only show a single correct perspective at a time. Nevertheless with a small number of users distributed at different displays the effect is mitigated, and applications can be tuned so that each user is at least able to view a primary display, even if peripheral displays which "belong" to other users are lost.

6 Conclusions

In this short paper we reported on development of the VxPortals platform, including integration with an existing visualization framework, SAGE2, and some short application case studies. The results to date, including applications developed, are a novel and promising use of VR technology which we intend to explore further. The combination of flexible display layouts with perspective correction based on head tracking to suit different applications, with the SAGE2 collaboration and web-based deployment platform, is novel and has not been documented before. We also demonstrated an application prototype for spatial reasoning applied in the industrial domain and deployed on the VxPortals in a format targeted towards intuitive spatial interpretation, and utilizing Microsoft Kinect technology. Among the ideas for future work are the use of new middleware technologies, such as SAGE2, to enable collaboration in a distributed VR context across different types of devices.

References

1. Blech, J.O., Peake, I., Schmidt, H., Kande, M., Rahman, A., Ramaswamy, S., Sudarsan S.D., Narayanan, V.: Efficient incident handling in industrial automation through collaborative engineering. In: Emerging Technologies and Factory Automation (ETFA). IEEE (2015)
2. Blech, J.O., Schmidt, H.: BeSpaceD: Towards a Tool Framework and Methodology for the Specification and Verification of Spatial Behavior of Distributed Software Component Systems, (2014). http://arxiv.org/abs/1404.3537.arXiv.org
3. Blech, J.O., Spichkova, M., Peake, I., Schmidt, H.: Cyber-Virtual Systems: Simulation, Validation & Visualization. In: Evaluation of Novel Approaches to Software Engineering. SciTePress ISBN 978-989-758-030-7 (2014)
4. Paul, B.: Virtual Containment Vessel now known as VROOM. http://paulbourke.net/exhibition/vroom/. Accessed 21 Mar 2016
5. Cruz-Neira, C., Sandin, D., Defanti, T., Kenyon, R., Hart, J.: The CAVE: audio visual experience automatic virtual environment. Commun. ACM **35**(6), 64–72 (1992)
6. DeFanti, T.A., et al.: The future of the CAVE. Cent. Eur. J. Eng. **1**(1), 16–37 (2011)
7. Febretti, Alessandro, et al.: CAVE2: a hybrid reality environment for immersive simulation and information analysis. In: IS&T/SPIE Electronic Imaging. International Society for Optics and Photonics (2013)
8. Greuter, S., Roberts, D.J.: Controlling viewpoint from markerless head tracking in an immersive ball game using a commodity depth-based camera. J. Simul. **9**(1), 54–63 (2015)
9. Henry, P., Krainin, M., Herbst, E., Ren, X., Fox, D.: RGB-D mapping: using Kinect-style depth cameras for dense 3D modeling of indoor environments. Int. J. Robot. Res. **31**(5), 647–663 (2012)
10. Kenderdine, S., Hart, T.: This is not a peep show. the virtual room at melbourne museum (VROOM). In: ICHIM (2003)
11. Khoshelham, K., Elberink, S.: Accuracy and resolution of kinect depth data for indoor mapping applications. Sensors **12**(2), 1437–1454 (2012)
12. Kooima, R.: Generalized perspective projection. LSU Computer Science and Engineering Division (2009). http://csc.lsu.edu/kooima/articles/genperspective/June
13. Marrinan, T., et al.: SAGE2: a new approach for data intensive collaboration using scalable resolution shared displays. In: 2014 International Conference on Collaborative Computing: Networking, Applications and Worksharing (CollaborateCom). IEEE (2014)
14. Machida, E., Cao, M., Murao, T., Hashi, H.: Human motion tracking of mobile robot with Kinect 3D sensor. In: Proceedings of SICE. IEEE (2012)

15. Popolin Neto, M., Remo Ferreira Brega, J.: A survey of solutions for game engines in the development of immersive applications for multi-projection systems as base for a generic solution design. In: 2015 XVII Symposium on Virtual and Augmented Reality (SVR). IEEE (2015)
16. Oikonomidis, I., Kyriazis, N., Argyros, A.: Efficient model-based 3D tracking of hand articulations using kinect. BMVC 1(2), 3 (2011)
17. Peake, I., Blech, J.O., Fernando, L., Schmidt, H., Sreenivasamurthy, R., Sudarsan S.D.: Visualization facilities for distributed and remote industrial automation: VxLab. In: ETFA. IEEE (2015)
18. Sandin, D.J., et al.: The varrier^{TM} autostereoscopic virtual reality display. ACM Trans. Graph. (TOG) 24(3), 894–903 (2005)
19. Peake, I.D., Vuyyuru, A., Blech, J.O., Vergnaud, N., Fernando, L.: Cloud-based analysis and control for robots in industrial automation. In: Automated Testing of Cyber-Physical Systems in the Cloud. IEEE (2015)
20. VROOM at RMIT GEElab. http://www.geelab.rmit.edu.au/content/vroom. Accessed 21 Mar 2016

Virtual Reality for Product Development in Manufacturing Industries

Laura Schina, Mariangela Lazoi[✉], Roberto Lombardo, and Angelo Corallo

Università del Salento, Via per Monteroni s.n., Lecce, Italy
{laura.schina,mariangela.lazoi,
roberto.lombardo,angelo.corallo}@unisalento.it

Abstract. Currently, Virtual Reality (VR) systems give industries in different domains the possibility to interact with and work into a simulated environment in order to improve their processes, efficiency and effectiveness, fast introducing new products in the market in a cost effective way.

The fundamental idea is to identify the main applications of Virtual Reality in the manufacturing domain and provide valuable insights for future research and trends concern the application of this technology along the whole product development process.

This paper aims to propose a set of new emerging scenarios, composed of Virtual Reality technologies, tools and systems used in manufacturing industries with a focus on the aerospace sector. The proposed scenarios are based on projects and initiatives carried out for applying the VR to industries in order to optimize internal processes and the overall supply chain.

Keywords: Virtual reality · New product development · Manufacturing industries · Aerospace · Emerging scenarios

1 Introduction

The development of a product is a complex and articulated process that requires to work both on its conceptual model and on its functional components. A common used abstraction in this context is the definition of (and the mapping between) functional and physical elements, that work together to provide new products architectures, configurations and features (Ulrich and Eppinger 2008). In particular, the design of physical elements has important and direct consequences on all the phases of the product lifecycle and on the product performance. Moreover, it has a significant impact on the time and costs needed to develop and manufacture the product.

An important feature of the product data is their interlinks with different activities and lifecycle phases (Ameri and Dutta 2005), that require appropriate tools and methodologies to be efficiently managed. In this aim, specialized technologies can be used to support the different stages of the product design, and the manipulation and analysis of the data related to physical and functional elements. The set of most used technologies in manufacturing industries, consists of Computer Aided Technologies (CAx) used to define engineering, manufacturing or testing data, including CAD systems for the design

© Springer International Publishing Switzerland 2016
L.T. De Paolis and A. Mongelli (Eds.): AVR 2016, Part I, LNCS 9768, pp. 198–207, 2016.
DOI: 10.1007/978-3-319-40621-3_15

activities and CAM for the manufacturing ones. Centralized data management is often implemented for the product data in the form of Product Data Management (PDM) software. PDM are commonly used to store mainly CAD data enriched with other product data, that may include advanced features such as workflow definition, query definition, etc. (Grieves 2006).

In this context, the use of the most adequate and valid technology can support the reduction of errors during the design stage and of the high costs of re-works.

Virtual Reality is one of the most promising and growing technology for supporting product design. Using VR, companies can digitalize, analyze and simulate all the aspects of a product, as its geometric structure, physical behavior, etc., including the simulation of all the processes related to the product lifecycle (i.e. manufacturing, design, etc.). VR receives a lot of attention from the manufacturing industry, in particular from the transportation one, and this is because its potential in the resolution of many problems in product design and in the general manufacturing industry applications (Caputo and Di Gironimo 2007).

Based on evidences coming from the literature and from the industrial practices, the paper aims to propose five industrial scenarios in which the virtual reality can play a relevant role in terms of performance improvement for the product design process of manufacturing companies.

The rest of the paper is organized in four sections. In the next section, it is introduced the relevant literature of reference for the paper background. A following section introduces the research approach and the relevant scenarios are described. A set of conclusions ends the paper.

2 Background

Virtual reality (VR) represents a widely diffused technology able to provide an immersive and interactive experience for users creating virtual spaces that overcome spatial and physical constraints of the real environment (ETRI 2001).

VR technologies exist since the early 1960s, and their usage in manufacturing industries has been increased in order to: improve their effectiveness along the whole product development process; gain in cost competitiveness; reduce the time to market; enhance systematic routines; analyze and create interactions among users, objects and operations (Shiratuddin and Zulkifli 2001; Ong and Nee 2004; Dorozhkin et al. 2012).

Nowadays, VR technology has various fields of application from industry to education, training and entertainment, including a vast number of manufacturing companies that apply VR at different stages of the "New Product Development" (NPD) process (Choi et al. 2015; Bernabei et al. 2015; Ottosson 2002). In this sense the efforts and the research undertaken to apply new technologies in manufacturing industries, lead to the definition of a variety of terms for identifying the VR application according to both the type of technology applied (i.e. smart manufacturing systems, Industry 4.0, Factory for the Future, Cyber-Physical System, etc.) (Wahlster 2012; Lee 2008) and the stage of the NPD at which it occurs.

Merging all these elements, the literature review shows different cases of VR application in manufacturing industries that can be addressed as follows:

Virtual Manufacturing (VM), represents the approach that enterprises can use to improve their processes, introducing new products more quickly in the market and in a cost effective way (Souza et al. 2006). In this aim, VR offers the opportunity to virtually explore objects allowing a variety of 2D and 3D representations that are able to reduce the level of abstraction increasing the possibility for users to interact with the multi-dimensional space as if they were part of the same environment (Shiratuddin and Zulkifli 2001; Carr and England 1995). Moreover, VR can support the representation of objects, processes, activities and principles (Marinov 2001) providing enhanced graphic interfaces for achieving rapid understanding and decisions by visualization and experience (Shiratuddin and Zulkifli 2001; Choi et al. 2015).

Finally, VM includes the Virtual Assembly defined as "the use of computer tools to make or "assist with" assembly-related engineering decisions through analysis, predictive models, visualization, and presentation of data without physical realization of the product or supporting processes" (Jayaram et al. 1997).

Leading industries in many sectors such as aerospace and automotive companies are making use of VM to support different stages of their product development process (Souza et al. 2006).

Virtual Training (VT), is considered as an advanced method to teach and transfer manufacturing skills and processes to employees in a realistic and simulated environment (Shiratuddin and Zulkifli 2001). In this aim VR based training is a way to make less difficult, dangerous and expensive or impossible the real type of training. VT also supports the training at wide audience and the possibility to reply processes to: better understand manufacturing processes and issues (Shiratuddin and Zulkifli 2001); reduce errors and risks on the shop floor and helps the transfer of technical skills; increase benefits and reducing the training time; learn 3D printing; and reduce time and cost of a print (Renner et al. 2015). The emergent need for cooperation between industrial robots and humans in modern manufacturing industries had led to the development of training system that uses VR to enable this type of virtual collaboration (Matsas and Vosniakos 2015), not only in training stage but along the whole product development process.

In the past VT was highly adopted within software companies working on the manufacturing of integrated circuits (i.e. Motorola, Samsung, IBM and Lucent Technologies).

Virtual Prototyping (VP). There are different understandings of what exactly virtual prototyping is, but it is possible to distinguish between: the "computer graphics" (virtual prototyping) and the "manufacturing" (digital mock-up) point of view (De Sa and Zachmann 1999). In line with this work, we refer to VP as the way to understand the application of virtual reality for prototyping physical mock-ups (PMUs) using product and process data. The VR system simulates and renders all characteristics relevant to the particular context as precisely and realistically as possible in an immersive environment. VP software are able to simulate and visualize 3D motion behaviors under real-world operating conditions, and to refine/optimize the design through iterative design studies prior to building the first physical prototype (Shiratuddin and Zulkifli 2001). In manufacturing industries, VP enables designer to simulate not just the way things look but also the way things run. VP can then be used to identify potential problems in a faster, less expensive, and safer way than with traditional physical proto-types, thus shortening design cycle times and reducing overall costs.

During the years there were a high numbers of applications of VP in automotive and aerospace companies. For example, automotive companies investigate the use of VR for styling reviews and other mere walk-through applications. At Daimler Benz the body of a car can be reviewed in an immersive virtual environment (Buck 1998). Since VR provides an intuitive and immersive human–computer interface, it is perfectly suited to do ergonomics studies. For example, Ford employs virtual prototypes with several proposed dashboard configurations to verify visibility and reachability of instrument (De Sa and Zachmann 1999).

In aerospace, Rolls-Royce Aero Engine Services Ltd., used a VR demonstrator for the company's Trent 800 engine, which was used in the Boeing 777 (Greenfield 1996).

Virtual Factory (VF), represents the way to apply VR to the design of production facilities, leading benefits in creating computer-based environments that accurately simulate individual manufacturing processes and total manufacturing enterprises, opti-mizing the time-to-market, shortening the development time, etc. (Shiratuddin and Zulkifli 2001). In its initial stage, this would could be considered as a first attempt to provide suitable virtual environment for both intra and inter organizational collabora-tions, in line with the aim to enable virtual co-working environments.

This literature review intended to provide an overview on the state of the art about the application of VR in manufacturing industries. In this aim we will provide a set of new emerging scenarios for applying VR in manufacturing industries integrating Computer Aided technologies (CAx) along the overall NPD process.

3 Research Approach

The research has followed an inductive approach based on gaps in the research literature and on the observation of organizational practices, from which the general scenarios and solutions have been developed (Bryman and Bell 2007; Thomas 2006).

The paper aims to answer at the research questions: Which are the main innovative scenarios for Virtual Reality applications in manufacturing companies for supporting new product development?

The authors initially investigated the research problem as a result of working on a research project named KHIRA (Knowledge Holistic Integrated Research Approach), which started in 2013, with the aim to develop a set of industrial solutions for the inte-grated management of data and information along the product lifecycle and mainly during the product design phase. Partners of the project KHIRA are relevant Italian manufacturing companies and universities. A PLM framework is proposed in order to be knowledge driven and enable a holistic integration for including persons, processes, practices, rules and technologies. Virtual Reality was the enabling technologies for collaborative and review processes.

Based on the experience matured in the project through the collaboration with indus-trial partners and based on references and applications available in literature, to address the research question, five emerging scenarios are proposed: (a) PLM integration in

Virtual Design; (b) Immersive Virtual Testing; (c) Virtual Training for Maintenance; (d) Collaborative Virtual Review in Design Chain; (e) Virtual Manufacturing Process review. Their wide spread in the company and their further exploration will lead future industrial and research applications.

4 Emerging Scenarios

This section describes the main features of the proposed five emerging scenarios regarding the utilization of Virtual Reality technologies in the manufacturing industry. These scenarios mainly concern the extension of the Virtual Design Review for improving analysis, evaluation and decision process operated on the design, in a virtual immersive environment. Our main purpose is to suggest integrated solutions able to optimize the results obtained from the review process, containing engineering information and knowledge from other phases of the product lifecycle, in order to foresee the successive decisions and reduce the time-to-market. A distinctive feature of the proposed scenarios is the tight integration with the embedded enterprise software applications that allow the direct access from the VR environment. Moreover, this enables the continuous update of data and information during and after the review process.

Table 1. Emerging scenarios

VR scenario	Technological components	Disciplines	Processes (PCF)
PLM integration in Virtual Design	PDM (Product Data Management); CAD	Change/lifecycle management; configuration management	2.2.1 Design, build, and evaluate products and services (10080)
Immersive Virtual Testing	CAE	Design and simulation	2.2.1 Design, build, and evaluate products and services (10080)
Virtual Training for Maintenance	HRM; PDM; Custom software with MRO activities	Human resources; maintenance, repair and overall	6.3 Develop and counsel employees (10411); 4.3 Produce/Manufacture/Deliver Product (10217)
Collaborative Virtual Review in Design Chain	CAD; PDM	Product design; supply chain	2.2.1 Design, build, and evaluate products and services (10080); 4.2.4 Manage suppliers (10280)
Virtual Manufacturing Process review	CAM	Manufacturing processes engineering	2.2.3 Prepare for production (10082)

The scenarios are classified according to three criteria: (1) the technological components of a company IT architecture with which the VR is interrelated through the exchange of data and information; (2) the disciplines impacted by the use of the VR that can also correspond with organizational unit; (3) the organizational processes involved in the scenarios. The specification of the processes is done considering the Cross Industry Process Classification Framework (PCF) of the American Productivity and Quality Center (APQC) v.6.1.1. These three criteria are relevant for having a clearer and more immediate view on the impacts and relationships in the proposed scenarios.

The Table 1 summarizes the five emerging scenarios and their classification.

The following sub-sections provide a detailed description of the emerging scenarios.

4.1 Product Lifecycle Management (PLM) and Virtual Reality

The first scenario concerns the integration between PLM software and VR technology that enables the possibility to navigate data and information along the whole NPD. The creation of this connection is essential to create the Virtual Design Review Environment (hierarchically organized in 3D geometric data to form a product structure) including data (read and saved) stored within the Product Lifecycle Management software.

One of the most important feature of the PLM is to allow the centralized and historized management of data related to the product lifecycle. This could be very useful to enable the navigation of different configurations of the product structure in the same design session, ideally recovering the data in real-time. The recovery of this information during the virtual design review brings the following benefits:

– Enable the consultation under the Configuration Management perspective (i.e. compared to different versions and configuration of the product);
– Reduce the need of manual procedures (i.e. data extraction and preparation) and enable the direct import of data from the PLM to Virtual Reality software;
– Make potentially available data related to each phase of the product lifecycle.

4.2 Immersive Virtual Testing

The second scenario includes simulation aspects in the virtual design review. In our vision, the integration of simulation and virtual reality software should allow the use of both non real-time systems (requiring long computation time) and systems that allow the real-time variation of simulation parameters, during the review process.

The main benefits resulting from this scenario can be addressed as follows:

– VR is an important visual tool able to facilitate the synthesis and comprehension of simulation data, and to make more effective product behavior analysis;
– The high level of interaction of VR technology allows to simply modify simulation parameters of a product (i.e. altering its geometric structure), and provide a more intuitive analysis of the dynamic behavior of the same product;
– Reduce errors and the time during the design process with the consequent reduction of re-work needed to develop an item.

4.3 Virtual Training for Maintenance

The third scenario suggests the enrichment of the geometric data with information concerning maintenance, assembly and disassembly processes. A proper use of a virtual training system should include mechanism to capture the training sessions, allowing for example the simply creation of VR animations (i.e. images and videos) representing assembly/disassembly and maintenance processes. These animations referred to the training sessions could be then compared with the real behavior of the operators in order to identify potential errors and suggest corrections and improvements. In this context, the use of haptic interfaces is highly recommended to reproduce the limitation to the movements due to the real product restrictions.

The integration of VR and training activities allows to accurately reproduce the required manual activities, with the following main benefits:

- Analyze the impact of human intervention (i.e. in terms of postural features or visibility of the parts) during the maintenance activities;
- Enhance the fast adaptation of the design to the maintenance requirements, allowing a more efficient identification of errors during the design phase, affecting the time and quality of assembly/disassembly processes;
- Build direct training paths in line with the workers' experience.

4.4 Collaborative Virtual Review in the Design Chain

The fourth scenario intends to provide insights for better integrating all the suppliers of the product design and impacting on the reduction of time, costs and errors.

Outsourcing activities require the continuous exchange of updated data for the prompt identification of manufacturing problems, that can bring added and unexpected costs and waste of time. In this sense, the Design Chain can benefit of VR technology building virtual collaborative working environments remotely connected, that enables the interaction of the designer with third party suppliers.

The main advantages of this scenario can be addressed as follows:

- Facilitate the collective virtual design review among actors geographically different located;
- Enhance the interaction between manufacturing and design experts in order to increase the expertise involved during the review process;
- Enable the implementation of automatic update of intra-organizational systems (i.e. ERP software) leading saving in terms of time and mistakes during the resource planning process.

4.5 Virtual Manufacturing Process Review

The fifth and last scenario concerns the integration of manufacturing data into the virtual design review process. This allows the virtual view of movements and operations carried out by the processing tools. In this aim, an interesting feature is the possibility for users to define/modify the sequences of the machining processes during the review, and to simulate/analyze different behavior of the product.

The use of VR in this phase can generate the following positive effects:

- Simplify and reduce the work required to optimize the manufacturing processes through the preventive check of feasibility, correctness and applicability of these processes;
- Support the transition from product design to manufacturing, by ensuring that the results of the design phase closely reflect the manufacturing requirements;
- Reduces the possibility of errors during the manufacturing phase.

5   Conclusions

The increasing competitiveness of companies in manufacturing domain requires the utilization of new methodologies and technological tools able to improve their processes. In this sense Virtual Reality technologies represent a key factor for companies in order to optimize the development processes, integrate systems and data and interactively simulate operations at different stages of the New Product Development Process.

This paper summarized the background concerning the application of VR in manufacturing industries in order to identify the most applied solutions.

The literature review showed that VR technologies mainly support the design stage and refer to the simulation of the manufacturing and prototyping processes; moreover VR supports also training activities and tends to support the virtualization of physical plants. The main benefits of the simulation before the real implementation phase are well-known and move towards the reduction of defects, errors and time to market.

The research method, integrating findings from the literature and the results collected during the KHIRA research project, has allowed to build an holistic knowledge base on persons, processes, practices, rules and technologies, and to enable the creation of a shared perspective between researchers and professionals about the best areas of application of VR in real industrial context with the possibility to propose an advancement in line with the future trends.

Indeed, following the proposed scenarios, several future research initiatives have been planned and will be the object of future studies. They will aim to test the validity of these applications in multiple industrial contexts, measuring the impacts in terms efficiency, performance and quality of the Virtual Reality against the most common and general used technologies. The overall added value of the proposed scenarios is the strong integration with company's technological systems (PLM, ERP, etc.) that allows to update and access data and information in real time, and work on real test case.

In details, the first scenario suggested the use of VR jointly with the PLM software. In this case, the main innovation from the integration of these technologies resides in the creation of a logic tighter and closer in line with the change management perspective, that allows a more effective virtual review process.

The second scenario suggested the use of VR with CAE technologies, that could be interpreted as an attempt to overcome the current lack of integration between these two technologies. In this sense the main innovations consist in the possibility to provide a graphical view of statistical analysis and simulation, increasing the understandings about the product simulated behavior (also for no expert users).

Moreover, VR technology allows to simplify the operations required to modify parameters and data, impacting on the total processing time.

The third scenario refers to the Virtual Training applications as defined in the background. In this sense our contribution is in line with the suggested future trends and is addressed to increase the collaboration within the new immersive training environments. Even if a lot of industrial contexts support this type of application, the practical experience suggested that there is a certain degree of resistance to change acquired and consolidated routines, especially related to internal skills and expertise.

The fourth suggested scenario overcomes the concept of Virtual factory and proposes the virtualization of effective collaboration among all the suppliers of a design chain. This could be able to improve the collaborative environment increasing the interaction of different participants also working on technical tasks that usually require the main changes.

Finally, the fifth scenario is in line with the previously defined Virtual Prototyping. In this area, the main innovation of our proposal resides in the introduction of specific manufacturing processes and data in the virtual environment and in the design review process, that lead to obtain design results more fitting to the manufacturing requirements.

References

Ameri, F., Dutta, D.: Product lifecycle management: closing the knowledge loops. Comput.-Aided Des. Appl. 2(5), 577–590 (2005)

Bernabei, G., Corallo, A., Lombardo, R., Maci, S., Galli, V., Cannoletta, D., Notaro, A.: Development of a framework to support virtual review within complex-product lifecycle management. In: De Paolis, L.T., Mongelli, A. (eds.) AVR 2015. LNCS, vol. 9254, pp. 449–457. Springer, Heidelberg (2015)

Bryman, A., Bell, E.: Business Research Methods. Oxford University Press, Oxford (2007)

Buck, M.: Immersive user interaction within industrial virtual environments. In: Dai, F. (ed.) Virtual Reality for Industrial Applications, Computer Graphics: Systems and Applications, pp. 39–59. Springer, Berlin (1998)

Caputo, F., Di Gironimo, G.: La Realtà Virtuale nella Progettazione Industriale. Aracne, Rome (2007)

Carr, K., England, R. (eds.): Simulated and Virtual Realities: Elements of Perception. CRC Press, Boca Raton (1995)

Choi, S., Jung, K., Do Noh, S.: Virtual reality applications in manufacturing industries: past research, present findings, and future directions. Concurrent Eng. 23(1), 40–63 (2015).

Greenfield, D.: Virtual prototyping at rolls-royce. Intell. Manufact. 2(1) (1996)

De Sa, A.G., Zachmann, G.: Virtual reality as a tool for verification of assembly and maintenance processes. Comput. Graph. 23(3), 389–403 (1999)

De Sa, A.G., von Praun, S.: Virtual prototyping – a fundamental building block of the digital mock-up strategy. VR NEWS Virtual Reality Worldwide 7(7), 15–19 (1998)

Dorozhkin, D.V., Vance, J.M., Rehn, G.D., Lemessi, M.: Coupling of interactive manufacturing operations simulation and immersive virtual reality. Virtual Reality 16(1), 15–23 (2012)

Electronics and Telecommunications Research Institute (ETRI): Virtual Reality Technology/Market Report. Daejon, pp. 12–29, 30 December 2001

Grieves, M.: Product Lifecycle Management: Driving the Next Generation of Lean Thinking. McGraw-Hill, New York (2006)

Jayaram, S., Connacher, H.I., Lyons, K.W.: Virtual assembly using virtual reality techniques. Comput.-Aided Des. **29**(8), 575–584 (1997)

Lee, E.A.: Cyber physical systems: design challenges. In: 2008 11th IEEE International Symposium on Object Oriented Real-Time Distributed Computing (ISORC), pp. 363–369. IEEE, May 2008

Marinov, V.: What Virtual Manufacturing is? Part I: Definition, 9 July 2001

Matsas, E., Vosniakos, G.C.: Design of a virtual reality training system for human–robot collaboration in manufacturing tasks. Int. J. Interact. Des. Manufact. (IJIDeM), 1–15 (2015)

Ong, S.K., Nee, A.Y.C.: A brief introduction of VR and AR applications in manufacturing. In: Ong, S.K., Nee, A.Y.C. (eds.) Virtual and Augmented Reality Applications in Manufacturing, pp. 1–11. Springer, London (2004)

Ottosson, S.: Virtual reality in the product development process. J. Eng. Des. **13**(2), 159–172 (2002)

Pratt, M.J.: Virtual prototypes and product models in mechanical engineering. In: Rix, J., Haas, S., Teixeira, J. (eds.) Virtual prototyping – virtual environments and the product design process, pp. 113–128. Chapman & Hall, London (1995)

Renner, A., Holub, J., Sridhar, S., Evans, G., Winer, E.: A virtual reality application for additive manufacturing process training. In: ASME 2015 International Design Engineering Technical Conferences and Computers and Information in Engineering Conference (2015)

Shiratuddin, M.F., Zulkifli, A.N.: Virtual reality in manufacturing (2001)

Souza, M.C.F., Sacco, M., Porto, A.J.V.: Virtual manufacturing as a way for the factory of the future. J. Intell. Manufact. **17**(6), 725–735 (2006)

Thomas, D.: A general inductive approach for analyzing qualitative evaluation data. Am. J. Eval. **27**(2), 237–246 (2006)

Ulrich, K.T., Eppinger, S.D.: Product Design and Development, 4th edn. McGraw Hill, New York (2008)

Wahlster, W.: From industry 1.0 to industry 4.0: towards the 4th industrial revolution (forum business meets research). In: 3rd European Summit on Future Internet Towards Future Internet International Collaborations Espoo, Finland, 31 May 2012

Virtual Reality Pave the Way for Better Understand Untouchable Research Results

Eva Pajorova[✉] and Ladislav Hluchy

Institute of Informatics, Slovak Academy of Sciences,
Bratislava, Slovakia
utrrepaj@savba.sk

Abstract. Virtual reality (VR) is the "last medium". VR achieves presence and becomes "real", we don´t need any other communication medium. We can communicate anything within VR, using just code. VR will also pave the way for better understanding of the micro world, cosmos world, underground world and lot of world environments, which pupil is not able in real world visit, because by zooming we are able to see cells function, we can fly by virtual space ship between stars, in front to the Sun and visit life under ground and so on. The best form, how present untouchable or abstract research results is to put them to the Virtual Reality form. Our research in institute is oriented on high performance computing like GRID and Cloud computing, clusters computing. Usually we compute with a big data and the results are large. The paper describe the tool for converting final outputs data to VR. The paper present VR tool for untouchable research results in the field of astrophysics research and in the field of underground water management. Tool is composed of several modules which all of them have individual role. The paper describe also the functionality of the singular module.

Keywords: Virtual reality · High performance computing · 3D visualization

1 Introduction

Research is excited about Virtual Reality, because many problems and many new frontier by using VR will be unlock. VR need to combine lot of technologies and visual depiction. Progress in VR technologies is splitting. This will create opportunities in many areas. There is creation of VR content like are tourist content, games, research…; technology to help capture the content; 360 degree camera rigs to capture VR ready videos; apps to help us create VR videos using us phone, etc.

In a field of programming architectures to write code for VR and tools, frameworks. VR could be the next *big thing* [1].

Computing with a big data usually ended with visual service [4]. We have developed lot of visualization tool. Research simulations are from different areas. Some of them requires the information visualization, some needs to show only the development over time, some only hierarchy. An interesting group of simulations are such,

© Springer International Publishing Switzerland 2016
L.T. De Paolis and A. Mongelli (Eds.): AVR 2016, Part I, LNCS 9768, pp. 208–217, 2016.
DOI: 10.1007/978-3-319-40621-3_16

where we are not able to go, and we have never been there, so it is up to us, how we perceive such an environment of knowledge available.

The best form, how present untouchable or abstract research results is to put output simulations data to the Virtual Reality form. Virtual Reality provide us all decision for the visual service of research result. The paper describe some of visualization of research results in environment as are cosmos and underground water management. The conversion of these results to the Virtual Reality provides the represent form of the scientific results for such community like are the students and scientists who are interested in this domain.

Visual service is usually post process. After high performance computing like are Grid, Cloud, Clusters the outputs data are stored on storage element and waiting for next process – visualization process. There are lot of VR technics.

"VizMove" [1] is a complete hardware and software solution designed to cost-effectively meet and scale to the needs of the user. Industry's first out-of-the-box wide-area-walking virtual reality solution that is well suited for a broad range of applications including design visualization, architectural walk-throughs, industrial training and behavioral research.

"Vizard's" [2] tools and script libraries are optimized for the most demanding simulations with unrivaled input and output device support. Create engaging virtual worlds and immersive applications with the most comprehensive virtual reality development platform in the industry.

"Tracking for VR Motion" tracking system combines advanced optical and inertial tracking technology and is capable of expanding to cover large spaces at an affordable cost.

"VR Design Solutions" [3] provides Art design and custom application development services for professionals and academics. From research to concept creation to collaboration and execution. VR Design Solutions make you better, faster and cheaper decisions. VR mission is to make the world more open and connected.

Virtual reality was once the dream of science fiction. But the internet was also once a dream, and so were computers and smartphones. The future is coming and we have a chance to build it together. I can't wait to start working with the whole team at Oculus to bring this future to the world, and to unlock new worlds for all of us [5].

Lot of technics are builds on Oculus platform. Not only games, but "Oculus platform" is for many other experiences. Imagine enjoying a court side seat at a game, studying in a classroom of students and teachers all over the world or consulting with a doctor face-to-face – just by putting on goggles in us home.

At present, there are lot of VR technologies. Each of them is sewn to the other problems. For our research, we have chosen the path of own design tools, because requirements for visualization of results of simulations are too specific. The article describes two examples of us developed VR tool. Both are from the area where the human foot step in not. One of which is a tool for visualizing the results of simulations of the cosmos. This is about the evolution of protoplanetary disk. The second is a description of the creation of VR tools for underground water management Both are composet from the same modules.

2 Virtual Reality Tool

VR tool is compose from 6 modules which be able working separately or together.

- Module for reading outputs data from storage element
- Module for sorting of data and creating the useful 3D models
- Module for clearing the composition of routes – scenes module
- Module for composing the scenes – the main module
- Module for synchronization all components
- Module for creating final VR video file

2.1 Reading Data and Converting to the Uniform Format

Downloading data from a resource, which can be a file (located on a local disk or on a network), database, web page, and so on. After computing process the output data are on storage element and waiting for next process. Data are in different format. As a continued process is to read them and to use them as an input data to the process of test and sort data. We have started with reading the data from storage element and to translate them to the uniform format which we use at the VR tool.

2.2 Sorting Module

Sorting data (Parse): the adaptation of the structure of the data, in order to meet the targets for visualization, data partitioning into categories, converting data types, Module is composed from sorting programs. How are sorted the data depend of architecture of tool and of the scenes which we want to build in the end.

2.3 Scenes Module

Data filtering (Filter), data normalization and knowledge mining (Mine): the use of methods of mathematical statistics and data analysis. Scenes module project the all scenes to the useful final VR. It depend of client. Client specify the scenes require-ments. The developer of VR scenes also specify the standards for VR scenes and revaluate software and hardware decision. Conjunction of the two is final scheme of scenes.

2.4 Composing Module

Module working on background. The appropriate Visual representation for data selection. Our goal is to develop the background as a 3D model of the objective environment in which have been visualize the outputs. The last one composition depend of final scheme of scenes.

2.5   Synchronization All Components

Module for synchronization all components is able to synchronize for example virtual speaking head with synthesis speech and with a text and all is synchronize with the developed scenes. For us tool we use free Unity system. Unity is a distributed computing environment available to NC State faculty, staff, and students. A distributed computing environment provides users with access to an ever-increasing wealth of resources, such as software applications, electronic resources on the Internet, and other hardware and software (such as printing and disk space). The Unity realm uses the client-server model for interaction between workstations. A client is usually the user's machine that sends a request to a program on another machine and awaits a response. The responder is the server. There are several server machines in the Unity realm that take requests from the servers and deliver the requested item(s).

2.6   Final VR Scenes

In the case of the development of a broader project focused on the needs of the users, the process of evaluating comprise more activities. For visualization as the user interface working with information's it is necessary to take account on serviceability and on the amiability of the creativity. We must take attention on:

- Specification of the context of use
- Specification users requirements, depend also on the proposal
- Design of solution
- Evaluation and comparison with project

3   Evaluation of Protoplanetary Disk – VR

As the example the VR tool is visualization in level of VR of the evaluation of Protoplanetary disk. The design is tested on the astronomical simulations in the scope of collaboration between Astronomical Institute of SAS, Catania Observatory and Adam Mickiewicz University in Poznan. Client naturally wants to see the intermediate and final results. The described tool is able to visualize the partial results of the application. The user can completely control the job during execution, and can change the input parameters while execution is still running. There are some reasons for that scientist in different disciplines are using VR representations of datasets.

- For a Visual control of the execution process
- Know-how discovery and for presentations the research academic results
- Formal publication of research results
- As the directly visual education form

The visualization tool is designed as a plug in module. Client asking for visualization is as a "visualization client". Output data on the storage element are the inputs data for visualization jobs. Visualization workers are to modify data to visualize - able formats, but also to prepare the typical visualization scenes. Client can render such scenes on the browser, can make the visual control and modify executions. For example in order to understand immediately the evolution of the investigated protoplanetary disc we have developed (VR) tool. The VR tool is composed of several modules, which are responsible for creating scenes and converting data to visualize - able format. The VR is designed as a plug-in module. The components generating rendering scenes are easy to exchange, according to the requirements of the given application. Our example looks on first main way for that scientist use visual representation. Actually the research community needs not only "traditional" batch computations of huge bunches of data but also the ability to perform complex data processing and this requires capabilities like on-line access to databases, interactivity, fine real-time job control, sophisticated visualization and data management tools (also in real-time), remote control and monitoring. The user can completely control the job during execution and change the input parameters, while the execution is still running. Both tools, the tool for submission designed before and continued sequential VR tool - provided complete solution of the specific main problem how is showed on Fig. 1.

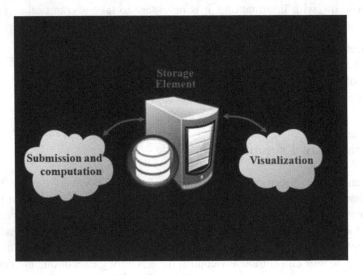

Fig. 1. Example when is visualization using as a control of execution process.

Result of dynamical evolution of Oort cloud as a part of Protoplanetary disk after his evolutionary epoch which was first Gyr (giga year) show Fig. 2.

Evolution of protoplanetary disc in the time of 1 Myr show Fig. 3. We can see that during the 1000 Myr time the particles were replaced from inside to outside of the spheres.

Fig. 2. Picture show the result of dynamical evolution of Oort cloud.

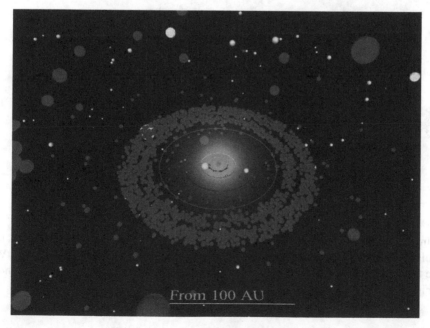

Fig. 3. Picture show the evolution of protoplanetary disc in the time of 1 Myr.

4   VR Tool for Visualization Research Results from Underground Water Management

Environment that provides sufficient information for calculations and simulations in water management required to design a 3D virtual reality terrains of Bratislava and its surroundings and the underground water supply pipes, water towers 3D buildings, which are different high, Orto photomap of Bratislava and surroundings. By using our Virtual reality tool we have developed a digital 3D model - TIN of the Bratislava and surroundings. In such model we have planed the Orto-photomap and for us simulations we have cover the terrain by buildings [6]. All pipes are underground, but advantage is that we are able to see them and watch the all process. We are able to take them over the grand. Examples show (Figs. 4 and 5).

Fig. 4. VR terrain and water pipes.

In this field we already prepared by the ability to view all the results of the simulations. This is a simulation of the water pressure, water flow, water loss, etc. We have tested these scenarios with data calculated every hour during 24 h as we can show on Fig. 6.

Fig. 5. VR terrain with pipes and all components.

Fig. 6. VR tool – research results from water pleasure.

5 Conclusion

This research convincingly shows the extreme potential of virtual reality to create truly impactful experiences with which viewers can engage. The specific features of virtual reality lead to a higher perception of immersion and increases the subjective feeling of being present in a non-physical world. In the future we plan to expand the VR by including in information visualization [7]. We want to make the VR tools which will include all current new trends in visualization, VR and visualization of information. The aim of research in our Institute is to propose a presentation form, which will be suitable for our purposes, research and presentation of the research results.

Acknowledgements. This work is supported by projects VEGA 2/0167/16.

References

1. SANTA BARBARA, Calif.–(BUSINESS WIRE)—WorldViz: WorldViz Introduces VizMove™: The Industry's First Out-of-the-Box Virtual Reality Solution for the Enterprise, 28 April 2015
2. http://www.worldviz.com/vizard-virtual-reality-software/VizardVirtualRealitySoftware
3. http://www.kantarretail.com/virtual-reality/vr-solutions/

4. Czajkowski, K., Fitzgerald, S., Foster, I., Kesselman, C.: Grid information services for distributed resource sharing. In: 10th IEEE International Symposium on High Performance Distributed Computing, pp. 181–184. IEEE Press, New York (2001)
5. Cuckerberk, M.: Foster. https://www.facebook.com/zuck/posts/10101319050523971
6. National Center for Biotechnology Information. http://www.ncbi.nlm.nih.gov
7. Carson, E.: VR in 2016, December, 2015. http://www.techrepublic.com/article/virtual-reality-in-2016-the-10-biggest-trends-to-watch/

Visualization of the Renewable Energy Resources

Ravil Muhamedyev[1,3], Sophia Kiseleva[2], Viktors I. Gopejenko[3(✉)],
Yedilkhan Amirgaliyev[1,4], Elena Muhamedyeva[1], Aleksejs V. Gopejenko[5],
and Farida Abdoldina[6]

[1] Institute of Information and Computational Technologies, Almaty 050010, Kazakhstan
ravil.muhamedyev@gmail.com
[2] Moscow State University, Moscow 119991, Russia
[3] ISMA University, Riga, 1019, Latvia
viktors.gopejenko@isma.lv
[4] Suleyman Demirel University, Kaskelen 040900, Kazakhstan
[5] Institute of Solid Sate Physics, University of Latvia, Riga, 1063, Latvia
[6] Kazakh National Research Technical University, Almaty 050013, Kazakhstan

Abstract. The methods of the renewable energy resources visualization are analysed in this work, the examples of the systems and possible architecture of the renewable energy monitoring systems of the Republic of Kazakhstan are considered. Successful practices are analysed, the leading scientific organization in the field of green energy are considered, a comparative analysis of geographic information systems and data sources in the field of green energy is performed. Possible software architecture of the system based on 3M paradigm of geographic information system (multilayer views, multilayer architecture and multi-agent interaction) is considered.

Keywords: Visualization · Renewable energy sources (RES) · Geographic information system (GIS) · Taxonomy · Information and communication technologies · Scientometrics

1 Introduction

The technologies of the energy production from RES have been actively developed in the recent years and in the long term they are going to significantly reduce the usage of non-renewable resources (such as oil, gas, coal, peat), to improve the ecological indicators of the energy production systems and living areas, reduce the energy production costs, increase the autonomy of the life support systems and the country's energy security. By the year 2050 the share of extracted sources will slightly exceed 40 % of the global energy producing [1].

The problems of the Republic of Kazakhstan are related to the depreciation and wearing of the equipment, dependence on electricity supply from nearby countries and low efficiency of energy usage require the establishment of a monitoring system of energy security of different regions and the country as a whole [2].

At the same time prospects of RES (primarily solar, wind and geothermal plants) are very high. Evaluation of technical and economic efficiency of new technologies

© Springer International Publishing Switzerland 2016
L.T. De Paolis and A. Mongelli (Eds.): AVR 2016, Part I, LNCS 9768, pp. 218–227, 2016.
DOI: 10.1007/978-3-319-40621-3_17

requires special approaches that are yet to be developed for the conditions of the Republic of Kazakhstan.

Modern information and communication technologies provide wide spectrum of approaches to solve the tasks estimation, monitoring and visualization of heterogeneous energy sources and storage systems [3].

Wireless sensor networks, inter-machine communication system (Machine-to-Machine - M2 M), developing a promising direction of the Internet of Things [3, 4] and broadband networks based on new communication protocols will become the technological basis for such systems. Combining disparate technologies within smart grids presents strong interest for researchers both in terms of system architecture, economic indicators [5], security [6, 7] and visualization [8].

These new technologies are characterized by considerable interosculation and intercommunication that is possible to present as semantic network [9]. Participation of Kazakh researchers in the domain of the global research cooperation has a good perspective.

The key element of the presented taxonomy is the visualization domain, which offers a wide range of methods, technologies and software. Visualization of the complex processes is one of the most important ways of aggregating multidimensional and heterogeneous information. Correct visualization and aggregation of the information facilitates the decision-making process. In this case, the construction of the RES monitoring system of the Republic of Kazakhstan is based on the GIS that are complemented by an appropriate functionality, allowing evaluating the possibilities of the new energy technologies application in different areas, the risks, economic costs, environmental impacts, etc. Combining heterogeneous technologies into a single system is of a significant interest to researchers in terms of both hardware and software architecture and impact on the region's economic performance. One of the components in the system is decision support system, which contains the visualization unit. Visualization methods and general architecture of the system are the subject of this paper.

2 Renewable Energy Sources and Their Visualization

Usage of RES is a modern powerful trend in energy development. "Green energy" technologies (i.e. the technologies of gathering energy from the renewable sources) are actively developed and will allow to significantly reduce the usage of non-renewable resources (such as oil, gas, coal, peat, etc.), to improve the ecology around the populated areas, to reduce the cost of obtaining energy in some cases, to increase the autonomy of life support systems and energy security of the country in the future.

At the same time, there is no reasonable alternative to the development of the renewable energy sources and energy efficiency according to the experts as decarbonization of the energy sector will allow to avoid the catastrophic consequences of global warming. In the best case scenario of the development it is planned to reduce the demand for oil (by 30 %), coal and gas with the overall growth of energy supply by 60 %. By the year 2050 the share of use of fossil fuels will slightly exceed 40 % of the total energy.

According to the expert calculations the potential of the renewable energy sources in the Republic of Kazakhstan exceeds one trillion kWh yearly, of which less than 0.1 % are used (as mentioned below). The use of RES is associated with a certain complexity due to the dependence of the systems performance from random natural factors.

RES usage allows improving the national energy system and is an important Successful examples of systems and portals in domain of RES.

Let us note that the idea of renewable energy source monitoring using GIS is not new. Such systems have a social and industrial demand. These systems are developed in Russia, in the United States, and in other countries. The systems include data for resource assessment of RES, technical specifications of installations, economic and social preconditions, and nature preservation aspects. They are divided into local, regional, national, and global.

There are currently no analogues to foreign Renewable Energy GIS in the Republic of Kazakhstan. Unlike Russia, where there are GIS projects on water resources for individual areas, an atlas of solar energy resources and a climatic database, as well as a portal for RES, the information base for the Republic of Kazakhstan is presented poorly. There is a wind atlas [10], however other RES are apparently not represented in the form of web resources.

3 Data Sources

Energy resources monitoring tasks imply collecting data from different sources. Weather stations, autonomous sensors, remote sensing data, surface images from satellites, results of mathematical modelling can serve as the data sources for the parameters of the environment. Besides crowd source data-mining gradually becomes of more importance. SETI@home, Galaxy Zoo, Citizen Weather Observer Program (CWOP) serve as the examples of such projects. E.g. OpenWeatherMap project uses the data from private weather stations in order to improve the accuracy of the weather forecasts as the number of measuring points is more important in predicting than the accuracy of the measurements.

The problem of collecting data for the territory of the Republic of Kazakhstan is quite actual as data itself is not sufficient for full-scale analysis. E.g. in order to assess the energy potential of wind and solar energy it is necessary to get the data about the weather conditions on the territory of the whole country with the best possible resolution in the first place. This data should also contain information about time, the force of wind, illumination and temperature affect the performance of energy plants of the given type directly. In order to assess the parameters, the weather stations are placed on the territory of interest.

However, according to the NASA Global Surface Summary of Day (GSOD) data for the year 2015 the territories of the Republic of Kazakhstan covered by the World Meteorological Organization (WMO) are about 1 km^2 for each 7590 km^2. This cannot even be compared with the coverages in Europe and in the USA and does not allow assessing the weather conditions accurately enough. The presence of a large number of the weather stations should allow improving the weather forecasting models assessing the energy potential more precisely.

Currently, the data provided by numerous subsidiaries of NASA and NOAA are of the highest interest. This data is mostly received from the remote probing of the surface. NCDC (National Climatic Data Center) stands out of these organisations as they offer a possibility to order the data in a certified printed form, so in this case the authenticity is guaranteed.

In addition to the text and numerical information, spatial data may be stored in the form of maps (layers of maps). There is a significant amount of map sources on different subjects. Lately, online map suppliers such as OpenStreetMap (OSM), OpenWeatherMap (OWM) mentioned above, Google Maps etc. are becoming popular.

In order to use the data sources mentioned above their consolidation and subsequent processing depending on the RES domain is required (Fig. 1).

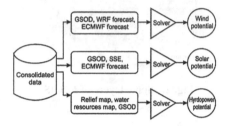

Fig. 1. Data consolidation usage scheme in different domains of green energy

The main problem of the data consolidation is the absence of the unified information exchange standard regarding the parameters of the environment including the climate data. Taking this into account one is forced to work with heterogeneous data sources as well as with the different data formats. Semi-automated data pre-processing, their conversion to the required format and subsequent usage is a typical practice. Even if it is possible to automate the process of the data acquisition (using client web-services, FTP loaders etc.), the process of the data conversion to the universal format requires expenses both for the development of such format and for the resources for the conversion itself. The creation of such system requires the development of:

- The mechanisms of the data input (separate for each type of the source);
- The data update planner (in order to identify outdated data and to launch the whole ETL process for the source);
- The converter for each type of the data sources.

4   System Architecture

To create the architecture for the system that ensures the acquisition and processing of large volumes of heterogeneous data in real time, additional research is required.

Currently, there are yet no standardized methods and systems to provide representation of large heterogeneous data sources, resources, analysis and reporting within the multilayer intelligent GIS (MLGIS) (Fig. 2).

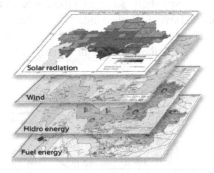

Fig. 2.   Some layers of MIGIS

Such system should provide: the choice of an energy production technology platform; evaluation of the economic feasibility of the new technological schemes for energy production; assessment of the accompanying risks; environmental impacts of the transition to the new energy sources; assessment of the possibilities of transition to the intelligent systems of the redistribution and energy storage, etc. Basic layers of MLGIS are:

- Energy sources
- Maps
- Energy consumers
- Energy transport system
- Energy gathering systems
- Energy storage systems
- Ecological condition, caused harm and dangers
- Economic evaluations
- Data protection

By the principles of its operations the planned system is different because of the spatial distribution, large volume of data, and asynchronous work of its components. For the systems design and implementation, the 3M paradigm is proposed: multilayer views, multilayer architecture, multi-agent interaction.

Multilayer system architecture can be illustrated by Fig. 3.

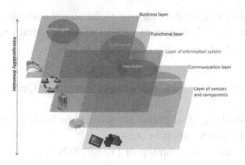

Fig. 3. Multilayer system architecture

It is proposed to develop and implement a prototype system providing a layered view of monitoring data and other graphical data (with different levels of detail and zoom) within this paradigm. Implementation of the system architecture is also contemplated to be multi-layered. This meets the modern approaches in software engineers on the construction of such systems [10]. Asynchronous communication of the system components is presumed to be provided by using the multi-agent approach, which has a number of successful applications, including at the micro level in the monitoring of the wind turbines.

The proposed goal and objectives are not only regional, but also have a general application. When implementing the system, there is a need to find approaches to solve scientific problems that are important in a number of areas of the study in the scientific schools of Europe, Russia and the United States.

These include monitoring resources on a national scale, the development of multi-agent intelligent system architecture, design and/or testing of methods for collecting and processing large amounts of heterogeneous data, the formation of methods to ensure the adaptability of the system to the new communication technologies, providing visualization of large data in the knowledge domain, information security, development of methods of economic analysis of the use of new technologies.

One of the possible prototype described in [11] presents an approach to the creation of the web-based system based on the cloud platform for the integration of the heterogeneous spatial information for the environmental monitoring coal mines. It should be noted that due to a large extent on the territories, point forms of measurements, significant delay of the event registration, and the lack of a unified picture of the environment, the assessment of the environmental status does not provide satisfactory results. It is proposed to use cloud technology in order to deal with the challenges of distributed data processing. The following components are involved in the system: cloud service Google App Engine, authentication service Google Users API, the mapping service Google Map API, database management system PostgreSQL. The data is collected using crowd sourcing methods. Authors are supposed to collect technological data, spatial ecological data, data continuously updated by remote sensing (radar and hyper spectral pictures). Analytical processing can be built using the data from the other sources (such as meta descriptions and cloud services). Computational module is formed as a tree. Computational steps are performed during the "motion" on this tree.

Summing all up we can derive a stack of technologies which can make it possible to build own GIS-based decision support system in RES domain. Current vision of the technologies stack is as follows:

- Map server - Google maps;
- Front-end - Play framework (Java, HTML5, Javascript), JQuery; Javascript mapping libraries;
- Middleware - Akka (Java, distributed asynchronous business logic, actors model), Apache Spark (in-memory data processing;
- Back-end - PostGIS databases (on top of PostgreSQL).

Current technologies stack has been chosen for multiple reasons. Firstly, there are no such systems implemented yet.

Secondly, it is planned to use modern approaches for data collecting including crowd sourcing and web services. Another reason is the requirement for the modularity. In order to provide flexibility and extendibility it is better to break unnecessary dependencies between different layers and modules. So, it is planned to implement the frontend using Play framework. It is a modern web MVC framework, which supports Java and SCADA.

This tool can save the developers a lot of time. Applications written using Play can be easily deployed.

The proposed middleware technologies are suitable for building asynchronous, distributed applications with the ability to scale in the future. The major part of the business logic is planned to be implemented using Akka, which is well suited for building asynchronous applications. This will break the dependency between frontend and backend, and so going to make it possible to parallelize the tasks. During the early stages of the project only Play framework will be used, however later with the growth of the functionality it will be better to implement business logic in middleware.

Data layer (which is situated on both the backend and middleware levels) consists of Apache Spark for fast in-memory data processing, for example, for real-time analysis tasks. Persistence will be implemented basing on the PostgreSQL RDBMS. RDBMS is free and it offers a powerful set of extensions for working with spatial data structures (Post GIS extension). PostgreSQL is also able to connect to different data sources and web services to easily import data from them using foreign data wrappers, i.e. another set of extensions. Google maps can be used in order to display spatial data on the map. It provides rich mapping and visualization functionality, good resolution and well documented Java script API.

On the bottom level we have multiple PostgreSQL databases for data storage, data collecting from different sources, PostGIS database for storing operational spatial data (Fig. 4).

On the upper level the data analysis will be implemented using Spark for the fast in-memory analysis tasks and Akka for the rest of the business logic. Frontend servers will run Play based web application that will be loosely connected with the middleware. Finally, JavaScript-based mapping will reside on the client side.

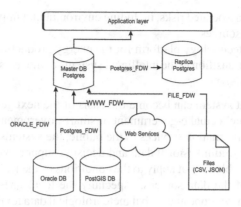

Fig. 4. The realisation of the heterogeneous data sources' connection to PostgreSQL

5 Conclusion

Approaches for the realisation of the RES monitoring system in the Republic of Kazakhstan were considered. The main attention was paid to the visualization data methods and to the architecture of the system. To fulfil this task, the visualization technologies, GIS, information technologies stacks were considered.

Monitoring of the country's resources status allows making the informed decisions in the field of government regulation and the sustainable and safe development of the territory. To develop such system a complex application of some modern concepts and information technologies is required (cloud computing, big and heterogeneous data, machine learning, next generation of communication protocols and other).

Renewable energy resources in the Republic of Kazakhstan are quite high. The accurate assessment of the potential and data aggregation in the easily perceived form facilitates the formation of the solution for their application. Currently, the search for the best methods of the data transformation of the energy systems basing on RES is being performed.

For the decisions on the use of the various mechanisms of the state regulation in the transition to the RES and the use of other useful resources a decision support system at national and regional levels is necessary.

This problem is actual in many countries, which develop the national systems as well as participate in the work of the supranational organizations.

Some successful examples of the monitoring systems are discussed above. These realisations show us several ways to construct the system architecture and to integrate different technologies.

The new system should provide:

- Monitoring of energy sources and delivery systems
- Evaluation of the economic feasibility of the new technological schemes for the energy production

- Assessment of the associated risks, including environmental impacts of the transition to the new energy sources
- The choice of the technology platform for the energy production
- Assessment of the transition to the intelligent systems of the redistribution and energy storage (Smart grids)

Such an intelligent system can become the basis of the next generation of the electronic government (intellectual e-government or smart-government) where, along with the provision of the information services to the public, the systems for the analysis and visualization of the multidimensional data and decision support will appear.

One of the main problems that apply to the conditions of the Republic of Kazakhstan is the low quantity of the data sources, especially the local ones. Nevertheless, it is possible to use the remote probe and global meteorological data for the initial assessment of the resources.

In order to implement the system, it is necessary to solve some important problems related to the detailed system architecture, services, data collection, integration and processing, functionality provided to users, aggregation of the heterogeneous data and the methods of their storage.

Acknowledgment. The work was funded by grant No. 0168/GF4 of the Ministry of Education and Science of the Republic of Kazakhstan and Smart Technology Research Centre of Ventspils University College, Latvia.

References

1. International Energy Agency. Energy Technology Perspectives. Executive Summary, 17 p. (2014). http://www.iea.org/publications/freepublications/publication/name-51003-en.html
2. Mustafina, R.M.: The issue of energy security in Kazakhstan regions. Vestnik PSU **2**, 110–116 (2010)
3. Muhamedyev, R.I., Alihodzhaev, I., Ishmanov, A., Muhamedijeva, J.: Monitoring of renewable energy sources in RK: technological preconditions, architecture of system and market volume. In: Proceedings of 16th International Symposium on Advanced Intelligent Systems, ISIS 2015, pp. 777–791 (2015)
4. Vermesan, O.: Peter Friess Internet of Things: Converging Technologies for Smart Environments and Integrated Ecosystems. River Publishers, Denmark (2013). ISBN 978-87-92982-96-4
5. Ardito, L., Procaccianti, G., Menga, G., Morisio, M.: Smart grid technologies in europe: an overview. Energies **6**, 251–281 (2013). doi:10.3390/en6010251
6. Wang, D., Guan, X., Liu, T., Yun, G., Shen, C., Zhanbo, X.: Extended distributed state estimation: a detection method against tolerable false data injection attacks in smart grids. Energies **7**, 1517–1538 (2014). doi:10.3390/en7031517
7. Alkaras, C., Zidalli, S.: Protecting of critical control systems. Open systems, No. 01, p. 10. (2014). http://www.osp.ru/os/2014/01/13039680/
8. Muhamedyev, R.I., Gladkikh, V., Gopejenko, V.I., Daineko, Y.A., Mansharipova, A.T., Muhamedyeva, E.L., Gopejenko, A.V.: A method of three-dimensional visualization of molecular processes of apoptosis. In: De Paolis, L.T., Mongelli, A. (eds.) AVR 2014. LNCS, vol. 8853, pp. 103–112. Springer, Heidelberg (2014)

9. Muhamedyev, R.I., Kalimoldaev, M.N., Uskenbayeva, R.K.: Semantic network of ICT domains and applications. In: Proceedings of the 2014 Conference on Electronic Governance and Open Society: Challenges in Eurasia, pp. 178–186. ACM, New York, NY, USA (2014). ISBN: 978-1-4503-3401-3. doi:10.1145/2729104.2729112

10. Gridasov, M.V., Kiseleva, S.V., Nefedova, L.V., Popel, O.S., Frid, S.E.: Development of geographic information systems, "renewable energy resources of Russia": statement of the problem and selection of methods. Therm. Eng. **11**, 38–45 (2011)

11. Smarsly, K., Law, K.H., Hartmann, D.: Multiagent-based collaborative framework for a self-managing structural health monitoring system. J. Comput. Civ. Eng. **26**, 76–89 (2012)

Transparency of a Bilateral Tele-Operation Scheme of a Mobile Manipulator Robot

Víctor Hugo Andaluz[1,2(✉)], Washington X. Quevedo[1],
Fernando A. Chicaiza[1], José Varela[2], Cristian Gallardo[2],
Jorge S. Sánchez[1], and Oscar Arteaga[1]

[1] Universidad de las Fuerzas Armadas ESPE, Sangolquí, Ecuador
{vhandaluzl, wjquevedo, fachicaiza, jssanchez,
obarteaga}@espe.edu.ec
[2] Universidad Técnica de Ambato, Ambato, Ecuador
jazjose@hotmail.es, cmgallardop@gmail.com

Abstract. This work presents the design of a bilateral tele-operation system for a mobile manipulator robot, allowing a human operator to perform complex tasks in remote environments. In the tele-operation system it is proposed that the human operator is immersed in an augmented reality environment to have greater transparency of the remote site. The transparency of a tele-operation system indicates a measure of how the human feels the remote system. In the local site an environment of augmented reality developed in Unity3D is implemented, which through input devices recreates the sensations that the human would feel if he were in the remote site, for which is considered the senses of sight, touch and hearing. These senses help the human operator to "transmit" their ability and experience to the robot to perform a task. Finally, experimental results are reported to verify the performance of the proposed system.

Keywords: Transparency · Bilateral tele-operation · Virtual reality · Augmented reality · Mobile manipulator

1 Introduction

Since remote times, man has been seeking tele-operated tools to enable it to increase the scope of its manipulations. At present there are devices that allow to reach and manipulate objects in places that are inaccessible or hazardous environments [1, 2]. The most significant application fields of tele-operation are in experimentation and planetary exploration, maintenance and operation of satellites; in the nuclear industry for the handling radioactive substances; exploration of dangerous environments with unmanned robots [3–9], among others. A tele-operation system consists of the following elements: *(i) The human operator* is the one who performs the operation control remotely. Their action can range from continuous control to an intermittent intervention, which only deals with monitoring and indicate objectives and plans from time to time; *(ii) Interface* is the set of devices that allow operator interaction with the system of tele-operation. The manipulator master is considered as part of the interface, as well

© Springer International Publishing Switzerland 2016
L.T. De Paolis and A. Mongelli (Eds.): AVR 2016, Part I, LNCS 9768, pp. 228–245, 2016.
DOI: 10.1007/978-3-319-40621-3_18

as video monitors, or any other device enabling the human operator to send and receive information to the system; *(iii) Communication channel* is the set of devices that modulate, transmit and adapt the set of signals transmitted between the remote and the local zone; *(iv) Tele-operated device* may be a robot, a vehicle or similar device, *i.e.,* the machine working at the remote site and is being controlled by the operator; and finally, *(v) Sensors* is the set of devices that collect information from both the local area and the remote area to be used by the interface and control.

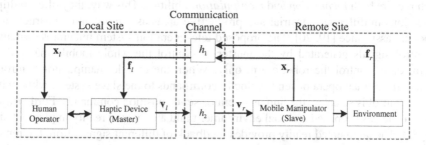

Fig. 1. General block diagram of a bilateral tele-operation system

In Fig. 1 it can be seen a general diagram of a bilateral teleoperation system. The human operator drives a robot through a haptic device generating velocity or position commands to be sent to the remote site, which will be executed by the robot [9]. The robot's state and its environment are visually back-fed to the human operator and a force is also back-fed to the human operator through the haptic device. The forces can be real or fictitious and are generated by the robot contact or non-contact interaction with the environment. The evolution of robotics and advancement of computers have helped increase the capabilities of tele-operated systems, especially as regards transparency in the local site, thus improving the performance of the human-machine interface [10–12].

Among recent works, presents a feasibility study of a time domain passivity approach for bilateral tele-operation of robots [13]. The Tele-operation in the beginning do not consider the feedback, currently applying tele-operated systems need greater sensitivity so the feedback becomes a very important element in the teleoperation especially when there are haptic devices [14, 15], for which the concept of transparency is introduced, so that the operator is able to perceive the forces occurring on the remote during teleoperation robot. In this sense, we often speak of tele-operated system with force reflection, as it is intended that the forces acting on it appear somehow reflected on the controller so that the operator is able to feel and take corrective action if appropriate. So, the infinite transparency would be a feature of a teleoperation system was able to make the operator feel exactly the same forces that feel if manipulate directly the environment [16]. There are different types of haptic interfaces, depending on the type of information that the operator is sent: visual, tactile numeric, among others [17]. These interfaces can be anything from a simple joystick to the most sophisticated virtual reality device. The use of haptic tools is increasing in industrial applications [18].

In this context, this article proposes a bilateral tele-operation scheme in which considers the human operator is immersed in an augmented reality environment to increase the transparency of the remote site. The remote site is the workplace where a mobile manipulator robot performs a task. Mobile manipulator robot is nowadays a widespread term that refers to robots built by a robotic arm mounted on a mobile platform. This kind of system, which is usually characterized by a high degree of redundancy, combines the manipulability of a fixed-base manipulator with the mobility of a wheeled platform. Such systems allow the most usual missions of robotic systems which require both *locomotion* and *manipulation* abilities. This way, they offer multiple applications in different industrial and productive areas as mining and construction or for people assistance [19, 20]. The proposed tele-operation system integrates switching of control signals generated by the master to control the whole mobile manipulator system, or to control the robotic arm only. When the mobile manipulator control is selected, the human operator sends velocity commands to the slave system; while when the arm control is selected, the human operator sends position commands. Furthermore, the local site has proposed a virtual environment and augmented reality implemented in Unity3D. The augmented reality provides feedback of different signals from the remote site in real time, so that through different haptic devices stimulate the senses of sight, touch and hearing of the human operator so that it can "transmit" their skill, experience and expertise to the robot to perform a task. To validate the proposed tele-operation system, experimental results are included and discussed.

This paper is divided into 5 Sections including the Introduction. In Sect. 2 the modeling of the mobile manipulator robot and the bilateral tele-operation scheme are formulated. The design of the local site of the human operator is presents in Sect. 3; while the experimental results are presented and discussed in Sect. 4. Finally, the conclusions are given in Sect. 5.

2   Modeling and Control Scheme

This section presents the kinematic modeling of the mobile manipulator robot. In addition, it shows the proposed scheme to solve the bilateral Tele-operation of a mobile manipulator for task that require both locomotion and manipulation abilities.

The kinematic model of a mobile manipulator gives the derivative of its end-effector location as a function of the derivatives of both the robotic arm configuration and the location of the mobile platform,

$$\dot{\mathbf{h}}(t) = \mathbf{J}(\mathbf{q})\mathbf{v}(t) \tag{1}$$

where, $\mathbf{J}(\mathbf{q})$ is the Jacobian matrix that defines a linear mapping between the vector of the mobile manipulator velocities $\mathbf{v}(t)$ and the vector of the end-effector velocity $\dot{\mathbf{h}}(t)$. The Jacobian matrix is, in general, a function of the configuration $\mathbf{q}$; those configurations at which $\mathbf{J}(\mathbf{q})$ is rank-deficient are termed *singular kinematic configurations*. It is fundamental to notice that, in general, the dimension of operational space m is less than the degree of mobility of the mobile manipulator. In this case we recall that the problem, mobile manipulator and task, is redundant [21].

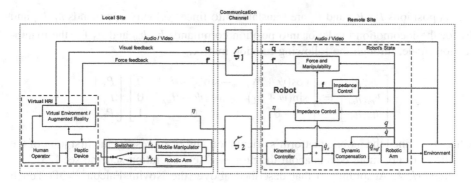

Fig. 2. Block diagram of the bilateral tele-operation system

In other hand, the proposed bilateral tele-operation system is shown in Fig. 2. In this system both the force back-fed to the human operator are considered.

A given mission is generally composed of several operation processes, and these commonly include three stages: approaching, manipulating and returning process. When the mission starts, the human operator should move the slave system closed to the target object within the r each of its robotic arm. This is the first stage: approaching. After the mobile base reaches the vicinity of the target object, the human operator changes the mode from locomotion to manipulation mode. When the manipulation mission is completed, the human operator changes again the mode from manipulation to locomotion and the slave would go back to a safe area (view Fig. 2).

When the | is selected, the human operator controls the mobile manipulator by sending velocity commands to the end-effector of the robot: h_l, h_m, and h_n, one for each axis, using a haptic device $\mathbf{\dot{h}_d} = \begin{bmatrix} \dot{h}_l & \dot{h}_m & \dot{h}_n \end{bmatrix}^T$; whereas, when the *manipulation* mode is selected, the human operator controls only the robotic arm by sending position commands to the end-effector: h_l, h_m, and h_n, one for each axis, using the same haptic device that in locomotion mode $\mathbf{h_d} = \begin{bmatrix} h_l & h_m & h_n \end{bmatrix}^T$.

The human operator commands are generated with the use of a Falcon™ haptic device from Novint Technologies Incorporated [22] as indicated in Fig. 3.

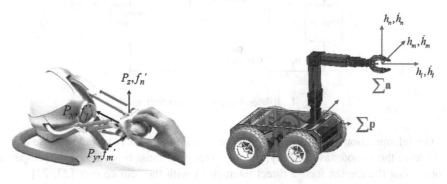

Fig. 3. Falcon ™ from Novint Technologies Incorporated

Its positions P_x, P_y, and P_z are translated into linear velocity commands $\dot{h}_l$, $\dot{h}_m$ and $\dot{h}_n$ for the locomotion mode; or into position commands h_l, h_m and h_n for the manipulation mode, through the following rotation matrix,

$$
\begin{bmatrix} h_l, \dot{h}_l \\ h_m, \dot{h}_m \\ h_n, \dot{h}_n \end{bmatrix} = \begin{bmatrix} \cos(\psi + \theta_1) & -\sin(\psi + \theta_1) & 0 \\ \sin(\psi + \theta_1) & \cos(\psi + \theta_1) & 0 \\ 0 & 0 & 1 \end{bmatrix} \begin{bmatrix} P_x \\ P_y \\ P_z \end{bmatrix}
$$

where ψ defined the mobile platform's orientation and θ_1 represents the first joint of the robotic arm. For more details about the proposed tele-operation scheme see [23].

Remark 1. According to that described above, the Novint Falcon™ 3D Touch Workspace allow the control of two ways of operation mode of robot for: *(a) locomotion mode,* the workspace of Novint Falcon™ is linearly related with the minimum and maximum velocities in the axis l, m, n of the reference system l, m, n Σa; while that *(b) manipulation mode* the workspace of Novint Falcon™ is linearly proportional to the workspace of the robotic arm, therefore the workspace of the arm depends of the length of the joints.

3   Transparency's Local Site

The transparency of a teleoperation system indicates a measure of how the human *feels* the remote system. In addition, the transparency gives an idea of how much the human controls the remote system; since the inclusion of delays, and control schemes makes that the human *takes smaller part* compared with a non-delayed direct teleoperation. In this section, we propose a definition of transparency in time and how it can be measured [24]. The transparency of a system define an equivalent system attached to the human such that it interacts with the human in the same way as the remote system. Figure 4 shows how the equivalent system is placed together with the human.

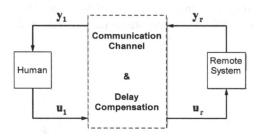

Fig. 4. Bilateral tele-operation system

The teleoperation systems search that the human operator is linked as close as it is possible to the remote task. Ideally, the tele-operation must be completely transparent in order that the human feels a direct interaction with the remote task [23, 24].

In order that the human operator have more transparency of the remote site, this work shows a Human Robot Interaction in 3D (HRI-3D) implemented on local site (view Fig. 1). For HRI-3D is considered 3D augmented reality through a graphical interface developed in Unity. The augmented reality 3D shows to the human operator the remote environment in which the robot is developing the task and the internal configuration of the robot, also it allows listening the environment's audio and feel through Falcon^{TM} haptic device the fictitious force feedback produced by the inter-action of the robot with the working environment (Fig. 5).

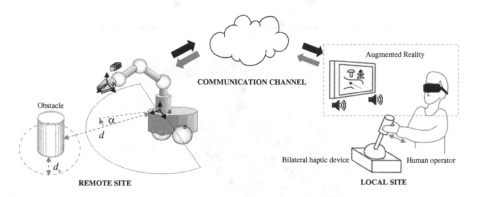

Fig. 5. Flow diagram of the system's transparency

3.1 Assembly Robot

The first step is to assemble a mobile manipulator robot that has the ability of loco-motion and manipulation, it should be formed of a unicycle type mobile platform and a robotic arm 6 DOF. The robot can be designed in any CAD (computer aided design) software for mechanical 3D modeling, *i.e.*, SolidWorks, Autodesk Inventor, etc. (Fig. 6)

3.2 Virtual Environment

The local site consists of a virtual reality and augmented to allow the human operator to have greater transparency in the remote site reality, as illustrated by the Fig. 7.

The Fig. 7 can be described in two stages, the first stage is *(A) Inputs,* These let read all the variables considered in the bilateral tele-operation of both the robot and the environment in which develops the task, entries that are processed in the script are: *(i) Output states of the robot,* represents the variables that describe the robot kinematics $\mathbf{q} = [q_1 \quad q_2 \quad \cdots \quad q_n]^T = [\mathbf{q}_a^T \quad \mathbf{q}_p^T]^T$. In the script, the data acquired from the platform $\mathbf{q}_p$ are assigned to the *Position* and *Rotation* features of the Game Object corresponding to the mobile robot manipulator simulated in the virtual scene; while the data arm rotation $\mathbf{q}_a$ are assigned to the characteristic of *Rotation* for each joint of the simulated arm Game Object.

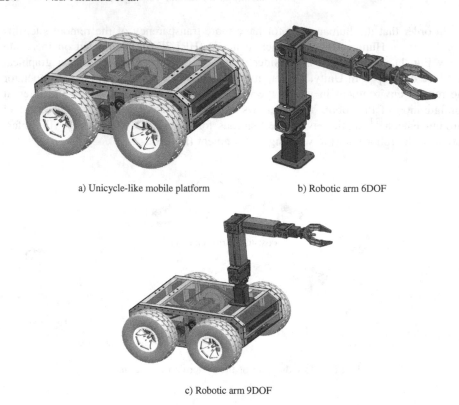

a) Unicycle-like mobile platform   b) Robotic arm 6DOF

c) Robotic arm 9DOF

Fig. 6. Mobile manipulator, assembly on SolidWorks

Remark 2. The kinematics of the robot represents the position-orientation of the mobile platform and orientation of each joint of the robotic arm.

(ii) Velocity or desired positions through the Falcon^{TM} haptic device emit the desired location $\mathbf{h_d} = \begin{bmatrix} h_l & h_m & h_n \end{bmatrix}^T$ for locomotion mode or desired velocity $\dot{\mathbf{h}}_\mathbf{d} = \begin{bmatrix} \dot{h}_l & \dot{h}_m & \dot{h}_n \end{bmatrix}^T$ for manipulation mode. The operational coordinates of the mobile manipulator define the position or velocity of the end-effector in R - environment in which it develops the task. The script obtains the variation of position in world coordinates by a Game Object that simulates the movement of the end-effector of Falcon^{TM} haptic device in space, as shown in Fig. 8.

Figure 9 shows the use of the Falcon^{TM} Game Object in Script "Control 2" linked to the 3D model of mobile robot manipulator.

Then part of the script of "Control 2" is shown where the change in position or speed Falcon^{TM} on the axes l, m, n of the reference system Σa allows controlling the movement of the mobile manipulator or only the robotic arm, depending on the mode selected by the human operator.

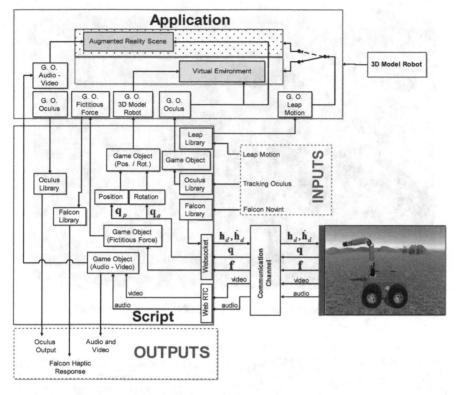

Fig. 7. Block diagram of the virtual environment

```
using UnityEngine;
...
public class Control2 : MonoBehaviour {
public GameObject GodFalcon;
...
void Update(){
...
fx = GodFalcon.transform.position.x;
fy = GodFalcon.transform.position.y;
fz = GodFalcon.transform.position.z;
... }}
```

(iii) Video and audio transmits the image and audio captured by the camera located at the end-effector of the robot. The image allows knowledge of the environment in which the task is performed, while the audio provides the sound of the medium and the sound generated by the robot motors; the audio information allows for greater transparency of the remote site because the human operator can know whether the robot is moving at high speeds based on the sound of the engines or can determine if the robot is entering a singularity configuration.; *(iv) Fictitious force* is produced by a sensor that

Fig. 8. Game Object: Simulates the FALCON™ position or velocity.

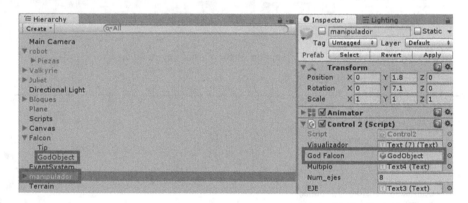

Fig. 9. Game Object: FALCON™ linked to the 3D model of mobile robot manipulator.

maps the area in which the robot can be moved freely. The fictitious force is denoted by $\mathbf{f} = \begin{bmatrix} f_l & f_m & f_n \end{bmatrix}^T$, review the previous section, *i.e.*, the robot will not collide with any fixed or mobile obstacle; *(v) Oculus Positional Tracking* modifies the position and rotation of the camera in the virtual and/or augmented environment, corresponding to the movement performed by the human operator when using the Head-mounted Display, HMD, in order to have a greater immersion in the experience of using the application; y finally *(vi) Leap Motion* allows a virtual model of the operator's hands in order to interact with the virtual environment and the user interface.

Remark 3. The Leap Motion device improves the usability of the user interface; while the joint use of Falcon™, Oculus Rift HMD and the Leap Motion device; allows the human operator to have greater transparency in the remote site and a more immersive experience in the virtual environment.

Furthermore, the second stage of Fig. 7 is *(B) Outputs Script* that recreates the sensations that the human operator should feel if he were at the remote site, this paper considers three ways that help the human operator to "transmit" their ability and experience to the robot to perform a task: *(i) Sense of vision,* to stimulate this sense is used the HMD Oculus Rift, to visualize an environment in virtual reality and augmented reality. The selection of these scenarios is performed through a user interface using the Leap motion; *(ii) Sense of touch,* this sense is created through the Falcon™ device, it generates a force in the three axes according to the existing fictitious forces at the remote site between robot - workspace. This force allows the human operator feel obstacles that cannot be displayed with the image transmitted by the camera placed at the remote site, the obstacles are simulated in the virtual environment, while in the augmented reality, the human operator can observe the actual object that produces the fictitious force detected by the sensor on the mobile platform; and *(iii) Sense of hearing,* to excite this sense in the augmented reality environment, the actual sound of the remote site is reproduced; while in the virtual reality, the fusion sound of the robot's engines is simulated and varies according to each engine rotating speed of the mobile platform and the robotic arm.

Remark 4. The data packets corresponding to the kinematics of mobile manipulator $\mathbf{q}(t)$, the fictional force between the robot - workspace $\mathbf{f}(t)$, and the position or velocity of the end-effector of the robot $\mathbf{h_d}(t)$, $\dot{\mathbf{h}}_\mathbf{d}(t)$ generated by the Falcon™ are transmitted through the WebSocket communication protocol, once the structure is standardized in JSON format.

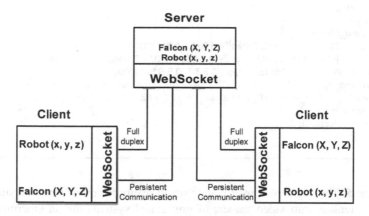

Fig. 10. Block diagram of the local site

Figure 10 illustrates the server-client communication via the WebSocket communication protocol, in this work it is considered like clients the Unity Script and Mobile

Platform. It is noted that the WebSocket protocol allows full duplex connection between the server and the client, occurs in real time and remains permanently open until closed explicitly, *i.e.*, when the client sends data to the server, the message is moved immediately, without the need to constantly initialize communication.

```
using WebSocketSharp;
...
public class Control2: MonoBehaviour {
public static int band_hilo;
public static int band_hilo2;
private Thread thread;
public static string mensaje;
static string botonstate;
public static JsonData itemData;
private static string jsonString;
public Text Visualizador;
void Start(){
    ...
    band_hilo2 = 1;
    jsonString = "{\"mot1\":\"0\",\"mot2\":\"0\",\"mot3\":\"0\"}";
    Thread.Sleep(20);
    thread = new Thread(new ThreadStart(socketInit));
    thread.Start();
}
void OnApplicationQuit(){
    band_hilo2 = 0;
    thread.Abort();
}
public static void socketInit(){
using (var ws = new WebSocket("ws://192.168.1.119:9300")){
ws.OnMessage += (sender, e) =>
jsonString = e.Data;
ws.Connect();
ws.Send("{\"cliente\":\"controlador\"}");
while (band_hilo2 == 1) {
    double PX= Convert.ToInt32(map(fx,-3,3,-0.5,0.5)*1000);
    double PY = Convert.ToInt32(map(fy,-3.2,3.2,-0.5,0.5) *1000);
    double PZ = Convert.ToInt32(map(fz,-1.8,3.1,-0.5,0.5) *1000);
    ws.Send("{\"origen\": \"controlador\", \"destino\": \"plataforma\", \"valor_x\": \""
    +PX+"\", \"valor_y\": \"" +PY + "\", \"valor_z\": \"" + PZ + "\",\"band\": \"" + botonstate + "\"}");
    band_hilo = 1;
    Thread.Sleep(50);
      ...}}
}
```

Remark 5. The augmented reality and virtual reality for robot's motion simulation and their extension into video games, of unmanned systems are an emerging topic. There are at least three motivations for robot simulators. One is the role of simulators in adoption of new technology, another is their potential for low cost training, and finally their utility in research. The range of robot computer simulations is economically and technically diverse.

4 Simulation Experimental Results

The feasibility of the proposed structure of bilateral tele-operation has been tested through real experiments using a mobile manipulator composed by a mobile platform and a robotic arm 6 DOFs. The robot is also equipped with a HD PRO WEBCAM C920 Video Sensor. The locate station consist in a desktop computer Core I7 3610QM running at 2.3 GHz, 8 GB RAM and a NVIDIA GeForce GT 630 M 1 GB dedicated graphics card; also the local site has a haptic device Novint Falcon™, Oculus Rift HMD and a LeapMotion device. Communication between the robot and the remote station is performed through of INTRANET using WebSocket protocol. According to [25] the Virtual Reality PC-Ready can run apps at least 60 fps. The configuration described above can run the app at 10/15 fps. The refresh rate of the HMD is 60/75 Hz independly of fps and the refresh rate of Novint Falcon is 1 kHz. The actual configuration setup is depicted in Fig. 11.

(a) Remote Site

(b) Local Site

Fig. 11. Experimental setup

The developed software consists of two different interfaces. The first interface displays a virtual scenario while the second is an augmented reality; each interface is based on actual experimental data.

4.1 Virtual Reality 3D

The 3D Virtual Reality scene shows the movement of the mobile robot manipulator based on experimental data transmitted from the remote site. The Virtual environment consists mainly in the lower right illustrated the online video captured by the camera located at the end-effector of the robotic arm, while in the upper right there is a menu that is controlled through the Leap Motion device with the hand movements of the human operator, view Fig. 12.

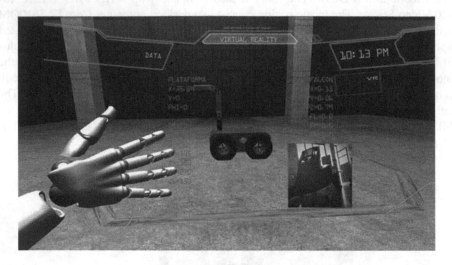

Fig. 12. Virtual Environment

Menu virtual environment controls the various camera angles of the virtual scene, displays the communication variables and Falcon^{TM} data input; also it allowed to pass Augmented Reality interface. Figure 13 shows snapshots of the experiment detailed in previous paragraphs, where different scenes are observed based on the modification of the different menu parameters.

Remark 6. Virtual reality allows the human operator to have a vision of the whole scenario where the experimental test is performed, but is useful as long as the environment of the remote site where it is to perform the task is known.

4.2   Augmented Reality

The Augmented Reality interface consists of a visual feedback where the video is captured by the camera located at the end-effector of the robot and transmitted in real time to the local site. The video provides information of the robot interaction with the environment Fig. 14(a) but does not show the internal configuration of the robot, *i.e.*, it is not known the position of each joint of the robot arm Fig. 14(b). This is a critical problem in robots that are made up of several chain links, - redundant robots - because they can enter a singularity configuration, which would cause an unstable control algorithm.

To prevent the mobile manipulator entering in a singularity configuration, a virtual model 3D of the mobile manipulator that simulates the internal configuration of the real

(a) Locomotion Mode: Find target

(b) Locomotion mode: Advance to target

(c) Manipulation mode: Open grippe

(d) Manipulation mode: Close gripper

(e) Locomotion mode: Transport of the target

(f) Locomotion mode: Return to point of origi

Fig. 13. Snapshots of the experiment on virtual environment

(a) Video image feedback

(b) Robot Internal configuration

Fig. 14. Visual feedback of the remote site

(a) Locomotion Mode: Find target   (b) Locomotion mode: Advance to target

(c) Manipulation mode: Open gripper   (d) Manipulation mode: Close gripper

(e) Locomotion mode: Transport of the target   (f) Locomotion mode: Return to point of origin

Fig. 15. Visual feedback of the remote site.

robot is plotted on the bottom right. The model simulates the movement based on the actual data transmitted from the local site. Additionally, the augmented reality allows the user to set the desired posture of the robotic arm and displays actual velocities of the robot and reference velocities sent by the user (Fig. 15).

Figure 16 shows a comparison between the reference generated by the human operator and the actual velocities of the end-effector.

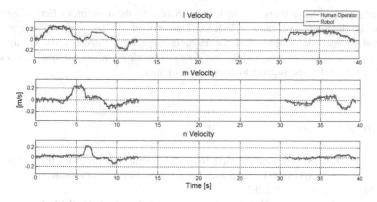

(a) Commands of velocity of the end-effector

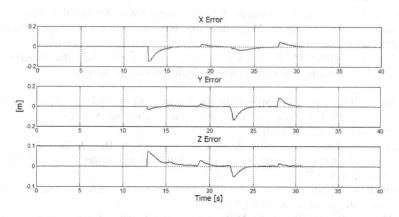

(b) Error position of the end-effector

Fig. 16. (a) Comparison between the reference generated by the human operator and the actual velocities and positions of the end-effector; while (b) depicts the time evolution of the control error of the robotic arm in manipulation mode

5 Conclusions

To increase the transparency of the proposed tele-operation system, two human-robot interface 3D were implemented, an interface shown a virtual environment while the second is an augmented reality; each interface is based on real experimental data. Experimental results were also presented showing the feasibility and the good performance of the proposed tele-operation structure. In this system is considers that human operator has greater transparency of the remote site. This system allows a human operator to perform complex tasks in a remote environment with a mobile manipulator robot. The teleoperation system integrates switching of control signals generated by the master to control the whole mobile manipulator system, or to control the robotic arm only.

Acknowledgment. The authors would like to thanks to the Consorcio Ecuatoriano para el Desarrollo de Internet Avanzado -CEDIA-, Universidad de las Fuerzas Armadas ESPE, Universidad Técnica de Ambato and the Escuela Superior Politécnica del Chimborazo for financing the project *Tele-operación bilateral cooperativo de múltiples manipuladores móviles – CEPRAIX-2015-05*, for the support to develop this paper.

References

1. Lawrence, D.A.: Stability and transparency in bilateral teleoperation. IEEE Trans. Robot. Autom. **9**(5), 624–637 (1993). 2015 24th IEEE International Symposium on Communication (RO-MAN), pp. 431–437. IEEE

2. Carlson, J., Murphy, R.R.: How UGVs physically fail in the field. IEEE Trans. Rob. **21**(3), 423–437 (2005)

3. Brunet, P., Vinacua, A.: Sistemas Gráficos Interactivos. Universidad Politécnica de Cataluña. Barcelona, España, Mayo de 2006. http://www.lsi.upc.edu/~pere/SGI/guions/ArquitecturaRV.pdf

4. Desbats, P., Geffard, F., Piolain, G., Coudray, A.: Force-feedback teleoperation of an industrial robot in a nuclear spent fuel reprocessing plant. Ind. Robot Int. J. **33**(3), 178–186 (2006)

5. Mukherjee, J.K.: Fast visualisation technique for view constrained tele-operation in nuclear industry. In: 2014 International Conference on Information Science and Applications (ICISA), pp. 1–4. IEEE (2014)

6. Sanchez, J.G., Patrao, B., Almeida, L., Perez, J., Menezes, P., Dias, J., Sanz, P.: Design and evaluation of a natural interface for remote operation of underwater robots. IEEE Comput. Graphics Appl. **1**, 1 (2015)

7. Christ, R.D., Wernli Sr., R.L.: The ROV manual: a user guide for remotely operated vehicles. Butterworth-Heinemann (2013)

8. Al Mashagbeh, M., Khamesee, M.B.: Unilateral teleoperated master-slave system for medical applications. IFAC-PapersOnLine **48**(3), 784–787 (2015)

9. Livatino, S., De Paolis, L.T., D'Agostino, M., Zocco, A., Agrimi, A., De Santis, A., Lapresa, M.: Stereoscopic visualization and 3-D technologies in medical endoscopic teleoperation. IEEE Trans. Ind. Electronics **62**(1), 525–535 (2015)

10. Andaluz, V.H., Salinas, L., Roberti, F., Toibero, J.M., Carelli, R.: Switching control signal for bilateral tele-operation of a mobile manipulator. In: 2011 9th IEEE International Conference on Control and Automation (ICCA), pp. 778–783. IEEE (2011)

11. Freund, E., Rossmann, J.: Proyetive virtual reality: Bringing the gap between virtual reality and robotic. IEEE Trans. Robot. Autom. **15**(3), 411–422 (1999)

12. Najmaei, N., Asadian, A., Kermani, M., Patel, R.: Design and Performance Evaluation of a Prototype MRF-based Haptic Interface for Medical Applications (2015)

13. Farkhatdinov, I., Ryu, J.H.: Switching of control signals in teleoperation systems: Formalization and application. In: IEEE/ASME International Conference on Advanced Intelligent Mechatronics, 2008, AIM 2008, pp. 353–358. IEEE (2008)

14. Pacchierotti, C., Tirmizi, A., Prattichizzo, D.: Improving transparency in teleoperation by means of cutaneous tactile force feedback. ACM Trans. Appl. Percept. (TAP) **11**(1), 4 (2014)

15. Song, G., Guo, S., Wang, Q.: A Tele-operation system based on haptic feedback. In: 2006 IEEE International Conference on Information Acquisition, pp. 1127–1131. IEEE (2006)

16. Willaert, B., Reynaerts, D., Van Brussel, H., Vander Poorten, E.B.: Bilateral teleoperation: quantifying the requirements for and restrictions of ideal transparency. IEEE Trans. Control Syst. Technol. **22**(1), 387–395 (2014)
17. Tanzini, M., Tripicchio, P., Ruffaldi, E., Galgani, G., Lutzemberger, G., Avizzano, C.A.: A novel human-machine interface for working machines operation. In: 2013 IEEE RO-MAN, pp. 744–750. IEEE (2013)
18. Okamura, A.M.: Methods for haptic feedback in teleoperated robot-assisted surgery. Ind. Robot Int. J. **31**(6), 499–508 (2004)
19. Khatib, O.: Mobile manipulation: The robotic assistant. Robot. Auton. Syst. **26**(2/3), 175–183 (1999)
20. Das, Y., Russell, K., Kircanski, N., Goldenberg, A.: An articulated robotic scanner for mine detection-a novel approach to vehicle mounted systems. In: Proceedings of the SPIE Conference, USA, pp. 5–9 (1999)
21. Andaluz, V., Roberti, F., Toibero, J., Carelli, R.: Adaptive unified motion control of mobile manipulators. Control Eng. Pract. **20**(12), 1337–1352 (2012)
22. Martin, S., Hillier, N.: Characterization of the novint falcon haptic device for application as a robot manipulator. In: Australasian Conference on Robotics and Automation (2009)
23. Andaluz, V., Salinas, L., Roberti, F., Toibero, J., Carelli, R.: Switching control signal for bilateral tele-operation of a mobile manipulator. In: 2011 9th IEEE International Conference on Control and Automation (ICCA), Santiago, Chile, pp. 778–783, 19–21 December 2011
24. Slawiñski, E., Mut, V.: Transparency in time for teleoperation systems. In: 2008 IEEE International Conference on Robotics and Automation, Pasadena, CA, USA, pp. 200–205, 19–23 May 2008
25. Oculus Ready PCs: Full Rift Experience System Recommendations, Abril de 2016. https://www.oculus.com/en-us/oculus-ready-pcs

Unity3D-MatLab Simulator in Real Time for Robotics Applications

Víctor Hugo Andaluz[1,2($\boxtimes$)], Fernando A. Chicaiza[1],
Cristian Gallardo[2], Washington X. Quevedo[1], José Varela[2],
Jorge S. Sánchez[1], and Oscar Arteaga[1]

[1] Universidad de las Fuerzas Armadas ESPE, Sangolquí, Ecuador
{vhandaluz1,fachicaiza,wxquevedo,jssanchez,
obarteaga}@espe.edu.ec
[2] Universidad Técnica de Ambato, Ambato, Ecuador
cmgallardop@gmail.com, jazjose@hotmail.es

Abstract. This paper presents the implementation of a new 3D simulator applied to the area of robotics. The simulator allows to analyze the performance of different schemes of autonomous and/or tele-operated control in structured environments, partially structured and unstructured. For robot-environment interaction is considered virtual reality software Unity3D, this software exchanges information with MATLAB to execute different control algorithms proposed through the use of shared memory. The exchange of information in real time between the two software is essential because the advanced control algorithms require a feedback from the robot-environment interaction to close the control loop, while the simulated robot updates its kinematic and dynamic parameters depending on controllability variables calculated by MATLAB. Finally, the 3D simulator is evaluated by implementing an autonomous control scheme to solve the problem of path following of a 6DOF robot arm, also the results obtained by implementing the tele-operation scheme for said robot are presented.

Keywords: Simulator 3D · Virtual reality simulator · Path following · Unity3d-MATLAB · Shared memory

1 Introduction

In recent years, robotics research has experienced a significant change. Research interests are moving from the development of robots for structured industrial environments to the development of autonomous mobile robots operating in unstructured and natural environments [1–5]. The robotic generally is classified according to their field of application, industrial robotics and service robotics [6–8]. In industrial and service applications it is necessary to avoid mistakes, they can cause economic and human losses; in this context it is necessary to have an environment in which to experience the performance of robots before they pass to perform any task in a real environment, for which it is considered a virtual simulation environment.

© Springer International Publishing Switzerland 2016
L.T. De Paolis and A. Mongelli (Eds.): AVR 2016, Part I, LNCS 9768, pp. 246–263, 2016.
DOI: 10.1007/978-3-319-40621-3_19

A virtual environment is an environment in which simulations activities found in everyday life are made, this is done with the purpose of bringing these activities to a controlled environment and analyze more deeply the stability and robustness of the systems designed, permitting in this virtual environment test, you may experience various system disturbances, and thus obtain a complete study of the operation of the system.

The advancement of technology has developed computers that let you simulations increasingly real and complex in different areas. A virtual environment would be divided into: *(i) interactive environment* it means that the user is "free" to navigate the virtual environment without having programmed the trajectory that you want to move, the system responds according to the user's wishes, this represents that the user can make decisions in "real time" in order to observe the scene from the selected viewpoint [9, 10]; *(ii) implicit interaction* this refers to the user must not learn commands or a procedure to perform some action in the virtual world, by contrast, the user performs movements that are natural to those used in the real world to move. It then searches the computer suits human nature and not the other, thereby ensuring that the experience in the virtual environment is as near as possible to the experience in the real world [9, 10]; and *(iii) sensory immersion* refers to disconnect sense the real world and the connection thereof to the virtual world [10].

The virtual environment was initially developed for application in computer games and consoles, recently the virtual environments are used to simulate different applications in the area of robotics. There are several commercial programs for the design and simulation of robots in virtual environments, between to simulate the behavior of any robot model are: Robcad, Robotstudio, Igrip, Workcell, Gazebo [11], etc.; specific for a robot in particular, *e.g.* V_CAT, V_TRAISIG y V_ISUAL of Staubli, not all programs are compatible with other CAD systems, do not support libraries all robots or other elements if any, and some are not sold under Windows, in this context, a software that is compatible with most CAD systems is sought, Unity3D for which the platform is analyzed.

Unity3D is a graphics engine developed by Unity Technologies in order to allow everyone to create attractive 3D environments, its creation was aimed at creating games. Unity3D possible to develop software for a wide range of platforms [12–14], so it is extremely attractive for a wide range of developers. For the simulation of a system is considered: *(i) 3D design*, this is done with special or general CAD programs; at this stage in addition to the three-dimensional drawing of the installation (environment modeling) the kinematic and dynamic characteristics of robots and other mobile elements of the system are defined; *(ii) trajectories following*, movements, velocities and sequences are determined; and *(iii) simulation of all movements,* the possibilities at this stage of the installation are checked, errors are corrected, the interference is detected and design are optimized.

As mentioned above, this paper presents a new 3D virtual reality simulator for robotic applications. The proposed simulator allows real-time communication between Unity3D and MATLAB software. For bilateral communication it proposes to use shared memory between these two software; the method of shared memory is a technique easy to apply, with short delays and low use of computer resources by not calling functions third. In addition, the simulator allows to evaluate real-time performance of different schemes of autonomous control and/or tele-operated in structured, partially structured environments, and unstructured; for tele-operation scheme 3D simulator accepts as input haptics devices that stimulate the senses of the human operator so that it can "transmit" their skill, experience and expertise to the robot to perform a task. Finally, to evaluate the performance of autonomous control simulator for monitoring roads proposed for a 6DOF robotic arm -system redundant-, as secondary objective is considered the maximum arm manipulability; also, the experimental test of a scheme bilateral tele-operation is performed.

This paper is divided into 6 Sections including the Introduction. In Sect. 2 the control problem is formulated. Next in Sect. 3 the modeling of the mobile manipulator robot and the controllers design for path following are presents. While the bilateral communication between MATLAB-Unity3D is present in Sect. 4. In Sect. 5 the experimental results for of autonomous control and tele-operated for a robotic arm are presented and discussed. Finally, the conclusions are given in Sect. 6.

2   Problem Formulation

The application development in the area of robotics requires accurately define the task to be performed to determine the needed characteristics of the robot. Determined these parameters, the execution of a task can be subdivided into the following steps: *(i) Modeling stage,* at this stage, it is essential to model the three-dimensional robot in a Computer Aided Design (CAD) software. The modeling lets to analyze the physical characteristics of the robot prior to the construction, in this context, there are tools such as SolidWorks, Autodesk Inventor, AutoCAD, among others, that allow to design mechanical elements and get results of mobility and strength of materials, among other mechanical characteristics, view Fig. 1;

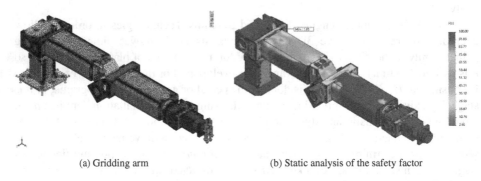

(a) Gridding arm   (b) Static analysis of the safety factor

Fig. 1. Ejemplo de un brazo robótico modelado en SolidWorks (Color figure online)

(ii) Construction stage, The main objective of this phase is to assemble each of the mechanical parts designed and incorporate the necessary electronics to move each joint, In addition to considering the signal conditioning for sensory perception of the external environment in which the robot will move, and internal sensors that must issue the

position, velocity, torque and strength of each link forming the robot. The information provided by the proprioceptive sensors and exteroceptive sensors will be used in the different advanced control algorithms proposed; *(iii) Controllers design stage,* to the design of advanced control algorithms it is essential to determine the mathematical model representing the robot kinematics and dynamics. The different mathematical models of robots are systems of multiple-input multiple-output, MIMO, so software tools that solve mathematical matrix operations to facilitate implementation of the proposed control scheme is required. MATLAB is a tool with its own programming language and development environment that offers the advantage of matrix manipulation and data processing. As a deployment scenario algorithms, MATLAB has libraries that can be extended according to programming needs [15]; *(iv) Simulation stage,* prior to the experimental implementation of the proposed control algorithms, it's necessary to check their performance in a three dimensional environment that emulates the actual conditions in which the robot operates, therefore, virtual development tools are required with the ability to support bilateral haptic devices, video output interfaces and audio, among others. Unity 3D is a tool for creating games, as well as development of virtual simulation and allows the incorporation of different haptic devices for manipulating its environment. Unity engine uses a script in C# language to manipulate the game objects with which you can modify the behavior of the simulated objects; and finally the *(v) Implementation stage,* it is the final phase in which the robot interacts with the environment where performs the task, this interaction is controlled via algorithms proposed control. The successful implementation of the planned task is based on compliance with each of the objectives of the above detailed steps; in this context, one can say that the design and simulation of control algorithms are the most critical stages for performing a task, so this work focuses on these two items.

In order to check the performance of control schemes in simulated/emulated environments, it is necessary to implement a communication channel between a bilateral graphics engine and mathematical software tool. The exchange of information in real time between the two applications is essential because the advanced control algorithms require the robot's feedback to close the control loop, while the emulated robot updates its kinematic and dynamic parameters depending on the robot-environment interaction, view Fig. 2.

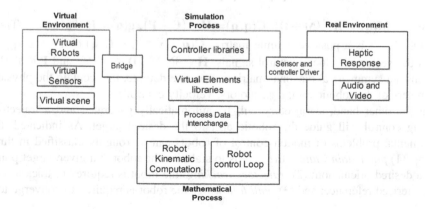

Fig. 2. Data interchange between Math software and 3D simulation software

In this context, the following sections show an emulator of advanced control algorithms implemented in MATLAB and displayed in real time in a virtual environment developed in Unity3D. It should be noted that the emulator allows bilateral interaction between MATLAB and Unity3D for any scheme or control technique implemented in MATLAB. As an example, autonomous control for tracking paths of a robotic arm 6 DOF is presented; and a tele-operated control from Unity's robotic arm.

Remark 1. A simulator represents reality in a similar way, while an emulator replica or improved conditions similar to the real ones.

3   Modeling and Control

The *instantaneous kinematic model of a robotic arm* sets the derivative of its location as a function of the derivative of its configuration (or its *operational velocities* as functions of its *generalized velocities*)

$$\dot{\mathbf{h}}(t) = \mathbf{J}(\mathbf{q})\dot{\mathbf{q}}(t). \tag{1}$$

It uses the Jacobian matrix $\mathbf{J}(\mathbf{q})$ of the function f: $\mathbf{J}(\mathbf{q}) = \frac{\partial f}{\partial \mathbf{q}}$. The configurations such that the rank of $\mathbf{J}(\mathbf{q})$ decreases are singular kinematic configurations and the problem, robotic arm and task, is redundant when $n > m$.

The mathematic model that represents the dynamics of a robotic arm can be obtained from Lagrange's dynamic equations, which are based on the difference between the kinetic and potential energy of each of the joints of the robot (energy balance). Most of the commercially available robots have low level PID controllers in order to follow the reference velocity inputs, thus not allowing controlling the voltages of the motors directly. Therefore, it becomes useful to express the dynamic model of the robotic arm in a more appropriate way, taking the rotational and longitudinal reference velocities as the control signals. To do so, the velocity controllers are included in the model. The dynamic model of the robotic arm, having as control signals the reference velocities of the system, can be represented as follows,

$$\mathbf{M}(\mathbf{q})\ddot{\mathbf{q}} + \mathbf{C}(\mathbf{q},\dot{\mathbf{q}})\dot{\mathbf{q}} + \mathbf{g}(\mathbf{q}) = \dot{\mathbf{q}}_{\mathbf{ref}} \tag{2}$$

where, $\mathbf{M}(\mathbf{q}) = \mathbf{H}^{-1}(\bar{\mathbf{M}} + \mathbf{D})$, $\mathbf{C}(\mathbf{q},\dot{\mathbf{q}}) = \mathbf{H}^{-1}(\bar{\mathbf{C}} + \mathbf{P})$, $\mathbf{g}(\mathbf{q}) = \mathbf{H}^{-1}\bar{\mathbf{g}}(\mathbf{q})$.   Thus, $\bar{\mathbf{M}}(\mathbf{q}) \in \Re^{\delta_n \times \delta_n}$ is a positive definite matrix, $\bar{\mathbf{C}}(\mathbf{q},\mathbf{v})\mathbf{v} \in \Re^{\delta_n}$, $\bar{\mathbf{G}}(\mathbf{q}) \in \Re^{\delta_n}$ and $\dot{\mathbf{q}}_{\mathbf{ref}} \in \Re^{\delta_n}$ is the vector of velocity control signals, $\mathbf{H} \in \Re^{\delta_n \times \delta_n}$, $\mathbf{D} \in \Re^{\delta_n \times \delta_n}$ and $\mathbf{P} \in \Re^{\delta_n \times \delta_n}$ are constant symmetrical diagonal matrices, positive definite, that contain the physical parameters of the robotic arm, *e.g.,* motors, velocity controllers.

In the other hand, a trajectory will be automatically generated and a trajectory tracking control will guide the robotic arm to the desired target. As indicated, the fundamental problems of motion control of robots can be roughly classified in three groups: (1) *point stabilization*: the goal is to stabilize the robot at a given target point, with a desired orientation; (2) *trajectory tracking*: the robot is required to track a time parameterized reference; and (3) *path following*: the robot is required to converge to a path and follow it, without any time specifications. For more details about the modeling and control see [16].

4   Bilateral Communication MATLAB-Unity3D

This section describes the methods of inter-process communication and exchange of information between MATLAB and Unity3D for control of an emulated manipulator with a haptic device.

4.1   Windows Inter-process Communication (IPC)

IPC is a feature enabled in the operating systems on which processes can exchange information through memory segments or through own communication tools, allowing resource sharing. Generally these processes are developed to low level – allowing to interact with the operating system resources – and according to the protocols for such communication.

Table 1. Windows Inter-process communication methods [17]

Method	Advantages	Disadvantages	Resources
Named Pipe	Easy to use and works across the network	The source code is platform dependent	Medium
WinSock	Works on the same computer as well as across networks. Moreover, it can be used across various platforms and protocols	Requires a knowledge of relatively advanced networking concepts	Low
Mailslots	Works across a network and supports broadcast	Provides one-way communication only	Medium
Shared Memory	**Linking processes using memory registers previously allocated, without functions of third party**	**Works on the same computer**	**Low**

The techniques to develop IPC vary depending on the application. This function can be used for the transmission of messages, synchronization, shared memory and remote procedures. The method used to communicate processes depends on the transfer rate required and the type of data to be treated. There are several ways to implement communication between processes, among which are: *(i) Named Pipe* is a method of channeling data by creating a memory space in the operating system explicitly declared before the execution of processes to communicate.; *(ii) WinSock* provides very high level networking capabilities, it supports TCP/IP (the most widely used protocol) along with many other protocols like AppleTalk, DECNet, IPX/SPX, etc.; *(iii) Mailslots* processes messages between applications via datagrams and allows to communicate unidirectionally, this method is useful for transmitting information to multiple clients;

and finally, *(iv) Shared memory* allows to create segments of memory to be accessed by multiple processes, access restrictions may be defined, *e.g.*, read only, read and write, execute, access over inheritance, among others. Table 1 presents the differences between the methods described for implementation of inter-processes communication.

Remark 2. Datagram is a data set of the communication protocol packet switched used to route information between nodes in a network.

In reference to illustrated in Table 1 and the proposed implementation guidance in this work, the method of *shared memory* is a technique easy to apply, with short delays and low use of computer resources by not calling third party functions.

4.2   MATLAB – Unity Communication

The bidirectional data communication between MATLAB - Unity3D is performed by a dynamic-link-library, dll, in which the Shared Memory method is implemented, SM, in RAM. The Fig. 3 illustrates the implementation of shared memory, where the dll manages the SM space, besides providing permits for the applications, label the memory space, provide functions to modify/obtain the stored information and liberate the space when the application is terminated.

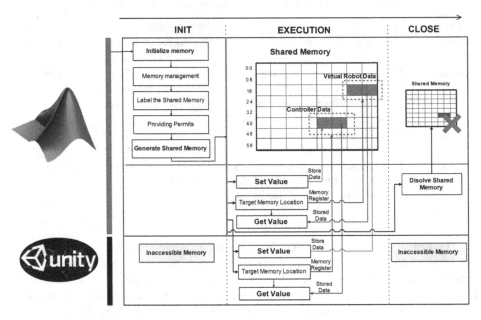

Fig. 3. Interprocess communication via shared memory

Using the dll between MATLAB and Unity3D is divided into three parts: *(i) Init phase,* the dll can be instantiated from an application through a handle, in which are set the security attributes and inheritance, permissions to read/write to memory registers reserved, RAM's space management and labeling. In this way, the client applications can reference data wishing to modify or capture, provided it have access permissions, aware of their existence and location where it is staying.

Remark 3. The characteristics of the dll allows that the generated memory can be started from MATLAB or Unity3D. From this step, both applications must use functions to identify dedicated spaces of memory, modify data or get them.

```
void CreateSharedMemoryArea()
{
        hFile = CreateFileMapping(INVALID_HANDLE_VALUE,        //Handle to instantiate the dll
created
                NULL,                                          //Null Security attributes and heritage
                0x40,                                          //Read&Write permissions
                0,
                1024 * 4,                                      //Memory Space Managed
                _T("memoriaza"));                              //Label the shared memory
        if (hFile == NULL)                                     // Memory Validation
        {
                printf("Unable to create a file.");
                exit(1);
        }
}
```

(ii) Execution phase, at this stage MATLAB and Unity3D must invoke the function *OpenSharedMemory()* to find the handle through the label and create a memory view, defining the read/write permissions, the point where the view begins and the number of bytes to be mapped, view Fig. 4. The view points to handle, from which a casting to LPINT type variables is made to locate the index of each of the stored data. The handle is referenced by the view when the application desires to read or write in memory.

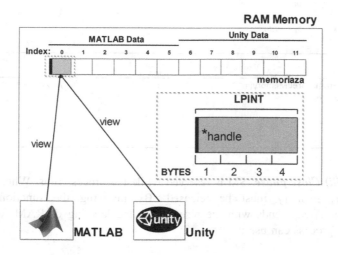

Fig. 4. Views of the Shared Memory

```
void OpenSharedMemory()
{
    hFile = OpenFileMapping(FILE_MAP_ALL_ACCESS,          // Search tag memory
                  FALSE,
                  _T("memoriaza"));

        if (hFile == NULL)                               // Validate the existence of
the memory
        {
                printf("Unable to open the shared area.\n");
                exit(1);
        }
        hView = (LPINT) MapViewOfFile(hFile,             // Creating view type LPINT
                FILE_MAP_ALL_ACCESS,                     // Read / Write definition
                0,                                       // Point where the view
begins
                0,
                0);                                      // All memory map

        if (hView == NULL)                               // View Validation
        {
                printf("Unable to create a VIEW.\n");
                exit(1);
        }
        aux = hView;                                     // Handle referenced to
Read or Write registers
}
```

The view allows update dedicated registers of each application. For writing data, the application is based on indexes that the dll provides in static manner for each of the variables.

```
void WriteOnSharedMemory(int data, int position)        // data defines the value,
position defines the index
    {
            aux[position] = data;
}
```

```
void ReadFromSharedMemory(int *data, int position)      // data defines the value,
position defines the index
    {
            *data = aux[position];
}
```

Finally *(iii) Close phase,* SM is reserved while the process runs. When the application *Close,* memory must be released. By invoking the function DestroySharedMemoryArea(), ends with the reservation and labeling of RAM for that any other system process can use it.

```
void DestroySharedMemoryArea ()                          // Free the shared memory
{
        if (!UnmapViewOfFile(hView))
        {
    printf("Could not unmap view of file.");
        }
        CloseHandle(hFile);
        printf("The end.\n");
}
```

4.3   Interaction MATLAB-Unity3D

The interaction between MATLAB and the graphics engine is divided into three stages, described in the following paragraphs as: import of three-dimensional design, interaction human-robot and bilateral communication processes (Fig. 5).

SolidWorks is the CAD tool used for mechanical design, but has no export formats supported by the virtual tool development. In the first phase, 3DS Max is used to modify parameters SolidWorks 3D modeling and hierarchies are established in the pieces that make up the assembly and supported file by Unity3D is exported. Once the three-dimensional model imported to Unity 3D environment, texture for each piece that makes up the prototype are established. In addition, the degrees of freedom of the 3D model is specified by activating the points of rotation and/or translation for objects that guides each.

In the second stage, the Unity3D environment performs the animation of virtual objects using Game Objects, scripts and plugins. The behaviour of Objects Game is controlled by scripts, which allow you to modify its properties and respond to user input as scheduled. The plugins allow you to use native functionality (support Oculus Rift) or include external code (support Novint Falcon). The human-robot interaction is achieved by information from input devices (Falcon encoders, Tracking Oculus HMD), the mathematical tool uses this data to return control actions and generate output responses (Falcon motors, Oculus HMD and audio).

Finally, in the third stage, information virtual robot is linked to MATLAB through the dll file and the invocation of the SM. When MATLAB requires send or retrieve information from the SM sector, its programming should include the lines:

```
loadlibrary('./dll64MATLAB.dll','./simple.h');            // Invoking the dll
calllib ('dll64MATLAB','initMemory');                     // Initialize memory
calllib ('dll64MATLAB','openMemory');                     // Create the view of the
shared memory
    calllib ('dll64MATLAB','setValue',v1,v2,v3,v4,v5,v6,v7,v8,v9,v10);        // Set values in the
memory
    val1 = calllib ('dll64MATLAB','getValue1');                      // Get values  from
memory
    calllib ('dll64MATLAB','destroy');                   // Free shared memory
```

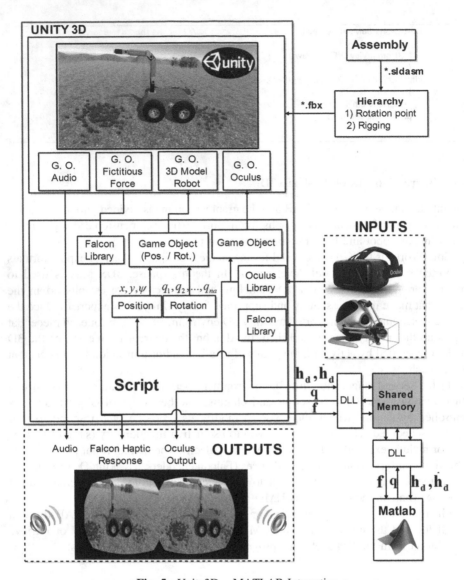

Fig. 5. Unity3D – MATLAB Interaction

While in each communication cycle, Unity receives velocities to control the rotation points and thus the operative end. Additionally, is sent the position of each actuator forming the modeled 3D robot and data human-robot, such as real interaction forces given by contact, effects of gravity, fictitious forces to avoid virtual obstacles, etc. Unity within the script, must contain the following lines of programming to invoke the read/write data in the SM.

```
[DllImport(@"C:\Users\Public\Documents\Unity
Projects\Animación\Assets\Plugins\dll64MATLAB.dll")]
    private static extern void openMemory();                    // Create the view of the
shared memory
    [DllImport(@"C:\Users\Public\Documents\Unity
Projects\Animación\Assets\Plugins\dll64MATLAB.dll")]
    private static extern int getValue1();                      // Get values from
memory
    PosX = -getValue1() / 100;                                  // Using the get value

    [DllImport(@"C:\Users\Public\Documents\Unity
Projects\Animación\Assets\Plugins\dll64MATLAB.dll")]
    private static extern int setValue(int v1, int v2,..., int v10);
    setValue(val1,val2,...,val10);                              // Set values in the
memory
```

Remark 4: The libraries developed for information sharing allow interaction between Unity Game Objects with any software package of MATLAB like Script, Simulink, etc., once initialized the SM.

Remark 5: In the case of robotic applications, update time data is relatively low due at time of sampling used. This work do not try to raise synchronization methods of information in shared memory.

5   Simulation Experimental Results

In order to illustrate the performance of the proposed simulator 3D of an arm robotic 6DOF, several experiments were carried out for path following autonomous control and bilateral tele-operation of a robotic arm; the most representative results are presented in this Section. The experiments were carried with the kinematic and dynamic models of a robotic arm 6 DOF, view Fig. 6.

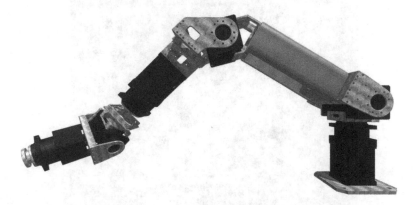

Fig. 6. Arm Robotic 6DOF developed in SolidWorks

On the other hand, the proposed simulator 3D consist in a desktop computer Core I7 3610QM running at 2.3 GHz, 8 GB RAM and a NVIDIA GeForce GT 630 M 1 GB dedicated graphics; also the local site has a haptic device Falcon^{MT} Novint. The evaluation of the latency in MATLAB takes into account the transmission, execution Unity and receiving data delay, which is within the desired sampling period of 100 [ms].

5.1   Autonomous Control

The performance of the control structure for path following is tested. The desired trajectory for the end-effector is described by $P(s) = (x_P(s), y_P(s), z_P(s))$, where $x_P = 0.35 \sin(0.2s + \frac{\pi}{2})$; $y_P = 0.35 \cos(0.2s + \frac{\pi}{2})$ and $z_P = 0.2 + 0.8 \sin(0.1s)$. Note that for the path following problem, the desired velocity of the end-effector of the robotic arm will depend on the task, the control error, the joint velocity of the arm, among other design specifications. In this experiment, it is considered that the reference velocity module depends on the desired velocity of the end-effector on path P and the control errors. Then, reference velocity in this experiment is expressed as $|\mathbf{v_{hd}}| = \frac{v_P}{1 + k\|\tilde{\mathbf{h}}\|}$, where k is a positive constant that weigh the control error module. Also, the desired location is defined as the closest point on the path to the end-effector of the experimental system.

Hence, Figs. 7, 8, 9 show the results of the experiment of autonomous control. Figure 7 shows the stroboscopic movement on the X-Y-Z space of Unity3D. It can be seen that the proposed controller works correctly; while the Fig. 8 shows the desired path and the current path of the end-effector of the robotic arm. It can be seen that the proposed controller presents a good performance;

Fig. 7. Stroboscopic movement of the robotic arm in Unity 3D.

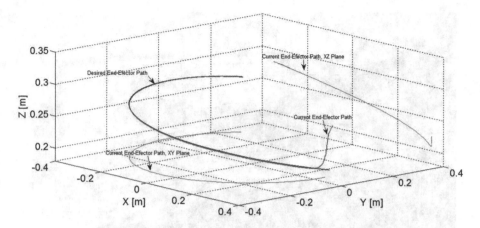

Fig. 8. Desired path and the current path of the end-effector

and finally Fig. 9 shows that the control errors of the robotic arm on the *X-Y-Z* space converge to values close to zero asymptotically.

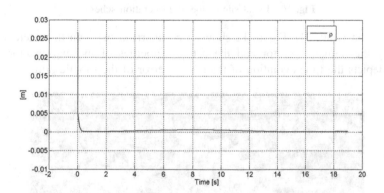

Fig. 9. Distance between the end-effector position and the closest point on the path

5.2 Tele-Operated Control

The feasibility of the proposed simulator 3D is tested through of bilateral tele-operation scheme using a robotic arm 6 DOFs. The local site has an Oculus and a haptic device Falcon^{MT} Novint. The human operator commands are generated with the use of a Falcon^{TM} haptic device from Novint Technologies Incorporated [18] as indicated in Fig. 10. Its positions are translated into desired velocities commands $P(s) = (x_P(s), y_P(s), z_P(s))$ of the end-effector of the robotic arm [19].

The simulation of a bilateral tele-operation scheme is presented, which consists on a grasping task. With this aim, the robot is guided near the object; then the user grasps the object opening the gripper; and finally the robot is guided to drop the object into a box. Obtained results are shown in Figs. 11, 12, 13. Figure 11 shows snapshots of the

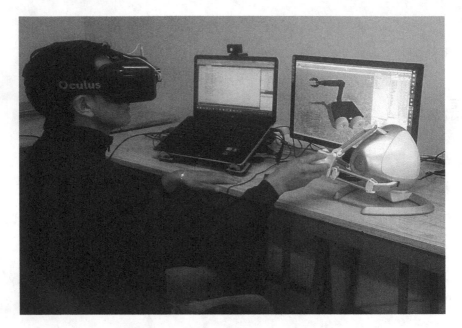

Fig. 10. Local site of the tele-operation scheme

experiment on Unity 3D. Figure 12 shows a comparison between the reference generated by the human operator and the actual velocities of the end-effector. While Fig. 13 depicts the time evolution of the control error of the robotic arm.

Fig. 11. Bilateral tele-operation: Grasping task on Unity 3D

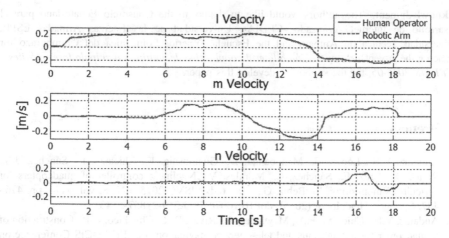

Fig. 12. Comparison between the reference generated by the human operator and the actual velocities of the end effector

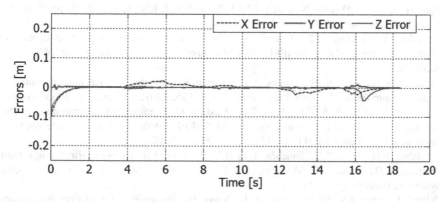

Fig. 13. Evolution of the control errors of the robotic arm. If $\lim_{t \to \infty} \tilde{x}(t) = 0$, $\lim_{t \to \infty} \tilde{y}(t) = 0$ and $\lim_{t \to \infty} \tilde{z}(t) = 0$ then $\lim_{t \to \infty} \rho(t) = 0$.

6 Conclusions

In this paper a 3D simulator in real time for robotics applications is proposed. This simulator considers the bilateral communication between MATLAB-Unity3D through of a dynamic-link-library, dll, in which the method of Shared Memory in RAM is implemented. The dll manages space SM, enable permissions to applications, puts the label to memory space, provide functions to modify/obtain the stored information and freeing the space when the application is terminated. Experimental results were also presented showing the feasibility and the good performance of the proposed simulator 3D; the experiments were carried out for path following autonomous control and bilateral tele-operation of a robotic arm 6DOF.

Acknowledgment. The authors would like to thanks to the Consorcio Ecuatoriano para el Desarrollo de Internet Avanzado -CEDIA-, Universidad de las Fuerzas Armadas ESPE, Universidad Técnica de Ambato and the Escuela Superior Politécnica del Chimborazo for financing the project *Tele-operación bilateral cooperativo de múltiples manipuladores móviles – CEPRAIX-2015-05*, for the support to develop this paper.

References

1. Andaluz, V.H., López, E., Manobanda, D., Guamushig, F., Chicaiza, F., Sánchez, J.S., Rivas, D., Pérez, F., Sánchez, C., Morales, V.: Nonlinear controller of quadcopters for agricultural monitoring. In: Bebis, G., et al. (eds.) ISVC 2015. LNCS, vol. 9474, pp. 476–487. Springer, Heidelberg (2015). doi:10.1007/978-3-319-27857-5_43
2. Andaluz, V.H., Chicaiza, F.A., Meythaler, A., Rivas, D.R., Chuchico, C.P.: Construction of a quadcopter for autonomous and tele-operated navigation. In: IEEE-DCIS Conference on Design of Circuits and Integrated Systems, Portugal (2015)
3. Andaluz, V.H., Canseco, P., Varela, J., Ortiz, J.S., Pérez, M.G., Roberti, F., Carelli, R.: Robust control with dynamic compensation for human-wheelchair system. In: Zhang, X., Liu, H., Chen, Z., Wang, N. (eds.) ICIRA 2014, Part I. LNCS, vol. 8917, pp. 376–389. Springer, Heidelberg (2014)
4. Andaluz, V.H., Ortiz, J.S., Roberti, F., Carelli, R.: Adaptive cooperative control of multi-mobile manipulators. In: IEEE–IECON Industrial Electronics Society, pp. 2669–2675, USA (2014)
5. Andaluz, V.H., Roberti, F., Marcos, T.J., Ricardo, C.: Adaptive unified motion control of mobile manipulators. J. Control Eng. Pract. 1337–1352 (2012). Elsevier Editorial System
6. Andersen, R.S.; Bogh, S.; Moeslund, T.B.; Madsen, O.: Intuitive task programming of stud welding robots for ship construction. In: 2015 IEEE International Conference on IEEE Industrial Technology (ICIT), pp. 3302–3307, March 2015
7. Andaluz, V.H., Ortiz, J.S., Sanchéz, J.S.: Bilateral control of a robotic arm through brain signals. In: De Paolis, L.T., Mongelli, A. (eds.) AVR 2015. LNCS, vol. 9254, pp. 355–368. Springer, Heidelberg (2015)
8. Ying, J.L., Peng, J.S., Qi, Z., Chang, C.L., Yong, H.: The review of workpiece loading and unloading robot in the catenary shot blasting. In: Research and Design of Machinery, Equipment and Technological Processes in Mechanical Engineering, Applied Mechanics and Materials, Vols. 496–500, pp. 578–581 (2014)
9. Freund, E., Rossmann, J.: Proyetive virtual reality: Bringing the gap between virtual reality and robotic. IEEE Trans. Robot. Autom. **15**(3), 411–422 (1999)
10. Brunet, P., Vinacua, A.: Sistemas Gráficos Interactivos. Universidad Politécnica de Cataluña, Barcelona, España, Mayo de 2006. http://www.lsi.upc.edu/~pere/SGI/guions/ArquitecturaRV.pdf
11. Meyer, J., Sendobry, A., et. al.: Comprehensive simulation of quadrotor UAVs using ROS and Gazebo. In: SIMPAR 2012 Proceedings of the Third International Conference on Simulation, Modeling, and Programming for Autonomous Robots, Berlin, Germany, vol. 12, pp. 400–411 (2015)
12. Oliveira, M., Pereira, N., Oliveira, E., Almeida, J.E., Rossetti, R.J.: A Multi-player Approach in Serious Games: Testing Pedestrian Fire Evacuation Scenarios. Oporto, DSIE15, January (2015)

13. Bartneck, C., Soucy, M., Fleuret, K., Sandoval, E.B.: The robot engine—Making the unity 3D game engine work for HRI. In: 2015 24th IEEE International Symposium on Robot and Human Interactive Communication (RO-MAN), pp. 431–437. IEEE (2015)
14. Indraprastha, A., Shinozaki, M.: The investigation on using Unity3D game engine in urban design study. J. ICT Res. Appl. 3(1), 1–18 (2009)
15. MATLAB and Simulink for Technical Computing. http://www.mathworks.com/
16. Andaluz, V., Salinas, L., Roberti, F., Toibero, J., Carelli, R.: Switching control signal for bilateral tele-operation of a mobile manipulator. In: 2011 9th IEEE International Conference on Control and Automation (ICCA), Santiago, Chile, 19–21 December 2011
17. Interprocess Communications. https://msdn.microsoft.com/en-us/library/windows/desktop/aa365574(v=vs.85).aspx
18. Andaluz, V., Roberti, F., Toibero, J., Carelli, R.: Adaptive unified motion control of mobile manipulators. Control Eng. Pract. 20(12), 1337–1352 (2012)
19. Martin, S., Hillier, N.: Characterization of the novint falcon haptic device for application as a robot manipulator. In: Australasian Conference on Robotics and Automation (2009)

Augmented and Mixed Reality

Mobile Augmented Reality Based Annotation System: A Cyber-Physical Human System

Constantin Scheuermann[1]($\boxtimes$), Felix Meissgeier[1], Bernd Bruegge[1], and Stephan Verclas[2]

[1] Department of Computer Science, Technical University Munich, Munich, Germany
{constantin.scheuermann,felix.meissgeier,bruegge}@in.tum.de
[2] T-Systems International GmbH, Frankfurt, Germany
stephan.verclas@t-systems.de

Abstract. One goal of the Industry 4.0 initiative is to improve knowledge sharing among and within production sites. A fast and easy knowledge exchange can help to reduce costly down-times in factory environments. In the domain of automotive manufacturing, production line down-times cost in average about $1.3 million per hour. Saving seconds or minutes have a real business impact and the reduction of such down-time costs is of major interest.

In this paper we describe MARBAS, a Mobile Augmented Reality based Annotation System, which supports production line experts during their maintenance tasks. We developed MARBAS as Cyber-Physical Human System that enables experts to annotate a virtual representation of a real world scene. MARBAS uses a mobile depth sensor that can be attached to smart phones or tablets in combination with Instant Tracking. Experts can share information using our proposed system. We believe that such an annotation system can excel current maintenance processes by accelerating them.

To identify applicable mesh registration algorithms we conducted a practical simulation. We used a 6 axis joint-arm robot to evaluate 7 different ICP algorithms concerning time and accuracy. Our results show that PCL non-linear ICP offers best performance for our scenario. Additionally, we developed a vertical prototype using a mobile depth sensor in combination with a tablet. We could show the feasibility of our approach augmenting real world scenes with virtual information.

Keywords: Augmented reality · Maintenance · Cyber-Physical Human System · Annotation system

1 Introduction

Horizontal and vertical knowledge sharing is a great challenge within the digital transformation of industries. Horizontal knowledge sharing refers to the exchange among industries at different locations, vertical knowledge sharing refers to hierarchical structures within one location. Challenges related to such knowledge

© Springer International Publishing Switzerland 2016
L.T. De Paolis and A. Mongelli (Eds.): AVR 2016, Part I, LNCS 9768, pp. 267–280, 2016.
DOI: 10.1007/978-3-319-40621-3_20

exchange are rooted in the usage of heterogeneous software frameworks with different data models, non-existing interfaces or even non-digitized processes. In case processes are not digitized, shareability, revision control as well as the analysis of data are difficult to accomplish.

In the domain of automotive manufacturing, production line down-times cost in average about $1,3 million per hour [16]. Efficient maintenance processes are of major importance for industries. In factory environments digitized knowledge sharing can contribute to faster reaction times and consequently has the potential to reduce down-times.

Typically, humans repair malfunctions. The role of humans in the domain of manufacturing covers production line experts, workers or specialized staff from the machine vendor. The experience to repair and set up a service as fast as possible might be distributed among these stakeholders. Therefore, they need to consult other experts and/or read manuals to repair the malfunctioning part. The knowledge is distributed among different parties and across different media. Some information is digitized, some is paper based and some information is only available as expert experience.

To address the problem of information and knowledge sharing in the domain of manufacturing we describe a Mobile Augmented Reality based Annotation System (MARBAS). The goal is to improve the cooperation and the knowledge sharing between experts that have to maintain machinery in factory environments. The information is stored together with a virtual representation of the real-world scene. Information is stored where it is needed and several experts can benefit from such information. As such information is digitized, a feedback-loop between experts and the machine manufacturer can be established with the goal to improve machinery according to the information.

We implemented MARBAS as a Cyber-Physical Human System, where the expert is able to scan a physical environment using an iPad with an attached structure.io[1]. After the real-world scene is scanned, the expert can annotate the environment with virtual stickies directly attached on the virtual representation of the physical objects. The virtual representation of the real-world scene including the annotation can be shared among experts. As soon as another expert scans the same environment, the previous scanned representation including the stickies is aligned with the newly scanned scene. The information is now visible to the expert again. Such information sharing can save time and reduce human error during down-time or maintenance scenarios.

For the described use case different scene meshes have to be compared and aligned. For this alignment different mesh registration algorithms exist. In this paper we conducted an experiment to estimate which algorithm performs best for our scenario, concerning registration time and accuracy. Additionally, we implemented a prototype that shows the feasibility of our approach. To the best of our knowledge a virtual annotation system, based on a depth sensor attached to a mobile device has not been implemented yet.

---

[1] First commercially available 3D depth sensor for mobile devices http://structure. io/.

Step	Description	Description	Step
1 — Scene Identification	Receive Module Identifier and Stored Depth Parameter (e.g. QR Code or BLE Device)	Mesh Registration and Annotation Reconstruction	Restore Annotations — 8
2 — Scene Scanning	Create Mesh of Real World Scene	Create Mesh of Real World Scene	Scene Scanning — 7
3 — Scene Annotation	Add Stickies to Scene Annotate Text or Audio Messages	Receive Annotation Set on his Tablet	Receive Annotation Set — 6
4 — Store and Share Annotation Set	Store Mesh and Annotations Share it with Experts	Comparism of Stored Scene Identifier	Scene Identification — 5

Fig. 1. MARBAS Workflow: The workflow is two folded as emphasized with red and green backgrounds. Steps 1 – 4 cover the initial annotation of a scene. Steps 5 – 8 cover the annotation recovery. (Color figure online)

The work is structured as follows: In Sect. 2 we describe the problem statement and our scenario. Section 3 summarizes existing frameworks and research efforts concerning augmented reality (AR) applications. Section 4 shows the overall system design. Section 5 introduces the simulation setup and Sect. 6 describes the results and the rationale concerning the choice of the mesh registration algorithm. Section 7 depicts the mobile application design and Sect. 8 offers limitations and future work of MARBAS. Section 9 concludes the work.

2 Problem Statement

The digitization of processes within production lines and more generally speaking within the domain of manufacturing is one of the great challenges within the Industry 4.0 movement. Maintenance tasks as well as the incident management is yet, in many cases, paper based [15]. Non-shareability as well as non-readability of handwritten notes are typical disadvantages relying on such processes. Digitized processes benefit from better shareability, searchability and better archiving capabilities. Using such advantages, efficiency and information transparency can be horizontally and vertically increased. In industries downtimes are costly and need to be reduced or avoided. Therefore, saving minutes by optimizing maintenance processes in factories is of major interest.

We propose a system that focuses on the maintenance of machinery in factory environments. Two types of maintenance need to be supported: preventive and corrective. Preventive maintenance wants to avoid failures or down-times of machinery in future. Typical tasks within this maintenance type are routine checks and the exchange of worn out materials. Corrective maintenance takes place in case a machine fails or is not operating properly. Machine failure results in cost intensive down-times and has to be fixed as fast as possible to restore the service. Production line experts perform maintenance tasks and therefore our goal is to assist and support experts during daily operations. Experience in maintenance tasks or of specific parts of machineries is not equally distributed among each production line expert. Thus, handovers between two working-shifts are a problem concerning information transfer. In case of preventive maintenance there might be no need to immediately fix the problem. Therefore, maintenance information must be available for days and handovers are a major point of failure.

To assist experts we propose a mobile-based real-time mesh-registration AR application. Using the application, an expert can capture a real world scene and annotate it with virtual stickies. Text and audio messages can be attached to each sticky. The expert can then share the mesh with other experts including the annotations. As soon as the expert scans the same scene previous annotations can be recovered and used for the analysis of the scene. The information is therefore digitally available, stored and shareable.

3   Related Work

In this section we discuss the existing approaches of AR applications. We shortly describe the approaches and describe advantages and disadvantages.

The use of markers for AR applications has a long tradition within research and applications. They are robust and have the advantage of low computational requirements. [9] Two types of two-dimensional fiducial markers exist: *ID-Markers* and *Picture-Markers*. *ID-Markers* are typically square-shaped black-white images that encode a binary identifier. To calculate the camera pose, the marker captured by the video device, will be converted to a binary image using adaptive threshold. After applying a corner and edge detection filter the pose will be estimated. *Picture-Markers* are used in many AR use cases using multiple methods for registration of 2D images, such as Scale Invariant Feature Transform (SIFT) and Speed Up Robust Features (SURF). *Picture-Markers* are used to excel print-media such as newspapers or magazines by projecting animations displayed on a see-through-device such as a smart phone.

The main disadvantage of marker-based tracking is that the real world scene has to be prepared before an AR application can be used. This includes the pose calibration of all equipment beforehand. Besides this, marker might be occluded by real objects which decreases reliability of the tracking [10].

To improve accuracy of marker based tracking, additional sensors such as a gyroscope or an accelerometer are used during the registration process. Such sensors are present in smart phones and tablets. You and Neumann [17] showed, that a hybrid concept including inertial and visual sensors "achieves high tracking stability and robustness". Also location based AR scenarios have been implemented such as the Augmented Reality Browser "Junaio" which showed geo-located POIs based on current compass and inertial sensor measurements [8]. Additionally, AR applications exist that use localization systems such as GPS for outdoor mesh registration [14] and indoor mesh registration [12]. Fiducial markers within industrial environments are not convenient [11]. Such markers have to be applied to each module or directly onto the machinery within a production line. Moreover, the user has to provide a permanent line-of-sight between marker and video see-through-device. Markerless tracking is a solution to this problem. Instead of using artificial markers as reference points, markerless AR approaches use the entire real world scene to estimate the pose and register the mesh. This is done by identifying and tracking prominent features within the real world scene. A common approach is edge based tracking in combination with simplified CAD models as input, as it demands low computational power and is robust to light changes [18]. According to Drummond et al. Edge based tracking consists of the following three steps: Location of visible edge in captured frame, find corresponding edges of predefined model, computation of pose [5]. To locate edges in a captured frame, intense transitions within the gray-image representation of the frame have to be identified. In the past, local gradient operators such as Sobel and Prewitt have been used to achieve the edge identification. Nowadays, the most common edge detector algorithms are derivatives of the smoothing filter such as Gaussian Edge Detection [1]. After the edge detection, the correlation between the calculated edge points of the real world scene and corresponding control points of the model's wireframe will be determined. After the pose estimation, the virtual predefined 3D model is projected onto the representation of the frame. The main benefit of Edge Based 3D Tracking Systems in comparison to marker-based tracking is that real world scenes do not have to be equipped with markers. The disadvantage of this approach is the necessity of 3D models representing the real world scene and the required preprocessing to create the wireframe.

A total independent approach has its origin in the field of robotics: Simultaneous Localization and Mapping (SLAM). SLAM was developed to navigate robots autonomously through unknown environments. The SLAM approach follows the idea of constructing a map of the real world scene while deducing the pose at the same time. The obvious chicken-and-egg situation of localizing the position of an entity within a scene, which is reconstructed during run-time, is called "SLAM problem". The SLAM concept is based on extraction and tracking of scene features commonly called landmarks. Such landmarks, which are captured by a camera or a laser-range-finder, are stored in a 3D map, which will be permanently updated. During this landmark update a data association check is performed which identifies correspondences between captured features and already observed landmarks. A widespread approach to solve the SLAM problem uses the Extended Kalman Filter (EKF) for estimating the pose based on the observed landmarks. Because this method abstracts "nonlinear motion and observation models" to linearity, it can lead to inconsistency [6]. FastSLAM addresses this problem. It is a SLAM algorithm based on Rao-Blackwellized particle filter that supports nonlinearity. Particle filters are used for discovering new landmarks instead of storing a history of previous observed features which results in a better performance than EKF algorithms but with higher computational costs [3,6].

Small, energy efficient and powerful devices such as smart phones in combination with the high quality of the integrated sensors allow the deployment of computing intensive SLAM algorithms within user-centric mobile software solutions. First achievements were made in reconstructing 3D information from a sequence of 2D images known as Structure from Motion (SFM). Since SFM systems are basically designed to be used for offline post-processing of image series, Davison et al. presented a real time SLAM algorithm for pose computation using a monocular camera as input via moving rapidly through an unknown scene [4]. They proposed a promising approach using a continuously refined probabilistic feature-based map which is updated by the extended Kalman filter. Monocular vision-based SLAM enables (mobile) AR experiences. New use cases become viable such as the navigation of autonomous vehicles (e.g. self-driving cars, drones, mars rover etc.), robust hybrid AR systems including model based initialization and continued SLAM tracking or development of AR 3D games using the real world as gaming environment.

The approach used in this paper is 3D SLAM or RGB-D SLAM (Real-Time Mesh-Registration). Endres et al. [7] presented an approach for simultaneous pose tracking and scene mapping using sensor input data from RGB-D cameras such as the Microsoft Kinect. The main difference to 2D SLAM is the possibility to process depth maps which are captured up to 30 times per second from the current field-of-view of the used depth sensor. All captured and slightly transformed depth maps have to be aligned in such a way, that a 3D mesh of the scanned environment can be reconstructed. This process is called mesh registration and has some advantages. No previous preparation of the real world scene is needed. The pose estimation and the 3D model are generated on the fly using a RGB-D sensor. The flexibility of this approach excels the before mentioned approaches and is therefore used for the described case study in this paper.

4   Sticky Annotation System

The Mobile Augmented Reality based Annotation System (MARBAS) focuses on an industrial maintenance use case. Within a production line, experts collaborate while maintaining machinery. A physical annotation with, for example sticky notes, is not applicable or even impossible because such machinery consists of movable parts. Taking pictures and attach notes to them has the disadvantage that experts need to transfer 2D information to a 3D real world scene. This paper describes a system that uses a 3D depth sensor (structure.io) in combination with an iPad. With this system the production line expert can create a virtual representation of the physical environment without any preliminary step. Neither a preparation of the scene with fiducial markers nor predefined 3D models of a certain scene are needed. With MARBAS an expert scans the scene with the iPad following the workflow as described in Fig. 1. As soon as an expert has to document a part of the production line the scene needs to be identified. This can be done by scanning a QR Code or by receiving beacon information such as BLE devices. This *Scene Identification* is not necessarily needed but facilitates the scene matching. For convenience we used a QR Code based scene identification. Within this *Scene Identification* phase the identifier carries the name of the module as well as the needed depth information used for the scanning process. In the second step the *Scene Scanning* takes place (see Fig. 4a). MARBAS creates a mesh, a virtual representation of the real world scene. As soon as enough features and mesh points have been collected the scene can be annotated (see Fig. 4b). Within the *Scene Annotation* virtual stickies can be attached to the virtual representation of the real word scene. Additionally, text as well as audio information can be attached to each sticky. After the annotation has been finished the mesh can be stored and shared. To *Store and Share the Annotation Set* the information of the *Scene Identification* is used. In the following step another expert wants to retrieve and recover the sticky information of the scene. By starting the *Scene Identification* the expert receives the stored and shared annotation set and then performs a *Scene Scanning*. As soon as enough features have been scanned the app can perform *Restore Annotations*. Within this step both meshes have to be aligned using the PCL non-linear ICP algorithm. As soon as this step has finished the virtual stickies can be aligned. Figure 4c shows the final result. The red dots are added for debugging purposes. For future tests we want to easily notice if the mesh alignment has worked properly.

5   Simulation Setup and Recorded Mesh

An evaluation of ICP algorithms for factory environments is to the best of our knowledge missing. Our use case aims on an expert that is scanning a real world scene on the fly. Additionally, the expert annotates the scene, stores it and shares it with another expert. The expert needs to scan the same scene to restore the previously stored annotations. We conducted a practical evaluation that offers an analysis of registration time and the mean square (RMS) distances in meters between two aligned meshes covering three distances.

Therefore, a six-axis joint-arm robot was used to simulate the six degrees of movement freedom, which are typical for a human arm holding an iPad while scanning the target scene. For this evaluation an iPad mini 2 was attached to a Comau SMART5 SiX 6-1.4 robot using a customized bracket. The joint-arm has six axes and a horizontal reach of 1.4 m. To get realistic meshes to evaluate the algorithms, a Festo module was used. It is used by the mechanical engineers to teach students how to program and deal with production line systems (see Fig. 2b). It is a functional module covering various sensors and actuators, cables and controllers, typical for production lines (see Fig. 4).

To generate the evaluation mesh data the iPad device was moved in a hemispheric trajectory around the target scene. Therefore, a fixed target scene reference point (framed point) as intersection point between the line-of-sight of the structure.io sensor and the target scan scene was defined. During the entire scan process the depth sensor focused this target reference point.

To estimate a realistic scan duration for each pose we conducted a short experiment, where we scanned three different environments each with different scene complexity. It started with a clean desk environment, a normal and finally a messy desk environment. Therefore, an iPad 2 Model A1490 running iOS 8.1 equipped with an external structure.io sensor that was fixed at a certain position, scanned each scene for 31s. Figure 2a shows the results. The scene complexity correlates with the total amount of vertices. The results show that more than

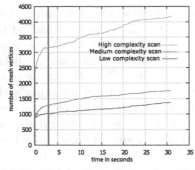

(a) **Estimate Scan Duration:** Experimental estimation of applicable scan duration for the ICP algorithm evaluation. The device is not moved while scanning. Red dashed line emphasizes that after three seconds 70% of the vertices have been captured.

(b) **Simulation Hardware Setup:** Six-axis joint robot arm capturing vertices following a trajectory around the real world scene. iPad with structure.io is attached to the arm. A Festo module used for teaching mechanical engineers at Technical University Munich represents the real world scene.

Fig. 2. Evaluation Setup and Preliminary Evaluation: (a) shows the results of the scan duration estimation conducted before the evaluation. (b) shows the simulation setup. (Color figure online)

70 % of all mapped vertices were computed within the first three seconds. We assume that using a scan duration of three seconds is suitable for our evaluation as most of the vertices have already been captured.

6 Simulation Results

Our practical evaluation compared 7 ICP algorithms: LibPoint Matcher, LIBICP, Sparse ICP, PCL Base ICP, PCL Generalized ICP, PCL ICP with normals and PCL Non-linear ICP. For all of these ICP algorithms Objective C implementations are available, that can be used for the intended iPad application.

The comparison framework is implemented in C++ using Qt[2] and OpenSceneGraph[3] for point cloud visualization. The framework is separated into a run-time module, quality analyzer and performance analyzer. The run-time module follows the adapter pattern to include ICP algorithms. Therefore, the process of adding a new ICP algorithm is simplified as only the register method, which takes two meshes as input must be implemented. The quality analyzer is used once a mesh registration procedure has finished. It analyzes the quality of the registration based on the overall average maximal point-to-point distance, minimal point-to-point distance, mean point-to-point distance and root mean square

---

[2] http://www.qt.io/.
[3] http://www.openscenegraph.org/.

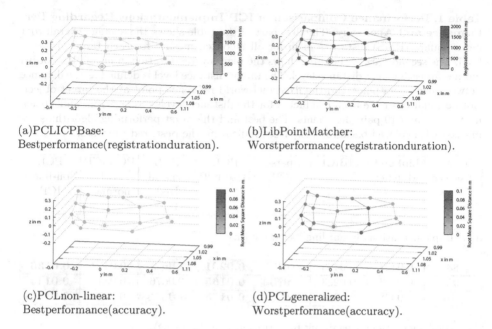

(a)PCLICPBase:
Bestperformance(registrationduration).

(b)LibPointMatcher:
Worstperformance(registrationduration).

(c)PCLnon-linear:
Bestperformance(accuracy).

(d)PCLgeneralized:
Worstperformance(accuracy).

Fig. 3. Evaluation Results: The four figures show the evaluation results for the best performing and the worst performing algorithms concerning register duration and accuracy based on RMS. The framed point marks the reference point. The remaining points represent the positions of the robot arm where a mesh has been taken for 3s. (Color figure online)

distance. Additionally, CPU as well as RAM usage will be logged. According to [2] and [13] the root-mean-square (RMS) distance is an accepted quantity to compare ICP algorithms. RMS is typically defined as standard deviation of the difference between predicted and observed values. Therefore, two characteristic quantities have been analyzed in detail and chosen for the evaluation: RMS (cm) and the registration duration (ms). As CPU and RAM usage differed slightly during the conducted evaluations those characteristics have not been considered.

The evaluation has been conducted on an Intel(R) Core(TM) i5-3337U 1.80 GHz with 4 GByte RAM running Windows 8.1 64 Bit. CPU usage as well as RAM usage was kept at a minimum by terminating additional programs and tasks. An assumption for our evaluations is that the performance of the ICP algorithms on an iPad will be worse but the results will be proportionally shifted. For the evaluation realistic distances between the scanning device and the scanned scene have been chosen: 88 cm, 95 cm and 110 cm.

All ICP algorithms have been used with their default configuration. Modifications from these presets have been made in case the performance could be improved using a different parameter set. The presented evaluation is therefore not an exhaustive evaluation of all possible configurations. The results are shown in Fig. 3 and Table 1. The results show that PCL Base ICP and PCL

Table 1. Performance Comparison of ICP Implementations Regarding Performance and Accuracy: The first part of the table shows the average overall root mean square (RMS) distances in m for all recorded meshes for each target distance level. The second part of the table shows the registration duration in ms of all recorded meshes for each target distance level. The target distance level is defined as the distance between each scan point and the fixed real-world reference point at the target object. Both evaluations have been conducted for the distance levels 88 cm, 95 cm and 110 cm using 7, 14 and 19 pair alignments. The best and the worst performing algorithms are marked with colored backgrounds. Green indicating the best, red the worst.

Target distance in cm	LibPoint Matcher	LIBICP	Sparse ICP	PCL Base ICP	PCL Generalized ICP	PCL ICP with normals	PCL Non-linear ICP
ICP Implementations Regarding Accuracy (m)							
88	0.0454	0.0433	0.0454	0.0201	0.0529	0.0453	0.0136
95	0.0223	0.0223	0.0700	0.0165	0.0676	0.0338	0.0144
110	0.0328	0.0324	0.0374	0.0175	0.0613	0.0300	0.0140
ICP Implementations Regarding Registration Duration (ms)							
88	9473.4	2524.3	88089.1	174.8	7344.6	752.5	474.1
95	9572.9	3555.4	90865.8	212.9	13774.6	848.4	733.0
110	11668.9	1697.6	74301.3	134.8	6559.3	710.8	655.2

Non-linear ICP outperform the other algorithms in terms of accuracy and registration duration. The worst algorithm concerning registration duration is the LibPoint Matcher algorithm. Concerning accuracy Sparse ICP has the lowest accuracy within the 95 cm distance. PCL Generalized ICP is the worst for both distances at 88 cm and 110 cm.

For MARBAS we have chosen PCL Non-linear ICP as an applicable algorithm. The alignment of the meshes is essential for the relocation of the annotations. According registration duration PCL Non-linear ICP is the second best algorithm. The registration accuracy is essential for the location of the annotations in MARBAS and therefore we prefer PCL Non-linear ICP.

7   User Interface Design

MARBAS is an iOS application designed for an iPad using the structure.io sensor. Figure 4 shows three essential screenshots following the workflow illustrated in Fig. 1: the *Scene Scanning Phase* (see Fig. 4a), the *Scene Annotation Phase* (see Fig. 4b) and finally the *Restore Annotation Phase* (see Fig. 4c). During the *Scene Scanning Phase* the expert scans the real-world scene of interest. While scanning the expert receives a visual and a numeric feedback telling how much

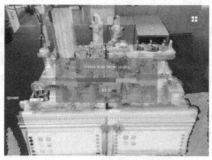

(a) Scene Scanning Phase   (b) Scene Annotation Phase

(c) Restore Annotation Phase

Fig. 4. MARBAS Application Screenshots: The screenshots from the application show the essential workflow steps and the User Interface Design. While scanning the plant modules from Festo the user can see, which structures have already been scanned. During the Scene Annotation Phase the environment can be annotated by clicking on the screen of the see-through-device. After the Restore Annotation Phase the annotations are located at the same position. Additionally, the mesh registration is visualized with red dots for debugging purposes. (Color figure online)

of the real-world scene has been scanned. The visual feedback is illustrated as a transparent white overlay on the objects. The numeric feedback refers to the minimum amount of vertices that have been scanned. Currently, a threshold of minimum 9000 vertices has been defined. We defined this threshold based on our experiences during the implementation phase. As soon as this minimum amount has been reached the scene annotation can start. During *Scene Annotation Phase* the expert can place virtual stickies to the objects. Additionally, text and/or audio comments can be added to each sticky. The *Scene Annotation Phase* finishes as soon as the expert has stored the annotations or leaves the annotation screen. For the *Restore Annotation Phase* the expert has to scan the scene again and choose a corresponding mesh that should be aligned with the scene. As soon as the scene is scanned a two-tier process is triggered. As a first approximation the Point Cloud Library is using Fast Point Feature Histograms (FPFH) to align the meshes. After that the fine mesh registration is triggered using the

PCL Non-linear ICP algorithm. As soon as these two processes have finished the stickies are aligned. For debugging and control purposes the reconstruction shows the stored mesh as overlay (red dots). The pin of the stickies defines the position of the sticky in the mesh. The orientation of the stickies depends on the pins' position and can slightly differ especially on uneven objects (compare Fig. 4b with c).

8   Limitations and Future Work

Within the scope of this paper we covered a rationale for the ICP algorithm selection and implemented a vertical prototype showing the potential of a virtual annotation system in factory environments.

Using an iPad as see-through-device in combination with a depth sensor, maintenance processes can be improved. In most cases both hands are occupied while holding the iPad. For the expert in many cases it is a disadvantage as the expert might want to use at least one hand to operate. From a technological point of view it simplifies the process, because no occlusion algorithm is needed that needs to deal with the presence of hands in the scene.

As depth sensors will soon be integrated in smart glasses such as Microsofts' HoloLens, MARBAS can be adapted and transferred to smart glasses following a hands-free paradigm. As soon as such sensors are integrated, applicable occlusion algorithms must be implemented that can handle the presence of hands within the real-world scene during the scanning process.

Rapidly changing environments can distort the mesh registration process. In case a scene changes in a way that the realignment will fail, a new scan and annotation is needed. Due to the fact that the process to scan and annotate a scene is fast, MARBAS is still applicable for production lines where scene changes are not that frequent.

With changing environments another problem needs to be addressed. Archiving historical annotation sets is an open challenge. The scene might have changed or it might even not be physically present anymore. One possible approach would be the aggregation of scanned meshes using the initial scene identifier in combination with several 2D images representing the real-world scene. Additionally, MARBAS can use feature detection algorithms to match existing 3D models of mechanical parts. Inferring the scene based on the detected features can improve the archiving mechanism.

The performance evaluation concerning the ICP algorithms on the iPad is missing but is part of our future work.

The real-world scene size and complexity is limited to the structure.io sensor capabilities. The structure.io sensor has a limited capture range of 0.4 to 3.5+ m. Smaller and larger scenes can not be scanned with one single scan. For that reason an empirical user study must be conducted. It should show the applicability in different factory environments. We also need evaluate the infra-red technology of the sensor as it is temperature sensitive and can only be used between $0° $ C - $35° $ C.

The battery consumption is yet very high. In our observations we could use the structure.io for about one hour using it 100 % of the time evaluating MARBAS. The root of this extensive power consumption are the ICP algorithms that have to register the different meshes on the iPad. In future scenarios such intense calculation can be handled by a cloud service.

The user interface evaluation and the workflow evaluation are missing. We are currently searching for a partner who is willing to pilot our approach. We want to gain an insight of the feasibility of this approach conducting a field experiment.

9 Conclusion

This paper describes the Mobile Augmented Reality based Annotation System (MARBAS) prototype. It is a vertical prototype using an iPad in combination with a RGB-D Sensor (structure.io) to annotate real-world scenes with virtual stickies. Such stickies can be text based or audio based annotations. The main goal is to support humans during industrial maintenance tasks. We believe that using virtual annotations can contribute to vertical as well as horizontal information and knowledge sharing. MARBAS offers a digital available data structure for the virtual stickies, their position within the captured mesh and the connected text as well as the audio annotations. This data structure can be shared easily and therefore meets one of the major goals of the fourth industrial revolution - shareability.

One of the main challenges within MARBAS is the mesh registration of the scanned real-world scenes. The mesh registration is done using ICP algorithms. To select an applicable algorithm we conducted an evaluation of common ICP algorithms in a realistic simulation environment using a 6-axis joint robot arm. Our results show that PCL Non-linear ICP performs best for our use case.

With MARBAS we showed the technical feasibility of our defined workflow and demonstrated it with the implementation of a vertical prototype. Industries can benefit from MARBAS as it defines a digitized process. All data can be shared, analyzed and stored. A captured mesh contains about 9000 vertices and is relatively small (approximately 70 kByte). Such meshes can be used for remote maintenance scenarios consuming less bandwidth as video based scenarios. Even in environments with a low bandwidth coverage this amount of data can still be transferred.

It is expected that RGB-D sensors will be integrated in smart glasses in near future. Using the advantage of hands-free operation in combination with applicable occlusion algorithms that can deal with moving hands within the scanned scene is part of our future work. Our approach can be transferred and adapted to smart glasses. We further want to evaluate the User Interface design and conduct an empirical study to test it within real factory environments.

Acknowledgments. The authors would like to thank Fortiss and especially Markus Rickert for providing the 6-axis joint robot arm used for the ICP algorithm evaluation.

References

1. Basu, M.: Gaussian-based edge-detection methods - a survey. IEEE Trans. Syst. Man Cybern. Part C Appl. Rev. **32**(3), 252–260 (2002)
2. Besl, P.J., McKay, N.D.: A method for registration of 3-d shapes. IEEE Trans. Pattern Anal. Mach. Intell. **14**, 239–256 (1992)
3. Bleser, G., Wuest, H., Stricker, D.: Online camera pose estimation in partially known and dynamic scenes. In: ISMAR, pp. 56–65. IEEE Computer Society (2006)
4. Davison, A.J., Reid, I.D., Molton, N.D., Stasse, O.: Monoslam: Real-time single camera slam. IEEE Trans. Pattern Anal. Mach. Intell. **29**, 1052–1067 (2007)
5. Drummond, T., Society, I.C., Cipolla, R.: Real-time visual tracking of complex structures. IEEE Trans. Pattern Anal. Mach. Intell. **24**, 932–946 (2002)
6. Durrant-Whyte, H., Bailey, T.: Simultaneous localisation and mapping (slam): Part i the essential algorithms. IEEE Robot. Autom. Mag. **13**(2), 99–110 (2006)
7. Endres, F., Hess, J., Engelhard, N., Sturm, J., Cremers, D., Burgard, W.: An evaluation of the rgb-d slam system, St. Paul, MA, USA (2012)
8. Jackson, T., Angermann, F., Meier, P.: Survey of use cases for mobile augmented reality browsers. In: Furht, B. (ed.) Handbook of Augmented Reality, pp. 409–431. Springer, New York (2011)
9. Klopschitz, M., Schall, G., Schmalstieg, D., Reitmayr, G.: Visual tracking for augmented reality. In: 2010 International Conference on Indoor Positioning and Indoor Navigation (IPIN), pp. 1–4 (2010)
10. Lima, J., Simões, F., Figueiredo, L., Teichrieb, V., Kelner, J.: Model based markerless 3D tracking applied to augmented reality. J. 3D Interact. Syst. **1**, 1–15 (2010)
11. Platonov, J., Heibel, H., Meier, P., Grollmann, B.: A mobile markerless ar system for maintenance and repair. In: IEEE/ACM International Symposium on Mixed and Augmented Reality 2006, pp. 105–108 (2006)
12. Reitmayr, G., Schmalstieg, D.: Location based applications for mobile augmented reality. In: Proceedings of the 4th Australasian User Interface Conference, pp. 65–73. Australian Computer Society (2003)
13. Rusinkiewicz, S., Levoy, M.: Efficient variants of the ICP algorithm. In: Third International Conference on 3D Digital Imaging and Modeling (3DIM), June 2001
14. Schall, G., Wagner, D., Reitmayr, G., Taichmann, E., Wieser, M., Schmalstieg, D., Hofmann-Wellenhof, B.: Global pose estimation using multi-sensor fusion for outdoor augmented reality. In: ISMAR, pp. 153–162. IEEE Computer Society (2009)
15. Scheuermann, C., Bruegge, B., Folmer, J., Verclas, S.: Incident localizationand assistance system: A case study of a cyber-physical human system. In: 2015 IEEE/CIC International Conference on Communications in China: 3rd IEEE ICCC International Workshop on Internet of Things (2015 ICCC IoT Workshop), Shenzhen, P.R. China, November 2015
16. Vadala, E., Graham, C.: Downtime costs auto industry $22k/minute - survey (2006). http://news.thomasnet.com/companystory/downtime-costs-auto-industry -22k-minute-survey-481017
17. You, S., Neumann, U.: Fusion of vision and gyro tracking for robust augmented reality registration. In: VR, pp. 71–78. IEEE Computer Society (2001)
18. Zhou, F., Duh, H., Billinghurst, M.: Trends in augmented reality tracking, interaction, display: A review of ten years of ISMAR. In: 7th IEEE/ACM International Symposium on Mixed and Augmented Reality (ISMAR). IEEE Computer Society (2008)

A Framework for Outdoor Mobile Augmented Reality and Its Application to Mountain Peak Detection

Roman Fedorov$^{(\boxtimes)}$, Darian Frajberg, and Piero Fraternali

Dipartimento di Elettronica, Informazione e Bioingegneria, Politecnico di Milano,
Piazza Leonardo da Vinci, 32, Milan, Italy
{roman.fedorov,darian.frajberg,piero.fraternali}@polimi.it

Abstract. Outdoor augmented reality applications project information of interest onto views of the world in real-time. Their core challenge is recognizing the meaningful objects present in the current view and retrieving and overlaying pertinent information onto such objects. In this paper we report on the development of a framework for mobile outdoor augmented reality application, applied to the overlay of peak information onto views of mountain landscapes. The resulting app operates by estimating the virtual panorama visible from the viewpoint of the user, using an online Digital Terrain Model (DEM), and by matching such panorama to the actual image framed by the camera. When a good match is found, meta-data from the DEM (e.g., peak name, altitude, distance) are projected in real time onto the view. The application, besides providing a nice experience to the user, can be employed to crowdsource the collection of annotated mountain images for environmental applications.

Keywords: Outdoor augmented reality · Mobile · Real-time · Mountain peak identification · Environment monitoring · Computer vision

1 Introduction

Outdoor augmented reality applications exploit the position and orientation sensors of mobile devices to estimate the location of the user and her field of view so as to overlay such view with information pertinent to the user's inferred interest. These solutions are finding a promising application in the tourism sector, where they replace traditional map-based interfaces with a more sophisticated user experience whereby the user automatically receives information based on what he is looking at, without the need of manual search. Examples of such AR apps include, e.g., Metro AR and Lonely Planet's Compass Guides[1]. The main challenge of such applications is providing an accurate estimation of the user's current interest, adapted in real-time to the changing view. Most commercial applications simplify the problem by estimating the user's interest based only

---

[1] http://www.lonelyplanet.com/guides.

© Springer International Publishing Switzerland 2016
L.T. De Paolis and A. Mongelli (Eds.): AVR 2016, Part I, LNCS 9768, pp. 281–301, 2016.
DOI: 10.1007/978-3-319-40621-3_21

on the information provided by the device position and orientation sensors, irrespective of the content actually in view. Examples are sky maps, which show the names of constellations, planets and stars based on the GPS position and compass signal. An obvious limit of these approaches is that they may provide information that does not match well what the user is seeing, due to errors in the position and orientation estimation or to the presence of objects partially occluding the view. These limitations, besides jeopardizing the user's experience, prevent the possibility for the AR application to create *augmented content*. If the overlay of the meta-data onto the view is imprecise, it is not possible for the user to save a copy of the augmented view, e.g., in the form of an image with captions associated to the objects. Such augmented content could be useful for several purposes: archiving the augmented outdoor experience, indexing visual content for supporting search and retrieval of the annotated visual objects, and even for the extraction of semantic information from the augmented content.

This paper describes *SnowWatch*, an outdoor mobile AR application for the automatic annotation of in-view mountain peaks with geographical meta-data (peak name, altitude, distance from viewer, etc.). Unlike other systems (e.g., PeakFinder), SnowWatch exploits a content-based reality augmentation algorithm, which takes in input not only the position and orientation of the user's device but also the content of the current view. The meta-data employed for reality augmentation derive from a Digital Elevation Model (DEM), which is a 3D representation of the Earth's surface. The augmentation process works in two steps. First, the DEM, the position and the orientation of the user are exploited to estimate a bi-dimensional projection of the panorama that should be viewed by the camera of the mobile device and to match such virtual panorama to the image currently captured by the camera. Second, when a high probability match is found, meta-data about mountain peaks are transferred from the DEM to the camera view; they are superimposed in real time to the camera view and can be saved as an augmented image of the mountain landscape.

The contributions of the paper can be summarized as follows:

- We introduce the problem of reality augmentation, specifically for mountain landscape views.
- We summarize our previous results in the offline detection of mountain peaks in static, geo-referenced images.
- We highlight the challenges of porting the offline algorithms to a mobile AR context, in terms of accuracy, stability of the registration of the camera view to the virtual panorama, and unreliable network connectivity.
- We describe a framework for the development and testing of outdoor mobile AR applications created for addressing the above-mentioned challenges.
- We illustrate the application of the framework to real-time peak detection and different optimization techniques that have been introduced in the generic framework to support the mountain peak identification task.
- We define a performance evaluation metrics based on a scalar value simulating the error that would be perceived in a real usage session.
- We report on the preliminary results of evaluating the SnowWatch app in real outdoor experimental conditions.

The rest of the paper is organized as follows: Sect. 2 overviews previous work in the areas of outdoor augmented reality applications, mountain image analysis, and environmental monitoring applications; Sect. 3 states the problem of outdoor AR application design and presents a generic architectural framework addressing the challenges of this class of applications; Sect. 4 shows the application of the framework to real-time mountain peak detection: it sets the background of the problem, briefly recaps our previous results for *offline* peak identification, highlights the challenges of the real-time AR version, and discusses the optimization techniques implemented, reporting the preliminary results of their evaluation; Sect. 5 concludes by presenting the outcome of using annotated mountain images for the resolution of a real-world environmental problem, and provides an outlook about the next research objectives.

2   Related Work

Augmented reality applications. AR is a well established research topic within the Human Computer Interaction field, which has recently attracted new attention due to the announcement by major hardware vendors of low-cost, mass-market AR devices. In particular, the recent trend of mobile devices as AR platforms benefits from the improved standardization (most AR software can now be used without ad hoc hardware), increased computational power and sensor precision [13]. The survey in [3] overviews the history of research and development in AR, introduces the definitions at the base of the discipline, and positions it within the broader landscape of other technologies. The authors also propose design guidelines and examples of successful AR applications and give an outlook on future research directions. An important branch of the discipline is the outdoor AR. Several works address the problem, usually to identify [5] and track [21] points of interest in urban scenarios. Although standard solutions for mobile AR already exist (e.g. Wikitude[2]), they rely only on compass sensors or the a priori known appearance of the objects. We present a novel framework for the fusion of the two techniques: refining the compass-based AR performance without knowing a priori the appearance of the objects.

Mountain image analysis. Image analysis in mountain regions is a well investigated area, with applications that support environmental studies on climate change and tourism [7]. Mountain image analysis research focuses on peak identification in public photographs [1,2] and the problem of segmenting the portion of the photograph corresponding to a certain mountain in snow covered areas [22,24]. A prominent application field of mountain image analysis is snow information extraction. Traditionally snow is monitored through manual measurement campaigns, permanent measurement stations, satellite photography, and terrestrial photography. Most approaches (e.g. [22,24]) rely on cameras designed and positioned ad hoc by researchers, and are not applicable to user-generated images created in uncontrolled conditions. Porzi et al. [18] propose an

---

[2] http://www.wikitude.com/app/.

app for mountain peak detection; the contribution focuses on the time efficient peak identification and does not address mobile AR requirements, such as real-time response, asynchronous dynamics of the algorithms and uncertain internet connection. Furthermore, the authors report the performance of the algorithms in terms of error vs time measures, so it is unclear which of the algorithms would provide a better user experience. In our work we propose a Capture and Replay testing framework that provides a unique performance measure capturing exactly the error that would be perceived by the user. SnowWatch has the potential of enabling a novel generation of mountain environment monitoring applications, in which the augmented images created by the users during tourist trips are reused for extracting information useful for environment management and planning problems. We report our first results in this direction in Sect. 5.

Environmental citizen science applications. "Citizen science" refers to the direct engagement of non-specialized people (the citizens) to help address scientific problems [15]. The massive diffusion of social media, with its powerful tools for public communication, engagement, and content sharing, has multiplied the ways to engage volunteers and exploit relevant public User-Generated Content (UGC). In particular, social media combined with mobile devices favored the collection of *geo-located* UGC in applications related to spatial information, so-called Volunteered Geographical Information Systems (VGIS), in which citizens help enhance, update or complement existing geo-spatial databases [11]. Several approaches have been applied to disaster management for e.g., earthquake mapping [29] and rapid flood damage estimation [19]. Applications monitoring hazards through the collection of user-generated content are also reported: tweet distribution analysis for monitoring is employed in [23] for earthquakes and in [25] for floods. Examples exist of continuous monitoring applications in the environmental field: bird observation network [26], phenological studies [20], hydrological risk assessment [6], plant leaf status assessment [17] and geological surveys (http://britishgeologicalsurvey.crowdmap.com). Besides text, also visual content, such as Flickr photographs [27] and public touristic webcams [16] have been used to monitor environmental phenomena, such as coarse-grained snow cover maps [27], vegetation cover maps [28], flora distribution [27], cloud maps [16] and other meteorological processes [12].

3   A Framework for Mobile Outdoor AR Applications

The problem addressed in this work is the design of mobile AR applications for the enrichment of outdoor natural objects. Restricting the focus to devices that support a bi-dimensional view, a generic architecture must be realized that receives as a first input a representation of the reality - in which the user is embedded - captured by the device sensors; such representation typically comprises a sequence of camera frames captured at a fixed rate, and the position and orientation of the device, captured by the GPS and orientation sensors; the second input is the information about the possible objects present in a region of interest. The output is the on-screen position of relevant objects and the association of relevant meta-data to such objects, computed at the same frequency of the input capture. Besides the near real-time execution time, the system must also cope with the following requirements:

- *Uncontrolled viewing conditions*: the objects to be identified have no fixed, known a priori, appearance, because the viewing conditions can drastically change due to weather, illumination, occlusions, etc.
- *Uncertain positioning*: position and orientation sensor errors make the location estimation potentially noisy; thus the identification of the relevant objects from these signals alone cannot be assumed to be fully reliable and must be corrected with information from the camera view.
- *Bi-dimensional reduction*: although the objects' position in the real world is estimated in the 3D space, the on-screen rendition requires a projection onto the 2D surface of the camera view, based on a model of the camera.
- *Uncertain internet connection*: especially for rural and mountain regions.

Figure 1 shows a representation, through an UML component diagram, of the reference architecture of a mobile outdoor AR application. The key idea is to enable the near real-time reality augmentation process thanks to a proper partition of functionality and a mix of synchronous and asynchronous communications among the modules. The architecture consists of four sub-systems: the Sensor Manager, the Data Manager, the Position Alignment Manager and the Bi-dimensional Graphical User Interface, which draws objects and their meta-data in provided on-screen coordinates.

3.1 Sensor Manager

The *Sensor Manager* coordinates data acquisition from the device sensors. It typically comprises one module per each signal processed by the application; the typical configuration comprises the GPS Sensor Manager, the Orientation Sensor Manager and the Camera Sensor Manager. The modules work asynchronously and provide input to the Position Alignment Manager and Data Manager, which subscribe to their interface and are notified when a new signal arrives from a sensor.

3.2 Data Manager

The *Data Manager* is responsible for providing to the other sub-systems the initial positions of the objects in view and the meta-data for enriching them. It receives as input the specification of an area of interest (typically, inferred from the user's position, which defines the region the user may be looking at, or may be moving within), and interacts with an external repository containing a virtual representation of the world (e.g., a sky map or a DEM). It produces as output *Object Positions*, which specify the (initially approximate) 3D coordinates of the candidate objects to display. Within the *Data Manager*, a *Data Provider*

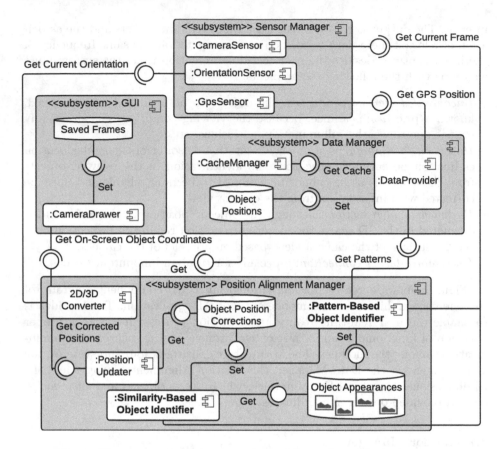

Fig. 1. The proposed architecture of a mobile outdoor AR application.

component queries one or more external geo-referenced data sources, with the current user's location, and extracts the coordinates of the objects that are likely to lie within the view of the user. For example, in a sky observation app, it queries the sky map for the celestial coordinates, plus meta-data such as type, name, distance, etc., of the potentially visible objects. The *Cache Manager* implements data pre-fetching and synchronization policies, based on information about current cache content, network availability, and cost of data transfer. Since data about the objects can be large the Cache Manager realizes a trade-off between on-demand transfer from external data sources and caching in the local storage of the device. Furthermore, it enables disconnected usage, as needed in the outdoor scenario, in which internet connection may not be always granted.

3.3   Position Alignment Manager

The Data Manager provides a *fast* computation of the initial Object Positions, to enable the immediate update of the GUI. But its output may be noisy, because the estimated user's position, the camera orientation and the virtual world representation may all contain errors. It is well-know that the GPS and orientation signal of mobile devices may be inaccurate; on the other hand, also the virtual world representation, e.g., a DEM describing the earth surface, may be affected by errors, e.g., due to low resolution. Therefore, the Position Alignment Manager comprises components for updating the positions of the objects, adapting them to the actual content of the camera view, and projecting them to the device's view. It takes in input the initial object positions provided by the Data Manager and produces in output the *corrected* on screen object coordinates. To support the trade-off between accuracy and speed, the (demanding) computations required for improving accuracy are delegated to separate modules, which provide asynchronous corrections to the initial candidate positions, by applying content-based object detection techniques. These modules feed the *Object Position Corrections* store (see Fig. 1) with the adjustments computed asynchronously, which the *Position Updater* and *3D/2D Converter* components exploit to correct the on screen coordinates used by the GUI. Examples of components for the content-based refinement of object positions are *Pattern-Based* and *Similarity-Based* Object Identifiers.

A *Pattern-Based Object Identifier* performs a frame-based match. It uses the virtual world representation as a pattern to search within the real world image. It takes in input the virtual representation of the world (e.g., the synthetic rendition of a constellation or of a piece of mountain skyline) and computes a ranked list of approximate matches between the virtual image and the real one, with respect to some similarity function. As a collateral output, the Pattern-Based Object Identifier can also extract from the real world image the regions that correspond to the identified objects, according to the best match. Such artifacts, cached in the *Object Appearance Store* of Fig. 1, denote the visual appearance of the objects of interest in the current view and can be used for accelerating the correction of objects' positions when the view changes.

A *Similarity-Based Object Identifier* performs object-based similarity search; it takes in input the object appearance artifacts and searches them in the frame, using computer vision techniques.

Finally, the *2D/3D Converter* projects 3D positions onto the bi-dimensional screen space. It takes in input the device position, orientation, and Field Of View (FOV), applies a prospective projection, determines the on-screen coordinates of the candidate objects and discards those out-of-view, e.g., due to micro-movements of the device. For example, it projects the celestial coordinates of the relevant sky objects into on-screen coordinates. The on-screen coordinates are used by the GUI for rendering the augmented reality view.

The asynchronous communication between the components that compute position corrections and those that project positions and render the virtual reality view aims at enabling a best effort, near real-time adjustment of the view. The prospective projection is a constant-time procedure, so that the total response time of the Position Updater and of the 3D/2D Converter is linear w.r.t. to the number of candidate objects. Since this number is reasonably bound, the resulting time complexity is constant, which allows the mobile device to call the Position Updater and the 3D/2D Converter *synchronously* at every frame arrival and redraw the view in near real-time based on the best available approximation of the object positions.

3.4   Capture and Replay Testing Framework

Testing an outdoor AR application is a complex task that requires evaluating simultaneously the precision of object positioning and the response time, two competing objectives, in a realistic setting that considers the sensor inputs (not available in the lab). The assessment criteria must also take into account usage conditions: if the user keeps the device steady, low error is the prominent goal, while higher execution time due to re-positioning after micro-movements is less relevant; conversely, if the device is subject to movement (e.g., during walking), fast execution can be more important than object positioning precision. Therefore, testing should be supported by an auxiliary architecture that helps achieve the following objectives:

- Perform lab testing in conditions equivalent to real outdoor usage.
- Contrast different designs in the same operating conditions and assess the same designs under different operating conditions.
- Use the performance metrics best suited to a specific application and operating condition.

To support such requirements, we have extended the architecture of Fig. 1 with a testing framework based on a *Capture & Replay* approach:

- A *Capture application*: it is a mobile application that can be used to record an outdoor usage session, complete with all sensor data (camera, GPS and orientation) and user's activity (start, stop, video record, snapshot, etc.).
- An *Annotation application*: it is an application that allows one to annotate the frames of a usage session with the position of the visible objects, so to create a gold standard for evaluating the accuracy of object positioning.
- A *Replay test driver*: it is an application that can attach to the Position Alignment Manager sub-system of the architecture of Fig. 1 and measure its performance based on a plug-in metrics.

The Capture application collects execution traces. A trace consists of a sequence of entries that record all the events occurred during a usage session, including: information about the device manufacturer and model; the set of frame images taken at frequency F, with their acquisition timestamp; and the sequence of time-stamped sensor readings, i.e., the values of the position and orientation sensors acquired at the maximum frequency supported by the device. The above mentioned information, logged by default, is normally sufficient to reproduce the user activity for a typical outdoor AR application; however, the Capture application can be extended to support additional logging, if needed by a specific application. The Annotation application allows the developer to associate with each frame zero or more triples $< i, x_i, y_i >$, where i is the index of an object visible on that frame, and x_i, y_i are the on-screen coordinates of that object. The annotated frame sets can be used as the ground truth for the assessment of the Position Alignment Manager. The Replay test driver is an application stub that replaces the Sensor Manager, Data Manager and GUI of the architecture of Fig. 1, so to reproduce the sequence of events and sensor readings previously recorded by the Capture application. It takes in input one or more traces and supplies to the Position Alignment Manager the frame images, at the capture frequency F, and the corresponding values of the sensor readings; then, it retrieves from the Position Alignment Manager the estimation of on-screen object positions and evaluates them w.r.t. the ground truth and to a selected metrics. The Replay test driver utilizes a metric function (called Real-Time Average Angular Error, RTAAE) that considers the positioning errors of all the relevant objects. For each visible object $i = 1, \ldots, n$ let (x_i, y_i) be the on-screen coordinates predicted by the Position Alignment Manager, while $(\hat{x}_i, \hat{y}_i)$ be the ground truth coordinates. We define the angular error in the position of the i-th object as

$$\varepsilon(\hat{x}_i, \hat{y}_i) = \sqrt{d_x(\hat{x}_i, x_i)^2 + d_y(\hat{y}_i, y_i)^2},$$

where

$$d_x(\hat{x}, x) = min(360 - \frac{f}{w}|\hat{x} - x|, \frac{f}{w}|\hat{x} - x|)$$

is the angular distance (in degrees) between the predicted and ground truth coordinate along the azimuth axis, given the circular symmetry, f is the horizontal FOV (in degrees) of the camera and w is the width (in pixels) of the image. Similarly we define the angular distance along the roll axis:

$$d_y(\hat{y}, y) = \frac{f}{w}|\hat{y} - y|$$

Note than the same angular resolution in degrees/pixel is assumed for both axes, because the elevation angles are small. The angular error for an entire sequence can be defined as the average angular error of each frame. Finally, given N traces, the Real-Time Average Angular Error (RTAAE) is the average over all traces.

Note that the described Capture & Replay approach allows lab tests to assess the Position Alignment Manager in the same operating conditions that occur in an outdoor session, because it exploits the same frame acquisition rate and sensor sampling frequency experimented in the real time use.

4   SnowWatch: An Outdoor AR Application for Mountain Image Enrichment

This section describes how the architecture of Fig. 1 has been adapted to the development of a mobile AR application for real-time mountain peak detection, by porting existing algorithms developed for the offline identification of peaks in geo-tagged photographs to the mobile AR context[3]. Here, we highlight the challenges in adapting the algorithms to the mobile AR scenario, discuss the application-specific solutions, and report preliminary evaluation results obtained with the testing framework described in Sect. 3.4. The offline algorithms have been developed in the SnowWatch project [9][4], which tackles mountain monitoring with a Citizen Science application for the collection of public Alpine images and the extraction of snow indexes usable in water availability prediction models. To this aim, SnowWatch crawls a large number of images from content sharing sites and touristic webcams, classifies those images that portrait mountain peaks and contain the location of shooting, identifies visible peaks by automatically aligning each image to a synthetic rendition computed from a public DEM, finds the pixels of each peak that represent snow and calculates useful snow indexes (e.g., minimum snow altitude). These indexes are then used to feed existing water prediction models and compared with other official sources of information.

The SnowWatch Web architecture is mainly server-side and thus very different from the mobile AR architecture of Fig. 1: it combines data providers (photograph crawler and webcam crawler), data consumers (front-end web portal and environmental models) and back-end processes that analyze photographs and enrich them with landscape and environmental meta-data (orientation of the photograph, mountain peak positions, snow covered areas). The interaction of the user is similar to that of a sharing site: uploading one's photos, applying filters (for peak detection, in this case), correcting the position of peaks manually, and rating, sharing, and commenting the resulting pictures.

Fig. 2. Photo to panorama cylindrical and equivalent 2D Cartesian alignment.

4.1 Offline Peak Detection for the Web

One of the key algorithms of SnowWatch Web architecture is the offline peak identification. Peak positions are obtained through the alignment between the photo and the terrain model. Given a photograph and the meta-data extracted from its EXIF container (geo-tag, focal length, camera model and manufacturer), a matching is performed with a 360° panoramic view of the terrain synthesized from a public, Web-accessible DEM. The rendered panorama contains

---

[3] A detailed description of the offline algorithms can be found in [8,10].
[4] http://snowwatch.polimi.it/?lang=en.

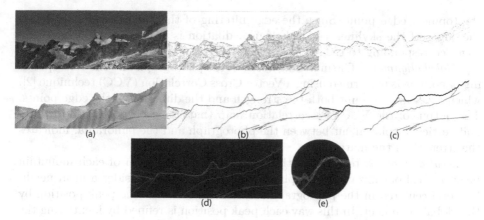

Fig. 3. An example of the photo-to-terrain alignment: (a) input photograph (top) and corresponding panorama (bottom), (b) edge extraction, (c) skyline detection, filtering and dilation (d) global alignment with refinement (e) local alignment. (Color figure online)

the mountain peak positions, so once a correct overlap is found, peak positions are projected from the panorama to the photo. The alignment can be seen as the search for the correct overlap between two cylinders (assuming the zero tilt of the photograph): one containing the 360° panorama and the other one containing the photo, suitably scaled. As Fig. 2 shows, this is equivalent to look for the offset between the photo and the unfolded 2D panorama that guarantees the best overlap. The alignment method proceeds in four steps, described below and illustrated in Fig. 3.

Preprocessing: The horizontal Field Of View (FOV) of the photograph is calculated from the focal length and the size of the camera sensor. Then, the photograph is rescaled considering that the width of the panorama corresponds to a FOV equal to 360°. After this step, the photo and the panorama have the same scale in degrees per pixel and thus matching can be performed without the need of scale invariant methods. Then an edge extraction algorithm is applied to both the photograph and the panorama to produce an edge map, which assigns to each pixel the strength of the edge at that point and its direction (Fig. 3b).

Matching edges of an image with those of a virtual panorama requires addressing the fact that there is not a one-to-one mapping between edge pixels extracted from the two sources. The photo generates many noisy edges that do not correspond to the mountain slopes, but to other objects in the foreground (e.g., rocks, trees, lakes, houses, etc.) and in the background (e.g., clouds, snow patches, etc.). Thus, a skyline detection algorithm is employed [14], and all the edge pixels above the skyline are removed, being considered obstacles or clouds. Then, a simple weighting mechanism is applied, which assigns decreasing weights to the edge pixels as the distance from the skyline increases (Fig. 3c - top). As for the panorama, the edges corresponding to the skyline can be simply identified as the upper envelope of the edge map, by keeping, for each column of pixels, the topmost edge point. Since the edge filtering of the photograph emphasizes the edges of the skyline, a morphological dilation is applied to emphasize the edges corresponding to the skyline of the panorama (Fig. 3c - bottom).

Global alignment: The matching between the photograph and the corresponding panorama is performed using a Vector Cross Correlation (VCC) technique [2], which takes into account both the strength and the direction of the edge points. The output of the VCC is a correlation map that, for each possible horizontal and vertical displacement between the photograph and the panorama, indicates the strength of the matching.

Local alignment: to improve the precision of the position of each mountain peak, a local optimization is applied. For each peak we consider a local neighborhood centered in the photograph location identified as the peak position by the global alignment. In this way each peak position is refined by identifying the best match in its local neighborhood. Overall, this is equivalent to applying a non-rigid warping of the photograph with respect to the panorama.

4.2   Mobile Peak Detection for AR Apps

The mobile version of the mountain peak detection task requires significant adaptations of the offline approach, to comply with the architecture of Fig. 1. The main challenges induced by the mobile and real-time AR requirements include:

- Lower computational power w.r.t. Web multi-tier architectures.
- Higher accuracy: while it is tolerable for a web-based application to misidentify mountain peaks (the image will be discarded, or manually adjusted by the Web user), an erroneous peak identification on a mobile application used live produces a disappointing user experience and the enriched image, once saved, can not be easily fixed on a small screen device.
- Faster response time: peak positions must be overlaid in real-time and no overhead for image processing initialization is acceptable, because mobile users do not tolerate delays in the order of seconds at app every start.
- Data storage and transfer: the whole data set for peak identification (the DEM) is too big to be stored entirely in the a mobile device; at the same time, the internet connection for downloading the needed data on the fly, can not be assumed always available. Indeed, a mountain peak AR app must be usable in mountain regions, where even today internet coverage is patchy.
- Technical constraints: mobile application development imposes numerous restrictions on the supported architectures, frameworks and libraries.

On the other hand, a significant advantage of the mobile version is the availability in real-time of the position and orientation sensor values, which, although subject to error, provides an estimate of the panorama in view.

The SnowWatch mobile AR application specializes the architecture of Fig. 1. In the sequel, we describe the application-specific concepts and component refinements introduced for the mobile context.

The *objects* to be identified are mountain peaks and the *object positions* are 3D global system coordinates laying on a unit sphere centered in the device location.

An application-specific *Cache Manager* has been implemented, responsible for pre-fetching and caching the DEM fragments corresponding to the geographical region the user is visiting. Pre-fetching is enabled when the WiFi connection of the device is on and cache data are used by the DataProvider component to compute the Object Positions during outdoor usage. When the user moves out of the region for which data are in the cache, a cache miss triggers the download of a new fragment, which, in case of cache full, replaces the fragment relative to the region visited earliest.

The *Similarity-Based Object Identifier* component is implemented with a state-of-the-art cross-correlation patch recognition technique [4], which has been ported to the mobile execution environment.

The component where the most relevant adaptations have been introduced is the Pattern-Based Object Identifier, described next.

4.3 Pattern-Based Object Identifier

The Pattern-Based Object Identifier implements the pattern matching between the skyline extracted from the DEM and the skyline visible in the camera view, and computes Object Position Corrections based on the outcome of such procedure. It has been realized starting from the experience for offline peak detection described in Sect. 4.1, introducing significant improvements.

Non-Zero Tilt. The web version of the matching algorithm assumes the camera tilt as negligible (equal to 0) and reduces the problem to the alignment between two cylinders, avoiding the (much more costly) spherical match. This assumption proved viable experimentally; mountain ranges are far from the position of the user and the error induced by a moderate tilt is compensated by the skyline matching algorithm. On a mobile device the assumption of zero or constant tilt must be relaxed, to cope with the movements of the mobile device made by the user during a viewing or shooting session. To avoid switching from 2D cylindrical to 3D spherical alignment, which would jeopardize the response time, we designed an approximate approach: the input image is rotated by the tilt provided by the orientation sensor, standard 2D alignment is performed, and the final peak coordinates are rotated in the inverse direction at the end. This method deals with tilting effectively and preserves the fast response time of the 2D alignment, to obtain corrections to the 3D object positions.

Edge Filtering and Skyline Detection. The heuristic methods described in Sect. 4.1 work well for offline peak detection, because they are applied to pre-filtered images (fixed webcams have a view that does not change and can be manually checked once and for all for suitability; user generated photos go through an offline binary classification step to retain only samples with obstacle-free skyline view). But they are not well suited to a mobile AR scenario, where it is more likely that the camera is used in adverse weather conditions and in presence of transient occlusions of the skyline. In these cases, a cloud, a high voltage cable, or a roof would be recognized as part of the mountain skyline; this would impact the heuristic edge filtering, e.g., a cloud edge would be treated as skyline and the mountain slope below it would be considered as noise. Such erroneous classification would hamper the alignment with the DEM and the positioning of peaks, yielding an unacceptable user's experience.

To increase robustness even to small, transient occlusions, we developed a new approach, based on the application of a Convolutional Neural Network (CNN) supervised learning algorithm, which finds the *landscape skyline*, i.e., the set of all points that represent the boundary between terrain slopes and the sky. First of all, a simple and fast Canny edge detector extracts a draft binary edge map. Then every pixel of such map is classified as positive or negative, where positive means that it belongs to the landscape skyline. The edge pixels classified negatively are removed from the edge map. For each edge pixel a $K \times K \times 3$ RGB patch centered at the pixel coordinates is extracted and classified with an image content-based classifier. The choice of the CNN over other machine learning algorithms (e.g. Logistic Regression, SVM, Random Forest) is motivated by the ability of the CNN to learn the best features to employ, which avoids their manual, and subjective, definition. Conversely, a typical downside of using CNN, the need of a very large amount of training data, is not an obstacle in our case, because the items to classify are small patches extracted from the neighborhood of image edges; in our experiments, an average 640×480 outdoor image contains tens of thousands of edge pixels. To build the training and test sets, it is sufficient to manually annotate the image with its landscape skyline. Then, all the patches corresponding to the edge points can be extracted and classified automatically (positive if the center is located no more than d pixels from a skyline point). With this semi-automatic procedure, it is possible to generate the massive amount of training data necessary to train the CNN, with low effort.

Figure 4 shows an example of alignment taken in very adverse conditions: the input image (top left) is taken from behind a window, the corresponding fragment of the panorama (middle left) contains two mountain peaks (red arrows). The edges extracted from the input image (top center) contain an enormous amount of noisy edges (mountain vegetation, houses, window frame) that would make the alignment with the panorama impossible; the CNN filtering procedure (top right, green points) successfully retains only skyline edge pixels. The panorama skyline to match is extracted simply by picking top points (middle center, red points); the alignment between the two skylines (middle right) allows us to project the two peak positions on the input image with high precision (bottom, augmented image). This resulted is computed in real time and the peak positions remain precise even when the user tilts or moves the mobile phone.

Occlusion Management. The virtual panorama view contains only the peaks that could be visible by an observer based on the elevation model; in the real image, virtually visible peaks can be occluded by irrelevant objects, such as houses, people or even clouds or fog. The CNN network used for edge filtering in the mobile AR scenario helps dealing with occlusions: the network is trained

Fig. 4. Example of the peak identification in presence of many noisy edges. (Color figure online)

to recognize the *landscape skyline*, i.e., the portion of the topmost edges that actually represent the boundary of a mountain slope. This capability supports effective occlusion detection. Given a correct alignment between the landscape skyline of the image and the virtual skyline of the panorama, the peaks that are actually visible in the image will have fragments of the landscape skyline in their vicinity, while occluded peaks will not. Thus, once the alignment is found, for each peak a visibility score v is defined as the number of landscape skyline points located no farther than d pixels from the peak position. A peak is considered visible if $v \geq \bar{v}$ (where $\bar{v}$ is a fixed threshold). If a peak is considered visible, its appearance patch is extracted and cached; otherwise no patch is extracted (or its patch is removed from the cache, if previously stored). In this way, the Similarity-Based Peak Identifier will not find the patch inside the future frames. Figure 5 shows an example of peak identification with 3 virtually visible peaks. In this case, peak n.2 is occluded by the bell tower; indeed, besides a few false positive pixels, the bell tower contour is absent in the overall identified landscape skyline (top right). After the alignment, the neighborhood of each peak is analyzed (bottom right): peaks n.1 and n.3 present a large number of landscape skyline points (green dots) in their vicinity, while peak n.2 does not, so it is marked as non-visible and not included in the augmented image (bottom left).

Fig. 5. Example of the peak identification in presence of occlusions. (Color figure online)

Sensor Orientation. The sensed orientation of the device can be used to improve the performance of the object identification. Since the match between the virtual panorama and image skyline is approximate, each candidate peak position receives a score, which is an estimate of the confidence of the match algorithm. Such score can be manipulated to take into account the agreement between orientation as sensed from the compass and estimated by the Position Alignment Manager. For example, a kernel function based on the difference between the sensed and estimated orientation can be used as a scale factor. Furthermore, the computation of peak alignment can be avoided in the areas of the image in which the kernel factor is equal to zero, because those regions would provide an unreliable peak position estimation. Such optimization decreases the computation time: we assume a maximum $15°$ orientation sensor error and perform the photo-to-panorama alignment not in the whole $360°$ panorama, but only in a $30° + FOV$ portion of it.

4.4 Experiments

This section presents the preliminary results of evaluating the landscape skyline detection algorithm and the accuracy of peak identification, in the mobile AR scenario. The experimental data set used for training the CNN comprises 158 mountain photos randomly crawled from Flickr and manually annotated with the landscape skyline. Out of these, 111 were included in the train set ($\sim 70\%$)

and 47 in the test set ($\sim 30\%$). Then, for each image the binary edge map was computed, and patches (of size $28 \times 28 \times 3$) were extracted for each edge point and labeled as positive or negative. To guarantee the balance of the patches data set, the same number of positive and negative samples was extracted from each image (by random sub-sampling the larger class); to avoid over-emphasizing edge-rich images, a maximum of 400 positive and 400 negative patches were derived from each image. The splitting into test and train data sets was performed at the image level, and not at the patch level, to ensure a bias-free estimation of the ability of the classifier to adapt to scenarios not seen before (patches from the same image could not belong to both the training and test set). The overall observed accuracy of the CNN trained on the training set and evaluated on the test set was 96%, which resulted also in a satisfactory subjective judgment of the resulting skylines.

The evaluation of the peak identifier accuracy was performed on the *VEN-TURI Mountain Dataset* [18]. The data set is a collection of 12 outdoor sequences accompanied with GPS positions and orientation sensor logs, resulting in 3117 frames. For each frame the position of the mountain peaks is manually annotated. We measured the performance of the Pattern-Based Peak Identifier in terms of average peak position angular error. The observed average peak position error was $1.32°$, which is lower than the minimum error obtained by the authors of [18] and defined suitable for mobile computation, namely $1.87°$. The average time currently required by the pattern- and similarity-based peak identifiers to process a frame is respectively less than 3" and less than 1". Such times are totally dependent on the architecture and characteristics of the device being used, which in this case correspond to a Motorola Nexus 6 with Chipset Qualcomm Snapdragon 805, CPU Quad-core 2.7 GHz Krait 450, GPU Adreno 420, RAM 3 GB, OS Android 5.1.1. On the other hand, due to the architecture of the system, the *on-screen peak positioning is always real-time* thanks to the sensor data, while the time complexity of peak identifiers influences only the update frequency of corrected peak positions.

Figure 6 shows an example of the mountain identification process in the mobile AR scenario. Initially, the on-screen peak positions are determined only through the orientation sensor data (top, red icons represent the predicted positions, arrows the real positions and the angular error is reported). After the photo-to-panorama alignment is performed, the peak positions are estimated more precisely (bottom left, green icons) and the corresponding mountain patches are extracted. The bottom right part of the figure shows how, in the next frames with a (slightly) different view, the same peaks can be quickly located by the similarity-based peak identifier.

Future experiments will collect a larger image data set, with occluded mountain skylines, which are missing in the Venturi data set. The described algorithms will be tested using the Capture and Replay framework of Sect. 3.4, to evaluate their response time with different mobile devices and RTAAE error.

Fig. 6. Example of an sensor-, pattern- and similarity-based peak identifications. Images from the Venturi dataset [18]. (Color figure online)

5   Conclusions and Future Work

We have presented a framework for the development of outdoor mobile AR applications and discussed its use in SnowWatch, an application for mountain image enrichment. SnowWatch has the primary goal of attracting the interest of tourists, who could use it to enhance their outdoor experience with virtual expert knowledge about the mountain peaks in view. However, the project has also a second, equally important, goal: producing a repository of annotated mountain images for supporting environmental research. This requires assessing the environmental utility of information derived from public mountain images; to this end, we have collected a large set of images contributed by users and automatically crawled from touristic webcams[5] and extracted automatically snow information to address a water management problem in which snow is a determinant factor. In particular, we exploited a water management simulation model for the regulation of the Como Lake and evaluated the impact of adding snow-related indexes (e.g., minimum snow altitude) extracted from annotated mountain images to its input. Lake Como is a regulated lake in Northern Italy with an Alpine hydro-meteorological regime characterized by scarce discharge in winter

---

[5] The data set is available at http://snowwatch.polimi.it.

and summer and water abundance in late spring and autumn due to rainfall and snow melt from catchment mountains. The lake inflow and effluent is the Adda River, which feeds hydroelectric power plants and serves five agricultural districts. The regulation model aims to support the decision makers in the daily setting of the lake level, so to prevent flooding in Como city, while ensuring water for agriculture. Farmers downstream would like to store water for the summer, but this increases the lake level and the flood risks. These competing goals generate a conflict between flooding and irrigation, which can be modeled using two quantitative objectives: 1. *Flooding*: the average annual number days when the lake is higher that the flooding risk threshold. 2. *Irrigation*: the daily average squared water deficit w.r.t. the daily downstream demand. Preliminary experiments with the two-objectives policy simulation model show that the virtual snow indexes computed from annotated mountain images help design more informed, and thus closer-to-the-optimum, water management policies. Specifically, the virtual snow indexes extracted from public mountain images have been compared with the official snow information of Region Lombardy, elaborated from ground stations and satellite data: even the snow information extracted from a single webcam stream in the lake catchment is capable of identifying policies with performance comparable to those conditioned on the official snow bulletin data. Our future plans aim at deploying the SnowWatch mobile app to the vast community of tourists and residents of the Lombardy region, to enlarge the mountain image data set and improve the predicting power of the mountain image information for lake regulation and for other environmental problems.

Acknowledgment. This work has been partially funded by European Commission and by the Lombardy Region through the PROACTIVE FESR Project (http://www. proactiveproject.eu) and by the FP7 CHEST Project (http://www.chest-project.eu) open call grant.

References

1. Baatz, G., Saurer, O., Köser, K., Pollefeys, M.: Large scale visual geo-localization of images in mountainous terrain. In: Fitzgibbon, A., Lazebnik, S., Perona, P., Sato, Y., Schmid, C. (eds.) ECCV 2012, Part II. LNCS, vol. 7573, pp. 517–530. Springer, Heidelberg (2012)
2. Baboud, L., Cadik, M., Eisemann, E., Seidel, H.P.: Automatic photo-to-terrain alignment for the annotation of mountain pictures. In: 2011 IEEE Conference on Computer Vision and Pattern Recognition (CVPR), pp. 41–48. IEEE (2011)
3. Billinghurst, M., Clark, A.J., Lee, G.A.: A survey of augmented reality. Found. Trends Hum. Comput. Interact. 8(2–3), 73–272 (2015)
4. Briechle, K., Hanebeck, U.D.: Template matching using fast normalized cross correlation. In: Aerospace/Defense Sensing, Simulation, and Controls, pp. 95–102. International Society for Optics and Photonics (2001)
5. Dähne, P., Karigiannis, J.N.: Archeoguide: system architecture of a mobile outdoor augmented reality system. In: null, p. 263. IEEE (2002)

6. Degrossi, L.C., Albuquerque, J., Fava, M.C., Mendiondo, E.M.: Flood citizen observatory: a crowdsourcing-based approach for flood risk management in brazil. In: 26th International Conference on Software Engineering and Knowledge Engineering (2014)
7. Dizerens, C., Hüsler, F., Wunderle, S.: Webcam imagery rectification and classification: potential for complementing satellite-derived snow maps over switzerland
8. Fedorov, R., Camerada, A., Fraternali, P., Tagliasacchi, M.: Estimating snow cover from publicly available images. IEEE Trans. Multimedia 18(6), 1187–1200 (2016)
9. Fedorov, R., Fraternali, P., Pasini, C.: SnowWatch: a multi-modal citizen science application. In: Bozzon, A., Cudré-Mauroux, P., Pautasso, C. (eds.) ICWE 2016. LNCS, vol. 9671, pp. 538–541. Springer, Heidelberg (2016). doi:10.1007/978-3-319-38791-8_43
10. Fedorov, R., Fraternali, P., Tagliasacchi, M.: Mountain peak identification in visual content based on coarse digital elevation models. In: Proceedings of the 3rd ACM International Workshop on Multimedia Analysis for Ecological Data (2014)
11. Goodchild, M.F.: Citizens as sensors: the world of volunteered geography. Geo J. 69(4), 211–221 (2007)
12. Hyvärinen, O., Saltikoff, E.: Social media as a source of meteorological observations. Mon. Weather Rev. 138(8), 3175–3184 (2010)
13. Jain, P., Manweiler, J., Roy Choudhury, R.: Overlay: practical mobile augmented reality. In: Proceedings of the 13th Annual International Conference on Mobile Systems, Applications, and Services, pp. 331–344. ACM (2015)
14. Lie, W.N., Lin, T.C.I., Lin, T.C., Hung, K.S.: A robust dynamic programming algorithm to extract skyline in images for navigation. Pattern Recogn. Lett. 26(2), 221–230 (2005)
15. Memarsadeghi, N.: Citizen science [guest editors' introduction]. Comput. Sci. Eng. 17(4), 8–10 (2015)
16. Murdock, C., Jacobs, N., Pless, R.: Webcam2satellite: estimating cloud maps from webcam imagery. In: 2013 IEEE Workshop on Applications of Computer Vision (WACV), pp. 214–221. IEEE (2013)
17. NatureServe, F.: Natureserve explorer: an online encyclopedia of life (2012)
18. Porzi, L., Buló, S.R., Valigi, P., Lanz, O., Ricci, E.: Learning contours for automatic annotations of mountains pictures on a smartphone. In: Proceedings of the International Conference on Distributed Smart Cameras, p. 13. ACM (2014)
19. Poser, K., Dransch, D.: Volunteered geographic information for disaster management with application to rapid flood damage estimation. Geomatica (2010)
20. Reddy, S., Shilton, K., Burke, J., Estrin, D., Hansen, M., Srivastava, M.: Evaluating participation and performance in participatory sensing. UrbanSense08, p. 1 (2008)
21. Reitmayr, G., Drummond, T.: Going out: robust model-based tracking for outdoor augmented reality. In: Proceedings of the 5th IEEE and ACM International Symposium on Mixed and Augmented Reality (2006)
22. Rüfenacht, D., Brown, M., Beutel, J., Süsstrunk, S.: Temporally consistent snow cover estimation from noisy, irregularly sampled measurements. In: Proceedings of the 9th International Conference on Computer Vision Theory and Applications (2014)
23. Sakaki, T., Okazaki, M., Matsuo, Y.: Earthquake shakes twitter users: real-time event detection by social sensors. In: Proceedings of the 19th International Conference on World Wide Web, pp. 851–860. ACM (2010)
24. Salvatori, R., Plini, P., Giusto, M., et al.: Snow cover monitoring with images from digital camera systems. Ital. J. Remote Sens. 43, 137–145 (2011)

25. Schnebele, E., Cervone, G., Waters, N.: Road assessment after flood events using non-authoritative data. Nat. Hazards Earth Syst. Sci. **14**(4), 1007–1015 (2014)
26. Sullivan, B.L., Wood, C.L., Iliff, M.J., Bonney, R.E., Fink, D., Kelling, S.: ebird: a citizen-based bird observation network in the biological sciences. Biol. Conserv. **142**(10), 2282–2292 (2009)
27. Wang, J., Korayem, M., Crandall, D.J.: Observing the natural world with flickr. In: 2013 IEEE International Conference on Computer Vision Workshops (ICCVW), pp. 452–459. IEEE (2013)
28. Zhang, H., Korayem, M., Crandall, D.J., LeBuhn, G.: Mining photo-sharing websites to study ecological phenomena. In: Proceedings of the 21st International Conference on World Wide Web, pp. 749–758. ACM (2012)
29. Zook, M., Graham, M., Shelton, T., Gorman, S.: Volunteered geographic information and crowdsourcing disaster relief: a case study of the haitian earthquake. Available at SSRN 2216649 (2010)

Augmented Industrial Maintenance (AIM): A Case Study for Evaluating and Comparing with Paper and Video Media Supports

Vincent Havard[1(✉)], David Baudry[1], Xavier Savatier[2],
Benoit Jeanne[1], Anne Louis[1], and Bélahcène Mazari[1]

[1] LUSINE, CESI School, Rouen, France
{vhavard, dbaudry, bjeanne, alouis, bmazari}@cesi.fr
[2] IRSEEM, ESIGELEC School, Rouen, France
xavier.savatier@esigelec.fr

Abstract. Maintenance is a crucial point to improve productivity in industry whereas systems to be maintained have an increasing complexity. Augmented Reality (AR) can reduce maintenance process time and improve quality by giving virtual information and assistance to the operator during the procedure. In this paper, a workflow is firstly presented allowing a maintenance expert to author augmented reality maintenance procedures without computer skills. Then the AR maintenance application developed is described. Based on it, we present a case study which aims to compare maintenance efficiency with respect to the market available media support used, i.e. paper, video, AR tablet or AR Smart Glasses. A set of experiments involving 24 persons is described and analyzed. The results show that augmented reality maintenance reduce number of errors done by operator than with paper for the same duration of maintenance. A qualitative analysis shows that AR systems are well accepted by the users.

Keywords: Augmented reality · Maintenance · Industrial application · Smart glasses · Modelling

1 Introduction

Maintenance efficiency is a key point for reducing its cost. For example maintenance of off-shore wind farm can cost up to 30 % of the kWh [1]. Moreover, as industrial systems becomes more and more complex, operator's skills are more difficult to find or they need longer training period to be autonomous. In this domain, industry has 2 major problematics: how to train a just-hired operator in an efficient way and how to capitalize and reuse the company expertise. Digitalization could help companies to be more efficient and to solve these problematics. As augmented reality (AR) can overlay real world with virtual content in real time, it has become a major topic in the research and industrial maintenance.

The term "augmented reality" was introduced by Caudell [2] in 1992. The author prototyped a head-mounted display providing information about the head position in the real world that could display, **real time**, virtual contents through a video see-through system. In 1994, Milgram proposed a mixed reality taxonomy [3]. He put

© Springer International Publishing Switzerland 2016
L.T. De Paolis and A. Mongelli (Eds.): AVR 2016, Part I, LNCS 9768, pp. 302–320, 2016.
DOI: 10.1007/978-3-319-40621-3_22

forward the hypothesis that there was no clear delineation between the real and the virtual world, and that it was possible to pass from one world to another through a continuum, called **mixed reality** (see Fig. 1).

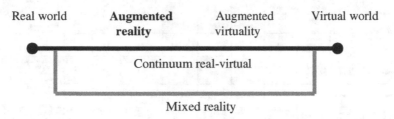

Fig. 1. Continuum real-virtual, called mixed reality

Following that, Azuma [4] proposed a more structured definition which was not technology dependent and commonly accepted by the community. Every augmented reality system should conform to these 3 rules:

1. A Combination of real and virtual
2. Interactive in real time
3. Registered in 3D

In order to be more concise in this paper, we define those virtual elements added to the real world as **augmentation** in the rest of the document. Augmented Reality is applied in several domains: games, leisure, medicine, tourism, training and maintenance [4–6]. This paper is focusing on the last topic since AR can be used as a tool to support a maintenance procedure. Interesting AR industrial projects for maintenance are detailed in [7] although no case study are formally presented.

Maintenance activity generally involves two kinds of collaborators: the maintenance expert and the operator, who respectively understands the failure and repairs it. Moreover, for large company or externalized services, operator is on site and is performing the maintenance while the expert could be remote. In literature we can distinguish two configurations of collaboration. One, where the expert is connected with the operator and explains him the process in a live conversation, we call it **assisted maintenance**. Another, where the operator is executing the process described on a specific media (paper, video or augmented reality) by the expert; there is no communication between each other's, we call it **guided maintenance**. Table 1 presents papers which focus on AR for maintenance and case studies done. Each paper is categorized by the tracking technology and the application domain used for their experiment. Moreover Table 1 presents how the expert authors the AR content, collaborates with the operator, then how the operator interacts with the AR system and which device is used during the experiment to see AR content. And last, Table 1 presents qualitative and quantitative results for case studies done. It displays completion time, number of errors, and qualitative criteria evaluated with the subjects.

Table 1. Augmented reality for maintenance in literature

Paper, year	Tracking technology	Use cases domain(s)	Expert - operator collaboration					Case study				
			Expert authoring and Interaction	Expert's system overview	Operator Interaction	Operator's Device(s)	Collaboration mode	Completion time	Completion time Standard deviation	Error	Qualitative criteria	Qualitative results
Bottechia, 2010 [8]	Template-based	Industrial maintenance	Mouse Keyboard Voice	Operator's video stream Voice	Voice	Smart Glasses - OST	Assisted	AR: 404 VISIO: 444 TEL: 441	AR.T.A.C: 91 VISIO: 123 TEL: 83	N/A	Easy conversation Speed estimated Understand expert explanation Comfort Easily fixing error Stress felt	AR is better
Friedrich, 2002 [10]	Marker-based Sensor-based Hybrid	Industrial Automotive Aircraft Assembly	Mouse Keyboard Remote laser	N/A	Microphone Remote laser	Head Mounted Display - VST	Assisted	N/A	N/A	N/A	Ergonomy Security Physiology	Eye troubles Headaches
Gonzalez-Franco, 2016 [16]	Sensor-based (Motion capture)	Industrial training	Mouse Keyboard	3D model	Motion tracked stick	Oculus Rift - VST	Guided	N/A	N/A	N/A	knowledge retention (QCM) knowledge interpretation	AR: 3.75/5 SD=1.21 Phys: 3.91/5 SD=1.41 AR: 35.4/43 SD=8.0 Phys: 39.5/43 SD=4.9
Henderson, 2011 [11]	Sensor based	Turret repair	Mouse Keyboard	3D model	No interaction	Head Mounted Display - VST	Guided	AR: 42s (loc 4.9) HUD: 55s(loc 11.1) LCD: 35s (loc 9.2)	boxplot (c.f paper)	N/A	Head movement Ease of use Satisfaction Intuitiveness	Less with AR LCD AR AR, LCD
Lamberti, 2014 [12]	3D model	Netbook repair	Mouse Keyboard	3D model (metaio)	Touchscreen	Tablet-VST	Guided	Paper: 671 s AR: 631 s	Paper: 105 s AR: 173 s	Paper: 8 AR: 3	N/A	N/A
Martinez, 2014 [20]	Marker Depth image	Automotive Education Phone repair	Mouse Keyboard	Photo	N/A	Tablet - VST	Guided	N/A	N/A	N/A	N/A	N/A
Syberfeldt, 2015 [15]	Template-based	Puzzle assembling	Mouse Keyboard	Unity 3D Editor	No interaction	Oculus Rift - VST	Guided	paper: 1'20" AR: 4 times as long	N/A	paper: 2 AR: 0	Easy to understand Easy to use Felt performance Adoptability Physically demanding Mentally demanding Frustration	Paper is better
Zhu, 2013 [13]	Marker	Industrial maintenance	Mouse Keyboard	3D model	Marker for editing	Tablet - VST	Guided	Better with AR	N/A	N/A	Intuitiveness Satisfaction Ease of use	All better with AR

Concerning the assisted maintenance, [8] presents an experiment where an operator has to repair a technical system. He wears smart glasses, optical see-through like, which displays the augmentation on. Therefore, the operator is sharing his view with the remote expert. The remote expert explains procedure with augmented reality which focuses the operator's view to the right piece to maintain. He compares AR support with pure phone conversation, and AR displayed on a side screen. Even if this is not statistically significant, he shows that AR on smart glasses maintenance is completed 10 % faster than the other version.

Concerning the guided maintenance, the earliest publication was the Feiner's one dealing with the KARMA project. He uses AR system to help repairing printer [9]. The ARVIKA project by Friedrich [10] proposes a stationary and mobile system to carry out augmented reality maintenance tasks and also evaluates ergonomic of the system.

In [11], author proposes an augmented reality system, with a Video See-Through head mounted display (HMD). It allows the operator to localize the task then to be guided, step by step, in the maintenance operation of a tank turret. The author demonstrates that the task localization is statically found 10 % quicker with the AR system, although the whole task is performed longer, due to the display device used during the experiment. During this experiment, the head movement registered shows that the operator is doing less head movement than with the LCD one. This is interesting for user to avoid musculoskeletal disorder.

In [12] a maintenance procedure is described by a succession of step. Each step contains the tracking configuration and the virtual elements to animate when the system recognizes elements. A procedure can be lively reconfigured if the operator asks the expert for advice. A case study shows that the completion time is not better with AR on tablet. But no experiment is done with smart glasses.

In [13], an authorable and context aware AR system is compared with a classical AR system (i.e. not authorable) and with paper instructions. The proposed system display AR information according to the operator level of expertise. The system is tested on tablet only and not glasses and the proposed system outperforms the two others for intuitiveness, satisfaction and ease of use criteria.

In [14], a case study shows that an assembly task is performed faster with explanation on paper than with the AR system. This result is explained by an experience made on Oculus Rift and on a very simple task (i.e. a puzzle game).

Another approach made in [15] is about how operators learn procedure of maintenance. Authors made a case study comparing people learning with augmented reality and learning on the real object. Authors show that the knowledge retention and the knowledge interpretation are the same for the both means. This is an interesting result since operator can learn without the real system, but only with a virtual representation of it. Therefore the learning process is less equipment dependent and allow to train new operators wherever they are and without reserving the system and make it unusable.

This literature review shows the great interest in AR to support maintenance tasks. This is confirmed by industrial companies which are already using AR for maintenance or manufacturing activities, like Volkswagen and the MARTA project [16] or Diota and their player [17]. However, the recent development of mass market smart glasses offers new opportunities to help operators in maintenance procedure that need to be investigated.

Consequently, this paper presents a case study comparing maintenance efficiency with respect to the media support used, i.e. paper, video, AR tablet or AR Smart Glasses. As the AR application used in this case study is developed with framework and devices available on the market, it will show the benefits and the limits of the market available AR technologies for industrial maintenance. The paper is organized as follows: Firstly, we present a workflow allowing to author AR application, from authoring content to performing the maintenance, passing by the devices choice (Sect. 2). Then, we present the experimental case study which compares several media supports: AR on tablet, AR on smart glasses, paper and video. Finally we discuss our results, before concluding.

2 From Application Authoring to Maintenance Operation

This section describes how a company can improve their maintenance efficiency by using AR in their procedures. First we describe a workflow to update an existing procedure described on paper to an AR procedure. Then we describe the devices available for developing AR application. Finally, we explain how we develop the mProd application, an AR maintenance application which describes a full maintenance procedure on the supply chain.

First and foremost, we need to precise the maintenance context. Two main jobs are involved:

- Operator

  His role is to physically go on site and maintain the system.

- Expert

  His role is to understand the system failures and the steps to follow to fix it. He is responsible for authoring the maintenance processes and for assisting the operator when he has to face an unexpected issue during the procedure.

  Both jobs need to collaborate and share experiences. AR allows improving the remotely sharing of expertise between them. Moreover the expertize remains in the company even if an expert is leaving it. Indeed all AR procedure are kept inside the information system of the company and can also be used as training scenarios for new operators. The next section describes how a company can little by little pass from paper procedures to AR ones.

2.1 Workflow from Paper to Augmented Reality Procedures

Industries have their own maintenance procedures described on paper (or electronic document). These procedures are part of the know-how of the company. A general and technical definition of a maintenance procedure is: "an ordered series of actions done on system objects. Those actions are done by an operator with a specific tool". A maintenance procedure aims to explain: where and what the operator must do and which tool to use.

The problematic for industry is: how to pass from paper version to AR maintenance procedure? As shown in Fig. 2, several job domains are involved in producing such an AR procedure. Each one produces or uses resources gathered in a Product Lifecycle Management (PLM) system so as to spread each update to the whole company. We modeled the workflow to produce AR procedures. The underlined texts focus on the subject that a company must develop in order to upgrade from paper to AR procedure. We are supposing that 3D or CAD model are mostly available: either because the company has designed it, or because the furnisher has sold it with the product the company has bought. However, if they do not have the 3D model of the element to maintain, the company can produce them by scanning the object. Last solution is to do without 3D model. Indeed AR can be made without any 3D model representing the object to act on. Classical image file can be used instead as in Fig. 3.

The AR authoring procedure is the most challenging step. Indeed, the expert in maintenance generally is not expert in IT. That is because he is only a user of the 3D model and the AR actions library (Fig. 2-2). Beforehand, the maintenance expert must collaborate with his IT department to fill the job specific AR actions library with the job specific actions, as unscrewing or controlling pressure value (Fig. 2-1b). They are produced once and adapted to the job specificities. Those AR actions are produced respecting the model proposed in a previous paper [18] which was adapted from work done by [13, 19, 20]. Given that actions are based on a model, different application can communicate by exchanging content produced through xml file export and import.

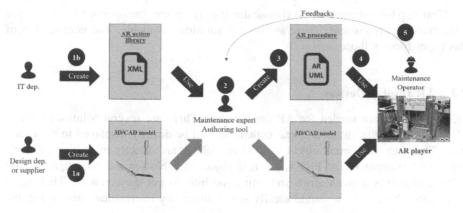

Fig. 2. Workflow from conception to effective AR maintenance procedure

Fig. 3. Op5: Turn off air valve of mProd application. AR maintenance step described without any CAD model representing the object to act on. The green turning arrow illustrates the action: "Turn the button to turn off air valve".

Once AR actions library is filled by the IT and the maintenance expert, the maintenance expert is able to author AR content by using a dedicated authoring tool which must also respect the model proposed to describe the maintenance. For instance, the authoring tool is conceived to display the system maintenance to maintain in a 3D view. Then the expert only needs to compose the AR procedure with the 3D model available and AR actions previously defined (Fig. 2-2). For each maintenance step, he simply choses the action to perform, parameterizes it and specifies which object it must act on.

Lastly, the operator uses the AR player to execute the procedure created by the expert (Fig. 2-4). Once done, the operator may give feedbacks about the procedure in order to continuously improve it (Fig. 2-5). The expert is in charge of validating these feedbacks and updating procedures. Moreover, it is worth to notice that AR application can be used as a means of automatically getting a big amount of statistics. As an example, the AR application presented below allows to automatically push up data on time spent by operators on each step of a procedure. With data analytics, it is possible to understand which step is worth to improve in the procedure.

Next step for a company is to choose the display devices the operator can use to see augmented reality content. There are several solutions available. The next section of this paper focuses those ones.

2.2 AR Display Devices

Display devices are needed for AR applications. There are several solutions for that [21, 22] Ideally, the virtual and real content should be directly displayed in the user's eyes. Therefore, the virtual object and the real object are directly mixed in the user's view. For example in the Fig. 4, the real object is a blower and the augmentation (virtual object) is a green arrow indicating the hole to put the screw in. That figure represents what a human should ideally see, without any intermediate device for displaying the augmentation.

Fig. 4. Ideal representation of augmented reality information from a human point of view. The green arrow represents the virtual content added to the user's view.

Mixing virtual and real content can be achieved by different devices: mobile, tablet, smart glasses, or projector. The Fig. 5 shows how a user is seeing augmented reality according to the device used. Each device has its own advantages and drawbacks.

Tablet has a wide enough screen size and an intuitive interface for the operator (Fig. 5 top-left). Therefore he can easily give his feedbacks, but it is not a hands-free device.

Optical glance monocular glasses can be used hands-free without obstructing the operator's view (Fig. 5 top-right). However the application interaction is only done with a few buttons, the device has a small screen size and the operator may need to close one eye to clearly see augmentations. Moreover he must constantly switch his direction of vision to the screen at the top right of his eye in order to see the augmentation. Once done, he must redirect his view back to the real scene and then mentally project what he has seen on the glance screen onto the real object. Therefore operators may experiment visual strain.

With the Optical See-Through smart glasses, as Epson Moverio BT-200, Meta spaceglasses or Microsoft Hololens (Fig. 5 bottom-left), virtual objects are naturally mixed with the real world. That is, the subject looks at the real object as usual and the

Fig. 5. Augmented reality viewed with different display devices from a human's point of view: (top left) tablet, (top right) Optical Glance glasses (Google Glass-like), (bottom left) optical See Through (Epson Moverio BT-200 like) and (bottom right) projective display.

augmented part is visible without the user needing to look at another screen. The virtual object remains registered (if the head movements are slow, less than 5° per second). If the movements are too quick, the computation time for keeping the augmentation registered creates synchronization difficulties between the reality and the virtual object. That shift generates mental and visual strain and can causes nausea. In addition to that drawback, we can add that the user sees the virtual object in semi-transparency since the screens are transparent in order to allow the user to see the real world. Moreover, for Moverio BT-200 the field of view (FOV) is small due to hardware limitations. In Fig. 5 bottom-left, the screen is symbolized by the green rectangle. So, if the user turns his head and the arrow moves out from the green rectangle, the arrow is not displayed anymore. The final most important drawback for this display method is physical security and safety. The augmentation can obstruct the user's view of the real world since they appear on the smart glasses screen. So, it is mandatory to design the application so as to guarantee user's security during the whole maintenance procedure.

Finally, with the projector (see Fig. 5 bottom-right), the virtual content is not displayed on a screen, but on the real world itself. It is the "other way round" working process compared to the other technologies. The advantage of the projective display is that the user can work hands free and does not need to wear anything to see the augmentation. However, the projection needs a support. For example, it is not possible to project a green arrow flying in the air whereas the other display modes can. That is why in the Fig. 5 bottom-right, the green arrow is a flat one displayed on the blower.

In fact, the blower acts as a projection support for the augmentation. To summarize, the projective display obviously limits the content type it is possible to display.

The AR usage strongly depends on the use case. Therefore, based on this analysis and work done by [21, 22], we have previously proposed a table allowing to choose display devices according to criteria such as mobility, interactivity, outdoor or hands free usage [23]. Based on that work, we have chosen to test the maintenance on Optical Glance device, Vuzix M-100 and tablet because there are devices which are the most mature for industrial usage. We choose not to evaluate optical See-Through device for security concerns. Moreover its rendering method is not mature enough for industrial usage.

2.3   mProd: Maintenance Production Application Developed

We develop the AR application called mProd (i.e. maintenance production). The application is developed with the Vuforia AR framework from PTC to track object and the Unity engine to perform 3D rendering. We transpose an existing maintenance procedure which was described on a document containing texts and photos to illustrate each action. The procedure occurs on a training assembly line dedicated to mobile phone manufacturing (see Fig. 6). The procedure occurs on the press module. It aims to replace an actioner which manages the press. This procedure contains 9 steps illustrated in Fig. 7:

Fig. 6. Assembly line where the maintenance is done (on left). Overview of the module maintained and the mProd application (on right).

- *Op1-Prepare yourself*: the operator checks if he has the 3 tools needed and can manipulate the AR application.
- *Op2-Lock the nut*: operator takes the screwdriver and block the nut on the back side.
- *Op3-Unscrew actioner*: while blocking the nut, operator unscrews with the Allen key.
- *Op4-Unscrew Electric Plugs*: operator removes the 2 electric plugs from the system.
- *Op5-Turn off the air*: operator turn off the air supply.

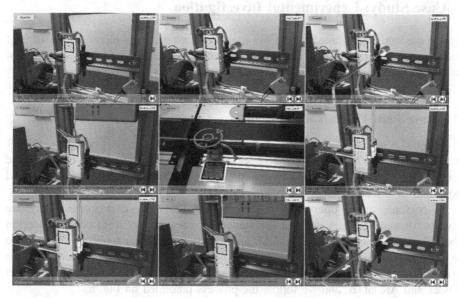

Fig. 7. Operations of the mProd application. It shows what to do with green elements. Full video available at https://www.youtube.com/watch?v=zmHkyFLNXhg&list=PLKxCeUO7RJly-ZqSjGKA6dJzBbMA2amokA&index=1

- *Op6-Remove hoses and substitute*: operator removes the hoses from the system and replace the actioner.
- *Op7-Plug hoses*: operator plugs back hoses inside the new actioner.
- *Op8-Screw Electric Plugs*: operator screws the electric plugs.
- *Op9-Screw actioner and supply air*: operator screws the actioner and supply the air.

This maintenance procedure contains a various type of AR actions, for instance unscrew, unplug, turn off air supplier… The AR actions are illustrated with 3D model, as in operation 3 and only with image, as in operation 5 (see Fig. 7). We use marker based detection because the template-based one is not stable since the actioner module is not textured enough. Therefore the tracking is sensible to illumination conditions. During the maintenance authoring the AR actions library is filled for our specific needs and those actions are now reusable for authoring other maintenance operations.

To summarize, the mProd application is explaining each maintenance step with AR animations, coupled with text explaining what to do at the bottom of the screen and with a Text-To-Speech also telling what to do (see Fig. 7). This application is used in the case study which we are going to discuss in the next section.

3 Case Study: Experimental Investigation

In this case study we wanted to test if a maintenance procedure is varying in term of time, error and operator's acceptability according to the media used to describe it. First we present the methodology used then we discuss results.

3.1 Case Study Evaluation Methodology

We compare 4 media which explain the procedure: paper, video, AR on tablet and AR on Smart Glasses Vuzix M100. The paper was our reference since it is currently the mostly used media. The study was based on the maintenance procedure described above and the mProd application.

24 persons, called **operators**, have participated to the experiment. They are between 19 and 43 years old and are students or researchers from our engineering school. Indeed we wanted to know if AR application is intuitive enough for people who are not used to do maintenance. We perform a between-group experiment. So, we divided them in 4 groups of 6, one group on each media: paper, video, AR Smart Glasses and AR tablet, and we follow the process presented on Fig. 8.

Fig. 8. Experiment methods process. Each step specifies the actors participating in.

During the brief sequence, we present 2 actors: the **operator** who is the subject of the experience and the maintenance **expert** who is callable by the operator if he does not understand a maintenance step. Only phone calls are permitted in order to simulate a remote expert. Besides the mProd application is demonstrated to operators in order to make them comfortable with it. However we do not present the application of the maintenance they are tested on in order to avoid making them learn the maintenance steps. The evaluated parameters are: 1-which media allows doing the maintenance the fastest? 2- Which media allows doing the maintenance with less error? 3- Which support offers the best ergonomic? 4- With which media the operator feels less stress and more confident? 5- For AR maintenance on mProd, which assistances among AR, audio or textual ones, are the most relevant and useful? In order to answer the first two questions, we are video recording the whole maintenance procedure performed by each operator.

By analyzing each video, the duration for each maintenance step for video and paper media are extracted: we consider that a new step is started when the operator looks at the media used and the current one is finished. For AR tablet and AR Smart Glasses, there is no need to analyze video recorded since each step duration are recorded by the mProd application.

The number of errors is extracted with this method: the operator takes the media to watch the current step, then he tries performing the gesture asked. If he performs the wrong gesture and passes to the next step, this is considered as an unfixed error. If he makes the wrong gesture, watches again the media and then performs the right gesture, this is considered as an error fixed alone. If he is doing the wrong gesture and calls the expert, this is considered as an error fixed with the expert.

To answer question 3 to 5 of this case study, an operator's interview is made just after the maintenance procedure is over. The operator gives his feedbacks on each question about, stress felt, ergonomic, usability and reliance. The questions asked are:

- What is the comfort felt during the maintenance operation?
- Is the media easy to use?

This question evaluates if the application is ergonomic and intuitive.

- What is the stress level during the operation (1 very stress, 5 very easy)?
- What is the reliance you give for the media used?

Both questions evaluate the stress and if operator feels confident in what he is doing.

- Do you think that the media is a good assistance mean?

This question allows evaluating the acceptability in the AR technology and if there will be resistance to change when adopting this technology.

- Fill in the augmented reality assistance, the audio assistance, the textual assistance.

This question evaluates the relative importance of each assistance in understanding the maintenance step to perform.

3.2 Results and Discussion

In this chapter, results are presented and discussed. Sometimes, AR Smart Glasses and AR tablet are grouped under the "AR media" denomination. The reference media is the paper.

3.2.1 Time and Error Results

Table 2 presents the mean maintenance duration time on each media basis and the Fig. 9 is focusing on the mean time distribution depending on the media. First, we can see that the mean duration to carry out the whole maintenance procedure with AR media application is shorter than with the paper or video media. In order to test if the result is statically significant, we performed a Lilliefors test to validate the data normality [24]. The results return a p-value of $0.099 > 0.05$. So mean completion duration

Table 2. Mean duration time to carry out maintenance. Percentage are calculated with paper as reference time

Maintenance media	Mean completion duration	Percent.	Std dev.
Paper	758 s	0 %	449
Video	992 s	31 %	440
AR tablet	735 s	−3 %	349
AR Smart Glasses	658 s	−13 %	294

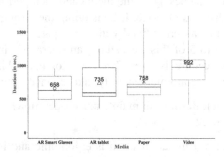

Fig. 9. Box plot of the duration time depending on the maintenance media

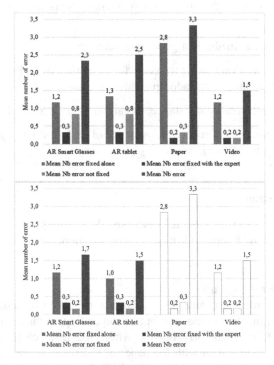

Fig. 10. Mean number of errors depending on the media used. (top) with all error taken into account for AR media. (bottom) without error due to the AR application implementation.

data can be considered as following a normal distribution. Then we do an ANOVA on mean completion duration, using $\alpha = 0.5$ $(F(3, 20) = 0.874 < F_{crit} = 3.10,$ $p - value = 0.471)$ [25]. Therefore we don't reject the null hypothesis. It means that difference in mean completion duration is not statically significant although AR tablet seems to perform 3 % better and AR Smart Glasses seems to perform 13 % better in term of duration compared to the paper media.

We could expect that AR media were statically faster than paper media to fulfill the maintenance. This results is firstly explained by the fact that operators were not trained to use the AR mProd application. They only had a demonstration on how to use it during the brief. Secondly, they were performing a task with 9 steps, which represents a rather short procedure. If operators had trained to use the mProd application and if we had made them act on a maintenance with more steps, we could have noticed a statically difference in duration. We will focus on that hypothesis in a future work.

On Fig. 9 the box plot displays the duration distribution by media used. We can see that the AR media is less spread than paper and video. This means the procedure is globally better understood by operators. In other word, the procedure is less operator dependent. Indeed, with AR media, operator can move himself to the point of view which let him better understand the step to do, whereas photo on paper media and video only show a specific point of view.

When we focus on the error done (Fig. 10. - top), the best media is the video one with only 1.5 errors done during the maintenance, followed by AR Smart Glasses (2.3 errors), AR tablet (2.5 errors) and paper (3.3 errors).

However, after a deep analysis of errors done by operators and their interviews, errors which were caused by a non-optimal AR implementation have been extracted. Indeed there are some errors which could have been avoided with a better implementation of the AR application. Actually, in order to compare all media together, the steps are similarly explained with AR than on paper. However, AR procedure must not be explained as paper ones. For example in *Op6-Remove hoses*, operators should remove 2 hoses on the right of the actioner and 1 on the left. Several operators removed only the both on the right and told during the interview they did not see the third one on the screen.

So, if we remove those kind of errors done due to AR implementation from the AR media, we can see on Fig. 10. - bottom that AR tablet (1.5 errors) is equivalent to Video followed by AR Smart Glasses (1.7 errors) and paper (3.3 errors). The most important point is that the number of error not fixed is the same for video, AR Smart Glasses and AR tablet (0.2 errors) whereas on paper (0.3 errors). This is an interesting result since it is obviously something an industrial want to minimize. Nevertheless maintenance done with AR media is more often asking answers from the expert: 0.3 errors is fixed with the expert whereas 0.2 errors for the video. This can be explained by the novelty of AR maintenance. Therefore operators needs more help. We expect that the more they will be used to the less they will need help from the expert. Moreover maintenance by video needs to be edited on site by the expert whereas AR maintenance can be remotely edited by the expert which reduce the production cost of such maintenance.

To conclude on this chapter, in term of errors done, AR maintenance allows doing less errors than paper and is similar than doing it with video explanation. This is true if the AR application is optimized for such media. That is why, we will provide our advice at the end of the results chapter allowing to adapt maintenance procedure from paper to AR ones. Following those advice, every AR media for maintenance application should reduce errors done by operator.

3.2.2   Operators' Feedbacks Results

As a reminder, all criteria displayed on Fig. 11-left are obtained with questions asked to the operator just after the maintenance procedure is carried out.

We can notice that AR media are globally well accepted by operators (Fig. 11-left - Good media). The first is the AR Smart Glasses, then the video on Smart Glasses, then AR tablet, then paper. The media which can be used hands-free are logically ranked first.

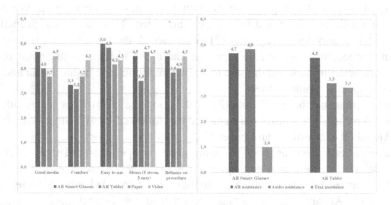

Fig. 11. (left) Operator's feedbacks interview results. Operator must give a mark from 1 as the worst answer and 5 as best answer. (right) Mark given by operator for each assistance for the AR devices.

When focusing on comfort criterion, it is better estimated with paper and video than with AR media (Fig. 11-left - Comfort). Indeed operator's interview reveal that they don't really know where to put the tablet when they work whereas with the paper they can put wherever they want with no accidental damage risk for the media. Concerning AR Smart Glasses, operators complain about the screen size which is not big enough to correctly distinguish augmentations. Moreover the video study reveals that operators need to close the left eye to see the Smart Glasses screen in front of their right eye. To adopt this kind of AR media, designer must particularly focus on comfort and ergonomic. Binocular devices or bigger screen size could be a good possible solutions.

For the criterion "Easy to use" (Fig. 11-left), AR Smart Glasses and tablet ranked first, respectively 20 % and 14 % better marked by operators than paper. This result is an encouraging point for the adoption of this kind of AR tool and it is reinforced since it was the first use for the operator and they feel to understand the AR content presented. This result is also explained by the application design since the mProd application was conceived with the intention to work with AR Smart Glasses, which can be handled with only 3 physical buttons. Buttons are used to navigate to previous step, next step and repeating the current step. We thus encourage AR application designer to use simple paradigm to control the application. It seems better to quickly and easily access important information than to have a lot of functionalities. Advanced functionalities, as operators' feedbacks, should be done after maintenance procedure.

For the "Reliance on procedure" criteria, it is 13 % better estimated by the operator with hands-free media, as AR or video on Smart Glasses, than with paper one (Fig. 11-left - Reliance on procedure). AR tablet is 5 % less estimated than the paper media. Indeed, with hands-free media, operators always have the information in front of their eyes, therefore they can always check in case of any doubt, whereas with paper and AR tablet; they must grab the media to check information for understanding and put it back.

With reference to "stress" felt by operators, paper remains the less stressing media, followed by video then AR media. The last is AR tablet and this result must be confirmed in a next experiment. As we can't explain the fact that AR tablet is 22 % more stressful than paper, we decided to compare the AR media results by grouping AR Smart Glasses and AR tablet in order to smooth the operators' distribution. Thus, the mark is 4, it is 15 % less estimated than paper. Operators feel less stress with paper since they are used to work with it whereas AR media are a new experience. Therefore operators feel anxious to correctly understand the augmentations displayed. Indeed, in this experiment, we wanted to test AR acceptance and usage without any training about this new technology. We can thus suppose that operators would be less stress if they carry out a training maintenance with AR media before being evaluated on the real maintenance.

So as to better understand assistance utility for guided maintenance application, we asked each operator to give a mark for each ones among AR, audio and text ones (Fig. 11-right). What is interesting is the fact that at least 2 of 3 assistances get a high value. The interviews confirm those marks. Operators explain that in spite of the fact they understand what they need to carry out only with the augmented reality assistance, they need a confirmation and/or a precision that is available by a secondary channel, which are text or audio. And as we must have thought, text assistance is useless since text is not readable on the small screen of the Smart Glasses. However it is important to notice that maintenance procedure are better understood by operator if information provided are redundant through several channel, vision, audio and sound. Moreover, the more you have, the better it is, since operators do not understand all in the same way.

Lastly, this experiment allows us to propose advice to obtain an efficient AR maintenance application. We can summarize them as this: (1) AR augmentation must be fully registered. Approximation on position or on the 3D model of the entity represented will be misunderstood by the operator. (2) Group maintenance steps if they focus on the same entity and are near enough, as 2 neighbor plugs in Op4 of mProd. (3) On the contrary, if you must act on 2 sides of an entity, split the step because operator could not see the augmentation on the other side. (4) Always specify the number of entity to act on for the specific step, for example "unscrew 2 electric plugs" or "remove 3 hoses". (5) Use AR to validate the tool to use for the specific step. (6) If an animation is out of the screen, it must be specified to the operator. Those advice have to be evaluated in future work in order to rank the most important ones.

4   Conclusion and Perspectives

In this paper, we have proposed a workflow allowing a maintenance service from a company to pass from paper to AR procedure. The workflow, based on a previous model proposed, allowed a maintenance expert to author maintenance procedure in augmented reality without having computer development skills. This workflow was based on AR actions library which was job specific and adaptable to all kind of existing and upcoming job. Based on this work, we developed an AR maintenance application on market available devices, we called mProd, which described an actioner industrial maintenance with AR, textual and audio assistance.

Based on the mProd application, we presented a case study comparing the maintenance efficiency with respect to the media support describing it: paper, video, AR tablet and AR Smart Glasses. The paper has shown that for the same maintenance duration, there were less errors made with AR media than with paper if we follow the advice given in this paper to create AR maintenance procedures. As the AR application used in this case study is developed with framework and devices available, it has showed the benefits, the limits of the market available AR technologies for industrial maintenance. Therefore there are still pending issues that researcher must work on, among AR object registration, AR devices and AR content authoring based on model like UML.

The operators' interviews after the maintenance revealed the good acceptance of the AR application and revealed the operators' reliance in it. As the AR technology was not yet used in everyday life, it remained considered as more stressful than paper or video media. The interviews also showed that AR application must use augmentation to explain procedure, but must also use another communication channel, like text or sound in order to be more understandable. Lastly, the AR application intuitive usage, even with smart glasses, gave this technology a great advantage for the adoption. The paper also gave best practices in order to pass maintenance procedures from paper to AR.

Future work will focus on developing a more complex maintenance procedure with more steps in order to evaluate if AR maintenance are statically faster and more reliable than other media. Operators will be trained to the mProd application we present in this paper in order to make them comfortable with the application and the evaluation will be performed on an advanced and more complex maintenance. We will also work on improving the AR maintenance UML model in order to make the AR content authoring easier to produce for maintenance expert.

Finally, as virtual reality can be used for training we will use this model to also describe maintenance procedure in virtual reality. Therefore, the procedure could be authored once and being used in virtual reality and augmented reality, respectively to virtually train new operator and to guide them during real maintenance procedure. Our future work will aim to merge those two worlds in a single model, adaptive to every jobs specificities.

References

1. Sahnoun, M., Godsiff, P., Baudry, D., Louis, A., Mazari, B.: Modelling of maintenance strategy of offshore wind farms based multi-agent system. In: CIE44 & ISSM14 (44th International Conference on Computers & Industrial Engineering & 9th International Symposiom on Intelligent Manufacturing and Service Systems), vol. 591, pp. 2406–2420 (2014)
2. Caudell, T., Mizell, D.: Augmented reality: an application of heads-up display technology to manual manufacturing processes. In: 1992 Proceedings of the Twenty-Fifth Hawaii International Conference on System Sciences. vol. 2, pp. 659–669 (1992)
3. Milgram, P., Kishino, F.: A taxonomy of mixed reality visual displays. IEICE Trans. Inf. Syst. **77**(12), 1321–1329 (1994)
4. Azuma, R., et al.: A survey of augmented reality. Presence **6**(4), 355–385 (1997)
5. Sanna, A., Manuri, F.: A survey on applications of augmented reality. Adv. Comput. Sci. Int. J. **5**(1), 18–27 (2016)
6. Zhou, F., Duh, H., Billinghurst, M.: Trends in augmented reality tracking, interaction and display: a review of ten years of ISMAR. In: Proceedings of the 7th IEEE/ACM International Symposium on Mixed and Augmented Reality, pp. 193–202 (2008)
7. Nee, A., Ong, S., Chryssolouris, G., Mourtzis, D.: Augmented reality applications in design and manufacturing. CIRP Ann. Manufact. Technol. **61**(2), 657–679 (2012)
8. Bottecchia, S.: Système TAC: Télé-Assistance Collaborative. Réalité augmentée et NTIC au service des opérateurs et des experts dans le cadre d'une tâche de maintenance industrielle supervisée. Ph.D. dissertation (2010)
9. Feiner, S., Macintyre, B., Seligmann, D.: Knowledge-based augmented reality. Commun. ACM **36**(7), 53–62 (1993)
10. Friedrich, W., Jahn, D., Schmidt, L., ARVIKA-augmented reality for development Production and Service. In: ISMAR vol. 2002 pp. 3–4 (2002)
11. Henderson, S., Feiner, S.: Exploring the benefits of augmented reality documentation for maintenance and repair. IEEE Trans. Vis. Comput. Graph. **17**(10), 1355–1368 (2011)
12. Lamberti, F., Manuri, F., Sanna, A., Paravati, G., Pezzolla, P., Montuschi, P.: Challenges opportunities and future trends of emerging techniques for augmented reality-based maintenance. Trans. Emerg. Top. Comput. **2**(4), 411–421 (2014)
13. Zhu, J., Ong, S., Nee, A.: An authorable context-aware augmented reality system to assist the maintenance technicians. Int. J. Adv. Manufact. Technol. **66**(9–12), 1699–1714 (2013)
14. Syberfeldt, A., Danielsson, O., Holm, M., Wang, L.: Visual Assembling Guidance Using Augmented Reality
15. Gonzalez-Franco, M., Cermeron, J., Li, K., Pizarro, R., Thorn, J., Hannah, P., Hutabarat, W., Tiwari, A., Bermell-Garcia, P.: Immersive Augmented Reality Training for Complex Manufacturing Scenarios. arXiv preprint arXiv:1602.01944 (2016)
16. Stanimirovic, D., Damasky, N., Webel, S., Koriath, D., Spillner, A., Kurz, D.: [Poster] A mobile augmented reality system to assist auto mechanics. In: 2014 IEEE International Symposium on Mixed and Augmented Reality (ISMAR), pp. 305–306 (2014)
17. Diota Soft: Home. In: Diota. http://www.diota.com/
18. Havard, V., Baudry, D., Louis, A., Mazari, B.: Augmented reality maintenance demonstrator and modelling associated. In: Proceedings of the IEEE Virtual Reality 2015, 25–27 March. IEEE (2015)
19. Martínez, H., Laukkanen, S., Mattila, J.: A new flexible augmented reality platform for development of maintenance and educational applications. Int. J. Virtual Worlds Hum. Comput. Interact. 2(1) (2014)

20. Su, C.-J., Liu, P.-T., Lin, Y.-C., et al.: Automatic generation of augmented reality enabled pedagogical system using object-oriented analysis and design in process modeling. In: Asia Pacific Industrial Engineering and Management Systems Conference (2012)
21. Van Krevelen, D., Poelman, R.: A survey of augmented reality technologies, applications and limitations. Int. J. Virtual Reality 9(2), 1 (2010)
22. Mallem, M., Roussel, D.: Réalité augmentée: principes, technologies et applications. Techniques de l'ingénieur. Télécoms (TE5920) (2014)
23. Havard, V., Sahnoun, M.: Offshore Wind Farms failures, e-maintenance using Augmented Reality (2014)
24. Dallal, G., Wilkinson, L.: An analytic approximation to the distribution of Lilliefors's test statistic for normality. Am. Stat. 40(4), 294–296 (1986)
25. Chambers, J., Freeny, A., Heiberger, R.: Analysis of variance; designed experiments. In: Chambers, J.M., Hastie, T.J. (eds.) Statistical Models in S, pp. 145–193. Wadsworth & Brooks/Cole, Pacific Grove (1992)
26. Syberfeldt, A., Danielsson, O., Holm, M., Ekblom, T.: Augmented Reality at the Industrial Shop-Floor. In: De Paolis, L.T., Mongelli, A. (eds.) AVR 2014. LNCS, vol. 8853, pp. 201–209. Springer, Heidelberg (2014)

Augmented Reality in the Control Tower: A Rendering Pipeline for Multiple Head-Tracked Head-up Displays

Nicola Masotti[✉], Francesca De Crescenzio, and Sara Bagassi

Department of Industrial Engineering, University of Bologna, Bologna, Italy
{nicola.masotti, francesca.decrescenzio,
sara.bagassi}@unibo.it

Abstract. The purpose of the air traffic management system is to accomplish the safe and efficient flow of air traffic. However, the primary goals of safety and efficiency are to some extent conflicting. In fact, to deliver a greater level of safety, separation between aircrafts would have to be greater than it currently is, but this would negatively impact the efficiency. In an attempt to avoid the trade-off between these goals, the long-range vision for the Single European Sky includes objectives for operating as safely and efficiently in Visual Meteorological Conditions as in Instrument Meteorological Conditions. In this respect, a wide set of virtual/augmented reality tools has been developed and effectively used in both civil and military aviation for piloting and training purposes (e.g., Head-Up Displays, Enhanced Vision Systems, Synthetic Vision Systems, Combined Vision Systems, etc.). These concepts could be transferred to air traffic control with a relatively low effort and substantial benefits for controllers' situation awareness. Therefore, this study focuses on the see-through, head-tracked, head-up display that may help controllers dealing with zero/low visibility conditions and increased traffic density at the airport. However, there are several open issues associated with the use of this technology. One is the difficulty of obtaining a constant overlap between the scene-linked symbols and the background view based on the user's viewpoint, which is known as 'registration'. Another one is the presence of multiple, arbitrary oriented Head-Up Displays (HUDs) in the control tower, which further complicates the generation of the Augmented Reality (AR) content. In this paper, we propose a modified rendering pipeline for a HUD system that can be made out of several, arbitrary oriented, head-tracked, AR displays. Our algorithm is capable of generating a constant and coherent overplay between the AR layer and the outside view from the control tower. However a 3D model of the airport and the airport's surroundings is needed, which must be populated with all the necessary AR overlays (both static and dynamic). We plan to use this concept as a basis for further research in the field of see-through HUDs for the control tower.

Keywords: Air Traffic Control Tower · Augmented Reality · Head-Up Display

© Springer International Publishing Switzerland 2016
L.T. De Paolis and A. Mongelli (Eds.): AVR 2016, Part I, LNCS 9768, pp. 321–338, 2016.
DOI: 10.1007/978-3-319-40621-3_23

1 Motivation

With the aim of increasing the air transport system efficiency and throughput, Europe has made plans for operating in Instrument Meteorological Conditions (IMC) as safely and efficiently as in Visual Meteorological Conditions (VMC) [1–3]. From a pilot perspective, the research on all-weather operations cockpits is already far advanced. Indeed, the integration of Head-Up Displays (HUDs) into modern civil flight decks has demonstrated many advantages. In modern cockpits, HUDs can be supplemented by Enhanced Vision Systems (EVS) and Synthetic Vision Systems (SVS) and a combination of these, the so-called Combined Vision Systems (CVS), is already being studied in the Single European Sky ATM Research (SESAR) for landing, take-off and taxi [4]. On the ground, a task that is still largely dependent on the visual observation of the surrounding area is the provision of Air Traffic Control (ATC) service by the control tower. Indeed, results of controllers' task analyses have shown the importance of the outside view for enhancing controllers' Situation Awareness (SA) [5–8]. Depending upon weather and lighting conditions, the visual contrast of controlled objects varies substantially, with possible detrimental impact on controllers' performances [9]. In particular, when bad weather, fog, smoke, dust or any other kind of environmental occlusion impairs the visibility from the control tower, the airport capacity is reduced and Low Visibility Procedures (LVP) must be applied. In addition, it is also possible for the airport, the surrounding airspace, and the controlled vehicles to be obscured by buildings, high-glare conditions and the cover of night [9]. LVP may include constraints, such as mandatory use of a Surface Movement Radar (SMR), taxiways that cannot be used, block spacing, limitation in pushback operations and use of a predefined runway. Consequently, as long as the operational capability is reduced, both carriers and Air Navigation Service Providers (ANSPs) incur in heavy financial losses. In [10], Shackelf and Karpe refer to large fuel savings and financial benefits if stable rates of airport capacity could be maintained in all visibility conditions. This also implies a higher arrival and departure rates and a more uniform and productive Air Traffic Flow Management (ATFM). Further, the increased reliability of the surface management service would improve metrics for taxi-times, departure queues, ground-delays, ground-holds and cancellations [10].

In recent years, many advances in Air Traffic Management (ATM) have come in the form of visualization tools for tower controllers. Movement maps, conformance monitoring, conflict detection and others Advanced Surface Movement Guidance & Control System (A-SMGCS) based solutions are a few examples of these tools. But there is a paradox in developing visual tools in order to increase the tower controllers' situation awareness (SA), which is that their sight is pulled away from the outside view and the head-down time is increased. Previous studies have already proven that tasks requiring frequent shifts of gaze back and forth between the outside and the inside view may become significantly slow and fatiguing, particularly after the fortieth years of age [11]. In other words, a constant refocusing between the far view and the head-down equipment contributes to the operator's workload and reduces his or her SA. The use of augmented reality tools (AR) that can safely enable tower operations in zero/low visibility conditions may be able to address this paradox.

2 Augmented Reality for the Airport Tower

The topic of Augmented Reality (AR) appears in the human factors' literature with increasing frequency, usually in conjunction with the more familiar subject of Virtual Reality (VR) [12]. Lloyd Hitchcock of the FAA firstly proposed the concept of using AR technology in the control tower over 25 years ago [13]. At that time, no prototype construction was attempted and little was published, though many recall Mr. Hitchcock speculating on several methods that could aid tower controllers [5]. For instance, he suggested that AR displays could provide air traffic controllers with useful status information, such as aircraft identification, barometer settings, wind conditions and runway/gate assignments. More recent studies suggest that also other spatially conformal information, such as flight tags, warnings, shapes and layouts, can be presented on AR displays [12, 14–21]. Displayed information may be extracted and synthesized from multiple data sources, such as radar-based surveillance systems (e.g. Airport Surveillance Radar and Surface Movement Radar), Differential Global Positioning System (DGPS), 3D digital maps and other ground based sensors (e.g. video or infrared cameras). Other information that can be displayed to the controller includes System Wide Information Management (SWIM) data, such as weather conditions, wind direction and speed, wind shear and wake vortexes visualization [22, 23]. These could be used to optimize separations between approaching and departing aircrafts, leveraging weather in a similar manner to what controllers did in SESAR Operational Service and Environment Definition (OSED) 06.08.01 – Time Based Separation [24]. In any case, a 3D airport model must be developed providing precise positioning for infrastructures and objects (both aerial and terrestrial). Similar technology was developed in SESAR Operational Focus Area 06.03.01 (Remote Tower) particularly in SESAR Project 06.09.03 (Remote & Virtual TWR) where visual overlays have been used to introduce or highlight relevant information on the out of the window view [25]. However, in this case, the AR layer has been placed on top of the video surveillance feed of a remote airport location instead of the actual tower's windows.

2.1 Expected Impacts

Using AR in the airport tower means that controllers will be no longer limited by what the human eye can see out of the tower's windows. Consequently, constraints in LVC could be reduced. For instance, when relying on visual augmentations, an exclusive use of taxiway blocks may not be necessary. Therefore, an aircraft could use a segment of a taxiway before the preceding aircrafts has left such segment. In other words, those tasks that can be negatively affected by poor visibility conditions will become weather-independent and the risk of creating bottlenecks in the traffic flow management system will be reduced.

AR overlays can also aid users by substantially reducing the amount of visual scanning needed to integrate various sources of information. This contrasts with the current practice of scanning multiple devices (screens, windows, flight strips, etc.), filtering the essential information from data that may not be relevant. As a result, the head-down time should be reduced.

On the whole, significant benefits are expected for the entire air traffic system, including (a) increased safety for passengers, (b) financial savings for carriers and ANSPs, (c) environmental pollution reduction, and (d) increased efficacy (and resilience) of the control tower IT system (Fig. 1) [5, 9, 10, 12, 19]. Also, the maintenance of operational capacity in all weather conditions should result in positive social impact on tourists, business travellers and the community living in the airport surrounding.

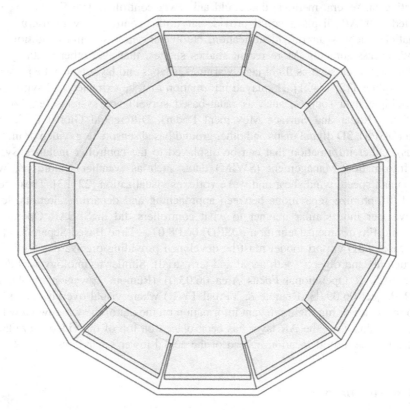

Fig. 1. A possible 360° deployment of spatial AR displays in the airport tower.

Finally, the development of AR tools will provide a technology bridge between the current tower systems and the 21st Century 'Remote & Virtual Tower' (R&VT) concept foreseen in both SESAR and NGATS (Next Generation Air Transportation System) visions. Over the last few years, several concepts for the provision of air traffic service from a distant/remote location have been proposed, including video-surveillance based systems (remote towers), and VR facilities in which a photo-realistic real-time rendering recreates a 360° tower view (virtual towers) [8, 9, 26, 27]. The first concept is actually far advanced in SESAR and has been proven ready for industrialization (leading to operational deployment). As for the second, this may take decades to refine. Nevertheless, there are strong financial reasons to develop this technology. One of the open issues associated with virtual towers is the assessment of the extent to which the 'digital world' can be trusted to resemble the referenced real world. In this sense, AR may become of critical importance for the R&VT research. If an augmented reality tool became certified and operational in the next several decades, it is expected that the community of tower controllers would generate discrepancy reports each time there is a mismatch between the real world that they observe and the virtual world that is presented via the AR Tower Tool [5]. Conversely, the inability of controllers to detect such discrepancies would become valuable data for the validation, verification and certification of R&VTs [5]. In this sense, AR towers will provide a suitable development path for designing the fully immersive virtual tower of the future [9].

2.2 Technologies

Many types of AR displays exist, all having specific areas of application. In [28] Bimber and Raskar provide a classification based on the AR display position along the optical path between the observed object and the viewer's eyes. Their classification includes head-attached displays (a.k.a. head-mounted displays), hand-held displays, spatial displays (a.k.a. head-tracked displays or head-up displays) and object-projected AR displays (head-attached, hand-held and spatial). Apart from the latter, that is so called because the virtual image is projected directly onto a real object, AR displays can be either of the see-through or the video-combined category. See-through AR displays combine the real and virtual images by means of mirrors, lenses, transparent screens or other optical components. This leaves the view of the real world nearly intact. Video-combined AR displays use cameras to covert the real view into a video feed, which is later merged with the virtual image. Spatial AR displays are typically fixed in space (e.g. attached to a desk, fixed on the floor or hung from the ceiling) and can be made to coincide with the tower windows (Fig. 2). These are often at an angle with each other and slope toward the tower at the base to avoid internal reflections. See-Through Head-Mounted Displays (ST-HMD) are worn by the user, resulting in a flexible but intrusive equipment. For both these systems to function properly, a head-coupled or eye-coupled perspective is needed. Thus, at any time, the underlying application (i.e. the one that generates the AR overlay) must know where the controller is and where s/he is looking. Indeed, the content of the screen is determined by the point of view of the observer, usually by tracking his or her head position and orientation. This differs from an aircraft HUD, where the displayed information is adjusted to the aircraft's perspective rather than the one of the pilot [29].

Also, because of its potentially large form factor, a spatial AR display can provide a considerably larger Field Of View (FOV) compared to a typical aircraft HUD.

2.3 Application Area

In this work, the application area is defined as panoramic, i.e. an egocentric environment where the observer is confined in a limited volume but experiences a panoramic

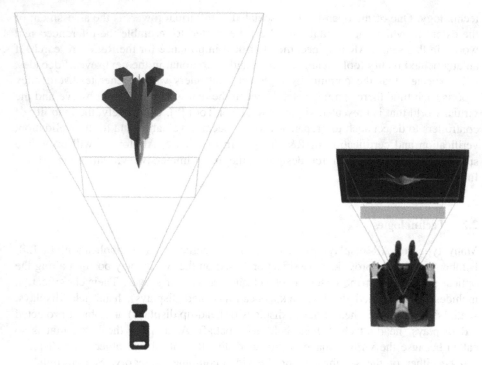

Fig. 2. The symmetrical frustum projection model, a.k.a. on-axis projection model.

view of the environment surrounding that volume [30]. Examples of panoramic environments include ATC towers and other control or supervision positions where complex visual tasks are performed from a distance (e.g. life guarding). Also, this work will focus on spatial see-through AR displays, primarily because they are less intrusive than head-attached (i.e. head-mounted) or hand-held displays. Object-projected AR will not be considered in this work because it doesn't fit the application area we have defined (real objects are far away, and potentially obstructed by other objects, therefore it is not possible to project images on them).

2.4   Open Issues

In the field of AR the concept of spatially matching the real and the virtual objects according to the user perspective is known as registration [30]. Alternate designations include 'object alignment', 'object connectivity', and 'conformal' or 'scene-linked' symbology [20, 21, 30]. As already mentioned, in order to achieve registration, one crucial factor is to have accurate spatial data (tracking) of the observed object, display device and observer (at all instances). This may be accomplished by means of depth from stereo, infrared tracking or many others techniques. Inaccurate measurements or latency in the tracking methodology lead to registration errors, which can seriously affects the system usability [30]. However, tracking is a widely researched topic

[31, 32] and will not be discussed further in this paper. Eventually, the tracking process must result in the head/eyes coordinates being fed (in real time) to the rendering pipeline.

Even assuming that an accurate tracking result is continuously fed to the AR content generator, there are still a number of significant issues in getting the real and virtual imagery to blend naturally. For instance, a digital model of the airport and the airport surroundings must be developed and populated with all the necessary overlays for both aerial and terrestrial object. Also, because in the airport tower multiple HUDs may be arbitrary oriented, any attempt to use a standard projection model would fail [33].

What we propose is a modified rendering pipeline that can be used in a first person, head-tracked (or eye-tracked), multi-screen, non-planar, panoramic environment, such as the AR control tower of the future. If all others prerequisites are met (i.e. accurate tracking and modelling) our algorithm will generate a spatially registered (i.e. conformal) overlay for an arbitrary number of anyway oriented HUDs. In other words, this is a flexible mechanism for generating AR contents that are (a) consistent with the display orientation and (b) constantly overlaid with the real view (i.e. spatially registered).

3   The Standard Projection Model

The majority of Virtual/Augmented Reality (V/AR) applications operate on some variant of the pinhole camera metaphor, i.e. a camera object exists in the virtual environment, which regularly takes bi-dimensional snapshots of a computer-generated scene, to be displayed on a physical device (Fig. 3). According to this model, programmers may simply select a horizontal FOV, specify an aspect ratio, declare the distances from the near clipping plane and the far clipping plane, and build the projection matrix.

For instance, the OpenGL[1] function *gluPerspective* [34] sets up a perspective projection matrix based on four user specified parameters (r, t, n and f). This entails the use a symmetrical frustum[2] such as the one represented in Fig. 3. You may find extensive information about the OpenGL projection matrix and *gluPerspective* input parameters either on the Internet [34, 35] or in the OpenGL Programming Guide, alias The Red Book [35, 36]. Also, be aware that alternatives to the OpenGL Application Programming Interface (API) exist [37]. However, as long as a 3D content must be displayed on a 2D media, rest assured that a projection matrix exists.

When *gluPerspective* is invoked, it builds a projection matrix that looks like this:

---

[1] OpenGL (Open Graphics Library) is a cross-language, multi-platform Application Programming Interface (API) for rendering 2D and 3D vector graphics.

[2] A *frustum* is a six-sided truncated pyramid that originates sectioning the shape the virtual camera FOV by means of two user-defined clipping planes. These are known as the 'far clipping plane' and the 'near clipping plane'. The latter is the one on which the scene must be projected as a necessary step of the rendering pipeline.

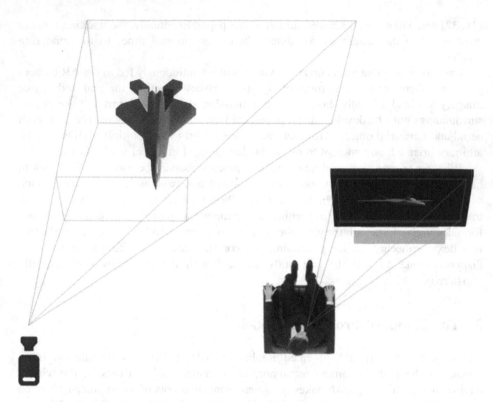

Fig. 3. The skewed frustum projection model, a.k.a. off-axis projection model.

$$P = \begin{bmatrix} \frac{n}{r} & 0 & 0 & 0 \\ 0 & \frac{n}{t} & 0 & 0 \\ 0 & 0 & \frac{n+f}{n-f} & -\frac{2fn}{f-n} \\ 0 & 0 & -1 & 0 \end{bmatrix} \tag{1}$$

Where r and t represent half of the horizontal and vertical near clip plane extents respectively, while n (nearVal) and f (farVal) refer to the distances between the viewpoint (i.e. the eye-space origin) and the near and far clipping planes respectively.

When (1) is used, a few underlying assumptions have been made, and that is that (a) the viewer is positioned in front of the screen, (b) facing perpendicular to it and (c) looking at the centre of it. This is also known as the 'on-axis' projection model (Fig. 3). As long as the projection matrix does not change, relative movements between the eyes and the screen (e.g. back and forward movements) are forbidden, as they modify the physical FOV whereas the projection model (i.e. the projection matrix) remains the same. In order to free up the viewpoint position from the screen normal[3],

---

[3] For the sake of readability, we refer to the straight line being <u>orthogonal</u> to the screen and passing by the centre of it simply as the screen normal.

OpenGL provides a second function (*glFrustum*) that sets up the projection matrix as follows:

$$
P = \begin{bmatrix} \frac{2n}{r-l} & 0 & \frac{r+l}{r-l} & 0 \\ 0 & \frac{2n}{t-b} & \frac{t+b}{t-b} & 0 \\ 0 & 0 & \frac{n+f}{n-f} & -\frac{2fn}{f-n} \\ 0 & 0 & -1 & 0 \end{bmatrix} \tag{2}
$$

Where l, r, b and t denote the distances between the near clipping plane edges and the straight line that goes from the camera origin to the plane itself (in a perpendicular manner). Again, you may find extensive information about *glFrustum* input parameters – namely l (left), r (right), b (bottom), t (top), n (nearVal) and f (farVal) – either on the Internet [38] or in the OpenGL Programming Guide [36].

Most importantly, a projection matrix such as (2) allows for asymmetric frusta to be used. In other words, the viewpoint position is freed from the screen normal. This is known as the off-axis projection model (Fig. 4). As a matter of fact, the projection model delivered by (2) is much more flexible than the one provided by (1). E.g., the frustum extents can be determined separately for each eye-screen pair, resulting in an much more accurate projection model for stereovision implementation [33]. However, there are still a few constraints. For instance, *glFrustum* assumes that the near clipping plane is orthogonal to the virtual camera depth axis (i.e. the eye-space coordinate system e_n axis). Also, relative movements between the screen and the viewpoint position are still forbidden (unless accounted for by the tracking system).

Eventually, the field of AR introduces circumstances under which the assumptions of both *glFrustum*() and *gluPerspective*() fail and the resulting incorrectness is not tolerable [33, 39, 40]. For instance, when dealing with very large format HUDs for the airport tower, the overlay between the scene-linked symbols and the background view strongly depends on the viewer's eyes position with respect to the HUD and on the HUD orientation. Hence, a far more generic perspective model is needed.

4 Formulation of a Custom Rendering Pipeline

Our first objective is to develop formulas allowing us to compute the parameters of a standard 3D perspective projection matrix (l, r, b and t) based on the relative position and orientation between the viewer's eyes and the screen. In order to constantly feed these parameters to the projection matrix a constant link between the tracking system and the projection matrix is needed. Also it is mandatory to know the exact transformation between the tacker-space coordinate system and the world space-coordinate system. However, this can be easily determined once the location and the orientation of the tracking device(s) are fixed and known.

Let's start reviewing the main characteristics of the AR system. These are the coordinates of the display corners, the origin of screen-space coordinate system, and the distance from the eye-space coordinate system origin to the screen (Figs. 5 and 6).

The coordinates of the head-up display corners, namely p_a (lower left corner), p_b (lower right corner), and p_c (upper left corner) are expressed with respect to

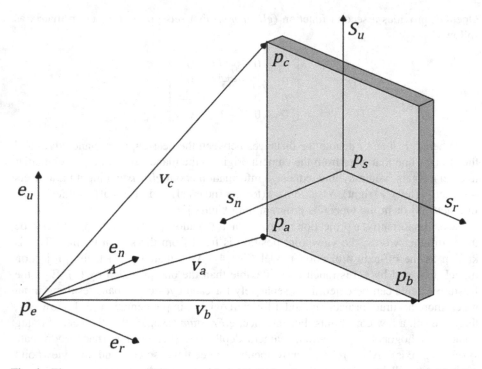

Fig. 4. The eye-space coordinate system (origin p_e), the screen-space coordinate system (origin p_s) and the screen corners vectors v_a, v_b and v_c.

world-space coordinate system. Assuming that flat screen is used, the position of the fourth point is implicit. Together these points encode the size of the screen, its aspect ratio, its position and orientation. Also, they can be used to compute an orthonormal basis for the screen-space coordinate system[4]. We refer to this basis as the triad of vectors composed by s_r (the vector toward the right), s_u (the vector pointing up), and s_n (the vector normal to the screen, pointing in front of it).

$$s_r = \frac{p_b - p_a}{|p_b - p_a|} \tag{3}$$

$$s_u = \frac{p_c - p_a}{|p_c - p_a|} \tag{4}$$

$$s_n = \frac{s_r \times s_u}{|s_r \times s_u|} \tag{5}$$

---

[4] In linear algebra an orthonormal basis for an inner product space is a basis whose vectors are all unit vectors orthogonal to each other.

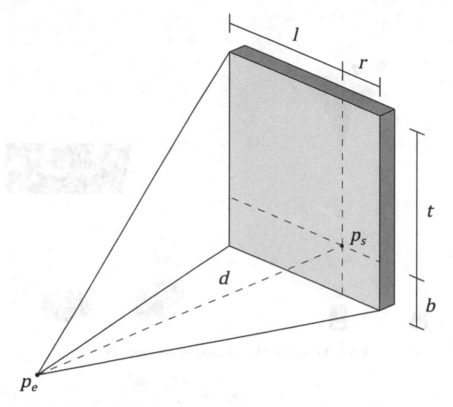

Fig. 5. The length of the frustum extents (l, r, b and t) at the plane of the screen.

The origin of the screen space coordinate system is the intersection between the perpendicular line drawn from p_e to the screen, and the plane of the screen itself. Since neither $\underline{p_e}$ nor p_s are fixed in space, when the viewer moves with respect to the screen, the screen-space origin changes accordingly. If s/he moves far to the side of the screen, then the screen space origin may not fall within the screen at all.

The distance from the eye-space origin p_e and the screen-space origin p_s may be computed by taking the dot product of the screen normal v_n with any of the screen vectors.

However, because these vectors point in quite opposite directions, their product must be negated.

$$d = -(s_n \cdot v_a) \tag{6}$$

In order to compute the frustum extents we need the vectors from the camera space origin (p_e) to the screen corners. Once again, these can be easily calculated using the screen corners.

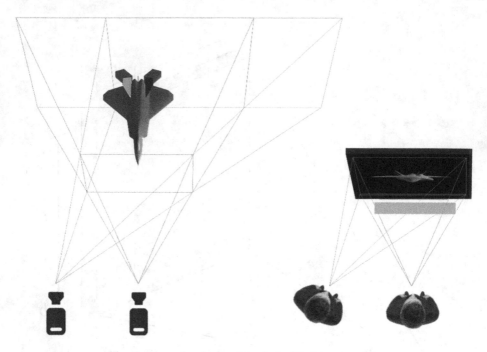

Fig. 6. Example of a head-tracked off-axis perspective.

$$v_a = p_a - p_e \tag{7}$$

$$v_b = p_b - p_e \tag{8}$$

$$v_c = p_c - p_e \tag{9}$$

Frustum extents may be interpreted (and computed) as distances from the screen-space origin to the edges of the screen (as shown in Fig. 6). However, because these are not specified at the near clipping plane, we must scale them back from their value at the plane of the screen, d units away from the eye-space origin, to their value at the near clipping plane, n units away from the eye-space origin.

$$l = \frac{(s_r \cdot v_a)n}{d} \tag{10}$$

$$r = \frac{(s_r \cdot v_b)n}{d} \tag{11}$$

$$b = \frac{(s_u \cdot v_a)n}{d} \tag{12}$$

$$t = \frac{(s_u \cdot v_c)n}{d} \tag{13}$$

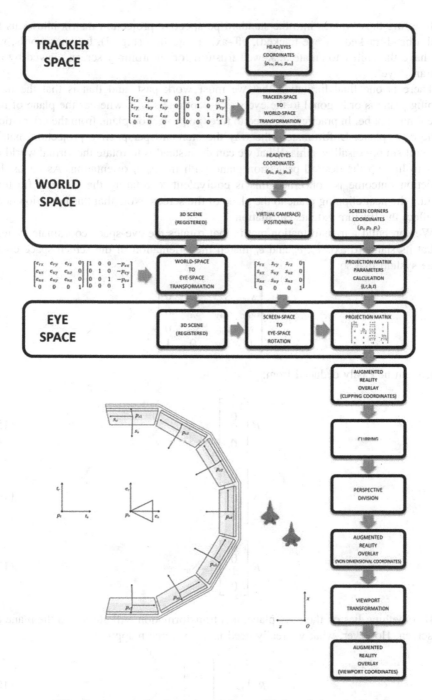

Fig. 7. An overall schematics of the modified rendering pipeline

Inserting these values into the standard perspective projection matrix allows us to build a head-tracked (or eye-tracked), off–axis projection (Fig. 7). In other words, we now have the ability to create a skewed frustum for an arbitrary screen viewed by an arbitrary 'eye'.

There is one final limitation that we must work past, and that is that the near clipping plane is orthogonal to the eye-space depth axis (e_n), whereas the plane of the screen may not be. In practice, we need to free the projection plane from the orientation of the e_u-e_r plane. Unfortunately the way the standard perspective projection matrix was built simply disallows this. What we can do instead is to rotate the virtual world in order to line up the desired projection plane with the e_u-e_r orientation. As far as the projection outcome is concerned this is equivalent to rotating the viewing frustum aligning the near clipping plane to the plane of the screen. Note that this operation does not affect the frustum extents calculation.

We can build a transformation matrix that rotates the eye-space coordinate system so that its standard axis e_r, e_u and e_n match the orientation of the screen-space coordinate system like so:

$$R = \begin{bmatrix} s_{rx} & s_{ux} & s_{nx} & 0 \\ s_{ry} & s_{uy} & s_{ny} & 0 \\ s_{rz} & s_{uz} & s_{nz} & 0 \\ 0 & 0 & 0 & 1 \end{bmatrix} \tag{14}$$

Which can be easily deduced from:

$$R \begin{bmatrix} 1 \\ 0 \\ 0 \\ 0 \end{bmatrix} = s_r \tag{15}$$

$$R \begin{bmatrix} 0 \\ 1 \\ 0 \\ 0 \end{bmatrix} = s_u \tag{16}$$

$$R \begin{bmatrix} 0 \\ 0 \\ 1 \\ 0 \end{bmatrix} = s_n \tag{17}$$

If something lies on the e_u-e_r plane, this transformation will align it to the plane of the screen. However, what we really need is the inverse mapping:

$$R^{-1} s_r = \begin{bmatrix} 1 \\ 0 \\ 0 \\ 0 \end{bmatrix} \tag{18}$$

$$R^{-1}s_u = \begin{bmatrix} 0 \\ 1 \\ 0 \\ 0 \end{bmatrix} \tag{19}$$

$$R^{-1}s_n = \begin{bmatrix} 0 \\ 0 \\ 1 \\ 0 \end{bmatrix} \tag{20}$$

Which is produced by the inverse of R:

$$R^{-1} = \begin{bmatrix} s_{rx} & s_{ry} & s_{rz} & 0 \\ s_{ux} & s_{uy} & s_{uz} & 0 \\ s_{nx} & s_{ny} & s_{nz} & 0 \\ 0 & 0 & 0 & 1 \end{bmatrix} \tag{21}$$

However, since R is orthogonal, R^{-1} is simply its transpose:

$$R^{-1} = R^T \tag{22}$$

Applying this transformation to all the objects in the virtual world will rotate the scene until the plane of the screen lines up with the e_u-e_r plane, which is exactly we needed.

If we compose the standard projection matrix P with the rotation matrix R^T, the resulting matrix M covers everything we need and will work under any circumstances.

$$M = R^T P \tag{23}$$

With this matrix, we are finally able to render the scene in order to generate the AR layered.

5 Conclusion

Various analysts have estimated the benefits of using AR tools in control tower operations. However it is unclear which one between the head-worn AR technology and the spatial AR technology will prevail. Also, it has been rarely specified how such tools should be designed and operated. Our review confirms that many problems must be addressed before these tools become operational. However, there is ample reason to believe that, eventually, this will happen.

With regard to the use of very large format AR displays, we have developed an advanced rendering pipeline that is capable of generating registered overplays for multiple, arbitrary oriented head-up displays, defined together in a common coordinate system (Fig. 8). Our concept is based on the excellent work by Robert Kooima (Electronic Visualization Laboratory, University of Illinois) [39]. However, because of a different target and development framework, the here-proposed implementation turned out to be a quite different thing. For instance, we do not consider the eye-space coordinate system to be bound to the world-space coordinate system (which probably seems quite reasonable to game engine developers).

In this document, the algorithm description has been deliberately mathematical, (i.e. not linked to any specific development framework or programming language). However, at our facilities, we have developed (and tested) a Python/C# code using an open source game engine and a Kinect^{TM} for Windows^{TM} tracking sensor. We plan to use this software as a basis for further research in the field of spatial see-through HUDs for the control tower.

References

1. Office for Official Publications of the European Communities: Single European Sky - Results from the transport research programme. http://www.transport-research.info/sites/default/files/brochure/20040617_111440_74437_singlesky.pdf
2. SESAR JU: Enhanced Ground Controller Situational Awareness in all Weather Conditions. https://www.atmmasterplan.eu/oisteps/AO-0201
3. Clean Sky JU: Clean Sky 2 - Joint Technical Programme. http://ec.europa.eu/research/participants/data/ref/h2020/other/guide-appl/jti/h2020-guide-techprog-cleansky-ju_en.pdf
4. SESAR JU: Honeywell in SESAR: Advancing ATM in the heart of Europe (2012). http://www.sesarju.eu/sites/default/files/documents/reports/SESAR_magazine_issue_7.pdf
5. Reisman, R., Brown, D.: Design of augmented reality tools for air traffic control towers. In: Proceedings of 6th AIAA Aviation Technology, Integration and Operations Conference (ATIO). American Institute of Aeronautics and Astronautics, Wichita, KS (2006)
6. Tavanti, M.: Control Tower Operations: A Literature Review of Task Analysis Studies. EEC Technical/Scientific Report No. 2006-013 (2006)
7. Pinska, E.: An investigation of the head-up time at tower and ground control positions. In: Proceeding of the 5th Eurocontrol Innovative Research Workshop, pp. 81–86 (2006)
8. Kunert, T., Krömker, H.: A pattern-based framework for the exploration of design alternatives. In: Jacko, J.A. (ed.) HCI 2007. LNCS, vol. 4550, pp. 1119–1128. Springer, Heidelberg (2007)
9. Ellis, S.R.: Towards determination of visual requirements for augmented reality displays and virtual environments for the airport tower. In: Virtual Media for Military Applications RTO-MP-HFM-136, pp. 31-1–31-10. RTO, Neuilly-sur-Seine (2006)
10. Shackelford, R., Karpe, P.: Low/Zero Visibility Tower Tools (L/ZVTT) Benefits Assessment., NASA Ames Research Center Technical Reports, Moffett Field, CA 94035 (1998)
11. Neveu, C., Blackmon, T., Stark, L.: Evaluation of the effects of a head-mounted display on ocular accommodation. Presence 7, 278–289 (1998)
12. Ellis, S.R., Adelstein, B.D., Reisman, R.J., Schmidt-Ott, J.R., Gips, J., Krozel, J.: Augmented Reality in a Simulated Tower Environment: Effect of Field of View on Aircraft Detection. NASA Ames Research Center Technical Reports (2002)
13. Weintraub, D.J., Ensing, M.J.: Human factors issues in head-up display and design: the book of HUD. Crew System Ergonomics Information Analysis Center, Wright-Patterson AFB, Ohio (1992)
14. Rediess, H.: An augmented reality pilot display for airport operations under low and zero visibility conditions. In: Guidance, Navigation, and Control Conference. American Institute of Aeronautics and Astronautics (1997)

15. Ruffner, J.W., Deaver, D.M., Henry, D.J.: Requirements analysis for an air traffic control tower surface surveillance enhanced vision system. Presented at the SPIE-The International Society for Optical Engineering (2003)
16. Fürstenau, N.: Virtual tower. In: 5th ATM R&D Symposium, Braunschweig (2005)
17. Azuma, R.: A survey of augmented reality. Presence: Teleoper. Virtual Env. **6**, 355–385 (1997)
18. Reisman, R.J., Feiner, S.K., Brown, D.M.: Augmented reality tower technology flight test. In: International Conference on Human-Computer Interaction in Aerospace (HCI-Aero), Santa Clara, CA (2014)
19. Reisman, R.J., Brown, D.M.: Augmented Reality Tower Technology Assessment. NASA Ames Research Center Technical Reports (2010)
20. De Crescenzio F., Bagassi S., Fantini M., Lucchi F.: Virtual Reality based HUD (Head Up Display) to simulate 3D conformal symbols in the design of future cockpits. Presented at the Council of European Aerospace Societies, Venice, Italy, 24–28 October 2011
21. Bagassi, S., De Crescenzio, F., Lucchi, F., Persiani, F.: Innovation in man machine interfaces: use of 3D conformal symbols in the design of future HUDs (Head-Up Displays). Presented at the 28th International Congress of the Aeronautical Sciences, Brisbane, Australia, 23 September 2012
22. SESAR JU: System Wide Information Management (SWIM). http://www.sesarju.eu/sesar-solutions/swim
23. SESAR JU: SWIM Concept of Operations. https://www.eurocontrol.int/sites/default/files/publication/files/del08.01.01-d41-swim_conops.pdf
24. SESAR JU: Time Based Separation. http://www.sesarju.eu/sesar-solutions/airport-integration-and-throughput/time-based-separation
25. SESAR: 06.09.03 Remote & virtual TWR. https://www.atmmasterplan.eu/projects/16484
26. Fürstenau, N., Schmidt, M., Rudolph, M., Möhlenbrink, C., Papenfuß, A., Kaltenhäuser, S.: Steps towards the virtual tower: Remote Airport traffic control Center (RAiCe). Presented at the ENRI International Workshop on ATM/CNS, Tokyo, Japan (2009)
27. Schulz-Rückert, D.: Future of aerodrome traffic control. Presented at the Aachen Aviation Convention, Aachen, Germany (2007)
28. Bimber, O., Raskar, R.: Spatial Augmented Reality: Merging Real and Virtual Worlds. A. K. Peters Ltd., Natick (2005)
29. Peterson, S.: Very large format stereoscopic head-up display for the airport tower. In: Proceedings of the Virtual Images Seminar, number 16. CNRS/Renault (2007)
30. Peterson, S., Pinska, E.: Human performance with simulated collimation in transparent projection screens. In: Proceedings of the Second International Conference on Research in Air Transportation (ICRAT) (2006)
31. Rolland, J.P., Baillot, Y., Goon, A.A.: A survey of tracking technology for virtual environments. Fundam. Wearable Comput. Augmented Reality **1**, 67–112 (2001)
32. Zhou, F., Duh, H.B.-L., Billinghurst, M.: Trends in augmented reality tracking, interaction and display: a review of ten years of ISMAR. In: 7th IEEE/ACM International Symposium on Mixed and Augmented Reality, ISMAR 2008, pp. 193–202 (2008)
33. Masotti, N., Persiani, F.: Gaze-coupled perspective for enhanced human-machine interfaces in aeronautics. Presented at the Conferences in Air Transport & Operations, Delft University of Technology, Delft, The Netherlands, 20 July 2015
34. OpenGL: gluPerspective. https://www.opengl.org/sdk/docs/man2/xhtml/gluPerspective.xml
35. Song Ho Ahn: OpenGL Projection Matrix. http://www.songho.ca/opengl/gl_projection matrix.html

36. Woo, M., Neider, J., Davis, T., Shreiner, D.: OpenGL programming guide: the official guide to learning OpenGL, Version 1.2. Addison-Wesley Longman Publishing Co., Inc., Boston (1999)
37. Microsoft: DirectX Graphics and Gaming. https://msdn.microsoft.com/en-us/library/windows/desktop/ee663274(v=vs.85).aspx
38. glFrustum – OpenGL. https://www.opengl.org/sdk/docs/man2/xhtml/glFrustum.xml
39. Kooima, R.: Generalized Perspective Projection. J. Sch. Electron. Eng. Comput. Sci. (2009)
40. Liverani, A., Persiani, F., De Crescenzio, F.: An Immersive Reconfigurable Room (I.R.R.) for virtual reality simulation. In: Electronic Proceedings of 12th International Conference on Design Tools and Methods in Industrial Engineering, Rimini, Italy, pp. E1-9–E1-16 (2001)

CoCo - A Framework for Multicore Visuo-Haptics in Mixed Reality

Emanuele Ruffaldi[✉] and Filippo Brizzi

TeCiP, Scuola Superiore Sant'Anna, Pisa, Italy
e.ruffaldi@sssup.it
http://www.percro.org

Abstract. Mixed Reality applications involve the integration of RGB-D streams with virtual entities potentially extended with force feedback. Increasing complexity of the applications pushes the limits of traditional computing structures, not keeping up with the increased computing power of multicore platform. This paper presents the CoCo framework, a component based, multicore system designed for tackling the challenges of visuo-haptics in mixed reality environment, with structural reconfiguration. Special care has been also given to the management of transformation between reference frames for easing registration, calibration and integration of robotic systems. The framework is described together with a description of two relevant case studies.

1 Introduction

Advancements in sensing, computing and display technologies is expanding the possibility of uses of Virtual, Augmented and broader Mixed Reality (MR) applications[1], in local or networked situation, involving robots or multiple users. Such variable Mixed Reality applications, in general, require the integration of sensing components, simulation and visuo-haptic feedback. The development of such applications is typically based on a computer graphics oriented framework, typically structured around a scene graph, and many of such frameworks do exist spanning from commercial ones to community or research developed. The scene graph is then paired with some form of application development based on explicit programming or visual programming following a data flow paradigm.

The abstraction level of a MR development tool allows the developer to easily create a prototype, but, due to the nature of high-latency, high-throughput nature of sophisticated MR applications it can soon impact into performance issues associated to frame rate and latency. The aspect of processing and output rate is even more relevant when the MR application needs to provide haptic feedback or timely feedback to a robot. In the end, as it is well known, a multimodal MR application is organized around multiple components exchanging data at different rates. The point is how to take advantage of recent multi-core systems for reasonably interesting MR solutions.

---

[1] We use the general term MR for all the applications in the Mixed Reality continuum.

© Springer International Publishing Switzerland 2016
L.T. De Paolis and A. Mongelli (Eds.): AVR 2016, Part I, LNCS 9768, pp. 339–357, 2016.
DOI: 10.1007/978-3-319-40621-3_24

This paper discusses the design choices and the implementation of the Compact Components (CoCo) framework that aims at providing abstractions concepts and specific components for addressing MR applications with modern multi-core systems. CoCo has been so far employed in the context of VR and MR applications with haptic feedback [1,2] or interfaced with robots [3]. CoCo is founded over three pillars that can be considered fundamental in such applications: integration, computing abstraction and transformations. The first pillar is provided by the component based approach, the second allows to control the use of resources after the development of components, and the third is an important mechanism that supports reference frames flexibility, registration and sensor fusion. Conceptually CoCo is based on three orthogonal graphs: *computational graph* that support the data flow between components (a DAG), a *scheduling graph* that supports the partitioning of components' execution in processes and threads (a tree), and a *transformation graph* (a general graph).

The following section provides the research context on the topic for better understanding the proposed innovation. Section 3 presents the concepts behind the design of CoCo, Sect. 4 describes the functionalities provided for supporting visuo-haptic applications. Section 5 discusses how Transformations between frames are addressed. Then Sect. 6 provides a case study followed by conclusions.

2   Background

There is a long history of frameworks for 3D graphics applications and their natural extension to Virtual Reality setup. Since the beginning the VR and in general MR applications have posed computing challenges, due to the requirement of high and regular output frame rates with minimal latency. In VR applications the main issues arise from integration with physics simulation and interaction devices. When moving to AR or MR applications the sensing component involves higher computing requirements due to the closed loop with imaging devices. Finally when moving to visuo-haptic devices there is the additional requirement of providing timely haptic feedback that, for rigid objects, requires update rates in the order of 1kHz or more.

Two main approaches are found in literature and in the implementation for structuring the application: scene graph-based and flow-based approaches. In scene-graph approaches the developer creates a hierarchy of entities spanning across the different modalities, then the framework organizes the processing in loops (graphics, physics, collision) with some flexibility for the developer. This approach is found in systems such as OpenSceneGraph [4], XVR [5] or Unity. Conversely flow-based approaches allow the developer to describe the application in terms of streams of data and events connected in a flow structure. The latter approach can be found in the X3D standard and derivatives like InstantReality [6] and other systems such as InTml [7] or FlowVR [8]. FlowVR is a notable example because it provides distributed computing capabilities for VR, introducing a very flexible mechanism for synchronization among modules that allows the implementation of several communication patterns. In general the use of declarative approaches, in comparison to immediate programming, allows for the underlying framework to perform certain optimizations based on the underlying platform, or for extending the rendering from single output to stereo or more.

When dealing with visuo-haptics the existing frameworks follow both patterns like scene-graph in CHAI3D [9,10], or flow-graphs derived from X3D in H3DAPI [11]. CHAI3D leaves to the developer the burden of organizing the loop, while internally performing traversal and computing, while H3DAPI and derived follow the event-based approach of X3D. In the above examples the control of execution loops is hidden in the framework or explicitly managed by the developer at low-level, with hard work for scalability or profiling.

CoCo contributes to the field by proposing a component based approach in which each component has an independent execution loop that is not directly controlled by the component developer. Instead the framework allows for structuring the scheduling of components at run-time providing space for reconfiguration depending on the users needs. This approach takes inspiration from the OROCOS robotic framework [12] introducing specific aspects aimed at visuo-haptic MR applications.

As discussed in the introduction the third pillar of CoCo is the transformation systems, an aspect that is fundamental in any MR or robotics application: how transformation between reference frames are generated and used by the components. In scene-graph based frameworks the scene-graph itself provides the structure of the transformations forcing a tree-like structure, while in data flow based approaches there is the need to stream the transformation along the structure.

CoCo provides a general declarative approach of transformations that is orthogonal to the information flow between components and based on a Spatial-Relationship Graph (SRG). Differently from the ROS [13] TF2 system, CoCo allows to associate semantics to transformations at run-time or at build-time, providing, in this way, the support for sensor fusion and moreover generalized registration, two aspects that are fundamental for AR/MR [14].

3   Concepts

The foundation of the CoCo framework is a component-based system in which each node is an independent unit of execution exchanging data, invoking operations or triggering the execution of other components. CoCo has been developed in C++11 with the objective of being lightweight and multi-platform. Components are loosely coupled to increase modularity and reduce development dependencies: in terms of C++ this means that the only common element between components is the data exchanged. Components are stored in dynamic or static libraries and they can be instantiated at run-time by name. A CoCo application is typically launched by providing an XML file that configures the components and connects them.

In general a CoCo component comprises the following elements:

- Callbacks, in particular with the loop callback *onUpdate*.
- Input and output data ports that are used for the main exchange of data.
- Declarative attributes that are configured via XML or at run-time.
- Operators that can be invoked in a thread-safe manner.

3.1   Components Lifetime

Components can be instantiated at any time although it is more typical to have main instantiations at application startup time. Two functions are used to perform initialization and configuration (*init*, *onConfig*) based on the parameters received via the configuration file. After initialization a component receives an execution request in the *onUpdate* function that, due to the execution abstraction of CoCo, can be periodic or not. In any case the *onUpdate* implementation should not block the execution.

3.2   Ports

Ports are the key mechanism for data exchange between components inside CoCo and they have been designed to support different patterns of exchange and moreover, the exchange of large entities such as images or pointclouds.

Each component can declare a set of input and output named ports which are templated against a C++ native type. Thanks to C++11 capabilities introspection of ports and their types is straightforward but at the moment no serialization capability between processes has been introduced. A port marked as event port is then used by the scheduling system to trigger aperiodic components.

The connection between ports is many-to-many meaning that a single element written to an output port can be received by multiple recipients. When an input port has multiple sources they are processed in a round robin fashion, although in a future timestamps could be used for chronological ordering.

An important principle of CoCo is that ports never block nor in reading or writing, because components should never block inside their looping step.

Two aspects, controlled in the XML file, specify the nature of the connection: buffering and synchronization policy. Three types of buffering are supported corresponding to recurring patterns in MR applications: for example a pipeline with different generation-consumption rates, or a window of the last valid values.

- **DATA**: The connection has a buffer of length 1 and new incoming data always overrides existing data even if it has not been read.
- **BUFFER**: The connection has a buffer of length as specified in the configuration file. If the buffer is full new incoming data is discarded without blocking.
- **CIRCULAR**: The connection has a circular FIFO buffer of length as specified in the configuration file. If the buffer is full new incoming data overrides the oldest one. A DATA buffering is equivalent to a CIRCULAR with length 1 except much more efficient.

The connections support two synchronization policies: **LOCKED** and **UNSYNC**. In the first case data access is regulated by mutexes while in the second case there is no resource access control policy. A lockless policy could be added providing high-efficient data access. The unsync policy applies for the connections between components inside the same activity.

CoCo ports and connections operate via value-copy of the received content. This solution is efficient for small sized types, and it allows to manage large entities via shared pointer solutions. The issue with shared pointer solution is that when the last user of the object releases the object this is destroyed. This is not the optimal choice for large objects produced at high rates for the effect on the memory manager. CoCo provides a pooled channel mechanism for supporting efficiently the exchange of large entities such as images, point clouds or meshes. Every slot of the pooled buffer has four states logically ordered: free, writing, ready, reading. This means that when a writer needs to write an entity, first it receives it from the pool, writes it and then it makes the entity available for ready. Similarly a reader receives the entity and needs to notify when it has finished using the content.

3.3 Scheduling

Execution of components in CoCo, and in a MR application in general, is periodic with fixed rate or aperiodic being triggered by some event, being it internal or external to the framework.

Whatever the nature of the component the execution takes place inside a container called *activity* that can hold multiple components. An activity corresponds, in practice, to an OS thread and, for this reason, it can be associated to system priority and processor affinity. At every step of the activity all the components are executed sequentially. Periodicity or triggering are specified at the level of activity: a triggered activity is activated when any of the contained components receive some data in a triggerable input port.

The XML configuration file of an application is organized per-activity each with the contained components. The activity configuration comprises the periodic nature as period in milliseconds or triggering. In addition one of the activity can be marked as "main" for being associated to the main thread of the CoCo application.

The component-activity separation allows the developer to reconfigure the flow of execution at run-time, without the need to customize or recompile the components. An improvement of the model discussed above relies on increasing the granularity of components activation, that is supporting multiple rates inside an activity or controlling the triggering.

3.4 Operations

In addition to the flow-based data exchange components can invoke operations of other components with the guarantee that the invoked operation is executed in a thread-safe manner: that is if the two components belong to the same thread no overhead is introduced otherwise a messaging system deals with the delivery of the function call.

Each component can bind any of its C++ methods to an operation. An operation is identified by a name and by the signature of the function it embeds. A task's operations can be called by any other task or can be enqueued in the task pending operations list. Every time an activity resumes its execution, either because the period timer expires or it is triggered by data reception, before executing the main loop function *onUpate*, it execute all the pending operations. The task invoking the function to enqueue an operation on another task can add to the call a function to get the return value of the operation.

3.5 Peers

There are some situations in which the activity-component hierarchy of execution is not enough, for this reason it is possible to nest components inside other components. CoCo calls them peers. Peers are used to extend the functionalities of a component preserving code encapsulation and reusability as they can be instantiated multiple times for different components and the binding is decided at run-time. Peers are components by themselves inheriting all the functionalities such as ports, attributes and operations. The main difference relies in the fact that peers execution is controlled by the owner component, and typically they are used via operations. Thanks to operations there is no limits in the number of peers that can be associated to a component or to another peer giving the possibility to create a tree of peers with any desired depth or width.

3.6 Patterns

From the scenarios of MR applications it is possible to identify several patterns of components usage. A common pattern is the one of sensor source that produces a stream of data triggered by an external source such as a socket, an external API or a USB file descriptor. A lightweight filtering component that needs to use the sensor source data, can be placed in the same activity to reduce latency, while heavier processing is better to be moved in a separate one. Another pattern is the one of state holders with fast query such as KD-Tree in which updates are expensive but queries are fast. In this case the update comes via an input port, while queries are realized with an operation.

3.7 Profiling

The CoCo libraries provides also an utility to easily calculate execution time of blocks of code. This functionality can be used by the user inside its components to quickly evaluate the computational load and it has been inserted inside the core of the library to obtain precise statistics on the components performance. The component profiling is activated passing a specific flag to the launcher and statistics of the execution are provided with a certain time interval. The measurements include, for each component, the number of executions and the total execution time; mean and variance of the average computation and service time. This last value is used to evaluate the feasibility of the application scheduling because it represents the mean time between two activations of a component and should be equal to the period for periodic components.

4   Visuo-Haptics for Mixed Reality

The CoCo framework has been used as the infrastructure for the realization of a set of libraries, called CoCo Mixed Reakity (CoCoMR), targeting the creation of visuo-haptics applications for MR scenarios. One of the complexity in this kind of applications stands in the different rates at which each component executes. A standard visuo-haptics application can be composed of a module reading frames from a camera at 30 Hz or more, the graphics renderer module that runs between 60 to 120 Hz depending on the visualization nature and a module controlling the haptic device running at least at 1 kHz. Three modules sets (Vision, Haptic and Display) have been developed to target each specific scenario and thanks to the CoCo features they can be combined and customized as desired at run-time. CoCoMR contains also common utilities and a shared interface to allow different components to exchange data through the CoCo ports. An overview of the core modules is shown in Fig. 1.

Each module set's components can be divided into two main categories: the ones that interacts with the external world, either devices or other applications, and the ones doing the internal computations. The components in the first group are all executed periodically and their period can be adjusted at run-time to synchronize it with a specific device or an external software (sources in the

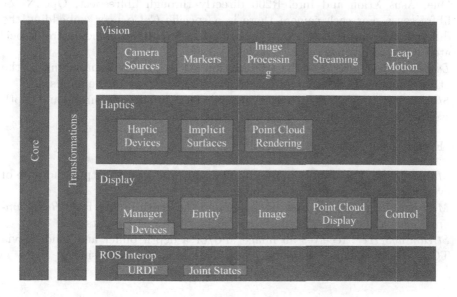

Fig. 1. Overall view of modules and components

computational graph). The second group, instead, contains the components that perform the internal calculations and their execution is usually triggered by the data received from the components in the first group.

The section continues with the features of each module that allow to understand the span of applications covered by CoCo and the approach described in the previous Concepts section.

4.1 Vision Module

The vision module provides the services for the computer vision part of a MR application, that is the acquisition of image sources, the tracking of features or fiducial markers, and, for the case of tele-presence applications, the streaming.

Components in the vision module exchange data structures that correspond to images, RGB-D images, and camera parameters (intrinsics matrix and distortion). In particular color images are encoded with the possibility of using several color formats (grayscale, RGBA, YUYV and YUV420) with the aim of limiting the conversion from sensors (typically producing images in YUYV) and toward computer vision algorithms that employ often grayscale images. The YUV420 is instead the layout of video compressors. GB-D data is stored as a combination of the color image and a depth image (float or signed int16).

Source components are the following:

- *CameraReader*: using gstreamer or OpenCV captures camera frames and share them with the other CoCo components.
- *RgbdCameraReader*: same as *CameraReader*, but captures also the depth buffer. The component supports multiple cameras such as Kinect 360 or One, Asus Xtion and Intel R200 directly through libfreenect, OpenNI or libfreesense. For each camera there is a specific CoCo peer embedding the different API for each vendor. If provided by the driver cameras are associated with the intrinsics.
- *LeapReader*: it interfaces the LeapMotion API with CoCo providing to the other components position, orientation and fingers pose of the hands.
- *StreamingReceiver*: it is used to receive via TCP and decodes image and depth streams in case of applications for tele-operation.

Filtering and sink components are:

- *MarkerTracker*: receives a camera buffer and produces in output the pose of eventual markers present in the image.
- *MeshReconstructor*: receives the image and the depth buffers from *RgbdCameraReader* and creates a mesh interpolating the missing points.
- *StreamingServer*: receives an image and/or a depth buffer and sends it via TCP. Must be coupled with *StreamingReceiver* at the client side.

4.2 Haptic Module

The haptic module provides *haptic rendering* that is the generation of force feedback following the convention of computer graphics rendering [15]. There are several challenges in haptic rendering tasks mainly related to the high rate of the update loop, 1 kHz, and especially when the interacting surface is dynamically updated as coming from a RGB-D camera. CoCo provides internally the support for the haptic rendering of implicit surfaces or point clouds (used in [2]). Other techniques can be integrated such as volumetric voxel models [16] or the 3DOF spherical Proxy algorithm [17] for triangular meshes to external libraries such a CHAI3D.

The rendering of implicit surfaces is based on the Salisbury algorithm [18] that updates a contact proxy based on an implicit surface described as a distance to the surface and the local gradient. CoCo supports the creation of procedural implicit surfaces expressed on constructive solid geometry over building blocks such as cylinders, planes and spheres. The *HapticImplicitSurf* component is configured over a functional description of the surface, and then it tracks the proxy over the surface, generating force feedback with friction parameters.

Contact rendering of live point clouds, or point-sampled meshes, is based on the identification of the points around the proxy via KD-Tree and the creation of a local surface from such points. The *KDTreeBuilder* component is responsible for the creation of the KD-Tree either from a point cloud or the vertices of a meshes provided by the adapter *MeshReconstruction* component. The *HapticCloud* component provides haptic rendering over these points using the KD-Tree emitted by the *KDTreeBuilder*. This is an example of the large resource management of CoCo: the KDTreeBuilder has an input port with the new point cloud and inside the loop it performs the slow update, while, at the same time, the last value of the KD Tree is available over the output port. The port mechanism allows the reuse of the values in the ports, much like happens in a classical front-back buffer, but only in a more general way.

For a complex scene with multiple surfaces (or layered materials) it is possible to coordinate different rendering components, or aggregate them inside a single component, called *HapticRenderer*, that invokes the various renderers using the peer mechanism. As discussed, anyway, the peers share the same activity, meaning the same OS thread.

4.3 Display Module

The Display module has been developed to provide a reasonably good visualization capability for MR applications with the main idea of displaying images or point clouds produced by set of cameras looking more at performance than display visual effects. There is no intention to replicate features found in more sophisticated 3D engines, such as shadows or large complex models.

The display module is based on OpenGL 3.3 and it is responsible for the rendering of 3D objects and the eventual images obtained from cameras.

It is composed of a single component and several peers, mainly due to the single-thread nature of the OpenGL API. Multi-threaded OpenGL could be an option but it is known to impact the performance of the overall 3D rendering, and multi-threading can be exploited only for the memory transfer between CPU and GPU buffers, e.g. for uploading point cloud or texture data. The recent introduction of the Vulkan API has opened the way for multi-threading with GPU and it could be an interesting enhancement for the graphics part of CoCo. The component (*GLManager*) is the graphics manager and it is in charge of initializing the OpenGL context and the rendering window across a variety of devices. The OpenGL camera and every element that has to be rendered are associated to a peer. *GLManager* queries the camera peer for the projection/view matrices and then iterates over all the other peers calling their rendering function.

When instantiating the *GLManager* component it is possible to specify the frame rate, setting the desired period in the activity containing it, the window resolution and the visualization type covering 2D, 3D stereo or Oculus Rift DK2. CoCoMR supports the creation of multiple visualization windows in Linux by instantiating at run-time one *GLManager* component for each desired display. Furthermore *GLManager* can render on texture and produce the result through a port allowing the streaming of the visualization scene or using CoCoMR as the input for some computer vision algorithms that requires the synthetic rendering of the estimated entity (e.g. hand's pose).

Camera. The *GLCameraManager* peer, one per *GLManager* at the moment, is in charge of managing the OpenGL camera, specifying the initial position of the camera through CoCo attributes and the type of camera through additional peers. The camera system supports oblique projections because they emerge in the common situation of head-tracking systems with precise co-location as in the encountered system work [2], or multi screen systems [19]. Camera controllers are also expressed as peers: first person shooter style camera (*FPSCamera* peer) and arcball camera (*ArcBallCamera* peer). Camera can be moved either using mouse and keyboard or by sending the desired position to the *GLCameraManager* dedicated port.

Camera Images. To render images provided by cameras two peers are available. *GLImage*: renders a 2D image in the background of the virtual world. The image is scaled to fit the resolution of the window. *GLRGBDImage* renders the 3D scene obtained from the *MeshReconstructor* component. In case of very noisy meshes it supports the possibility to average the position of the mesh points among multiple sequential frames. Furthermore with the support of a geometric shader it is possible to clean the scene removing the big triangles that connect objects far from each others.

3D Objects. The *GLEntity* peer is used to render any mesh into the 3D world. It supports all the standard formats and provides a set of basic shaders to support textures and lights. *GLEntity* exposes several attributes to set the object initial pose and scale, the eventual color if not present in the mesh file and the possibility to run a subdivision algorithm on the object surface. *GLEntity* can be further specialized associating custom peers to it. A peer, to be supported, has to expose an operation named *preRender* that takes in input a pointer to the *GLEntity* object. The operation is called by the component before the OpenGL draw function and can be used to modify the standard behavior of the virtual object. For example it could be possible to alter its color according to external information, to change the mesh shape or to modify the pose.

The display module also supports the rendering of Universal Robot Description Format (URDF) objects from ROS through the *GLUrdf* peer. This feature is very useful when performing robot teleoperation because it allows to easily check that the camera mounted on the robot and the robot itself are correctly registered. Details of registration are provided in the following section. Furthermore it allows to have a clear idea of the robot pose when the camera only focuses the end-effectors. It can also be used to simulate a robot in a pure virtual environment.

4.4   ROS Interface

The integration and interoperability with ROS is a mandatory requirement when developing robotic applications. ROS has become the de facto standard in robotics and many vendors provides the control software of their devices directly as ROS nodes. Thanks to the simplicity and versatility of CoCo it is very straightforward to transform a component so that it can be used as a bridge between ROS and CoCo. To do so the user has to simply create a CoCo component inside a standard ROS package and compile it as a library. In this way the component can declare a *ros::NodeHandle* object and use it to register or publish in topics. Received data can be transformed to be exchanged trough CoCo ports. When an application contains a ROS component a different launcher has to be used, that is a ROS node embedding the same functionalities and the same behavior of the standard launcher.

5   Transformations

Transformation between reference frames are a fundamental element of any MR application in particular when multiple image sources are used together with other tracking devices. CoCo approaches the problem by providing a general **transformation graph** that is orthogonal to the other graphs of the CoCo structure (components and scheduling). The nodes of the graphs are reference frames that are connected via edges that express relative poses.

The components publish transformations between pairs of frames and these are used to update the internal graph. The transformation query mechanism is based on a path resolution over the graph: the transformation between two frames corresponds to one of the paths between them in the transformation graph. The path associated to each query is cached for future requests avoiding repetition of the path resolution and it is updated every time one of the edges change.

The transformation information flows inside the computational graphs via the CoCo ports as long as the rest of the data. The *TransformationInterface* is a single component in the computational graph that receives all the transformations between frames, updates the internal graph, and propagates information to the other components. Two type of propagation are supported, via callback or operations. Each component can register a callback function to a query, that is, when any of the edges in the query's path changes and after the computation of the new transformation all the registered callbacks are called receiving the new result. In addition *TransformationInterface* exposes an operation that can be called by any other component to retrieve the transformation between two frames. Internally a readers-writer lock is implemented to avoid concurrency problems.

In contrast to ROS TF2 that is fully dynamic, CoCo allows to declare in advance the structure of the graph, in particular describing the nature of the edges that can be static, or dynamic, or projected from the 6DOF space to a single axis. The declarative feature is useful during development for controlling the different transformations, and, at the same time, at run-time, to optimize the execution of the internal processing of the graph.

5.1   Robotics Support

Single axis is specifically useful for robotics or human tracking in which the update value is the single joint value and the 6DOF transformation is the resulting application of a Denavit-Hartenberg transformation or equivalent. URDF provides a hierarchical, joint based, description of the robot and it can be directly loaded into the transformation graph.

5.2   Registration

The declarative approach allows for the automatic support for the registration between two disjoint frames (A,B). The registration is obtained by the introduction of a new temporary path between A and B that is produced by an external source, e.g. a chessboard or a fiducial marker that is not present during the execution. Multiple measures of the transformation between A and B are accumulated during the registration phase, and then the final value is obtained by 6DOF averaging.

This approach has been successfully used for registering the camera of a robotic head wrt the rest of the robot body by placing a fiducial marker over the robot arm and moving the arm (Fig. 2). In practice the approach is quite flexible and can take into account multiple temporary paths.

5.3   Diagnostics

A fundamental aspect of the CoCo management of transformation is diagnostics. First it is possible to serialize the graph over JSON at any time and to generate

Fig. 2. Result of the registration of the Kinect with the robot kinematics. The image part is a rendering of the Kinect point cloud, while the colored parts are meshes from the URDF controlled by robot joints. Finally in the lower left the calibration fiducial marker is visible.

a graphical representation of the graph using graphviz. Secondly it is possible to access the graph via a Web based REST interface in which all frames and the graph in general are accessible. The interface supports also Websockets for continuous streaming of transformations.

This is specifically useful for interfacing CoCo with other frameworks such as WebGL based frameworks or Unity.

6   Case Study

The CoCoMR libraries have been used for several applications both involving haptic devices and robot tele-operation. In the following two examples will be provided, showing the component structures and the performance measurements.

6.1   Visuo-Haptic Application

This section will describe how CoCoMR has been used in an application [2] for virtual remote palpation examination. Figure 3 shows the different hardware components involved in the setup. The whole system comprehends a Kinect 360 streaming via *StreamingServer* the RGB-D image of a mannequin laying on a table and representing a patient; a 3-DOF haptic device; the Leap Motion sensor to track the position of the hand and a 3D screen to visualize the remote scene. The user moves the hand below the screen and his movements are captured by the Leap Motion. The hand's pose is used to display on screen the 3D model of an hand superimposing it on the remote scene obtained through TCP (ZeroMQ) from the Kinect. The position of the hand is also sent to *HapticDeviceInterface*, an ad hoc component used to interact with the haptic device. *HapticDeviceInterface* communicates with a Simulink module performing the low level control of the device. The module uses the hand position to place the end-effector exactly below the user hand; in this way when the user lowers the hand and touches the virtual surface it will find the end-effector of the device providing force feedback based on the indentation with the virtual remote scene. To improve the visual feedback the virtual hand gradually shifts its color towards a red shade the deeper the end-effector is inside the surface; this is performed thanks to the *UpdateColor* peer assigned to the *GLEntity* component responsible for the virtual hand.

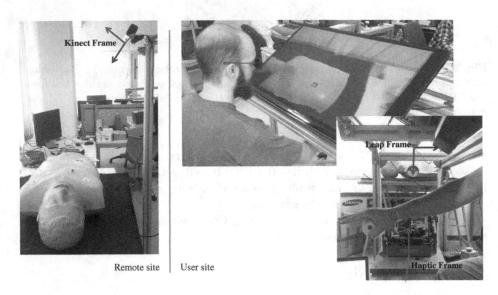

Fig. 3. The virtual palpation system. The hardware components are shown along with their reference frames.

The system is composed of multiple components each one running at different rates: 60 Hz the graphics, 30 Hz for reading images from the Kinect streaming, 100 Hz the LeapMotion and 1 kHz the haptic interface. As shown in Fig. 3 each device produces its data in its own reference system; to allow the various component to communicate the pose informations are all gathered by the *TransformationInterface* component that provides to the other components the position information in the desired reference frames. *TransformationInterface* is also in charge of performing the calibration between the different reference frames, in particular between the remote virtual scene, the hand pose and the device end-effector pose. This is done by putting a marker on the belly of the remote mannequin and its pose is associated with the one of the hand from the Leap Motion, the user has also to grasp the haptic device end-effector so that it is possible to assume that the three reference systems are aligned.

Figure 4 shows all the components and peers involved in the application. The components are divided per activity and the scheduling policy is shown. Given they high number of connections the lines have not been drawn but the assumption is that connection with the same name are linked. This apart from the pose transformations data that all flow trough *TransformationInterface*.

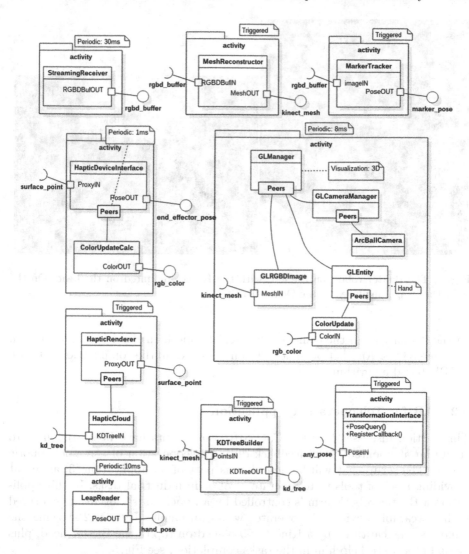

Fig. 4. CoCoMR components involved in the visuo-haptic application. Port with the same name type are connected to each other. Every poses pass through *Transforma-tionInterface* to be transformed in the correct reference system.

Performance. The application run on an Intel PC (Core i7 4770R 3.2 GHz, 8 GB RAM, embedded GPU) running Ubuntu Linux 14.04. The estimated sensor to display average latency is 75 ms, computed after synchronizing the robot and graphics computers with the Precision Time Protocol (PTP). The *HapticRender* component was able to calculate the surface proxy position at 1 kHz while some optimization were required to manage the kd-tree update at 30 Hz. The *KDTreeBuild* component performed a filtering on the received points based

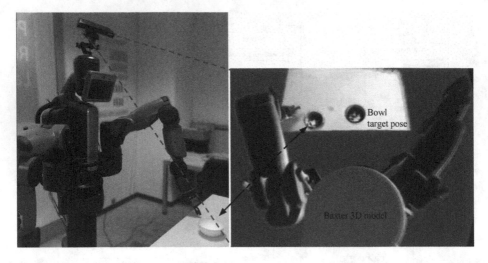

Fig. 5. The Baxter robot, on the left, with the Kinect mounted on the head. On the right the image displayed in the Oculus Rift

on the distance from the camera to reduce the mesh size and be able to run in less than 33 ms. Another possible solution to speed up the computation is to use a GPU-based algorithm.

6.2   AR for Teleoperation Application

This section discusses how the CoCoMR components have been combined to create an augmented visual feedback during teleoperation of a remote robotic device. The setup that will be described is part of an application [3] aimed at providing a set of tools to teleoperate a robot in industrial tasks. In this application a Baxter robot's arm is controlled by an operator's movements captured with a wearable device. The operator wears an Oculus Rift DK2 showing the remote scene, captured by a Kinect 360 placed on top of the Baxter head, plus virtual objects to help him in the tasks completion, see Fig. 5.

The task to be performed by the operator is to grasp a bowl and move it to a target position. The bowl to be picked is identified by a colored mesh that overlay the real bowl in the rendered image. The virtual mesh helps the user to identify the object which is of the same color of the table; in addition the mesh color changes the closer the robot end-effector is to the bowl easing the task. The target position, where to move the object, is indicated by another mesh of the bowl allowing the operator to be more precise in the placement. The visual feedback is augmented also by the 3D model of the Baxter robot, allowing the user to know the position of the end-effector even when it exits from the Kinect field of view. In addition it helps the operator predicting the remote robot arm movements and its pose in the environment given the high movement latency of the robot arm.

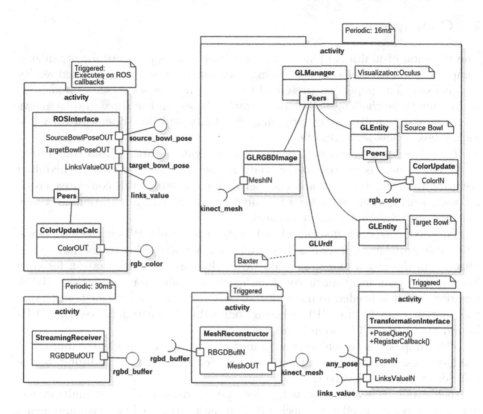

Fig. 6. CoCoMR components involved in the teleoperation application. Port with the same name type are connected to each other. Every pose passes through *TransformationInterface* to be transformed in the correct reference system.

The components structure is showed in Fig. 6. Several of the components are the same of the ones used for the application described before, proving the reusability capability of the framework. The *ROSInterface* component collects from the ROS topics the information regarding the Baxter joints position and the bowl location, obtained from the *object_recognition_tabletop* package[2], and delivers them to the *TransformInterface* component. The *UpdateColorCalc* peer calculates the distance between the robot end-effector and the bowl to correctly update its color. There are two *GLEntity* peers, one for each rendered bowl and a *GLUrdf* peer to display the Baxter 3D model.

Performance. The application runs on quad-core Intel i7 CPU (2.3 GHz) and a NVIDIA GeForce GT 650 MacBook Pro. The estimated sensor to display average latency is 89 ms, computed after synchronizing the robot and graphics computers with the Precision Time Protocol (PTP). Compared with the previous application the computational load is lower and the execution is smooth also on a laptop.

---

[2] http://wg-perception.github.io/tabletop/.

7 Conclusions

The diffusion of multicore platform is requiring new approaches for organizing computation in particular in demanding tasks such as visuo-haptic mixed reality applications. The paper has presented the CoCo framework as an approach for addressing these challenges. The organization based on the three graphs allows to tackle these challenges by providing flexibility and developer control while hiding several low-level aspects.

There are several aspects that can be investigated starting from the present work. One aspect is related to the analysis and optimization of the scheduling resulting from the data flow and the user-defined schedule, this could give space for the identification and reuse of common patterns and adaptation to a new machine with different number of cores.

The second aspect is instead related to the support of GPUs in the data flows. The most promising solution is based on CUDA mainly due to the number of libraries in the vision and simulation world that provide optimization for such library. The port mechanism could be easily extended for supporting CUDA pointers, but it is needed to introduce an automatic mechanism for transferring the content from/to the GPU when a connection is created between a GPU-bound port and a CPU-bound port.

This proposed solution, currently under investigation, is clearly limited to single-process architecture and it is also subject, in terms of scheduling, to the policies of the CUDA driver.

Incidentally it is worth discussing that the extension of CoCo to multiprocess is viable, provided an efficient mechanism for data exchange between components in different processes is found. ZeroMQ is an optimal candidate, while reduced or no-serialization could be employed for efficient data exchange.

Acknolwedgments. This work has been carried out within the framework of the European Project REMEDI, grant number 610902, and the Tuscany Regional Project TAUM.

References

1. Ruffaldi, E., Brizzi, F., Filippeschi, A., Avizzano, C.A.: Co-located haptic interaction for virtual usg exploration. In: Proceedings of IEEE EMBC, pp. 1548–1551 (2015)
2. Filippeschi, A., Brizzi, F., Ruffaldi, E., Jacinto, J.M., Avizzano, C.A.: Encountered-type haptic interface for virtual interaction with real objects based on implicit surface haptic rendering for remote palpation. In: 2015 IEEE/RSJ International Conference on Intelligent Robots and Systems (IROS), pp. 5904–5909. IEEE (2015)
3. Peppoloni, L., Brizzi, F., Ruffaldi, E., Avizzano, C.A.: Augmented reality-aided tele-presence system for robot manipulation in industrial manufacturing. In: Proceedings of the 21st ACM Symposium on Virtual Reality Software and Technology, pp. 237–240. ACM (2015)

4. Burns, D., Osfield, R.: Tutorial: open scene graph a: introduction tutorial: open scene graph b: examples and applications. In: Proceedings of the IEEE Virtual Reality, p. 265 (2004)
5. Carrozzino, M., Tecchia, F., Bacinelli, S., Cappelletti, C., Bergamasco, M.: Lowering the development time of multimodal interactive application: the real-life experience of the XVR project. In: Proceedings of the 2005 ACM SIGCHI International Conference on Advances in Computer Entertainment Technology, pp. 270–273. ACM (2005)
6. Behr, J., Bockholt, U., Fellner, D.: Instantreality – a framework for industrial augmented and virtual reality applications. In: Ma, D., Fan, X., Gausemeier, J., Grafe, M. (eds.) Virtual Reality & Augmented Reality in Industry, pp. 91–99. Springer, Heidelberg (2011)
7. Figueroa, P., Bischof, W., Boulanger, P., Hoover, H., Taylor, R.: InTml: a dataflow oriented development system for virtual reality applications. Presence 17(5), 492–511 (2008)
8. Allard, J., Gouranton, V., Lecointre, L., Limet, S., Melin, E., Raffin, B., Robert, S.: FlowVR: a middleware for large scale virtual reality applications. In: Danelutto, M., Vanneschi, M., Laforenza, D. (eds.) Euro-Par 2004. LNCS, vol. 3149, pp. 497–505. Springer, Heidelberg (2004)
9. Conti, F., Morris, D., Barbagli, F., Sewell, C.: Chai 3d (2006). http://www.chai3d.org
10. Ruffaldi, E., Frisoli, A., Gottlieb, C., Tecchia, F., Bergamasco, M.: A haptic toolkit for the development of immersive and web enabled games. In: ACM Symposium on Virtual Reality Software and Technology (VRST), pp. 320–323. ACM (2006)
11. Eck, U., Sandor, C.: Harp: a framework for visuo-haptic augmented reality. In: 2013 IEEE Virtual Reality (VR), pp. 145–146, March 2013
12. Bruyninckx, H.: Open robot control software: the orocos project. In: Proceedings of the 2001 IEEE International Conference on Robotics and Automation, ICRA 2001, vol. 3, pp. 2523–2528. IEEE (2001)
13. Quigley, M., Conley, K., Gerkey, B., Faust, J., Foote, T., Leibs, J., Wheeler, R., Ng, A.Y.: ROS: an open-source robot operating system. In: ICRA Workshop on Open Source Software, vol. 3(3.2), p. 5 (2009)
14. Seichter, H., Looser, J., Billinghurst, M.: Composar: an intuitive tool for authoring AR applications. In: Proceedings of the 7th IEEE/ACM International Symposium on Mixed and Augmented Reality, pp. 177–178. IEEE Computer Society (2008)
15. Salisbury, K., Conti, F., Barbagli, F.: Haptic rendering: introductory concepts. IEEE Comput. Graph. Appl. 24(2), 24–32 (2004)
16. Ruffaldi, E., Morris, D., Barbagli, F., Salisbury, K., Bergamasco, M.: Voxel-based haptic rendering using implicit sphere trees. In: Symposium on Haptic Interfaces for Virtual Environment and Teleoperator Systems, Haptics 2008, pp. 319–325, March 2008
17. Ruspini, D.C., Kolarov, K., Khatib, O.: The haptic display of complex graphical environments. In: Proceedings of the 24th Annual Conference on Computer Graphics and Interactive Techniques, pp. 345–352. ACM Press/Addison-Wesley Publishing Co. (1997)
18. Salisbury, K., Tarr, C.: Haptic rendering of surfaces defined by implicit functions. ASME Dyn. Syst. Control Div. 61, 61–67 (1997)
19. Cruz-Neira, C., Sandin, D.J., DeFanti, T.A.: Surround-screen projection-based virtual reality: the design and implementation of the cave. In: Proceedings of the 20th Annual Conference on Computer Graphics and Interactive Techniques, pp. 135–142. ACM (1993)

Design of a Projective AR Workbench for Manual Working Stations

Antonio Emmanuele Uva[1(✉)], Michele Fiorentino[1], Michele Gattullo[1],
Marco Colaprico[2], Maria F. de Ruvo[2], Francescomaria Marino[2,3], Gianpaolo F. Trotta[1],
Vito M. Manghisi[1], Antonio Boccaccio[1], Vitoantonio Bevilacqua[3],
and Giuseppe Monno[1]

[1] DMMM, Polytechnic University of Bari, Bari, Italy
{antonio.uva,michele.fiorentino,michele.gattullo,
gianpaolofrancesco.trotta,vitomodesto.manghisi,
antonio.boccaccio,giuseppe.monno}@poliba.it
[2] APIS srl, Bari, Italy
{m.colaprico,mf.deruvo}@spinoffapis.com
[3] DEI, Polytechnic University of Bari, Bari, Italy
{francescomaria.marino,vitoantonio.bevilacqua}@poliba.it

Abstract. We present the design and a prototype of a projective AR workbench for an effective use of the AR in industrial applications, in particular for Manual Working Stations. The proposed solution consists of an aluminum structure that holds a projector and a camera that is intended to be mounted on manual working stations. The camera, using a tracking algorithm, computes in real time the position and orientation of the object while the projector displays the information always in the desired position. We also designed and implemented the data structure of a database for the managing of AR instructions, and we were able to access this information interactively from our application.

1 Introduction

Looking at the different phases of the product lifecycle and how AR has already been used for each, those that are less dependent from the product itself, are manufacturing, commissioning and inspection, and maintenance. In particular, in those three phases, except for certain product categories (e.g. cars, planes, plants), the product is handled into a Manual Working Station (MWS). Common operations that are accomplished into a MWS are assembly, welding (especially spot welding), packing, testing, repairing, inspecting. In all these tasks, the worker has to follow some strict procedures and s/he is supported by information that can be provided in an AR mode, with all the benefits, which are widely discussed in the literature [1–8]. This work aims to confirm and make substantial the opportunity to use AR in the industrial sector. The motivation for this optimism arise from the literature and was strengthen by our previous work, where we found that AR instructions reduced significantly participants' overall execution time and error rate in manual assembly tasks.

© Springer International Publishing Switzerland 2016
L.T. De Paolis and A. Mongelli (Eds.): AVR 2016, Part I, LNCS 9768, pp. 358–367, 2016.
DOI: 10.1007/978-3-319-40621-3_25

The scenario of the MWS allows us to develop a prototype that can easily meet the requirements requested by Navab [9] for developing applications for industrial augmented reality, i.e.:

- reliability: high accuracy, fall-back solutions;
- user-friendliness: AR system safe and easy to set up, learn, use, and customize;
- scalability: setup easy to reproduce and distribute in large numbers.

The MWS scenario is effortlessly reproducible in a laboratory, so we can look for all the possible bottlenecks and try to solve them in order to have a reliable application. We can test the application with focused user tests, and thanks to their feedbacks, it would be possible to create a user-friendly solution. Finally, about the scalability, we aim to find all the hardware and software solutions that are the less dependent as possible to the product and operations to be accomplished in the MWS.

Most of the AR solutions in literature employ Head Mounted Displays (HMDs), which have several drawbacks in terms ergonomics, cost, limited field of view, low resolution, encumbrance and weight. After several years of research in this field [10, 11] and after different meeting with interested enterprises, we decided to use projected AR. It is based on digital projectors to superimpose virtual data (text, symbols, indicators, etc.) directly on the real environment [12]. However, projected AR, as all new technologies, requires some feasibility studies and optimization processes before it can be introduced in the industrial environment. One of the most important issues is the correct visualization of technical information. In particular, we evaluated the possibility to project text directly on workbench surfaces (without the need to calibrate the scene), comparing users' performance with that deriving from the use of a normal LCD monitor [13]. This because, in a real working environment, the operator stands in front of the workbench and is currently assisted by instructions on monitors usually placed on their workbenches or on tool carts. As far as the authors know, there are few studies on this topic and there are no widely accepted guidelines to follow in the design of this kind of system.

In the next section we label the system requirements and in Sect. 3 we describe the proposed system and the prototype. Section 4 presents preliminary results and possible future works.

2 Requirements

In the previous section, we motivated the choice of the main application scenarios: maintenance, inspecting, repairing, testing, etc. In our previous works, we collected several feedbacks from the industrial world.

The first lesson learned is that Head Worn Displays (HWD) should not be used in this scenario. The worker does not have a real perception of the objects that s/he is handling, and this could be very dangerous. Furthermore, HWDs are connected via cable to the computer where the application is running. This physical link, along with wearing issues may cause ergonomic problems.

We also found [13] that the projection of text on real industrial workbench surfaces produces the same performance of text displayed on a LCD monitor (except for the blue text). Furthermore, reading of text projected on wooden surfaces is better than reading of text displayed on a LCD monitor.

Vision-based tracking methods are highly sensitive to lighting changes [14]. For this reason, a fine control of the environmental lighting should be taken into account. This led to the need of an external lighting system.

As regards contents, our experience demonstrates that the use of animated 3D virtual objects is not essential. The time required to create an animation is often more than the benefit that the animation gives, especially for experienced workers. This encouraged us to the use of projective AR and the consequent use of 2D graphic signs to indicate objects or operations to accomplish in the real scene.

2.1 System

The main technical features that we defined for the prototype are:

- A light frame to be clasped on a normal workbench of a Manual Working Station; the dimensions of the reference workbench are 1200 mm (L) × 1000 mm (D). The frame should be designed to hold multiple cameras and projectors at an adjustable distance.
- A turntable where the product to be assembled/maintained should be fixed. In many cases, this additional frame is already present to facilitate the operators in the maintenance tasks. We decided to use it in our system also to locate the tracking markers. This is because marker position on the product may vary during the working steps, e.g. assembly.
- The optical tracking is based on fiducial markers that are glued on the turntable. A multi-marker technique is used with the markers placed so that it is always visible from the camera at least one of them.
- An additional lighting system must be provided, to have a uniform lighting on the markers.
- The virtual contents that the projector should display are 2D graphic signs as circles, arrows, squares, crosshairs, etc.
- The user interface is projected directly on the workbench and contains a menu with the tree of the operations performed/to perform and the possible subtasks of the current operation.
- The contents navigation could be done with virtual buttons or other Natural User Interfaces like voice recognition and gesture recognition [15].

2.2 Contents

The application framework developed for this prototype is based on the general structure of an assembly/maintenance manual. In our previous experiences [1], we have successfully reorganized the information about the maintenance steps in a tree-like structure with different levels of detail. This allowed the technicians to gain in efficiency as compared to paper manual, skipping well known details while accessing specifics only if needed (learning, troubleshooting, etc.). Therefore, we assumed that the following four commands may be sufficient to effectively navigate the manual:

- Next. A maintenance task, at the current level of detail, is clear or completed. The user wants to access the information about the next task at the same level of detail.
- Previous. The user wants to access the information about the previous task at the same level of detail.
- Go down (to a lower level). A more detailed information is required, therefore the current task is expanded in a more detailed sequence of sub-tasks (e.g., unknown task or troubleshooting).
- Go up (to an upper level). The user needs less details, therefore s\he navigates through a sequence of a less detailed tasks.

Going up to the first level brings the user to the root node of the manual. Considering this structure of manual, the user of the application can go back and forth from a step to the previous/following, up a level to go the main menu, down a level to access further details for that step.

3 Our System

The system architecture is schematized in Fig. 1. The hardware side is composed by a camera for tracking and a projector for visualizing info on the workbench. The device under maintenance is located on a tracking board with optical markers which is supported by four wheels allowing for easy translation and spinning on the workbench. The beamer projects also a GUI for managing the procedure and the info. The software side, running on one PC, is composed by an application based on Unity 3D and the tracking module based on ARToolkit. In our framework, each working step is a Unity scene file that includes all the contents needed for the display of the information, namely

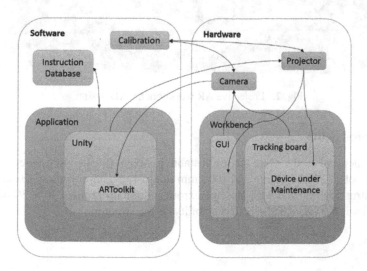

Fig. 1. System architecture.

CAD models of the virtual objects, their placement on the scene (position/orientation), their possible animation, text list of tools needed, and text instructions. Each scene component is conveniently stored in a SQL database managed by a MySQL RDBMS, linked using a MYSQL connector for Unity 3D. Each interaction between operator and the system correspond to a SQL query. The result of a query is a collection of data used to instantiate at run-time a scene component.

According to the requirements, we designed the physical structure in CATIA (see Fig. 2), using a team work approach. We took in consideration structural issues and geometrical location of components for visibility and occlusions.

Fig. 2. Projective AR workbench CAD design.

3.1 Physical Setup

As workbench, we used a white table adjustable in height (the height was set at 750 mm from the floor), 1200 mm large and 1000 mm deep. The components are installed on a physical structure realized with Bosch Rexroth aluminum profiles 30 × 30 (shown in Fig. 3) allowing a very good physical stability of the structure.

Fig. 3. The prototype.

As tracking board, we used a square table (side 650 mm) where we put on the product to be maintained; it can freely move on the table due to four wheels mounted beneath the base. At the corners of the table we fixed four 140 mm markers used for the tracking. In this way, the markers move jointly to the product, but they are not fixed on it, so this solution is scalable to different products to be maintained.

We used a Benq W1080ST + projector mounted at a distance of about 1300 mm from the table and from the side of the user. In this way the projector illuminate mainly the area in front of the user. The distance from the table is set in order to illuminate all the width of the table, whereas part of the height is not illuminate. The resolution used is 1600 × 1200. The projector was fixed at the end of an aluminum bar whose height can be changed, in order to have a scalable solutions, i.e. we can use the same frame even if we change the projector. The projector used in this prototype was set at a height of 1330 mm. For tracking purpose, we used an Imaging Source DFK 23U445 (1/3" CCD sensor, resolution 1280 × 960, USB 3.0) with a 4 mm optic. The camera was mounted on a horizontal bar at a height of 1000 mm from the table to frame the entire table.

We also add two lamps (30 W energy-saving, 5200 K), mounted inside an aluminum reflector (Ø 26 cm) with a diffuser to have a softer light and very uniform illumination, at an height of 1150 mm.

3.2 Graphical User Interface

We designed the Graphical User Interface (see Fig. 4) including the following elements:

- Graphic signs (arrows, circles, etc.) are projected to point at the parts of the product where to operate. Their placement is computed in the authoring phase by overlapping the virtual object on the CAD model of the object to be maintained. The CAD model is also used in the Unity scene as occlusion model to have a more realistic rendering of the scene.
- A textbox at the bottom of the table with instructions for the operator. A navigation tree, to understand which step of the maintenance procedure the operator has reached and if there are any sublevels for that step.
- At what point of the procedure is the operator, and if there are sublevels for that step.
- A panel with the list of needed tools; in this panel, also additional information or images can be provided.
- Indicators of the marker occluded for the navigation of the user interface.

Fig. 4. The Graphical User Interface.

As to the interface navigation, we used a technique based on marker occlusion. We used four different markers for the four directions of the application: next, previous, up a level, down a level. When the user occludes with his/her hand the marker, the corresponding trigger is activated and the corresponding scene is loaded. We inserted also a control on the GUI to check if a marker has been occluded. It consists of four squares; a square is red if the related marker is not occluded, green otherwise.

Just as an example, on each new step, the system suggests the operator to move the rotating base in order to adjust the point of view to optimize the projected information. A virtual red circular arrow indicates the direction of rotation, and it disappears when the correct position of the rotating base is reached (see Fig. 5).

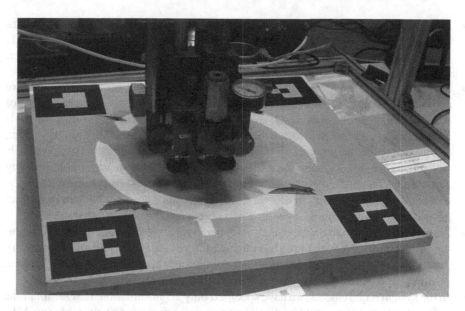

Fig. 5. The red circular arrow suggests the operator to rotate counterclockwise the rotating base. (Color figure online)

4 Preliminary Results and Discussion

As a first test case, we implemented the maintenance procedure of an oleodynamic valve (model GMV 3010 ¾"). The maintenance procedure was quite simple with four macro-steps, with several sub-levels.

Nevertheless, the test case was able to test the functionality of the complete system. In this case, we measured a working volume of about 600 mm (L) × 500 mm (D) × 600 mm (H). Common assembly/maintenance instructions usually contain information about the localization of the sub-product involved in the operation (e.g., a screw), the tools needed, and the operation itself to accomplish. Our system proved to be very effective to locate specific points or objects in our product, for example heads of screws, holes, sensors, buttons, etc. However, these points must lie on a surface, which is directly illuminated by the projector.

As to the interface navigation, in this initial prototype we were not able to create a reliable solution. This type of navigation of the interface it is not reliable because an occlusion occurs whenever something (often user's arm) stands between the marker and the camera, leading to frequent false positives (unwanted triggers).

We are currently planning several research activities as future works, in particular:

- For the localization tasks of points directly illuminated by the projector, we want to measure the accuracy of our system in the localization of these points to determine the dimensions of the virtual objects to use.
- Find which is the virtual object that ensures higher reliability and is more user-friendly: circle/square, filled/empty, fixed/flashing.

- For those points that do not lie on a surface directly illuminated by the projector (e.g., vertical objects, undercut points, etc.), we suggest to test two possible solutions: (1) use of multiple projectors; (2) use of a portable camera coupled with a pico-projector, to be handled by the operator as a torchlight.
- As regards tools, the information can be showed in different ways: the simpler are codes of the tools or images projected on the table. Nevertheless, if we have a set of the working tools in a wall stand, we could mount a projector in front of the tools and project a graphic sign to locate the tools needed. For the reliability of this system, all the tools must be put back at their correct place after their use. Therefore, it is possible to position a camera near the projector to compare, using simple imaging processing techniques, the actual image of the tools with a reference one with all the tools at their correct place. In this way, if a tool has not been put back in its correct position after the operation, a warning message would be shown to the operator.
- As regards information on the operation to perform, this can be provided in different ways: text, arrows (for example to indicate un/screwing, insertion, and extraction). As to the text, the optimal location and formatting should be find. As to arrows, position, type, color, dimensions, animation should be determined.
- In the system requirements, we have specified only 2D information. If 3D animations are really needed, they could be displayed as a video projected on the table (no AR).
- We have to find which is the more reliable and user-friendly way to navigate the User Interface among those proposed in the description of the prototype: voice recognition, gesture recognition, hand recognition, others [16].
- Finally, in order to have also a more scalable solution, we intend to optimize the frame creating a less heavy and intrusive as possible structure.

5   Conclusion

We were able to design and build a prototype for an effective use of the AR in the industrial world, in particular for Manual Working Stations. It consists of an aluminum frame with a camera and a projector that dynamically projects information on the real object to be maintained on the workbench. The virtual environment engine uses the frames captured by the camera as input to its tracking algorithm; it computes in real time the position and the orientation of the object. In the meanwhile, the projector displays the information in the desired position even if moving the target object. We also designed the data structure of a database for the managing of AR instructions, and we were able to access this information interactively from our AR application.

With this work, we created the basis for the development of an effective AR application for the industrial environment. Further tests and experiments should be done to implement reliable, user friendly and scalable solutions as suggested by Navab.

The prototype designed in this work is still to be optimized, in particular as regards the use of graphic signs, the navigation of the User Interface, the frame optimization, the projection of information on undercut points.

References

1. Fiorentino, M., Uva, A.E., Gattullo, M., Debernardis, S., Monno, G.: Augmented reality on large screen for interactive maintenance instructions. Comput. Ind. **65**(2), 270–278 (2014)
2. Tang A., Owen C., Biocca F., Mou W.: Comparative effectiveness of augmented reality in object assembly. In: Proceedings of the SIGCHI Conference on Human Factors in Computing Systems, pp. 73–80. ACM (2003)
3. Ganier, F.: Factors affecting the processing of procedural instructions: implications for document design. IEEE Trans. Prof. Commun. **47**(1), 15–26 (2004)
4. Watson, G., Curran R., Butterfield J., Craig C.: The effect of using animated work instructions over text and static graphics when performing a small scale engineering assembly. In: Curran, R., Chou, S.-Y., Trappey, A. (eds.) Collaborative Product and Service Life Cycle Management for a Sustainable World. Advanced Concurrent Engineering, pp. 541–550. Springer, London (2008)
5. Fiorentino, M., Monno, G., Uva, A.: Interactive "touch and see" FEM simulation using augmented reality. Int. J. Eng. Educ. **25**(6), 1124–1128 (2009)
6. Webel, S., Bockholt, U., Keil, J.: Design criteria for AR-based training of maintenance and assembly tasks. In: Shumaker, R. (ed.) Virtual and Mixed Reality, HCII 2011, Part I. LNCS, vol. 6773, pp. 123–132. Springer, Heidelberg (2011)
7. Henderson, S., Feiner, S.: Exploring the benefits of augmented reality documentation for maintenance and repair. IEEE Trans. Visual Comput. Graphics **17**(10), 1355–1368 (2011)
8. De Marchi, L., Ceruti, A., Marzani, A., Liverani, A.: Augmented reality to support on-field post-impact maintenance operations on thin structures. J. Sens. **2013**, 1–10 (2013)
9. Navab, N.: Developing killer apps for industrial augmented reality. IEEE Comput. Graph. Appl. **24**(3), 16–20 (2004)
10. Debernardis, S., Fiorentino, M., Gattullo, M., Monno, G., Uva, A.E.: Text readability in head-worn displays: color and style optimization in video versus optical see-through devices. IEEE Trans. Vis. Comput. Graph. **20**(1), 125–139 (2014)
11. Fiorentino, M., Debernardis, S., Uva, A.E., Monno, G.: Augmented reality text style readability with see-through head-mounted displays in industrial context. Presence: Teleoper. Virtual Env. **22**(2), 171–190 (2013)
12. Bimber, O., Raskar, R.: Spatial augmented reality: merging real and virtual worlds. CRC Press (2005)
13. Di Donato, M., Fiorentino, M., Uva, A.E., Gattullo, M., Monno, G.: Text legibility for projected augmented reality on industrial workbenches. Comput. Ind. **70**, 70–78 (2015)
14. Bajana, J., Francia, D., Liverani, A., Krajčovič, M.: Mobile tracking system and optical tracking integration for mobile mixed reality. Int. J. Comput. Appl. Technol. **53**(1), 13–22 (2016)
15. Fiorentino, M., Radkowski, R., Stritzke, C., Uva, A.E., Monno, G.: Design review of CAD assemblies using bimanual natural interface. Int. J. Interact. Des. Manufact. (IJIDeM) **7**(4), 249–260 (2013)
16. Bevilacqua, V., Barone, D., Suma, M.: A multimodal fingers classification for general interactive surfaces. In: Huang, D.-S., Jo, K.-H., Wang, L. (eds.) ICIC 2014. LNCS, vol. 8589, pp. 513–521. Springer, Heidelberg (2014)

A Taxonomy for Information Linking in Augmented Reality

Tobias Müller[1]([⊠]) and Ralf Dauenhauer[2]

[1] Robert Bosch GmbH, 71272 Renningen, Germany
tobias.mueller8@de.bosch.com
[2] Reutlingen University, 72762 Reutlingen, Germany
ralf.dauenhauer@student.reutlingen-university.de

Abstract. A key challenge in augmented reality is the precise linking of virtual information with physical places or objects to create a spatial relationship. The visual presentation of these links can have many forms like direct overlays or connection lines. In spite of its importance, this topic has never been systematically addressed by existing approaches. As a first step in this direction, we suggest a taxonomy for such visualizations to facilitate their detailed analysis in terms of graphical properties. It consists of the three artifact types spatial anchor, information object and information connection as well as the three dimensions reference system, visual connection and context. Additionally we surveyed literature to collect the knowledge on how these dimensions and their combinations affect user performances. To explain the application of our taxonomy, we classified user interfaces from literature. We also conducted an empirical experiment regarding the effects on task performance of different classes from our dimension visual connection, i.e. the type of visual connection that is presented to the user. The outcomes give important guidance for augmented reality interface design in a part, which has not been researched before. The results show that the preferred method for visualizing information linking is using a close spatial proximity, followed by a continuous visual connection, a color coded symbolical connection and a shape coded symbolical connection.

Keywords: Augmented reality · User interface · Perception

1 Introduction

Augmented reality is about embedding virtual objects in the physical world and creating relationships with spatial anchors. In many cases this is simply done by overlaying them. However, this is not always feasible, e.g. due to moving parts that may not be covered by any virtual objects. When using a handheld combiner a user might just put the device aside but for head mounted displays this would be very cumbersome. As a result, multiple ways of presenting information as linked to an anchor have been developed. Examples are connection lines between virtual objects and anchors or colored highlights around anchors.

© Springer International Publishing Switzerland 2016
L.T. De Paolis and A. Mongelli (Eds.): AVR 2016, Part I, LNCS 9768, pp. 368–387, 2016.
DOI: 10.1007/978-3-319-40621-3_26

To facilitate research on the different ways of visualizing information linking in augmented reality, we propose a taxonomy that allows to analyze and compare them and also provides a common vocabulary to describe them. As part of our ongoing work on a conceptual framework to support the execution of manual tasks with augmented reality, we intend to use it as a guidance in application design [18]. The goal is to support reducing the mental and sensory effort of a user so that for each application context the appropriate visualization can be chosen. In order to achieve this, the influence of the dimensions on user performance has to be known.

Our approach is the following. First we survey existing work in the field of taxonomies for augmented reality and visualization of information linking in 3D environments and augmented reality. Then we suggest a taxonomy and collect information on the influence of its dimensions on user performance. We show its applicability by classifying examples from scientific publications. To deepen the knowledge on the effect on users, we present a first empirical experiment on the dimension visual connection whose results can be used to inform design.

2 Related Work

Many approaches to classify augmented reality applications have already been made based on their various aspects. A widely recognized taxonomy was suggested by Milgram et al. that contains three dimensions by which an augmented reality application can be classified [17]. Extent of world knowledge classifies how much of the users environment is digitally modeled, reproduction fidelity classifies how close the virtual objects come to a physical representation and the extent of presence metaphor classifies how well the user is embedded in the virtual world. Tönnis et al. surveyed literature on augmented reality classifications and taxonomies and use it as a foundation to propose their taxonomy [29]. It contains the dimensions "temporality: continuous versus discrete representation of virtual objects; dimensionality: the number of features (dimensions) that virtual and physical objects possess as well as methods to visualize and render them; viewpoint reference frame: ego-centric versus exo-centric ego-motion-based control of viewpoints; mounting/registration: spatial relationships between objects [and] type of reference: concepts regarding the visibility of referred-to physical objects" [29]. Wither et al. present a detailed classification schema for annotations in augmented reality [33]. Their dimensions are location complexity, location movement, semantic relevance, content complexity, interactivity and annotation permanence. Location complexity classifies whether the location the augmentation is attached to, is a 3D point, a 6DoF point or a 2D or 3D region. Location movement classifies if the location of the annotation moves. Semantic relevance classifies how close the relation of the annotation to the annotated physical object is. Content complexity classifies how complex in terms of information amount or visual complexity the content of one annotation is. Interactivity classifies how interactive in terms of manipulation an annotation is. Finally, annotation permanence classifies how permanently visible an annotation is. In none of the previously mentioned works, visualization of information linking has been addressed in detail and none of the taxonomies is appropriate to approach this topic. Only the taxonomy by Wither et al., with the dimension location complexity, has some relation to it. Also in none of these publications the influence of the dimensions on sensory or mental effort is collected.

Visual information linking has been intensively studied as a labeling-problem, e.g. as part of explaining 3D illustrations, connecting labels to 3D models or maps etc. Often this is approached with a focus on layout algorithms and not on visualizations of links [5]. For augmented reality a rich body of publications exists concerning label placement, e.g. [1,2,15,27], but research on how to present virtual and physical objects as belonging together is mostly missing.

For information-rich virtual environments (IRVE) this topic has been researched more thoroughly. A schema for classifying the way abstract information is embedded into IRVEs has been proposed by Bowman et al. [3]. Their three dimensions are display location, association and level of aggregation. Display location classifies the position of abstract information and can either be world-fixed, display-fixed, object-fixed or user-fixed. Association classifies how abstract data, i.e. textual annotations, is connected to perceptual data, i.e. parts of a 3D scene, of the virtual environment. It can either be spatially explicit with a direct visual link or visually implicit with a symbolic connection. Level of aggregation classifies how much data is combined into a single visualization. Even though their work is following a similar goal, we cannot simply adopt their approach. The dimension association is not granular enough for our goal to classify visualizations of information linking. Level of aggregation is not in our focus because we want to stay agnostic of the actual information transported.

Some empirical experiments on connecting abstract information to perceptual data have already been conducted for IRVEs. Polys et al. investigated how displaying information in object space or viewport space and a changing field of view influenced user performance in spatial search tasks [20]. In their study they used two kinds of tasks. In the first one users had to identify spatial objects based on a description and then find information on a label attached to them. In the second one users had to identify two spatial objects based on a description and then compare the attached labels. The authors found that in the wide field of view configuration object space resulted in better test results in terms of accuracy while in the small field of view configuration viewport space resulted in better test results. They attribute this to short lines and a close proximity of the labels to their related 3D objects when a small field of view is used. With an increased software field of view and a small physical field of view, object space resulted in worse results and viewport space resulted in better results. In a follow up study the same authors researched the role of the Gestalt cues proximity and connectedness [19]. The task was the same as in the previous experiments and they measured the participants task performance based on the independent variables proximity in viewport space and connection visualization. The result was that static positions of the abstract information in the viewport space were more important than spatial proximity. Also the shape of the visual connection, which could either be a triangle or a simple line, influenced the performance based on the task. Chen et al. also conducted a similar study in which they evaluated two interaction techniques in combination with two text layout techniques within-the-world display (WWD) and heads-up display (HUD) [4]. For the WWD condition they placed the texts in the virtual environment in close proximity to the corresponding object while in the HUD condition they positioned the texts fixed to the user's viewpoint and connected them with the corresponding 3D objects via connection lines. They found that the HUD condition showed generally favorable results and account this to the clear layout. Sonnet et al. published a study on visualizations of connections of textual annotations with 3D objects in IRVEs [28]. They conducted three empirical tests on a test bed [23] of which two are relevant in this context. In the first one they compared three conditions: (a) labels which are spatially attached to objects, (b) annotations that are attached via the shadow of objects and (c) separated annotations that did not have an optical connection to 3D objects. The second experiment covered the conditions: (a) object and text only linked with a line, (b) highlighting of the shadow in greyscale additionally to the line and (c) highlighting of the shadow in the objects color additionally to the line. Their study showed that no visualization technique performed best in all situations and each had certain drawbacks. While these studies provide a good starting point for our work on visualization of information linking, they are only partly applicable to augmented reality. The reason is that augmented reality does not allow a full control of the environment. In many cases the experiments also included conditions during which text comprehension was tested, which is not relevant here.

This work on visualization of information linking is part of our ongoing work on a conceptual framework for information presentation in augmented reality [18]. Part of the framework are five conceptual layers each representing a different graduation of spatial connection that information can have. The lowest two levels contain information from the physical world, which the user either perceives directly or mediated, e.g. via a video see-through HMD. The next two layers contain information which can either be spatially referenced or spatial. While spatial objects can be integrated into the physical world so that there is one matching position and size, this is not possible spatially referenced objects. In other words, every point of a spatial virtual object can only be assigned to one point or a strictly constrained set of points in the physical space without loss of information for the user. Examples for spatial objects are 3D models of machine parts or wiring diagrams that match physical layouts. Examples for spatially referenced objects are simple texts or arbitrary 3D animations. The top most layer contains information that does not have any spatial connection to the physical world.

3 Proposed Taxonomy

In the following we propose a taxonomy for visualizations of information linking in augmented reality. First we describe which artifacts are included and how they relate to each other. Based on this, we present the three independent dimensions reference system, visual connection and context that allow classifying visualizations of information linking.

3.1 Included Artifacts

For augmented reality an *anchor* in the physical world is needed. It can either be a *point* or a *3D object* in the physical world, which serves as a reference for the augmentation. Wither et al. included anchors in their taxonomy as location complexity [33].

The *information object* is the virtual object that is supposed to be linked to the anchor and provides the actual information. It can range from simple texts to complex animated 3D models. We differentiate between spatial and spatially referenced objects [18]. This definition allows a distinction between using position and orientation of the information object as a meaningful way of connecting information. Wither et al. include content complexity as a similar concept in their taxonomy, which covers the amount of information and its visual complexity [33]. Tönnis et al. describe this as dimensionality of represented features and differentiate between 2D and 3D objects [29].

Every visualization that is included to make a connection between one information object and one anchor is an *information connection*. It can also be nonvisual by positioning information objects in such a way that unambiguous connections are made. The information connection is the part that is classified by the three dimensions of the taxonomy. In [32] a similar concept called pointer is described where the anchors are highlighted to connect various types of multimedia information to it. However, our concept of information connection is more general and does not describe only one specific visualization for information linking.

3.2 Reference System

The dimension *reference system* classifies the coordinate system an information object is positioned and oriented in. We differentiate two types of coordinate systems, the world coordinate systems (WCS), which are bound to the environment or an object in the environment and the spectator coordinate systems (SCS), which are bound to the users viewpoint or a device controlled by the user, e.g. a tablet. An information object can have one of the four combinations of position and orientation:

- *WCS Positioned / WCS Oriented*
- *WCS Positioned / SCS Oriented*
- *SCS Positioned / WCS Oriented*
- *SCS Positioned / SCS Oriented*

Similar concepts for augmented reality have been previously proposed. Tönnis et al. include mounting dimension as part of their taxonomy, which acts as the the reference system an object can be bound to in augmented reality [29]. It contains the classes human, environment, world and multiple mountings. For IRVEs the dimension display location with the classes world-fixed, display-fixed, object-fixed and user-fixed has been proposed [3]. It is based on earlier work on positioning information in augmented reality that uses the classes surround-fixed, display-fixed and world-fixed for location [8]. In contrast to this, we differentiate only between two types of coordinate systems based on their relation to the user but include location and orientation separately. This keeps the differentiation simple and comprehensive. For textual labels these two types of coordinate systems are often called object space and screen space [14,20] respectively within-the-world display technique and heads-up display technique [4]. Information objects in the class WCS positioned / SCS oriented are usually called billboards.

Examples. In an augmented reality application an information object is connected to an anchor. A tablet is used as combiner. If the tablet is moved but the information object appears at a position fixed to the world and moves relative to the screen it is WCS positioned. When the tablet is moved and the information object appears at a position fixed to the screen and moves relative to the anchor it is SCS positioned. If the tablet is turned around the anchor and the information object makes the same rotation in the opposite direction it is WCS oriented. Finally, if the tablet is turned around the anchor and the virtual object does not rotate but always shows the same side to the user, it is SCS oriented.

Human Factors. As previously mentioned, research on positioning information objects has already been conducted for IRVEs. Especially when a small field of view is used, SCS positioning is preferred, particularly with a wide software field of view [20]. So far this has only been researched for objects that we classify as spatially referenced. Positioning information in SCS prevents guaranteeing proximity, so that the user has to mentally bridge the distance [20]. In case the information object and the anchor are far away from each other, this can result in a reverted law of Gestalt proximity. However, SCS positioning allows better screen management which can support the visualization of information linking. A fixed position from the user's perspective might even be more important than a close proximity of information objects to their anchors [19]. A study conducted by Madsen et al. suggests that users perform best in augmented reality environments when labels are part of the scene, i.e. WCS positioned / WCS oriented [15]. The differences to the previous studies might arise from the different tasks or the different general layout of the user interfaces. When an object is WCS positioned, depth cues have to be given or the user might have problems to estimate the correct position and make a connection to its anchor. This is especially important when the visual connection is non-visual and only proximity is used to present the link [6,9,13].

3.3   Visual Connection

The dimension *visual connection* classifies how the link from an information object to its anchor is visualized for the user. Some of its classes are similar to Gestalt laws which is not unexpected because the Gestalt laws describe how humans perceive objects as belonging together [26]. An example is a continuous connection, e.g. a line, that is an instance of the Gestalt law connectedness. However, the Gestalt laws are not fully transferable, e.g. good continuation not applicable here. They describe perception phenomena while visual connection describes classes of visualizations. The following ones can be differentiated:

- *Spatially assigned*: The connection is made via an unambiguous spatial assignment
- *Continuously connected*: A connecting line or shape goes from the information object to the anchor or vice versa. It may only be interrupted by smaller gaps that allow an unproblematic and unambiguous continuation. Subclasses are based on the way the shapes or lines are different from each other:
  - *None*
  - *Color*
  - *Style*
  - *Both*
- *Symbolically connected*: A connection can be made in a symbolic way which means that the user has to make a connection from the anchor to the information object based on a common coding. Subclasses are based on the way the symbolic connection is presented to the user:
  - *Color*
  - *Shape*
  - *Both*

For SCS positioned information objects the spatial assignment can be done by using a spatial order, e.g. positioning information objects from left to right in the same order like as anchors. In contrast to the dimensions reference system and context, a specific visualization can have more than one class of visual connection. E.g. it is possible to have an unambiguous spatial assignment and still include a symbolic connection as well.

Examples. When an information object is WCS positioned and shown close to the anchor and no other visual connection exists, it is connected via spatial assignment. When an information object is SCS positioned and a continuous line connects it to an anchor, a continuous connection is used. When a continuous connection between an anchor and an information object is dotted and yellow, while the line for the only other connection is solid and red, the visualization is in the subclass both. When both the anchor and the information object are marked with a star without showing another connection, e.g. being close together or having a connection line, the visualization is in the class symbolic connection with the subclass shape. When each connection uses a different color but all have the same symbol, the visualization is in the subclass color.

Human Factors. In multimedia learning the success rate during learning is higher if corresponding elements are positioned in close proximity to each other as described by Mayer's contiguity principle [16]. This gives a hint that using a spatial assignment with a close proximity of the anchor and information object supports understanding the link. However, the research was not about augmented reality nor a closely related field and thus it can only be considered as a hint. It is usually assumed in view management for augmented reality that close proximity to the anchor is best for linking information to a 3D object, followed by a continuous connection (e.g. [2,20]). This is supported by the fact that the human fovea is relatively small and larger distances between anchor and information object require eye movement. When an anchor is visualized, depth cues must be given for non trivial environments or it will be difficult for the user to recognize its correct position [6,9,13].

3.4   Context

The dimension *context* classifies if an additional context is visualized around the anchor, the information object or around both. A context is a stylized representation of the physical world in a given area that is included in the computer-generated image. The following classes are possible:

- *Both without context*: Neither around the anchor nor the information object a context is shown
- *Anchor with context*: A context is shown around the anchor but not the information object
- *Information object with context*: A context is shown around the information object but not around the anchor
- *Both with context*: A context is shown around the information object and the anchor

This dimension is in so far special that if the information object is WCS positioned at the anchor position, only the two classes both with and both without are possible. The reason is that it is no longer possible to differentiate between the context for the anchor or the information object.

Examples. An information object is displayed as SCS positioned / SCS oriented and visually connected to an anchor via a continuous connection. If a line drawing of the area around the anchor is shown around the information object the visualization is in the class information object with context. If a context is also added around the anchor, the class is both with context.

Human Factors. A context around the anchor helps to ameliorate the effects of imperfect tracking and helps a user to make less errors and complete tasks faster. Even if the tracking is so error prone that the task is not performable due to incorrect positioning, context can make this task doable [25]. Even in case of perfect tracking, the user's confidence is increased in this case [25]. Context around an information object which is not positioned at the anchor can

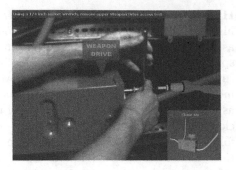

Fig. 1. Image taken from [2]   **Fig. 2.** Image taken from [10]

help a user to link information when it is oriented with the user's view of the workspace, i.e. WCS oriented and aligned in correct perspective [24]. Also if a spatial information object is WCS positioned at the position of the anchor, a context visualization can help to integrate it into the scene [12].

3.5 Direct Spatial Mapping

Direct spatial mapping is a special case of information linking visualization which is very common in augmented reality. It means that a spatial virtual object which is WCS positioned / WCS oriented is positioned in such a way that it has its matching position and size. Usually this is the case when a spatial virtual object is embedded into the physical world which has a (possible) physical counterpart that is simulated. Examples ares a part that must be mounted to a machine or a not yet finished part of a newly constructed building. The position of a spatially referenced object, e.g. a text label, on the other hand may very well not have a meaning and only the anchor's position is relevant. It can be freely moved and resized as long as the connection to the anchor is unambiguous. Thus direct spatial mapping is not possible for spatially referenced objects.

4   Classification Examples

When we started working on the taxonomy, we considered using it to classify existing systems from scientific publications. However, we encountered the problem that within one application a lot of different ways to visualize information linking are used and that they are often not described in sufficient detail. So instead we opted for using images from selected publications and give explanations for their classification.

In Fig. 1 two visualization types of information linking are used, the direct overlays of texts on the buildings and the texts connected to the buildings via a line. The texts are non-spatial information objects, and the buildings serve as the anchors. In both cases the information objects' reference systems are WCS positioned / SCS oriented and all anchors and information objects are displayed without context. For the directly overlaid texts the visual connection is spatially assigned while for the texts connected by line this is continuously connected with the subclass none, because all lines have the same shape and color.

Two visualization types are included in Fig. 2. The first one is used for the weapon drive label. The text is a non-spatial information object. The anchor could either be the whole weapon drive and thus a 3D object or the point where the tip is pointing at. Its reference system is WCS positioned / SCS oriented, the visual connection is continuous but the subclass can not be identified because only one text label is shown here. The second type is used for the two washers, the bolt and the wrench, which are all spatial objects. The anchors are the positions the objects must be mounted to and they are continuously connected to them vial the yellow dotted line. Even though all models are WCS positioned / WCS oriented, this is not a case of direct spatial mapping because they are not positioned at their anchors. In both cases no context is used.

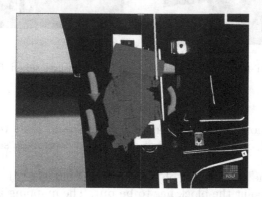

Fig. 3. Image taken from [22] (Color figure online)

In Fig. 3 only direct spatial mapping is used. While it is obvious for the car part (purple), it is not for the arrows because there is no natural size or position for them. However, because of their orientation and the limited range of possible positions they can be placed at without a loss of information, they are considered spatial objects. Therefore they are classified as direct spatial mapping as well. This is certainly a borderline case and one could also argue for not classifying them as such.

The upper image of Fig. 4 is an example of direct spatial mapping of the 3D model from the sensor and the arrow on the physical model. The physical sensor acts as the anchor. The additional textual instruction in the upper right hand corner is redundant information and is not considered here. In the lower image a symbolically connected visual connection is used as indicated by the yellow circle around the anchor. The information object is SCS Positioned / SCS Oriented. In this case it is unambiguous that the highlighted area belongs to the textual

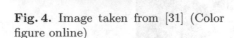

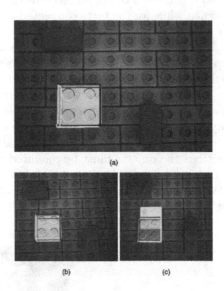

Fig. 4. Image taken from [31] (Color figure online)

Fig. 5. Image taken from [25] (Color figure online)

description. It is not clear how this connection would scale to more than one information object or anchor and thus a subclass cannot be selected for visual connection. In both cases no context is used.

In Fig. 5 (a) the information object is the 3D model of the Lego block and the anchor is the point the block has to be put. The mapping is a direct spatial mapping because the virtual block is positioned like the physical block would be placed. While in Fig. 5 (a) no context is present, it has been added in (b) and (c) with the 3D models of the two blocks. Because of the WCS positioning it cannot be decided whether the context is placed around the anchor or the information object and thus the class is both with. Image (b) shows context without error, image (c) with an already set physical yellow block and an error.

Figure 6 is again an example of direct spatial mapping. Each virtual Lego block is an information object that has an anchor at the position it shall be set. The virtual model in the overlay at the upper right corner however is not connected to the physical world and thus no information linking is made. Context is used but only hardly visible. In the left corner of the green baseplate an edge of the virtual model of the plate can be seen, probably due to a tracking error.

In Fig. 7 two different types of visualizations for information linking are used. The labels are non-spatial information objects which are WCS positioned / SCS oriented. They are continuously connected (dotted line) with their corresponding anchors. The anchors are at the positions of the the blue or green dots. Even though the lines and the dots are colored, the color does not allow an assignment

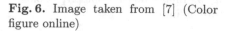

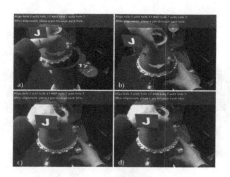

Fig. 6. Image taken from [7] (Color figure online)

Fig. 7. Image taken from [11] (Color figure online)

because multiple anchors may be marked with the same color (see Fig. 7 b). The arrows are also non-spatial information objects because they could be changed in position and size without losing any meaning. They are WCS positioned / WCS oriented and spatially assigned. The shown bolts are spatial information objects and are WCS positioned / WCS oriented. Their anchor is the same as the one of the labels and they are as well continuously connected. No context is used in all three cases.

In Fig. 8 non-spatial information objects are used as descriptions of the buttons. They are WCS positioned / SCS oriented. The anchors are highlighted in the form of blue and red dots. Depending if only the marked points or the whole knobs are seen as anchors, they are either points or 3D objects. Here they only serve as point anchors. The visual connection is continuously connected with the subclass none (yellow lines). Even though the labels are close to the anchors, its not possible to infer a connection via the position of an information object.

In all images of Fig. 9 the text labels are non-spatial information objects which are WCS positioned / WCS oriented. The WCS orientation is especially visible in the right hand side images where the labels are clearly not oriented towards the user. The anchors are the red, yellow and blue stones which are 3D objects. The difference is that in the upper images the visual connection is created via spatial assignment while in the lower two images it is done in a continuously connected way with the subclass none. No context is used.

5   Experiment

In addition to the classification schema we were also interested in using the proposed taxonomy to inform design of augmented reality applications. Even though some information on human factors could already be derived from existing literature, it is still not fully understood how the different ways to visualize information linking effects user task performance and the mental and sensory effort

Fig. 8. Image taken from [1] (Color figure online)

Fig. 9. Image taken from [27] (Color figure online)

to understand the relations. As a starting point we conducted a first experiment that is focused on the dimension information connection.

For the experiment we designed a simple task. Shapes of five animals (fish, rabbit, bird, crab, pig) were printed out and attached to a wall in front of the participants. To each of these animals a random number ranging from one to five was displayed via AR in varying ways, e.g. via spatial assignment. Each participant had to name the pairs (e.g. bird three, crab one, fish two, ...) as quickly as possible. Overall four types of visual connection were tested as independent variables. Examples are shown in Figs. 10, 11, 12 and 13:

- PROX: Spatially assigned (via proximity)
- CONT: Continuously connected (subclass none)
- COLO: Symbolically connected (subclass color)
- SYMB: Symbolically connected (subclass shape)

This is only a subset of all possible classes from the tested dimension. The reason is that we were especially interested in the basic options and left out other variations (e.g. combinations of color and shape) for the sake of simplicity. In the case of symbolic connections, it is not possible to link information without a shape or a color. We had no conclusive indication which would perform better before we conducted the experiment and thus tested both variations.

The animals were used as anchors, thus having object anchors. The displayed numbers represented non-spatial WCS positioned / WCS oriented information objects. We did not include any context. Three common device types were used for the experiment to assure that our findings are device independent. The tests were performed with an optical see-through HMD (OST), a video see-through HMD (VST) and a tablet (HAR). For the handheld setup a Microsoft Surface Pro 3 was used. A Lumus DK-32 with an attached camera was used for optical and video see-through. For the video see-through condition a cover against external light was attached to the DK-32.

We conducted a within-subject experiment, so each participant had to experience the four selected types of visual connection under all device conditions.

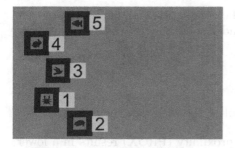

Fig. 10. Spatially assigned (PROX)

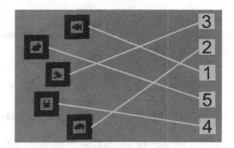

Fig. 11. Continuously connected (CONT)

Fig. 12. Symbolically connected with color (COLO)

Fig. 13. Symbolically connected with shape (SYMB)

At the beginning of each experiment, the participants were asked to complete a questionnaire to provide some basic information including their age, gender, debility of sight and previous experience with AR/VR environments. Each participant was instructed to name all animals and their corresponding number as fast as possible but care for correctness. Before the actual tests were conducted, a trial run was made for each device. All of the four conditions were shown and it was checked if the subject could clearly see and understand the information in order to perform the tasks.

For each device and each variation of the visual connection the participants had to solve a task block consisting of 10 random assignments. This resulted in a total number of 120 tasks (12 blocks) for each participant. After completing a block, the participants were asked to estimate their mean subjective mental effort during that block on the Rating Scale of Mental Effort (RSME) [34]. The conditions and the tested devices were in random order. In contrast to the type of visual connection, the device type did not serve as an independent variable. We were not interested in the influence of the device on the result but instead if the differences between the conditions are consistent over all devices. The dependent variables were the time to complete the task in milliseconds and the perceived mental workload (RSME-value) for each block. From pretests we knew that people sometimes correct themselves during the test but hardly any mistakes pass unnoticed by them. This influences the completion time and we opted for not taking corrected errors into account and instead rely on the extra time the corrections need.

5.1 Hypothesis

Our hypothesis regarding the time to complete the tasks are the following:

- H1: The use of spatial assignment with proximity (PROX) results in a lower mean time to map the information than all other variations across all devices.
- H2: The use of continuously connected visual connections (CONT) results in a lower mean time to map the information than the use of symbolically connected (subclasses shape and color) visual connections (COLO, SYMB) across all devices.
- H3: The use of symbolically connected visual connections with subclasses color (COLO) results in a lower mean time to map the information than symbolically connected visual connections with subclasses shape (SYMB) across all devices.

Our hypothesis regarding the subjective mental workload are the following:

- H4: The use of spatial assignment with proximity (PROX) results in a lower subjective mental workload than all other variations across all devices.
- H5: The use of continuously connected visual connections (CONT) results in a lower subjective mental workload than symbolically connected (subclasses shape and color) visual connections (COLO, SYMB) across all devices.
- H6: The use of symbolically connected visual connections with subclasses color (COLO) results in a lower subjective mental workload than symbolically connected visual connections with subclasses shape (SYMB) across all devices.

5.2 Results

A total number of 26 persons participated in the experiment (7 females and 19 males) who were mostly students recruited from the department. The mean age of the participants was 26,4 years (SD = 6,8) and ranged from 19 to 47 years. 12 subjects had a debility of sight corrected by either contact lenses or glasses and one was colorblind. 88.5 % of the subjects noted an affinity to technology. 63.1 % of the subjects had no or very little experience with augmented reality and half of the subjects experience with virtual reality. 57.7 % of the subjects did not play video games on a regular basis.

For each trial the dependent variable time in milliseconds and for each block, consisting of ten trials, the dependent variable RSME-value were collected. Technical errors and mistakes made by the subjects (e.g. wrong number or animal) have been manually classified. 22 trials have been marked as invalid due to technical problems or other interference. A total number of 69 trials have been identified where participants corrected themselves and thus resulted in a higher task completion time. Only 45 mistakes were made unnoticed by the participants, which results in a low overall error rate of 1.45 %.

Completion Times. For the subsequent calculations the mean time of each test run (10 tasks for each variation, or less if invalid) was calculated. A one-way ANOVA with repeated measures and a pairwise comparison using t-tests with Bonferroni correction revealed significant differences in task completion time between the four variations. Spatially assigned (PROX) significantly outperformed ($p_{total} < 0.001$) all other variations on all devices and thus H1 can be accepted. The use of continuously connected visualizations (CONT) resulted in a significant ($p_{total} < 0.001$) lower mean task completion time on all devices (HAR, VST, OST) than symbolically connected visualizations with color (COLO) or shape (SYMB) and thus H2 can be accepted. The comparison between the the subclasses color (COLO) and the subclass shapes (SYMB) of the continuously connected conditions revealed a significant ($p_{total} < 0.001$) lower mean for color, again consistent across all tested devices. Thus H3 can be accepted. An overview of the mean task completion times in milliseconds and the 95 % confidence intervals for all variations and devices is given in Fig. 14.

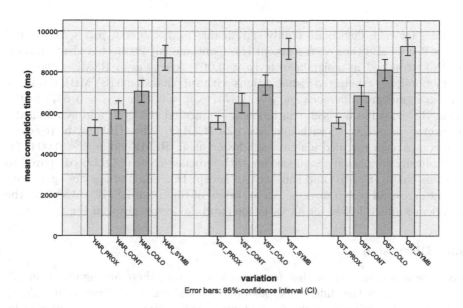

Fig. 14. Mean task completion times in milliseconds of all variations and 95 % confidence intervals (CIs)

RSME. A one-way ANOVA with repeated measures and a pairwise comparison using t-tests with Bonferroni correction was conducted to test hypothesis H4 to H6. The tests revealed a significant lower mean RSME-value for spatial assignment (PROX) compared to all other conditions. Even the highest

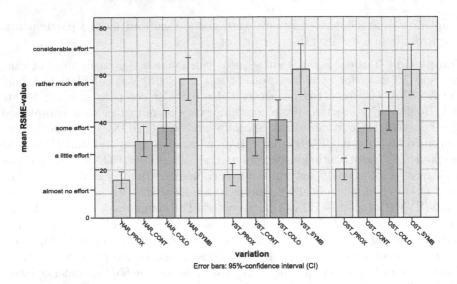

Fig. 15. Mean RSME-values of all variations and 95 % confidence intervals (CIs)

p-values for each device are highly significant ($p_{har} < 0,001$, $p_{vst} < 0,001$ and $p_{ost} < 0,001$) and thus we can accept H4. Continuously connected visualizations (CONT) resulted in a significantly ($p < 0.001$) lower mean RSME-value than the symbolically connected visualizations with subclass shape (SYMB), but there was no significant difference ($p_{har} = 0,374$, $p_{vst} = 0,112$, $p_{ost} = 0,637$) in the mean RSME-value between continuously connected (CONT) and symbolically connected visualizations with subclass color (COLO). Thus H5 must be rejected. The comparison revealed a significant lower mean RSME-value ($p < 0.003$) for symbolically connected visualizations with subclass color (COLO) compared to subclass shape (SYMB) and thus we can accept H6. The findings are again consistent across all tested devices. An overview of the mean RSME-values and the confidence interval 95 % for all variations and devices is given in Fig. 15.

5.3   Discussion

These results clearly show that for our selected task, there are signification differences between the different types of visualizations for information linking. Close spatial proximity results in the lowest task completion times, followed by continuous visual connections, color coded symbolical connections and, with the longest times, shape coded symbolical connections. Except for the combination of continuous visual connections and color coded symbolical connections this order is also the result for subjective mental workload. Even though the task is quite simple, the results are probably transferable to other areas, e.g. labeling of machine parts, because they of their similarities. Due to existing but not augmented reality related research on visual search, we also have reason to believe that results scale well for varying numbers of anchors and information objects

[21,30]. These outcomes give important guidance for augmented reality interface design. Where possible, a visual connection should be made with a spatial assignment and where not, a continuous connection should be made. Symbolic connections should only be used when the other possibilities are not feasible. However, with changes of the task or the other two dimensions, reference system and context, the results may change.

5.4   Summary and Outlook

With this work we proposed a taxonomy for visualizations of information linking in augmented reality. Included artifacts are *anchor*, *information object* and *information connection*. Based on these, three independent dimensions to classify different types of visualization were presented: *reference system*, *visual connection* and *context*. For each of these dimensions we were able to collect information on their effect on user performance. We also showed the applicability of the taxonomy on examples taken from selected publications. To deepen the understanding of the influence of the dimension visual connection on user performance, we conducted an experiment to compare four of its classes. We were able to show that in terms of completion time for WCS positioned and WCS oriented information objects a spatial assignment in close proximity to the anchor is the fastest followed by a continuous connection, a symbolical connection with color and as slowest a symbolical connection with shapes. These findings are consistent across all three tested devices (HAR, VST, OST). Considering the subjective mental work loads we were able to show that the spatial assignment condition resulted in the lowest mean RSME-value and the symbolical connection with shapes in the highest value compared to all other conditions. However, we found no significant difference in terms of mental workload between a continuous visual connection and a symbolical connection with colors. We also have reason to believe that the results will not change significantly with different numbers of information objects and anchors. From these findings we were able to derive guidelines for augmented reality interface design.

In the future we plan to extend our taxonomy. So far it only addresses static scenes and does not include animations, especially those that change how the scene must be classified, e.g. by moving the information objects from WCS positioned to SCS positioned. We also plan to conduct further experiments to gain a better understanding how the three dimensions can be used to inform design.

References

1. Azuma, R., Furmanski, C.: Evaluating label placement for augmented reality view management. In: Proceedings of the 2nd IEEE/ACM International Symposium on Mixed and Augmented Reality, p. 66. IEEE Computer Society (2003)
2. Bell, B., Feiner, S., Höllerer, T.: View management for virtual and augmented reality. In: Proceedings of the 14th Annual ACM Symposium on User Interface Software and Technology, pp. 101–110. ACM (2001)

3. Bowman, D.A., North, C., Chen, J., Polys, N.F., Pyla, P.S., Yilmaz, U.: Information-rich virtual environments: theory, tools, and research agenda. In: Proceedings of the ACM Symposium on Virtual Reality Software and Technology, pp. 81–90. ACM (2003)
4. Chen, J., Pyla, P.S., Bowman, D.A.: Testbed evaluation of navigation and text display techniques in an information-rich virtual environment. In: Proceedings of the IEEE Virtual Reality, pp. 181–289. IEEE (2004)
5. Christensen, J., Marks, J., Shieber, S.: An empirical study of algorithms for point-feature label placement. ACM Trans. Graph. (TOG) 14(3), 203–232 (1995)
6. Drascic, D., Milgram, P.: Perceptual issues in augmented reality. In: Electronic Imaging: Science & Technology, pp. 123–134. International Society for Optics and Photonics (1996)
7. Engelke, T., Webel, S., Gavish, N.: Generating vision based lego augmented reality training and evaluation systems. In: 2010 9th IEEE International Symposium on Mixed and Augmented Reality (ISMAR), pp. 223–224. IEEE (2010)
8. Feiner, S., MacIntyre, B., Haupt, M., Solomon, E., Windows on the world: 2d windows for 3d augmented reality. In: Proceedings of the 6th Annual ACM Symposium on User Interface Software and Technology, pp. 145–155. ACM (1993)
9. Furmanski, C., Azuma, R., Daily, M., Augmented-reality visualizations guided by cognition: perceptual heuristics for combining visible and obscured information. In: Proceedings of the International Symposium on Mixed and Augmented Reality, ISMAR 2002, pp. 215–320. IEEE (2002)
10. Henderson, S.J., Feiner, S.: Evaluating the benefits of augmented reality for task localization in maintenance of an armored personnel carrier turret. In: 8th IEEE International Symposium on Mixed and Augmented Reality, ISMAR 2009, pp. 135–144. IEEE (2009)
11. Henderson, S.J., Feiner, S.K.: Augmented reality in the psychomotor phase of a procedural task. In: 2011 10th IEEE International Symposium on Mixed and Augmented Reality (ISMAR), pp. 191–200. IEEE (2011)
12. Kalkofen, D., Mendez, E., Schmalstieg, D.: Interactive focus and context visualization for augmented reality. In: Proceedings of the 2007 6th IEEE and ACM International Symposium on Mixed and Augmented Reality, pp. 1–10. IEEE Computer Society (2007)
13. Kruijff, E., Swan II, J.E., Feiner, S.: Perceptual issues in augmented reality revisited. In: Proceedings of the International Symposium on Mixed and Augmented Reality, ISMAR 2010, vol. 9, pp. 3–12 (2010)
14. Maass, S., Düllner, J.: Embedded labels for line features in interactive 3d virtual environments. In: Proceedings of the 5th International Conference on Computer Graphics, Virtual Reality, Visualisation and Interaction in Africa, pp. 53–59. ACM (2007)
15. Madsen, J.B., Tatzgern, M., Madsen, C.B., Schmalstieg, D., Kalkofen, D.: Temporal coherence strategies for augmented reality labeling. Trans. Vis. Comput. Graph. 22, 1415–1423 (2016)
16. Mayer, R.E.: The Cambridge Handbook of Multimedia Learning. Cambridge University Press (2005)
17. Milgram, P., Takemura, H., Utsumi, A., Kishino, F.: Augmented reality: a class of displays on the reality-virtuality continuum. In: Photonics for Industrial Applications, pp. 282–292. International Society for Optics and Photonics (1995)
18. Müller, T.: Towards a framework for information presentation in augmented reality for the support of procedural tasks. In: De Paolis, L.T., Mongelli, A. (eds.) AVR 2015. LNCS, vol. 9254, pp. 490–497. Springer, Heidelberg (2015)

19. Polys, N.F., Bowman, D.A., North, C.: The role of depth and gestalt cues in information-rich virtual environments. Int. J. Hum. Comput. Stud. **69**(1), 30–51 (2011)
20. Polys, N.F., Kim, S., Bowman, D.A.: Effects of information layout, screen size, and field of view on user performance in information-rich virtual environments. In: Proceedings of the ACM Symposium on Virtual Reality Software and Technology, pp. 46–55. ACM (2005)
21. Quinlan, P.T., Humphreys, G.W.: Visual search for targets defined by combinations of color, shape, and size: an examination of the task constraints on feature and conjunction searches. Percept. Psychophys. **41**(5), 455–472 (1987)
22. Reiners, D., Stricker, D., Klinker, G., Müller, S.: Augmented reality for construction tasks: doorlock assembly. Proc. IEEE and ACM IWAR **98**(1), 31–46 (1998)
23. Ritter, F., Sonnet, H., Hartmann, K., Strothotte, T.: Illustrative shadows: integrating 3d and 2d information displays. In Proceedings of the 8th International Conference on Intelligent User Interfaces, pp. 166–173. ACM (2003)
24. Robertson, C.M., MacIntyre, B., Walker, B.N.: An evaluation of graphical context when the graphics are outside of the task area. In: Proceedings of the 7th IEEE/ACM International Symposium on Mixed and Augmented Reality, pp. 73–76. IEEE Computer Society (2008)
25. Robertson, C.M., MacIntyre, B., Walker, B.N.: An evaluation of graphical context as a means for ameliorating the effects of registration error. IEEE Trans. Vis. Comput. Graph. **15**(2), 179–192 (2009)
26. Rock, I., Palmer, S.: The legacy of Gestalt psychology. Sci. Am. **263**, 84–90 (1990)
27. Shibata, F., Nakamoto, H., Sasaki, R., Kimura, A., Tamura, H.: A view management method for mobile mixed reality systems. In: IPT/EGVE, pp. 17–24. Citeseer (2008)
28. Sonnet, H., Carpendale, S., Strothotte, T.: Integration of 3D data and text: the effects of text positioning, connectivity, and visual hints on comprehension. In: Costabile, M.F., Paternó, F. (eds.) INTERACT 2005. LNCS, vol. 3585, pp. 615–628. Springer, Heidelberg (2005)
29. Tönnis, M., Plecher, D.A., Klinker, G.: Representing information-classifying the augmented reality presentation space. Comput. Graph. **37**(8), 997–1011 (2013)
30. Treisman, A.M., Gelade, G.: A feature-integration theory of attention. Cogn. Psychol. **12**(1), 97–136 (1980)
31. Webel, S., Bockholt, U., Engelke, T., Gavish, N., Olbrich, M., Preusche, C.: An augmented reality training platform for assembly and maintenance skills. Robot. Auton. Syst. **61**(4), 398–403 (2013)
32. Webel, S., Bockholt, U., Engelke, T., Gavish, N., Tecchia, F.: Design recommendations for augmented reality based training of maintenance skills. In Recent Trends of Mobile Collaborative Augmented Reality Systems, pp. 69–82. Springer, New York (2011)
33. Wither, J., DiVerdi, S., Höllerer, T.: Annotation in outdoor augmented reality. Comput. Graph. **33**(6), 679–689 (2009)
34. Zijlstra, F.R.H.: Efficiency in Work Behaviour: A Design Approach for Modern Tools. TU Delft, Delft University of Technology (1993)

Mobile User Experience in Augmented Reality vs. Maps Interfaces: A Case Study in Public Transportation

Manousos Kamilakis[1], Damianos Gavalas[2,4(✉)],
and Christos Zaroliagis[3,4]

[1] School of Science and Technology, Hellenic Open University, Patras, Greece
mankamilakis@gmail.com
[2] Department of Cultural Technology and Communication,
University of the Aegean, Mytilene, Greece
dgavalas@aegean.gr
[3] Department of Computer Engineering and Informatics,
University of Patras, Patras, Greece
zaro@ceid.upatras.gr
[4] Computer Technology Institute and Press 'Diophantus' (CTI), Patras, Greece

Abstract. This article comprises a study on user experience when interacting with different modes of mobile interfaces. Our emphasis is on application instances commonly found in mobile app stores, which utilize sensor-based augmented reality or two-dimensional zoomable maps to visualize points of interest (POIs) in the vicinity of the user. As a case study, we developed two variants of an Android application addressed to public transportation users. The application displays nearby transit stops along with timetable information of transit services passing-by those stops. We report findings drawn from an empirical field study in real outdoors conditions. The evaluation findings have been cross-checked with logged (usage) data. We aim at eliciting knowledge about user requirements related to mobile application interfaces in this context and evaluating user experience from pragmatic and affective viewpoints.

Keywords: Augmented reality · Map interface · Public transportation · Mobile application · User experience · User evaluation

1 Introduction

Recent developments in mobile computing (such as the wide penetration of mobile devices equipped with camera, GPS receiver and inertial sensors) shaped a favorable technology landscape for mobile augmented reality (MAR) applications. MAR services provide a novel interface to the ubiquitous digital information in the physical world, hence serving in great variety of contexts such as tourism, cultural heritage, games, advertising, etc. [1]. The ongoing rise of AR is evidenced from the large body of

© Springer International Publishing Switzerland 2016
L.T. De Paolis and A. Mongelli (Eds.): AVR 2016, Part I, LNCS 9768, pp. 388–396, 2016.
DOI: 10.1007/978-3-319-40621-3_27

publications describing MAR demonstrators [1], the multitude of MAR apps in the mobile application markets, as well as the proliferation of publicly available MAR frameworks, such as Wikitude[1], Android Augmented Reality Framework[2], etc.

A considerable share of MAR applications are location (sensor)-based. The majority among them inherently provide means for superimposing virtual objects on the physical environment framed by the device's camera; for instance, floating markers placed upon nearby points of interest (POIs). Such MAR interfaces become more and more prevalent, commonly substituting conventional map visualizations.

The research questions addressed in this article are: (a) whether the MAR paradigm indeed involves a more natural and intuitive interface than that of conventional two-dimensional maps; (b) what is the actual quality of experience perceived by mobile users; (c) what are the most desired characteristics of each paradigm, i.e. what makes a practical, intuitive and stimulating user interface. Our focus is on outdoors, 'on-the-go' applications; namely, on instances aiming at assisting users to easily locate and consume information of interest.

To support our research objectives, we have implemented the mobile application *Transit Assistant* addressed to the users of the Athens (Greece) metropolitan public transit network. Transit Assistant is offered in two variants, one featuring a standard 2D zoomable map interface and another based on sensor-based MAR technology to display transit stops. Note that another MAR-based application tailored to public transportation users (solely indicating bus stop locations) has been recently presented by Nurminen et al. [3]. Unlike our work, the aim of the authors has been to compare the MAR application against a variant based on augmented virtuality.

Our emphasis has been on studying the utility and experience perceived by users interacting with those two mobile application interfaces. We have conducted user evaluation trials with 22 participants in realistic outdoors conditions, aiming at answering the above discussed research questions; to the best of our knowledge, this is the first empirical study that compares the two mobile interface paradigms (i.e. MAR vs. Map-based interfaces) under real-world conditions in this particular setting.

The remainder of this article is structured as follows: Sect. 2 reviews research relevant to our work. Section 3 discusses design considerations and implementation details about the two variants of Transit Assistant. Section 4 discusses evaluation results and analyzes logged data, while Sect. 5 concludes the paper.

2 Related Work

A key advantage of mobile digital maps compared to the 'traditional' paper-based map forms (further to offering multiple zoom levels and map data search) is their capacity to display layers of dynamic geolocative information [7] such as POIs in the vicinity of the user's estimated position. Efforts have been made to improve the usability of mobile map interfaces (from rendering, interaction and performance points of view) [8], support

---

[1] http://www.wikitude.com/.

[2] https://code.google.com/p/android-augment-reality-framework/.

non-visual space perception means for visually impaired users [2], incorporate waypoint navigation instructions [5], investigate appropriate means of interaction for pedestrian navigation applications [6], etc.

The MAR paradigm suggests an alternative way for visualizing information about nearby POIs via mobile interfaces. Numerous mobile applications adopting this paradigm are already in offer through app marketplaces. Recent research involved usability studies on MAR applications aiming at understanding the expectations of potential end users, their perceived experience and factors affecting user acceptance when using MAR services [1, 4, 10].

Nevertheless, empirical studies comparing the relevant (dis)advantages of MAR vs. map-based mobile interfaces are still scarce. So far a few relevant studies have been reported in the specific domain of pedestrian navigation [6, 9]. Our research focuses on a -very common- application scenario which involves the display of nearby POIs. The properties of this scenario are essentially different than those of navigation. Firstly, the (AR) virtual content superimposed on the device's camera is interactive (clickable) in our case. Secondly, pedestrian navigation applications are rather task-intensive and engage the user attention for prolonged time; on the other hand, the locate-nearest-POIs applications suggest a more relaxed interaction model with shorter usage sessions and could be used to mediate the experiential exploration of the surrounding environment.

3   *Transit Assistant*: Design Considerations and Implementation Issues

The mobile application developed in the framework of our research aims at providing assistance to the users with regard to accessing and receiving timetable information about the transport network of Athens, Greece. In particular, it includes two independent environments for locating nearby transit (bus, metro, tram, suburban railway) stops; it also provides information about departure times of transit services passing by selected stops in the ensuing time period, along with their end-to-end routes (i.e. resembling the information typically projected on dedicated monitors mounted on 'smart stops'). The application is compatible with timetable data formatted based on the GTFS (General Transit Format Specification[3]) standard and provided by local transport operators or transportation authorities.

App Architecture. Most mobile applications that leverage GTFS data adopt the client-server model, where the data tier is kept at the server side (due to its considerable size[4]) and queried by remote clients. Instead, we investigated the feasibility for implementing a standalone application (i.e. storing the GTFS data locally in order to relax the requirement for network connectivity), as dictated in the user requirements specification phase. Having set appropriate database indices, performance tests on the

---

[3] https://developers.google.com/transit/gtfs/.

[4] For instance, the GTFS feeds for the metropolitan transport networks of Athens and Paris are 151 MB and 721 MB, respectively. The database storing the Athens GTFS data occupies 278 MB (due to the redundancy introduced by indices used to speedup information search).

standalone application indicated satisfactory responsiveness even on fairly modest mobile devices.

App Design. The MAR environment is rendered on the mobile device interface through superimposing virtual objects over real-world POIs. The screen displays a real-time -rear- camera view and visual indications of POIs (markers) are overlaid on the real transit stop locations. The marker icons illustrate the type of the respective transit stops and are accompanied by an info window indicating the transit stop name as well as its distance from the current user's location.

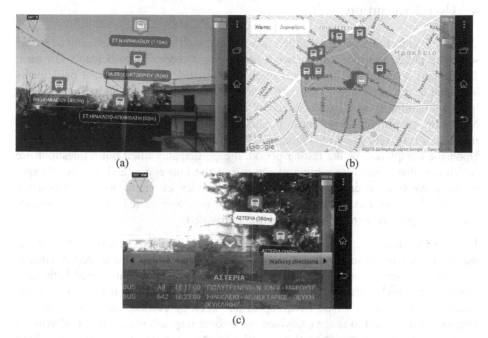

(a)   (b)

(c)

Fig. 1. (a) The MAR interface; (b) the map interface; (c) transit services' schedule information for a selected bus stop.

A 'collision avoidance' method has been employed to avoid overlaps among marker icons in environments overcrowded with POIs. A 'radar' in the upper left side of the screen informs the user about nearby stops, including those which fall out of the user's field of view. Finally, a scrollbar on the right adjusts the maximum range for locating stops around the user, hence filtering the MAR markers and the pointers shown in the radar accordingly (see Fig. 1a). The implementation of the MAR prototype has been based on the Android Augmented Reality Framework.

The map-based environment is based on a 2D Google Maps interface superimposed by markers similar to those used for the MAR environment; due to the high overlap among markers associated with neighbouring stops, we opted to omit information about the stop's name and the distance from the user (this can be displayed by tapping on the markers). A shaded circle centred at the user's location clearly denotes the search range for locating stops, similarly to the radar used in the MAR view (see Fig. 1b).

In both environments, the tapping upon a marker triggers the opening of a sliding drawer which contains information about the departure times of transit services scheduled to pass through the respective stop (see Fig. 1c). Last, the application offers auxiliary functions such as filtering stations by transit service type, walking directions towards a selected transit stop, or public transport directions to an arbitrary location pointed on the map. A demo of Transit Assistant is available from: https://www.youtube.com/watch?v=dOfltVo7_Eo.

4   User Evaluation

We have conducted a field trial of the two mobile application variants using as a case study the public transportation network of Athens, Greece. 22 participants (10 men, 12 women) installed and tested the application in their own devices. 8 participants belonged to the age group 21–30 and 14 in the age group 31–40. Only 5 participants have had familiarity with the MAR technology (they had used at least once in the past a MAR application, yet, irrelevant to public transportation). The participants have had moderate (9) to very good (13) familiarity with the transportation network in Athens. Upon the completion of the testing period, the participants filled out a questionnaire which contained questions aiming at comparing the impression and quality of experience perceived by utilizing the two offered modes of interaction. Although the questions have been closed-ended, most allowed to attach short free text to elaborate further and provide explanations on answers provided.

Indirect Comparison. Firstly, the participants have been asked to separately evaluate the two environments responding to a common set of questions. That served as a means of 'indirect' comparison among the two interfaces. The participants found both environments relatively pleasant, usable and useful (see Table 1). Their in-between comparison shows that the MAR environment has been appreciated more than the map interface with respect to usage enjoyment with some respondent comments referring to original and uncommon interaction experience. No significant difference has been reported as regards to the perception of usability among the two environments, although some respondents underlined their higher degree of familiarization and confidence with map environments. Yet, the utility of the map interface has been valued more, on average, with a few participants justifying their view by the better perception of the surrounding area (topographic information, street names) conveyed by maps. Last, no significant difference has been measured as regards the cognitive effort required to determine the location of stops relatively to the user's location.

When prompted to characterize each environment in one sentence, the verbalization has been around the concepts of entertainment and innovation for MAR (e.g. 'fun', 'interesting', 'original', 'groundbreaking') and around the concepts of intimacy and usefulness (e.g. 'familiar', 'ordinary', 'helpful') for the map interface.

Direct Comparison. The next section of the questionnaire involved a more direct comparison in the sense that respondents have been invited to explicitly compare the two evaluated environments with respect to several criteria (see Table 2). Participants appeared bifurcated as regards the easiness in using the two interfaces. The MAR

Table 1. Indirect comparison among the two environments, using a Likert scale: 1–5 (1:Not at all, 5: Very much).

	Statement	Median		Average	
		MAR	Map	MAR	Map
S1	The environment has been pleasant to use	4	4	4.2	3.7
S2	The environment has been usable	4	4	3.8	3.9
S3	The environment has been useful	4	4	3.6	4.5
S4	The environment required cognitive effort to identify the location of stops relatively to my location	3	3	2.6	2.7

environment clearly prevailed as regards the fun element of application usage (although the fact that it has been new to most users could have somewhat biased their response). Notably, half of the participants indicated preference on the map environment (mainly due to the higher level of familiarity with alike applications) with a 30 % favoring the MAR environment.

Table 2. Direct comparison among the two environments.

	Question	MAR	Map	Equally
Q1	Which environment did you find more easy to use?	45.5 %	45.5 %	9 %
Q2	Which environment did you find more pleasant to use?	90.9 %	9.1 %	0 %
Q3	Which environment did you prefer?	30 %	50 %	20 %

A next set of questions focused on the users' perception of markers due to their critical standing as the main means of interaction in both interfaces (see Table 3). The participants found the MAR markers more functional and conspicuous with some arguing that they have been more informative (as they additionally included bus stop name and distance info) and discernible (due to being more sizeable and not over-lapping among them). On the other hand, the participants indicated -slight- preference on the map environment as regards the ease in interacting with (tapping on) the markers with some stressing out their 'stability' as opposed to the floating MAR markers whose positioning has been very sensitive to devices' orientation changes (yet, some opposite views highlighted the significant overlap often noticed in the map interface which required the adjustment of the zoom level in order to distinguish individual markers). The MAR interface has been favored by the majority of respondents as regards to the ease in locating nearby transit stops, with some respondents stressing the more natural orienteering offered by MAR (as it directly conveys the direction towards a transit stop) and the fact that it displayed stop names without having to tap on a marker. Some users expressed opposite views arguing that the map interface offered a broader view of area illustrating all nearby stops without requiring any rotation (also noting that the radar of the MAR environment did not compensate that deficiency). Finally, most evaluators found it easier to reach specific transit stops using the map environment, especially when being in unfamiliar settings or in areas with complicated street layouts which are

Table 3. Comparison among the markers of the MAR and map-based environments.

	Question	MAR	Map	Equally
Q4	Which environment's markers did you find more usable?	54.5 %	27.3 %	18.2 %
Q5	Which environment's markers did you find more conspicuous?	63.6 %	27.3 %	9.1 %
Q6	Which environment's markers did you find most easy to tap on?	27.3 %	45.4 %	27.3 %
Q7	Which environment did you find easier to locate nearby transit stops?	50 %	40 %	10 %
Q8	Which environment did you find easier to reach a specific transit stop?	27.3 %	45.4 %	27.3 %

hidden in the MAR view. On the other hand, the MAR interface has been found more convenient to reach stops which lied within the users' field of view.

A last question elicited the evaluators' attitude with regards to the prospect of a third application variant featuring a dual (combined) MAR/map view. Most (72.7 %) participants appeared positive towards such a design approach with the remaining 27.3 % arguing that the offering of a single environment serves adequately the application purposes.

Interpretation of Logged Data. Aside the qualitative evaluation conducted through compiling questionnaire data, we have complemented our study by analysing -application usage- logged data. These include (separately for each evaluated environment) recording the usage session duration, the number of successful and unsuccessful taps on available markers and the number of zoom level adjustments on the map interface.

Most participants spent more time in the MAR environment (67.6 % of the overall application usage, on average). However, this should probably not be interpreted as an indication of preference but, rather, as a sign of experimentation with an unfamiliar environment which requires more time to explore.

The logging of (un)successful taps on markers demonstrates prevalence of the map environment. Note that an 'unsuccessful tap' is the one that does not trigger the event handler of any consumable interface control (e.g. markers, buttons, menu items, etc.). Specifically, only a 26.6 % of taps have been successful in the MAR environment, a lot lower than the 75.6 % measured in the MAR interface. However, it must be taken into account that most evaluators have been inexperienced with MAR applications, hence, it would be possibly fairer to observe those numbers over longer periods of usage. Besides, the assumption that unsuccessful taps could be attributed to experimentation with the interface's behaviour should not be excluded. The same holds for the possibility that several unsuccessful taps on the map interface have not been captured as such; for instance, the case of tapping a wrong marker due to the common overlaps among markers in the map environment should be investigated. In any case, the significant difference measured among the two interfaces should somewhat reveal the difficulty of users to target the floating MAR markers despite their bigger size, as also claimed in some questionnaire forms. Another explanation could be the typically inconvenient use of MAR applications which engage one hand for holding the device in a rather unstable position letting the other to tap on the user interface. On the other hand, the map interface (and markers) are not affected from changes on devices' orientation; besides, it may comfortably be used by placing the device on a fixed stand (e.g. a table) without compromising its functionality.

5 Discussion

In this article we presented design decisions and implementation details relevant to Transit Assistant, a mobile application which addresses practical requirements of public transport users (visualization of nearby transit stops along with timetable information of transit services passing-by those stops). Our emphasis has been on studying the utility and experience perceived by users interacting with MAR vs. map-based mobile application interfaces. To some extent, our empirical findings controvert the enthusiastic views widespread among the mobile developers community which suggest the unreserved use of MAR in any application context, mainly motivated by its unique natural interaction model. Our field study revealed some of the strong and weak traits of each evaluated interface paradigm when employed in alike applications.

MAR interfaces have been shown to offer an enjoyable, intuitive interaction model (still commonly unknown to mobile users); this serves well the purpose of directly linking digital content with the user's physical environment thereby enabling the experiential exploration of the surrounding elements. The offering of improved sense of orienteering relatively to surrounding physical elements (e.g. unambiguous interpretation of the direction towards a POI) should be regarded as another strong aspect of sensor-based MAR applications. Last, existing MAR frameworks may well address the -undesirable- effect of overlaps among markers; this frees space in the device's screen and allows to accompany the marker with additional useful information (e.g. stop name and distance information in the case of Transit Assistant).

Map interfaces suggest a well-established interface mode, fairly familiar to the majority of mobile web users. To this end, map-based environments represent a reliable and practical option for POI-searching mobile applications. The map interface has been shown to be susceptible to marker congestion problems especially in settings featuring dense presence of POIs (yet, this problem could be mitigated through employing marker grouping techniques); in turn, this compels the adjustment of the zoom level so as to separate individual markers. Furthermore, map environments overcrowded with POIs allow no visual space to attach extra information to the markers; hence, the users are often required to tap on several markers only to display their respective info window and be able to locate a particular POI. On the other hand, mobile maps help users not to miss important information and obtain an overview of a larger territory (e.g. perceive the topological context, view street names, etc.). This feature (along with the higher degree of familiarization) has been mostly appreciated by the evaluators of the map-based interface involved in our field trials.

Overall, the two environments tied with respect to usability criteria. Nevertheless, the field study participants highlighted the fun element and the natural interaction model of the MAR application, but also appreciated the familiarity and practicality aspects of the map interface. It appears that the practical qualities of the map-based mode have been valued more as the majority of users argued that it would be more useful to support their everyday activities.

In conclusion, MAR interfaces still need to resolve major usability issues until they can be regarded as undisputable substitute of traditional map-based interfaces. Until then, mobile developers should be cautious when deciding upon the appropriate interaction mode, carefully evaluating their application requirements per case and weighing all involved human/usability factors. Furthermore, current developments in mobile and wearable computing set new standards and create opportunities for the effective employment of MAR. Most likely, emerging devices like smart glasses (which involve principally different methods for interacting with digital content) will essentially affect the quality of experience perceived by users. As a next step in our research, we intend to investigate this issue.

Acknowledgement. This work has been supported by the CIP-ICT-PSP-2013-2017 Programme under grant agreement no. 621133 (HoPE - "Holistic Personal public Eco-mobility").

References

1. Carmigniani, J., Furht, B., Anisetti, M., Ceravolo, P., Damiani, E., Ivkovic, M.: Augmented reality technologies, systems and applications. Multimedia Tools Appl. **51**(1), 341–377 (2011)
2. Jacobson, R.D.: Navigating maps with little or no sight: an audio-tactile approach. In: Proceedings of the Workshop on Content Visualization and Intermedia Representations (1998)
3. Nurminen, A., Järvi, J., Lehtonen, M.: A mixed reality interface for real time tracked public transportation. In: Proceedings of the 10th ITS European Congress (2014)
4. Olsson, T., Kärkkäinen, T., Lagerstam, E., Ventä-Olkkonen, L.: User evaluation of mobile augmented reality scenarios. J. Ambient Intell. Smart Environ. **4**(1), 29–47 (2012)
5. Pielot, M., Boll, S.: Tactile wayfinder: comparison of tactile waypoint navigation with commercial pedestrian navigation systems. In: Floréen, P., Krüger, A., Spasojevic, M. (eds.) Pervasive 2010. LNCS, vol. 6030, pp. 76–93. Springer, Heidelberg (2010)
6. Rehrl, K., Häusler, E., Leitinger, S., Bell, D.: Pedestrian navigation with augmented reality, voice and digital map: final results from an in situ field study assessing performance and user experience. J. Location Based Serv. **8**(2), 75–96 (2014)
7. Sarjakoski, L.T., Nivala, A.M.: Adaptation to context-a way to improve the usability of mobile maps. In: Meng, L., Reichenbacher, T., Zipf, A. (eds.) Map-Based Mobile Services, pp. 107–123. Springer, Heidelberg (2005)
8. Setlur, V., Kuo, C., Mikelsons, P.: Towards designing better map interfaces for the mobile: experiences from example. In: Proceedings of the 1st International Conference and Exhibition on Computing for Geospatial Research & Application (2010)
9. Wen, J., Helton, W.S., Billinghurst, M.: A study of user perception, interface performance, and actual usage of mobile pedestrian navigation aides. Proc. Hum. Factors Ergon. Soc. Annu. Meet. **57**(1), 1958–1962 (2013)
10. Yovcheva, Z., Buhalis, D., Gatzidis, C.: Smartphone augmented reality applications for tourism. e-Review Tourism Res. (eRTR) **10**(2), 63–66 (2012)

GazeAR: Mobile Gaze-Based Interaction in the Context of Augmented Reality Games

Michael Lankes[1(✉)] and Barbara Stiglbauer[2]

[1] Department of Digital Media, University of Applied Sciences Upper Austria,
Softwarepark 11, Hagenberg, Austria
Michael.Lankes@fh-hagenberg.at
[2] Department of Education and Psychology, Johannes Kepler University Linz,
Altenbergerstr. 69, Linz, Austria
Barbara.Stiglbauer@jku.at
http://www.fh-ooe.at/campus-hagenberg/
http://aom.jku.at/

Abstract. Gaze-based interaction in the gaming context offers various research opportunities. However, when looking at available games supported by eye tracking technology it becomes apparent that the potential has not been fully exploited: a majority of gaze-based games are tailored for static settings (desktop PC). We propose an experimental setting that transfers approaches of mobile gaze-based interactions to the augmented reality (AR) games domain. It is our main aim to find out if the inclusion of gaze input in an AR game has a positive impact on the User Experience (UX) in comparison to a solely touch-based approach. By doing so designers and researchers should receive insights in the design of gaze-based mobile AR games. To find answers we carried out a comparative study consisting of two mobile game prototypes. Results show that the inclusions of gaze in AR games is very well received by players and this novel approach was preferred in comparison to a design without gaze interaction.

Keywords: Gaze-based interaction · Augmented reality games

1 Introduction

During the last years the diversity of game input devices has increased dramatically. Nowadays game controllers are able to capture nonverbal communication channels (finger gestures, body postures, etc.) and promise players to interact with games "in simpler, more natural ways" [12]. Just recently also eye tracking systems have found their way into the games domain as the technology can now be efficiently integrated into games at an affordable price [13]. Companies, such as Tobii[1] or the Eye Tribe[2] encourage developers to identify and create

---

[1] www.tobii.com/en/eye-experience/.
[2] theeyetribe.com.

© Springer International Publishing Switzerland 2016
L.T. De Paolis and A. Mongelli (Eds.): AVR 2016, Part I, LNCS 9768, pp. 397–406, 2016.
DOI: 10.1007/978-3-319-40621-3_28

concepts for future gaze-based games. However, when looking at the available games and research projects supported by eye tracking technology it becomes apparent that the potential has not yet been fully exploited: a majority of gaze-based games and prototypes are tailored for static settings (interaction via a desktop PC). The design possibilities in regard to mobile games remain to a large extent untouched. Most research in the context of gaze-based interaction and mobile devices can only be found outside of games (for instance: [4,9]) ranging from gaze-based interaction with wearable (such as Head Mounted Displays) to handheld devices (smartphones or tablets).

We are of the opinion that gaze-based mobile games prove to be an interesting field of games research – especially in the context of augmented reality (AR) games – as these games combine real and virtual elements without confining the players operation to a particular location [1]. Several design challenges can be found within this area: for example while interacting with a mobile device with a large touch display players tend to hold the device with one hand as the game elements are out of their fingers' reach [8]. Consequently, the players cannot maintain the optimal viewing position of the game scenery as the device becomes unstable. This issue becomes even more visible in AR game designs that require players to move in the physical world during play and are based on so called "twitch skills" (i.e. players have to react quickly to game situations, game mechanics require frequent input to reach the game goal).

Gaze-based interaction techniques provide solutions to these issues as they can be used to efficiently replace actions that are currently carried out via touch input. We want to find out if the integration of gaze input into a mobile AR game yields beneficial aspects in comparison to mobile AR games that rely only on touch-based interaction. Thus, we propose a comparative study – made up of two prototypes (gaze with touch interaction and touch only) – that should shed some light concerning the user experience (UX) of gaze-based AR games. By identifying and highlighting risks as well as potentials designers should receive knowledge in the design and creation of this specific type of game.

2   Mobile Gaze-Based Games

The use of AR technology in mobile games can be found in various research projects. [2], for instance, propose a game concept developed with the aim of studying and developing mobile augmented reality applications for tablets using face recognition interaction techniques. The publication of [5] explores the design space of sketching within in-place AR with particular attention to AR games. The researchers describe different case studies of sketch-based AR games based on their sketch-based 3-D game engine and introduce guidelines for AR game designers focusing on sketch-based interaction. [11] discusses the design of a mobile AR system that engages students to practice the doing of history in an AR real-world context. They created and conceptualized multiple AR activities within an instructional unit using a local historic site. [3] introduce an AR installation, coined VirtualTable, where players are engaged in an interactive tower defense game. It runs permanently and has the design goal to attract people to a table, where the game is shown.

Studies dealing with mobile AR games supported by eye tracking technology (including handheld or wearable devices as well as interaction concepts) are very hard to find. Many studies in the context of mobile gaze-based interactions employ handheld devices without integrating playful aspects (game mechanics, game goals): for example [10] propose a continuous gaze tracking and non-touch gesture recognition based interaction method for 3D virtual spaces on tablet devices. Users can turn their viewpoint or select objects with gaze and grab and manipulate objects with non-touch hand gestures. They created a comparative study and evaluated the completion times of a combined gaze tracking and non-touch gesture interaction method. Subjects mentioned that gaze tracking was more interesting and showed potential. However, eye tracking would require more stability to be suitable for use with mobile devices.

[8] note that handheld touch-based mobile devices are awkward to use with one hand. They propose a novel user interface called "MobiGaze" that utilizes the gaze of users to operate a handheld mobile device. [7] introduce a system coined "GazeProjector" that combines accurate point-of-gaze estimation with natural feature tracking on multiple displays. These examples should have briefly shown the potential of mobile gaze-based interactions. Until now no transfer of the approaches to playful AR scenarios and interactions has been carried out.

3   Experiment Description

Based on the previously described opportunities we propose an experimental setting that transfers approaches of mobile gaze-based interactions to the AR games domain. We want to find out if the inclusion of gaze input in an AR game (touch and gaze) has a positive impact on the user experience (UX) in comparison to an approach that is solely based on touch interaction techniques. By doing so designers and researchers should receive insights in the design of gaze-based mobile AR games. Since our game concepts are tailored for AR settings with a high degree of mobility we employed a handheld device scenario (smartphone or tablet). Tablets in this regard can be utilized as a "magic lens" through which an alternate non-immersive perspective on the world is provided, which emphasizes the applicability of gaze-based interactions. Furthermore, handheld AR has generally been viewed as more practical for wide-scale adoption [1]. To create a game design that fulfills the design requirements of a mobile AR game supported by eye tracking we formulated the following 3 design considerations:

- *Physical game space:* the game design should consider the physical space in which the game takes place; the physical space should be an integral part of the game mechanics; the inclusion of AR elements should consider both the virtual and the physical dimension;
- *Player mobility:* players should have the possibility to physically explore the game space; the game design should address the way how players can explore

the game world and should clearly communicate the consequences of the players' presence via the virtual game interface;

- *Gaze integration:* the inclusion of gaze input should be seamless and made plausible for the player; it should augment the players' ability to act within the game world;

3.1 Scenarios

To investigate and find an answer to the stated research question we created two scenarios (resembled through 2 game prototypes) based on the previously described 3 design requirements (called scenario 1 and 2). The only difference between the scenarios is the way players interact with the game prototypes (scenario 1: touch, scenario 2: touch and gaze). As a first step, the overall game concept will be described in detail. Our game is called *Block!Block!* and references different mechanics from various games such as table tennis, *Pacman* or *Edge*. To play the game a tablet device (plus an attached eye tracker) as well as a physical game board that is placed on the floor are required. The player uses the tablet's built in camera to focus on the game board in order to observe the game world. It is important to note that our game concept is very flexible regarding the complexity of AR elements. The approach allows the integration of various objects (such as tables, exterior architecture elements that resemble grid-like structures) and can be transferred to different locations (indoor, outdoor, private but also public spaces such as parks).

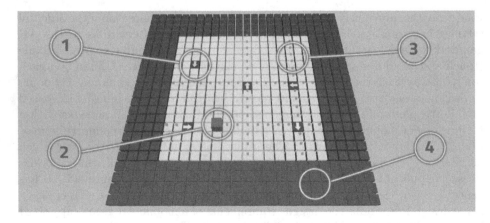

Fig. 1. Screenshot of the game *Block!Block!*: 1. arrow cube, 2. mover cube, 3. coin, 4. active sector. (Color figure online)

The game itself takes place on a grid-based board. On that grid a cube (called mover cube) translates automatically from one end of the board to the other (discrete and step by step moves). One goal of the game is to prevent the mover cube from moving out of the game board by changing its direction.

This is achieved by interacting with the mover cube via touch and gaze-based interaction (dependent on the given scenario which is described later). However, this can only be done at one of the four blue sections that are located at the outer areas of the grid (see Fig. 1).

Players are required to physically go to the blue area to change the mover cube's direction (see Fig. 2). If the mover cube resides in this blue section and the player interacts with the mover cube, than its directional movement is altered by 180 degrees (resemblance to table tennis). The player gets also feedback of his/her current position via the green highlight in the blue area.

Apart from preventing the mover cube to move out of the grid players have to collect yellow cubes with the mover cube to complete a game level successfully. Yellow cubes are not only placed from top to bottom, but also from left to right. Players are able to rotate the mover cube by 90 degrees via the blue cubes with a white arrow (called arrow cubes). If the mover cube collides with an arrow cube than the mover cube changes its movement into the direction indicated by the direction of the arrow.

Fig. 2. Players use the tablet's built in camera to focus on the game board in order to observe the current game situation. It is required to constantly move in order to be successful in the game. (Color figure online)

As mentioned in the beginning of this Sect. 2 scenarios are derived from the described game concept. In scenario 1 players use only touch input to interact with the game, while scenario 2 (see Fig. 3) combines gaze and touch input. In scenario 1 players tap on game objects with their fingers to change their state. Regarding scenario 2 players look at the game elements that they want to manipulate (gaze as pointer) and confirm their action via touch (tap gestures) – independent from the location of the touch position.

402 M. Lankes and B. Stiglbauer

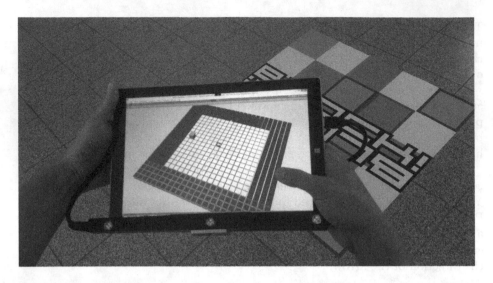

Fig. 3. Scenario 2 – players use both gaze and touch interaction to play the game. The eyeX eye tracking device is mounted on the Surface Pro tablet.

With the exception of this aspect there is no difference between the scenarios. Regarding our research question we assume that scenario 2 (gaze and touch) will receive higher UX ratings as it provides players a more efficient way of interaction (no need for pointing via touch), a stable position of the device and the game view by constantly using two hands. Furthermore, we expect that the scenario 2 will arouse a more pleasant and novel experience.

3.2 Participants and Procedure

The study was conducted at the Playful Interactive Environments (PIE) Lab of the University of Applied Sciences Upper Austria. The sample consisted of 24 participants (50.0 % male, 50.0 % female), aged 16 to 33 years (M = 24.63, SD = 4.12). Most of the participants played video games occasionally (58.3 %) or several times a week to daily (29.2 %). The procedure itself took between 25 to 30 min per participant.

The experimental setting was made up of a Microsoft Surface Pro 3 tablet device and a Tobii EyeX tracker[3] that was mounted on the bottom of the tablet PC. The Surface tablet was chosen as it includes an USB 3.0 port for the eye tracker as well as sufficient computing power to grant players an enjoyable experience. The two prototypes were created using the Unity3D game engine[4] in conjunction with the vision-based augmented reality software Vuforia[5].

---

[3] http://www.tobii.com/xperience/.
[4] http://unity3d.com/.
[5] https://www.qualcomm.com/products/vuforia.

The evaluation was divided into two parts based on the previously described two scenarios. By choosing a *within-subject design*, all participants had to play the two scenarios (average play time per scenario: approx. 8 to 10 min). The order in which participants were confronted with the prototypes was randomized to take possible interaction effects into account. To grant players the opportunity to get used to the game mechanics 5 levels were created that gradually increased in difficulty (3 levels with one mover cube, 2 levels with two mover cubes, 1 level with 3 mover cubes).

3.3   Measures

When the interaction with one scenario was completed, the experimenter instructed the participants to fill out the questionnaire ("AttrakDiff" by [6]) followed by a brief interview (questions: which aspects of the game could be improved, what do players like or dislike, how would players describe the game experience with the eye tracking device, etc.).

The AttrakDiff assess the overall UX during product use and enables researchers and designers to measure implications of the attractiveness. Users indicate their impression of a given product by bipolar terms that reflect 4 dimensions. The first dimension, the Pragmatic Quality (PQ), describes tradi-tional usability aspects, while the dimension Hedonic Quality-Stimulation (HQ-S) refers to the need of people for further development concerning themselves. Hedonic Quality-Identification (HQ-I) allows measuring the amount of identifi-cation a user has towards a product. Attractiveness (ATT) resembles an overall judgment based on the perceived quality.

4   Results

A within subjects ANOVA indicated a significant main effect of scenario type on the AttrakDiff scores, $F(1, 23) = 118.19$, $p < .001$. Post-hoc comparisons using paired samples T-tests further revealed significant differences between the two scenarios for all four subscales (cf. Table 1). Thus, participants evaluated sce-nario 2 significantly better in terms of hedonic quality, pragmatic quality, and attractiveness. These differences were large in size (cf. Cohen's d), particularly for the HQ-S dimension, and remained significant after controlling for sociode-mographic characteristics and gaming habits or when using more conservative non-parametric tests. Concerning the interviews that were carried out after each scenario was played participants generally gave very positive feedback for both scenarios. They were pleased by the overall game design (integration of move-ment) as well as the combination of gaze-based interaction with an AR setting. A majority of players had a very positive impression in regard to the eye tracking device. Negative feedback was mainly based on technical issues (tracking was lost in some cases, touch input was not recognized by the system).

Table 1. Differences between the two scenarios in the AttrakDiff scale scores.

Scale	Scenario 1		Scenario 2		t	Cohen's d
	M	SD	M	SD		
ATT	5.44	0.47	6.03	0.63	-4.82***	-1.04
PQ	4.31	0.45	4.85	0.32	-5.95***	-1.36
HQ-I	5.07	0.39	5.76	0.56	-5.22***	-1.44
HQ-S	5.75	0.42	6.47	0.36	-8.81***	-1.83
Total	5.14	0.30	5.78	0.38	-10.87***	-1.80

*** $p < .001$.

5   Discussion

From a general point of view the integration of gaze (scenario 2) led to a better UX than scenario 1. Subjects perceived the interaction via the eye tracking device as very intuitive and engaging. This can be especially seen when looking at the hedonic qualities. Several players noted in the interviews that the playful interaction via gaze on a tablet was a novel and fresh idea, and it gave them a feeling of being able to act in the game ("I can use my gaze to change something in game"). Furthermore, they liked the combination of movement and gaze interaction as it supported players to keep the game situation under control and to maintain the device in a stable position. One player also said that scenario 2 is much more convenient and efficient ("There is no need to touch the mover cube – I simply have to look at it and touch anywhere on the pad".). Players also pointed out that mobile gaze interaction fitted very well for playful purposes and that the design would also be applicable for multiplayer games ("I can try things out – I like to play the game with my friends").

However, players also criticized several aspects in regard to the gaze-based interaction. Most negative feedback was related to technical difficulties and to ergonomic factors (as measured by PQ). The device was perceived as heavy in comparison to conventional tablet devices (weight of surface tablet: 453 g). Additionally, in some situations the Surface Pro 3 tablet became fairly hot making it difficult for players to hold the device comfortably. Since the EyeX eye tracker was originally designed for static scenarios (desktop PC) some issues arose: in order to make the eye tracking device work properly players had to keep track of the distance between their eyes and the tracking device. The wrong viewing angle also led in some cases to technical difficulties. Due to these limitations 4 evaluation sessions had to be canceled (and were left out of the study) as the gaze tracking abruptly stopped working on several occasions.

Concerning the gaze feedback two subjects noted that visual and audio cues might help players to identify if a game element was focused or not. The inclusion of more pronounced cues has to be handled with care: in level 1 (tutorial) the current gaze position was visualized via a small red rectangle in order to get players used to the gaze interaction and reassure them that the device is actually working. In the following levels no information on the gaze position was shown.

Some players noted that they were annoyed by the red dot ("I know where I am looking!"). Thus, visual cues in regard to gaze have to be very subtle to avoid player distraction. This could be done via highlighting or a color change of the focused game object. However, apart from these negative aspects the inclusion of gaze in the context of mobile AR games appears to be very promising and offers players and interesting and engaging game experience.

6   Conclusions

This submission introduced an experimental setting that transfers approaches of mobile gaze-based interactions to the AR games domain. We created two game prototypes (scenario 1: touch only, scenario 2: touch and gaze) in order to find out if the inclusion of gaze input in an AR game would have a positive impact on the UX in comparison to a traditional approach. Results showed that the gaze interaction was positively received by players – both in regard to hedonic and pragmatic aspects.

Although the gathered findings appear to be very promising, several improvements and variations of our concept could be made. Subjects mentioned that the device was too heavy, and it became hot after some playtime. Thus, it would be feasible to evaluate the game concept *Block!Block!* with other devices (lighter tablets or smartphones) that have the required computing power. Another way to improve the game interaction would be using eye tracking technology that is better integrated in the device in order to identify its effects on UX (tracking of gaze via built-in camera as introduced in [14]).

We think that it also would make sense to evaluate our experimental setup with different AR elements (interior and exterior objects such as tables, walls, etc.) and genres (strategy and tactics, puzzle solving, etc.). Also the setting itself could be modified for further investigation (private, semi-public, public settings). Additionally, our setup could also be transferred to other scenarios to investigate the design opportunities in regard to mobile gaze-based interaction (film and photography, guidance systems, collaboration scenarios, etc.).

References

1. Burnett, D., Coulton, P., Murphy, E., Race, N.: Designing mobile augmented reality interfaces for locative games and playful experiences. In: Proceedings of the Digital Games Research Conference 2014 (2014). http://eprints.lancs.ac.uk/69998/1/DiGRA_Scarecrows_Full_paper.pdf
2. Cordeiro, D., Correia, N., Jesus, R.M.: Arzombie: a mobile augmented reality game with multimodal interaction. In: 7th International Conference on Intelligent Technologies for Interactive Entertainment, INTETAIN 2015, Torino, Italy, 10–12 June 2015, pp. 22–31 (2015). http://ieeexplore.ieee.org/xpl/freeabs_all.jsp?arnumber=7325481

3. Dal Corso, A., Olsen, M., Steenstrup, K.H., Wilm, J., Jensen, S., Paulsen, R.R., Eiríksson, E., Nielsen, J., Frisvad, J.R., Einarsson, G., Kjer, H.M.: Virtualtable: a projection augmented reality game. In: SIGGRAPH Asia 2015 Posters, SA 2015, pp. 40:1–40:1. ACM, New York (2015). http://doi.acm.org/10.1145/2820926. 2820950

4. Dybdal, M.L., Agustin, J.S., Hansen, J.P.: Gaze input for mobile devices by dwell and gestures. In: Proceedings of the Eye Tracking Research and Applications, ETRA 2012, pp. 225–228. ACM, New York (2012). http://doi.acm.org/10.1145/2168556.2168601

5. Hagbi, N., Grasset, R., Bergig, O., Billinghurst, M., El-Sana, J.: In-placesketching for augmented reality games. Comput. Entertain. **12**(3), 3:1–3:18 (2015). http://doi.acm.org/10.1145/2702109.2633419

6. Hassenzahl, M., Burmester, M., Koller, F.: Attrakdiff: Ein fragebogen zur messung wahrgenommener hedonischer und pragmatischer qualitt. In: Szwillus, G., Ziegler, J. (eds.) Mensch & Computer 2003: Interaktion in Bewegung, pp. 187–196. B. G. Teubner, Stuttgart (2003)

7. Lander, C., Gehring, S., Krüger, A., Boring, S., Bulling, A.: GazeProjector: Location-independent Gaze Interaction on and Across Multiple Displays. DFKI Research Report 15–01, DFKI, Saarbrücken (2015). http://www.dfki.de/web/research/publications?pubid=7618

8. Nagamatsu, T., Yamamoto, M., Sato, H.: Mobigaze: development of a gaze interface for handheld mobile devices. In: CHI 2010 Extended Abstracts on Human Factors in Computing Systems, CHI EA 2010, pp. 3349–3354. ACM, New York (2010). http://doi.acm.org/10.1145/1753846.1753983

9. Patidar, P., Raghuvanshi, H., Sarcar, S.: Quickpie: an interface for fast and accurate eye gazed based text entry. In: India HCI 2013. ACM (2014)

10. Pouke, M., Karhu, A., Hickey, S., Arhippainen, L.: Gaze tracking and non-touch gesture based interaction method for mobile 3d virtual spaces. In: Proceedings of the Australian Computer-Human Interaction Conference, OzCHI 2012, pp. 505–512. ACM, New York (2012). http://doi.acm.org/10.1145/2414536.2414614

11. Singh, G., Bowman, D., Hicks, D., Cline, D., Ogle, J., Johnson, A., Zlokas, R., Tucker, T., Ragan, E.: Ci-spy: designing a mobile augmented reality system for scaffolding historical inquiry learning. In: 2015 IEEE International Symposium on Mixed and Augmented Reality - Media, Art, Social Science, Humanities and Design (ISMAR-MASH'D), pp. 9–14, September 2015

12. Smith, J.D., Graham, T.C.N.: Use of eye movements for video game control. In: Proceedings of the Advances in Computer Entertainment Technology, ACE 2006. ACM, New York (2006). http://doi.acm.org/10.1145/1178823.1178847

13. Sundstedt, V.: Gazing at games: using eye tracking to control virtual characters. In: ACM SIGGRAPH 2010 Courses, SIGGRAPH 2010, pp. 5:1–5:160. ACM, New York (2010). http://doi.acm.org/10.1145/1837101.1837106

14. Wood, E., Bulling, A.: Eyetab: model-based gaze estimation on unmodified tablet computers. In: Proceedings of the Eye Tracking Research and Applications, ETRA 2014, pp. 207–210. ACM, New York (2014). http://doi.acm.org/10.1145/2578153.2578185

Visualization of Heat Transfer Using Projector-Based Spatial Augmented Reality

Karljohan Lundin Palmerius[✉] and Konrad Schönborn

Linköping University, Linköping, Sweden
karljohan.lundin.palmerius@liu.se

Abstract. Thermal imaging cameras, commonly used in application areas such as building inspection and night vision, have recently also been introduced as pedagogical tools for helping students visualize, interrogate and interpret notoriously challenging thermal concepts. In this paper we present a system for Spatial Augmented Reality that automatically projects thermal data onto objects. Instead of having a learner physically direct a hand-held camera toward an object of interest, and then view the display screen, a group of participants can gather around the display system and directly see and manipulate the thermal profile projected onto physical objects. The system combines a thermal camera that captures the thermal data, a depth camera that realigns the data with the objects, and a projector that projects the data back. We also apply a colour scale tailored for room temperature experiments.

Keywords: Spatial Augmented Reality · Thermal imaging · Real-time projection mapping · Science education

1 Introduction

Thermal imaging cameras, also referred to as infrared thermography (IRT) cameras, are utilised to detect mid- and longwave infrared radiation emitted from objects. The resulting images are rendered in various pseudo-colour scales to enable human perception of the warmest and coolest parts of viewed surfaces. Thermography is used in multiple applications that include building inspection, automotive night vision, search and rescue, and medical diagnosis. More recently, IRT cameras have been empirically investigated as pedagogical tools for helping students visualize, interrogate and interpret notoriously challenging thermal concepts [7]. Herein, the use of IRT cameras for learning offers a form of educational technology that makes otherwise invisible processes visible [12,14]. In this regard, we have used IRT cameras in science education contexts [6,7] for direct macroscopic visualization of thermal concepts related to heat transfer (e.g. conduction and thermal insulation), energy transformations (e.g. kinetic to thermal), and other dissipative processes (e.g. dry friction).

To date, our investigations have involved students viewing the thermal camera display of the hand-held camera while performing different tasks to interpret

© Springer International Publishing Switzerland 2016
L.T. De Paolis and A. Mongelli (Eds.): AVR 2016, Part I, LNCS 9768, pp. 407–417, 2016.
DOI: 10.1007/978-3-319-40621-3_29

thermal phenomena, or where the image feed is projected onto a screen. As an alternative approach, we hypothesise that an Augmented Reality (AR) system could offer a more natural visual feedback and intuitive learning experience for interpreting abstract science concepts (e.g. [13]). In this manner, instead of having to physically direct a hand-held camera toward an object of interest, and then view the display screen as the graphical overlay of the thermal world, what if the thermal image could be projected directly onto the object surface? In addition, we are of the view that an augmented display may also open up opportunities for novel collaborative learning spaces [8], where more than one participant can simultaneously manipulate thermal phenomena during physical interaction with the AR system.

In this paper we present a system for Spatial Augmented Reality (SAR), displaying thermal data onto real objects, as a part of our ongoing efforts on exploring the use of thermal imaging in education. The main contributions of the paper are

- the presentation of a technique for displaying thermal data onto real objects through real-time projection mapping,
- the presentation of a complete hardware and software concept for a fully 3D thermal projection system, including mounting and discussion of shadow concepts, and
- a colour scheme specially designed for the projection of thermal data for heat-related experiments at ±10°C of room temperature.

2   Related Work

Spatial Augmented Reality (SAR) was first introduced by Raskar et al. in [11], as an approach to provide Augmented Reality without introducing head-mounted display systems. The use of structured light projection to extract surface geometries was cited as a technique to compensate for the shape of the projection surface. Today this is encapsulated as consumer-available depth cameras. Two of the authors later published a book on the subject [2]. A more recent example of projector-based SAR is the work by Benko et al. [1], in which multiple projectors are used to turn all surfaces in a room into a 3D display system.

When it comes to thermal imaging, there has been some work on the use of projector-based Augmented Reality, however to the authors current knowledge, nothing has yet been published in the scientific literature. For example, Ken Kawamoto presented in both a blog and an online video what he terms a *ThermalTable* [9]. He used a FLIR C2 camera to record thermal data from a table that were then projected back using a projector. The camera and the projector are aligned so that the recorded thermal profile is projected back to its origin, at least on the table surface. For objects above the surface, the projection becomes increasingly misaligned with increasing distance from the surface.

Gladyszewski et al. posted a video [5] showing their "thermal video projection system", initially part of the choreographic project *Corps Noir*. This system uses a co-located thermal camera, video projector and video camera to create a live video feed that shows thermal information projected onto the bodies of dancers. Since the three devices are co-located their different views can be adjusted to align without taking the shape of the projection surface into account. In continuation of that work, Gladyszewski recently posted a new video of a related artwork [4]. This work is similar to that of Kawamoto, and the thermal image is instead projected back onto a table-top clay surface.

While the former aesthetically attractive examples certainly represent the many possible applications of projector-based thermal AR, the challenge still remains of automatically aligning any 3D object viewed from any angle. Our work presented here aims to use depth information to create a dynamically updated projection mapping of the thermal information onto any object placed on, or held above the table surface. In turn, such a solution will make the concept more accessible for education purposes.

3   Display System

Our projector-based spatial AR display system for thermal data uses a thermal camera to capture thermal data in a region above a small table surface, and a data projector to project those data back to the recorded object. The theoretical optimum is to co-locate the thermal camera and the projector, so that the projection can be perfectly aligned with the recorded data. However, with the current hardware available for this project we also faced the challenge of solving a more complicated placement. This is further explained below.

To obtain correct alignment between the recorded thermal data and the projection, regardless of the presented geometry, we use a depth camera that captures the geometry and enables dynamic, real-time projection mapping [11]. Thus, our system consists of a rig with three imaging devices: a thermal camera, a depth camera and a projector, see Fig. 1.

3.1   Projector

The purpose of the projector is to augment objects with visual thermal information by projecting colours onto them as part of a natural educational environment. The most important aspects of the projector are colour reproduction and static contrast. Since the projection area is smaller compared to other applications, brightness is of less importance.

We selected an Epson EB-1940W, a three-panel LCD projector, for our prototype. Since it is recommended not to be mounted vertically, like most projectors of that type, we use a mirror to redirect the projection towards the table surface, see Fig. 1(d).

3.2   Depth Camera

The depth camera used in our system is a Microsoft Kinect Version 2, which is an active camera based on structured light in the N-IR spectrum. It is factory

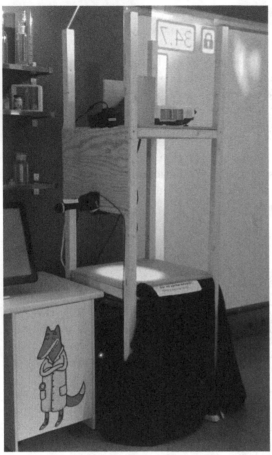

(b) The mounted FLIR E4.

(a) The full rig with all equipment mounted, placed in a public exhibition at a digital science centre.

(c) The calibration target.

(d) The Kinect and the projector with accompanying mirror.

Fig. 1. Photographs of the thermal SAR display system, and comprising components.

calibrated but requires a minimum distance of approximately 400 mm to the nearest objects. Therefore, to allow users of the system to hold objects above the table surface, we mounted the depth camera at a height of about 750 mm.

We have designed and 3D printed holders to mount the camera as close as possible to the origin of the projection, see Fig. 1(d).

3.3 Thermal Camera

The thermal camera included in our display system is a FLIR E4, an entry level device with 80×60 pixels sensor resolution, which is much lower than a conventional camera. The camera provides live video streaming via USB Video Class (UVC) standard, and includes both thermal scale legend and other information. These do not represent thermal data and should thus be masked out for a better user experience.

Due to the low resolution, we cannot afford to record a large area of the table and since the camera has a fixed lens, this means that the camera has to be mounted close to the table surface. This means that the thermal camera has to be mounted to the side, to avoid it occluding the two other imaging devices. We decided on a distance of 350 mm, resulting in a pixel size of ~4 mm over a surface of 300 by 250 mm after masking out non-thermal video features.

The camera is designed for hand-held use and therefore has no mount. To fix it to the display system we again designed and 3D printed appropriate holders, see Fig. 1(b).

3.4 Projection Calibration

There are three different imaging devices in this system that need to be calibrated and co-registered to the same coordinate system: the projector, the depth camera and the thermal camera. All three devices have their own special features making it a non-trivial task to find the correspondances necessary for the calibration. The depth camera only detects depth differences, the thermal camera requires a target with a higher or lower temperature than the surroundings, and the projector cannot detect anything.

The depth camera defines the coordinates of the system. Thus, the depth camera/projector and the depth camera/thermal camera registration needs to be estimated. We did this by first finding corresponding points both in 3D on the depth camera and in 2D on the projector and thermal camera, respectively. There are ways to automatically find correspondences between a projector and a calibration target (see e.g. [10]). However, since the thermal camera requires separate solution anyway, we chose to use a manual method for the projector: we manually move graphics projected by the projector to align it with a target visible to the depth camera, see Fig. 1(c).

The target we use consists of a soaked paper sheet, placed on top of a plastic surface for stability. The paper cools due to evaporation and a hole in the surface can be detected by both the depth camera and the thermal camera, while it is also easy to align a projected pattern to it.

The manually collected correspondences are then used in OpenCV's calibrateCamera function to find the intrinsics and extrinsics of the projector and the thermal camera, respectively, relative to the 3D space defined by the depth camera.

4   Colour Scheme

The primary purpose of the prototype presented here is to visualize thermal processes occuring near room temperature. So, the most important feature is to visualize where the temperature diverges from ambient room temperature. For this purpose we have specially designed a colour scale that represents room temperature as black, so that the projector leaves those objects unaugmented.

To obtain high colour contrasts while allowing for a high dynamic range, we have selected four colours to represent temperatures 10°C below, 5°C below, 5°C above and 10°C above room temperature, respectively, see Fig. 2. This temperature range covers educational thermal experiments that we have conducted to date [7].

The FLIR E4 uses a dynamic scale. To realize this colour scale, the video feed data have to be converted. First, the camera is set to display a gray scale representation of the thermal data. The video feed contains a numeric scale showing the range of the data, which we read off using OCR. Every gray scale thermal pixel, $t_{i,j}$ in the range 0–255, can then be converted to its corresponding absolute temperature value, $T_{i,j}$, by

$$T_{i,j} = \frac{t_{i,j}}{255}\left(T_{\max} - T_{\min}\right) + T_{\min} \tag{1}$$

where $T_{\min}$ and $T_{\max}$ are the minimum and maximum temperature in the scale, respectively. It is then straightforward to apply the colour scale described above.

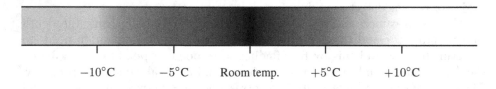

Fig. 2. Our colour scale designed for projector-based augmentation with thermal data. The scale is centered on room temperature, which is rendered black, and ranges from 10°C below to 10°C above room temparature, respectively, through cyan-blue-black-red-white. This means that the projector only augments objects that are affected by heat transfer outside of room temperature. (Color figure online)

5 Software Implementation

The software that generates the projector output is implemented with Open-SceneGraph (OSG), a high performance, OpenGL-based scenegraph library. It uses two main components encoded into scenegraph nodes: the DepthMesh node, providing a 3D mesh that leads to correct projection mapping, and the Thermal-Texture node, which maps the thermal imaging onto that mesh as a texture. The software also applies special lighting effects to remove artifacts, which is discussed further in Sect. 6.

5.1 The ThermalTexture Node

The ThermalTexture node reads off the video feed from the thermal camera, applies the colour scale described above and encodes the image as an OSG texture. The FLIR E4 communicates via USB as a UVC device where we use OpenCV to capture for cross platform support. The temperature scale, needed for the colour scale as described above, is extracted from the video feed using the Tesseract OCR library.

5.2 The DepthMesh Node

Our DepthMesh node uses libfreenect2 [3] to read off depth data from the Kinect camera, for cross platform support. Each pixel, (i, j) with depth $d_{i,j}$, in the depth image is then mapped to a 3D position, p, through

$$p_x = d_{i,j} \frac{i - W/2}{f_x} \tag{2}$$

$$p_y = d_{i,j} \frac{j - H/2}{f_y} \tag{3}$$

$$p_z = -d_{i,j} \tag{4}$$

where W and H are the image width and height, respectively, and f_x and f_y are the camera's focal length in pixels in x and y, respectively, taken from the camera intrinsics obtained in the calibration step described above. For each square of four pixels, if at least three of them contain valid depth data, then this square can be triangulated into a patch. When all sets of 2×2 pixels have been triangulated, we have a mesh representing the depth data from the camera, which is encoded as a OSG geometry.

It is possible to use hole filling algorithms to compensate for missing data from the depth camera. However, our experience with the current system is that incorrect data, which cannot be corrected this way, is more common than missing data.

The ThermalTexture, described above, is applied to colour the DepthMesh geometry. The correct texture coordinates, (u, v), for the thermal data on the mesh, are calculated using the thermal camera's intrincis and extrinsic matrices,

$$w \begin{pmatrix} u \\ v \\ 1 \end{pmatrix} = M_{\text{intr}}\, M_{\text{extr}} \begin{pmatrix} p_x \\ p_y \\ p_z \\ 1 \end{pmatrix} \tag{5}$$

where M_{extr} is the 4×4 camera extrinsics matrix and M_{intr} is the 3×4 camera intrinsics matrix.

6 Shadows in the System

Any 3D object placed in the system will cast shadows. The most intuitive shadow is that appearing behind the object from the projector's point of view, because of the occlusion of the projector light. However, the two cameras will also generate shadows. First, the depth camera cannot see behind a solid object and there will therefore be a "shadow", actually a hole in the 3D mesh, behind the object from the depth camera's point of view.

Second, the thermal camera cannot detect thermal data behind non-transparent objects. However, the texture coordinates that map the thermal data onto the mesh are directly calculated from the 3D position of the mesh and therefore do not take this into account. Thus, the thermal data of an object is cast onto background surfaces as a *ghost image* of that object. This projection does not represent the thermal signature of that surface and needs to be digitally removed.

Fortunately, the OpenSceneGraph library used for the software has support for real-time shadow rendering. We deploy the ShadowMap functionality, which implements the shadow map algorithm, to cast shadows configured as black.

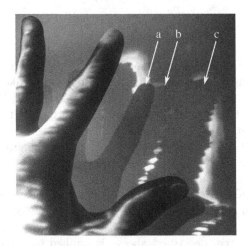

Fig. 3. The three shadows cast behind an object in our display system, from the point of view of (a) the projector, (b) the depth camera and (c) the thermal camera.

This algorithm supports self-shadowing, which is necessary since it is the part of the mesh that represents the object in front of the camera that should cast shadows onto another part of the same mesh. The result is black shadows behind objects with respect to the thermal camera, which removes most of the ghost image that was otherwise fully visible, see Fig. 3. The shadow and ghost image will never match perfectly due to discretization and also, in particular, due to the low resolution of the thermal camera.

7   Results

This work has resulted in a thermal Spatial Augmented Reality display system that superimposes thermal information onto objects, using a colour scheme that focusses on visualizing heat phenomena near room temperature range. Objects placed on the table or held above are augmented only on surfaces facing all imaging devices and within all their respective fields of view. This is not a large volume, partly because of the placement of the thermal camera, but is still sufficient for exploration and basic experimentation, see Fig. 4.

Non-reflective, non-transparent objects work best with both the thermal camera and the depth camera. All resonably bright objects adequately reflect the colours displayed by the projector, but white or bright gray objects are augmented more accurately, since this system does not apply any surface colour compensation [2].

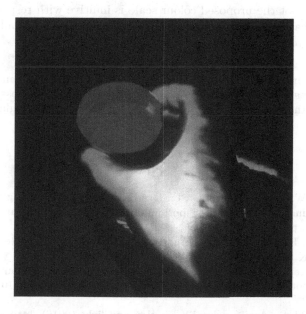

Fig. 4. The AR system projecting real-time thermal data onto a hand holding a cup of water. Warmer areas on the surface of the hand are displayed in red and white, relative to the cooler water surface in blue. The surroundings are at room temperature (black). (Color figure online)

The projector produces hot air and early experiments indicate that it is important that the air stream is directed away from the rig to avoid it heating the table surface.

Our preliminary observations indicate that the AR system allows for real-time visualization of various heat phenomena. For example, we have used the system to conduct tasks envisioned for public (e.g. science center) and formal (e.g. school) science learning contexts. These include the thermal visualization of the surface of one's hand, heat transfer from one's palm to the wooden table surface, liquid water at different temperatures (and the subsequent mixing thereof), latent heat of evaporation, and rubbing an eraser across a rough surface.

8   Conclusions and Future Work

We conclude that the presented hardware combination—Kinect depth camera, FLIR E4 thermal camera and Epson EB-1940W projector—used with the described software constellation results in thermal data intuitively presented on the objects in the Spatial Augmented Reality system. The proposed colour scale effectively highlights objects or regions with temperatures that diverge from room temperature. Multiple experiments can be carried out to demonstrate the educational implications of the system for visualizing thermal concepts. Future work will explore the role of the AR system in communication, learning and teaching in this regard.

Whether or not the proposed colour scale is inuitive with respect to what is warmer and what is cooler is yet to be formally examined and shall constitute a forthcoming perception study.

Acknowledgments. We thank Anna-Karin Lindblom, Product Manager at FLIR Systems AB, for supporting this work. We also thank Dr. Fredrik Jeppsson, Linköping University, for the loan of a FLIR E4 camera, and Dr. Jesper Haglund for useful discussions.

References

1. Benko, H., Wilson, A.D., Zannier, F.: Dyadic projected spatial augmented reality. In: Proceedings of The ACM Symposium on User Interface Software and Technology (UIST), pp. 645–655 (2014)
2. Bimber, O., Raskar, R.: Spatial Augmented Reality - Merging Real and Virtual Worlds. A K Peters/CRC Press, Wellesley (2005)
3. Blake, J., Kerl, C., Echtler, F., Xiang, L.: libfreenect2: Open-source library for kinect v2 depth camera. Zenodo, January 2016. http://dx.doi.org/10.5281/zenodo.45314
4. Gladyszewski, S.: Argile et lumière — clay and light (2016). https://vimeo.com/152905116
5. Gladyszewski, S., Burton, A., Ricard, J., Grenier, É.: Live thermal video projection system (2013). https://vimeo.com/60292952. accessed 12 Feb 2016

6. Haglund, J., Jeppsson, F., Hedberg, D., Schönborn, K.J.: Students framing of laboratory exercises using infrared cameras. Phys. Rev. ST Phys. Educ. Res. **11**(2) (2015)
7. Haglund, J., Jeppsson, F., Melander, E., Pendrill, A.M., Xie, C., Schönborn, K.J.: Infrared cameras in science education. Infrared Phys. Technol. **75**, 150–152 (2016)
8. Johnson-Glenberg, M.C., Birchfield, D.A., Tolentino, L., Koziupa, T.: Collaborative embodied learning in mixed reality motion-capture environments: Two science studies. J. Educ. Psychol. **106**, 86–104 (2014)
9. Kawamoto, K.: Thermaltable, December 2014. http://kenkawamoto-works.tumblr.com/post/106298696083/thermaltable-2014-dec-link-using-flir-one-an
10. Lee, J., Dietz, P.H., Maynes-Aminzade, D., Raskar, R., Hudson, S.: Automatic projector calibration with embedded light sensors. In: Proceedings of the ACM Symposium on User Interface Software and Technology (UIST), October 2004
11. Raskar, R., Welch, G., Fuchs, H.: Spatial augmented reality. In: Proceedings of the IEEE International Workshop on Augmented Reality (1998)
12. Vollmer, M., Möllmann, K.P., Pinno, F., Karstädt, D.: There is more to see than eyes can detect – visualization of energy transfer processes and the laws of radiation for physics education. Phys. Teach. **39**(6), 371–376 (2001)
13. Wu, H.K., Lee, S.W.Y., Chang, H.Y., Liang, J.C.: Current status, opportunities and challenges of augmented reality in education. Comput. Educ. **62**, 41–49 (2013)
14. Xie, C., Hazzard, E.: Infrared imaging for inquiry-based learning. Phys. Teach. **49**(6), 368–372 (2011)

An Efficient Geometric Approach for Occlusion Handling in Outdoors Augmented Reality Applications

Vlasios Kasapakis[1,2], Damianos Gavalas[1,2(✉)],
and Panagiotis Galatis[3]

[1] Department of Cultural Technology and Communication,
University of the Aegean, Mytilene, Greece
{v.kasapakis, dgavalas}@aegean.gr
[2] Computer Technology Institute and Press 'Diophantus' (CTI), Patras, Greece
[3] School of Science and Technology, Hellenic Open University, Patras, Greece
galatisp@gmail.com

Abstract. Mobile location-based AR frameworks typically project information about real or virtual locations in the vicinity of the user. Those locations are treated indiscriminately, regardless of whether they are actually within the field of view (FoV) of the user or not. However, displaying occluded objects often misleads users' perception thereby compromising the clarity and explicitness of AR applications. This paper introduces an efficient geometric technique aiming at assisting developers of outdoors mobile AR applications in generating a realistic FoV for the users. Our technique enables real time building recognition in order to address the occlusion of physical or virtual objects by physical artifacts. Our method is demonstrated in the location-based AR game *Order Elimination*. The latter utilizes publicly available building information to calculate the players' FoV in real-time. Extensive performance tests provide sufficient evidence that real-time FoV rendering is feasible by modest mobile devices, even under stress operation conditions. A user evaluation study reveals that the consideration of buildings for determining FoV in mobile AR games can increase the quality of experience perceived by players when compared with standard FoV generation methods.

Keywords: Augmented reality · Mobile games · Occlusion · Field of view · Line of sight · Raycasting · OSM · Performance analysis · User evaluation

1 Introduction

Outdoors mobile augmented reality (AR) applications require only a limited amount of the user's field of view (FoV) to be superimposed with computer-generated graphics, while rest of the user's view perceives the physical world [1]. Viewing the physical world augmented by digital information provides the user with a better sense of her location and surroundings, thus improving her overall perception. Outdoors mobile (location-based) games often involve virtual characters hiding from (or chasing) the user. When playing in urban settings, though, surrounding buildings are highly likely to

© Springer International Publishing Switzerland 2016
L.T. De Paolis and A. Mongelli (Eds.): AVR 2016, Part I, LNCS 9768, pp. 418–434, 2016.
DOI: 10.1007/978-3-319-40621-3_30

occlude a virtual character. In cases that occlusion is not appropriately handled (e.g., when all virtual characters are visualized identically, regardless of whether they are actually within the players' FoV or not), the depth judgment of players is compromised, thereby resulting in misconceptions and wrong pursuance of tasks amongst users [2].

The occlusion problem has received considerable attention in the field of AR research. The approaches proposed for handling the occlusion problem in AR are mainly classified into two types [3]: model-based and depth-based approaches. Model-based methods require the accurate (offline) 3D modeling of the real environment's objects [4], hence, limiting their portability. Depth-based methods rely on some sort of image processing (e.g. stereo matching) to acquire depth information of real objects, which is computationally expensive, hence, not applicable to real-time applications [5, 6]. Recently, several studies have investigated a number of visual metaphors to convey the depth (i.e. the positioning) of the graphical entities relative to the real objects, considering handheld AR in outdoors environments [7].

The occlusion problem has only be addressed in indoors AR games with most prototypes relying on the Microsoft Kinect sensor to receive depth cues [8]. To the best of our knowledge, none of the existing outdoors AR games sufficiently addresses the occlusion problem. In those games, players are typically allowed to interact with virtual objects provided that their in-between distance is below a certain threshold [9, 10]; some prototypes also require players to point their device towards the targeted virtual object in order to enable interaction [11–13].

In classic video games, the visibility of virtual objects is estimated utilizing the *raycasting* technique. Raycasting refers to the act of casting imaginary light beams (rays) from a source location (typically the point of view of the character or object controlled by the player) and recording the objects hit by the rays [14]. Herein, we extend this idea in mobile gaming wherein, unlike video games, the game space is not pre-registered and occlusion is typically due to surrounding buildings. Our focus is on methods for determining LoS (Line of Sight) and FoV, which satisfy critical requirements of mobile games: real-time performance; anytime/anywhere game play; suitability for execution on average mobile equipment; support of popular map platforms.

Along this line, we introduce a *geolocative raycasting* method which allows mobile game developers to detect buildings (or custom-generated obstacles) in location-based and AR game environments, thereby reliably resolving the object occlusion issue. Our method receives inspiration from the raycasting technique utilized in video games to detect objects hit by bullets. Similarly to the standard raycasting technique, our method involves casting a sequence of rays (consecutive rays are separated by a specific angle). However, it does not progressively generate virtual locations (ray steps) along the ray until a ray step 'hits' a (building) polygon. Instead, it employs an efficient geometric technique to calculate the intersection of the ray segments with the building polygons. Note that, through casting a number of rays covering a specific angle (e.g. 15 rays separated by a 2° angle cover an overall angle of 28°) this technique may calculate the device's FoV, namely the 2D polygon which approximates the player's sight.

The performance of our method has been thoroughly evaluated under realistic game play conditions. Building-related data are yield from open map data repositories. Hence, our raycasting technique suggests a portable scheme which may be incorporated in any outdoors AR application and be utilized at any urban setting, provided that sufficient topographical data exist. As a case-study, we have prototyped the proposed geolocative raycasting technique in the context of *Order Elimination*, an outdoors AR game.

Note that our work is regarded as complementary to research dealing with occlusion detection in AR applications. Most existing works enable the user to see virtual representations of physical objects whose positions are occluded in real scenes. Rather, we tackle the problem of detecting the occlusion of virtual objects hidden by physical obstacles (mainly buildings). We also take into account the mobility of both the players and the virtual characters which makes occlusion management harder as it poses real-time execution requirements. Furthermore, our approach determines the FoV of handheld devices, which is regarded as a more generic problem than occlusion handling and may be applicable to several AR applications, other than gaming. Nevertheless, our method is also suitable to estimate the LoS, i.e. whether the virtual character is along the device's exact direction and not occluded by any building. The determination of LoS would be crucial in 'first-person shooter[1] -like mobile games where the player would have to point his device directly towards a virtual character to enable interaction.

The remainder of this article is structured as follows: Sect. 2 presents previous research related to our work. Section 3 describes the game mechanics of Order Elimination. Section 4 introduces our geolocative raycasting algorithm. Section 5 reports the results of the performance tests conducted upon the proposed FoV determination method. Section 6 presents the evaluation results of a game incorporating geolocative raycasting as well as alternative FoV determination techniques. Finally, Sect. 7 concludes our work.

2   Related Work

Notably, most existing mobile games utilizing maps to visualize the game space neglect the LoS/FoV issue and enable the interaction of the player with in-game entities by solely considering their in-between straight line distance [9, 10, 15]. A number of mobile games have been developed in the past utilizing AR to visualize and allow interaction with in-game objects registered to geographical coordinates. For instance, in Epidemic Menace II [12] players used a HMD to view 3D models of virtual viruses according to their location. The interaction of players with a virus has been solely based on their in-between distance and the device's orientation, without checking the LoS condition. TimeWarp [16] adopted a similar principle utilizing a mobile PDA AR system to augment the real environment with projected virtual robots. The evaluation trials of TimeWarp revealed the need to address the occlusion of virtual objects (e.g. to hide a virtual robot when a building interleaves among the robot and the player).

To the best of our knowledge, ManHunt [13] is the only mobile game addressing the occlusion problem between players and in-game entities. In ManHunt the player

---

[1] The term 'first-person shooter' refers to a video game genre centered on gun and projectile weapon-based combat through a first-person perspective; that is, the player experiences the action through the eyes of the protagonist.

acts as a Knight who has to run after and kill a runaway (virtual) Pirate before the latter reaches an escape point. ManHunt utilizes Google Maps to display the location of the player (Knight) and the Pirate. The Knight needs to approach the Pirate in distance less than 60 m and shoot him, by tapping a 'cannon' button, provided that he is in LoS with him.

In order to check the LoS condition, the ManHunt game engine requests walking directions (from the Knight's to the Pirate's location) from the Google Directions API. It is assumed that no LoS exists if there is a 'turn' direction in the Google Directions API JSON route response (i.e. it is assumed that a building lies in between). The above described technique may be a useful instrument in a variety of outdoors location-based games. However, it fails to detect situations wherein LoS exists even if a 'turn' is in between two locations (e.g. when a park or a parking lot lies in the corner). This is illustrated in the example scenarios of Fig. 1, wherein the gray line denotes the route followed by the Pirate, while the black dashed line denotes the route recommended by the Google Directions API, which is invoked when the player attempts to shoot the Pirate. While in the first two cases the game engine correctly determines the visibility among the player and the Pirate, in the third case it erroneously assumes lack of LoS although the park lying in between the player and the Pirate ensures FoV clearance.

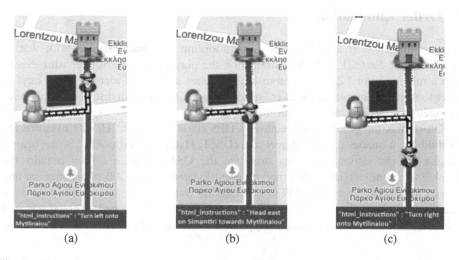

(a)   (b)   (c)

Fig. 1. Screenshots taken from the ManHunt mobile application: (a) The player is not in LoS with the Pirate (a building blocks the player's FoV); (b) the player is in LoS with the Pirate; (c) the player is in LoS with the Pirate although they are not on the same road (a park lies in between clearing the player's FoV).

The requirement to function anytime/anywhere becomes increasingly common among mobile game prototypes [10, 11, 13, 17]. This trend highlights the need for a LoS/FoV determination technique suitable for diverse outdoors locations (e.g. city streets or parks) and different time periods (e.g. during daytime or nighttime), namely under various lighting conditions. Typically, LoS/FoV determination methods should satisfy strict real-time requirements even when executed in resource-constrained mobile devices. Additionally, recent advances in mobile gaming should be carefully taken into consideration: smartphones have become the most favorable platform for mobile games development; interactive maps are widely used to visualize the game space; AR glasses are expected to have profound impact in gaming in the near future [17]. Therefore, any LoS/FoV determination method addressed to mobile games should appropriately address the above listed trends.

To the best of our knowledge existing FoV calculation and occlusion handling techniques fail to address the above discussed requirements either featuring short FoV distance [18]; lacking support for smartphones [19]; being only applicable to indoors environments [20]; being sensitive to environmental light to perform accurate FoV determination (often using cameras), thereby failing to function during nighttime [21]; exhibiting poor performance to be considered as real-time FoV rendering options [22]. Notably, several relevant commercial products have been released recently, like Arduino Ping[2], Project Tango[3] and Structure Sensor[4], which may be easily integrated with smartphones and utilized for FoV determination. Nevertheless, those products feature short FoV determination distance (maximum 4 m); thus, they would not be applicable to outdoors mobile games.

3   Order Elimination

Order elimination[5] is a mobile AR game adopting a scenario similar with that of ManHunt (see Sect. 2). In Order Elimination the player acts as a Soldier who tries to stop a running virtual Zombie, before it approaches a group of victims in the city. In order to stop the Zombie, the Soldier has to approach it in a 50 m distance and shoot it, provided that the Zombie is within the player's FoV.

On startup, the game engine requires a GPS fix of the player. Having obtained the location fix, it queries the OpenStreetMap (OSM) Overpass Turbo API[6], wherefrom it obtains the surrounding buildings stored in the OSM database[7]. Then it pairs the Zombie's current location with a random point located at least 300 m distance far and queries the Google Directions API to generate the walking route to be followed by the Zombie. The directions' turning points (contained in the Google Directions API response) are utilized to construct a waypoint line and animate the Zombie's marker on

---

[2] https://store.arduino.cc/product/SEN136B5B.

[3] https://www.google.com/atap/project-tango/.

[4] http://structure.io.

[5] A commercial version of *Order Elimination* is available in Google Play (https://play.google.com/store/apps/details?id=bl.on.mi.en).

[6] http://overpass-turbo.eu/.

[7] The OSM Overpass API provides textual description of buildings in a certain area, essentially a list of polygons, each comprising a series of latitude/longitude points.

the map interface, visualizing a smooth movement along their routes (see the dashed line in Fig. 2). Except from map visualization, Order Elimination utilizes the Beyon-dAR framework[8] to generate an AR view of the Zombie. The main contribution of this work is the replicable method used by the system to determine whether the Zombie lies within the player's FoV. The FoV of the player is determined utilizing a form of geolocative raycasting, based on the algorithmic technique presented in Sect. 4.

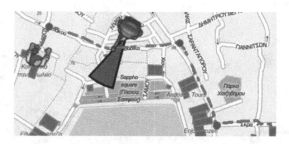

Fig. 2. Visualization of the Zombie's route (obtained from the Google Directions API). The red line represents the Zombie's route while blue dots represent the intermediate turning points along the route. (Color figure online)

4 FoV Determination Algorithm

This section introduces our novel FoV determination algorithm, titled *Ray-Polygon Intersection* (RPI). It is noted that, in addition to the device's exact location, RPI requires the calculation of the device's orientation (bearing[9]) based on measurements taken from the accelerometer and magnetometer sensors of the device. Thereafter, the bearing is set as the center of the player's FoV. The precise estimation of the player's FoV (i.e. the exact 2D polygon which delimits the player's sight) may then be undertaken by the approach discussed in the sequel.

Our FoV determination approach employs an efficient, geometric ray intersection method. Initially, building polygons are deconstructed to pairs of vertices, each referring to a polygon side (line segment). We then generate a sequence of ray segments (consecutive rays are $angle_s$ degrees far from each other) from the leftmost to the rightmost FoV's angle ($angle_l$ and $angle_r$, respectively) considering the current bearing of the device as the bisector of the FoV's angle. The edges of each ray segment are set to the device's location and the ray's endmost point being d_{max} far (maximum FoV distance). To determine FoV we then calculate the intersection points among each ray segment and the building polygon side lines. For each ray segment, the intersection point which is nearest to the device is regarded as the furthest FoV point along this particular ray.

---

[8] http://www.beyondar.com/.

[9] Bearing refers to the angle of a moving object's direction from the North.

Figure 3 demonstrates our method through a simplified scenario which involves five rays and a building polygon. The green circles denote the endmost points of the five ray segments while the red circles denote the intersection points of the rays with the building polygon sides. The yellow-shadowed area (ABCDEF) represents the estimated FoV polygon. Note that the accuracy of FoV estimation depends on the density of rays (i.e. their in-between angle). For instance, the triangle CC_1C_2 is erroneously considered to be within the player's FoV (the triangle's area would be smaller if rays were denser).

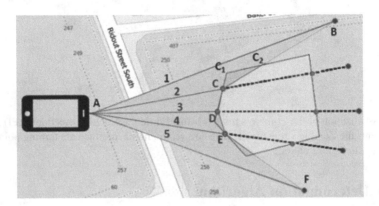

Fig. 3. FoV determination utilizing the ray intersection approach. (Color figure online)

A pseudocode implementation of the RPI algorithm is presented in Algorithm 1. The computational complexity of the RPI algorithm is $O(r \cdot p)$, where r denotes the number of rays covering the FoV (depends on the overall FoV angle and the incremental step for the FoV angle) and p denotes the number of buildings considered in the raycasting process (depends on the maximum ray length and the buildings' density).

Algorithm 1 (Ray-Polygon Intersection)

1.	initialize $angle_l$, $angle_r$ // The left and right angles (edges) of FoV (in degrees)
2.	initialize $angle_s$ // The incremental steps for the FoV angle
3.	initialize d_{max} // The maximum FoV distance (ray length)
4.	$\vartheta = angle_l$ // Current FoV angle
5.	measure *azimuth* // Measured by the device's magnetometer sensor (in degrees)
6.	measure *lat, lon* // User (i.e. device) geo-coordinates measured by the device's GPS receiver
7.	initialize P /* Polygons (buildings) extracted from OSM data whose centroid is within a specified radius from the user (in ascending order of distance between the polygon's centroid and the user's location) */
8.	initialize *FoV* // The FoV polygon (initially empty)

```
9.        while ϑ < angle_r do
10.           bearing = azimuth + angle
11.           lat_r = asin(sin(lat)*cos(d_max) + cos(lat)*sin(d_max)*cos(bearing))  /* Latitude of the ray's
                                                                              endmost point */
12.           a = atan2(sin(bearing)*sin(d_max)*cos(lat), cos(d_max)-sin(lat)*sin(lat_r))
13.           lon_r = ((lon + a + 3π) % 2π) - π   // The longitude of the ray's endmost point
14.           for each b ∈ P  // iterate through polygons (buildings)
                     {lat_int, lon_int}=nearest_intersection (lat, lon, lat_r, lon_r, b)  /* Returns the
15.                       intersection point among b and the ray segment nearest to {lat, lon}, if
                          exists; returns {lat_r, lon_r} otherwise. */
16.                   FoV = FoV ∪ {(({lat_int, lon_int})}  /* insert the vertex (intersection point or ray's
                                                          endmost point) into the FoV polygon */
17.                   if ! (({lat_int, lon_int} ≡ {lat_r, lon_r})  /* The ray has been blocked (do not consider
                          remainder buildings) */
18.                      break
19.                   end if
20.           end for
21.           ϑ = ϑ + angle_s
22.        end while
```

In Order Elimination, the intersection points among blocked rays and their nearest polygons (or the endmost points of the non-blocked ray segments) are saved in a vector; upon the completion of the raycasting process, those points are utilized to draw a polygon on the OSM map, providing a visual representation of the player's FoV. Finally, utilizing the Google Maps Android API library, the game engine easily inspects whether the Zombie marker lies inside the FoV's polygon, thus determining whether the Zombie is within the Soldier's sight. If this condition holds, both the Zombie's AR and map markers turn red, allowing the players to shoot the Zombie so as to win and end the game[10]. In Fig. 4a, a nearby building only partially occludes the player's FoV (the Zombie is viewed via the in-between road segment). In Fig. 4b, though, the Zombie is occluded by a nearby building, therefore, the player is not allowed to shoot.

5 Performance Tests

FoV determination is subject to real time constraints in most outdoors mobile games as the time required to render the simulated FoV considerably affects the overall quality of experience perceived by players. The real time execution requirement also derives from the dynamics of such applications, considering the mobility patterns of both the players and the virtual characters; namely, implemented FoV determination methods are expected to execute fast enough to update FoV upon any change of the player's or virtual character's location and/or the player's orientation.

---

[10] As reported in the *TimeWarp* evaluation results, the virtual artifacts in AR games should be preferably hidden when the player has no LoS with them. Even though we could effortlessly hide the AR content when eye contact with the *Zombie* was infeasible, we chose not to for game design purposes.

(a)   (b)

Fig. 4. (a) Zombie lying within the player's FoV; (b) Zombie lying out of the player's FoV. The AR view of the Zombie is generated by the BeyondAR framework.

This section reports the results of performance tests executed on Order Elimination in order to assess the impact of various performance parameters under realistic game play conditions. In order to better evaluate the performance if our RPI method, we compare it against that of an alternative raycasting (RC) method. The implemented RC approach is analogous to the raycasting method using in classic video games. In particular, it progressively generates virtual locations along a straight line (each virtual location is at distance d_s far from the previous one, along a ray of d_{max} length) towards the player's facing direction. When one of the ray steps (i.e. virtual location) is found to lie inside a polygon (building) of the surrounding buildings' list, it is inferred that the ray has been blocked by a building, hence, further ray steps along that line are unnecessary. Therefore, it becomes evident that RC method is less accurate than the RPI method with respect to the estimation of the 'collission' points: in the RPI technique, intersection points are precisely determined through a simple geometric calculation (see points C, D, E in Fig. 3), while in the RC approach accuracy depends on the distance among the consecutive ray steps. The RC method has been implemented and also incorporated in Order Elimination in order to serve as a baseline for evaluating the performance of our RPI algorithm.

Experimental Setup. Both the implemented FoV determination methods involve some sort of preprocessing of the OSM building data which are then stored in a memory structure. Upon the startup of Order Elimination, data (vertices of building polygons) are yield by the Overpass Turbo API and utilized to generate a list of polygons, then overlaid on the OSM map interface. We apply a distance threshold to filter out polygons whose centroid is located further than a specified distance threshold from the player's location. Nearby buildings are re-calculated upon every change on the player's position. The application of a distance threshold slightly longer (~ 20 m) than the ray length ensures that: (a) the corners of buildings whose centroids are slightly further from the ray's reach are also detected, (b) the list of polygons do not need to be updated upon minor displacement of the player or the virtual character.

The test game space has been set in the center of Brussels (Belgium), as the OSM database contains a large number of registered buildings in that area. The game space has been a square with side length of 500 m, and the ray step (in the RC method) has been set to 3.8 m to minimize the possibility of missing even small buildings. The angle step (among successive rays) has been set to 1° to enable highly accurate building detection. The player's location has been switched every 2 s between 2 fixed locations. Upon each relocation the list of nearby buildings is updated (the overall number of buildings considered during the tests have been 1000).

The duration of all testing sessions has been 60 s; the device has been constantly rotated throughout each testing session (12 degrees/s, namely 2 full rotations/session). We have conducted performance tests for both the RPI and RC approaches evaluating the effect of several performance variables, such as the ray length, the overall FoV angle and the number of buildings. The figures reported below represent the average among ten (10) performance test measurements. All performance tests have been executed using a middle-range Android device (Samsung S3 Neo, 4 core 1400 MHz CPU, 1.5 GB RAM).

Performance Tests on LoS Estimation. Our first experiment involved the performance analysis of LoS estimation for the RPI and RC approaches. On this test we casted a single ray along the device's bearing, aiming to determine whether the moving Zombie has been hit by this ray. The test involved 1000 buildings and 100 m ray length, where the ray has not been occluded by any building. We measured average performance of 18.1 and 4.4 ms for the RC and RPI methods, respectively (these only refer to the time required to determine LoS without taking into account the time needed to perform the processing of building data). The above reported measurements indicate a clear performance advantage of the RPI method.

Performance Tests on FoV Determination. The remainder experiments focused on FoV determination. The first testing session evaluates the impact of the ray length on the measured performance. We conducted tests with the ray length spanning from 20 m to 100 m. Note that the maximum distance allowed to enable interaction in previous mobile game studies has been 50 m [10–13], hence, the 100 m maximum distance used in our tests far exceeds this requirement. The FoV angle has been set to 28° (see Fig. 5a) and 45° (see Fig. 5b); this has been decided not only to provide sufficient FoV for in-game use but also to meet the visual field specifications of popular AR glasses[11] and AR frameworks[12], respectively. Our reported results refer to the average execution time required to complete the whole FoV determination process employing the two evaluated methods.

---

[11] Vuzix M100 Smart Glasses (https://www.vuzix.com/Products/M100-Smart-Glasses) supports a FoV angle of 15°, while Epson Moverio BT-200 (http://global.epson.com/newsroom/2014/news_20140107.html) supports 28°. Both products fully support smartphone integration.

[12] The Android Augment Reality Framework (https://github.com/phishman3579/android-augment-reality-framework) and Mixare (http://www.mixare.org/) support a FoV angle of 45°.

RC outperforms the RPI approach when considering ray lengths below 40 m as on those cases the ray points inspected in the RC method are still few. However, when the ray length becomes longer than 40 m, the RPI approach performs better. As expected, the execution time increases with the ray length: the evaluated methods consider a larger number of buildings in the FoV calculation while the RC method undertakes a larger number of ray steps. However, the RPI method scales remarkably well. Interestingly, the expansion of the FoV angle (from 28° to 45°) does not much affect the average execution time, thus indicating the domination of the building's processing time which is independent of the FoV angle. Note that the measured performance of RPI comfortably meets the requirements of real-time game applications (e.g. $\sim$ 5 FoV calculations/s for FoV angle of 28° and ray length of 100 m). On the other hand, the RC approach can be safely applied to game scenarios where the maximum interaction distance between a player and an in-game entity is below 50 m.

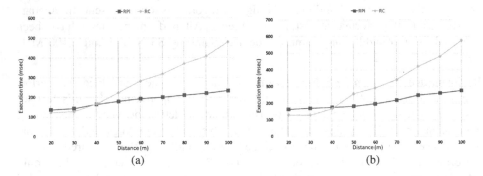

Fig. 5. Performance of the evaluated FoV techniques as to the ray length for FoV angle set to (a) 28°; (b) 45°.

Another critical factor of FoV determination is the overall FoV angle. Wide viewing angles are definitely desirable, however they require more rays to cover the respective visual spectrum, hence, more computational cycles. In order to assess the impact of FoV angle on the overall performance we have conducted two tests, setting the ray length to 50 m and 100 m, accordingly. In both tests the FoV angle ranges from 5° up to 45°. This allows testing the proposed FoV determination techniques for diverse game scenarios. For instance, the 5° angle would suit games that involve shooting a bullet or casting a spell towards an enemy, wherein targeting must be fairly accurate (traditionally, classic video games utilize a single ray to confirm accurate targeting)[13]. On the other hand, wider FoV angles would suit games which should inform players that a virtual or physical object is 'within sight' along the player's moving direction.

---

[13] The intuition for choosing the 5° angle has been, firstly, to create a sufficient FoV polygon for the Zombie to be included in and, secondly, to allow sufficiently wide FoV (than that of a single ray) so as to compensate for GPS location fix inaccuracies, which do not allow precise positioning calculations as in computer games.

Out tests involved several FoV angles spanning from 5° to 45° (see Fig. 6). The results verify the prevalence of RPI against RC. Both methods scale well as the increased FoV angle only determines the number of rays casted and does not affect the number of buildings processed. Note that the effect of the ray length (i.e. the extension of the ray length from 50 m to 100 m as shown in Fig. 6a and b, respectively) is marginal in both the evaluated approaches. In RC, this is because the -longer- rays typically hit a nearby building in their first steps (hence, the next steps are not examined). In the RPI method, the added computational overhead for checking the intersection of each ray with a larger number of buildings is very little. The test results demonstrate that the RPI technique can be safely incorporated in AR frameworks (i.e. with 45° FoV angle) and meets the requirements of real-time applications.

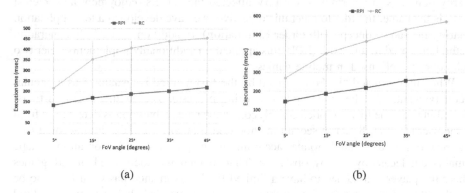

(a)   (b)

Fig. 6. Performance of the evaluated FoV techniques as to the FoV angle for ray length set to (a) 50 m; (b) 100 m.

On our last set of experiments we study the extent to which the number of buildings around the player affects the performance of the examined FoV determination approaches. We tested various building set scales (varying from 200 to 800 buildings) with ray length of 100 m and FoV angle of 28°. Obviously, bigger building density scales decrease the average performance of RC and RPI (see Fig. 7) as a larger number

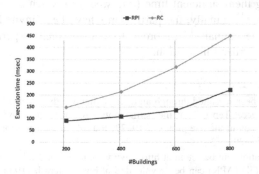

Fig. 7. Performance of the evaluated FoV techniques as to the number of surrounding buildings for ray length of 100 m and FoV angle of 28°.

of buildings is examined to determine potential collision events. This effect is more noticeable in the RC algorithm which examines all buildings on every ray step. Certainly, when considering larger number of buildings, the ray steps in RC are typically interrupted early as they are more likely to hit a nearby building. Nevertheless, the RC performance deteriorates as the processing of building data (undertaken every 2 s in our tests) dominates the overall execution time.

6 Evaluation

The FoV generation technique presented in this article has been evaluated by 12 players[14]. Our emphasis has been to investigate the extent to which the consideration of nearby buildings in determining the FoV affected the players' enjoyment and interest towards the game. In order to meet this objective, we have developed a test application (sharing the same concept with Order Elimination). In addition to the FoV generation method proposed in this work (RPI), this application additionally implements other two techniques widely used in mobile games.

When unobstructed, the FoV derived by the first method is visualized as a circular sector (generated by the multi-angle raycasting process). The circular sector is transformed in real-time to a complicated polygon shape when a building is detected in front of the user (see Fig. 8a). The second method does not take buildings into account (see Fig. 8b). Hence, the triangle rotates according to the player's orientation and its shape remains unaffected by nearby obstacles. That method is widely used in AR games where the player is assumed to have a limited FoV; this method has been found to be mostly affected by the occlusion problem in past studies [11–13]. The third method involves a circle denoting the area where the Zombie should lie in order to allow the player shooting it (see Fig. 8c). The latter method is also commonly employed in mobile games where the distance circle might be visible (like in Ingress [10]) or invisible (like in CYSMN? [9]); that method aims at determining players' proximity with important in-game entities (like enemies), where the player is only required to approach them in order to interact with them, disregarding the player's direction [13].

In order to evaluate the usability and quality of experience aspects of Order Elimination, the test application presented above has been handed to the evaluation trial participants, allowing them sufficient time (one week) to watch an introductory video and test the application[15]. Finally, the participants have been invited to fill in anonymously an online questionnaire[16] in order to convey their experience and assess qualitative aspects of Order Elimination.

---

[14] The participants have been recruited through an open invitation advertised in the University of the Aegean, Mytilene, Greece. Ten (10) of the participants have been male and two (2) female. Six (6) participants have been in the age group of 19–23, four (4) in the age group of 24–33 and two (2) in the age group 34–39.

[15] A video of the application can be found at https://www.youtube.com/watch?v=D–A3fEghbA. The Android Application File (APK) can be downloaded at http://zarcrash.x10.mx/OrderEliminationc.apk.

[16] The questionnaire can be found at http://zarcrash.x10.mx/OrderEliminationGoogleForm.pdf.

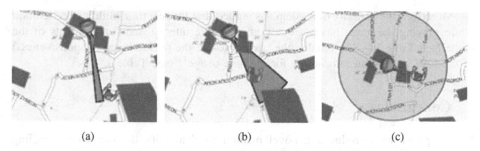

(a)   (b)   (c)

Fig. 8. FoV generation types: (a) geolocative raycasting (the Zombie is 'hidden' behind a building); (b) limited FoV generation method that neglects occlusion due to nearby buildings; (c) interaction with virtual objects enabled when the proximity condition holds.

Firstly, we invited participants to rank (denote their preference among) the three implemented visualization methods. All (12) players denoted preference to the first method (i.e. the one which adapts the FoV according to the detected surrounding buildings). Interestingly, the two other visualization modes tied in the overall ranking list, namely they received the same preference ratio by participants.

Proceeding to the evaluation of FoV aspects, we asked the participants to assess the simulation of a certain FoV versus the use of the distance circle in the context of a mobile game. To a large extent, the players argued that the use of a limited FoV made the game more realistic, interesting and enjoyable (see Table 1 – S1). Moreover the consideration of surrounding buildings in adapting the players' FoV has been positively perceived by the participants as it increased their interest towards the game and their enjoyment while playing due to being more consistent with humans' cognitive perception of the physical environment (see Table 1 – S2).

Table 1. Order elimination evaluation results using a Likert scale: 1–5 (1: Not at all, 5: Very much).

Statement		Median	Average
S1	Having a visual representation of a certain field of view that I should put the Zombie into to shoot has been more interesting than using the distance circle	5	4.5
S2	Taking nearby buildings into account made the game more interesting and fun	5	4.58
S3	The recognition of the buildings in real-time is important for the game to be interesting and fun	5	4.4
S4	The responsiveness of the field of view generation was satisfactory for in-game use	5	4.6

Moreover, the majority of participants argued that the real time building recognition while playing the game has positively affected the interest and fun elements of the game (see Table 1 – S3). Finally, the players found the performance (responsiveness) of the FoV generation satisfactory for in game usage[17] (see Table 1 – S4).

7 Conclusions

In this paper we introduced a novel method to deal with the occlusion handling problem in outdoors AR applications. Our RPI method is able to efficiently generate a realistic FoV (consistent with the device's location and orientation) through the real-time detection of buildings in the vicinity of the player. The generated FoV may be subsequently used to verify whether a single or multiple virtual objects are 'within sight' or occluded by nearby buildings. Our method involves casting of a sequence of rays (covering a specific FoV angle) and accurately estimates the location where each ray hits a nearby (building) polygon utilizing an efficient geometric technique.

The performance of our geolocative raycasting method has been tested in real settings and compared against a baseline approach which is analogous to the raycasting employed in video games (the baseline approach progressively generates virtual locations along consecutive ray segments until a hit is detected). The measured performance (i.e. the execution time required to complete the FoV generation process) has been evaluated with respect to several performance variables (ray length, FoV angle, number of surrounding buildings). We have found evidence that real-time FoV rendering is feasible even by modest mobile devices for ray lengths up to 100 m and FoV up to 45°, under stress conditions (densely built urban areas, constant device rotation). Our test results demonstrated that our RPI method better meets the requirements for real-time performance and anytime/anywhere game play.

The RPI algorithm has been incorporated within Order Elimination, an outdoors AR game. The user evaluation of Order Elimination revealed that the consideration of surrounding buildings may significantly improve the quality of experience perceived by players. The FoV determination method presented in this work is applicable to mobile games in order to resolve the occlusion problem, by hiding virtual objects when not within the player's sight. Similarly, our methods could be useful in a variety of location-based applications (e.g. games, tourist guides, special-purpose navigators, etc.) which need to draw the user's FoV (or adjust the appearance of POI markers) on a map interface, play appropriate audio/video clips and so on.

Acknowledgement. This work has been supported by the CIP-ICT-PSP-2013-2017 Programme under grant agreement no. 621133 (HoPE - "Holistic Personal public Eco-mobility").

---

[17] The application distributed to participants has been configured with the ray length set to 100 m, the FoV angle set to 28° and a game space of 250,000 m^2 (square with side length of 500 m) while the mobile devices used by players varied in technical specifications (Sony Xperia S, Samsung (Galaxy S4 Mini, Beam, Note 4, S4), Nexus (4 & 6), F&U Tablet and Motorola Moto G 2nd Generation).

References

1. Billinghurst, M., Clark, A., Lee, G.: A survey of augmented reality. Found. Trends Hum. Comput. Inter. **8**, 73–272 (2014)
2. Tian, Y., Long, Y., Xia, D., Yao, H., Zhang, J.: Handling occlusions in augmented reality based on 3D reconstruction method. Neurocomputing **156**, 96–104 (2015)
3. Tian, Y., Guan, T., Wang, C.: Real-time occlusion handling in augmented reality based on an object tracking approach. Sensors **10**, 2885–2900 (2010)
4. Hayashi, K., Kato, H., Nishida, S.: Occlusion detection of real objects using contour based stereo matching. In: International Conference on Augmented Tele-Existence, pp. 180–186. ACM (2005)
5. Kim, H., Yang, S.-J., Sohn, K.: 3D reconstruction of stereo images for interaction between real and virtual worlds. In: IEEE and ACM International Symposium on Mixed and Augmented Reality, pp. 169–176. IEEE (2003)
6. Ohta, Y., Sugaya, Y., Igarashi, H., Ohtsuki, T., Taguchi, K.: Client/server depth sensing for see-through head-mounted displays. Presence: Teleoperators Virtual Environ. **11**, 176–188 (2002)
7. Dey, A., Sandor, C.: Lessons learned: Evaluating visualizations for occluded objects in handheld augmented reality. Int. J. Hum Comput Stud. **72**, 704–716 (2014)
8. Clark, A., Piumsomboon, T.: A realistic augmented reality racing game using a depth-sensing camera. In: 10th International Conference on Virtual Reality Continuum and Its Applications in Industry, pp. 499–502. ACM (2011)
9. Benford, S., Crabtree, A., Flintham, M., Drozd, A., Anastasi, R., Paxton, M.: Can You See Me Now? ACM Trans. Comput. Hum. Interact. **13**, 100–133 (2006)
10. Hodson, H.: Google's ingress game is a gold mine for augmented reality. New Sci. **216**, 19 (2012)
11. Herbst, I., Braun, A.-K., McCall, R., Broll, W.: TimeWarp: interactive time travel with a mobile mixed reality game. In: 10th International Conference on Human Computer Interaction with Mobile Devices and Services, pp. 235–244. ACM (2008)
12. Fischer, J., Lindt, I., Stenros, J.: Final Crossmedia Report (part II) – Epidemic Menace II Evaluation report (2006)
13. Kasapakis, V., Gavalas, D.: Blending history and fiction in a pervasive game prototype. In: 13th International Conference on Mobile and Ubiquitous Multimedia, pp. 116–122. ACM (2014)
14. Schroeder, J.: AndEngine for Android game development cookbook. Packt Publishing Ltd., Birmingham (2013)
15. Cheok, A.D., Sreekumar, A., Lei, C., Thang, L.M.: Capture the flag: mixed-reality social gaming with smart phones. IEEE Pervasive Comput. **5**, 62–63 (2006)
16. Wetzel, W., Blum, L., McCall, R., Oppermann, L., Broeke, T.S., Szalavári, Z.: Final prototype of TimeWarp application (2009)
17. Kasapakis, V., Gavalas, D.: Pervasive gaming: status, trends and design principles. J. Netw. Comput. Appl. **55**, 213–236 (2015)
18. Behzadan, A.H., Kamat, V.R.: Scalable algorithm for resolving incorrect occlusion in dynamic augmented reality engineering environments. Comput. Aided Civ. Infrastruct. Eng. **25**, 3–19 (2010)
19. Fischer, J., Huhle, B., Schilling, A.: Using time-of-flight range data for occlusion handling in augmented reality. In: IPT/EGVE, pp. 109–116 (2007)
20. Zhu, J., Pan, Z., Sun, C., Chen, W.: Handling occlusions in video-based augmented reality using depth information. Comput. Animation Virtual Worlds **21**, 509–521 (2010)

21. Yang, T., Pan, Q., Li, J., Li, S.Z.: Real-time multiple objects tracking with occlusion handling in dynamic scenes. In: IEEE Computer Society Conference on Computer Vision and Pattern Recognition, pp. 970–975. IEEE (2005)
22. Lepetit, V., Berger, M.-O.: Handling occlusion in augmented reality systems: a semi-automatic method. In: IEEE and ACM International Symposium on Augmented Reality, pp. 137–146. IEEE (2000)

Improving the Development of AR Application for Artwork Collections with Standard Data Layer

Emanuele Frontoni[1], Roberto Pierdicca[1(✉)], Ramona Quattrini[2], and Paolo Clini[2]

[1] Department of Information Engineering, Università Politecnica Delle Marche, Via Brecce Bianche 12, 60131 Ancona, Italy
{e.frontoni,r.pierdicca}@univpm.it
[2] Department of Civil Engineering, Building and Architecture, Università Politecnica Delle Marche, Via Brecce Bianche 12, 60131 Ancona, Italy
{r.quattrini,p.clini}@univpm.it

Abstract. Museums and art galleries are called to preserve and promote their collections. Mobile technologies like Augmented Reality would transform visitors from passive observers to protagonists, creating engaging and personal art experience for the audience. However, the hurdles preventing Augmented Reality from becoming a widespread medium to convey virtual information about the Cultural Heritage, lies in the limitations in adopting fast and agile tools of development. The paper presents an ongoing research, aimed at the creation of a framework to serialize the development of Augmented Reality application, based on a standard data layer. The core of the application is designed to augment artworks, while the standardization of data will permit a fast multi-app development. This framework is useful to bridge the gap between designers and developers, and will facilitate a semi-automatic development of Augmented Reality applications for Cultural Institutions.

Keywords: Standard · Augmented reality · Museums · Artworks · Mobile development

1 Introduction

Augmented Reality (AR) is a promising cutting-edge technology that gives the possibility to see computer generated data, overlaid above a screen, with the same point of view of the user. This permits to know details and curiosities of an object, that otherwise would not be visible. This tool is extremely powerful for Cultural Heritage (CH) domain and, in particular, to augment artworks. In the literature there are several examples of using AR as an instrument to discover conceived details of a painting [1]; further, we witnessed to an impressive growing of research project in this direction [2]. The advantages are manifold, since this approach helps both insiders and visitors of a museum. The first, like scientists,

© Springer International Publishing Switzerland 2016
L.T. De Paolis and A. Mongelli (Eds.): AVR 2016, Part I, LNCS 9768, pp. 435–443, 2016.
DOI: 10.1007/978-3-319-40621-3_31

could for example make in-depth analysis on the technical aspects behind an artwork, while visitors can switch from a passive status to an active one, to feel themselves as a part of the painting, to enter virtually in the scene and to live in a more interactive way the experience of this work of art [4,14]. Besides, the use of AR for CH purposes is also widespread for the visualization of 3D models through portable devices [6]. Several studies demonstrate that, the introduction of new ways of interaction inside exhibitions, but also before and after the visit, entails several benefits and impacts from several standing points: the social, the cultural and the economic one [7]. The use of AR may also produce unexpected benefits, such as providing users with a new perspective of the artwork, as well as increasing their curiosity and encouraging them to experiment with the technology [8]. In [10], the authors state that virtual museums need to have an always more integrated approach between cultural contents, interfaces and social studies. In this work, we present a research, at an early stage, aimed at the development of a framework for an agile development of mobile apps, specifically developed to augment artworks. Previous researches ([3] and [11]) delivered meaningful results in terms of quality of contents usability and appreciation. However, the hurdles preventing Mobile Augmented Reality (MAR) acceptance and diffusion for CH purposes encompasses several aspects, one of which being development limitations (i.e. cross-platform, aspect-ratio, format, development environment etc.). In this light, our study is aimed at delivering a fast configuration service, scalable for multi-app development, allowing multi-user cooperation and contamination between computer scientists and content designers. The design of this framework will be based on a standard data layer, specifically designed to overcome with the lack of standards for AR application. Nowadays in fact, there is no standard way to create Augmented Reality applications, neither PCs nor mobile devices. In addition, the proposed application will allow the user to interact with three masterpieces preserved at Galleria Nazionale delle Marche of Urbino and in particular: The Ideal City by unknown author, La muta by Raffaello and Portrait of Guidobaldo and son by Pedro Berruguete. The app, actually under development, is structured to augment conceived details of the artworks, following the same clear and usable interface. In the following, the wireframe concept of the app will be presented, with particular emphasis on contents, usability and data structure.

2   Data Standardization

The presence of standards provides a common base for developers. Currently, there are numerous standards that can be used not only in the development but also in the deployment of open AR applications and services [9]. However, due to the lack of an unique standard, there are still important interoperability gaps in the Augmented Reality chain which lead to hard communications between the operations. To meet the needs of all the people involved in this technology, all of them must collaborate in order to create this common standard. Thus, developers, experts in hardware or content publishers, for example, must "talk the same language" if they want to make possible the standardization of Augmented Reality. So, the enhancement of existing protocols used in different steps of the whole system will yield a common way to manipulate data for augmented reality services. There is clearly a lack of standards for implementing mobile AR applications for users of multiple, different platforms and in different use scenarios which will make harder the growth of the technology in next years if no common standard is created. To create a more efficient interoperable AR, avoiding expensive errors, it is necessary to take into account the most popular standard yet in use for AR and AR-like applications (OpenGL ES, JSON, HTML5, KML, GML, CityGML,X3D, and so on). From the point of view of mobile device, a lot of sensor technologies have been developed and integrated, providing sensor data for mobile AR application with new capabilities. The acceleration in the growth of several mobile AR applications made clear the lack of standards for the implementation of mobile AR applications for different platforms and different scenarios. For this purpose we present our proposal of creating a knowledge base applied to AR paintings. The idea is to propose a standard method which has the task of augmenting the real world through multimedia objects (such as image, text, audio, video). For the creation of data model we applied XML since it is the most widely used language for network computing.

3   The Project

The applications described in this work fall within the activities of "DUCALE" (Digital Urbino: Cultural Augmented Learning Experience). The name of the project is an Italian term meaning goal/aim but recalling also the idea of view, and has the main objective of developing three mobile application with Augmented Reality and static functions, to improve the knowledge of the visitors. The paintings that have been used for our study are reported in Fig. 1.

The framework, under development, is intended to be headed by a configuration tool, in order to provide the museum with an agile instrument to update contents independently. The three sub-areas are the static application, for in-depth analysis of the painting, the AR section to discover conceived details of the painting, and a statistic tools to monitor the usability of the system. Data Standardization is aimed at providing a unique instrument of management. The target of this approach is on a high level developer who is interested in fast and scalable multiapp developing. This is a nice tool also for multi user development and for contamination between computer scientist and content designers. A schematic representation of the proposed architecture can be found in Fig. 2.

In terms of development, we faced with two main challenges. The first one consisting in the creation of a smart configuration tool for multi app development. Configuration utility allows application's administrator to design multiple apps for the large collection of paintings. The second one consisting on the functionalities implementation. Thanks to the "DUCALE" project, an expandable framework is conceived as a structure in which are allowed not only applications and tourist tools about paintings but also about architecture and specific themes (see Fig. 2).

(a) The Ideal City unknown author (1480-1490)

(b) Portrait of a Gentlewoman
Raffaello (1507)

(c) Federico and Guidobaldo's
portrait, Pedro Berreguete
(1476-1480)

Fig. 1. Paintings subject of the applications and used as the references images for
Augmented Reality section.

4   Methodology and Technology

Designing applications considering the interaction with the real world is a hard
task. Especially for artworks, contents should be presented in a clear and intuitive
way, to make the app educative end enjoyable at the same time. To achieve this
result, we divide the application in two sections:

- Static contents section: it allows users to make in-depth analysis of the painting, to know its history, restorations and to share the visit on social networks.
  The High Resolution of the painting have been acquired and tells some highlights through magnifications in some portion of the paining. Furthermore,

exploits spherical photogrammetric acquisition the user can navigate the entire museum collection, switching among different rooms.
- Augmented Reality section: by framing the painting with the built-in camera of the device, virtual contents like video or images appear in overlay above the screen, creating a seamless interaction between real and virtual.

The concept of the application "La Muta". The Augmented Reality tool, tailored for the painting "La Muta", has been designed to be educative and enjoyable at the same time. For this, we developed proved contents, highlighting information to raise the interest of the viewer. These contents have been

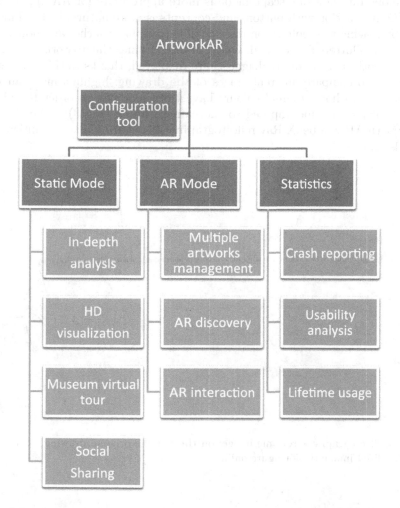

Fig. 2. Schematic representation of the application functionalities and tools. Main functionalities are divided into three main colours: Blue represents the whole framework. Red blocks are the main sections of the framework. Green blocks are the functionalities to be implemented with the standard data layer. (Color figure online)

developed and scientifically validated by historians of art. While the choice of contents to be deepened has been done after a focus group among people with different backgrounds and different cultural and professional interests. Considering the recent restoration, driven by a huge amount of preliminary investigations, AR section is mainly focused on the explanation of the artwork's conservation before the restoration. This is particularly effective for the visitors, since they will visualize old images compared with the actual renewed beauty. This kind of contents are particularly suitable to be overlaid in AR as virtual layers; besides, we gained several feedbacks from previous experiences on similar applications [12], so that the improvement will be focused on a User Centric design. Usability testing demonstrate how landscape mode is more appropriate for AR applications, since the interaction with buttons and contents is more natural [5,13]. Furthermore, by placing the toolbars on the side of the display, touches are more simple while visual clutters are avoided. Once the user frames the artwork, the images obtained with reflectography diagnosis are displayed; thanks to this contents, it is possible to compare different stages of the drawing, highlighting changes of mind of the author. Original colours have been modified in order to enhance the visibility once superimposed to the camera frame (Fig. 3). Other features visible with AR will be: X Ray reflectography, side lighting image, multispectral analysis and so on.

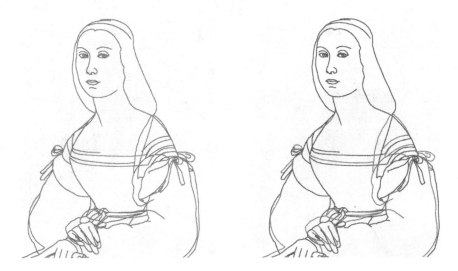

Fig. 3. Reflectography wireframe image: on the left the original drawing, on the right the AR edited image (Color figure online)

Standard Data Layer. The proposed framework is meant to be used with a suite of different artworks and is an innovative approach to create a standardization of data for artworks enhanced using augmented reality. This underpins a crucial aspect: in order to fulfil a common structure for all the paintings, a current practice is to carry out countless attempt until reaching the best solution. To overcome this problem, we introduce our approach, based on configuration tool, built on top of a generic object model to allow future serializations and future extensibility for the whole museum collection. More in deep, we propose a standard data structure and, for the AR section, we used as starting point the ARML 2.0, the most updated existing standard provided by OGS7[1].

The data layer describes the components of the ARtworkAPP class:

– PICTURE data: with the type="ImageType" we describe physical parameters of the background that consists of the image parameters (e.g.name, dimensions, resolution, and so on).
– TRACKABLE data: with the type="ARAnchorType" we describe the location of a feature in the real world (coordinates and orientation), zoom of the first appearance and the AR engine. This Anchor is used for virtual objects that are registered in the real world and move around on the screen as the user moves around.

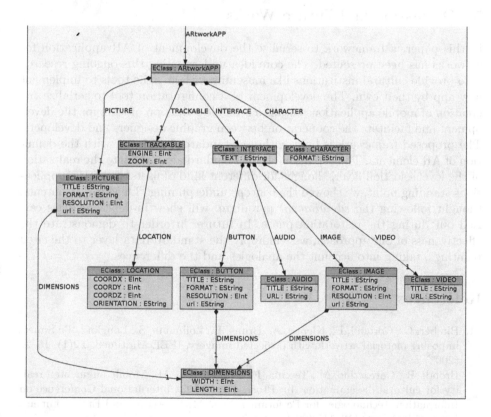

Fig. 4. Json representation of the ARtwork class components.

[1] https://portal.opengeospatial.org/files/?artifact_id=62131, last accessed: April 12, 2016.

- INTERFACE data: the type="ScreenAnchorType" has been defined for the user interface and describes all the elements that appears in AR mode. In other words, a fixed location of a feature on the screen that will not move when the user is moving.
- CHARACTER data: with the type="ARElementType" we describe the digital contents that appears in AR. This underpins a series of variables such as format, data type (e.g. audio, text, image, video and so on).

Figure 4 shows the Json schema of the standard data structure of the ARtworkAPP dynamic components. Each property of the ARtworkAPP class is represented by identifying the individual components and their elements. We create an AR application based on a structure that can be used as a standard method to create any AR application for different paintings. Each AR artwork application can be designed taking into account the components that forms ARrtworkAPP class.

5   Discussion and Future Works

In this paper, a framework to serialize the development of AR application for artworks has been presented. The core idea underpinning this ongoing research is to provide cultural institutions like museums with an agile tools to implement new app by their own. The development of a configuration tool to serialize the creation of mobile applications entails a sensible reduction of time for the development and facilitate the cooperation between graphic designers and developers. The proposed framework is built within a standard data layer, with the definition of AR elements. The definition of this standard also facilitate the realization of the level selection layer, thought for different kind of users. From the applications standing point, we showed the concept underpinning "La Muta". Contents, thought following the *edutainment* paradigm, will show in-depth analysis carried out during the restoration phase. In future, in order to demonstrate the effectiveness of our approach, we will apply the standard data layer to the cited paintings, taking into account the analogies and the differences.

References

1. Bimber, O., Coriand, F., Kleppe, A., Bruns, E., Zollmann, S., Langlotz, T.: Superimposing pictorial artwork with projected imagery. IEEE Multimed. **12**(1), 16–26 (2005)
2. Brondi, R., Carrozzino, M., Tecchia, F., Bergamasco, M.: Mobile augmented reality for cultural dissemination. In: Proceedings of 1st International Conference on Information Technologies for Performing Arts, Media Access and Entertainment, Firenze, Italy, pp. 113–117 (2012)
3. Clini, P., Frontoni, E., Quattrini, R., Pierdicca, R.: Augmented reality experience: From high-resolution acquisition to real time augmented contents. Advances in Multimed. **2014**, 18 (2014)

4. Clini, P., Quattrini, R., Frontoni, E., Pierdicca, R., Nespeca, R.: Real/not real: Pseudo-holography and augmented reality applications for cultural heritage. In: Handbook of Research on Emerging Technologies for Cultural Heritage (2015, in press)
5. Cooper, D.: User and design perspectives of mobile augmented reality. Ph.D. thesis, Ball State University (2011)
6. Giovanni, M., Fratarcangeli, M., Empler, T.: Augmented visualization on handheld devices for cultural heritage, pp. 97–103 (2013)
7. Laudazi, A., Boccaccini, R.: Augmented Museums Through Mobile Apps, vol. 1336, pp. 12–17 (2014)
8. Lu, W., Nguyen, L., Chuah, T., Do, E.: Effects of mobile ar-enabled interactions on retention and transfer for learning in art museum contexts. In: 2014 IEEE International Symposium on Mixed and Augmented Reality-Media, Art, Social Science, Humanities and Design (IMSAR-MASH'D), pp. 3–11. IEEE (2014)
9. Perey, C., Engelke, T., Reed, C.: Current status of standards for augmented reality. In: Recent Trends of Mobile Collaborative Augmented Reality Systems, pp. 21–38. Springer, New York (2011)
10. Pescarin, S., Wallergird, M., Hupperetz, W., Pagano, A., Ray, C.: Archeovirtual 2011: An evaluation approach to virtual museums. In: 2012 18th International Conference on Virtual Systems and Multimedia (VSMM), pp. 25–32. IEEE (2012)
11. Pierdicca, R., Frontoni, E., Zingaretti, P., Sturari, M., Clini, P., Quattrini, R.: Advanced interaction with paintings by augmented reality and high resolution visualization: a real case exhibition. In: De Paolis, L.T., Mongelli, A. (eds.) AVR 2015. LNCS, vol. 9254, pp. 38–50. Springer, Heidelberg (2015)
12. Quattrini, R., Pierdicca, R., Frontoni, E., Clini, P.: Mobile e realtà aumentata al palazzo ducale di urbino: Il museo è digitale. Archeomatica 6(1) (2015)
13. Santos, B., Romão, T., Dias, A.E., Centieiro, P., Teixeira, B.: Changing environmental behaviors through smartphone-based augmented experiences. In: Nijholt, A., Romão, T., Reidsma, D. (eds.) ACE 2012. LNCS, vol. 7624, pp. 553–556. Springer, Heidelberg (2012)
14. Sdegno, A., Masserano, S., Mior, D., Cochelli, P., Gobbo, E.: Augmenting painted architectures for communicating cultural heritage. SCIRES-IT-SCIentific RESearch Inf. Technol. 5(1), 93–100 (2015)

Augmented Reality for the Control Tower: The RETINA Concept

Nicola Masotti[✉], Sara Bagassi, and Francesca De Crescenzio

Department of Industrial Engineering, University of Bologna, Bologna, Italy
{nicola.masotti,sara.bagassi,francesca.decrescenzio}@unibo.it

Abstract. The SESAR (Single European Sky Air Traffic Management Research) Joint Undertaking has recently granted the Resilient Synthetic Vision for Advanced Control Tower Air Navigation Service Provision project within the framework of the H2020 research on High Performing Airport Operations. Hereafter, we describe the project motivations, the objectives, the proposed methodology and the expected impacts, i.e. the consequences of using virtual/augmented reality technologies in the control tower.

Keywords: Air Traffic Control · Airport tower · Virtual/Augmented Reality · Synthetic Vision

1 Overview

In the latest years, many of the technological advancements designed to improve the airport operational safety have come in the form of innovative visualization tools for tower controllers. Surface Movement Guidance and Control System (SMGCS) based solutions, such as movement maps, conformance monitoring, and conflict detection are a few examples of these tools. However, there is a paradox in developing these tools to increase the control-tower air traffic controller's situational awareness. By creating additional computer displays that show the runway and taxiway layout, aircrafts and vehicles position, and detect actual and foreseen conflicts, the controller's vision is pulled away from the out of the window view and his or her 'head-down' time is increased[1]. This reduces their situational awareness by forcing them mentally to repeatedly switch between these two ways of interpreting the working environment. In order to be able to address this paradox, Lloyd Hitchcock introduced the idea of using AR in the control tower when the Augmented Reality technology was still in the very early stages of its industrialization. At that time, no prototype construction was attempted and little was published, though many recall Mr. Hitchcock speculating on several methods that could aid tower controllers fulfilling their tasks [1–5]. For instance, he suggested that AR displays could provide air traffic controllers with useful status information, such as aircraft identification, barometer settings, wind conditions and runway or gate

---

[1] The 'head-down' time is the time spent by the air traffic controller looking at his/her desk equipment or managing flight strips.

© Springer International Publishing Switzerland 2016
L.T. De Paolis and A. Mongelli (Eds.): AVR 2016, Part I, LNCS 9768, pp. 444–452, 2016.
DOI: 10.1007/978-3-319-40621-3_32

assignments. More recent studies suggest that other spatially conformal information, such as flight tags, warnings, shapes and layouts can also be presented on AR displays [2, 6–12]. Indeed, the scientific community has already performed many experiments with by now out-dated hardware [1, 13].

The Resilient Synthetic Vision for Advanced Control Tower Air Navigation Service Provision (RETINA) project is one of the selected Single European Sky ATM Research (SESAR) projects on High Performing Airport Operations that will investigate the potential and applicability of Virtual/Augmented Reality (V/AR) technologies for the provision of Air Traffic Control (ATC) service by the airport control tower. The project will assess whether those concepts that stand behind tools such as Head-Mounted Displays (HUDs), Enhanced Vision Systems (EVSs) and Synthetic Vision Systems (SVS) can be transferred to ATC with relatively low effort and substantial benefits for controllers' Situational Awareness (SA). In doing so, the project Consortium (Fig. 1) will investigate two different augmented reality systems: Conformal-Head-Up Displays (C-HUDs) – which, potentially, can be made to coincide with the tower windows – and See-Through Head-Mounted Displays (ST-HMD). This will be done by means of out-off-the-shelf AR hardware components. A dissimilar third tool, i.e. a virtual reality based Table-Top interface, will be conceived as well, since the upper view is the easiest way to visualize the airport digital model (Fig. 2).

Fig. 1. The RETINA project consortium.

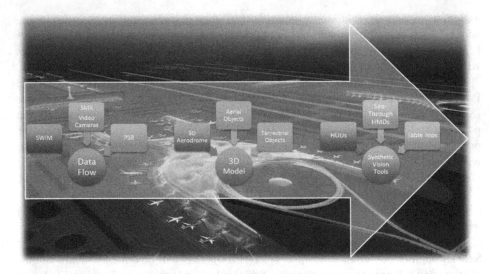

Fig. 2. The overall RETINA concept.

Because the focus of the project will be the placement of information over the actual window view, the relationship between conformal (registered) information and the user's perspective is a major issue. This subject has been widely studied in other fields such as cultural heritage, entertainment and virtual interaction. For instance, several studies have demonstrated that, at any time, the conceived AR environment must be aware of the user's eyes position with respect to the Virtual/Augmented Reality (V/AR) screens [14–16]. This is mandatory in order to generate (render) the best AR content for each eye and achieve the best registration possible. Within the RETINA project this concept will be implemented and demonstrated by means of non-intrusive, out-of-the-shelf, body-tracking sensors (e.g. MicrosoftTM KinectTM) or taking advantage of the tracking capabilities of certain HMDs (e.g. MicrosoftTM HoloLensTM). Thus, the AR screens would know where the controller is and where s/he is looking, allowing the interface to present the most beneficial information without adding needless clutter. Cues to critical situations that take place outside of the controllers view can also be placed in controllers' peripheral vision, to draw their attention in that direction. Overall, the information that is currently displayed on the head-down computer screens (flight tags, runway layout, intrusion warnings) could be displayed on either the see-through glasses or the head-up displays, therefore superimposed to the controller's line of sight.

As a common database between the V/AR systems, a three-dimensional Aerodrome Traffic Zone (ATZ) model will be developed and implemented, providing precise positioning for simulated aerial and terrestrial objects. Multiple simulated or recorded data sources such as Airport Surveillance Radar, Surface Movement Radar or other ground-based sensors (e.g. video or infrared cameras) will provide the displayed information (Fig. 2). In this respect, the RETINA project foresees a technology transfer between remote and on-site tower operations. Indeed, a proper 2D camera distribution within the simulated environment can provide reliable data regarding the positioning, speed, speed direction and size of ground-based objects. This is particularly convenient for smaller airports, where installing an Advanced Surface Movement Guidance and Control System (A-SMGCS) is deemed too much expensive. In larger airports, such sensors could still be useful to cover distant and blind spots, improving the controllers' SA of the surrounding area.

Other information that can be displayed to the controller includes SWIM (System Wide Information Management) related data, such as weather conditions, wind direction and speed, wind shear and wake vortexes visualization. Within the SESAR, the SWIM concept is the enabler for ensuring the delivery of the proper information, with the required quality, to the appropriate person at the right time [17]. RETINA will look at SWIM standards and services that can support the need for information of the planned V/AR tower tools. For example, RETINA will investigate how SWIM services can consume and visualize meteorological data using the data exchange format WXXM, one of the AIRM-based data model standards. Weather related information (such as wake vortexes, wind and wind shears) information could be used to optimize separations between approaching and departing aircrafts, leveraging weather related phenomena in a similar manner to what has been done in the SESAR Operational Service and Environment Definition (OSED) 06.08.01 (Time Based Separation) [18, 19].

This adds to the SWIM's overall objective of achieving global Air Traffic Management (ATM) interoperability and standardization.

Finally, the RETINA project will investigate the impact of the newly conceived tools on the control tower traffic management procedures. For instance, in low visibility or bad weather conditions, ad hoc Low Visibility Procedures (LVP) must apply. In many airports, this entails the use of a Surface Movement Radar (SMR), which provides only primary positioning for the ground traffic (without any identification support system). Moreover, depending on the airport layout, Low Visibility Procedures might include constraints, such as taxiways that cannot be used, block spacing, limitation in start-up and pushback operations, runway closure or use of a predefined runway. In this context, the use V/ARTT could possibly reduce restraints, producing benefits in terms of safety and capacity. For instance, when relying on Synthetic Vision (SV), an exclusive use of taxiway blocks should not be necessary – i.e. an aircraft could use a segment of a taxiway before the preceding aircrafts has left such segment. Whenever a new technology is used, ATC procedures must change accordingly. Therefore, the RETINA project will define when, why and how controllers will make use of augmented visual observation in order to manage the aerodrome traffic. Ad hoc recovery procedures will be proposed and validated, in order to demonstrate the real world applicability of the proposed solutions. Indeed, in case of a sudden SV failure, controllers must be able to return to standard Low Visibility Procedure in a quick manner, with no real threat to safety.

2 Methodology

In Air Traffic Control, operators must deal with easy tasks and familiar events, as well as with unfamiliar, time consuming and unexpected events. Besides talking to pilots, controllers need to extract information from the PVD, check weather, consult Flight Strips (FS), elaborate long term strategies, detect potential conflicts, make tactical decisions, coordinate with each-other and look out of the tower window (if any) [20, 21]. In addition, controllers need to balance cognitive resources and carefully time-table actions [20, 21]. Under these circumstances, human-computer interaction designers cannot only focus on the user but must consider the complexity of the work domain. Within the RETINA project, the interface design will draw from the Ecological Interface Design (EID) approach (Fig. 3).

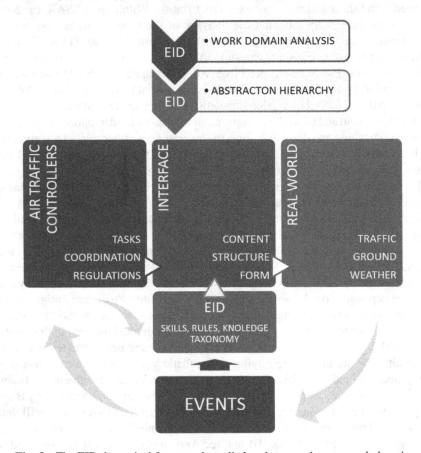

Fig. 3. The EID theoretical framework applied to the control-tower work domain.

EID is a theoretical framework for designing human-machine interfaces in complex, real-time and dynamic systems. This methodology differs from User-Cantered Design (UCD) insofar it focuses on the analysis of the work domain (a.k.a. Work Domain Analysis - WDA) rather than on the end-user or his/her specific tasks. EID attempts to provide the operators with the necessary tools and information to become active problem solvers as opposed to passive monitors, particularly during the development of unforeseen events [22]. Interfaces designed following the EID approach aim to decrease the mental workload when dealing with unfamiliar and unanticipated events, which are attributed to increased psychological pressure [22]. Doing so, EID makes use of two theoretical pillars from cognitive engineering research: the Abstraction Hierarchy (AH) and the Skills, Rules, Knowledge (SRK) taxonomy.

The Abstraction Hierarchy (AH) is a 5-level functional decomposition used for modelling the work environment (a.k.a. the work domain). In the EID framework, the AH is used to determine what kinds of information should be displayed on the system interface and how the information should be arranged. In doing so the designers attempts to make constraints and complex relationships in the work environment perceptually evident (e.g. visible, audible) to the end user (i.e. the air traffic controller) in order to free up cognitive resources that might support efficient problem solving [5]. As an example, the reader can easily refer to the use of tunnels or highways-in-the-sky for aircraft governance.

The Skills, Rules, Knowledge (SRK) framework (a.k.a. SRK taxonomy) defines three types of behaviour or psychological processes which are present in the operator information processing. The three categories essentially describe three possible ways in which information can be extracted and understood from a human-machine interface [6]. The categories can be weighted according to the user needs. For example, by supporting skill and rule based behaviour in familiar tasks, more cognitive resources may be devoted to knowledge-based behaviour, which are important for managing unanticipated events.

3   Expected Impacts

In 2014, within the European Civil Aviation Conference Area (ECACA), an average delay per flight of 9.7 min was developed [23]. Further analysis of the rationale behind the delay show that 0.51 min were due to weather, mainly strong wind, snow and low visibility conditions, whilst 0.96 min were due to restrictions at the departing or arrival airport, including the typical LVP restrictions defined in Sect. 1 [23]. Also, please notice that these data do not account for cancelled or redirected flights.

If the RETINA concept will ever become operative the proposed solutions will provide concerned actors with high-quality 4D information (position, height and speed over time) in any operational condition (traffic, weather, airport complexity, etc.). Thus the resilience and efficacy of the control tower IT system will be improved as well as the controllers' SA. This will allow Instrument Landing System (ILS) or SV equipped aircrafts to seamlessly operate under any visibility condition at synthetic vision equipped airports.

Complex airports will benefit from the implementation of the RETINA concept by preserving airport capacity in all weather conditions, even when LVP apply. This will result in financial savings for carriers and larger incomes for Air Navigation Service Providers (ANSP). In addition, nearby airports will not face the risk of saturation. With fewer delay, a reduction of the environmental impact of flights in terms of fuel burnt, emissions, CO_2, etc. will be achieved.

New advancements in the design of a camera-based tracking system will benefit smaller airports by enabling a ground control system through limited investments with respect to those required for a conventional A-SMGCS system. Such implementation will allow extending the provision of cost-effective Air Traffic Services (ATS) to those airports where only the Aerodrome Traffic Information Service (AFIS) is provided (either remotely or locally operated).

Definitely, the RETINA concept could highly contribute to establish a satisfactory level of safety for smaller airports, where traffic volume is simply too low to pay back for the initial investment in a SMR equipment. Side effects, such as the increase of traffic volume at smaller or peripheral airports due to a better level of quality of service must not be neglected. Passengers and couriers could use small aircrafts on a more frequent basis, with positive social impact on the community living in the airport surrounding. Consequently, the number of operations would increase and more airport equipage may be needed (Fig. 4).

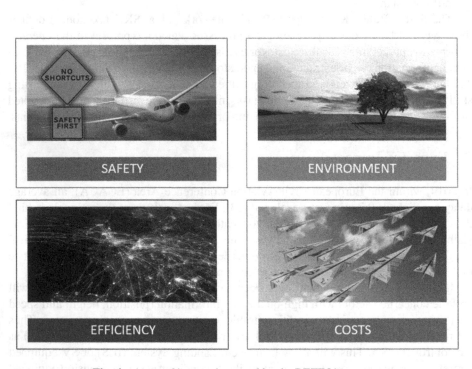

Fig. 4. Areas of interest impacted by the RETINA concept.

The project will also exploit the SWIM concept allowing for a cost effective stand-ardization and better re-use of data sets and services between the control tower IT systems. With no need for duplicates, significant savings for all ANSP will be achieved.

Overall, the RETINA project is expected to push the Technology Readiness Level (TRL) for V/AR technologies in the control tower from 1 to 2 and consolidate the leading role of European companies (ANSP and industries) into the field of air navigation.

References

1. Reisman, R., Brown, D.: Design of augmented reality tools for air traffic control towers. In: Proceedings of 6th AIAA Aviation Technology, Integration and Operations Conference (ATIO). American Institute of Aeronautics and Astronautics, Wichita, KS (2006)
2. Ellis, S.R., Adelstein, B.D., Reisman, R.J., Schmidt-Ott, J.R., Gips, J., Krozel, J.: Augmented Reality in a Simulated Tower Environment: Effect of Field of View on Aircraft Detection. NASA Ames Research Center Technical reports (2002)
3. Reisman, R.J., Brown, D.M.: Augmented Reality Tower Technology Assessment. NASA Ames Research Center (2010)
4. Peterson, S.: Very large format stereoscopic head-up display for the airport tower. In: Proceedings of the Virtual Images Seminar, number 16. CNRS/Renault (2007)
5. Ellis, S.R.: Towards determination of visual requirements for augmented reality displays and virtual environments for the airport tower. In: Virtual Media for Military Applications RTO-MP-HFM-136, pp. 31–1–31–10. RTO, Neuilly-sur-Seine, France (2006)
6. Rediess, H.: An augmented reality pilot display for airport operations under low and zero visibility conditions. In: Guidance, Navigation, and Control Conference. American Institute of Aeronautics and Astronautics (1997)
7. Ruffner, J.W., Deaver, D.M., Henry, D.J.: Requirements analysis for an air traffic control tower surface surveillance enhanced vision system. Presented at the SPIE - The International Society for Optical Engineering (2003)
8. Fürstenau, N.: Virtual Tower. In: 5th ATM R&D Symposium, Braunschweig (2005)
9. Azuma, R.: A survey of augmented reality. Presence Teleoperators Virtual Environ. **6**, 355–385 (1997)
10. Reisman, R.J., Feiner, S.K., Brown, D.M.: Augmented reality tower technology flight test. In: International Conference on Human-Computer Interaction in Aerospace (HCI-Aero), Santa Clara, CA (2014)
11. De Crescenzio F., Bagassi S., Fantini M., Lucchi F.: Virtual reality based HUD (Head Up Display) to simulate 3D conformal symbols in the design of future cockpits. Presented at the Council of European Aerospace Societies, Venice, Italy, 24–28 October 2011
12. Bagassi, S., De Crescenzio, F., Lucchi, F., Persiani, F.: Innovation in man machine interfaces: use of 3D conformal symbols in the design of future HUDs (Head Up Displays). Presented at the 28th International Congress of the Aeronautical Sciences, Brisbane, Australia, 23 September 2012
13. Reisman, R.J., Ellis, S.R.: Air traffic control tower augmented reality field study. In: ACM SIGGRAPH Posters. ACM, New York (2005)
14. Solari, F., Chessa, M., Garibotti, M., Sabatini, S.P.: Natural perception in dynamic stereoscopic augmented reality environments. Displays **34**, 142–152 (2013)
15. Masotti, N., Persiani, F.: Gaze-coupled perspective for enhanced human-machine interfaces in aeronautics. Presented at the Conferences in Air Transport & Operations, Delft University of Technology, Delft, The Netherlands, 20 July 2015
16. Rolland, J.P., Baillot, Y., Goon, A.A.: A survey of tracking technology for virtual environments. In: Fundamentals of Wearable Computers and Augmented Reality, chap. 3, pp. 67–112 (2001)
17. SESAR JU: System Wide Information Management (SWIM). http://www.sesarju.eu/sesar-solutions/swim
18. SESAR JU: Time Based Separation. http://www.sesarju.eu/sesar-solutions/airport-integration-and-throughput/time-based-separation

19. Matayoshi, N.: Reduced wake vortex separation using weather information. In: Electronic Navigation Research Institute (ENRI), Air Traffic Management and Systems. LNEE, vol. 290, pp. 49–68. Springer, Japan (2014)
20. Masotti, N., Persiani, F.: On the history and prospects of three-dimensional human–computer interfaces for the provision of air traffic control services. CEAS Aeronaut. J., 1–18 (2016)
21. Harper, R.H.R., Hughes, J.A.: "What a f-ing system! Send 'em all to the same place and then expect us to stop 'em hitting": making technology work in air traffic control. In: Button, G. (ed.) Technology in Working Order: Studies of Work, Interaction, and Technology, pp. 127–144. Routledge, London (1993)
22. Vicente, K.J., Rasmussen, J.: Ecological interface design: theoretical foundations. IEEE Trans. Syst. Man Cybern. **22**, 589–606 (1992)
23. EUROCONTROL: All-Causes Delay and Cancellations to Air Transport in Europe. https://www.eurocontrol.int/publications/coda-digest-annual-2014

Automatic Information Positioning Scheme in AR-assisted Maintenance Based on Visual Saliency

Miko May Lee Chang[2(✉)], Soh Khim Ong[1,2],
and Andrew Yeh Ching Nee[1,2]

[1] Mechanical Engineering Department, National University of Singapore,
9 Engineering Drive 1, Singapore 117576, Singapore
{mpeongsk,mpeneeyc}@nus.edu.sg
[2] NUS Graduate School for Integrative Sciences and Engineering,
National University of Singapore,
28 Medical Drive, Singapore 117456, Singapore
mikochang@nus.edu.sg

Abstract. This paper presents a novel automatic augmentation of pertinent information for Augmented Reality (AR) assisted maintenance based on a biologically inspired visual saliency model. In AR-assisted maintenance, the human operator performs routine service, repair, assembly and disassembly tasks with the aid of information displayed virtually. Appropriate positioning of virtual information is crucial because it has to be visible without hindering the normal maintenance operation at the same time. As opposed to conventional positioning approaches based on discretization and clustering of the scene, this paper proposes a novel application of a graph-based visual saliency model to enable automatic positioning of virtual information. Particularly, this research correlates the types of information with the levels of activation on the resulting visual saliency map for different scenarios. Real life examples of the proposed methodology are used to evaluate the feasibility of using visual saliency for information positioning in AR applications.

Keywords: AR-assisted maintenance · Augmentation · Positioning scheme · Visual saliency · View management

1 Introduction

Augmented reality (AR) is an emerging human-computer interaction technology that augments real scene with computer-generated virtual information. Since the emergence of AR technology in the 90's, it has been applied to many domains, e.g., medical visualization, manufacturing, repair, entertainment and military aircraft navigation [1]. AR is like a bridge connecting the virtual and the real world, providing an intuitive interaction interface for users in the real world to communicate with the virtual world. As technology advances, the virtual world contains increasing amount of information. Easy access and retrieval of such information will help users solve real world problems efficiently. Generally, a typical AR system consists of five major modules:

© Springer International Publishing Switzerland 2016
L.T. De Paolis and A. Mongelli (Eds.): AVR 2016, Part I, LNCS 9768, pp. 453–462, 2016.
DOI: 10.1007/978-3-319-40621-3_33

(i) registration; (ii) rendering and tracking; (iii) interaction; (iv) content generation; and (v) collaboration. In short, computer-generated information, e.g., text labels, 3D models and images, should be registered and rendered on the real life scene at appropriate positions. In AR visualization and guidance, the easiest and most straightforward augmentation method is pre-defined positioning with respect to markers or corresponding features. For example, one can define a virtual menu to be on top left and 3D models to be on top of the marker position at all times. However, this is not ideal as such inflexible positioning might affect the visibility of important structures during maintenance. In addition, AR-assisted maintenance requires full user attention on specific tasks at hand because maintenance operations, e.g., disassembly or unfastening, are both physically and cognitively demanding. With appropriate positioning of virtual information that considers both the visibility of important structures and human attention, AR-assisted maintenance can achieve its intended goal in providing optimal guidance of the users throughout the maintenance process. Considering both human attention and appropriate positioning, this paper describes a novel application of visual saliency for information visualization in AR-assisted maintenance. A correlation model is constructed to map the levels of activation in the saliency map to different types of visual information.

2   Related Work

Positioning of virtual information is always a crucial problem in AR visualization and guidance. Depending on the types of virtual information, e.g., annotation, animation, etc., the corresponding position has to be appropriate so that it can provide intended guidance without affecting the overall visibility of the users in real life. There are many reported works that investigate spatial layout of annotations, e.g., text labels and images, in AR environment, also known as view management. One of the earliest reported works by Azuma et al. evaluated four different placement algorithms including clustering, greedy depth first search, discrete gradient descent and adaptive simulated annealing for general AR views management [2]. Shen et al. worked on product information visualization and described a cluster-based greedy algorithm to prevent overlapping of annotations in a collaborative design environment [3]. Chen et al. presented an adaptive guiding scene display method based on optimal viewpoint selection for automatic positioning of virtual scene in an AR-based assembly and disassembly guidance system [4]. Most of the work reported considered positioning from the scene perspective and less from the user perspective. Recognizing the importance of considering human attention especially in maintenance, this paper explores the suitability of using visual saliency to enhance user experience in AR-assisted maintenance.

Visual saliency, a biologically inspired research problem, has been actively studied over the past three decades. Given the vast amount of visual information that human perceives each day, the visual system has evolved biologically to detect abnormalities and recognize threat immediately based on rapid scene analysis. In a complex object recognition scene, human processes the scene from one small patch to another subsequently. This scene analysis based on serialization is achieved through attention.

In computational modelling of visual attention, there are two mechanisms, namely, stimulus-driven bottom-up and task-driven top-down. "Saliency" is the core component in the stimulus-driven bottom-up approach because it is expected that human will be attracted by something that is salient, outstanding and different from the rest in a given scene [5]. Being able to predict human eye fixations to certain extent, visual attention models have been applied widely in many research fields, e.g., computer vision, human-robot interaction, and advertisement. Several innovative AR research based on saliency have also been reported especially in AR visualization. Sandor et al. developed an AR X-ray system based on visual saliency to address occlusion [6]. Meanwhile, Grasset et al. presented an image-driven view management based on saliency-inspired importance map for label placements in an AR browser and suggested its potential application for AR in heritage or maintenance [7].

3 Methodology

In this paper, a bottom-up visual saliency model, namely, graph-based visual saliency is implemented. The proposed algorithm consists of two parts, namely, generation of a saliency map followed by automatic positioning of virtual information. Firstly, a static scene image is captured from a camera. Next, a saliency map of the input scene is generated using a graph-based visual saliency method. Depending on the class that the virtual information is categorised into, this virtual information will be placed in the respective region that has the saliency score for that class.

3.1 Saliency Model

Graph-based visual saliency (GBVS) is a bottom-up saliency model based on the Markovian approach, which consists of three stages, namely, feature extraction, activation and normalization [8]. Firstly, the feature maps, e.g., colour, intensity and orientation, are extracted from input image at multiple spatial scales (Fig. 1). Each feature map is modelled as a fully connected graph, where nodes represent pixels and weighted edges are proportional to the similarity of feature values and corresponding spatial distance. The dissimilarity for two nodes (i, j) and (x, y) given by their respective feature values $M(i, j)$ and $M(x, y)$ is defined in Eq. (1), where $\sim$ refers to "similarly represented". The weight of a directed edge from node (i, j) to (x, y) is proportional to their dissimilarity and distance as defined in Eq. (2).

$$d((i, j) \| (x, y)) \triangleq \left| \log \frac{M(i, j)}{M(x, y)} \right| \sim |M(i, j) - M(x, y)| \tag{1}$$

$$w((i, j), (x, y)) \triangleq d((i, j) \| (x, y)) \cdot F(i - x, j - y)$$
$$\text{where } F(a, b) \triangleq \exp\left(-\frac{a^2 + b^2}{2\sigma^2} \right) \tag{2}$$

Next, the resulting graphs are formulated as Markov chains by normalizing the weights of the outbound edges of each node to 1, and by drawing a correspondence between nodes and states, and edge weights and transition probabilities. The equilibrium distribution is computed by repeated multiplication of the Markov matrix with an initially uniform vector. The resulting principal eigenvector of the matrix is adopted as the activation and saliency maps [8]. In the equilibrium distribution, nodes that have high dissimilarity with surrounding nodes will be assigned larger values, contributing to high

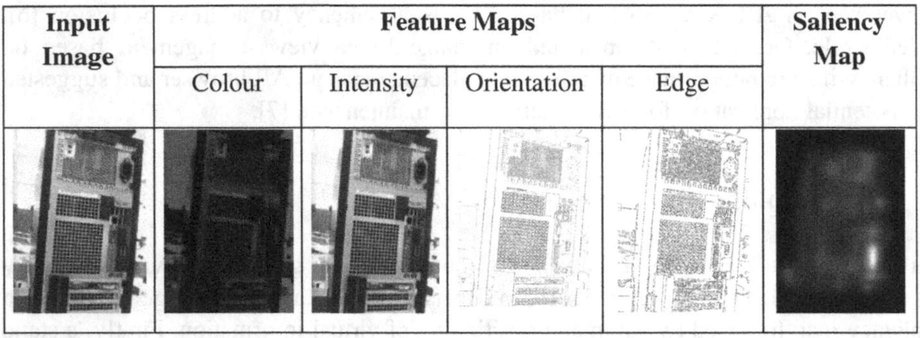

Input Image	Feature Maps				Saliency Map
	Colour	Intensity	Orientation	Edge	

Fig. 1. Examples of features and saliency maps

saliency. Lastly, the activation maps are combined and normalized into a single map to emphasize saliency.

3.2   Virtual Information

There are many types of visual information, e.g., labels for product visualization, virtual menus, images and 3D guiding scenes. As shown in Fig. 2, visual information can be categorized into two types: static (S) and dynamic (D) information. Static information refers to general information that will be displayed consistently throughout a particular maintenance task, e.g., virtual menus, product information and prompts, which only appear when necessary. Dynamic information refers to information that has to be updated regularly during maintenance, e.g., 3D guiding scenes and step-by-step maintenance instructions. Generally, only the required types of information need to be rendered for a specific maintenance task. In other words, it is not necessary to augment all four types of information on a scene simultaneously.

3.3   Positioning Scheme

Due to inherent centre bias in a human vision system, it is inevitable that important information should always be positioned at the centre and less important on the peripheral. However, in some cases, setting a default position/region is not ideal because that position might contain important structures as compared to other regions when viewing from a certain perspective. Thus, this paper proposes an automatic

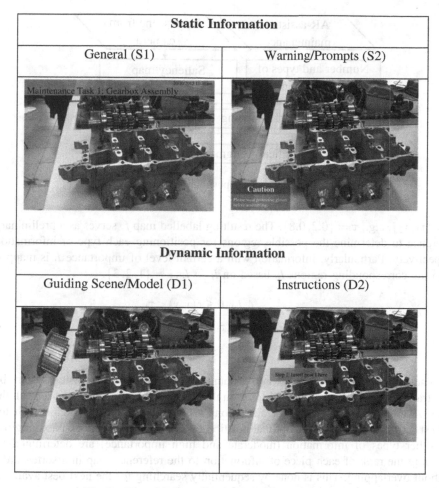

Static Information	
General (S1)	Warning/Prompts (S2)

Dynamic Information

| Guiding Scene/Model (D1) | Instructions (D2) |

Fig. 2. Virtual information in AR-assisted maintenance

positioning scheme (Fig. 3) based on the number and types of virtual information. First, a saliency map for an input scene is generated. Next, virtual information will be ranked and mapped to corresponding regions with certain levels of activation in the saliency map.

All input virtual information is first categorized into one of the four sub-types (Fig. 2). After categorization, each piece of information will be ranked accordingly and assigned a level of low, moderate or high importance. D1 and S2 information are assigned high importance, D2 information are assigned moderate importance, and S1 information are assigned least importance. All the information with assigned level of importance is now ready to be mapped to the saliency map for positioning and augmentation.

Based on the normalized saliency score, each pixel (x, y) on the saliency map f will be labelled L_1, L_2 or L_3 in Eq. (3), according to a set of predefined thresholds

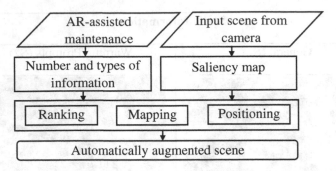

Fig. 3. Proposed positioning scheme

$\tau = \{\tau_1, \tau_2\}$, e.g., $\tau = \{0.2, 0.8\}$. The resulting labelled map f' serves as a preliminary reference to determine the possible regions for positioning each type of information respectively. Particularly, information with a certain level of importance I_i is mapped onto the corresponding regions L_i based on $I_i \rightarrow L_i, i = \{1, 2, 3\}$.

$$f'(x, y) = \begin{cases} L_1, 0 \leq f(x, y) < \tau_1 \\ L_2, \tau_1 \leq f(x, y) < \tau_2 \\ L_3, \tau_2 \leq f(x, y) \leq 1 \end{cases} \quad (3)$$

The positioning scheme takes into account centre bias in human vision system by constraining information of type S1 to be on the least salient regions of the scene all the time. Average saliency scores for all regions are computed and the region with the lowest score is deemed as the optimal position for S1 (low importance). Next, regions for other types of information (moderate and high importance) are determined by mapping the rank of each piece of information to the reference map in a sorted order without overlapping. This is done by sequentially searching for the next best available position in the reference map until all information has been processed.

In summary, general information (S1), e.g., virtual menus, product name, date and time, is considered least important and will be placed on least salient regions. Text-based or image-based instructions (D2) are considered moderately important and will be placed next to guiding scenes (D1). Warning messages and prompts (S2) are considered as important as guiding scenes (D1), e.g., 3D models, and will be placed on the most salient regions that exhibit the highest level of activation.

4 Preliminary Results

The proposed algorithm has been tested using several scenarios; the scenarios consist of the same maintenance scene from different viewing angles and positioning of multiple types of information on the given scene.

4.1 Multiple Perspectives Given a Scene

In maintenance, the viewing angles are limited by the accessibility of the machine and the surrounding environment. For example, when there is more than one technician on-site, each of them will have different viewing perspectives depending on their locations. In this example, automatic augmentation of static information is illustrated by assuming that there are three technicians working on a gearbox assembly at the same time. As shown in Fig. 4, setting a default position for general information, e.g., virtual menu, on a certain region is not always ideal. Considering real life physical constraints in maintenance that may limit the viewing angle of the technicians, the proposed augmentation scheme based on saliency values could help define a suitable position for static information (S1), e.g., virtual menus, so that it will not occlude important structures.

4.2 Multiple Types of Information

Given multiple types of information to be rendered, the positioning scheme will process the information in ascending order of importance (low, moderate, high). Firstly, static information (S1) will be positioned on the least salient region. Next, instructions of moderate importance (D2) will be placed on the grey region L_2. Similarly, important warning messages (S2) and guiding scenes (D1) will be placed on white regions L_3 with highest saliency values. As shown in Fig. 5, saliency map could predict the best

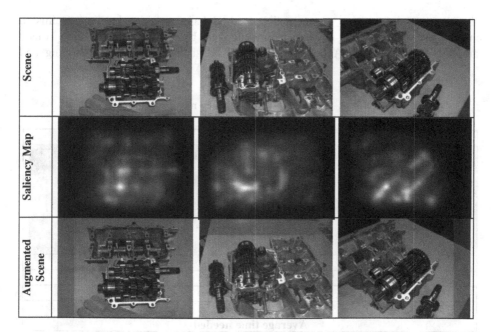

Fig. 4. Same maintenance scene with three viewing angles

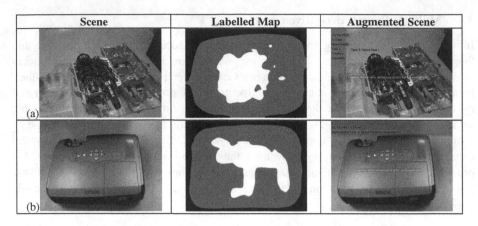

Fig. 5. Multiple types of information in: (a) Gearbox assembly, (b) Product inspection

region accurately for positioning the virtual menu, e.g., on the left for (a) and top for (b). Next, guiding instructions are placed on moderately salient regions without blocking important structures. Lastly, user attention is attracted as intended by placing warning messages (red box) on regions with high saliency values.

5   Discussion

The proposed information augmentation method based on visual saliency aims to enhance user experience in AR-assisted maintenance by predicting distribution of user attention given a scene. A positioning model consisting of ranking, mapping and

Table 1. Time required for saliency map generation

Scene 1	Scene 2	Scene 3
Image size (pixel)		
1024x768	1024x768	1024x768
Time needed (sec)		
1.08	1.06	1.07
Average time needed		
1.07 sec		

positioning has been developed to correlate the types of virtual information with levels of activation in the saliency map.

Notably, one major requirement for AR system is to achieve real time performance. For the preliminary results presented in this paper, the saliency maps are generated based on graph-based visual saliency Matlab algorithm running on a laptop with 2.5 GHz Intel Core i7. The time needed to generate each saliency map is recorded as shown in Table 1.

Given an image size of 1024 × 768, the average time needed to generate the corresponding saliency map is about 1 s. In AR-assisted maintenance, it is expected that the user's point of view is not static because the user may need to move around to perform a task. However, it is not desirable to change the positions of the information constantly as it may cause more distraction than provide helpful guidance to the user. Hence, it is suggested that the proposed positioning scheme to be activated during the initial registration phase, or upon user request only when there are changes in the viewing angles.

In general, the proposed model works well in predicting the most suitable regions for general information positioning, e.g., virtual menus. It also defines preliminary regions for the respective types of information, e.g., L_2 region for instructions and L_3 region for guiding scene. However, actual positioning of the information requires incorporation of exhaustive algorithms, such as sequential search or clustering. Hence, the proposed scheme is not intended for exact positioning of guiding scene or accurate parts labelling because the resulting labelled map only serves as a rough reference for view management. Exact positioning requires accurate tracking based on markers or object detection which are beyond the scope of this paper. Due to the inherent limitation of the saliency map, the model might not work well for a complex scene. In future work, the model can be integrated with other positioning methods, such as tracking to form a hybrid view management approach and implemented in a fully functional AR-system to test the actual applicability of the methodology.

6 Conclusion

An ideal AR system should provide seamless integration between computer-generated information and the real physical environment. In AR-assisted maintenance, proper organization of virtual information is essential to convey instructions to users effectively without hindering the maintenance operations. The proposed algorithm is able to identify suitable regions for appropriate positioning of virtual information based on visual saliency and a correlation model. Preliminary results of the augmented scene have successfully demonstrated the applicability of the methodology. Since there is an active on-going research in visual saliency modelling, new visual saliency algorithms can be further investigated and compared in future study.

References

1. Azuma, R., Baillot, Y., Behringer, R., Feiner, S., Julier, S., MacIntyre, B.: Recent advances in augmented reality. IEEE Comput. Graph. Appl. **21**(6), 34–47 (2001)
2. Azuma, R., Furmanski, C.: Evaluating label placement for augmented reality view management. In: Proceedings of the 2nd IEEE/ACM International Symposium on Mixed and Augmented Reality (ISMAR 2003), p. 66. IEEE Computer Society, Washington (2003)
3. Shen, Y., Ong, S.K., Nee, A.Y.C.: Product information visualization and augmentation in collaborative design. Comput. Aided Des. **40**(9), 963–974 (2008)
4. Chen, C.J., Hong, J., Wang, S.F.: Automated positioning of 3D virtual scene in AR-based assembly and disassembly guiding system. Int. J. Adv. Manufact. Technol. **76**(5), 753–764 (2015)
5. Borji, A., Itti, L.: State-of-the-art in visual attention modeling. IEEE Trans. Pattern Anal. Mach. Intell. **35**(1), 185–207 (2013)
6. Sandor, C., Cunningham, A., Dey, A., Mattila, V.V.: An augmented reality X-Ray system based on visual saliency. In: 2010 9th IEEE International Symposium on Mixed and Augmented Reality (ISMAR), Seoul, pp. 27–36 (2010)
7. Grasset, R., Langlotz, T., Kalkofen, D., Tatzgern, M., Schmalstieg, D.: Image-driven view management for augmented reality browsers. In: Proceedings of the 2012 IEEE International Symposium on Mixed and Augmented Reality (ISMAR 2012), pp. 177–186. IEEE Computer Society, Washington (2012)
8. Harel, J., Koch, C., Perona, P.: Graph-based visual saliency. In: Proceedings of Neural Information Processing Systems (NIPS) (2006)

Interactive Spatial AR for Classroom Teaching

YanXiang Zhang[✉] and ZiQiang Zhu

Department of Communication of Science and Technology,
University of Science and Technology of China, Hefei, Anhui, China
petrel@ustc.edu.cn, monster@mail.ustc.edu.cn

Abstract. The authors fuse the virtual objects in science and the action of teachers on real podium by developing an interactive spatial AR system, in which teachers could interact with virtual objects by their gesture in real-time presentation, and the images of virtual objects that projected on a transparent projection screen were aligned and matched to calibrate with their body part's position. The students will see virtual objects are seamlessly matched on the real teachers on podium space as if they are real things that are just under the control of the teachers. The students will immerse into the presentation more deeply, hence enhance the cognitive effect of classroom teaching and learning.

Keywords: Spatial AR · Classroom · Transparent projection screen

1 Introduction

There have been a number of researches about how use augmented reality technologies in through augmented reality book [1, 2] or mixed reality book [3] and in classrooms [4–14] that focus on allowing students to interact with content. Most of these researches utilized HMD and mark recognition based augmented reality technologies, and usually each student should interact with the system himself or herself. However, it may be not suitable for many traditional classrooms to apply this scenario mechanically, especially if there are many students and only few equipments then the students will have to take many time to learn the related contents by interacting with the system one by one, on the other hand, usually there is a schedule that teacher should teach some specified contents to the students in a certain period of time.

This paper aimed to provide the teachers with a more effective way to communicating knowledge to the students by allowing the teachers to present the educational 3D contents interactively with spatial AR technology [15]. In this scenario, 3D virtual objects is displayed on a transparent projection screen [16, 17] that arranged in front of the podium, while students will see their teacher is interacting with the 3D virtual objects just like in the air, so the students could get much deeper immersive experience than that in traditional mode.

L.T. De Paolis and A. Mongelli (Eds.): AVR 2016, Part I, LNCS 9768, pp. 463–470, 2016.
DOI: 10.1007/978-3-319-40621-3_34

Both half-mirror [16] and transparent projection screen [17, 18] could generate "in air" planar illusion, while the pyramid-shaped virtual showcase [19] could supports up to four viewers, and the cone-shaped virtual showcase [20] could supports multiple users and provides a seamless surround-view illusion. Thereby the technological progress that is being made within these areas allows shifting interactive storytelling more and more into the third dimension [21] and into the physical world.

By using the above technologies to present information within a unique aura of a real environment [22], information communication could be more vividly and effectively. In the field of calibrate virtual objects with the real people's body part position in spatial AR, several research groups are using Kinect sensor or infrared camera to track and respond to actors' movements in a 3D projection environment [23, 24] to merges live action with a virtual world.

However, applying technology to classroom on real podium to achieve and vividly and immersive experience for the students is the direction that this paper is concerned with.

Microsoft Kinect sensor was used to catch the skeleton, gesture and motion of the teacher, and then images of virtual objects displayed on transparent projection screen could be matched and aligned to calibrate with the body part's position of the teacher. Finally, the virtual objects and real teacher were seamlessly and interactively integrated.

2   System Design and Implementations

In our design (Fig. 1), in order to calibrate and composite virtual objects with teacher's body part accurately, transparent projection screen is arranged on podium just in front of or behind the teacher, a Kinect sensor is used to capture the teacher's skeleton, gesture, motion, and body part position, computer will match virtual objects on the related body part, as shown in Fig. 2, and the detailed steps of calibration of reality and Kinect is

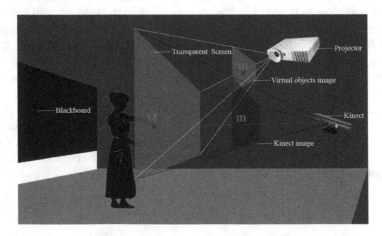

Fig. 1. System design, a transparent projection screen is arranged on podium just in front of or behind the teacher, a Kinect sensor is used to capture the teacher's skeleton, gesture

shown in Fig. 3. then we could achieve our aim of fuse real people and virtual objects through spatial registration on the transparent projection screen.

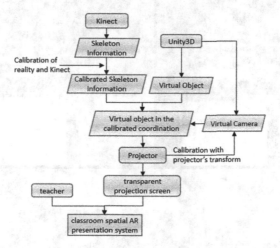

Fig. 2. Overview of the steps of classroom spatial AR presentation system

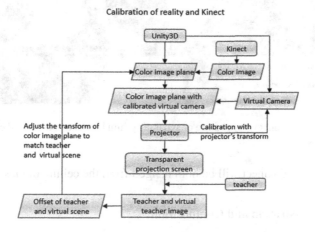

Fig. 3. The steps of calibration of reality and Kinect

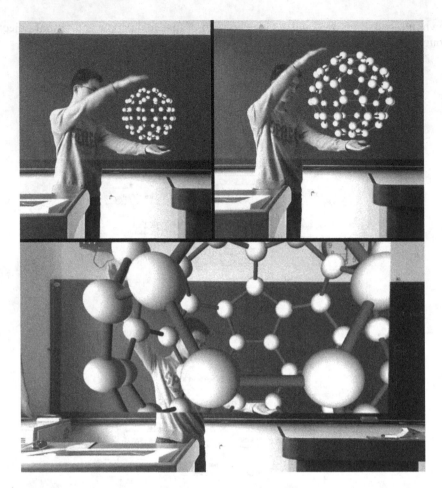

Fig. 4. Zoom in and zoom out by gesture of separating him hands, teacher could even zoom into the virtual objects

The projector and Kinect will be both hanged from the ceiling of classroom.

2.1 Spatial Registration and Composition

Kinect could capture depth image and color image, and acquire teacher's skeleton from depth image, but we will use its color image as reference in Unity 3D software to align and match virtual objects with real teacher on the podium.

In the first step of spatial registration on transparent projection screen, Kinect's skeleton image will be used as background of rendering camera in Unity 3D, and then projected on the transparent screen to match and align the teacher and image of teacher on screen, from the view of students, the teacher and his/her skeleton on screen should be in same size and same position and the teacher should just in a plane with skeleton image of himself and also the Kinect, so that virtual objects could appear just on his body parts, show as Fig. 5.

Fig. 5. Translating the virtual object by gesture of move hands

After spatial registration, we will remove Kinect skeleton image in Unity 3D and only left the virtual objects with black background, so when it was projected on the transparent screen, the black background area will still keep transparent and students could see teacher and the environment behind him.

2.2   Interact with Virtual Objects

It will also be very wonderful to allow teacher to interact with virtual objects, which could bring much more real feel and deeper immersive experience to the students also for the teacher. We made scripts in Unity 3D to build interaction between Kinect skeleton and virtual objects, which allowing teacher to interact with virtual objects on transparent screen by using his hands or feet and achieve highly attractive performance. Figures 4, 5 and 6 shows the process of a user interacting with a virtual objects, zoom in or zoom out, translate, and rotate them. Here different gestures will be used to realize different manipulations.

Fig. 6. Rotating the virtual object by gesture of turning over the two hands

3   Discussion

By using this system, teachers could communicate knowledge more vividly and effectively to the students with immersive experience in classroom teaching, although the target user is teacher, students could also interact with this system in the break between classes.

Acknowledgments. The research was sponsored by China National Key Technology Support Program project, project number: 2014BAH15F02.

References

1. Bazzaza, M.W., Al Delail, B., Zemerly, M.J., Ng, J.W.P.: iARBook: An immersive augmented reality system for education. In: International Conference on Teaching, Assessment and Learning (TALE), Wellington, pp. 495–498 (2014)
2. Dünser, A., Walker, L., Horner, H., Bentall, D.: Creating interactive physics education books with augmented reality. In: Farrell, V., Farrell, G., Chua, C., Huang, W., Vasa, R., Woodward, C. (eds.) Proceedings of the 24th Australian Computer-Human Interaction Conference (OzCHI 2012), pp. 107–114. ACM, New York (2012)
3. Grasset, R., Dunser, A., Billinghurst, M.: The design of a mixed-reality book: Is it still a real book? In: 7th IEEE/ACM International Symposium on Mixed and Augmented Reality, ISMAR 2008, Cambridge, pp. 99–102 (2008)
4. Billinghurst, M., Duenser, A.: Augmented reality in the classroom. Computer **45**(7), 56–63 (2012)

5. Bodén, M., Dekker, A., Viller, S., Matthews, B.: Augmenting play and learning in the primary classroom. In: Proceedings of the 12th International Conference on Interaction Design and Children (IDC 2013), pp. 228–236. ACM, New York (2013)
6. Balaam, M., Fitzpatrick, G., Good, J., Luckin, R.: Exploring affective technologies for the classroom with the subtle stone. In: Proceedings of the SIGCHI Conference on Human Factors in Computing Systems (CHI 2010), pp. 1623–1632. ACM, New York (2010)
7. Cuendet, S., Bonnard, Q., Do-Lenh, S., Dillenbourg, P.: Designing augmented reality for the classroom. Comput. Educ. **68**, 557–569 (2013). ISSN 0360-1315
8. Bodén, M., Dekker, A., Viller, S., Matthews, B.: Augmenting play and learning in the primary classroom. In: Proceedings of the 12th International Conference on Interaction Design and Children (IDC 2013), pp. 228–236. ACM, New York (2013)
9. Bai, H., Lee, G., Billinghurst, M.: Free-hand gesture interfaces for an augmented exhibition podium. In: Ploderer, B., Carter, M., Gibbs, M., Smith, W., Vetere, F. (eds.) Proceedings of the Annual Meeting of the Australian Special Interest Group for Computer Human Interaction (OzCHI 2015), pp. 182–186. ACM, New York (2015)
10. Cuendet, S., Bonnard, Q., Do-Lenh, S., Dillenbourg, P.: Designing augmented reality for the classroom. Comput. Educ. **68**, 557–569 (2013)
11. Budhiraja, R., Verma, S., Pandey, A.: Designing interactive presentation systems for classrooms. In: Proceedings of the 28th ACM International Conference on Design of Communication (SIGDOC 2010), pp. 259–260. ACM, New York (2010)
12. Bodén, M., Dekker, A., Viller, S., Matthews, B.: Augmenting play and learning in the primary classroom. In: Proceedings of the 12th International Conference on Interaction Design and Children (IDC 2013), pp. 228–236. ACM, New York (2013)
13. Schwerdtfeger, B., Pustka, D., Hofhauser, A., Klinker, G.: Using laser projectors for augmented reality. In: Proceedings of the 2008 ACM Symposium on Virtual Reality Software and Technology (VRST 2008), pp. 134–137. ACM, New York (2008)
14. Kaufmann, H., Schmalstieg, D.: Mathematics and geometry education with collaborative augmented reality. In: ACM SIGGRAPH 2002 Conference Abstracts and Applications (SIGGRAPH 2002), pp. 37–41. ACM, New York (2002)
15. Bimber, O., Raskar, R.: Spatial Augmented Reality: Merging Real and Virtual Worlds. A K Peters/CRC Press, Wellesley (2005)
16. Laser Magic Productions. Holograms, Transparent Screens, and 3D Laser Projections. Available from World Wide Web (2016). http://www.laser-magic.com/transscreen.html)
17. Bimber, O., Fröhlich, B., Schmalstieg, D., Encarnação, L.M.: The Virtual Showcase. IEEE Comput. Graphics Appl. **21**(6), 48–55 (2001)
18. Bimber, O.: Interactive Rendering for Projection-Based Augmented Reality Displays, Ph.D. Dissertation, Darmstadt University of Technology (2002)
19. Bimber, O., Fröhlich, B., alstieg, D.S., Encarnação, L.M.: The Virtual Showcase. IEEE Comput. Graphics Appl. **21**(6), 48–55 (2001)
20. Bimber, O., Fröhlich, B., Schmalstieg, D., Encarnação, L.M.: Real-time view-dependent image warping to correct non-linear distortion for curved virtual showcase displays. Comput. Graph. Int. J. Syst. Appl. Comput. Graph. **27**(4), 512–528 (2003)
21. Janet Horowitz Murray: Hamlet on the Holodeck: The Future of Narrative in Cyberspace. MIT Press, Cambridge, MA (1998)
22. Bimber, O., Encarnação, L.M., Schmalstieg, D.: The virtual showcase as a new platform for augmented reality digital storytelling. In: Proceedings of the Workshop on Virtual Environments (EGVE 2003), pp. 87–95. ACM, New York (2003)

23. Marner, M.R., Haren, S., Gardiner, M., Thomas, B.H.: Exploring interactivity and augmented reality in theater: A case study of Half Real. In: 2012 IEEE International Symposium on Mixed and Augmented Reality (ISMAR-AMH), Atlanta, GA, USA, pp. 81–86 (2012)
24. Low, K.-L., Welch, G., Lastra, A., Fuchs, H.: Life-sized projector-based dioramas. In: Proceedings of the ACM Symposium on Virtual Reality Software and Technology (VRST 2001), pp. 93–101. ACM, New York (2001)

Third Point of View Augmented Reality for Robot Intentions Visualization

Emanuele Ruffaldi[✉], Filippo Brizzi, Franco Tecchia, and Sandro Bacinelli

TeCiP, Scuola Superiore Sant'Anna, Pisa, Italy
e.ruffaldi@sssup.it
http://www.percro.org

Abstract. Lightweight, head-up displays integrated in industrial helmets allow to provide contextual information for industrial scenarios such as in maintenance. Moving from single display and single camera solutions to stereo perception and display opens new interaction possibilities. In particular this paper addresses the case of information sharing by a Baxter robot displayed to the user overlooking at the real scene. System design and interaction ideas are being presented.

A new generation of robotic systems is being introduced in working environments from small to large factories. These robots, thanks to advancements in actuation and perception, are capable to cooperate with human workers in the execution of task, rather than performing their own task independently inside a highly structured workflow. Examples of such robotic system are the Baxter [1] from Rethink Robotics and ABB Yumi, anticipated in the research world by many projects [2].

With the increased capability of these robots and the expected cooperative interaction, there is a need for the operator to understand the robot intention and current state as much as the robot needs to understand operator intentions. The former for supervision, the latter for safety and proactivity. The nature of the Human-Robot Communication (HRC) between these robots and human workers needs to take into account the specificities of working environment that limits traditional communication channels [3]: possibly over the average sound levels, direct manipulation of touch devices limited by gloves or by the working activity.

A specific need for the operation is the possibility of understanding the intention of the robot contextualized over the working environment, that is to understand if the chosen object to be manipulated is the correct one or the target location. There are several display options for providing this information spanning from the traditional ones, such as display panels placed in the environment, on the robot, wear by the operator or simply in the hand, to projective or presented in eye- or head- mounted displays. In any of this case we are interested in presenting the selection highlighted in the real world by means of the capabilities offered by Augmented Reality (AR).

Industrial plants commonly require specialist maintenance expertise; as a consequence, plants located in remote sites and away from where the compo-

L.T. De Paolis and A. Mongelli (Eds.): AVR 2016, Part I, LNCS 9768, pp. 471–478, 2016.
DOI: 10.1007/978-3-319-40621-3_35

nents were produced can be difficult to service effectively. Addressing major equipment failures often requires specialist on-site intervention, which can result in significant down-time and cost, but, more importantly, some maintenance and corrective procedures are so complicated or site-specific that a local engineer often is not able to proceed without complex instructions. The potential of Augmented Reality and Robotic Assistance in these frequent situations is therefore potentially disruptive, as both can greatly decrease the perceived complexity of the tasks.

The paper presents and discusses a stereo Augmented Reality eye-wear integrated in a working helmet for HRC with a humanoid robot for collaborative applications, a Baxter, discussing the supporting components, system architecture and calibration issues. The long term research question is on which information is better to be displayed, how it can be overlaid on the real scene, and which are the usability challenges. The specific research question of this short paper is on the challenges in calibrating the different point of view, and supporting the augmentation on a low power system such the one proposed.

Section 2 presents the State of the Art, Sect. 3 discusses the helmet and architecture, followed by the augmentation in Sect. 4. Then, follows Discussion in Sect. 5.

1   Background

There is recent strong technological trend in eye-level AR that is moving from research prototypes to high-quality displays for wearable AR such as HoloLens [4], Meta, Canon MREAL, Epson Moverio, Dahiri, followed by more unknown technology such as Magic Leap. All these systems are characterized by some form of pass-through display technology that allows to overlay the information over the field of view of the operator coupled with a wearable computer vision subsystem that acquires information about the external environment and allows to provide gesture recognition, object recognition and more over information for the correct overlay of augmented models over the real world.

The AR helmet presented in this work is not providing a see-through experience, but it is instead based on a display that is located in the upper part of the field-of-view of the operator. The choice of this solution is coming from the experience in tele-maintenance with helmets in which the operator is interested in an augmented view only in certain phases of the work while keeping the clear site of the environment. The motivation is also in the compactness of the solution and integration in a regular safety helmet.

The interaction between human and robots in cooperative environments has been investigated in several projects looking at specific aspects of safety, physical interaction, coping also with cognitive capabilities for the collaboration. The communication part has been typical based on the audio channel or regular display. In the area of Augmented Reality many works have been devoted to the overlay of information coming from a database or a running system such as examples in industrial or automotive maintenance [5]. An example of alternative communication from robots is based on projective augmented reality [6].

An important aspect is the physical co-location of the human operator with respect to the robot. When such co-location is not necessary it is possible to employ more immersive display techniques such as a Head Mounted Displays (HMD) as the authors employed in a Mixed Reality (MR) setup with a Baxter robot [7].

The present work proposes the setup to explore the HRC in collaborative robotics by means of a industrial helmet augmented with a non-see through display that is connected with the robot system, being capable, in this way, to show the results from the perceptual and cognitive subsystems of the robot.

2 Helmet for Industrial AR

In this section we are discussing the design and realization of a video see-trough Augmented Reality helmet as shown in Fig. 1. This device has been explicitly designed to fit over a standard safety helmet without the need of modifications or an adapter. This is a key aspect to comply to safety regulations in many industrial environments. There are two main snap-on parts, kept together by elastic bands: the main part contains a wireless, battery-powered module equipped with a stereo display, a stereo camera subsystem with interchangeable lenses and on-board computing. The display module is constituted by two compact LCD displays with LED retro-illumination. The field of view (FOV) for each eye is 32 degrees, with a 100 % overlap. The display block is structured along a plastic pipe that contains a mechanism to allows the adjustment of the intra-ocular distance. An unique characteristic of the displays is their placement: the design of the unit was carefully chosen to occlude only a small portion of the worker field of view. In this way it is still easy to navigate into the environment without the encumbrance usually associated to video see-trough solutions. The computer vision part is characterized by two 5 M pixel cameras that support Full HD video streaming at 30 Hz. Anyway in this setup they have been scaled down to VGA resolution (640 × 480) at 30 Hz in order to limit the potential effects of WiFi interferences. The on-board processing is provided by two ARM modules based on the BCM2835 chipset, running at 700 MHz and equipped with 512 MB of RAM, that have been conceived exactly for compact high efficiency processing. This architecture allow to access the cameras using a low-latency Mobile Industry Processor Interface (MIPI). to control the output display via HDMI and to perform compression and decompression of the image streams in real-time. The helmet has been designed for a general purpose of tele-presence and its main software capability is to stream and receive compressed video images, encoded in low-latency h.264, to a target computer or to another helmet over WiFi with a end-to-end latency comparable (or inferior) to what is usually allowed by standard USB cameras. The device is also equipped with a 6-DOF motion sensor based on the Invensense MPU-9150, although it was not used in the setup discussed in this work.

An unique characteristic of the displays is their placement: the design of the unit was carefully chosen to occlude only a small portion of the worker

Fig. 1. Helmet concept

field of view, as discussed in [8]. In this way it is still easy to navigate into the environment without the encumbrance usually associated to video see-trough solutions

3   System Setup

The HRC case discussed in this paper has been realized with a Baxter robot that is provided with two arms. The Baxter has natively one VGA camera at each arm end-effector and it has been augmented with an Asus xTion Live Pro RGB-D camera that has characteristics similar to the original Kinect 360. The robot has an internal computer running the Robotic Operating System (ROS), while a separate computer is bridging the robot with the Helmet performing all the necessary augmentation computations. The bridging is performed by using the CoCo framework for Mixed Reality [9,10] that has been extended for supporting the Helmet: the helmet appears as a stereo camera source and as a stereo display output. The low-level driver of the Helmet exposes two shared memory buffers that are polled/updated dealing with compression and decompression of the image stream. System architecture is shown in Fig. 2.

The resulting interaction in the experimental environment is shown in Fig. 3.

4   Augmentation

The objective of the augmentation discussed in this work is to provide information about the status of the robot represented in the field of view of the operator. In particular the robot localizes an object, and if it is also in the field of view of the operator it is highlighted in the head-up display. The head-up shows the images coming from the helmet cameras augmented with the object highlight. The augmentation is performed by transferring the pose of the object from the robot reference systems to the operator ones without the need of performing object recognition in the helmet. The outcome is shown in Fig. 5.

The relevant reference frames and their connections are discussed here for clarifying the proposed approach: a frame is named by an upper case letter,

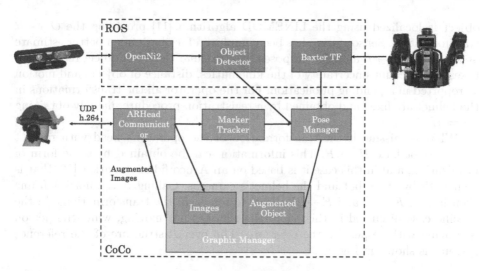

Fig. 2. System Architecture: on the top part the Baxter robot is shown with the ROS nodes supporting object recognition. The lower part shows the CoCo based processing that acquires the camera images, augment them using the information from the robot and send them back to the ARHead.

Fig. 3. Experimental environment with Baxter and operator

while the associated transformation is expressed by an arrow, that is simple as in $A \rightarrow B$ for dynamic transformations and double as in $A \Rightarrow B$ for static ones. Let's call (R) the robot root at the hip, (C_i) is the i-th camera of the robot, (O) is the object, (H) is the operator helmet, (Q_i) is the i-th camera of the helmet. For the robot cameras can be fixed $C_i \Rightarrow R$, as for the RGB-D at the torso, or $C_i \rightarrow R$ kinematic-based as for the cameras at end-effectors. The object is localized using the LINEMOD algorithm [11] providing the $O \rightarrow R$ transformation. Sensor fusion has been employed for obtaining a better estimate of the object $O \rightarrow R$ and $H \rightarrow R$ poses. In particular the robot object recognition takes into account uncertainty of the kinematics, distance of objects and motion as reported in a pending publication. For the operator all the transformations in the helmet are fixed and obtained by a registration procedure, namely obtaining $Q_i \Rightarrow H$.

What is missing is the transformation of the operator's head with respect to the robot base $H \rightarrow R$. This information can be obtained by some form of localization, and in this case it is based on an Aruco fiducial marker [12] that is seen both by the robot and the helmet's cameras. Calling F the marker frame then having $F \Rightarrow R$ and $F \rightarrow H$ allows to relate all the transformations. In the specific case discussed in this paper the robot is not moving, while the person is moving with respect to the reference. The overall structure of the reference systems is shown in Fig. 4.

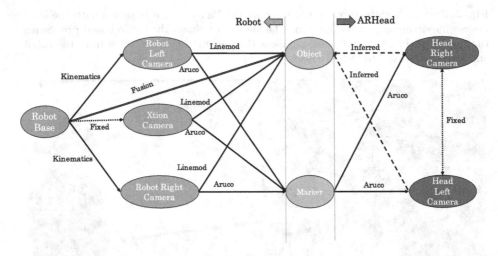

Fig. 4. Reference systems and connections. On the left the ones of the robot, in the middle the working environment, on the right the ARHead. Object position is obtained by sensor fusion and shown as double line.

The helmet pose is obtained by fusing the two estimates $F \rightarrow Q_1$ and $F \rightarrow Q_2$ in SE3 and weighted by the reprojection errors.

At present the resulting augmentation is limited to representing a reference system over the target object as shown in Fig. 5. Several types of augmentations can be investigated as briefly listed in the discussion section.

5   Discussion

Augmentation elements have been only sketched in this work, while most of focus has been on reference systems and architecture. Possible types of feedbacks that

Fig. 5. System Augmentation from two different point of views of the left eye. The robot frames have been highlighted and the object identified has been marked with a red cylinder. The direction of motion of the robot arm is shown with an arrow (Color figure online)

are being investigated are: (1) robot trajectory, (2) target position for moved object, (3) better highlight of the object, (4) robot workspace, (5) information about the object. Robot trajectory is useful for programming by demonstration task or in any case in which the robot is going to execute a motion path and the operator would like to see it in advance [13]. Object highlighting can be used to identify which is the object that is going to be picked by the robot, or that the robot suggests to the operator [7,14].

6   Conclusions

The paper has presented the system setup, the architecture and the reference frame issues that emerge from the possibility of creating a third point of view augmented reality feedback based on robot state. Basic augmentation has been presented as the result of the system design.

The main challenge in present setup is the quality of the tracking to obtain the common integrated reference system with the robot. The VGA resolution of the ARhead cameras could be raised up to Full HD at the cost of higher bandwidth requirements. Anyway, due to the fact that the head tracking information is based on the marker, while most of the computer vision part is done on the robot the tracking could be processed locally.

The next stage of the work is the investigation of effectiveness of the feedbacks, and the understanding on feedbacks that can be adapted depending on the level of uncertainty of the tracking.

Acknolwedgments. This work has been carried out within the framework of the Tuscany Regional Project TAUM. We also acknowledge Erika Di Stefano for having provided the Baxter setup and the computer vision algorithm, and Alessandro di Fava for the robot control.

References

1. Guizzo, E., Ackerman, E.: How rethink robotics built its new baxter robot worker. IEEE Spectrum (2012)
2. Heyer, C.: Human-robot interaction and future industrial robotics applications. In: 2010 IEEE/RSJ International Conference on Intelligent Robots and Systems (IROS), pp. 4749–4754. IEEE (2010)
3. Mavridis, N.: A review of verbal and non-verbal human-robot interactive communication. Robot. Auton. Syst. **63**, 22–35 (2015)
4. Chen, H., Lee, A.S., Swift, M., Tang, J.C.: 3d collaboration method over hololens and skype end points. In: Proceedings of the 3rd International Workshop on Immersive Media Experiences, pp. 27–30. ACM (2015)
5. Regenbrecht, H., Baratoff, G., Wilke, W.: Augmented reality projects in the automotive and aerospace industries. IEEE Comput. Graph. Appl. **25**(6), 48–56 (2005)
6. Chadalavada, R.T., Andreasson, H., Krug, R., Lilienthal, A.J.: Thats on my mind! robot to human intention communication through on-board projection on shared floor space. In: European Conference on Mobile Robots (ECMR) (2015)
7. Peppoloni, L., Brizzi, F., Ruffaldi, E., Avizzano, C.A.: Augmented reality-aided tele-presence system for robot manipulation in industrial manufacturing. In: Proceedings of the 21st ACM Symposium on Virtual Reality Software and Technology, pp. 237–240. ACM (2015)
8. Huang, W., Alem, L., Tecchia, F.: HandsIn3D: supporting remote guidance with immersive virtual environments. In: Winckler, M. (ed.) INTERACT 2013, Part I. LNCS, vol. 8117, pp. 70–77. Springer, Heidelberg (2013)
9. Ruffaldi, E., Brizzi, F., Filippeschi, A., Avizzano, C.A.: Co-located haptic interaction for virtual USG exploration. In: Proceedings of IEEE EMBC, pp. 1548–1551 (2015)
10. Ruffaldi, E., Brizzi, F.: CoCo - a framework for multicore visuo-haptic in mixed reality. In: De Paolis, L.T., Mongelli, A. (eds.) AVR 2016, Part I. LNCS, vol. 9768, pp. 339–357. Springer, Switzerland (2016)
11. Hinterstoisser, S., Holzer, S., Cagniart, C., Ilic, S., Konolige, K., Navab, N., Lepetit, V.: Multimodal templates for real-time detection of texture-less objects in heavily cluttered scenes. In: 2011 IEEE International Conference on Computer Vision (ICCV), pp. 858–865. IEEE (2011)
12. Garrido-Jurado, S., Muñoz-Salinas, R., Madrid-Cuevas, F.J., Marín-Jiménez, M.J.: Automatic generation and detection of highly reliable fiducial markers under occlusion. Pattern Recogn. **47**(6), 2280–2292 (2014)
13. Zaeh, M.F., Vogl, W.: Interactive laser-projection for programming industrial robots. In: IEEE/ACM International Symposium on Mixed and Augmented Reality, ISMAR 2006, pp. 125–128, October 2006
14. Olwal, A., Gustafsson, J., Lindfors, C.: Spatial augmented reality on industrial CNC-machines. In: Electronic Imaging 2008. International Society for Optics and Photonics, p. 680409 (2008)

Optimizing Image Registration for Interactive Applications

Riccardo Gasparini, Stefano Alletto, Giuseppe Serra$^{(\boxtimes)}$, and Rita Cucchiara

University of Modena and Reggio Emilia, Modena, Italy
giuseppe.serra@unimore.it

Abstract. With the spread of wearable and mobile devices, the request for interactive augmented reality applications is in constant growth. Among the different possibilities, we focus on the cultural heritage domain where a key step in the development applications for augmented cultural experiences is to obtain a precise localization of the user, i.e. the 6 degree-of-freedom of the camera acquiring the images used by the application. Current state of the art perform this task by extracting local descriptors from a query and exhaustively matching them to a sparse 3D model of the environment. While this procedure obtains good localization performance, due to the vast search space involved in the retrieval of 2D-3D correspondences this is often not feasible in real-time and interactive environments. In this paper we hence propose to perform descriptor quantization to reduce the search space and employ multiple KD-Trees combined with a principal component analysis dimensionality reduction to enable an efficient search. We experimentally show that our solution can halve the computational requirements of the correspondence search with regard to the state of the art while maintaining similar accuracy levels.

1 Introduction

Augmented user experiences in the cultural heritage domain are in increasing demand by the new digital native tourists of 21st century. With the widespread of wearable and mobile devices, modern tourists are inherently equipped with the hardware needed to provide multimedia and augmented reality content, and while in the academic community a renewed focus rises toward this problem, consumer market is increasing its demand for fast and accurate algorithms.

In this paper, we focus on the task of obtaining precise user localization from a query image (i.e., a photo acquired by the user) with respect to a known environment. For example, a tourist visiting a cultural heritage building could acquire an image using his smartphone or a wearable camera, send it to a processing server that elaborates it registering it to a pre-built Structure from Motion (SfM) 3D model of the scene and returns the localization. A precise (6 degree-of-freedom) localization is a key step in augmented reality applications [2,5,21], furthermore the process of localizing an image on a 3D model can be used to propagate on the image any annotation present on the 3D point cloud such as the presence

© Springer International Publishing Switzerland 2016
L.T. De Paolis and A. Mongelli (Eds.): AVR 2016, Part I, LNCS 9768, pp. 479–488, 2016.
DOI: 10.1007/978-3-319-40621-3_36

of relevant architectural details that may be subsequently browsed by the user on a screen [1].

While the registration of a query image to a SfM model has been tackled in the past [13,19,20], it is usually approached from an algorithmic point of view, e.g. focusing on large-scale datasets or trying to solve issues like matching under different viewpoints and lighting conditions. Many of these works disregard execution times in favor of high accuracies under challenging conditions, but in order to be able to build interactive consumer applications based on the localization on a 3D model the correspondence search between 2D features and 3D points has to be performed in semi-real time. The standard pipeline employed in the registration of a query image is based on the extraction of local discriminative features (e.g. SIFT keypoints) from the query image and the search for correspondences of these keypoints into the 3D point cloud. This search is often addressed as a nearest neighbor problem and the most popular data structure employed to speed up this phase is the KD-Tree. Once 2D-3D correspondences are established, the query is localized using standard Perspective-n-Point methods [6].

In this work, we propose to intervene on the correspondence search aiming at speeding up the most onerous component of the registration pipeline. In particular, we perform initial experiments exploiting the heavy parallelism of modern multi-core CPUs and GPGPUs. These experiments, highlighting the parallelization difficulties inherent to the structure of the problem, show that approaching the problem from an hardware point of view may not be sufficient to achieve the interactive requirements of an end-user application. Hence, we propose to address the main limitation of the KD-Tree data structure, i.e. its poor scalability under high dimensional data points. By reducing the dimensionality of the data points before constructing the KD-Tree, we can achieve matching times under half a second, which are suitable for interactive cultural heritage applications.

2   Related Work

Large-scale image-based localization is often treated as an image retrieval task, where a query image is matched with a database of geo-localized images [13,19,20]. Schindler et al. [20] present a method for city scale localization based on the bag of visual words representation using street side images. Hay and Efros [8] propose an approach that is able to extract coarse geographical information from a given image exploring a set of Flickr images. Recently some approaches have started addressing the problem of severe changes in lighting conditions between reference images and query. Hauagge et al. [7] propose the use of outdoor illumination models for estimating appearance and timestamps from a large set of images of an outdoor scene. Torri et al. [24] propose a place recognition method that combines synthesis of new virtual views with densely sampled image descriptors. After finding the images most similar to a query, the localization is determined using the GPS localization of those images. In most of the cases, the results are evaluated in terms of registration performance or matching quality, but execution times or scalability are rarely considered. Furthermore, these approaches have shown high performance in scenarios of very large-scale datasets; however, the major problem is that the achieved localization accuracy cannot be better than the precision of the GPS position of the images in the database, which is not suitable for augmented reality applications.

To obtain a better localization accuracy, various techniques have explored the use of the 3D structure of the environment [14,18]. The significant progress achieved in Structure from Motion (SfM) makes it possible to build models on a city-scale. Essentially, localization is obtained by identifying correspondences between 2D local features in the query image and 3D points of the point-cloud. A common strategy to address this matching problem is to use local-invariant features, such as SIFT [15]. In [14], the authors deal with the task of registering images to multiple 3D point clouds, possibly modeling places in different parts of the world. To address the ambiguity in the nearest neighbor search resulting from having millions of 3D points, they propose to employ co-occurrence priors and incorporate them into the RANSAC loop, effectively sampling hypotheses in a statistically significant way. Once 2D-3D correspondences are identified and filtered from outliers, a standard 3-point pose solver is used to compute the camera location. Sattler et al. [18] propose to exploit the advantages of direct 2D-3D matching by creating a codebook of SIFT visual words and use it to limit the search space. Instead of matching every descriptor in the query image to the entire space of the point cloud, they approximate this search by clustering descriptor into visual words and, once a query descriptor is identified as belonging to a cluster, exhaustive linear search is performed inside the cluster to retrieve the exact correspondence.

3   Proposed Method

Structure from Motion (SfM) techniques aim at building a 3D point cloud of a scene from an unordered set of images exploiting keypoint correspondences (e.g. SIFT features) between pictures capturing similar viewpoints of the same object [4,17,22,23]. After finding a set of geometrically consistent matches, their projecting points into the 3D space and the camera parameters (intrinsic and extrinsic, i.e. focal length, location and orientation) are jointly estimated running the Bundle Adjustment (BA) algorithm [23]. Iteratively, after each new image is matched and added to the point cloud, the algorithm minimizes the sum of the distances between the projection of the 3D points and their relative 2D keypoints (i.e. the reprojection error). This allows to use non-linear least squares solvers reducing the risk of incurring in local minima, an otherwise significant issue when trying to find the minimum cost in a single run. Figure 1 shows an example of 3D model obtained using the aforementioned process.

While using SfM to recover the 3D structure of an environment provides accuracies often used as ground-truth for other methods [12], performing the feature extraction, the exhaustive matching and the iterative BA often requires computation times beyond any real-time applications. Hence, given a pre-built 3D model, we analyze how to perform the registration of a single image under the constraints of a cultural heritage interactive applications, in which the user can only wait for a few seconds of processing time.

Fig. 1. 3D sparse reconstruction using image acquired by wearable cameras.

3.1   Image Registration Under Time Constraints

The task of registering or localizing a single image to a pre-built 3D point cloud has been recently addressed in literature [13,18–20]. In particular, the standard pipeline used to obtain precise localization of a query image is the following. First, SIFT keypoints are extracted from it: the usage of this descriptor allows to match with the 3D points of the model, where every point is described with the list of SIFT descriptors that matched to produce that point in the SfM phase. To obtain a set of 2D-3D correspondences, the SIFT features on the query image are matched with the 3D point cloud. A match is considered correct if the distance ratio (distance from the closest neighbor to the distance of the second closest)

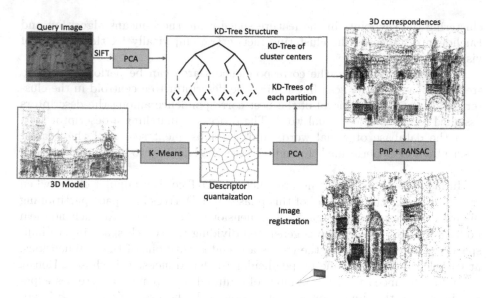

Fig. 2. Summarization of the proposed approach.

is lower than a fix threshold (often set at 0.8). Once that 2D-3D correspondences are established, Perspective-n-Point (PnP) algorithm can be used to retrieve the extrinsic camera parameters [6,9]. In particular, the PnP algorithm finds the 6 degrees-of-freedom (DoF) pose of a calibrated camera by exploiting the projective model:

$$\mathbf{p} = \mathtt{K}[\mathtt{R}|\mathbf{t}]\mathbf{P} \tag{1}$$

where $\mathbf{p}$ is the 2D point on the image place (in homogeneous coordinates), $\mathbf{P}$ is the 3D point in the world reference system and $\mathtt{K}, \mathtt{R}$ and $\mathbf{t}$ are respectively the intrinsic parameters, rotation and translation matrices. Since the presence of possible outliers in the correspondences can compromise the results of the PnP algorithm, its execution is often enclosed in a RANSAC loop formulating transformation hypotheses and minimizing the reprojection error that such hypotheses result in.

Matching the 2D descriptors of a query that potentially features several thousands keypoints to a 3D point cloud composed of hundred of thousands of points requires some strategies to reduce the search space in order to be computationally feasible. In fact, our experiments showed that, despite the recent advancements in hardware quality, approaching the problem in terms of multi (CPU) or many-core (GPU) parallelization is not sufficient to satisfy the requirements of an interactive application (see Sect. 4).

To achieve fast 2D-3D correspondences, we follow the strategy adopted in [18] that builds a vocabulary of visual words quantizing SIFT descriptors. First of all, a visual vocabulary is obtained through vector quantization of the local SIFT features of the 3D point cloud. The visual vocabulary is generated by clustering the keypoints in the feature space using the k-means algorithm and Euclidean distance as the clustering metric (we empirically fix the number of visual words to 1000).

Given a query image, the correspondence search can be performed in two steps: first, a similarity search assigning the descriptor to a centroid in the cluster, followed by the retrieval of the best correspondence among the descriptors assigned to the selected visual word. The process of matching a descriptor with both the database of visual words and the subsequent search of the nearest descriptor can be performed through the use of a KD-Tree to improve the search speed.

In fact, the use of tree structures such as KD-Trees is a popular choice when trying to reduce the workload of this phase [3]. KD-Trees are space-partitioning binary trees designed to organize k-dimensional data points. At each non-leaf node, a splitting hyperplane is generated dividing the search space in two half-spaces. Since every node in the tree is associated with one of the k dimensions, at each level an hyperplane perpendicular to that dimension is chosen. Hence, to build a balanced tree, the number of required data points n increases exponentially with the dimension k of such points. If the property $n >> k$ is not satisfied, the search based on a KD-Tree degenerates to an $O(n)$ linear search instead of the $O(\log n)$ property of a binary tree.

To overcome this issue of KD-Trees, where in practice given the dimension of the 3D point cloud of a structure the theoretical average search cost is never reached, we propose to reduce the dimensionality of the quantized descriptors via Principal Component Analysis (PCA) [10]. PCA is a statistical approach that, through orthogonal transformations maps a set of correlated data points into a lower dimensional space where the resulting variables are linearly independent. Recent literature demonstrated that the use of PCA to reduce the dimensionality of local SIFT descriptors allows to obtain compact and informative feature vectors [11,16].

Applying dimensionality reduction to both the first level KD-Tree (cluster centroids) and the second level KD-Trees (one for each visual word) allows to exploit the advantages of quantizing the descriptors while jointly reducing the dimensionality of the data points and improve the search performance. Differently from [18], the usage of dimensionality reduction techniques has a major impact on the computational time while still resulting in a similar number of valid matches. In fact, given the size of the 3D model employed in our experiments, the high dimensionality of the SIFT descriptor is not ideal and the improvements tied to the use of a KD-Tree with respect to the Brute Force approach are otherwise negligible. Figure 2 summarizes the proposed solution.

4   Experimental Evaluation

To evaluate the impact on both performance and matching quality of our search strategy, we adopt the publicly available dataset presented in [1]. This dataset, which revolves around the romanic Cathedral of Modena, features 743 images captured from different points of view and in unconstrained lighting and weather conditions. These images have been employed, using the structure from motion tool presented in [25], to build a sparse 3D model of the structure. The 3D point cloud contains more that 220.000 points obtained from more than 1.000.000 SIFT correspondences and it is in line with models built in recent state of the art techniques [12, 23]. All the presented results were performed on an Intel Core2 Quad q9550 2.83 GHz CPU and a Nvidia GeForce GTX660 2 GB GDDR5 GPU.

Table 1. Execution times of retrieving the 2D-3D matches of a query image with 2000 SIFT keypoints. The number of 3D Points have been subsampled from the complete point cloud and different sampling sizes are reported. The methods reported are: Brute Force (BF) on CPU (multi-core), BF on GPU, KD-Tree on CPU, KD-Tree on GPU.

Method	3D Points	Time(s)
BF	10^3	0.083
	10^4	0.770
	10^5	7.472
KD-Tree	10^3	0.911
	10^4	8.467
	10^5	83.885
BF-GPU	10^3	0.532
	10^4	6.493
	10^5	76.896
KD-GPU	10^3	0.699
	10^4	8.944
	10^5	104.854

Given the recent improvements achieved by hardware producers, the first option evaluated to improve the performance of the 2D-3D matching is to exploit multi-core parallelization in the algorithms. In particular, we present an evaluation of the parallelization of the two main exhaustive strategies in 2D-3D matching: the brute-force approach and the nearest neighbor search based on KD-Trees. Table 1 reports the results exploiting both CPU and GPU parallelization. It can be noticed that due to the high dimensionality of SIFT descriptors, the adoption of a KD-Tree to speed-up the search for a match does not provide the expected improvement. Moreover, given the nature of the problem, where both the query data and the KD-Tree must be transferred from the local memory to the GPU, adopting a GPU does not provide any improvement with respect to the brute force strategy. On the contrary, since due to the memory requirements of the search it is not possible to transfer all the required data together to the GPU memory, it can be seen how the communication time dominates the actual computation and results in an overall execution time worst than running on CPU. Based on these results, it clearly appears how tackling the problem from

Table 2. Comparison between the approach proposed by Sattler et al. [18] and the presented solution with different dimensionality reduction.

Method	Dimensionality	Time (s)	Valid Matches
Sattler et al. [18]	128	1.2538	22.6
Our approach	64	0.6690	22.2
	32	0.3996	19.2
	16	0.2634	7.8
	8	0.1766	6.4

an hardware point of view by parallelizing existing exhaustive search algorithms is not sufficient to achieve the required performance for interactive applications.

To evaluate the impact in performance and accuracy of our solution we compare it with a similar approach proposed in [18] that performs an approximate 2D-3D matching strategy. To perform a fair comparison for both methods we use the same experimental setting (same query images, local features, clustering procedure and 3D model). The results are reported considering queries with an average of 2500 SIFT keypoints and the full 3D point cloud. Table 2 shows the results in terms of required time and matching performance. In particular, we evaluate the impact of the reduction of the SIFT vector dimensionality through PCA. The objective of this dimensionality reduction is to scale the SIFT feature vector to a dimensionality that enables the use of balanced KD-Trees. In fact, given the amount of 3D points in our dataset, obtaining a balanced KD-Tree from 128-d descriptor is not possible since it would theoretically require 2^{128} points. It can be noticed the lower the number of considered principal components is, the fastest the method gets at the price of a lower matching performance. In particular, the results show that depending on the desired accuracy and the particular interaction requirements the dimensionality of the resulting vector can be adjusted to either speed up the method or increase its accuracy. For example, reducing the descriptor dimensionality from 128 to 64 halves the required time to perform the search using the KD-Tree while keeping the number of resulting matches substantially unchanged.

Since, in general, the minimum number of required 2D-3D correspondences needed by PnP methods is 4, it can be noticed how dividing the descriptor dimensionality by a factor of 4 still produces sufficient correspondences to robustly (i.e., in a RANSAC loop) perform the query registration. Thanks to the reduction to 32-d vectors, the matching process takes in average less than 0.4 s which is an acceptable value for an interactive application. Dimensionality reduction below 32, while still providing significant speed-up and achieving an average of more than 4 matches, is not guaranteed to enable the execution of multiple RANSAC iterations and should therefore be discarded.

5   Conclusions

In this paper we presented an analysis of the standard image registration pipeline, focused on finding the bottlenecks of the procedure and provide a solution that enables the use of registration techniques when requiring interactive response times. In particular, we experimentally showed that exploiting hardware parallelism does not result into improvements. We hence proposed to cluster the descriptors in the 3D point cloud to reduce the search space approximating the results. Through the use of KD-Trees, both the search for the nearest visual word and the retrieval of the closest descriptor belonging to the given visual word are speeded up. To overcome the most critical issue of KD-Trees, i.e. their inability to effectively deal with high dimensional data points, we performed principal component analysis and reduced the resulting descriptor to a dimensionality more suitable. The experimental evaluation on a public benchmark dataset showed that our solution is capable of obtaining a significant speed-up compared to a state of the art approach while maintaining similar levels of matching quality, a key step in the design of interactive augmented reality applications.

Acknowledgments. This work was partially supported by the Fondazione Cassa di Risparmio di Modena project: "Vision for Augmented Experience" and the PON R&C project DICET-INMOTO (Cod. PON04a2 D).

References

1. Alletto, S., Abati, D., Serra, G., Cucchiara, R.: Exploring architectural details through awearable egocentric vision device. Sensors **16**(2) (2016)
2. Arth, C., Wagner, D., Klopschitz, M., Irschara, A., Schmalstieg, D.: Wide area localization on mobile phones. In: Proceedings of IEEE International Symposium on Mixed and Augmented Reality (2009)
3. Bentley, J.L.: Multidimensional binary search trees used for associative searching. Commun. ACM **18**(9), 509–517 (1975)
4. Brown, M., Lowe, D.G.: Unsupervised 3D object recognition and reconstruction in unordered datasets. In: Proceedings of International Conference on 3-D Digital Imaging and Modeling (2005)
5. Castle, R., Klein, G., Murray, D.W.: Video-rate localization in multiple maps for wearable augmented reality. In: Proceedings of IEEE International Symposium on Wearable Computers (2008)
6. Hartley, R.I., Zisserman, A.: Multiple View Geometry in Computer Vision, 2nd edn. Cambridge University Press, Cambridge (2004). ISBN: 0521540518
7. Hauagge, D., Wehrwein, S., Upchurch, P., Bala, K., Snavely, N.: Reasoning about photo collections using models of outdoor illumination. In: Proceedings of British Machine Vision Conference (2014)
8. Hays, J., Efros, A.: IM2GPS: estimating geographic information from a single image. In: Proceedings of CVPR (2008)
9. Irschara, A., Zach, C., Frahm, J., Bischof, H.: From structure-from-motion point clouds to fast location recognition. In: Proceedings of IEEE International Conference on Computer Vision and Pattern Recognition (2009)

10. Jolliffe, I.: Principal Component Analysis. Wiley Online Library (2002)
11. Ke, Y., Sukthankar, R.: PCA-SIFT: a more distinctive representation for local image descriptors. In: Proceedings of IEEE International Conference on Computer Vision and Pattern Recognition (2004)
12. Kroeger, T., Van Gool, L.: Video registration to SfM models. In: Proceedings of IEEE European Conference on Computer Vision (2014)
13. Li, Y., Snavely, N., Huttenlocher, D., Fua, P.: Worldwide pose estimation using 3D point clouds. In: Fitzgibbon, A., Lazebnik, S., Perona, P., Sato, Y., Schmid, C. (eds.) ECCV 2012, Part I. LNCS, vol. 7572, pp. 15–29. Springer, Heidelberg (2012)
14. Li, Y., Snavely, N., Huttenlocher, D., Fua, P.: Worldwide pose estimation using 3D point clouds. In: Proceedings of IEEE European Conference on Computer Vision (2012)
15. Lowe, D.G.: Distinctive image features from scale-invariant keypoints. Int. J. Comput. Vis. $60(2)$, 91–110 (2004)
16. Perronnin, F., Sánchez, J., Mensink, T.: Improving the fisher kernel for large-scale image classification. In: Proceedings of IEEE European Conference on Computer Vision (2010)
17. Pollefeys, M., Van Gool, L., Vergauwen, M., Verbiest, F., Cornelis, K., Tops, J., Koch, R.: Visual modeling with a hand-held camera. Int. J. Comput. Vis. $59(3)$, 207–232 (2004)
18. Sattler, T., Leibe, B., Kobbelt, L.: Fast image-based localization using direct 2D-to-3D matching. In: Proceedings of IEEE International Conference on Computer Vision (2011)
19. Sattler, T., Weyand, T., Leibe, B., Kobbelt, L.: Image retrieval for image-based localization revisited. In: Proceedings of British Machine Vision Conference (2012)
20. Schindler, G., Brown, M., Szeliski, R.: City-scale location recognition. In: Proceedings of IEEE Conference on Computer Vision and Pattern Recognition (2007)
21. Schops, T., Engel, J., Cremers, D.: Semi-dense visual odometry for AR on a smartphone. In: Proceedings of IEEE International Symposium on Mixed and Augmented Reality (2014)
22. Snavely, N., Seitz, S.M., Szeliski, R.: Photo tourism: exploring photo collections in 3D. ACM Trans. Graph. 25, 835–846 (2006). ACM
23. Snavely, N., Seitz, S.M., Szeliski, R.: Modeling the world from internet photo collections. Int. J. Comput. Vis. $80(2)$, 189–210 (2008)
24. Torii, A., Arandjelovic, R., Sivic, J., Okutomi, M., Pajdla, T.: 24/7 place recognition by view synthesis. In: Proceedings of IEEE Conference on Computer Vision and Pattern Recognition (2015)
25. Wu, C., Agarwal, S., Curless, B., Seitz, S.: Multicore bundle adjustment. In: Proceedings of IEEE Conference on Computer Vision and Pattern Recognition (2011)

A System to Exploit Thermographic Data Using Projected Augmented Reality

Saverio Debernardis[✉], Michele Fiorentino, Antonio E. Uva, and Giuseppe Monno

DMMM, Politecnico di Bari, Bari, Italy
{s.debernardis,michele.fiorentino,antonio.uva,
giuseppe.monno}@poliba.it

Abstract. We present a prototype system composed practically of an IR camera and a video projector with the purpose to create a device that projects the thermal map directly on the observed surface. The novelty of this work lies on the building of a portable tool, the development of software and the proposing of a calibration procedure to be used in industrial and construction sites from thermal inspectors.

1 Introduction

Infrared thermography [13] inspection is a very used technique applied by technicians and engineers, with different methods and modalities [22, 35], to understand conditions of mechanical parts on machines [19, 20], to make building diagnoses [2–4, 14], to investigate pipeline conditions [9, 10, 18], archaeological ruins [6, 7, 16], to create systems for medical applications [5, 6, 17], or for military investigation [28], and whatever is possible to find out by thermal information [22, 27, 31]. A typical use of an infrared thermography system is to have a thermal map of the considered surface, to observe or an exact temperature distribution or a temperature gradient, depending on different methods applied to extract information from thermal detector [30]. Infrared thermal imaging is crucial to provide video data which show the correct observed phenomenon.

In the building industry, thermography inspections, allow to obtain a global vision about structure conditions, and being no-destructive, give almost easily information about the state of structures, the orientation of load-bearing platforms of floors, the counterthrust chains of facades, masonry textures underneath the plaster, about what causes moisture and water seeping, and help to detect thermal anomalies like heat bridges, loss of heat through and around doors and windows.

Industry makes full use of IR inspections to prevent halts in production, to monitor high temperature pipe-lines, electrical machines and wires, thermal and chemical processes, to detect corrosion phenomena, and to predict fatigue fractures.

Imaging techniques can set different parameters of the overall system, for example the use of different filters on thermal detector signals, different lens, different frame rates, different color palettes, different color scales associated to an observed temperature range, and so on. For operators, one of the most important issue in this application is the difficult association between real world points and temperature map on the screen of the device. Thermal maps may differ from the visible space and therefore users have no

© Springer International Publishing Switzerland 2016
L.T. De Paolis and A. Mongelli (Eds.): AVR 2016, Part I, LNCS 9768, pp. 489–499, 2016.
DOI: 10.1007/978-3-319-40621-3_37

visual clues for correct and quick diagnose. This problem is critical in flat, even surfaces like walls, steel plates, etc., very common in industry and building. In these situations, an exact identification of some anomalies on surfaces is required, for example to locate a broken pipe in a long and large wall without the possibility to easily approach it. These particular cases necessarily need an important image processing, evidently not in the construction site, before having a criterion of a good positioning. All that means high costs due to multiple inspection services before taking action on the real cause of the problem.

One interesting approach to this issue is to register thermal images on the 3D reconstruction, as proposed by [29]. They created a system with a thermal camera and a depth sensor to obtain 3D reconstruction of a thermal map. The IR device detects the temperature map and the depth sensor the 3D environment. The algorithm they developed, based on KinectFusion [24] and ray casting, provides a correct association between each point detected by the depth sensor and pixel of the thermal map detected by the IR sensor. Considering the cheap depth sensors like Microsoft Kinect, they have also an RGB camera so they can merge three type of information: 3D surface reconstruction, the RGB color mapping texture and the thermal colored map. In this manner, they are able to show information they need also partially in the scene. As regards ray casting, 5 are the factors that they considered in assigning the thermal data: the speed of the thermal sensor,

(a) the position of the pixel in the visual field,
(b) the angle between the ray and the normal vector to the surface,
(c) the distance of the vertex from the camera,
(d) and the validity of the radiometric model considered.

Our approach is to use Spatial Augmented Reality, an emerging technology in the field of digital art and media, as many of the applications in events, concerts, theater, advertising, museums and videogames are showing [36]. The first example of projection on non-planar surfaces dates back to 1969, i.e. for the opening of the Haunted Mansion at Disneyland. Other pioneering experiments on the projection have been conducted since 1980 by Naimark [23]. Actually, the SAR acronym was introduced by Raskar and Colleagues [25, 26], with the definition as a technique in which virtual objects are graphically rendered directly inside or on the user's physical space, that is, the physical environment of user is increased with embedded images directly with the user's environment, and not only in his visual field. Their first application was 'The office of the future', a conceptual prototype that includes the use of projectors in place of lights within a very similar way to a CAVE for the tele-collaboration in the workplace.

The purpose of our work is to create a product based on the paper presented by Iwai and Sato [15]. They presented a novel infrared thermography visualization technique where a sequence of captured thermal images is optically and simultaneously superimposed onto the target object via video projection in real time. We think this idea is interesting because, while in conventional thermography visualization, observers have to frequently move their eyes from the object to a 2D screen where a thermal image is displayed, in this proposed method the heat distribution of the object's surface emerges directly onto its physical surface. As a result, the observer can intuitively understand the object's heat information just by looking at it in the real space. Practically, in accordance to the above example of the long and large wall, with our tool we can cancel further image processing and inspections, and visualize easily and exactly where anomalies are located.

In our experience, we explored how information could be perceived using projected Augmented Reality [8], and how they could improve industrial uses [11, 12, 21]. Now what the authors present is a prototypal tool based on the idea of [15] to be applied in the building industry to detect warm/cold tube under plaster or heat no homogeneity distribution surfaces. To be a practical tool, ready to be tested, we thought to study an adequate calibration procedure to make it with changeable instruments, that is different projectors and IR camera, and an experimental frame to assemble them. Different calibration procedures, to calibrate similar system, were proposed ([1, 32–34]), but what we propose here is a tool that can be used by technicians and engineers and not only in a laboratory.

2   Requirements

We identified the following requirements for the tool we want to develop according to the purpose of our work:

- Portable
- Calibration procedure should be easy to do everywhere and no in lab
- IR camera and projector should be replaceable
- It is enough to project the thermal map on a plan surface, without considering different surface in the same scene.

These requirements were considered for a first prototype tool to be validated in the building construction field. Future development should go over that to become more specific as a new product. A description of the developed system follows in the next sections with the reached results. In the last two sections we show what are the final purposes about the characteristics of our product.

3   Our System

In order to make the device portable, as hardware we utilized a pico video projector, an IR camera, and a frame with handles to locate them. The pico projector is an Asus S1 with the following main features:

- Physical Dimensions (WxHxD): 110.5 × 30.7 × 102 mm
- Weight: 342 g
- Resolution: 854 × 480px (WVGA)
- Illuminance: 200 lm
- Contrast: 1000: 1
- Colors: 16.7 M
- Light source: RGB LED

- Video Compatibility: NTSC, PAL, SECAM, 480i, 480p, 576i, 576p, 720p, 1080i, 1080p

The thermal camera available in our laboratory is a FLIR A20 M with the following main features:

- Output: CVBS, IEEE 1394 DCAM monochrome (1:0:0) 320 × 240, IEEE 1394 DCAM color (4:2:2) 640 × 480, IEEE 1394 (FFF) 16-bit monochrome
- Camera control: keyboard, RS-232, IEEE 1394 interface, IEEE 1394 TCP/IP interface
- Lens: IR lens 17 mm
- Physical dimensions (W × H × D): 72 × 84 × 161 mm

To operate the system, we developed a software that receives the signal from the camera and sends it to the projector appropriately deformed. As a starting point, the geometric parameters were given by the built prototype scheme. A constructive criterion followed in this phase was to obtain the maximum possible proximity between the two optical axes, so as to obtain the maximum overlap between cone of vision of the IR camera and projection cone of the video projector. Fixed as the prototype operating distance 1,2 m, the following geometrical characteristics for the IR camera were calculated (Fig. 1):

- Captured area (HxV): 500 × 370 cm
- Capture area symmetric respect to its optic axis both vertically and horizontally
- Horizontal capturing angle $\alpha = 23.5°$
- Vertical capturing angle $\beta = 17.5°$

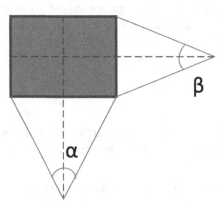

Fig. 1. Section of the vertical and horizontal planes relative to the IR camera as well as composition of the captured area

As regards the video projector, at the same distance of 1.2 m, with an aspect ratio of 16:9, the following features result (Fig. 2):

- Projection area no symmetric to its optic axis
- Horizontal projection angle: α = 39°
- Vertical projection angle: β = 28.4°

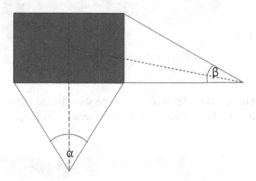

Fig. 2. Section of the vertical and horizontal planes relative to the video projector as well as composition of the captured area

Finally, our prototype system is composed by two wooden sideburns, one swiveling, connected by two aluminum bars, as shown in (Fig. 3)

Fig. 3. Prototype system composed by Bosch aluminum profiles and wooden sideburns to house the FLIR A20 M and the video projector ASUS S1

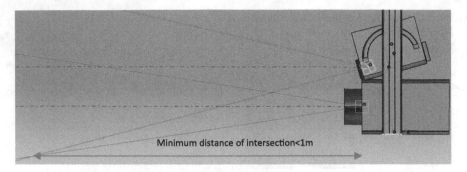

Fig. 4. Visualization of the CAD model of our prototype showing the minimum distance required to have a complete inclusion of captured cone of IR camera in the projection cone of the video projector

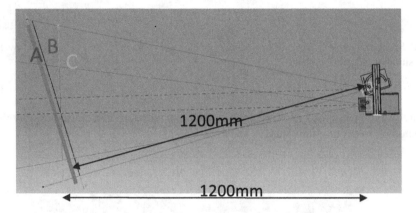

Fig. 5. Cad model of the device with indication of the plane used to align the detected area and the projection plane

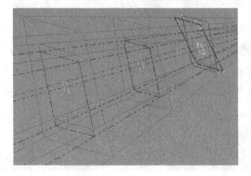

Fig. 6. CAD model of the detected area from the IR camera (red rays) at different distances, and its correspondent space (blue rays), included in full projection space (green rays). (Color figure online)

The developed system has the parallelism between the optical axis of the IR camera and the bisector of the angle of video projection, and the cone of projection includes as much as possible the capturing cone of the IR camera (Fig. 7).

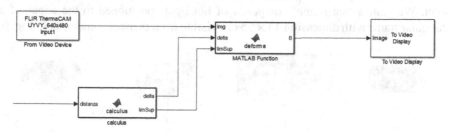

Fig. 7. Workflow of Simulink tool: IR camera signal and ultrasound distance sensor are the two inputs, the output video is the projected one

Considering a plane of 1.2 m as in Fig. 5, the IR camera detects the temperature on the plane C whereas the projector project on plane A, on plane B if the distance is considered on the axis of the IR camera. We developed a software with Matlab/Simulink to adapt the image detected and elaborated of the IR camera, and to send it appropriately deformed to the video projector.

3.1 II Phase Development

In a second phase we added an ultrasound distance sensor to our device and our software calculates in-time the correct deformation according to our geometric scheme, as described in Fig. 6.

Important to observe is that for every distance, over the minimum one indicated in the Fig. 4, the projection cone includes the IR detected cone (Fig. 8).

Fig. 8. 'Hot frame' built with IR emitting light with dimensions of 43 × 25 cm visible from thermal camera

3.2 Calibration Procedure

We present here a prototype of a calibration algorithm different from the other ones present in literature [1, 32–34], because we do not use a RGB camera, external to the system. We built a 'hot frame' composed of hot lights positioned to the edges of a rectangular frame with dimension 43×25 cm visible from thermal camera, as in Fig. 9.

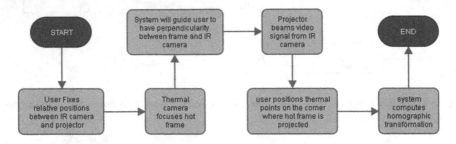

Fig. 9. Description of the proposed calibration procedure

The procedure consists of six operations:

(1) The relative position between IR camera and video projector is blocked. User has to assure that the area of projection enormously includes the taken IR camera area.
(2) Fixed the position of the hot frame on a wall, the thermal camera has to focus it.
(3) The developed system guides the user to orient it (IR camera + video projector) perpendicular to the captured frame, basing on its shape.
(4) Projector beams video signal from thermal camera on the wall. According to condition (1), the projected frame should be around the real one but deformed
(5) User has to position each thermal point on each corner of the projected frame. Thermal points are simple small circular hot plates visible from the thermal camera
(6) Developed system calculates homographic transformation between hot frame and projected frame. The homographic matrix will be used from the system up to a new calibration.

We consider this procedure useful to be utilized almost everywhere, it is simple and fast to do. What a user needs is some accessories (hot frame and hot points) and a wall on which to fix the hot frame.

4 Results and Future Developments

The results obtained were satisfactory enough to be ready to organize a series of experiments appropriate to validate the usability of the instrument and its benefits of utilization in industry and in the building field.

The images in Fig. 10 show the case of the considered prototyping, i.e. the coupling of the pico projector ASUS S1 and the FLIR A25. The different tests carried out, even at different distances have demonstrated the robustness of the implemented models and the high accuracy achieved in the overlap between real and projected. The built prototype has the main feature to be a portable framework, apart from the computer, even if a notebook could be an interesting solution.

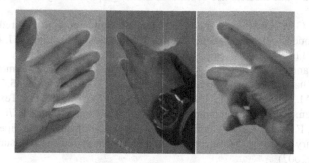

Fig. 10. The system working on a wall where is superimposed a hand with a higher temperature than the wall

Future works will validate the usefulness of the projection mapping against a common visualization of a thermal map on a video screen to locate hot piping lines under plaster with experiments with users. In these future experiments we intend also to do a validation of the calibration procedure about how users consider that in term of easiness of use and the utility of the GUI interface. In the validation process should be also considered also the visibility of the thermal map with different enlightenment conditions commons in the specific sites of use, where 200 lm of the ASUS S1 projector are may be not ever enough.

5 Conclusions

The purpose of this paper is to show the building of a system composed of a thermal camera and a video projector with the idea to use the projection mapping techniques in the qualitative thermal inspections common in the industrial and building fields. Even if we used an already proposed idea, what is here described is a practical tool built not only to satisfy research laboratory needs but handy and portability requirements useful to engineers and technicians in industrial and building sites. More attention is considered about the calibration of the system, not in terms of new algorithms, but in terms of easiness and handiness.

References

1. Amano, T.: Projection center calibration for a co-located projector camera system. In: Proceedings of the IEEE Conference on Computer Vision and Pattern Recognition Workshops, pp. 443–448 (2014)
2. Avdelidis, N.P., Moropoulou, A.: Emissivity considerations in building thermography. Energy Build. **35**(7), 663–667 (2003)
3. Balaras, C.A., Argiriou, A.A.: Infrared thermography for building diagnostics. Energy Build. **34**(2), 171–183 (2002)

4. Barreira, E., de Freitas, V.P.: Evaluation of building materials using infrared thermography. Constr. Build. Mater. **21**(1), 218–224 (2007)
5. Berz, R., et al.: The medical use of infrared-thermography history and recent applications (2007)
6. Carlomagno, G.M., Di Maio, R., Fedi, M., Meola, C.: Integration of infrared thermography and high-frequency electromagnetic methods in archaeological surveys. J. Geophys. Eng. **8**(3), S93 (2011)
7. Casana, J., Kantner, J., Wiewel, A., Cothren, J.: Archaeological aerial thermography: A case study at the Chaco-era Blue J community, New Mexico. J. Archaeol. Sci. **45**, 207–219 (2014)
8. Di Donato, M., Fiorentino, M., Uva, A.E., Gattullo, M., Monno, G.: Text legibility for projected augmented reality on industrial workbenches. Comput. Ind. **70**, 70–78 (2015)
9. Fan, C., Sun, F., Yang, L.: An algorithm study on the identification of a pipeline's irregular inner boundary based on thermographic temperature measurement. Measur. Sci. Technol. **18**(7), 2170 (2007)
10. Fan, C., Sun, F., Yang, L.: Investigation on nondestructive evaluation of pipelines using infrared thermography. In: The Joint 30th International Conference on Infrared and Millimeter Waves and 13th International Conference on Terahertz Electronics, 2005. IRMMW-THz 2005, pp. 339–340 (2005)
11. Fiorentino, M., Debernardis, S., Uva, A.E., Monno, G.: Augmented reality text style readability with see-through head-mounted displays in industrial context. Presence: Teleoperators Virtual Environ. **22**(2), 171–190 (2013)
12. Fiorentino, M., Uva, A.E., Gattullo, M., Debernardis, S., Monno, G.: Augmented reality on large screen for interactive maintenance instructions. Comput. Ind. **65**(2), 270–278 (2014)
13. Gaussorgues, G., Chomet, S.: Infrared Thermography. Springer, Netherlands (2012)
14. Hart, J.M.: A Practical Guide to Infra-red Thermography for Building Surveys. Building Research Establishment, Watford (2010)
15. Iwai, D., Sato, K.: Optical superimposition of infrared thermography through video projection. Infrared Phys. Technol. **53**(3), 162–172 (2010)
16. Kordatos, E.Z., Exarchos, D.A., Stavrakos, C., Moropoulou, A., Matikas, T.E.: Infrared thermographic inspection of murals and characterization of degradation in historic monuments. Constr. Build. Mater. **48**, 1261–1265 (2013)
17. Lahiri, B.B., Bagavathiappan, S., Jayakumar, T., Philip, J.: Medical applications of infrared thermography: A review. Infrared Phys. Technol. **55**(4), 221–235 (2012)
18. Liu, Z., Kleiner, Y.: State of the art review of inspection technologies for condition assessment of water pipes. Measurement **46**(1), 1–15 (2013)
19. Maillard, S., Cadith, J., Eschimese, D., Walaszek, H., Mooshofer, H., Candore, J., Bodnar, J.: Towards the use of passive and active infrared thermography to inspect metallic components in the mechanical industry. In: 10th International Conference on Quantitative InfraRed Thermography (2010)
20. Maldague, X.P.: Nondestructive Evaluation of Materials by Infrared Thermography. Springer Science & Business Media, London (2012)
21. de Marchi, L., Ceruti, A., Marzani, A., Liverani, A.: Augmented reality to support on-field post-impact maintenance operations on thin structures. J. Sens. **2013** (2013)
22. Meola, C., Christophe, A., Carlomagno, G.M., Klaus, G., Ermanno, G., Ivana, K., Petr, K., Carosena, M., Rocco, P., Roberto, R., et al.: Infrared thermography recent advances and future trends (2012)
23. Naimark, M.: Two unusual projection spaces. Presence **14**(5), 597–605 (2005)

24. Newcombe, R.A., Davison, A.J., Izadi, S., Kohli, P., Hilliges, O., Shotton, J., Molyneaux, D., Hodges, S., Kim, D., Fitzgibbon, A.: KinectFusion: Real-time dense surface mapping and tracking. In: 2011 10th IEEE International Symposium on Mixed and Augmented Reality (ISMAR), pp. 127–136 (2011)
25. Raskar, R., Welch, G., Cutts, M., Lake, A., Stesin, L., Fuchs, H.: The office of the future: A unified approach to image-based modeling and spatially immersive displays. In: Proceedings of the 25th Annual Conference on Computer Graphics and Interactive Techniques, pp. 179–188 (1998)
26. Raskar, R., Welch, G., Fuchs, H.: Spatially augmented reality. In: First IEEE Workshop on Augmented Reality (IWAR 1998), pp. 11–20 (1998)
27. Schaefer, A., Cook, N., Church, J., Basarab, J., Perry, B., Miller, C., Tong, A.: The use of infrared thermography as an early indicator of bovine respiratory disease complex in calves. Res. Vet. Sci. **83**(3), 376–384 (2007)
28. Thanh, N.T.: Infrared thermography for the detection and characterization of buried objects. Uitgeverij VUBPRESS Brussels Univ. Press **23** (2007)
29. Vidas, S., Moghadam, P.: HeatWave: A handheld 3D thermography system for energy auditing. Energ. Build. **66**(2013), 445–460 (2013)
30. Vollmer, M., Möllmann, K.P.: Infrared Thermal Imaging: Fundamentals, Research and Applications. Wiley, Weinheim (2010)
31. Yahav, S., Giloh, M.: Infrared Thermography-Applications in Poultry Biological Research. INTECH Open Access Publisher (2012)
32. Yang, R., Chen, Y.: Design of a 3-D infrared imaging system using structured light. IEEE Trans. Instrum. Meas. **60**(2), 608–617 (2011)
33. Yang, R., Yang, W., Chen, Y., Wu, X.: Geometric calibration of IR camera using trinocular vision. J. Lightwave Technol. **29**(24), 3797–3803 (2011)
34. Zhang, X., Li, J., Zhang, Z., Du, Y.: Region registration of large-scale IR/visual images based on improved SC algorithm. In: 7th International Symposium on Advanced Optical Manufacturing and Testing Technologies (AOMATT 2014), pp. 928225–928225 (2014)
35. Živčák, J., Hudák, R., Madarász, L., Rudas, I.J.: Methodology, Models and Algorithms in Thermographic Diagnostics. Springer, Heidelberg (2013)
36. Projection Mapping. http://projection-mapping.org/. Accessed 12 Feb 2016

Cloud Computing Services for Real Time Bilateral Communication, Applied to Robotic Arms

Cristian Gallardo[1] and Víctor Hugo Andaluz[1,2(✉)]

[1] Universidad Técnica de Ambato, Ambato, Ecuador
cmgallardop@gmail.com
[2] Universidad de Las Fuerzas Armadas ESPE, Sangolquí, Ecuador
vhandaluz1@espe.edu.ec

Abstract. This work presents the design of a bilateral teleoperation system for a robotic arm. It proposes a new prototype communication protocol with Websockets for the communication and Json for data structuration on a cloud computing environment with OpenStack and Openshift Origin. The human operator receives visual and force feedback from the remote site, and it sends position commands to the slave. Additionally, in the tele-operation system it is proposed that the human operator is immersed in an augmented reality environment to have greater transparency of the remote site. The transparency of a tele-operation system indicates a measure of how the human feels the remote system. Finally, the experimental results are reported to verify the performance of the proposed system.

Keywords: Cloud computing · Bilateral teleoperation · Robotic arm · Path following · Virtual reality

1 Introduction

During the last decades, various models of field robots have been developed to take the place of humans in dangerous tasks, such as rescue missions, Mars exploration, airport patrols, and missions in war [1–3]. In order to operate in highly variable, unstructured, unknown, or dynamic environments, an advanced tele-robotic system with increased adaptability and human like manipulation capabilities is required. In general, a tele-operation system is composed of a local site, where a human operator drives a hand-controller named master; a remote site, where a robot named slave follows the motion of the master to execute a given task in interaction with the environment; and a communication channel that links both sites. The master is used to generate velocity or position commands which are sent to the remote site, while the force due to the interaction between the slave and the environment is back-fed to the human operator through the actuators of the master [4–7].

Cloud computing is a paradigm in the way that the computing resources and applications are used and delivered as a services. These main resources as a service are computing, storage and the network infrastructure. Cloud computing refers to providing these resources as a service over the Internet to the public or in an organization

L.T. De Paolis and A. Mongelli (Eds.): AVR 2016, Part I, LNCS 9768, pp. 500–514, 2016.
DOI: 10.1007/978-3-319-40621-3_38

that is of private use [8]. There are three types of cloud services and they differ in the approach on how the resources are made available. The first approach is to make the hardware infrastructure available as a service and is called Infrastructure as a Service (IaaS). The second approach is to provide a platform (the OS along with the necessary software, frameworks and tools) over the hardware infrastructure. This is called Platform as a Service (PaaS). The third approach is to provide the application as a service and is called Software as a Service (SaaS) [9–12].

Recently, many researches about cloud communication are taking an increasing interest in the field of robot services for manipulation and getting information from them, *e.g.*, Cloud-Based Robot services [13] that examining previous implementations RT-Middleware, ROS and make a new proposal (RSNP) that is based on web service technologies, similarly many researches have been made about cloud computing and how we can interact with it, but almost all of this interactions are by standard protocol http like http polling: that make a request to the server and the server answer this request, other protocols that give more interaction client-server are: push comet, long polling, flash, XMR, htmlfiles and others technologies like webservice. Cloud computing is a new wave in the field of technology information. Some see it as an emerging field in computing. They it consists of a set of resources and services offered by In-Internet. Therefore, "cloud computing" is also called "computer on the Internet. "The word" cloud "is a metaphor to describe the Web as a space where the computer was preinstalled and exists as a service. (Cloud Computing: Opportunities and Challenges) the main characteristic of cloud computing is the virtualization of network, storage and compute [14–17].

In such context, this work proposes a bilateral teleoperation system in order to allow the handling of objects. It comprises a robotic arm (slave) so that it can move and manipulate objects. The human operator receives visual and force signals and sends position commands generated by a haptic device (master) to the remote site; furthermore, the local site has proposed a virtual environment and augmented reality implemented in Unity3D. The augmented reality provides feedback of different signals from the remote site in real time, so that through different haptic devices stimulate the senses of sight, touch and hearing of the human operator so that it can "transmit" their skill, experience and expertise to the robot to perform a task. Whereas for the channel communication is proposed a new implementation of teleoperation-communication (Robot + Cloud) but in the communication using WebSockets and Json data Structure unlike in the works found in the literature. On the other hand, the design of the teleoperation system structure is mainly composed by two parts, each one being a controller itself. The first one is a minimum norm controller to solve the path following problem which considered the desired position of the person to move of the arm. The second one is a dynamic compensation controller, which receives as inputs the velocity references calculated by the kinematic controller. To validate the proposed teleoperation system, results are included and discussed.

The work is organized as follows: in Sect. 2 describes the bilateral teleoperation system proposed. Section 3 presents the implementation of communication channel through the cloud computing services; while that the kinematic and dynamic modeling of the robotic arm are shown in Sect. 4, also of the controllers design and the analysis of the system's stability. Next in Sect. 5 the design of the local site of the human operator developed, and finally the results are presented and discussed in Sects. 6 and 7, respectively.

2   Bilateral Teleoperation System

A bilateral tele-operation system for a robotic arm is proposed, in which forward and backward delay between local and remote sites are assumed to be irrelevant ($\zeta_1(t) = 0$ and $\zeta_2(t) = 0$). The proposed tele-operation system is shown in Fig. 1. In this system both the force back-fed to the human operator are considered.

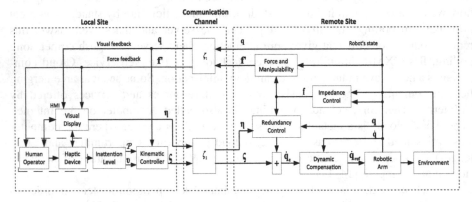

Fig. 1. Block diagram of the bilateral tele-operation system

For communication channel of the bilateral tele-operation system this work proposed a new implementation of teleoperation-communication (Robot + Cloud) with a communication using websockets and Json data Structure as shown in Fig. 2. Websockets is a standardized communication protocol that give a full-duplex, bidirectional channel communication and help to make scalable applications giving a high performance communication through Internet in this case on a cloud computing infrastructure; while that Json Data Structure (JavaScript Object Notation) is a light weight format for data interchange.

On other hand, a given mission is generally composed of several operation processes, in this context the human operator controls the robotic arm by sending position commands to the end-effector of the robot: h_l, h_m, and h_n, one for each axis in respect to the inertial frame $\mathcal{R}(\mathcal{X}, \mathcal{Y}, \mathcal{Z})$, using a haptic device $\mathbf{h_d} = \begin{bmatrix} h_l & h_m & h_n \end{bmatrix}^T$. The human operator commands are generated with the use of the FALCON^{TM} from Novint Technologies Incorporated as indicated in Fig. 3. Its positions P_x, P_y, and P_z are translated into position commands h_l, h_m and h_n for the manipulation mode, through the following rotation matrix,

$$
\begin{bmatrix} h_l \\ h_m \\ h_n \end{bmatrix} = \begin{bmatrix} \cos(q_1) & -\sin(q_1) & 0 \\ \sin(q_1) & \cos(q_1) & 0 \\ 0 & 0 & 1 \end{bmatrix} \begin{bmatrix} P_x \\ P_y \\ P_z \end{bmatrix} \tag{1}
$$

where q_1 represents the first joint of the robotic arm that rotates about the axis Z.

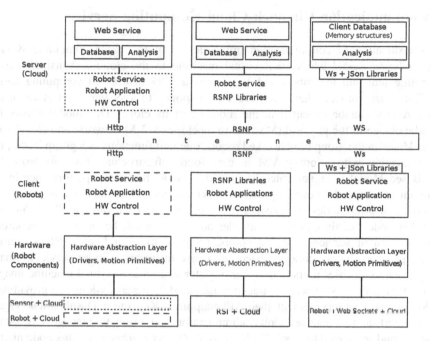

Fig. 2. Block diagram of the bilateral tele-operation system

In the case of robotic manipulators, the force feedback is the result of a physical interaction with the environment.

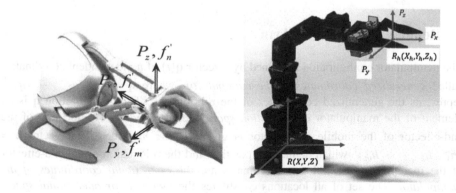

Fig. 3. FALCON^{TM} Novint Technologies Incorporated

On the other hand, the human operator has the possibility of changing the desired internal configuration of the robotic arm at any time during the execution of a mission, through the visual display (HMI), *i.e.*, $\eta = [q_{1d} \quad q_{2d} \quad \cdots \quad q_{nd}]^T$. This desired configuration vector may or may not have the values that maximize manipulability of the robotic arm.

3   Communication Channel: Cloud Computing Services

The classification of communication infrastructure of the cloud computing is [13] *(i) Peer-based model* where each virtual machine in the cloud is considered as a computing unit and the robots and Vms form a fully distributed computing mesh; *(ii) Clone-based model* where each robot corresponds to a system level clone in the cloud. A task can be executed in the robot or in its clone. This model allows for sporadic outage in the physical (Machine to machine) M2 M network; and *(iii) Proxy-Based Model* in the group of networked robots, one unit functions as a group leader, the communication with a proxy VM in the cloud infrastructure. For this work the roxy-Based Model is implemented because this model has a best performance in the communication speed. In our proposed model considers an internal cloud infrastructure composed of three nodes, as shown Fig. 4., where, *(a) Controller & Block Storage node* this node mainly contain: Controller administrate all the openstack resources, administration of services, api end points, projects, users and roles. Block storage service provides block storage devices to guest instances (Cinder service). Image Storage service enables users to discover, register and retrieve virtual machine images (Glance). Identity service perform tracking users and their permissions and providing a catalog of available services with their API endpoints (Keystone). Dashboard service is a web interface that enables cloud administrator and users to manage OpenStack resources and services (Horizon); *(b) Network & Object storage node* this node mainly contain: Network service allows to create and attach interface devices managed by other OpenStack services to network (Neutron). Object Storage Service work together to provide object storage and retrieval through a REST API (Swift); and finally *(c) Compute Node* this node contain Compute Service allow to host and manage cloud computing systems this host contain the Hypervisor (Nova).

4   Remote Site: Robotic Arm

The manipulator configuration is defined by a vector $\mathbf{q}(t)$ of n independent coordinates, called *generalized coordinates of the manipulator*, where $\mathbf{q} = [q_1 \quad q_2 \quad \cdots \quad q_n]^T$ represents the generalized coordinates of the robotic arm. The configuration $\mathbf{q}$ is an element of the manipulator *configuration space*; denoted by $\mathcal{N}$. The location of the end-effector of the mobile manipulator is given by the m–dimensional vector $\mathbf{h} = [h_1 \quad h_2 \quad \cdots \quad h_m]^T$ which defines the position and the orientation of the end-effector of the manipulator in $\mathcal{R}$. Its m coordinates are the *operational coordinates of the manipulator*. The set of all locations constitutes the *manipulator operational space*, denoted by $\mathcal{M}$.

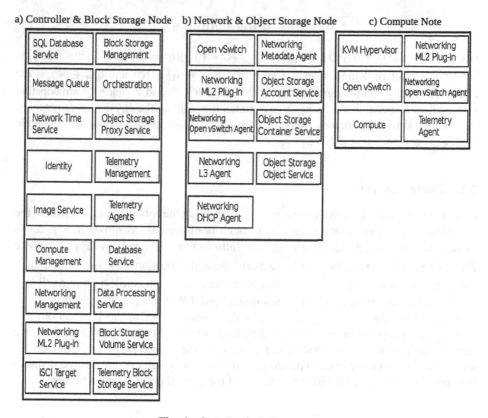

Fig. 4. OpenStack: Infrastructure

4.1   Kinematic and Dynamic Model

The kinematic model of a robotic arm gives the derivative of its end-effector location as a function of the derivatives of both the robotic arm configuration and the location of the mobile platform,

$$\dot{\mathbf{h}}(t) = \mathbf{J}(\mathbf{q})\dot{\mathbf{q}}(t) \tag{2}$$

where $\mathbf{J}(\mathbf{q})$ is the Jacobian matrix that defines a linear mapping between the vector of the robotic arm velocities $\dot{\mathbf{q}}(t)$ and the vector of the end-effector velocity $\dot{\mathbf{h}}(t)$.

On the other hand, the mathematic model that represents the dynamics of a robotic arm can be obtained from Lagrange's dynamic equations, which are based on the difference between the kinetic and potential energy of each of the joints of the robot (energy balance) [18]. The dynamic model of the robotic arm, having as control signals the reference velocities of the system, can be represented as follows [19],

$$\mathbf{M}(\mathbf{q})\ddot{\mathbf{q}} + \mathbf{C}(\mathbf{q}, \dot{\mathbf{q}})\dot{\mathbf{q}} + \mathbf{g}(\mathbf{q}) = \dot{\mathbf{q}}_{\mathbf{ref}} \tag{3}$$

where, $\mathbf{M}(\mathbf{q}) = \mathbf{H}^{-1}(\bar{\mathbf{M}} + \mathbf{D})$, $\mathbf{C}(\mathbf{q}, \dot{\mathbf{q}}) = \mathbf{H}^{-1}(\bar{\mathbf{C}} + \mathbf{P})$, $\mathbf{g}(\mathbf{q}) = \mathbf{H}^{-1}\bar{\mathbf{g}}(\mathbf{q})$. Thus, $\mathbf{M}(\mathbf{q}) \in \Re^{\delta_n \times \delta_n}$ is a positive definite matrix, $\bar{\mathbf{C}}(\mathbf{q}, \mathbf{v})\mathbf{v} \in \Re^{\delta_n}$, $\bar{\mathbf{G}}(\mathbf{q}) \in \Re^{\delta_n}$ and $\dot{\mathbf{q}}_{\mathbf{ref}} \in \Re^{\delta_n}$ is the vector of velocity control signals, $\mathbf{H} \in \Re^{\delta_n \times \delta_n}$, $\mathbf{D} \in \Re^{\delta_n \times \delta_n}$ and $\mathbf{P} \in \Re^{\delta_n \times \delta_n}$ are constant symmetrical diagonal matrices, positive definite, that contain the physical parameters of the robotic arm, *e.g.*, motors, velocity controllers. More details about the dynamic model (5) can be found in [19].

4.2   Control Design

From the viewpoint of control theory, the end-effector of the robotic arm must follow the path desired by a person and generated through brain signals, as shown in Fig. 5. As represented in Fig. 5, the path to be followed is denoted as $\mathcal{P}(s)$, where $\mathcal{P}(s) = (x_p(s), y_p(s), z_p(s))$; the actual desired location $P_d(s_D) = (x_P(s_D), y_P(s_D)z_P(s_D))$ is defined as desired point of the person, *i.e.*, the closest point on $\mathcal{P}(s)$, with s_D being the curvilinear abscissa defining the point P_d; $\tilde{x} = x_P(s_D) - x$ is the position error in the X direction; $\tilde{y} = y_P(s_D) - y$ is the position error in the Y direction; $\tilde{z} = z_P(s_D) - z$ is the position error in the Z direction; ρ represents the distance between the end-effector position of the robotic arm $h(x, y, z)$ and the desired point for the person P_d, where the position error in the ρ direction is $\tilde{\rho} = 0 - \rho = -\rho$, *i.e.*, the desired distance between the end-effector position $h(x, y, z)$ and the desired point P_d must be zero.

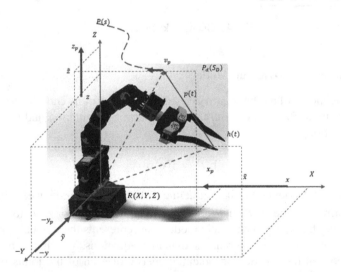

Fig. 5. The orthogonal projection of the point of interest over the path

Hence, the path following problem is to find the control law for the robotic arm as a function of the control errors (position and orientation of the end-effector) and the desired velocities of the end-effector

$$\dot{\mathbf{q}}_{ref}(s_D, h) = f(\rho(t, s), \upsilon_P(s_D, h)) \tag{4}$$

such that $\tilde{x} = 0$, $\tilde{y} = 0$ and $\tilde{z} = 0$. Therefore, if $\lim_{t \to \infty} \tilde{x}(t) = 0$, $\lim_{t \to \infty} \tilde{y}(t) = 0$ and $\lim_{t \to \infty} \tilde{z}(t) = 0$ then $\lim_{t \to \infty} \rho(t) = 0$.

4.2.1 Kinematic Controller

The design of the kinematic controller of the robotic arm is based on the kinematic model of the arm (4). The following control law is proposed

$$\dot{\mathbf{q}}_c = \mathbf{J}^\# \left(\upsilon_d + \mathbf{L_K} \tanh\left(\mathbf{L_K^{-1}K\,\tilde{h}}\right)\right) + \left(\mathbf{I} - \mathbf{J}^\#\mathbf{J}\right)\mathbf{L_B}\tanh\left(\mathbf{L_B^{-1}B}\,\Lambda\right) \tag{5}$$

where $\mathbf{J}^\# = \mathbf{W}^{-1}\mathbf{J}^T\left(\mathbf{JW}^{-1}\mathbf{J}^T\right)^{-1}$, being $\mathbf{W}$ a definite positive matrix that weighs the control actions of the system, υ_d is the desired velocities vector of the end-effector $\mathbf{h}$, $\tilde{\mathbf{h}}$ is the vector of control errors, defined as $\tilde{\mathbf{h}} = \mathbf{h_d} - \mathbf{h}$, $\mathbf{B}$ and $\mathbf{L_B}$ are definite positive diagonal matrices that weigh the vector Λ. In order to include an analytical saturation of velocities in the robotic arm the use of the $\tanh$ (.) function is proposed, which limits the error in $\tilde{\mathbf{h}}$ and the magnitude of the vector Λ. The second term of (5) represents the projection on the null space of $\mathbf{J}$, where Λ is an arbitrary vector which contains the velocities associated to the robotic arm. Therefore, any value given to Λ will have effects only on the internal structure of the arm, and will not affect the final control of the end-effector at all. By using this term, different secondary control objectives can be achieved effectively [20].

4.2.2 Controller with Dynamic Compensation

The proposed kinematic controllers presented in Subsect. 4.2.1 assume perfect velocity tracking; nevertheless this is not true in real contexts, i.e., $\dot{\mathbf{q}}(t) \neq \dot{\mathbf{q}}_c(t)$, mainly when high-speed movements or heavy load transportation are required. Therefore, it becomes essential to consider the robot's dynamics, in addition to its kinematics. Then, the objective of the dynamic compensation controller is to compensate the dynamics of the system, thus reducing the velocity tracking error. This controller receives as inputs the desired velocities calculated by the kinematic controllers, and generates velocity references for the mobile platform and robotic arm. Hence, relaxing the perfect velocity tracking assumption, there will be a velocity error defined as, $\dot{\tilde{\mathbf{q}}}(t) = \dot{\mathbf{q}}_c(t) - \dot{\mathbf{q}}(t)$. This velocity error motivates the dynamic compensation process, which will be performed based on the inverse dynamics of the system. With this aim, the exact model of the system without disturbances is considered, thus the following control is proposed,

$$\dot{\mathbf{q}}_{ref} = \mathbf{M}(\mathbf{q})\sigma + \mathbf{C}(\mathbf{q}, \dot{\mathbf{q}})\dot{\mathbf{q}} + g(\mathbf{q}) \tag{6}$$

where $\sigma = \ddot{\mathbf{q}}_c + \mathbf{L_v}\tanh\left(\mathbf{L_v^{-1}K_v}\dot{\tilde{\mathbf{q}}}\right)$. Now, Replacing (6) in (5) it results $\ddot{\tilde{\mathbf{q}}} + \mathbf{L_v}\tanh\left(\mathbf{L_v^{-1}K_v}\dot{\tilde{\mathbf{q}}}\right) = \mathbf{0}$. For the stability analysis the following Lyapunov's candidate function is considered $V\left(\dot{\tilde{\mathbf{q}}}\right) = \frac{1}{2}\dot{\tilde{\mathbf{q}}}^{T}\dot{\tilde{\mathbf{q}}}$, its time derivative is $\dot{V}\left(\dot{\tilde{\mathbf{q}}}\right) = -\dot{\tilde{\mathbf{q}}}^{T}\mathbf{L_v}\mathbf{tanh}\left(\mathbf{L_v^{-1}}\mathbf{K_v}\dot{\tilde{\mathbf{q}}}\right) < 0$. Thus it can be immediately concluded that the error vector $\lim_{t\to\infty}\dot{\tilde{\mathbf{q}}}(t) = 0$ asymptotically, provided that $\mathbf{K_v}$ and $\mathbf{L_v}$ are symmetrical positive definite matrices.

5 Local Site

The local site consists of a virtual reality and augmented to allow the human operator to have greater transparency in the remote site reality, as illustrated by the Fig. 6. The Fig. 6 can be described in two stages, the first stage is *(A) Inputs,* These let read all the variables considered in the bilateral tele-operation of both the robot and the environment in which develops the task, entries that are processed in the script are: *(i) Output states of the robot,* represents the variables that describe the robot kinematics $\mathbf{q} = \begin{bmatrix} q_1 & q_2 & \cdots & q_n \end{bmatrix}^{T}$. In the script, the data acquired from the platform $\mathbf{q}$ are

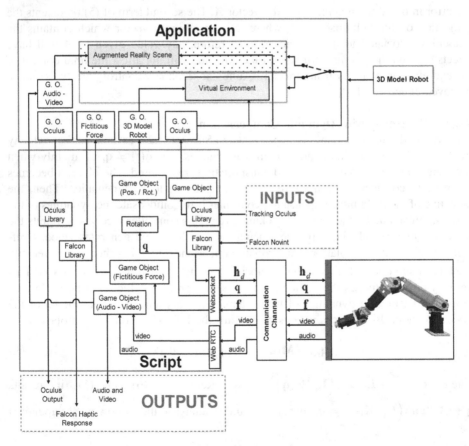

Fig. 6. Block diagram of the virtual environment

assigned to the characteristic of *Rotation* for each joint of the simulated arm Game Object; *(ii) Desired positions* through the FALCON^{MT} haptic device emit the desired location $\mathbf{h_d} = [h_l \quad h_m \quad h_n]^T$ for manipulation mode. The script obtains the variation of position in world coordinates by a Game Object that simulates the movement of the end-effector of FALCON^{MT} haptic device in space. *(iii) Video and audio* transmits the image and audio captured by the camera located at the end-effector of the robot; *(iv) Fictitious force* is produced by a sensor that maps the area in which the robot can be moved freely; y finally *(v) Oculus Positional Tracking* modifies the rotation of the camera in the virtual and / or augmented environment, corresponding to the movement performed by the human operator when using the Head-mounted Display, HMD, in order to have a greater immersion in the experience of using the application.

Furthermore, the second stage of Fig. 6 is *(B) Outputs Script* that recreates the sensations that the human operator should feel if he were at the remote site, this paper considers three ways that help the human operator to "transmit" their ability and experience to the robot to perform a task.

6   Experimental Results

In order to illustrate the performance of the proposed tele-operation structure, several simulation experiments are carried out for control of a robotic arm, most representative results are presented in this section. The experiments were carried with the kinematic and dynamic models of a robotic arm 6 DOF which was developed at the University of the Armed Forces ESPE (only 3 DOF of the 6 available DOFs are used in the experiments, see Fig. 7). The links of the robotic arm are controlled by a network of servomotors Dinamixel communicated via a RS-485 interface. Therefore to give greater scalability for future functions of the cloud computing environment are used three computers with the same characteristics, intel core i7-3770 Processor, 6 GB ram memory, two Hard disk sata connection of 750 GB for each computer, CentOS Linux 7 X64 with minimal install for the base system, the network connection are using Cat6a devices, for The IaaS infrastructure of the Cloud-Computing environment was used

Fig. 7. Rootic arm 6DOF developed at the University of the Armed Forces ESPE

OpenStack Kilo, then created a OpenShift project with php5.4 support on the cloud infrastructure for the communication service and presentation of the data.

The local site has an Oculus Rift HMD and a haptic device FALCON™ Novint. To transmit the comands generated by humans with was used a FALCON™ haptic device from Novint Technologies Incorporated as indicated in Fig. 8; while the Fig. 9 shown a robotic arm 6DOF developed in SolidWorks.

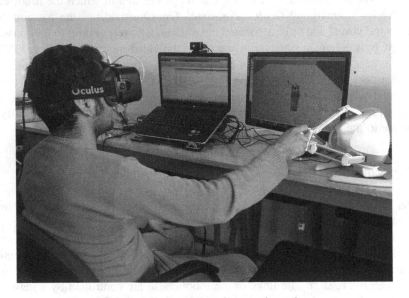

Fig. 8. Local site of the tele-operation scheme

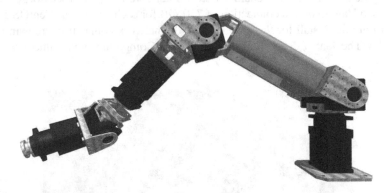

Fig. 9. Rootic Arm 6DOF developed in SolidWorks

The FALCON™ Novint communication functions were developed in C ++ language to create dynamic link libraries to use on LabView environment to get FALCON™ signals, for testing of FALCON™ hosts were used windows 8.1 X64 and windows 7 X86, for test of C ++ dll compatibility on each Operative System. On labView was created some operations and functions, the data that will be send are set in Json data structure, to encapsulate and send to the cloud was used websocket protocol, for keeping the connection on the cloud with all the clients, each client must set a id and store the connection in a structure list in memory where the data will be decoded and will show information of the origin, the destination and the message, on the server for manage all the connections thread, the service on the host were developed with php + javascript + html languages with phpwebsockets, the fancywebsocket libraries and codeigniter framework. The connection to the cloud of the arm and the functions are developed with C ++ language on GNU/Linux Operative System.

Hence, Figs. 10–12 show the results of the experiment of bilateral tele-operation. Figure 10 shows the stroboscopic movement on the X-Y-Z space of Unity3D. Figure 11 shows a comparison between the reference generated by the human operator and the

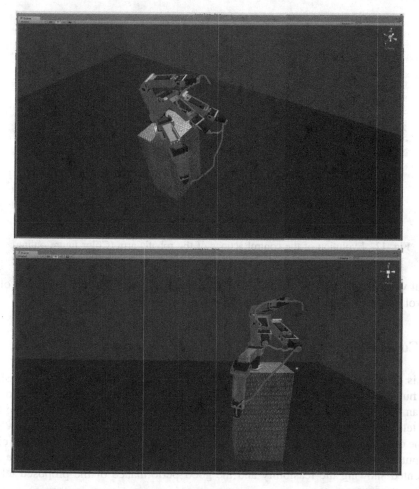

Fig. 10. Stroboscopic movement of the robotic arm in Unity 3D.

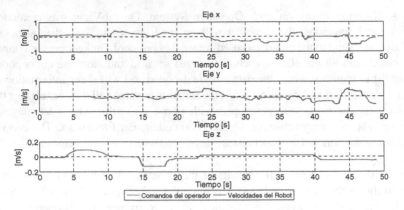

Fig. 11. Comparison between the references generated by the human operator and the actual velocities of the end effector (Color figure online)

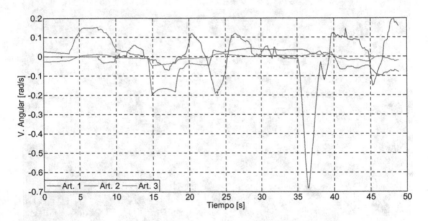

Fig. 12. Evolution of the control actions of the robotic arm (Color figure online)

actual velocities of the end effector; while the Fig. 12 depicts the time evolution of the control actions for the joints of the robotic arm.

7 Conclusions

In this paper a bilateral tele-operation system is proposed, in this system is considers that human operator has greater transparency of the remote. This system allows a human operator to perform complex tasks in a remote environment with a robotic arm. The teleoperation system use a communication channel that implements a new prototype of communication protocol with WebSockets and Json data structures on a cloud computing environment with OpenStack. Therefore, experimental results were also presented showing the feasibility and the good performance of the proposed teleoperation structure.

Acknowledgment. The authors would like to thanks to the Consorcio Ecuatoriano para el Desarrollo de Internet Avanzado -CEDIA-, Universidad de las Fuerzas Armadas ESPE and the Universidad Técnica de Ambato for financing the project *Tele-operación bilateral cooperativo de múltiples manipuladores móviles – CEPRAIX-2015-05*, for the support to develop this paper.

References

1. Andaluz, V.H., Canseco, P., Varela, J., Ortiz, J.S., Pérez, M.G., Morales, V., Robertí, F., Carelli, R.: Modeling and control of a wheelchair considering center of mass lateral displacements. In: Liu, H., Kubota, N., Zhu, X., Dillmann, R. (eds.) ICIRA 2015. LNCS, vol. 9246, pp. 254–270. Springer, Heidelberg (2015)
2. Slawinski, E., Mut, V.: PD-like controllers for delayed bilateral teleoperation of manipulators robots. Int. J. Robust Nonlinear Control **25**(12), 1801–1815 (2015)
3. Voth, D.: A new generation of military robots. Intell. Syst. **19**(4), 2–3 (2004)
4. Sheridan, T.B.: Telerobotics, Automation, and Human Supervisory Control. The MIT Press, Cambrige (1992)
5. Stramigioli, S., Mahony, R., Corke, P.: A novel approach to haptic tele-operation of aerial robot vehicles. In: Proceedings of the IEEE International Conference on Robotics and Automation (ICRA 2010), pp. 5302–5308, May 2010
6. Niculescu, S.-I., Taoutaou, D., Lozano, R.: Bilateral teleoperation with communication delays. Int. J. Robust Nonlinear Control **13**(9), 873–883 (2003)
7. Yin, S., Ding, S.X., Xie, X., Luo, H.: A review on basic datadriven approaches for industrial process monitoring. IEEE Trans. Ind. Electron. **61**(11), 6414–6428 (2014)
8. Griffith, R., Joseph, A.D., Katz, R., Konwinski, A., Lee, G., Patterson, D., Rabkin, A., Stoica, I., Armbrust, M., Fox, A., Zaharia, M.: Above the clouds: A berkeley view of cloud computing [white paper] (2009). http://www.eecs.berkeley.edu/Pubs/TechRpts/2009/EECS-2009-28.pdf
9. Amazon ec2. amazon elastic compute cloud (2009). http://aws.amazon.com/ec2/
10. Google app engine (2009). http://code.google.com/appengine/
11. Wurm, K.M., Stachniss, C., Burgard, W.: Coordinated multi-robot exploration using a segmentation of the environment. In: International Conference on Intelligent Robots and Systems (2008)
12. Fox, D.: Distributed multi-robot exploration and mapping. In CRV 2005: Proceedings of the 2nd Canadian Conference on Computer and Robot Vision, pp. 15–xv. IEEE Computer Society, Washington, DC (2005)
13. Dhiyanesh, B.: Dynamic Resource Allocation for Machine to Cloud Communications Robotics Cloud. In: IEEE International Conference on Emerging Trends in Electrical Engineering and Energy Management, pp. 451–454 (2012)
14. Guizzo, E.: Robots with their head in the clouds. IEEE Spectrum, Robotics, March 2011
15. Asaro, P.: Remote-control crimes: roboethics and legal jurisdictions of tele-agency, Special issue on Roboethics, Veruggio, G., Van der Loos, M., Solis, J. (eds.) IEEE Robot. Autom. Mag. **18**(1), 68–71 (2011)
16. Shiraz, M., Sookhak, M., Gani, A., Shah, S.A.A.: A Study on the critical analysis of computational offloading frameworks for mobile cloud computing. J. Netw. Comput. Appl. **47**, 47–60 (2015)
17. Riazuelo, L., Civera, J., Montiel, J.M.M.: C2TAM: a cloud framework for cooperative tracking and mapping. Robot. Auton. Syst. **62**(4), 401–413 (2014)

18. Siciliano, B., Sciavicco, L., Villani, L., Oriolo, G.: Robotics: Modeling, Planning, and Control. Springer, London (2009). ISBN 978-1-84628-641-4
19. Andaluz, V., Roberti, F., Carelli, R.: Robust control with redundancy resolution and dynamic compensation for mobilemanipulators. In Proc. of the IEEE-ICIT International Conference on Industrial Technology, pp. 1449–1454 (2010)
20. Bayle, B., Fourquet, J.-Y.: Manipulability analysis for mobile manipulators. In: Proceedings of the IEEE International Conference on Robots & Automation, pp. 1251–1256 (2001)

Author Index

Printed in the United States
By Bookmasters